Principled Pragmatism in Practice

Studies in EU External Relations

Edited by

Marc Maresceau (*Ghent University*)

Editorial Board

Marise Cremona (*European University Institute*)
Günter Burghardt (*former EU ambassador Washington*)
Alan Dashwood (*University of Cambridge*)
Frank Hoffmeister (*European Commission*)

VOLUME 19

The titles published in this series are listed at *brill.com/seur*

Principled Pragmatism in Practice

The EU's Policy towards Russia after Crimea

Edited by

Fabienne Bossuyt and Peter Van Elsuwege

BRILL
NIJHOFF

LEIDEN | BOSTON

Cover illustration: Cracked brick wall painted with an European Union flag on the left and a Russian flag on the right. Stockfoto ID:1155146162 ©Gwengoat.

Library of Congress Cataloging-in-Publication Data

Names: Bossuyt, Fabienne, editor. | Elsuwege, Peter Van, editor.
Title: Principled pragmatism in practice : the EU's policy towards Russia after Crimea / edited by Fabienne Bossuyt and Peter Van Elsuwege.
Description: Leiden ; Boston : Brill | Nijhoff, 2021. | Series: Studies in EU external relations, 1875-0451 ; volume 19 | Includes bibliographical references and index. |
Identifiers: LCCN 2020058686 (print) | LCCN 2020058687 (ebook) | ISBN 9789004423916 (hardback) | ISBN 9789004453715 (ebook)
Subjects: LCSH: European Union countries–Foreign relations–Russia (Federation) | Russia (Federation)–Foreign relations–European Union countries. | Crimea (Ukraine)–Annexation to Russia (Federation)
Classification: LCC D2025.5.R8 P75 2021 (print) | LCC D2025.5.R8 (ebook) | DDC 341.242/20947–dc23
LC record available at https://lccn.loc.gov/2020058686
LC ebook record available at https://lccn.loc.gov/2020058687

Typeface for the Latin, Greek, and Cyrillic scripts: "Brill". See and download: brill.com/brill-typeface.

ISSN 1875-0451
ISBN 978-90-04-42391-6 (hardback)
ISBN 978-90-04-45371-5 (e-book)

Copyright 2021 by Koninklijke Brill NV, Leiden, The Netherlands.
Koninklijke Brill NV incorporates the imprints Brill, Brill Hes & De Graaf, Brill Nijhoff, Brill Rodopi, Brill Sense, Hotei Publishing, mentis Verlag, Verlag Ferdinand Schöningh and Wilhelm Fink Verlag.
All rights reserved. No part of this publication may be reproduced, translated, stored in a retrieval system, or transmitted in any form or by any means, electronic, mechanical, photocopying, recording or otherwise, without prior written permission from the publisher. Requests for re-use and/or translations must be addressed to Koninklijke Brill NV via brill.com or copyright.com.

This book is printed on acid-free paper and produced in a sustainable manner.

Contents

Preface IX
List of Abbreviations XII
List of Figures and Tables XVII
Notes on Contributors XVIII

General Introduction
From Strategic Partner to Strategic Challenge: In Search of an EU Policy towards Russia 1
   Peter Van Elsuwege and Fabienne Bossuyt

PART 1
The Minsk Agreements and the Sanctions Regime in EU-Russia Relations

1   The Minsk Agreements
   Has the Glimmer of Hope Faded? 17
      Sebastiaan Van Severen

2   The Role of EU Member States and the Future of EU-Russia Relations
   Disentangling the Role of Germany and the Netherlands in EU Decision-Making on Relations with Russia since the Ukraine Crisis 40
      Tony van der Togt

3   Two Monologues Don't Make a Dialogue
   The EU's and Russia's Strategic Narratives about the Minsk Agreements and Sanctions Regime 62
      Irina Petrova

4   The Punitive Effect of the EU's Restrictive Measures against Russia
   A Help or a Hindrance for Principled Pragmatism? 86
      Alexandra Hofer

5   The EU-Russia Sanctions Regime before the Court of Justice of the EU 104
      Kirill Entin

6   The Impact of the Adjudication of Sanctions against Russia before the Court of Justice of the EU   125
    Celia Challet

PART 2
EU-Russia Relations and the Shared Neighbourhood

7   Armenia
    A Precarious Navigation between Eurasian Integration and the European Union   143
    Laure Delcour and Narine Ghazaryan

8   The EU and the *De Facto* States of the East European Periphery
    Constraints in International and European Law   163
    Benedikt Harzl

9   The EU's and Russia's Visa Diplomacy in a Contested Neighbourhood   180
    Igor Merheim-Eyre

PART 3
EU Resilience to Russian Threats

10 The EU's Concept of Resilience in the Context of EU-Russia Relations   201
    Elena Pavlova and Tatiana Romanova

11 The EU's Energy Relationship with Russia
    Between Resilience and Engagement   216
    Marco Siddi

12 Addressing Cyber Security Threats from Russia in the EU   234
    Andreas Marazis

PART 4
Selective Engagement with Russia

13 Countering Transnational Security Threats
   Prospects for EU-Russia Cooperation in an Era of Sanctions   257
      Olga Potemkina

14 Conditions for Effective Selective Engagement
   Greening Russia's Energy Sector   277
      Niels Smeets

15 The Arctic as a Micro-Cosmos for Selective Engagement between the EU and Russia?   290
      Thomas Kruessmann

PART 5
Supporting Russian Civil Society and People-to-People Contacts

16 Principled Pragmatism and Civil Society in the EU Policies towards Russia   313
      Elena Belokurova and Andrey Demidov

17 A Crisis or a Turning Point? EU Cultural Relations with Russia after Crimea   332
      Domenico Valenza

18 The Integration of Russia in the European Higher Education Area
   Challenges and Opportunities   352
      Natalia Leskina

   General Conclusion
   The Five Guiding Principles for the EU's Relations with Russia: In Need of Revision?   370
      Fabienne Bossuyt and Peter Van Elsuwege

   Studies in EU External Relations   383
   Index   385

Preface

The origins of this book go back to the colloquium 'EU-Russia Relations: How to Get Out of the "Midlife" Crisis?' organised under the auspices of Ghent University's Russia Platform on 22 September 2017. This initiative brought together a number of scholars and practitioners from various disciplines to present their research on the evolution of relations between the European Union (EU) and Russia after the conflict in Ukraine and the adoption of the EU Global Strategy on Foreign and Security Policy. To take stock of the most recent developments in the field, a follow-up workshop was organised in Ghent in October 2018. The present volume is the result of in-depth discussions on draft papers presented during those events. The organisers of the workshops, also being the editors of this book, would like to express their deep appreciation to all the contributors for their cooperation and commitment.

The aim of this book is to take stock of the implementation of the EU's Global Strategy and the five principles that are currently guiding EU-Russia relations. In particular, it seeks to examine the implications of each of these principles for the EU's relations with Russia and aims to assess the state of implementation and its challenges. In doing so, the book provides a forward-looking angle, in the sense that it wants to contribute to a better understanding of the current EU-Russia relationship and the prospects for overcoming the existing deadlock. By adopting an interdisciplinary perspective on EU-Russia relations, combining insights from EU studies, international relations, and European and international law, the book provides a comprehensive and holistic view to the current state of affairs.

Recent academic contributions to the literature on EU-Russia relations paint a rather bleak picture of the EU-Russia relationship, and see little scope for improvement due to the absence of a long-term concept of cooperation and lack of a common vision of the future.[1] There is wide acknowledgement among scholars that the current crisis in EU-Russia relations is the culmination of a longer process of downward descent that had already been going on for more than a decade.[2] In trying to explain this gradual deterioration and

---

[1] M. David and T. Romanova, 'The EU in Russia's House of Mirrors', *Journal of Common Market Studies* 57 (1), 2009, 128–140; T. Bordachev, 'Russia and Europe: Between Integration and Diplomacy', *Russia in Global Affairs* 17 (3), 2019, 38–63.

[2] H. Haukkala, 'From Cooperative to Contested Europe? The Conflict in Ukraine as a Culmination of a Long-term Crisis in EU-Russia Relations', *Journal of Contemporary European Studies* 23 (1), 2015, 25–40; T. Hoffmann and A. Makarychev (eds.), *Russia and the EU: Spaces of Interaction* (Routledge 2018); A. Maass, *EU-Russia Relations, 1999–2015: From Courtship to*

the current deadlock of EU-Russia relations, several theoretical perspectives and lenses have been applied. While constructivists have pointed to the normative discord between the EU and Russia and their clash of identity,[3] realists emphasise the power competition (especially in the shared neighbourhood),[4] whereas others see an explanation in domestic factors.[5]

In line with previous studies, which have revealed the importance of images and perceptions in understanding EU-Russia relations,[6] it has been a deliberate choice of this book to bring together academics working in different disciplines and in different academic environments. In particular, the inclusion of several Russian authors was deemed important to understand the various perspectives on the recent developments in EU-Russia relations. This is especially important considering that diverging images and perceptions can be major obstacles to the enhancement of relations between the EU and Russia.[7] As demonstrated specifically in the chapter by Irina Petrova in this volume, the EU's and Russia's views on the events in Ukraine, the Minsk agreements and the sanctions regime differ significantly. The existence of diverging views and approaches is also reflected in other chapters. The extent – as well as the implications – of this profound discord between the EU and Russia is discussed in the concluding chapter, where an overall assessment is made of the five guiding principles for the development of EU-Russia relations.

In full respect of the authors' personal preferences, and as an illustration of the divergent perceptions existing in the Russian and European academic worlds, the editors chose not to impose any harmonised rules with respect to the use of either Ukrainian or Russian spelling of terms (e.g., *Kyiv* versus *Kiev*; *Donbas* versus *Donbass*) nor with respect to the qualification of the events that unfolded in eastern Ukraine and Crimea.

The structure of the book is based on the five guiding principles for EU-Russia relations. The *first* part is devoted to an analysis of the sanctions regime and the Minsk agreements as a crucial condition for the further development of EU-Russia relations. Sebastiaan Van Severen sketches the rocky road of the

---

Confrontation (Routledge 2017); T. Forsberg and H. Haukkala, *The European Union and Russia* (Palgrave Macmillan 2016).

3   A. Makarychev, *Russia and the EU in a Multipolar World: Discourses, Identities, Norms* (Ibidem 2014); T. Casier and J. DeBardeleben (eds.), *EU-Russia Relations in Crisis: Understanding Diverging Perceptions* (Routledge 2017).

4   I. Busygina, *Russia-EU Relations and the Common Neighborhood: Coercion vs. Authority* (Routledge 2017).

5   Maass, *op.cit.*, note 2.

6   Casier and DeBardeleben, *op.cit.*, note 3.

7   *Ibid.*

Minsk peace process and the challenges surrounding its implementation. Tony van der Togt focuses on the role of EU Member States, in particular Germany and the Netherlands, in EU decision-making on relations with Russia since the Ukraine crisis. Irina Petrova unravels the EU's and Russia's strategic narratives about the Minsk agreements and the sanctions regime, whereas Alexandra Hofer critically discusses the punitive effect of the EU's restrictive measures against Russia. The final contributions of the first part, written by Kirill Entin and Celia Challet respectively, involve a legal analysis of the EU-Russia sanctions before the Court of Justice of the EU.

The *second* part looks at the EU's objective to develop strengthened relations with its Eastern partners. Laure Delcour and Narine Ghazaryan look into the specific case of Armenia as a country balancing between European and Eurasian integration. Benedikt Harzl focuses specifically on the EU's engagement with frozen conflicts and *de facto* states in the post-Soviet region. Finally, Igor Merheim-Eyre deals with the EU's and Russia's visa diplomacy in the shared neighbourhood.

The *third* part tackles the issue of 'resilience to Russian threats' as one of the principles guiding the EU's policy towards Russia after the crisis in Ukraine. Elena Pavlova and Tatiana Romanova offer a critical assessment of the EU's understanding of the concept of 'resilience' in the context of EU-Russia relations. Marco Siddi addresses the EU's energy relationship with Russia, whereas Andreas Marazis focuses on the question of cyber security.

The *fourth* part touches on the EU's ambition of 'selective engagement' with Russia in a number of specific policy areas; namely, cooperation in countering transnational security threats (Olga Potemkina), developing renewable energy strategies (Niels Smeets) and cooperation in relation to the Arctic (Thomas Kruessmann).

The *fifth* and last part relates to the EU's approach towards Russia's civil society and the promotion of people-to-people contacts. This includes contributions about evolving strategies towards the involvement of Russia's civil society (Elena Belokurova and Andrey Demidov), the development of the EU's cultural relations with Russia (Domenico Valenza) and EU-Russia cooperation in the sphere of higher education (Natalia Leskina). The book concludes with a number of general reflections about the implications of the Ukraine crisis and the challenges surrounding the implementation of the five guiding principles for the development of EU-Russia relations.

Fabienne Bossuyt and *Peter Van Elsuwege*
September 2020

Abbreviations

AA	Association Agreement
AFD	Alternative für Deutschland
AFSJ	Area of Freedom, Security and Justice
AIIB	Asian Infrastructure Investment Bank
AP	Action Plan
APEC	Asia-Pacific Economic Cooperation
APT28	Advanced Persistent Threat 28
BAR	Barents Regional Council
bcm	billion cubic metres
BEAC	Barents Euro-Arctic Council
BRI	Belt and Road Initiative
BRICS	Brazil, Russia, India, China and South Africa
CBC	cross-border cooperation
CDA	critical discourse analysis
CDU	Christlich Demokratische Union
CEPA	Comprehensive and Enhanced Partnership Agreement
CERT-EU	Computer Emergency Response Team for the EU
CFSP	Common Foreign and Security Policy
CGES	Centre for German and European Studies
CIS	Commonwealth of Independent States
CJEU	Court of Justice of the European Union
CNPC	China National Petroleum Corporation
CoE	Council of Europe
cPPP	contractual public-private partnership
CPSU	Communist Party of the Soviet Union
CSCE	Conference on Security and Cooperation in Europe
CSDP	Common Security and Defence Policy
CSF	Civil Society Forum
CSFSJ	Common Space of Freedom, Security and Justice
CSIRTs	Computer Security Incident Response Teams
CSO	civil society organisation
CSR	Common Strategy on Russia
DCFTA	Deep and Comprehensive Free Trade Area
DDoS	distributed denial-of-service
DG NEAR	Directorate-General for Neighbourhood and Enlargement Negotiations
DGAP	Deutsche Gesellschaft fuer Auswaertige Politik
DPR	Donetsk People's Republic

DSB	Dispute Settlement Body
EACEA	Education, Audiovisual and Culture Executive Agency
EAEU	Eurasian Economic Union
EaP	Eastern Partnership
EBRD	European Bank for Reconstruction and Development
EC	European Commission
ECFR	European Council on Foreign Relations
ECHR	European Convention on Human Rights and Fundamental Freedoms
ECJ	European Court of Justice
ECtHR	European Court of Human Rights
ECTS	European Credit Transfer System
EDA	European Defence Agency
EEA	European Economic Area
EEAS	European External Action Service
EHEA	European Higher Education Area
EIB	European Investment Bank
EIDHR	European Instrument for Democracy and Human Rights
EITI	Extractive Industries Resource Initiative
EMCDDA	European Monitoring Centre for Drugs and Drug Addiction
ENI	European Neighbourhood Instrument
ENISA	European Union Agency for Network and Information Security
ENP	European Neighbourhood Policy
ENPI	European Neighbourhood and Partnership Instrument
EPCA	Enhanced Partnership and Cooperation Agreement
ERDF	European Regional Development Fund
EU	European Union
EUCAM	Europe-Central Asia Monitoring
EUMM	EU Monitoring Mission
EUNIC	European Union National Institutes for Culture
EurAsEC	Eurasian Economic Community
EUSR	EU Special Representative
FDCS	Federal Drug Control Service
FIIA	Finnish Institute for International Affairs
FOM	Foundation Public Opinion
FPI	Foreign Policy Instrument
Frontex	European Border and Coast Guard Agency
FTF	foreign terrorist fighters
GATS	General Agreement on Trade in Services
GATT	General Agreement on Tariffs and Trade
GC	General Court

GCTF	Global Counter-Terrorism Forum
GHG	greenhouse gas
GRU	Russian military intelligence unit
GSP	Generalised Scheme of Preferences
H2020	Horizon 2020 Research and Innovation Framework
HEI	higher education institution
HR/VP	High Representative of the Union for Foreign Affairs and Security Policy and Vice-President of the European Commission
IBPP	Institution Building Partnership Programme
ICJ	International Court of Justice
ICR	international cultural relations
IEA	International Energy Agency
IMF	International Monetary Fund
IP	intellectual property
IPRM	Incident Prevention and Response Mechanism
IRENA	International Renewable Energy Agency
ISIS	Islamic State in Iraq and Syria
IT	information technology
JCC	Joint Control Commission
JCPOA	Joint Comprehensive Plan of Action (JCPOA)
JHA	Justice and Home Affairs
JIT	Joint Investigation Team
JLS	Justice, Liberty, Security
JPO	Joint Police Operation
LBT	Local Border Traffic
LGBT	lesbian, gay, bisexual and transgender
LNG	liquefied natural gas
LPR	Luhansk People's Republic
LTV	Limited Territorial Validity
MA	managing authority
MENA	Middle East and North Africa
MEP	Member of European Parliament
MFA	Ministry of Foreign Affairs
NATO	North Atlantic Treaty Organisation
ND	Northern Dimension
NDICI	Neighbourhood, Development and International Cooperation Instrument
NDTPL	Northern Dimension Partnership on Transport and Logistics
NGO	non-governmental organisation
NIS	Network and Information Security
NSR	Northern Sea Route

ABBREVIATIONS

NWP	Northwest Passage
OCHA	United Nations Office for the Coordination of Humanitarian Affairs
ODIHR	Office for Democratic Institutions and Human Rights
OECD	Organisation for Economic Co-operation and Development
OLAF	European Anti-Fraud Office
OSCE	Organisation for Security and Co-operation in Europe
P4M	Partnership for Modernisation
PAME	Protection of the Arctic Marine Environment
PCA	Partnership and Cooperation Agreement
PESCO	Permanent Structured Cooperation
PI	Partnership Instrument
PNR	passenger name records
PPC	Permanent Partnership Council
R&D	research and development
RA	Readmission Agreement
RAO UES	Unified Energy System of Russia
RE	renewable energy
REPS	renewable energy policies
RES	renewable energy sources
RF	Russian Federation
RWGTL	Regional Working Group on Transport and Logistics
SAO	Senior Arctic Officials
SCO	Shanghai Cooperation Organisation
SINNEA	Switzerland, Norway and the EU-Iceland and European Economic Area Joint Parliamentary Committees
SMES	small and medium enterprises
SMM	Special Monitoring Mission
SMREES	small- and medium-sized renewable energy enterprises
SPD	Sozialdemokratische Partei Deutschlands
SPS	sanitary and phytosanitary standards
TACIS	Technical Assistance for Newly Independent States
TBT	technical barriers to trade
TEMPUS	Trans-European Mobility Programme for University Studies
TEN-E	Trans-European Networks for Energy
TEN-T	European Transport Network
TEU	Treaty on European Union
TFEU	Treaty on the Functioning of the European Union
TO	Thematic Objective
TRIPS	Trade-Related Aspects of Intellectual Property Rights
UAVS	unmanned aerial vehicles

UN	United Nations
UNCLOS	UN Convention on the Law of the Sea
UNHCR	United Nations High Commissioner for Refugees
US	United States
USSR	Union of Soviet Socialist Republics
VEB	Vnesheconombank
VFA	Visa Facilitation Agreement
VLAP	Visa Liberalisation Action Plan
VTsIOM	Russian Public Opinion Research Center
WTO	World Trade Organisation

Figures and Tables

Figures

18.1 Number of selected capacity-building projects involving Russia within TEMPUS and Erasmus+ programmes   360
18.2 Russian universities in Erasmus+ capacity building in higher education   366
18.3 Participation of Russian universities in Jean Monnet activities   366

Tables

3.1 Attitudes towards the European Union among the Russian population   77
3.2 Attitudes towards Ukraine among the Russian population   78
3.3 Perceived impact of EU sanctions against Russia   79
3.4 Expressed concern about sanctions among the Russian population   79
3.5 How much confidence do you have in Russian President Vladimir Putin to do the right thing regarding world affairs?   81
3.6 Favourable attitudes towards Russia among the EU Member States   82
5.1 Overview of key judgments in relation to the EU-Russia sanctions regime   108
12.1 Russian hybrid operations: characteristics, objectives and toolkit   237
12.2 List of reported Russian cyber operations targeting different EU Member States from 2016 until 2018   240
17.1 CBC programmes (2014–2020) with cultural objectives and involving Russian regions   343

Notes on Contributors

Elena Belokurova
is Lecturer at the Faculty of International Relations and Political Science, North-West Institute of Management, the Russian Academy of National Economy and Public Administration. At the same time, she is also Director of the German-Russian Exchange in St. Petersburg, Russia. She has studied sociology and defended her candidate dissertation in Political Science in 2000. She worked in 2000–2014 as co-founder and researcher at the Centre for European Studies – EU Centre at the European University St. Petersburg; in 2008–2013 she also worked as Russian Deputy Director of the Centre for German and European Studies and in 2004–2019 she taught at St. Petersburg State University. Her research interests include civil society, EU-Russia cross-border cooperation and local politics.

Fabienne Bossuyt
is Professor at the Centre for EU Studies, Department of Political Science, at Ghent University (Belgium). She holds a PhD in Politics and International Relations from Aston University and a PhD in EU Studies from Ghent University. Her main area of expertise is the EU's foreign policy and, in particular, the EU's relations with the post-Soviet space. Her most recent research projects focus on various aspects of the EU's relations with and policies towards post-Soviet countries, including democracy promotion, development policy and human rights promotion. She has published articles in, among others, *Democratization, Cambridge Review of International Affairs, Journal of International Relations and Development, Eurasian Geography and Economics, East European Politics & Societies,* and *Communist and Post-Communist Studies*. She is currently co-editing a book on the EU's and China's engagement with Central Asia (Routledge) and a double special issue on the Sino-Russian relationship for the journal *Eurasian Geography and Economics*.

Celia Challet
is Academic Assistant at the College of Europe in Bruges in the European Legal Studies Department. She holds an LLM in EU Law from the College of Europe (2018–2019 Manuel Marín promotion) and a master's degree in European Business Law from the University Paris II Panthéon-Assas. She is a PhD candidate at the University of Ghent, where she is preparing a PhD thesis devoted to the judicial review of EU sanctions adopted in response to the crisis in Ukraine.

Laure Delcour

is Associate Professor at Université Paris 3-Sorbonne nouvelle and Visiting Professor at the College of Europe. Her research interests focus on the EU's and Russia's policies in their 'contested neighbourhood', domestic change in Eastern Europe and the South Caucasus as well as region-building processes in Eurasia. She has taken part in EU-FP7/H-2020 projects and published extensively on these topics.

Andrey Demidov

works as Scientific Coordinator at the Institute for Advanced Study at the Central European University (CEU). He obtained his PhD from the same institution in 2014 and since then he has worked as Visiting Professor at the CEU Department of Public Policy, as Postdoctoral Fellow at ACCESS Europe (Amsterdam Center for European Studies) and as Lecturer at the University of Amsterdam. His research interests include civil society, EU-Russia relations and EU public policy.

Kirill Entin

is Deputy Registrar – Head of the Legal Research and Analysis Department at the Eurasian Economic Union Court. He graduated in EU Law with honours from the Moscow State Institute of International Relations (MGIMO University) and the College of Europe (Bruges) in 2008. In 2011, he defended a PhD thesis in EU Law. He also completed research projects on the legal aspects of EU autonomous restrictive measures at the Institute of European Law in Fribourg (Switzerland) in 2015 and on the comparison between the case law of the Eurasian Economic Union (EAEU) Court and the Court of Justice of the European Union (CJEU) at the Ghent European Law Institute in 2019. Before taking his position at the EAEU Court, he worked as Associate Professor at Higher School of Economics (HSE) developing and teaching courses on EU law, EU-Russia relations and public international law. In 2012–2013, he became the first Russian paid trainee at the CJEU. He is currently Head of the Eurasian Sector at the Centre for Comprehensive European and International Studies at HSE and is a Member of the board of editors of the International Justice journal (*Mezhdunarodnoe pravosudie*).

Narine Ghazaryan

is Associate Professor in Law at the School of Law, University of Nottingham. She specialises in EU international relations law with an interest in the EU's relations with its neighbouring countries. She has published a monograph, journal articles and book chapters in the field. Ghazaryan has acted as an expert on the subject of the EU's human rights policies in its neighbouring countries in EU-funded projects.

Benedikt Harzl
is Assistant Professor at the Russian East European Eurasian Studies Centre (REEES) of the Law Faculty of the University of Graz. He has worked in various research institutions across Europe, among them the European Academy of Bozen/Bolzano (Italy) in 2007–2012. While the University of Graz is Harzl's alma mater, he completed his PhD in Law at the University of Frankfurt. His research interests cover issues pertaining to international and EU law in the post-Soviet space as well as ethnic conflicts in the South Caucasus.

Alexandra Hofer
is Assistant Professor in Public International Law at Utrecht University School of Law, Department of International and European Law. She is a member of the Utrecht Centre for Regulation and Enforcement in Europe (RENFORCE). She received her PhD in international law from Ghent University and is an affiliated member of the Ghent Rolin-Jaequemyns International Law Institute (GRILI).

Thomas Kruessmann
is Academic Director of the Master of Arts programme 'International Corporate Compliance and Business Ethics' at the Higher School of Economics (Moscow). In addition, he is co-ordinator of the Erasmus+ Capacity Building in Higher Education Project 'Modernisation of Master Programmes for Future Judges, Prosecutors, Investigators with respect to European Standard on Human Rights' for Ukraine and Belarus with the University of Graz. As President of the Association of European Studies for the Caucasus, he devotes himself to European Studies in the wider Caucasus region, including by acting as Series Editor of the book series 'European Studies in the Caucasus'. He is Founding Director of the Russian, East European & Eurasian Studies Centre at the University of Graz (2010–2015) and Visiting Professor at Kazan Federal University (2015–2016). Beyond the Caucasus, his research interests extend to issues of comparative, European and international criminal law, as well as corruption and compliance.

Natalia Leskina
is Doctoral Researcher at the Department of International Relations at Ural Federal University, Russia. Her research interest is higher education regionalism with a regional focus on the post-Soviet space.

Andreas Marazis
is Head of Research for Eastern Europe and Central Asia at the European Neighbourhood Council (ENC). His research deals with the post-Soviet space, particularly sociopolitical developments in Central Asia and the South Caucasus. Marazis is also Affiliated Researcher at Vrije Universiteit Brussel (VUB) and Associate Researcher for Europe-Central Asia Monitoring (EUCAM). Before joining ENC, he worked as Junior Researcher and EUCAM Programme Officer for the Foundation for International Relations and Foreign Dialogue (FRIDE), and as Project Manager for Eurasian Dialogue. Marazis holds a MLitt in Middle East, Caucasus and Central Asian Security Studies from the University of St. Andrews (Scotland) and an MA in Black Sea Cultural Studies from the International Hellenic University (Thessaloniki, Greece).

Igor Merheim-Eyre
works in the European Parliament as Head of Office of an MEP. He focuses mainly on issues related to foreign policy, security and defence, and the EU's relations with its Eastern neighbours. He is also Research Fellow at the Global Europe Centre (University of Kent), and within the Global Challenges Research Fund (GCRF) Comprehensive Capacity Building in Eastern Neighbourhood and Central Asia (COMPASS) Project. Merheim-Eyre publishes regularly on issues related to wider European security. He received his PhD from the University of Kent in 2017, and has previously worked in international democracy support.

Elena Pavlova
is Associate Professor at St. Petersburg State University and Senior Researcher at the University of Tartu. She obtained her PhD from St. Petersburg State University in 2000. Her research interests include contemporary political philosophy, theory of international relations, Russian foreign policy and EU-Russian normative competition. She has published widely on these issues, including in the *Journal of International Relations and Development, Problems of Post-Communism, Scando-Slavica* and *Perspectives on European Politics and Society*.

Irina Petrova
is Postdoctoral Researcher at the GCRF COMPASS project, School of Politics and International Relations, University of Kent. She holds a doctoral degree in Social Sciences from the University of Leuven. Previously, Petrova worked as Assistant at the 'Master of European Studies' programme at the University of Leuven, Adjunct Lecturer at the Vesalius College (Vrije Universiteit Brussel) and Research Associate at the Brussels School of International

Studies (BSIS) at the University of Kent. Her research interests focus on the interaction of external and internal actors in international relations, particularly the development of the novel approach of resilience-based governance anchored in local preferences and perceptions. Geographically, her research focuses on the European Union, Russia, Eastern Partnership and Central Asian states.

Olga Potemkina
is Head of the European Integration Studies at the Institute of Europe, Russian Academy of Sciences (IE RAS). She graduated from the Faculty of History, Moscow State University (MGU), holds a PhD in history (1990) and is Doctor of Political Science (2013). Previously, she worked at the Institute of International Labour Movement (later the Institute of Comparative Political Studies), RAS. Since 1994, she has been working at the Institute of Europe. Her teaching experience includes MGIMO University, Faculty of International Relations, and Moscow State University, Faculty of World Politics. She is Board Member of the Russian Association of European Studies (AES) and Editorial Board Member of the journals *Contemporary Europe* (IE RAS), *Vestnik MGU: World Politics*. Her main research areas are the European Union and Russia, European cooperation on internal security, migration processes in Europe, and integration processes in Europe.

Tatiana Romanova
is Associate Professor at St. Petersburg State University and at the Higher School of Economics. She obtained her PhD from St. Petersburg State University in 2002. She was Jean Monnet Chair holder in 2011 and Director of the Jean Monnet Centre of Excellence at St. Petersburg State University in 2015. Her research interests include EU-Russia relations, European integration and Russian foreign policy. She has published widely on these issues, including in *European Foreign Affairs Review, Journal of Contemporary European Studies, International Spectator, Europe-Asia Studies* and *Geopolitics*.

Marco Siddi
is Senior Research Fellow at the Finnish Institute of International Affairs, where he focuses primarily on EU-Russia relations and EU energy policy. He is also Visiting Professor at the University of Cagliari, and he regularly lectures at the Universities of Helsinki and Tampere. His publications include the monograph *National Identities and Foreign Policy in the European Union* (ECPR Press, 2017) and articles in various journals, including *Europe-Asia Studies, Politics, Geopolitics, The International Spectator, Journal of Contemporary European*

Studies and *International Politics*. He holds a PhD in Politics from the University of Edinburgh.

Niels Smeets

is Postdoctoral Research Fellow at the Leuven International and European Studies institute (LINES), KU Leuven, Belgium. He holds a PhD in Social Sciences from KU Leuven on explaining Russia's renewable energy policies. During his field research, he was Visiting Scholar at the Primakov Institute of World Economy and International Relations, and the Institute of Europe, both of the Russian Academy of Sciences in Moscow during the pivotal years 2014–2015. He has a multidisciplinary background, holding master's degrees in Comparative and International Politics, Management, and Slavonic Studies. In this last field, he published the first Ukrainian grammar for Dutch speakers, as well as a dictionary. He served as Intern in the EU Commission Support Group for Ukraine, gaining firsthand experience in EU policy-making. Currently, he is Energy Policy Officer at the Belgian Federal Public Service (FPS) Economy.

Domenico Valenza

is PhD Fellow at the United Nations University – Institute on Comparative Regional Integration Studies (UNU-CRIS) and at the Department of Political Science at Ghent University (Belgium). In his PhD research, he enquires into the role of culture in foreign affairs and analyses the EU's and Russia's cultural diplomacy discourses and practices towards the post-Soviet space. Valenza holds an MA in European Studies from Université Paris 8 Saint Denis and Université libre de Bruxelles, and an MSc in 'Russia in Global Systems' from King's College London. Prior to joining UNU-CRIS and Ghent University, he worked at No Peace Without Justice as Programme Officer and at the College of Europe, Bruges, as Senior Academic Assistant.

Tony van der Togt

is Associate Senior Research Fellow at the Russia Centre of the Clingendael Institute in The Hague, and Strategic Policy Adviser for the Europe Department at the Netherlands Ministry of Foreign Affairs. After studying contemporary history in Amsterdam (Free University) and Nijmegen, he had a long career as a Dutch diplomat, dealing with Eastern Europe and Central Asia, in The Hague and in Moscow, Almaty and St. Petersburg. In 2013, he acted as Dutch Co-ordinator of the Netherlands-Russia bilateral year. He has published widely on EU-Russia relations, the EU's Eastern Partnership, Dutch-Russian bilateral relations and the Eurasian Economic Union. He is also a regular contributor to a number of dialogue platforms with Russian and other international experts, including in the framework of the EU-Russia Expert Network, the Minsk Dialogue and the Cooperative Security Initiative.

Peter Van Elsuwege
is Professor in EU Law and Jean Monnet Chair holder at Ghent University, where he is Co-director of the Ghent European Law Institute (GELI). He is also Visiting Professor at the College of Europe (Natolin Campus) and Board Member of the Centre for the Law of EU External Relations (CLEER) at the Asser Institute in The Hague. His research activities essentially focus on the law of EU external relations and EU citizenship. Specific attention is devoted to the legal framework of the relations between the European Union and its East European neighbours. He is, among others, the author of *From Soviet Republics to EU Member States: A Legal and Political Assessment of the Baltic States' Accession to the EU* (Brill 2008) and Editor (together with R. Petrov) of the books *Legislative Approximation and Application of EU Law in the Eastern Neighbourhood of the European Union: Towards a Common Regulatory Space?* (Routledge 2014) and *Post-Soviet Constitutions and Challenges of Regional Integration* (Routledge 2018).

Sebastiaan Van Severen
is PhD Researcher in International Law at Ghent University and a member of the Ghent Rolin Jaequemyns International Law Institute (GRILI). He conducts research on themes of comparative international law, self-determination and nationhood, with a particular interest in Russia and the Commonwealth of Independent States.

GENERAL INTRODUCTION

From Strategic Partner to Strategic Challenge: In Search of an EU Policy towards Russia

Peter Van Elsuwege and Fabienne Bossuyt

1 Introduction

In a Joint Declaration, adopted on 3 December 1993, Russia and the European Union (EU) laid down the foundations for a new partnership that was expected to 'enhance stability, security and prosperity for the whole of Europe'.[1] For this purpose, a Partnership and Cooperation Agreement (PCA) was signed in Corfu in June 1994 and entered into force in December 1997 for an initial period of ten years.[2] The PCA aimed to establish an appropriate framework for close political and economic relations leading to 'the gradual integration between Russia and a wider area of cooperation in Europe'.[3] However, it soon became clear that notwithstanding its attractive title and ambitious objectives, the PCA *as such* was insufficient to handle the multifaceted challenges of EU-Russia cooperation. The impossibility to adopt legally binding decisions within the PCA institutional structures as well as the general nature of most provisions quickly revealed the limits of this legal instrument. Moreover, the PCA essentially aimed to support Russia's economic and political transition after the demise of the Soviet Union without offering concrete perspectives for the long-term development of EU-Russia relations.[4]

As a complement to the PCA, the June 1999 Cologne European Council adopted the Common Strategy on Russia (CSR) within the framework of the

---

1   Joint Political Declaration on Partnership and Cooperation between the Russian Federation and the European Union, 9 December 1993, IP/93/1102, available at: <https://ec.europa.eu/commission/presscorner/detail/en/IP_93_1102> (last accessed 1 September 2020).
2   Agreement on Partnership and Cooperation establishing a Partnership between the European Communities and their Member States, of one part, and the Russian Federation, of the other part, *OJ*, 1997, L 327/3.
3   *Ibid.*, Art. 1 PCA.
4   P. Van Elsuwege, 'Towards a Modernisation of EU-Russia Legal Relations?', *CEURUS EU-Russia Papers* 2012 (5), 3–7, available at: <http://ceurus.ut.ee/wp-content/uploads/2011/06/EU-Russia-Paper-51.pdf> (last accessed 1 September 2020).

EU's Common Foreign and Security Policy (CFSP).⁵ The CSR identified the EU's ambitions for the development of a 'Strategic Partnership' with Russia. However, despite high expectations and good intentions, the CSR scarcely concealed the lack of a strategic vision on the part of the EU, particularly with respect to the implications of the EU's eastward enlargement.⁶ The document simply observed that this process would bring benefits and opportunities to all countries in Europe, including Russia, without addressing its specific economic, legal and political consequences for EU-Russia relations. The limits of this approach became obvious in the discussions surrounding sensitive issues such as Kaliningrad transit and the protection of Russian-speaking minorities.⁷

Whereas the PCA institutional structures, in particular the organisation of biannual EU-Russia summits, proved instrumental in reaching last-minute compromises, the absence of a possibility to adopt legally binding decisions implied that any progress in EU-Russia relations was essentially based on the adoption of joint statements with a purely political value. Often, those political statements turned out to be nothing more than vague diplomatic declarations without any tangible content.⁸ Accordingly, there appeared to be an increasing gap between the political discourse of 'Strategic Partnership' and the reality of growing distrust on the ground. This became very visible with respect to the implementation of the so-called 'four Common Spaces', which had been launched on the occasion of the May 2003 Saint Petersburg EU-Russia Summit as the new strategic framework replacing the CSR. For the first time, the EU and Russia agreed on a joint and comprehensive agenda for future cooperation on a wide variety of issues ranging from, among others, the deepening of trade relations and energy cooperation to internal and external security, the fight against organised crime, migration and asylum, as well as culture and education.⁹ However, the legal framework of EU-Russia relations

---

5   Common Strategy of the European Union of 4 June 1999 on Russia, 1999/414/CFSP, *OJ*, 1999, L 157/1.
6   See, for example, M. Maresceau, 'EU Enlargement and EU Common Strategies on Russia and Ukraine: An Ambiguous yet Unavoidable Connection', in C. Hillion (ed.), *EU Enlargement: A Legal Approach* (Hart 2004), 181–219.
7   See: P. Van Elsuwege, *From Soviet Republics to EU Member States: A Legal and Political Assessment of the Baltic States' Accession to the EU* (Brill | Nijhoff 2008), 335–346 and 399–410.
8   K. Böttger, 'Interdependence as a Leitmotiv in the EU's Russia Policy: A Failure to Live Up to Expectations', in: K. Raik and A. Racz (eds.), *Post-Crimea Shift in EU-Russia Relations: From Fostering Independence to Managing Vulnerabilities* (Tallinn, International Centre for Defence and Security 2019), 50–51.
9   P. Van Elsuwege 'The Four Common Spaces: New Impetus to the EU-Russia Strategic Partnership?', in: A. Dashwood and M. Maresceau (eds.), *Law and Practice of EU External*

was not adapted to the implementation of this ambitious cooperation agenda. The weak dispute settlement mechanism, the impossibility to adopt legally binding decisions within the Permanent Partnership Council and the absence of formal legal provisions on issues such as energy and investment protection were the most obvious shortcomings.[10] Moreover, the so-called 'coloured revolutions' in Georgia and Ukraine revealed the growing geopolitical tensions in the region. A series of disputes with several EU Member States further complicated the development of EU-Russia relations.[11] In this context, EU-Russia relations reached a first freezing point in May 2007 when, in contrast to previous practice, the summit meeting held in Samara ended without a joint declaration.

It was only on the occasion of the 26–27 June 2008 EU-Russia Summit in Khanty-Mansiysk that a new atmosphere in the bilateral relationship could be perceived. This gathering, for the first time chaired by the new Russian President, Dmitry Medvedev, and organised under the auspices of Slovenia as the first new EU Member State to hold the Presidency of the EU, formally launched the negotiations for a new bilateral framework agreement to replace the outdated PCA.[12] Unfortunately, the new enthusiasm quickly received a major blow with the outbreak of the military conflict between Russia and Georgia in August 2008 and Russia's unilateral decision to recognise the independence of Abkhazia and South Ossetia. In response, the EU decided at an extraordinary European Council meeting to postpone the negotiations on the new partnership agreement.[13] However, the European Commission quickly suggested the resumption of the negotiating process,

---

Relations: Salient Features of a Changing Landscape (Cambridge University Press 2008), 334–359.

[10] P. Van Elsuwege, 'The Legal Framework of EU-Russia Relations: *Quo Vadis?*', in: I. Govaere, E. Lannon, P. Van Elsuwege and S. Adam (eds.), *The European Union in the World: Essays in Honour of Marc Maresceau* (Brill | Nijhoff 2014), 446.

[11] Reference could, for instance, be made to the Russian import ban on Polish agricultural products, the Litvinenko affair in the United Kingdom, the Mazeikiu refinery dispute with Lithuania and the Estonian monument crisis. See: M. Roth, 'Bilateral Disputes between EU Member States and Russia', CEPS Working Document No. 319/2009, available at: <https://www.ceps.eu/ceps-publications/bilateral-disputes-between-eu-member-states-and-russia/> (last accessed 1 September 2020).

[12] Joint Statement on the launch of negotiations for a new EU-Russia agreement, Khanty-Mansiysk, 27 June 2008, available at: <http://www.consilium.europa.eu/ueDocs/cms_Data/docs/pressData/en/er/101524.pdf>.

[13] Presidency Conclusions Extraordinary European Council, Brussels, 1 September 2008, *Bulletin EU* 9 (2008), I.2.11.

arguing that an open dialogue on issues of disagreement would be a better option than a simple suspension of the negotiations.[14] This position was later confirmed by the General Affairs and External Relations Council, which opened the gates towards the formal start of negotiations for a new strategic agreement in December 2008.[15] Subsequently, the EU and Russia also launched the so-called 'Partnership for Modernisation' at the 2010 Rostov-on-Don EU-Russia Summit. This new initiative supplemented the Common Spaces road maps with a joint programme for pragmatic bilateral cooperation.[16]

However, these efforts to reinvigorate the EU-Russia Strategic Partnership could not conceal the growing divergence between the positions and interests of both parties. This became particularly visible with respect to their competing paradigms for the development of relations within the so-called 'shared neighbourhood' of post-Soviet republics. Whereas the EU launched the Eastern Partnership (EaP) as part of its European Neighbourhood Policy (ENP) to promote the export of its own values and norms, Russia increasingly promoted the process of Eurasian regional integration within the framework of the Eurasian Economic Union (EAEU). In this regard, the EU's offer of political association and economic integration in the form of Deep and Comprehensive Free Trade Areas (DCFTAs) on the basis of a far-reaching process of legislative approximation clashed with the logic of Eurasian economic integration within the EAEU.[17] Against this background of opposing approaches, 'a serious conflict was waiting to happen', as a former Head of the European Commission Delegation to Russia put it.[18]

---

14   Communication from the Commission to the Council, *Review of EU-Russia Relations*, COM (2008) 740 final, Brussels, 5 November 2008, 5.
15   Council of the EU, Doc. 15396/08, 10–11 November 2008.
16   Joint Statement on the Partnership for Modernisation, EU-Russia Summit, 1 June 2010, Doc. 10546/10.
17   In particular, for the EaP countries, the establishment of a bilateral DCFTA with the EU is legally not compatible with participation in the customs union of the EAEU. See further: G. Van der Loo and P. Van Elsuwege, 'Competing Paths of Regional Economic Integration in the Post-Soviet Space: Legal and Political Dilemmas for Ukraine', *Review of Central and East European Law* 37 (4), 2012, 421–447; and P. Van Elsuwege, 'The European Union and the Eurasian Economic Union: Searching for the Lowest Common Denominator', in: O. Potemkina (ed.), *The EU Global Strategy: Implications for Russia* (RAS-Egmont Institute 2017), 63–81.
18   M. Franco, 'EU-Russia Relations: From Hope to Despair. Can the New EU Global Strategy Make a Difference?', in: O. Potemkina (ed.), *The EU Global Strategy: Implications for Russia* (RAS-Egmont Institute 2017), 34.

2 The Ukraine Crisis: A Critical Juncture in EU-Russia Relations?

In anticipation of the Vilnius EaP Summit, scheduled to take place in November 2013, Armenian President Serzh Sargsyan declared that his country would join the customs union between Russia, Belarus and Kazakhstan – and later the EAEU – instead of concluding an Association Agreement (AA) with the EU. The Armenian U-turn was the prelude of a similar scenario in Ukraine. A few days before the EaP Summit in Vilnius, the Ukrainian government decided to suspend the process of preparation for signature of the AA 'to ensure the national security of Ukraine and to recover trade and economic relations with the Russian Federation'.[19] This news sparked mass demonstrations and became the start of the so-called 'Maidan revolution', leading to the ousting of President Viktor Yanukovych on 22 February 2014.[20]

In the wake of the Maidan revolution, pro-Russian demonstrations were held in the Crimean city of Sevastopol. By the end of February 2014, so-called 'little green men' (armed men in uniforms without insignia) captured strategic positions and the Supreme Council of Crimea decided to organise a referendum, which paved the way to the incorporation of the Crimean Peninsula in the territory of the Russian Federation. Subsequent unrest in the Donetsk and Luhansk Oblasts (regions) of Ukraine, commonly known as the Donbas area, escalated into an armed conflict and the creation of the self-declared Donetsk and Luhansk People's Republics.

These events formed the background for a unprecedented crisis in EU-Russia relations. On the occasion of an extraordinary Council meeting held on 3 March 2014, the EU Ministers for Foreign Affairs not only strongly condemned 'the clear violation of Ukraine's sovereignty and territorial integrity by acts of aggression by the Russian armed forces' but also warned that 'in the absence of de-escalating steps by Russia, the EU shall decide about consequences for bilateral relations between the EU and Russia'.[21] This included, in the first place, the suspension of bilateral talks on visa matters and a new bilateral legal framework to replace the largely outdated PCA. Subsequently, and in response to the increasing violence in the Donbas region and the downing of

---

19 Decision of the Cabinet of Ministers of Ukraine from 21st November 2013, N 905-p.
20 Also known as the 'Euromaidan Revolution' or the 'Revolution of Dignity' in Ukraine. It is noteworthy that Russia holds an entirely different view of the events and considers the Maidan protests as an anti-constitutional coup d'état. See on these divergent views, the contribution by I. Petrova (chapter 3) in this volume.
21 Council of the EU, Conclusions of the Foreign Affairs Council of 3 March 2014, Doc. 7208/14, Brussels, 4 March 2014.

Malaysian Airlines flight MH17 in the area controlled by pro-Russian separatists, the EU progressively adopted a wide range of restrictive measures in the framework of its CFSP.[22] Russia responded with the adoption of countersanctions such as an import ban on agricultural products and the blacklisting of EU officials and politicians.[23]

The sanctions policy largely paralysed the existing framework for cooperation and significantly affected the EU's discourse towards Russia. Federica Mogherini, EU High Representative for Foreign Affairs and Security Policy at the time, was the first to state that 'Russia is no longer the EU's strategic partner'.[24] Instead, the relationship with Russia is defined as 'a strategic challenge' in the sense that the EU needs to find a new approach, which is no longer based on the assumption that Russia necessarily shares the same norms and values.[25] Hence, the Ukraine crisis may well be regarded as a 'critical juncture' in the development of EU-Russia relations.[26] The paradigms of the past, which were largely based on a belief that Russia is gradually transforming in the direction of a Western-style liberal democracy, no longer hold true and are replaced by a return to *Realpolitik*.[27] The Ukraine crisis has thus led to a paradigm shift in how the EU views Russia, whereby the annexation of Crimea and Russia's military intervention in eastern Ukraine are perceived as fundamental breaches of international law and are considered to mark an end to the post–Cold War European security order.[28]

---

22   For an overview, see: <https://www.consilium.europa.eu/en/policies/sanctions/ukraine-crisis/> (last accessed 25 October 2019). For comments, see the contributions by K. Entin (chapter 5), C. Challet (chapter 6) and A. Hofer (chapter 4) in this volume.

23   P. Kalinichenko, 'Post-Crimean Twister: Russia, the EU and the Law of Sanctions', *Russian Law Review* 5 (3) 2017, 21.

24   See: 'Mogherini: Russia Is No Longer the EU's Strategic Partner', *Euractiv*, 2 September 2014, available at: <https://www.euractiv.com/section/global-europe/news/mogherini-russia-is-no-longer-the-eu-s-strategic-partner/>. See also the Report of the European Parliament Committee on Foreign Affairs from 13 March 2015 (A8-0162/2015, para. 2), which also stressed that 'Russia, because of its actions in Crimea and in Eastern Ukraine, can no longer be treated as, or considered as, a Strategic Partner'.

25   The term *strategic challenge* in relation to Russia is used in the Global Strategy for the EU's Foreign and Security Policy, available at: <http://eeas.europa.eu/archives/docs/top_stories/pdf/eugs_review_web.pdf>.

26   House of Lords European Union Committee, 'The EU and Russia: Before and beyond the Crisis in Ukraine', 6th Report of Session 2014–15, 9.

27   S. Biscop, 'The EU Global Strategy and the Great Powers of Realpolitik Revisited', in: O. Potemkina (ed.), *The EU Global Strategy: Implications for Russia* (RAS-Egmont Institute 2017), 7.

28   T. van der Togt, 'In Search of a European Russia Strategy', *Atlantisch Perspectief*, 1, 2020, 36.

3 The EU's Global Strategy and the 'five guiding principles' for the Development of EU-Russia Relations

A key point of reference for the EU's new approach towards Russia is the *Global Strategy for the European Union's Foreign and Security Policy*, adopted in June 2016.[29] This document provides that:

> A consistent and united approach must remain the cornerstone of EU policy towards Russia. Substantial changes in relations between the EU and Russia are premised upon full respect for international law and the principles underpinning the European security order, including the Helsinki Final Act and the Paris Charter. We will not recognise Russia's illegal annexation of Crimea nor accept the destabilisation of eastern Ukraine. We will strengthen the EU, enhance the resilience of our eastern neighbours, and uphold their right to determine freely their approach towards the EU. At the same time, the EU and Russia are interdependent. We will therefore engage Russia to discuss disagreements and cooperate if and when our interests overlap.[30]

Hence, the EU's approach towards Russia follows the new guideline of '*principled pragmatism*' as the central tenet of the EU's external action.[31] This approach means that the EU will stand firm on key principles, such as respect for international law, democracy and human rights, while at the same time allowing sufficient leeway for the development of pragmatic cooperation in certain areas. Translated to the specific context of EU-Russia relations, this implies that, on the one hand, the EU will not change its position on Crimea or eastern Ukraine but, on the other hand, the door is left open to cooperate with Russia in relation to issues of common interest such as climate change, the situation in the Middle East and the fight against terrorism.

In this respect, the Global Strategy reiterates the so-called '*Five Guiding Principles for the Development of EU-Russia Relations*', as adopted by the General Affairs Council in March 2016.[32] These principles may be regarded as the EU's attempt to develop a new framework for EU-Russia cooperation after the Ukraine crisis and provide a perspective beyond the policy of sanctions.

---

29 EU Global Strategy, *op. cit.* note 25.
30 *Ibid.*, 33.
31 *Ibid.*, 8.
32 Council of the EU, Conclusions of the Foreign Affairs Council, Doc. 7042/16, Brussels, 14 March 2016.

Principle 1: Full Implementation of the Minsk Agreements

According to the first principle, the implementation of the Minsk agreements, which were signed in September 2014 and February 2015 with a view to end the conflict in eastern Ukraine, remains the key condition for any substantial change in the EU's stance towards Russia.[33] In March 2015, the European Council decided that 'the duration of the restrictive measures against the Russian Federation ... should be clearly linked to the complete implementation of the Minsk agreements'.[34] Ever since, this has been the consistent position of the EU and its Member States.[35] It also serves as a point of reference for the periodic extension of the restrictive measures within the framework of the CFSP.[36] However, as argued by Sebastiaan Van Severen in this volume, the implementation of the Minsk agreements is proving extremely cumbersome, and prospects for any improvements are grim. Moreover, the EU and Russia hold entirely different perspectives on the sequencing of the implementation process of the Minsk agreements and on the responsibilities of the parties involved. Whereas the EU's policy focuses on the role of Russia in the de-escalation process in eastern Ukraine, Russia for its part essentially blames Ukraine and the EU for the lack of progress.[37] Hence, the Minsk agreements and the policy of sanctions clearly illustrate the current paradoxes and challenges of EU-Russia relations.[38]

Principle 2: Strengthened Relations with the EU's Eastern Partners and Other Neighbours

Significantly, the second principle for the development of EU-Russia relations does not concern Russia itself but the EU's relations with its Eastern partners and other neighbours, including in Central Asia. This is linked to the understanding that the development of bilateral EU-Russia relations

---

33 See the contribution by S. Van Severen (chapter 1) in this volume.
34 European Council conclusions, 19–20 March 2015, EUCO 11/15, para. 10.
35 On the role of EU Member States, see the contribution by T. van der Togt (chapter 2) in this volume.
36 See, for example, Council Decision (CFSP) 2019/2192 of 19 December 2019 amending Decision 2014/512/CFSP concerning restrictive measures in view of Russia's actions destabilising the situation in Ukraine, *OJ* (2019) L 330/71.
37 See the contribution by I. Petrova (chapter 3) in this volume.
38 On the legal and political questions surrounding the effectiveness, legality and legitimacy of the sanctions regime, see the contributions by A. Hofer (chapter 4), K. Entin (chapter 5) and C. Challet (chapter 6) in this volume.

cannot be disconnected from the wider neighbourhood of former Soviet republics and the process of regional integration within the EAEU. The latter significantly affects the legal and political framework of EU-Russia relations in the sense that the transfer of Russia's trade competences to the EAEU level limits the scope for bilateral trade integration. In principle, Russia's World Trade Organisation (WTO) membership could have opened the gates to negotiations on a bilateral free trade agreement as foreseen under Article 3 of the PCA. However, this option was never really on the negotiating table and, as a consequence of the common customs policy of the EAEU, it is now even no longer possible. The only alternative option is to work towards a free trade agreement between the EU and the EAEU leading to a situation of 'free trade from Lisbon to Vladivostok', as suggested by Vladimir Putin on several occasions.[39] However, such a scenario is not very realistic. From an EU perspective, there is a clear pitfall that a formalisation of EU-EAEU relations creates a 'bloc' to 'bloc' dynamic which is potentially detrimental for the EU's bilateral relations with the countries in the region. Hence, the right of every country to freely choose the level of ambitions and the goals to which it aspires with the EU is of fundamental importance in the context of EU-Russia relations.[40]

Finding a balance between accepting the EAEU as a new reality in the region without undermining the scope for the development of differentiated bilateral relations with the countries of the post-Soviet space is an important challenge for the EU. In this respect, the conclusion of new bilateral agreements with the EAEU countries of Kazakhstan, Kyrgyzstan and Armenia is of particular significance in the sense that it illustrates that EAEU membership is reconcilable with close bilateral links with the EU.[41] The Comprehensive and Enhanced Partnership Agreement (CEPA) with Armenia deserves particular attention, taking into account that this country is an active participant of the EaP, which initially started negotiations on a more far-reaching Association Agreement but later decided to join the EAEU. Accordingly, as Laure Delcour and Narine Ghazaryan observe in this volume, Armenia became 'a litmus test for both the

---

39   See, for example, V. Putin, 'A New Integration Project for Eurasia: The Future in the Making', *Izvestiia*, 3 October 2011, available at: <https://russiaeu.ru/en/news/article-prime-minister-vladimir-putin-new-integration-project-eurasia-future-making-izvestia-3-> (last accessed 1 September 2020).
40   P. Van Elsuwege, *op. cit.* note 17, 75.
41   L. Delcour, H. Kostanyan, B. Vandecasteele and P. Van Elsuwege, 'The Implications of Eurasian Integration for the EU's Relations with the Countries in the Post-Soviet Space', *Studia Diplomatica* 68 (1) 2015, 25–26.

EU's ability to strengthen ties with its Eastern partners and Russia's acceptation thereof'.[42]

Apart from the development of new bilateral relations with all post-Soviet countries, certain specific issues also fall within the scope of the second principle for the development of EU-Russia relations. This concerns, among others, the unresolved question of the so-called 'frozen conflicts' and *de facto* states in the post-Soviet space.[43] Whereas most of these conflicts go back to the ethnopolitical upheavals shortly before and after the collapse of the Soviet Union, the self-proclaimed Donetsk and Lugansk People's Republics (DPR and LPR) in eastern Ukraine create a new security challenge at the EU's Eastern borders. In this context, phenomena such as 'passportisation' and 'visa diplomacy' play an increasingly important role in the contested neighbourhood between Russia and the EU.[44]

Principle 3: EU Resilience to Russian Threats

According to the third guiding principle, the EU should strengthen its resilience to Russian threats, including military and hybrid threats.[45] The longest standing threat remains the EU's energy dependence on Russia. While EU resilience in this field has improved since the Russian-Ukrainian gas crisis in 2009,[46] several EU Member States are still highly dependent on the supply of Russian gas for their energy provision. The Ukraine crisis of 2013–2014 only reinforced the importance of energy security as one of the key issues on the agenda of EU-Russia relations. This resulted in new initiatives, such as the Energy Union, to reduce the independence from Russia's energy supplies. At the same time, however, the energy relationship with Russia remains important, implying that energy cooperation also forms a certain form of 'selective engagement' as defined under the EU's fourth guiding principle (cf. *infra*).[47]

---

42   See the contribution by L. Delcour and N. Ghazaryan (chapter 7) in this volume.

43   See the contribution by B. Harzl (chapter 8) in this volume.

44   Whereas 'passportisation' involves the issuance of passports for foreign policy goals, 'visa diplomacy' entails the use of visa as an instrument to facilitate or complicate travel to influence relations with neighbouring countries. See the contribution by I. Merheim-Eyre (chapter 9) in this volume.

45   On the concept of 'resilience' and its application in the context of EU-Russia relations, see the chapter by E. Pavlova and T. Romanova (chapter 10) in this volume.

46   S. De Jong and S. Sterkx, 'The 2009 Russian-Ukrainian Gas Dispute: Lessons for European Energy Crisis Management after Lisbon', *European Foreign Affairs Review* 15 (4) 2010, 511–538.

47   See the contributions by M. Siddi (chapter 11) and N. Smeets (chapter 14) in this volume.

More recently, new threats have emerged. Since the Ukraine crisis, Russia has significantly scaled up its military activities along its border with the Baltic countries and has not been afraid of sending Russian warplanes into North Atlantic Treaty Organisation (NATO) airspace. However, given that NATO's military capabilities and resources are far more extensive than those of Russia, the EU is much more wary of the arsenal of non-military tools that Russia seems to have at its disposal. These tools include cyber attacks and the dissemination of fake news through mass media and social media. Hence, protection against these types of 'hybrid warfare' has risen significantly on the security agenda of the EU.[48]

Principle 4: Selective Engagement with Russia

The fourth guiding principle spells out the need for 'selective engagement' with Russia over matters of common interest. Although the conflict in Ukraine and the ensuing introduction of restrictive measures disrupt the potential for cooperation on several issues, the EU acknowledges that the high level of interdependence means that it needs to find a common language again with Russia to address common challenges. Therefore, as highlighted also in the EU's Global Strategy of June 2016, the EU wants 'selective engagement' with Russia both on pressing foreign policy issues, such as Syria and counter-terrorism, and in other areas where there is a clear EU interest such as climate, the Arctic, maritime security, education, research and cross-border cooperation.[49]

Hence, the EU's approach towards Russia is not limited to a policy of sanctions but also involves a certain level of cooperation in specific areas of common interest. This fully reflects the spirit of 'principled pragmatism' as outlined above. Of course, such a policy is not without challenges in the sense that the sanctions regime and the lack of trust complicate the level of engagement in practice. This can, among other things, be illustrated with respect to the tackling of transnational security threats, cooperation around the Arctic region and in the field of renewable energy.[50]

Principle 5: Supporting Russian civil society and engaging in people-to-people contacts

---

48 See the contribution by A. Marazis (chapter 11) in this volume.
49 Global Strategy, *op. cit.* note 25, 33.
50 See the contributions by O. Potemkina (chapter 13), N. Smeets (chapter 14) and T. Kruessmann (chapter 15) in this volume.

According to the fifth guiding principle, the EU should continue to support Russian civil society and engage in people-to-people contacts. In a context of strained official relations between the EU and Russia, it is deemed important to invest in strengthening societal ties through student exchanges, civil society cooperation, research and cross-border cooperation and business contacts. As Russia's civic space is under pressure, assistance to civil society and people-to-people contacts requires new approaches with a growing emphasis on cultural relations and public diplomacy.[51] Last but not least, it is noteworthy that Russia's integration in the European Higher Education Area (EHEA) remains on the agenda and the EU even increasingly focuses on cooperation in the area of education and research as part of the development of EU-Russia relations.[52]

4   Conclusion

EU-Russia relations have gone a long way. After an initial period of high expectations about the development of a Strategic Partnership based on shared values, a growing list of legal, political and economic irritants gradually undermined the prospects for close cooperation. Domestic developments in Russia and the EU, as well as diverging perspectives on the implications of the EU's eastward enlargement and ENP, formed the background for a climate of political distrust in which it became impossible to modernise the largely outdated PCA.

In this context, the events of 2013–2014 with the Maidan revolution, the Russian annexation of Crimea and the outbreak of violence in the Donbas region may be regarded as the result of a long-term process where both the EU and Russia gradually alienated from each other and largely followed their own logic and strategic narratives. At the same time, the Ukraine crisis is also a critical juncture in the development of EU-Russia relations. It made an abrupt end to the discourse of Strategic Partnership and entailed a return to a more realist approach and a policy of sanctions. Whereas the adoption of restrictive measures appears a logical, short-term response to the dramatic events, the key challenge is to define a new long-term strategy for the future of EU-Russia relations, which is able to overcome the current deadlock and lay the basis for a more positive and sustainable bilateral relationship.

For the time being, the five guiding principles for the development of EU-Russia relations adopted by the EU Foreign Affairs Council in March 2016,

---

51   See the contributions by E. Belokurova and A. Demidov (chapter 16) and D. Valenza (chapter 17) in this volume.
52   See the contribution by N. Leskina (chapter 18) in this volume.

continue to provide the framework for cooperation. The principles may be seen as an operationalisation of the new mantra of 'principled pragmatism', as introduced in the Global Strategy. This implies, on the one hand, the strict observance of the EU's basic values such as respect for the rule of law and principles of international law and, on the other hand, sufficient leeway to cooperate with Russia in areas of common interest. It is increasingly clear that this is only an intermediate solution, in between a policy of confinement based on sanctions and a potential return to 'business as usual'.

PART 1

The Minsk Agreements and the Sanctions Regime in EU-Russia Relations

CHAPTER 1

The Minsk Agreements
Has the Glimmer of Hope Faded?

Sebastiaan Van Severen

1   Introduction

Since March 2014, the EU has steadily extended and increased its sanctions against Russia including diplomatic measures, asset freezes, travel restrictions and multiple types of economic sanctions.[1] At the basis of this sanctions regime lie two interrelated crises. The first one is Russia's annexation of the Autonomous Republic of Crimea following a disputed referendum. The second is the armed conflict in the Donbas region in eastern Ukraine. EU sanctions have officially been imposed on the Russian Federation as a reaction to both crises.[2] However, the EU treats the possible relaxation of the sanctions separately in relation to both cases. EU leaders repeatedly insisted that the restrictive measures imposed on Russia and its citizens can be loosened only on the condition that the Minsk agreements be implemented.[3] This course of action is also mentioned in the first principle of the five guiding principles of the EU's policy towards Russia. Significantly, despite the EU's commitment to the principle of non-recognition[4] and to UN General Assembly Resolution 68/

---

1 For a more extensive discussion of the EU's sanctions against Russia, see the contributions of K. Entin (chapter 5) and A. Hofer (chapter 4) in this volume.
2 See: Council of the EU, 'EU restrictive sanctions in response to the crisis in Ukraine', at: <https://www.consilium.europa.eu/en/policies/sanctions/ukraine-crisis/> (accessed 18 September 2020).
3 'The European Council agreed that the duration of the restrictive measures against the Russian Federation, adopted on 31 July 2014 and enhanced on 8 September 2014, should be clearly linked to the complete implementation of the Minsk agreements', see: European Council on External Relations, Conclusions 19–20 March 2015, EUCO 11/15, available at: <www.consilium.europa.eu/en/press/press-releases/2015/03/19/conclusions-russia-ukraine-european-council-march-2015/> (accessed 7 April 2019).
4 European Council conclusions, 13–14 December 2018, Doc. No. 789/18, available at: <www.consilium.europa.eu/en/press/press-releases/2018/12/14/european-council-conclusions-13-14-december-2018/pdf> (accessed 7 April 2019).

262,[5] there is no reference to Crimea in the Minsk agreements. This not only suggests Russia's solid negotiation position on the Crimean issue, if not a *fait accompli* with regard to Russian control over the peninsula, but also indicates the careful balancing act by the EU, in which it attempts to facilitate partial solutions by compartmentalising the conflict.

This chapter aims to provide the necessary background to contextualise the Minsk agreements. The war in Donbas is not retold exhaustively, so any political developments or major military events that are not strictly relevant to the Minsk agreements are omitted for the purpose of clarity. The consecutive diplomatic efforts are used as points of reference to narrate the chain of events leading up to the agreements, as they introduced many of the core objectives that were eventually incorporated into the Minsk agreements. Readers will note that the seemingly separate attempts at peace negotiations in fact form one continuous process towards the February 2015 Minsk II agreement. Furthermore, this chapter lays out the contents, status and implementation of said agreements. It is concluded that virtually none of the provisions in the Minsk agreements have been truly implemented. Nevertheless, it is argued that the Minsk process remains the only viable point of reference for the EU.

1.1   *Geneva Statement*

On 17 April 2014, Russia, the United States and the European Union adopted a joint declaration on the Ukrainian crisis in Geneva. During the meeting, the representatives agreed on initial steps to de-escalate tensions and restore security for the civilian population in eastern Ukraine. From the start, the Geneva Statement had to contend with a cautious wait-and-see attitude from the parties involved, as well as with its own vagueness. US President Barack Obama stated: 'I don't think we can be sure of anything at this point, but there is a chance that diplomacy may de-escalate the situation.'[6] Secretary of State John Kerry described the measures as an important first step to avert 'a complete and total implosion' in Ukraine.[7] According to Russian Foreign Minister

---

5 General Assembly Resolution 68/262, Territorial Integrity of Ukraine, A/RES/68/262, available at: <https://undocs.org/a/68/262> (accessed 7 April 2019).
6 P. Bump, 'Obama sums up Ukraine: "I don't think we can be sure of anything at this point"', available at: <www.theatlantic.com/politics/archive/2014/04/obama-sums-up-ukraine-i-dont-think-we-can-be-sure-of-anything-at-this-point/360847/> (accessed 19 September 2020).
7 M.R. Gordon, 'U.S. and Russia agree on pact to defuse Ukraine crisis', available at: <www.nytimes.com/2014/04/18/world/europe/ukraine-diplomacy.html> (accessed 19 September 2020).

Sergei Lavrov, the deal was 'largely based on compromise', and a settlement of the crisis was primarily Ukraine's responsibility.[8] The Statement entailed five elements to de-escalate the crisis: namely, (1) all sides must refrain from any violence, intimidation or provocation; (2) all illegal armed groups must be disarmed and buildings must be returned; (3) there would be amnesty for the protestors; (4) there would be monitoring by the Organisation for Security and Co-operation in Europe (OSCE) Special Monitoring Mission (SMM); and (5) there would be an inclusive and transparent 'constitutional process'.[9] Each of these objectives would eventually be reflected in both Minsk agreements to some extent.

That the Geneva Statement was marred by its own vagueness, is exemplified in several instances. For one, it introduced to the discourse on Ukraine the key phrase 'all parties to the conflict', which is interpreted differently *by all parties*. It left room for the denial of Russian involvement but could equally be understood as the condemnation of that involvement, without explicitly mentioning Russia. Moreover, the obligation to 'refrain from any violence, intimidation or provocation', however praiseworthy, served Russian strategic aims. After all, it meant that the Ukrainian government could no longer use force against the Russian-backed rebels while, at the same time, bearing the implied responsibility to put in place reforms to provide parts of eastern Ukraine with more autonomy. In that regard, the Russian Foreign Ministry clearly wanted to stress that 'this crisis ... must be settled by Ukrainians.'[10] When US, EU and Ukrainian officials alluded to possible Russian interference, its Foreign Ministry promptly rejected any statements containing 'traces of ultimatum':[11] 'In this regard, we would like to emphasise that exclusively the internal situation in Ukraine was discussed in Geneva.'[12] It was, and still is, crucial for the Kremlin to deny material involvement in the war in Donbas. The Geneva Statement did not make any reference to the sizeable contingent

---

8   *Ibid.*
9   U.S. Mission to Geneva, 'Text of the Geneva Statement on Ukraine released by the US, EU, Ukraine and Russia', available at: <https://geneva.usmission.gov/2014/04/18/text-of-the-geneva-statement-on-ukraine-released-by-the-us-eu-ukraine-and-russia/> (accessed 7 April 2019).
10 Russian Ministry of Foreign Affairs, 'Speech by the Russian Foreign Minister Sergey Lavrov ...', 17 April 2014, available at: <www.mid.ru/en/web/guest/maps/ua/-/asset_publisher/ktn0ZLTvbbS3/content/id/64910> (accessed 7 April 2019).
11 Russian Ministry of Foreign Affairs, 'Comment by the Information and Press Department ...', 18 April 2014, available at: <www.mid.ru/en/web/guest/maps/ua/-/asset_publisher/ktn0ZLTvbbS3/content/id/64830> (accessed 7 April 2019).
12 *Ibid.*

of Russian troops amassed at the Russo-Ukrainian border, nor did it impose any obligations on Russia.

Pro-Russian rebels mostly rejected the deal.[13] A shoot-out in rebel-held Slavyansk on 20 April was the first real threat to the Geneva Statement. Ukrainian authorities accused the Russian military intelligence unit (GRU) of staging the attack, while pro-Russian rebels accused Ukrainian neo-Nazis of a deliberate provocation.[14] By the end of April 2014, both the EU[15] and the United States had adopted targeted sanctions against Russian individuals and several Russian-backed Ukrainian rebels. Western leaders vowed further sanctions if Russia interfered with the Ukrainian presidential elections at the end of May 2014.[16] Coinciding with the European warning in early May, Russian President Vladimir Putin stated that, following the Ukrainian military operations in Slavyansk, the Geneva Statement was no longer viable.[17] A further deterioration of the situation in May 2014 showed that the Statement had indeed exceeded its expiry date.

1.2 *Trilateral Contact Group and the Normandy Format*

In the late spring of 2014, two diplomatic 'formats' emerged in the attempt at de-escalating the Ukrainian crisis. The OSCE-based Trilateral Contact Group would form the basis for the first Minsk Protocol, while the so-called 'Normandy format' would later serve as the negotiation platform for the second Minsk Protocol.

First, on 25 May 2014, Petro Poroshenko was elected as the new Ukrainian President. On the day of his inauguration in the Verkhovna Rada, Poroshenko set out a peace plan entailing, among other goals, amnesty measures and a controlled corridor in the war zone, constitutional reform and decentralisation

---

13   ABC News, 'Ukraine agreement: armed pro-Russian separatists vow to stay in public buildings despite US, EU deal', available at: <www.abc.net.au/news/2014-04-18/pro-russian-separatists-stay-put-despite-deal/5399532> (accessed 7 April 2019).

14   L. Harding, 'Slavyansk shootout threatens to bury Ukraine peace deal', available at: <www.theguardian.com/world/2014/apr/20/ukraine-agreement-falters-shoot-out-slavayansk> (accessed 18 September 2020).

15   Council of the European Union, 'Implementing Regulation 433/2014 of 28 April 2014', OJ (2014) L 126/48.

16   Reuters, 'Obama, Merkel vow broader Russian sanctions if Ukraine election derailed', available at: <www.reuters.com/article/us-ukraine-crisis-obama-merkel/obama-merkel-vow-broader-russian-sanctions-if-ukraine-election-derailed-idUSBREA410UI20140502> (accessed 18 September 2020).

17   A. Luhn, 'Putin says Geneva agreement no longer viable after Ukrainian military action', available at: <www.theguardian.com/world/2014/may/02/putin-geneva-agreement-not-viable-ukraine-military-action> (accessed 18 September 2020)..

of power.[18] To facilitate talks between Russia and Ukraine under auspices of the OSCE, the Trilateral Contact Group on Ukraine was created on 8 June 2014 with a meeting in Kyiv between the Ambassador of Russia to Ukraine Mikhail Zurabov, the Ambassador of Ukraine to Germany Pavlo Klimkin and the Special Representative of the OSCE General Secretary Heidi Tagliavini.[19] The Trilateral Contact Group discussed President Poroshenko's peace plan, which entailed a ceasefire to facilitate peace talks. Poroshenko unveiled his 15-point peace plan on 20 June 2014, while also unilaterally declaring a one-week ceasefire.[20] He stated that this was intended to give rebels the time to disarm.[21] Russia welcomed the plan but stated, at the same time, that 'the proposed plan [would] not be viable or realistic if no practical steps are taken to commence [the] negotiation process.'[22] Furthermore, President Putin stressed that 'the peace plan proposed by President Poroshenko should not take the form of an ultimatum to militia groups.'[23] The pro-Russian separatists agreed to honour the ceasefire and released captive OSCE observers on 23 June 2014.[24] On the same day, the Trilateral Contact Group met in Donetsk with rebel leaders to discuss the situation in eastern Ukraine.[25] Representatives of the self-proclaimed Donetsk and Luhansk People's Republics refused to consider actual peace talks until Ukraine pulled all of its armed personnel and artillery out of Donbas.[26]

---

18   Ukraine, 'The Ministry of Foreign Affairs of Ukraine calls on the international community to support the President of Ukraine', available at: <https://mfa.gov.ua/en/press-center/comments/1567-ministerstvo-zakordonnih-sprav-ukrajini-zaklikaje-use-mizhnarodne-spivtovaristvo-pidtrimati-kroki-prezidenta-ukrajini-petra-porshenka> (accessed 18 September 2020).

19   NB-news, 'Ogon na vostokye dolzhen bit' na etoy nedele – Poroshenko', available at: <https://web.archive.org/web/20140908234650/http://nbnews.com.ua/ua/news/123688/> (accessed 18 September 2020).

20   Ukraine, 'In Donbas, Petro Poroshenko presented the peaceful plan on the settlement of the situation in the east of Ukraine', available at: <https://www.president.gov.ua/en/news/petro-poroshenko-predstaviv-v-donbasi-mirnij-plan-z-vregulyu-33044> (accessed 18 September 2020).

21   Ukraine, 'President of Ukraine commanded to cease fire', available at: <https://www.president.gov.ua/en/news/prezident-ukrayini-viddav-nakaz-pro-pripinennya-vognyu-33043> (accessed 18 September 2020).

22   Russia, 'On the plan for peaceful settlement in Ukraine', available at: <http://en.kremlin.ru/events/president/news/45952> (accessed 18 September 2020).

23   *Ibid.*

24   *The Guardian,* 'Pro-Russian separatists agree to honour Ukraine ceasefire', available at: <www.theguardian.com/world/2014/jun/23/ukraine-separatists-ceasefire-luhansk-donetsk> (accessed 18 September 2020).

25   TASS, 'Next round of consultations on south-east Ukraine crisis may be held June 27', available at: <http://tass.com/world/737938> (accessed 18 September 2020).

26   *Ibid.*

Alongside the formation of the Trilateral Contact Group, a second diplomatic effort at peace in Ukraine was launched in early June. During the remembrance events of the 70-year anniversary of the Allied landings in Normandy, leaders of France, Germany, Russia and Ukraine met at a chateau in Bénouville, where French President François Hollande hosted a breakfast meeting. Before the gathering, Hollande, together with German Chancellor Angela Merkel, had a conversation with President Poroshenko and Russian President Putin and their respective Foreign Affairs Ministers, in an effort to realise a diplomatic breakthrough on the escalating conflict in Ukraine. The conversation was reportedly brief[27] but served as the basis for recurrent talks between the four leaders at later stages. Its early impact on the crisis in Ukraine should probably not be overstated. Yet these talks served as the roots of the Minsk protocols, especially for the second Minsk agreement in February 2015, which was negotiated within the Normandy format, and its cooperation with the Trilateral Contact Group. The ministers of the four Member States issued a joint declaration on 2 July 2014, committing to sustainable peace and stability in Ukraine.[28] In the statement, the ministers urged for a resumption of the OSCE Trilateral Contact Group talks by 5 July 2014, 'with the goal of reaching an unconditional and mutually agreed sustainable cease-fire,' and for that ceasefire to be monitored by the OSCE Special Monitoring Mission. The Trilateral Contact Group held a meeting on 6 July 2014 in Kyiv but failed to produce substantial results.[29]

The Trilateral Contact Group convened on 17 July, after the crash of flight MH17 in the region of Donetsk. Representatives of the separatist groups in Donetsk committed to closing of the site, providing safe access to both the national investigation commission and OSCE monitors, as well as cooperating with Ukrainian authorities.[30] After that, a new round of negotiations started in Minsk, between Ukraine, Russia, the OSCE and representatives of separatist groups.[31] This would eventually lead to the first Minsk Protocol on 5 September 2017.[32]

---

27 Deutsche Welle, 'Putin vstretilsya s Poroshenko na torzhestvakh v normandiy', available at: <www.dw.com/ru/путин-встретился-с-порошенко-на-торжествах-в-нормандии/a-17689469> (accessed 18 September 2020).

28 German Ministry of Foreign Affairs, 'Joint Declaration by the Foreign Ministers of Ukraine, Russia, France and Germany, 2 July 2014', available at: <www.auswaertiges-amt.de/de/newsroom/-/263460> (accessed 18 September 2020).

29 OSCE, 'Press statement by the Trilateral Contact Group, 6 July 2014', available at: <www.osce.org/home/120863> (accessed 18 September 2020).

30 OSCE, 'Press statement by the Trilateral Contact Group, 18 July 2014', available at: <www.osce.org/home/121390> (accessed 18 September 2020).

31 OSCE, 'Press statement by the Trilateral Contact Group, 31 July 2014', available at: <www.osce.org/home/122142> (accessed 18 September 2020).

32 OSCE, 'Chairperson-in-Office welcomes Minsk agreement, assures President Poroshenko of OSCE support', available at: <www.osce.org/cio/123245> (accessed 18 September 2020).

2 Minsk Agreements

2.1 *Minsk Protocol of 5 September 2014*

The first Minsk Protocol was signed on 5 September 2014, as the synthesis of the peace talks held in the OSCE Trilateral Contact Group format.[33] The document was signed for the OSCE by Ambassador Heidi Tagliavini, for Ukraine by former President Leonid Kuchma, and for Russia by Mikhail Zurabov. The secessionist rebels were represented by Aleksandr Zakharchenko and Igor Plotnitskiy but were not granted any titles or descriptions, as to avoid questions about legitimacy or recognition. The main purpose was an immediate bilateral ceasefire between government forces and pro-Russian rebels in Ukraine. The text of the protocol consists of twelve points:

1. To ensure an immediate bilateral ceasefire.
2. To ensure the monitoring and verification of the ceasefire by the OSCE.
3. Decentralisation of power, including through the adoption of the Ukrainian law 'On temporary Order of Local Self-Governance in Particular Districts of Donetsk and Luhansk Oblasts'.
4. To ensure the permanent monitoring of the Ukrainian-Russian border and verification by the OSCE with the creation of security zones in the border regions of Ukraine and the Russian Federation.
5. Immediate release of all hostages and illegally detained persons.
6. A law preventing the prosecution and punishment of persons in connection with the events that have taken place in some areas of Donetsk and Luhansk Oblasts.
7. To continue the inclusive national dialogue.
8. To take measures to improve the humanitarian situation in Donbass.
9. To ensure early local elections in accordance with the Ukrainian law 'On temporary Order of Local Self-Governance in Particular Districts of Donetsk and Luhansk Oblasts'.
10. To withdraw illegal armed groups and military equipment as well as fighters and mercenaries from the territory of Ukraine.
11. To adopt a programme of economic recovery and reconstruction for the Donbass region.
12. To provide personal security for participants in the consultations.

---

33 OSCE, 'Protocol on the results of consultations of the Trilateral Contact Group, signed in Minsk, 5 September 2014', available at: <www.osce.org/home/123257> (accessed 18 September 2020).

The twelve points in the Minsk Protocol of September 2014 were concise, if not inadequately limited in scope. Nevertheless, they were an improvement compared to the Geneva Statement of April 2014.[34] Particularly the first point in the Minsk Protocol is less vague than its predecessor, with 'all sides must refrain' being replaced in favour of a call for a clear 'immediate bilateral ceasefire'. Furthermore, the role of the OSCE was outlined more clearly, with the monitoring of the ceasefire, the Russo-Ukrainian border and a specified security zone as its objectives. Additionally, whereas the Geneva Statement asked for a disarmament of all illegal armed groups, the Minsk Protocol speaks about withdrawal from the territory of Ukraine. The September 2014 Minsk Protocol also formally introduced the release of hostages and illegally detained persons, as well as adding a clause stressing the importance of the humanitarian situation in Donbas. Finally, the 'inclusive, transparent and accountable' constitutional process is specified by points 3 and 9. These points put the burden on the Ukrainian government to enact reforms to provide the insurgent areas with more self-governance.

The first of the two expressions of the constitutional process was the decentralisation of power. To this end, Ukraine was given the obligation to introduce a law 'On temporary Order of Local Self-Governance in Particular Districts of Donetsk and Luhansk Oblasts'. What that law would entail exactly was not specified in point 3. In contrast, point 9 is very clear in its demand for early local elections. This objective, too, would be guaranteed by Ukraine through the aforementioned law on local self-governance. Both points relating to the autonomy of the insurgent areas constitute the clearest obligations in the deal. And whereas Ukraine has obvious obligations, neither Russia nor the secessionist rebels are unequivocally assigned responsibilities, except for where such obligation might fall under the general clauses. This complicated EU and US demands for implementation, as Russia takes the position that Ukraine must fulfil its obligations first, while Ukraine insists on bona fide simultaneous execution of the deal on all sides.

2.2   *Follow-Up Memorandum of 19 September 2014*

At the time of signing, President Poroshenko was 'absolutely not confident' that any ceasefire would hold.[35] In the days following the Minsk Protocol,

---

34   *Op. cit.* note 68.
35   S. Walker, 'Ukraine ceasefire "agreed for east of country" at Minsk peace talks', available at: <www.theguardian.com/world/2014/sep/05/ukraine-ceasefire-east-minsk-peace-talks> (accessed 18 September 2020).

violations were reported on both sides. Russian Foreign Minister Lavrov stated that the ceasefire was mostly observed, but that some incidents were to be expected.[36] On 19 September 2014, two weeks after the Minsk Protocol was signed, an additional memorandum was signed in Minsk to support the fragile ceasefire with more concrete measures.[37] The OSCE Chairperson-in-Office, Didier Burkhalter, called the memorandum 'a significant step towards making the cease-fire sustainable and an important contribution in the efforts to peacefully settle the crisis in Eastern Ukraine.'[38] The follow-up memorandum contained the following nine points:

1. The ceasefire is to be considered general.
2. Halting of sub-divisions and military formations of the parties on the contact line as of 19 September 2014.
3. Ban on all offensive weapons and offensive operations.
4. Withdrawal of heavy weapons ... from the contact line at a distance of at least 15 km from each side ... which will make it possible to create a demilitarised zone no less than 30 km wide (security zone). ...
5. Ban on the deployment of heavy weapons and military equipment in the area bounded by the settlements of Komsomolskoye, Kumachevo, Novoazovsk, Sakhanka, that is to be monitored by the OSCE.
6. Ban on the installation of new mine barriers within the boundaries of the security zone. Obligation to remove previously installed mine barriers in the security zone.
7. Ban ... on flights of combat aviation and foreign unmanned aerial vehicles (UAVs), with the exception of UAVs used by the ... OSCE, along the entire contact line of the parties in the [security zone].
8. Deployment of the Special Monitoring Mission of the OSCE [in the security zone] ...

---

36 Russia, 'Foreign Minister Sergey Lavrov in an interview with the Right to Know program on TV Centre', available at: <http://www.mid.ru/en/web/guest/maps/ua/-/asset_publisher/ktn0ZLTvbbS3/content/id/670843>; Russia, 'Interview by Russian Foreign Minister Sergey Lavrov with Russia Beyond the Headlines', available at: <www.mid.ru/en/web/guest/maps/ua/-/asset_publisher/ktn0ZLTvbbS3/content/id/670288> (accessed 18 September 2020).

37 OSCE, 'Memorandum of 19 September 2014 outlining the parameters for the implementation of commitments of the Minsk Protocol of 5 September 2014', available at: <www.osce.org/home/123806> (accessed 18 September 2020).

38 OSCE, 'Memorandum on stabilizing ceasefire another important step towards de-escalation, OSCE Chairperson-in-Office says', available at: <https://www.osce.org/cio/123808> (accessed 18 September 2020).

9. Withdrawal of all foreign armed groups, military equipment, as well as militants and mercenaries from the territory of Ukraine, monitored by the OSCE.

The most prominent innovation in the follow-up agreement was the 30-kilometre security zone between the Ukrainian government forces and the separatist rebels. The withdrawal of the heaviest calibre guns had to serve the goal of lowering the intensity of occasional skirmishes. However, both the Minsk Protocol and its follow-up memorandum would eventually collapse over the battle for Donetsk Airport.[39] Late September reports[40] by the OSCE of heavy fighting and shelling near the airport heralded a fierce battle that would last until the eventual retreat of the Ukrainian army in January 2015.[41] In September 2014, too, bouts of heavy fighting broke out in the area of Debaltseve, a strategically located railroad town on the border between the self-proclaimed Donetsk (DPR) and Luhansk (LPR) Peoples' Republics.[42] In mid-January 2015, the city was in the hands of the Ukrainian army, surrounded by DPR and LPR forces. Most civilians had left Debaltseve by the time the rebels began shelling the city. A drawn-out battle erupted that lasted for more than a month and left most of the city completely destroyed, with rebel forces eventually seizing the city. The first Minsk Protocol had failed.

2.3 Minsk II – 'Package of Measures for the Implementation of the Minsk Agreements'

After months of ceasefire violations and the brutal battle for Donetsk Airport and Debaltseve, the original Minsk Protocol had lost any remaining authority that it had commanded before. But despite the Minsk agreement's failure, the next attempt at a ceasefire did not quite do away with the progress that had been made. 'The Minsk agreements' are commonly mentioned in tandem

---

39 S. Walker, 'Ukraine ceasefire breached in Donetsk and Mariupol', available at: <https://www.theguardian.com/world/2014/sep/06/eastern-ukraine-ceasefire-russia> (accessed 18 September 2020).

40 OSCE, 'Latest from OSCE Special Monitoring Mission (SMM) to Ukraine', available at: <www.osce.org/ukraine-smm/124699>; OSCE, 'Latest from OSCE Special Monitoring Mission (SMM) to Ukraine …, 30 September 2014', available at: <www.osce.org/ukraine-smm/124842> (accessed 18 September 2020).

41 BBC, 'Ukraine crisis: army retreats at Donetsk airport', available at: <www.bbc.com/news/world-europe-30929344> (accessed 18 September 2020).

42 OSCE, 'Spot Report by the OSCE Special Monitoring Mission to Ukraine (SMM), 15 September 2014: Monitoring to the east of Donetsk, SMM patrol vehicles hit by fire', available at: <www.osce.org/ukraine-smm/123587> (accessed 18 September 2020).

because the second Minsk agreement's chief goal is to clarify certain points or tweak others in the 5 September 2014 deal. What is commonly referred to as Minsk II was on 12 February 2015 given the official name 'Package of Measures for the Implementation of the Minsk Agreements'. Minsk II was not intended to replace, but to supplement and refine, the first agreement. Obligations from both documents must therefore be read together. Minsk II was the result of the cooperation between both the Normandy format and the Trilateral Contact Group. The OSCE Chairperson-in-Office, Serbia's Foreign Minister Ivica Dačić, noted the 'tireless work of the leaders of France, Germany, Russia and Ukraine',[43] as well as the OSCE Special Representative in the Trilateral Contact Group, Heidi Tagliavini, thanking her for her 'role in maintaining contact between all sides and thereby paving the way to an agreement has proven to be indispensable'.[44] Minsk II was signed by OSCE Special Representative Heidi Tagliavini, former President of Ukraine Leonid Kuchma, Russian Ambassador to Ukraine Mikhail Zurabov, and separatist leaders Alexander Zakharchenko (DPR) and Igor Plotnitsky (LPR).[45]

On 12 February 2019, four years after its signing, the UN Security Council held a meeting to assess the progress – or lack thereof.[46] Miroslav Jenča, OSCE Special Representative and one of four expert briefers, emphasised that 'there is an urgent need to agree on the additional measures that would make the ceasefire sustainable and irreversible'.[47] He added that advanced military positions on both sides of the contact line are also coming closer to each other in the so-called 'grey areas' (i.e., security zone). The Security Council debate was a poignant summary of the current status of the Minsk agreements: Russia[48] and Ukraine[49] accused each other of violating the agreements. Other states stressed the need for the OSCE to be able to fulfil its mandate, and for the parties involved to respect the ceasefire agreement.[50] Strong disagreements remained over who is to blame for the apparent inaction of parties on the ground to implement their commitments. Ukraine holds that Russian-backed rebels

---

43 OSCE, 'Cooperation between the Normandy format and the Trilateral Contact Group: OSCE Chairperson-in-Office gives full backing to Minsk package', available at: <www.osce.org/cio/140196> (accessed 18 September 2020).
44 *Ibid.*
45 Both Zakharchenko and Plotnitsky were not given official titles to go along with their signatures, most likely in the context of the non-recognition of DPR and LPR.
46 Security Council Verbatim Records, S/PV.8461, 8.
47 *Ibid.*, 3.
48 *Ibid.*, 7.
49 *Ibid.*, 22.
50 *Ibid.*

violated the Minsk agreements as soon as they were signed, by seizing the town of Debaltseve the very next day. It therefore demands that Russia comply *first* with the Minsk agreements by adhering to the first two paragraphs; that is, the 'immediate and full ceasefire' and the withdrawal of heavy weaponry. Russia, in opposition, insists that the 'agreements contain not a word about Russia',[51] and that it has no commitments to live up to, since it maintains it is not a party to the conflict. Furthermore, Russia accuses Kyiv of 'persistently evading its political commitments, trying to marginalise the mechanisms of the Trilateral Contact Group'.[52]

2.4   The Steinmeier Formula

Coinciding with Germany's OSCE Presidency in 2016, its then Minister of Foreign Affairs and current President, Frank-Walter Steinmeier, informally proposed a simplified sequence in which to execute the points of the Minsk protocols.[53] The goal of the so-called 'Steinmeier formula' was to facilitate the road map for both sides' obligations. It called for elections to be held in the territories under separatist control. The OSCE would serve as a neutral observer of the election process. After the OSCE's official approval of the elections, the territories would be granted a special self-governing status. Ukraine, in turn, would regain full control of its easternmost border. Whereas the Russian Federation has repeatedly confirmed its support for this proposal,[54] it has never been quite as popular on the Ukrainian side.

After the election of Volodymyr Zelenskiy as President in 2019, Ukraine seemed to adjust its position on the Steinmeier formula. At a meeting of the Trilateral Contact Group on 1 October 2019, the Ukrainian government and the separatist authorities agreed on a bilateral military withdrawal from the towns of Zolote and Petrivske, in exchange for 'special status' accorded to Donbas.[55]

---

51 *Ibid.*, 8.
52 *Ibid.*, 9.
53 On the role of Germany in EU-Russia relations, see also the contribution by T. van der Togt (chapter 2) in this volume.
54 See, for example, the joint press conference of 15 August 2016 with Mr. Lavrov and Mr. Steinmeier, available at: <www.mid.ru/en/web/guest/meropriyatiya_s_uchastiem_ministra/-/asset_publisher/xK1BhB2bUjd3/content/id/2392395>; or the remarks by the Permanent Representative of the Russian Federation to the OSCE Alexander Lukashevich at a meeting of the OSCE Permanent Council in Vienna on 23 June 2016, available at: <www.mid.ru/en/web/guest/maps/ua/-/asset_publisher/ktnoZLTvbbS3/content/id/2330364> (accessed 18 September 2020).
55 OSCE, Doc. PC.DEL/1070/19/Corr.1, 'Statement by Mr. Alexander Lukashevich, Permanent Representative of the Russian Federation, at the 1242nd meeting of the OSCE Permanent

Despite regular ceasefire violations in October, full military disengagement from Zolote and Petrivske started by the end of the month.[56] The Ukrainian government's endorsement of the Steinmeier formula resulted in some domestic protest, in which Zelenskiy was accused of capitulating to Russia.[57] At the same time, Russian officials noted that the ball was 'largely in Ukraine's court', stating that Ukraine needed to provide a legislative framework to grant special status to the Donbas region, and to organise elections.[58] Taking into account the potential pitfalls following the Ukrainian acceptance of the Steinmeier formula, the decision still marks a potential shift in the deadlocked negotiations on the Minsk protocols.

French President Emmanuel Macron made an attempt at rekindling the Minsk process with a Normandy Format Summit in Paris on 9 December 2019, in the presence of both Ukrainian President Zelenskiy and Russian President Putin, as well as German Chancellor Merkel. They concluded that the Minsk process was still the only basis to attain peace.[59] The parties agreed on demining efforts, additional areas to be demilitarised by the end of March 2020, and prisoner swaps, and reiterated the need for the OSCE monitors to be able to work without interference.[60] Furthermore, the parties 'expressed their interest' in an agreement on all legal aspects with regards to self-government in Donetsk and Luhansk. They considered it 'necessary' to integrate the Steinmeier formula in Ukrainian legislation. However, such an option is not self-evident, taking into account the opposition against the Steinmeier formula in Ukraine.

Council', available at: <www.osce.org/permanent-council/435176> (accessed 18 September 2020).

56 OSCE, 'OSCE SMM Chief Monitor Çevik welcomes beginning of disengagement from Zolote', 30 October 2019, available at: < www.osce.org/special-monitoring-mission-to-ukraine/437405> (accessed 18 September 2020).

57 J. Lynch, 'Zelensky flounders in bid to end Ukraine's war', available at: <www.foreignpolicy.com/2019/10/11/zelensky-pushes-peace-deal-ukraine-war-russia-donbass-steinmeier-formula/> (accessed 18 September 2020).

58 See the remarks made by Mr. Alexander Lukashevich, *op. cit.* note 114.

59 France, Ministry of Foreign Affairs, 'Conclusions Agréées – Sommet de Paris en Format "Normandie"', 9 December 2019, available at: <www.elysee.fr/front/pdf/elysee-module-14873-fr.pdf> (accessed 18 September 2020).

60 *Ibid.*

3 Status and Implementation

So far, the Minsk agreements remain the only agreed framework for a negotiated peace in eastern Ukraine. As most of the 13 provisions of Minsk II are related to points in the first Minsk Protocol, a thematic overview of the relevant additions and changes can be found below, accompanied by an analysis of their respective implementation status. It seems that most stakeholders can agree on only one thing; namely, that the Minsk agreements have not yet been implemented. It remains to be seen whether the acceptance of the Steinmeier formula by Ukrainian President Zelenskiy will be able to change that. The point-by-point analysis below roughly follows the sequence of obligations in the second Minsk Protocol. Considering the internal references and strong connection between points 4 and 12, and points 9 and 11 respectively, these obligations will be examined jointly.

Point 1 – Ceasefire. The core provision of both agreements, the ceasefire, was scheduled in Minsk II to take effect on 15 February 2015, 00:00 midnight, three days after its signing, to allow military forces and rebels to withdraw behind their respective side of the security zone. The word 'full' was added to the phrase 'immediate and full ceasefire'.

Fighting continues on a daily basis, well into the fifth year after the signing of the second Minsk agreement in February 2015. The OSCE Special Monitoring Mission to Ukraine regularly reports, among other things, landmines, ceasefire violations, restricted access to official disengagement zones, and civilian casualties due to shelling.[61] The agreement to withdraw from the contact line in October 2019 has not stopped the ceasefire violations.[62] Point 1 has not been implemented.

Point 2 – Withdrawal of heavy weapons. Minsk II's second provision was based on point 4 of the 19 September 2014 follow-up memorandum to the first Minsk Protocol. It expanded the minimal width of the regular safety zone from 30 to 50 kilometres. Moreover, it expanded the security zones for rocket launchers and tactical missile systems to 70 and 140 kilometres, respectively. The contact line was established in the memorandum. Both sides were given a time frame in which to complete their obligations: the pull-out was to start

---

61 See daily reporting by OSCE Special Monitoring Mission to Ukraine, available at: <www.osce.org/special-monitoring-mission-to-ukraine> (accessed 8 April 2019).

62 OSCE, 'Special Monitoring Mission to Ukraine (SMM) Daily Report 257/2019 issued on 30 October 2019', available at: <www.osce.org/special-monitoring-mission-to-ukraine/437456> (accessed 18 September 2020).

no later than two days after the start of the ceasefire (i.e., 17 February 2015) and had to finish within 14 days (i.e., 3 March 2015).

Ukraine demands that the ceasefire paragraph (point 1) has to be implemented before any other point can be addressed. The OSCE, meanwhile, reports the presence of heavy weaponry in government-controlled areas as well as non-government-controlled areas.[63] Nevertheless, the OSCE Special Monitoring Mission does not state to whom the heavy weaponry belongs. The mission has been severely hampered in its adequate monitoring of the situation. Point 2 has not been implemented.

Point 3 – Monitoring by the OSCE. This point clarified the means of the OSCE for its monitoring mission. Whereas point 2 of the first Minsk Protocol mandated only that the OSCE monitor and verify the ceasefire, corresponding point 3 in Minsk II prescribes any technical means necessary to carry out its task.

The Special Monitoring Mission to Ukraine reports daily impediments to the fulfilment of its mandate. Its monitoring and freedom of movement are restricted by 'security hazards and threats, including risks posed by mines, unexploded ordnance and other impediments' – which vary from day to day. The mandate supposedly provides for safe and secure access throughout Ukraine. Nonetheless, the armed formations in parts of Donetsk and Luhansk regions frequently deny the SMM access to areas adjacent to Ukraine's border outside control of the government.[64] The SMM's operations in the Donetsk and Luhansk regions remain restricted following the fatal incident of 23 April 2017 near Pryshyb;[65] these restrictions continue to limit the mission's observations. Point 3 has not been implemented.

Points 4 and 12 – Local elections and demarcation. Building on point 9 in Minsk I, the fourth provision ordered a dialogue on local elections, in accordance with the new self-governance law, resulting in a resolution to be approved by the Verkhovna Rada of Ukraine within 30 days. This resolution had to demarcate the territory that falls under the special regime in accordance with said law. In an attempt at further clarifying point 4, point 12 stated that questions related to local elections would be discussed and agreed on with

---

63   *Op. cit.* note 61.
64   OSCE, 'Restrictions of SMM's freedom of movement and other impediments to fulfilment of its mandate', available at: <www.osce.org/special-monitoring-mission-to-ukraine/412754> (accessed 18 September 2020).
65   OSCE, 'Spot Report: One SMM patrol member dead, two taken to hospital after vehicle hits possible mine near Pryshyb', <www.osce.org/special-monitoring-mission-to-ukraine/312971> (accessed 8 April 2019).

representatives of particular districts of the Donetsk and Luhansk Oblasts in the framework of the Trilateral Contact Group. The OSCE and its Office for Democratic Institutions and Human Rights (ODIHR) were given the role to monitor the local elections.

The *Law on Special Local Self-government Procedures in Donetsk and Luhansk Regions* was adopted in September 2014,[66] and was extended to 31 December 2019.[67] It provided that local self-government procedures in the Donbas region take effect only 'after the fulfilment of all conditions stated in Article 10 of the law, in particular, as regards the withdrawal of all illegal armed groups, their military hardware, and also militants and mercenaries from the territory of Ukraine.'[68] Since no significant progress was made with regard to the ceasefire and the withdrawal of weapons (points 1–3), there had been no noteworthy debate on local elections in Donetsk and Luhansk. Nevertheless, self-styled elections were held in these territories on 11 November 2018,[69] drawing sharp rebukes from Ukraine[70] and the European Union.[71] Pursuant to the non-recognition of the so-called 'elections', no talks on demarcation were held.

Following the agreement on the Steinmeier formula in October 2019, the Ukrainian government altered its principal position on local elections. However, at the time of this writing, a legislative framework to organise elections in the Donbas region was not in sight. President Zelenskiy stated that there would be 'no elections at gunpoint', indicating that a complete withdrawal of separatist

---

66 Ukraine, 'Law of Ukraine on Special Local Self-government Procedure in Specific Regions of Donetsk and Luhansk Oblasts', available in English at: <http://iplex.com.ua/index.php?page=english&name=3024_134_1>.

67 Kyiv Post, 'Rada prolongs law on special status of Donbas', available at: <www.kyivpost.com/ukraine-politics/rada-prolongs-law-on-special-status-of-donbas.html> (accessed 18 September 2020).

68 *Ibid.*

69 'Separatist-held regions hold elections in eastern Ukraine', available at: <www.reuters.com/article/us-ukraine-crisis-donetsk-election/separatist-held-regions-hold-elections-in-eastern-ukraine-idUSKCN1NG045> (accessed 18 September 2020).

70 Ukraine, 'Statement on illegal and fake so called "elections" in the Russia-occupied territories of the Donetsk and Luhansk regions of Ukraine', available at: <www.osce.org/permanent-council/403841?download=true> (accessed 18 September 2020).

71 European Union, 'Statement on the announcement of "elections" in the so-called "Luhansk People's Republic" and "Donetsk People's Republic"', available at: <https://eeas.europa.eu/headquarters/headquarters-Homepage/50243/statement-announcement-elections-so-called-luhansk-peoples-republic-and-donetsk-peoples_en> (accessed 18 September 2020).

and/or Russian troops would be required for elections to go ahead.[72] Point 4 and point 12 have not yet been implemented.

Point 5 – Amnesty. While similar to its corresponding point 6 in Minsk I, this point not only required a law 'forbidding persecution and punishment' but also stated explicitly that this law was meant to provide 'pardon and amnesty'.

To a certain extent, amnesty measures have been taken by the Ukrainian state. Coinciding with the adoption of the law on self-government, the Ukrainian Verkhovna Rada also adopted the *Law on Preventing Persecution and Punishment of Participants of Events on the Territories of Donetsk and Luhansk Oblasts* in September 2014.[73] The law would grant amnesty for a number of crimes against the Ukrainian state committed during the 'anti-terrorist operations', to certain members of armed groups and other separatists of the 'self-proclaimed bodies in Donetsk and Luhansk Oblasts.'[74] However, the law has never had much effect since it is to come into force only 'after the withdrawal of all illegal armed formations, their military equipment, as well as fighters and mercenaries from the territory of Ukraine.'[75] Point 5 has therefore not been implemented.

Point 6 – Release and exchange of hostages and prisoners. The new provision on the release of hostages and illegally held persons stated that an exchange was to be conducted based on the principle of 'all for all'. Furthermore, it provided a five-day deadline for this point to be executed. The sixth paragraph of Minsk II made explicit reference to the principle of 'all for all'. While there have been prisoner exchanges from time to time,[76] the 'all for all' principle has certainly not been maintained. Prisoners are still held on both sides. Point 6 has therefore been only partially implemented.

Point 7 – Humanitarian aid. Whereas the September 2014 Minsk Protocol asked for 'measures' to improve the humanitarian situation in Donbas, Minsk II prescribed safe access, delivery, storage and distribution of humanitarian aid

---

72   Kyiv Post, 'Ukraine agrees to 'Steinmeier formula,' green-lights elections in occupied Donbas', available at: <www.kyivpost.com/ukraine-politics/ukraine-agrees-to-steinmeier-formula-green-lights-elections-in-occupied-donbas.html> (accessed 18 September 2020).

73   'The Verkhovna Rada of Ukraine adopted the Law "On preventing persecution and punishment of participants of events on the territories of Donetsk and Luhansk Oblasts" ', available at: <https://rada.gov.ua/en/news/News/News/97825.html> (accessed 8 April 2019).

74   *Ibid.*

75   Kyiv Post, 'Rada prolongs law on special status of Donbas', available at: <www.kyivpost.com/ukraine-politics/rada-prolongs-law-on-special-status-of-donbas.html> (accessed 8 April 2019).

76   'Ukraine crisis: exchange of hundreds of prisoners takes place', available at: <www.bbc.com/news/world-europe-42493270> (accessed 18 September 2020).

to the needy, based on 'an international mechanism'. To the external observer, point 7 of Minsk II still lacks the clarity provided by other points, despite its change in formulation.

This ties in with the controversy over the many truck convoys sent to eastern Ukraine by Russia, without the consent of the Ukrainian government.[77] OSCE monitors have not been able to assess the contents of these convoys, although the Russian government states that they are merely for humanitarian purposes.[78] At most, Ukrainian border guards are allowed a 'visual observation of the vehicles from the outside (without entering the trucks' cargo space)'.[79] Between August 2014 and January 2019, Russia had sent more than 80 such convoys to Ukraine.[80] Despite point 7 arguing for an 'international mechanism', no such thing has transpired. While the EU and the United States provide considerable humanitarian aid to internally displaced persons from eastern Ukraine, their assistance is limited to government-controlled areas of Ukraine. Since no mechanism exists and Russian 'aid' cannot be monitored by the OSCE, it may well be argued that point 7 has not been implemented.

Point 8 – Restoration of social and economic connections. This provision was one of the substantial innovations of the second Minsk deal. Remarkably, it was another provision that imposed considerable burdens on the Ukrainian state. Point 8 requested the definition of the modalities of a full restoration of the social and economic connections between Ukraine and the secessionist regions, including social transfers such as payments of pensions and income and revenue taxes. Moreover, Ukraine has to restore management over the segment of its banking system in the districts affected by the conflict. The upside to this provision for Ukraine is obviously the recognition that the Donbas region is part of its sovereign territory. The downside is that it bears the responsibility of paying pensions and other social payments to areas where it is fighting

---

77   N. MacFarquhar, 'A Russian convoy carrying aid to Ukraine is dogged by suspicion', 13 August 2014, available at: <www.nytimes.com/2014/08/13/world/europe/russian-convoy-leaves-moscow-for-ukraine-bearing-aid.html> (accessed 18 September 2020).

78   OSCE, 'Latest from the OSCE Special Monitoring Mission to Ukraine (SMM), based on information received as of 19:30, 29 March 2018', available at: <www.osce.org/special-monitoring-mission-to-ukraine/376654> (accessed 18 September 2020).

79   OSCE, 'Spot Report by OSCE Observer Mission: The eighty-second Russian convoy of 22 vehicles crossed into Ukraine and returned through the Donetsk Border Crossing Point', 20 December 2018, available at: <www.osce.org/observer-mission-at-russian-checkpoints-gukovo-and-donetsk/407522> (accessed 18 September 2020).

80   Unian, 'Ukraine's Foreign Ministry condemns another Russian "humanitarian convoy" arrived in Donbas', 24 November 2018, available at: <www.unian.info/war/10350636-ukraine-s-foreign-ministry-condemns-another-russian-humanitarian-convoy-arrived-in-donbas.html> (accessed 18 September 2020).

insurgent rebels. The language used ('possibly') to refer to the establishment of another 'international mechanism' was never quite convincing.

No payments of pensions or other 'social and economic connections' have been restored, as no serious efforts were ever made to set up the mechanism. On 14 February 2019, the topic of providing pensions to residents of the Donetsk region was raised at a meeting of the Economic Working Group of the Trilateral Contact Group in Minsk. The 'Ministry of Foreign Affairs' of the self-proclaimed Donetsk People's Republic reported that during the conflict in the Donbas, the Ukrainian authorities owed residents of the DPR pension payments of UAH 71.6 billion ($2.6 billion).[81] Kyiv meanwhile insists that the payment of pensions in non-government-controlled territories is impossible due to the inability to verify the recipients and to avoid manipulation and abuse.[82] Since no concrete measures towards the restoration of social and economic connections have been taken, point 8 cannot be considered implemented.

Points 9 and 11 – Restoration of the state border and constitutional reform. In what seems like the most generous concession towards Ukraine, the restoration of the state border to the Ukrainian government in the whole conflict zone, point 9 of Minsk II was rather deceptive. The fulfilment of this provision depended on two conditions and was limited in time. First, local elections would have to be held before the start of the restoration procedure. Second, this procedure would have to end 'by the end of 2015', after the 'full political regulation', meaning that the local elections would have to be based on a constitutional reform law.

The constitutional reform required by point 11 entails a 'new constitution' to come into effect by the end of 2015. Its key reforms had to be 'decentralisation' and approval of permanent legislation on the special status of particular districts of Donetsk and Luhansk Oblasts. If these conditions were not relatively demanding by themselves, a footnote was attached to the Minsk II agreement, in which it was specified which measures had to be taken. In summary, there were eight elements to be included in the legislation: amnesty measures; right of choice of language; participation of local governments in the appointment of the heads of prosecutor's offices; the possibility to conclude agreements on economic, social and cultural development; Ukrainian support for socio-economic development in Donbas; assistance from central executive bodies for 'cross-border cooperation' with the Russian Federation; the freedom to create people's militia units by decision of local councils to maintain public order;

---

81 Kommersant, 'V Donetske zayavili, shto Kiev zadolzhal pensioneram DNR okolo $2,6 mlrd', available at: <www.kommersant.ru/doc/3882704> (accessed 8 April 2019).
82 *Ibid.*

and the impossibility to terminate the powers of local council deputies and officials by the Ukrainian state.

In short, the constitutional reforms demanded in Minsk II were targeting decentralisation of power. No significant changes have been made to Ukraine's constitution to comply with the Minsk agreements.[83] Nevertheless, Ukraine did alter its constitution to reflect other policy goals such as its intention to become a member of the European Union and of NATO.[84] President Zelenskiy's acceptance of the Steinmeier formula could signal a change in attitude towards constitutional reform. However, concrete adjustments have not surfaced. Since the restoration of the Russo-Ukrainian border (point 9) depended on the implementation of constitutional decentralisation (point 11), there have been no notable developments in that regard. Points 9 and 11 have not been implemented.

Point 10 – Pull-out of all foreign armed formations. Improving somewhat on the language in the preceding Minsk I agreement and the subsequent follow-up memorandum, this provision commanded the pull-out not only of mercenaries but also of foreign armed formations and military equipment. Moreover, supervision by the OSCE was added, supposedly to give the clause more strength. The Russian Federation maintains that it is not involved in the armed conflict in the Donbas region.[85] The phrasing of point 10 allowed the OSCE monitors, in theory, to identify violations of the ceasefire.

The Ukrainian army still finds itself fighting well-equipped Russian-backed forces. Daily reports[86] and status reports[87] by the OSCE Special Monitoring Mission give the observer an idea of the heavy weaponry that is available to both sides of the conflict. As long as Russia insists on the untruthful narrative that it does not have military forces and equipment in the east of Ukraine, no progress will be made on this point – or, arguably, any other point.

---

83 M. Marlin and A. Butts, 'Constitutional reform in Ukraine in 2016: Prospects for regional reintegration and reconciliation of dominant Eastern and Western ethnonationalist factions', *European Yearbook of Minority Issues* 15 (2018), 151–168.

84 Ukrinform, 'Poroshenko signs constitutional amendments on Ukraine's movement to EU, NATO', available at: <www.ukrinform.net/rubric-polytics/2643679-poroshenko-signs-constitutional-amendments-on-ukraines-movement-to-eu-nato.html> (accessed 8 April 2019).

85 Security Council Verbatim Records, S/PV.8461, 8.

86 All reports of the OSCE Special Monitoring Mission to Ukraine are available at: <www.osce.org/ukrainesmm/reports> (accessed 8 April 2019).

87 OSCE Special Monitoring Mission to Ukraine, 'Status report "as of 29 March 2019"', available at: <www.osce.org/special-monitoring-mission-to-ukraine/415469?download=true> (accessed 8 April 2019).

Point 13 – Working groups. The final point of Minsk II sets out the plan to establish working groups on the implementation of relevant aspects of the Minsk agreements. It calls for an intensification of the work of the Trilateral Contact Group. The working groups would reflect its composition, meaning that there would be representatives of Ukraine, Russia and the OSCE. Arguably, representatives of the secessionist rebels would have to be included as well, given their previous involvement in the Trilateral Contact Group talks.

Within the negotiation structure provided by the OSCE, four working groups have been established:[88] the Humanitarian Working Group, the Economic Working Group, the Security Working Group and the Political Working Group. They reflect the make-up of the Trilateral Contact Group, which also serves as its umbrella group for further discussion. In press statements by the OSCE Chairmanship, a brief summary of the topics discussed in the working groups is provided.[89] Despite the lack of tangible results from the working groups, it cannot be denied that working groups have been set up. Therefore, point 13 has been implemented.

4 Conclusion

Diplomatic efforts to stop the fighting in eastern Ukraine quickly followed after hostilities broke out in April 2014. The first attempt, the so-called 'Geneva Statement', was too vague and was not sufficiently backed up by its negotiators. After Petro Poroshenko's ascent to the Presidency of Ukraine, the OSCE, together with Ukraine and Russia, set up the Trilateral Contact Group. Simultaneously, Germany and France established the Normandy format. Both platforms eventually led to the Minsk agreements, improving and specifying at every stage, but to little avail. German negotiator Frank-Walter Steinmeier proposed a road map to address the conflict about the sequence in which the points of the Minsk agreements were to be executed. The so-called 'Steinmeier formula', wherein elections and special status for Donbas were to be exchanged for complete Ukrainian sovereignty over its borders was eventually accepted

---

[88] Interfax, 'OSCE Troika calls for setting up working groups to implement Minsk agreements', available at: <https://en.interfax.com.ua/news/general/263261.html> (accessed 8 April 2019).

[89] OSCE, 'Press statement of Special Representative of OSCE Chairperson-in-Office Sajdik after meeting of Trilateral Contact Group on 4 December 2018', available at: <www.osce.org/chairmanship/405266> (accessed 8 April 2019).

by the newly elected Volodymyr Zelenskiy, potentially allowing new diplomatic efforts to take place.

Minsk II still risks consolidating the status quo by allowing the line of contact to become a border of sorts, between Ukraine and the breakaway regions. Its non-implementation means Minsk could be on a road to nowhere.

One of the diplomatic solutions that has not yet been attempted is the deployment of a UN-mandated peacekeeping operation. Shortly after the second Minsk Protocol was signed in February 2015, Ukrainian President Petro Poroshenko had proposed the idea to an emergency Security Council meeting, following the seizure of Debaltseve by Russian-backed rebels.[90] Poroshenko reiterated the need for peacekeeping throughout his Presidency, even finding Vladimir Putin in agreement in September 2017.[91] However tempting, the mandate of such a peacekeeping mission would have to be precisely negotiated. For instance, Ukraine wanted a peacekeeping operation to guard not only the line of contact but also the Russo-Ukrainian border, a proposition to which the Kremlin objected. A mere presence at the contact line and protection of OSCE monitors could allow a freezing of the conflict, without offering a long-term perspective on restoring Ukrainian control over its own territory.

After comprehensive consideration of every point in the second Minsk Protocol, it must be concluded that the Minsk agreements are nowhere near 'full implementation.' Ukraine has long held that no substantial measures can be taken until the weapons are withdrawn and the ceasefire holds. Conversely, the secessionist rebels and Russia insist that constitutional reforms, amnesty and other measures are necessary to permit the cessation of hostilities. Furthermore, given the apparent deadlock of the past five years, it must also be concluded that the sanctions do not amount to their intended results. The costs of the status quo for Ukraine are immense, while Russia seems willing to bear the burden of Western sanctions to whip up unrest in Donbas. With that in mind, a merely legal solution (e.g., by means of a peace treaty) is highly unlikely in the current circumstances. Until the election of Volodymyr Zelenskiy in 2019, there seemed to be a lack of political will to concede on either side. From the start, German Chancellor Angela Merkel called Minsk II 'no more than a glimmer of hope'.[92] Five years later, it seems that only the

---

90   BBC, 'Ukraine conflict: Poroshenko calls for UN peacekeepers', available at: <https://www.bbc.com/news/world-europe-31527414> (accessed 18 September 2020).

91   EURACTIV, 'Russia asks UN to set up mission for east Ukraine', available at: <https://www.euractiv.com/section/europe-s-east/news/russia-asks-un-to-set-up-mission-for-east-ukraine/> (accessed 18 September 2020).

92   Reuters, 'Minsk meeting offers glimmer of hope, not more: Germany', available at: <www.reuters.com/article/us-ukraine-crisis-minsk-germany/minsk-meeting-offers-glimmer-of-hope-not-more-germany-idUSKBN0LF0YY20150211> (accessed 18 September 2020).

Steinmeier formula, an initiative by a compatriot of hers, has prevented the light from fading completely. This was again stressed by the Normandy Format Summit in Paris on 9 December 2019. It remains to be seen whether rekindled peace negotiations will result in sustained peace.

CHAPTER 2

The Role of EU Member States and the Future of EU-Russia Relations

Disentangling the role of Germany and the Netherlands in EU Decision-Making on Relations with Russia since the Ukraine Crisis

Tony van der Togt

1   Introduction

EU decision-making on the Common Foreign and Security Policy (CFSP) remains one of the most difficult puzzles inside the EU, as different actors all have their own roles to play in a complicated institutional arrangement which even after the Lisbon Treaty has not been settled in favour of a fully integrated and comprehensive European approach. In this context, dealing with EU-Russia relations not only is no exception to this puzzle but has always been shaped by a rather complex interplay of EU institutions and national governments with their own interests and diverging perspectives on relations with Moscow: past experience and the intensity of their respective bilateral relations with Russia would influence EU Member States to 'upload' some issues in their relations with Moscow to the European level, while reserving other topics mainly for direct bilateral discussions.[1]

This complexity in decision-making on a 'Russia policy' also applies to Germany, which has traditionally entertained the most intensive relationship with Russia and constitutes by far the most important EU Member State in defining the relationship with Moscow. Over time Berlin has uploaded some elements of its *Ostpolitik* to the EU level, while reserving especially energy relations mainly for its bilateral relationship with Russia, irrespective of the

---

1   T. Forsberg and H. Haukkala, *The European Union and Russia* (Palgrave 2016); M. David, J. Gower and H. Haukkala (eds.), *National perspectives on Russia: European foreign policy in the making?* (Routledge 2013); M. Leonard and N. Popescu, 'A power audit of EU-Russia relations' (2007), available at: <https://www.ecfr.eu/publications/summary/a_power_audit_of_eu_russia_relations> (accessed 14 March 2020). K. Liik, 'Winning the normative war with Russia: an EU-Russia power audit' (2018), available at: <https://www.ecfr.eu/publications/summary/winning_the_normative_war_with_russia_an_eu_russia_power_audit> (accessed 14 March 2020).

interests of other European states, both inside and outside the EU. In a number of aspects, the Netherlands has broadly followed the German Russia policy, albeit at a lower level of business and societal relations. Only on human rights has the Netherlands been more vocal, especially in the EU context. Until the Ukraine crisis, both countries had a mainly cooperative relationship with Russia with intensive business, cultural and societal contacts. The Russian annexation of Crimea, Moscow's involvement in destabilising eastern Ukraine and (especially for the Netherlands) the downing of Malaysian airliner MH17 by a Russian anti-air missile would lead to a paradigm shift in the relationship. Perspectives on Russia and on Russian policies changed fundamentally, preventing any early return to 'business as usual'.[2]

In this context, Germany was called on to exercise a leadership role within the EU, using its intensive relationship with Russia to act as a mediator and an honest broker in attempting to resolve the Ukraine crisis. Berlin already played such a role in early 2014 in a multilateral effort to mediate the internal crisis in Ukraine, resulting from the Euromaidan, and continued to contribute actively at the highest level in the framework of the 'Normandy format' in negotiating the Minsk agreements in 2014 and 2015.[3] As requested by Germany, the most important part of the EU sanctions against Russia was linked to full implementation by Russia of the provisions of the second Minsk agreement. Both inside the EU and as Organisation for Security and Co-operation in Europe (OSCE) Chairman in 2016, Germany was to play a central role in shaping decisions on the EU's relationship with Russia. For the Netherlands, the MH17 tragedy in July 2014 became henceforth the defining element in its relations with Moscow, and The Hague actively sought support from the EU and other international partners to bring the perpetrators to justice.

This chapter first looks more closely into the recent changes in German perspectives on Russia, as the Ukraine crisis constituted a *game changer* for many, although not all, German politicians, leading to the conclusion that the old *Ostpolitik* of *Wandel durch Annäherung* (change through rapprochement) had ultimately failed and that a new Russia policy was called for, on the national and on the EU level. This change of heart was also affected by the frustrating experience of attempting to negotiate a solution to the Ukraine crisis with

---

2 S.F. Szabo, *Germany, Russia and the rise of geo-economics* (Bloomsbury 2015); T. van der Togt, 'The impact of MH 17 on Dutch-Russian relations. International law versus hard Realpolitik: how MH 17 will impact Dutch-Russian relations for a long time to come' (2016), available at: <https://www.clingendael.org/publication/impact-mh17-dutch-russian-relations> (accessed 14 March 2020).

3 See the contribution by S. Van Severen (chapter 1) in this volume.

a Russian partner, who according to Chancellor Angela Merkel was 'living in another world'.[4] Russian disinformation and information warfare, targeting Germany and German politicians, only contributed to seriously damaging any remaining trust in a negotiated settlement, which would respect international law and European values.

Second, this chapter turns to the changing perspectives on Russia in the Netherlands, which had just organised a rather successful bilateral year with Russia in 2013 and was heavily and directly affected by the Ukraine crisis, as it lost around 200 of its own citizens, when Malaysian airliner MH17 was shot down above Donbas by a Russian Buk missile. Russian disinformation on the integrity and impartiality of the MH17 investigations and on the Dutch referendum on the EU-Ukraine Association Agreement also fundamentally undermined trust in dealing with Russian authorities. The 2015 Dutch Russia policy of 'pressure and dialogue' in fact minimalised (official) dialogue and negatively affected the broader relationship. According to the current Dutch Minister of Defence, the Netherlands even found itself in a 'cyber war with Russia'.[5]

Finally, this chapter concludes with some thoughts about the implications of the changing perspectives on Russia in both Germany and the Netherlands and, especially, how far they still attempt to *Europeanise* their relations with Russia. As the Netherlands has recently presented its 'new' Russia policy (which basically constitutes a continuation of its earlier policy of 'pressure and dialogue' with some openings for further dialogue) and Germany has held the EU Presidency in the second half of 2020, any changes that Berlin and The Hague would be making in their respective Russia policies could also have a fundamental impact on shaping EU-Russia relations in the near future. As Germany (like the Netherlands) continues to simultaneously *bilateralise* an important part of its energy relationship with Russia, especially in facilitating the construction of the Nord Stream 2 gas pipeline, this could negatively affect Germany's future leadership role in EU-Russia relations and damage chances to shape a more comprehensive EU-Russia policy, which could also count on the full support of Central and Eastern European Member States. With a new 'geopolitical' European Commission in office since December 2019 and French President Emmanuel Macron aspiring to launch new initiatives in dealing

---

4   See P. Baker, 'Pressure rising as Obama works to rein in Russia', 2 March 2014, available at: <https://www.nytimes.com/2014/03/03/world/europe/pressure-rising-as-obama-works-to-rein-in-russia.html?hp> (accessed 14 March 2020).
5   See J. Pieters, 'Netherlands in "cyber war" with Russia, Defense Minister says', 15 October 2018, available at: <https://nltimes.nl/2018/10/15/netherlands-cyber-war-russia-defense-minister-says> (accessed 14 March 2020).

with Russia, only in the near future will it become clear whether decision-making on EU-Russia relations will remain as heavily influenced by especially Germany, as in the recent past, or shift to other EU institutions or other EU Member States like France. The recent decision by the EU Foreign Ministers to revisit the implementation of the 'five principles for the relations with Russia' will reopen the debate on the future of EU-Russia relations and will also offer some further indications about the respective roles of EU Member States and institutions in decision-shaping in this respect.

2 Germany, the Ukraine Crisis and EU-Russia Relations

The original German *Ostpolitik*, as shaped in the late 1960s and the early 1970s by West German Sozialdemokratische Partei Deutschlands (SPD) politicians Willy Brandt and Egon Bahr, was aimed at developing constructive relations with both the Soviet Union and other states belonging to the Soviet-dominated East European block, which in the long term could lead to German reunification and in the short term to a decrease in tensions and an increase in contacts, including between East and West German populations. Trade relations, including in the energy sector, constituted an important element in building bilateral relations with Moscow, which already in the 1980s would regularly bring Bonn into conflict with the more hard-line and confrontational policies towards the Soviet Union, as pursued by different administrations in Washington.

East-West détente would gradually change the political configuration in Europe by pursuing a policy of rapprochement: *Wandel durch Annäherung*. In this context, Germans would envisage the eventual end of the Cold War, as mainly a result of such policies and not as a result of hard confrontation and outspending the Soviets in an expensive arms race. This German Eastern policy was implemented by different West German governments (also when lead by a Christlich Demokratische Union [CDU] *Bundeskanzler*, like Helmut Kohl), both bilaterally and multilaterally, the latter mainly in the context of the Conference on Security and Cooperation in Europe (CSCE) process, which later developed into the Organisation on Security and Co-operation in Europe (OSCE). At the time, European Political Cooperation had only just begun, and the European Communities and its Member States could not yet constitute an influential force in European politics.

After the fall of the Berlin Wall, German reunification and the disintegration of the Soviet Union, German governments continued to pursue constructive relations with Russia and other Newly Independent States (NIS) in an effort to integrate such states in a broader transatlantic and European security order, based on the principles enshrined in the Helsinki Final Act (1975) and the Charter of Paris (1990).

In the meantime, after the Maastricht Treaty (1992), the European Union did become a more powerful political player, which in the relations with Russia and other former Soviet states resulted in Partnership and Cooperation Agreements (PCAs), replacing older agreements between the European Communities and its Member States and the Soviet Union.

As Stefan Meister argues, 'Germany's bilateral relations with Russia have in the past undermined the construction of a coherent European Russia policy'.[6] Especially substantive German business interests, including in the energy sector, have put serious pressure on Berlin to *bilateralise* to a large extent economic and especially energy relations with Moscow. Although German policymakers were clearly interested in the EU's Common Strategy on Russia in 1999 and in developing the EU's Common Spaces with Russia and accompanying road maps in 2004/2005, it remained difficult for the EU to move beyond the lowest common denominator as long as energy relations, and also broader security issues, remained outside the EU framework. In this context, Moscow also strongly preferred to deal with the bigger European powers, like Germany, in a bilateral setting, which did not stimulate the development of an effective and comprehensive EU-Russia policy either.[7]

Some gradual changes could be identified, when then Foreign Minister Frank-Walter Steinmeier introduced in 2006 a modified concept for Germany's relations with Russia: *Annäherung durch Verflechtung* (rapprochement through linkage), which was later also called *Wandel durch Handel* (change through trade). This concept implied that the development of closer ties with Russia, not only economically but also by linking societies, would eventually lead to positive political change in Russia with an emphasis on rule of law and a strong civil society. In this context, German Chancellor Gerhard Schröder and President Vladimir Putin presented a new joint initiative, the *Petersburger Dialogue*, a platform linking German and Russian politicians and a broad range of non-governmental organisations (NGOs) in a dialogue format, which could present recommendations to the regular bilateral summit meetings at the highest level. Furthermore, under Dmitry Medvedev's Presidency in Russia (2008–2012), this new concept led to the active promotion by Germany of a

---

6   S. Meister, 'Reframing Germany's Russia policy – an opportunity for the EU', European Council on Foreign Relations, 24 April 2014, available at: <https://www.ecfr.eu/publications/summary/reframing_germanys_russia_policy_an_opportunity_for_the_eu306> (accessed 14 March 2020).

7   Forsberg and Haukkala, *op. cit.* note 1.

'Partnership for Modernisation' with Russia, which in the German view could stimulate such positive developments.[8]

This idea of *modernisation partnerships* has also been promoted and *uploaded* by Berlin *to the EU level* and has developed into an EU-Russia Partnership for Modernisation. It was also replicated by a whole range of additional bilateral partnerships between Russia and individual EU Member States, including the Netherlands. The main idea of such policies was that a modernising Russia could be more easily integrated in a broader European framework, where interests would mainly converge and conflict could be avoided or peacefully resolved. These concepts for the relations with Russia, which became the core of Germany's and of the EU's Russia policies, would be fundamentally challenged by the developing crisis in and around Ukraine.

3   The Ukraine Crisis and Its Impact on German Perceptions on Russia

Although the Ukraine crisis as such was unexpected and German and European policy-makers had not foreseen any Russian military intervention to halt Ukraine's closer association and integration with the EU, a more fundamental conflict between Russia and the West had already been building up at an earlier stage. After the return of Putin to the Presidency in 2012, Moscow had been gradually restricting the possibilities for civil society to operate freely and develop contacts and cooperation with Western counterparts. At first, it seemed that mainly links with US organisations were targeted but then German (and other European) political foundations and NGOs were also confronted by restrictive Russian 'foreign agent legislation'. Therefore, relations between Germany and Russia had started to deteriorate in 2012, when German President Joachim Gauck cancelled a celebratory meeting with President Putin and Moscow refused further contacts with the CDU Member of Parliament and Special Envoy for Russia, Andreas Schockenhoff. Furthermore, 'anti-[lesbian, gay, bisexual and transgender]LGBT-legislation' adopted by the Duma in 2013 also underlined once more, that Russian politics and society were not changing

---

[8] S. Stewart, 'Germany', in: M. David, J. Gower and H. Haukkala (eds.), *National perspectives on Russia: European foreign policy in the making?* (Routledge 2013); S. Meister, *op. cit.* note 6; T. Forsberg, 'From Ostpolitik to "frostpolitik"? Merkel, Putin and German foreign policy towards Russia', *International Affairs* 92 (1), 2016, 21–42; M. Siddi, 'German foreign policy towards Russia in the aftermath of the Ukraine crisis: a new Ostpolitik?', *Europe-Asia Studies* 68 (4), 2016, 665–677.

in a supposedly modern European direction, based on democratic values and rule of law. In that sense, any policy of 'rapprochement through linkage' or 'change through trade' seemed to approach its limits.[9]

Because one of the main tenets of post-war German foreign policy had been the prevention of war and the peaceful settlement of conflicts on the basis of international law, the Russian takeover and subsequent annexation of Crimea and Russia's military intervention in eastern Ukraine provided a huge shock to the German political establishment, demanding a forceful (albeit non-military) response. Moscow's handling of this conflict estranged many Germans, as reflected in such critical articles, as entitled 'How Russia Lost Germany' and 'Wie Putin Berlin verlor' ('How Putin Lost Berlin').[10] Even Gernot Erler, who had succeeded Schockenhoff as German Special Envoy for Russia (and who as an SPD politician had always been working intensively on improving relations with Russia) now experienced a profound feeling of estrangement in contacts even with close Russian friends.[11]

On changing security narratives in Germany, Wolfgang Zellner concluded that 'this expectation of a co-operative relationship in the framework of a shared order has been – and this marks the change – fundamentally destroyed' and he qualified this rupture as 'so deep, that almost nobody believes that such a relationship can be "re-established" in the short- or even medium-term perspective'.[12] Most authors seem to agree, although there continues to be debate on the degree to which relations have changed: was this really a paradigm shift in the relations? Or do converging economic interests still provide an underlying continuity in the relations as a basis for an eventual return to some form of business as usual?[13]

---

9 Forsberg, *op. cit.* note 8; Meister, *op. cit.* note 6; Siddi, *op. cit.* note 8.
10 S. Meister, 'How Russia lost Germany: and how it can win it back', *Russia in Global Affairs* (2), 2015, available at: <http://eng.globalaffairs.ru/number/How-Russia-Lost-Germany-17365> (accessed 14 March 2020). A. Rinke, 'Wie Putin Berlin verlor. Moskaus Annexion der Krim hat die deutsche Russland-Politik verändert', *Internationale Politik* (3), 2014, 33–45.
11 G. Erler, *Weltordnung ohne den Westen? Europa zwischen Russland, China und Amerika* [*World order without the West: Europe between Russia, China and the US*] (Herder Verlag 2018).
12 W. Zellner, 'German perceptions of Russian-Western relations', in: W. Zellner (ed.), *Security narratives in Europe: a wide range of views* (Nomos Verlag 2017), 59–70.
13 Forsberg, *op. cit.* note 8; M. Siddi, *National identities and foreign policy in the European Union: the Russia policy of Germany, Poland and Finland* (ECPR 2017); M. Siddi, 'Germany's evolving relationship with Russia: towards a norm-based *Ostpolitik*?', in: N. Helwig (ed.), *Europe's new political engine: Germany's role in the EU's foreign and security policy* (FIIA/Helsinki 2016), available at: <https://www.fiia.fi/en/publication/europes-new-political-engine> (accessed 14 March 2020).

However, a broad consensus seems to have emerged within the German political elite, that the old *Ostpolitik* had ultimately failed and that new policies towards Russia and the neighbouring states, like Ukraine, were needed. The frustrating experience of German diplomacy in attempting to solve the Ukraine crisis and to negotiate a settlement at the highest level has also further contributed to the feeling of estrangement between Germans and Russians and to the notion that quick fixes were no longer possible in the new political circumstances. Whereas post-war Germany had always been unwilling to take a strong leadership role within EU foreign and security policy, the crisis with Russia now pushed Berlin in that direction, as no alternative leadership was available, either within the EU or from the United States.

4   German Leadership Role, Including in EU-Russia Relations

The Euromaidan revolution, which was triggered by the refusal of Ukrainian President Viktor Yanukovich to sign an Association Agreement with the EU at the November 2013 Vilnius Summit, posed a serious challenge to both EU and German foreign policy. Whereas the EU hardly recognised the geopolitical risks involved in negotiating such an agreement against strong Russian opposition, Germany attempted to move away from turning negotiations into a fundamental binary choice, either in favour of closer relations with the EU or with the Russian-dominated Eurasian Economic Union. However, events in the streets of Kyiv and other Ukrainian cities gradually took their own course with both the authorities and the opposition taking more hard-line positions, leaving little room for compromise.[14]

Similar to mediation efforts by external parties during the Orange Revolution in Ukraine in 2004, the EU at first did not take any special diplomatic initiative in reaction to the developing crisis. It eventually fell to German Foreign Minister Steinmeier, teaming up with his French and Polish colleagues within the *Weimar Triangle*, to co-lead mediation efforts in an attempt to negotiate a compromise between opposing sides in Kyiv. To underline that their efforts were not in opposition to Russia, a Russian representative was also invited to observe the negotiations. However, as a compromise solution was turned down and violence erupted, it became clear, especially after the flight of President Yanukovich to Russia, that Russia would become more actively

---

14 For a useful account by former Council President Van Rompuy's speechwriter, see L. van Middelaar, *Alarums & excursions: improvising politics on the European stage* (Agenda 2019).

involved, starting with the takeover of Crimea. Germany tried at the highest level to warn Russia not to move forward with plans for a referendum and for annexation of the peninsula. At the same time, German diplomacy worked hard to involve the EU and elaborate a package of possible sanctions, in case Russia would not comply with broader Western efforts within the OSCE to reach a diplomatic solution.[15]

Also, Chancellor Merkel was involved from the start in trying to persuade President Putin to find an acceptable solution, which would fully respect the sovereignty and territorial integrity of Ukraine. However, multiple telephone conversations could not prevent Moscow from moving ahead and taking over Crimea with its notorious 'little green men'. The annexation of Crimea and Sevastopol by the Russian Federation in March 2014 caused Berlin to fundamentally change course and to move ahead with EU partners on a package of sanctions in three stages, as already established in principle by the European Council on 6 March 2014: starting in phase 1 with diplomatic sanctions (including cancellation of summit meetings and suspension of bilateral talks with Russia) and then moving to impose travel bans and asset freezes for those connected with Russian (military) actions (phase 2).

The most difficult negotiations within the EU would be about the more serious economic and financial sectoral sanctions (phase 3) to be implemented, in case Russia would press ahead with further destabilising Ukraine, especially in the Donbas region, but initially even broader from Kharkiv to Mariupol and on to Odessa.[16] The European Council, in which Germany played a prominent and active role, tasked the European Commission to present a balanced proposal, which would take into account Member States' vulnerabilities in relations with Russia and provide for fair burden sharing for any financial losses to be incurred by the imposition of sanctions (and possible Russian counter-sanctions).

In the German political elite, a discussion continued, to which extent a simultaneous threat of sanctions and a continuation of diplomatic efforts could present effective tools in crisis management. Whereas EU Member States like Poland and the Baltic states already pressed for tougher and more real sanctions, Berlin still seemed to be wavering under the pressure of a strong business lobby. Furthermore, to move forward, it had to be able to convince

---

15   For more detailed accounts of German diplomatic efforts, see M. Siddi, 'A contested hegemon? Germany's leadership in EU relations with Russia', *German Politics* 29 (1), 2020, 97–114; Rinke, *op. cit.* note 10.

16   Russian media in those days heavily speculated about establishing a 'Novorossiya' in the eastern and southern parts of Ukraine, which would give Moscow control over a large part of Ukrainian territory, directly linking Crimea to Russia.

other EU Member States, even those less favourable to such sanctions like France and Italy. Furthermore, France had taken a new diplomatic initiative in June 2014 to establish the Normandy format for direct negotiations between France, Germany, Russia and Ukraine.[17]

This sanctions debate was still inconclusive, when on 17 July 2014 Malaysian airliner MH17 was shot down by a Russian anti-air Buk missile from separatist-held territory in the eastern Ukrainian Donbas area. This event would have a profound impact and it is generally envisaged as a real 'game changer', further complicating the relations with Moscow. It also temporarily ended the debate on the need to impose phase 3 sectoral sanctions, both within the EU and in the German political and economic elite. For Germany, the escalation of the crisis in Donbas and the downing of flight MH17 had two major implications.

First, the German business community and, more particularly, those major companies involved in energy relations and other important business deals in Russia had finally come to the conclusion, albeit grudgingly, that the political imperative of opposing Russian violations of international law, and the challenge this implied for the post–Cold War security order, trumped any business interests. Therefore, sectoral sanctions would be implemented, although some sectors were partly exempted, including (for Germany, most importantly) bilateral gas relations.[18]

Second, as US President Barack Obama encouraged Germany to take the lead in trying to reach a negotiated settlement to the crisis within the Normandy framework, Chancellor Merkel became *de facto* the number one Western leader to take diplomatic initiatives forward. In return, the US President complied with the strong German wish to find a peaceful solution and refrain from any actions which could run contrary to diplomatic efforts, like arms deliveries to Ukraine. It was also Chancellor Merkel who *de facto* received a mandate from the EU to negotiate (together with French President François Hollande) with Russian President Putin and Ukrainian President Petro Poroshenko. This broad acceptance was more easily achieved after Germany finally supported selected phase 3 sectoral sanctions, as proposed

---

17　Forsberg, *op. cit.* note 8; W. Seibel, 'Arduous learning or new uncertainties? The emergence of German diplomacy in the Ukrainian crisis', *Global Policy* 6 (S1), 2015, 56–72; P. Daehnhardt, 'German foreign policy, the Ukraine crisis and the Euro-Atlantic order: assessing the dynamics of change', *German Politics* 27 (4), 2018, 516–538; L. Fix, 'The different "shades" of German power: Germany and EU foreign policy during the Ukraine conflict', *German Politics* 27 (4), 2018, 498–515.

18　Siddi, *op. cit.* note 13, 157–170; Forsberg, 'The domestic sources of German foreign policy towards Russia', in: N. Helwig (ed.), *Europe's new political engine: Germany's role in the EU's foreign and security policy* (FIIA/Helsinki 2016), 137–154.

by the European Commission. Thereby, Germany had built trust in its role as an honest broker and turned out to be acceptable as such to other EU Member States, as it showed its willingness to share in suffering from possible negative effects on German business. All this also implied that German-Russian relations had now been turned into a matter to be dealt with by the Chancellor personally, even more than before moving negotiations away from the Foreign Office and into Merkel's Chancellery.[19]

Although sanctions had in a formal sense not been taken in connection with Russia's responsibility for the downing of MH17 (which still had to be proven in further investigations), the escalation of violence in Donbas which led to MH17 galvanised public opinion within the EU that stronger EU actions were now called for. Merkel's own telephone calls with Putin and her call for an independent investigation and an immediate ceasefire in the area did not receive any positive response from Moscow.[20]

As developments had propelled Germany into taking a leadership role in negotiating a solution to the Ukraine crisis, it was Chancellor Merkel who personally played a central role in negotiations in summit meetings of the Normandy format, leading first to the Minsk Protocol (September 2014) and, after its failure to produce a lasting ceasefire in Donbas, to the Minsk agreement in February 2015.[21] Her strong personal involvement in these negotiations was reflected in both the memoirs of her co-negotiator French President Hollande and the account by EU Council President Herman Van Rompuy's speechwriter Luuk van Middelaar.[22] And on 19 March 2015, Merkel's personal involvement within the European Council lead to a Council decision to align the existing sanctions regime to the full implementation of the Minsk

---

19 W. Koeth, 'Leadership revised: how did the Ukraine crisis and the annexation of Crimea affirm Germany's leading role in EU foreign policy?', in *Lithuanian Annual Strategic Review* 14, 2015–2016, 101–116; M. Natorski and K. Pomorska, 'Trust and decision-making in times of crisis: the EU's response to the events in Ukraine', *Journal of Common Market Studies* 55 (1), 2017, 54–70; N. Wright, 'No longer the elephant outside the room: why the Ukraine crisis reflects a deeper shift towards German leadership of European foreign policy', *German Politics* 27 (4), 2018, 479–497; U. Speck, 'The West's response to the Ukraine conflict: a transatlantic success story', Transatlantic Academy Washington, 2016, available at: <http://www.gmfus.org/publications/wests-response-ukraine-conflict> (accessed 14 March 2020).

20 See S. Wagstyl, 'Merkel rethink of sanctions reflect loss of trust in Putin', 30 July 2014, available at: <https://www.ft.com/content/a29dfa7e-17d5-11e4-a82d-00144feabdc0> (accessed 14 March 2020).

21 See the contribution by S. Van Severen (chapter 1) in this volume.

22 F. Hollande, *Les leçons du pouvoir* (Stock 2018); van Middelaar, *op. cit.* note 14.

agreements, which should ultimately enable Ukraine to regain control over its borders in the East.[23]

This crucial Council meeting not only took place after the negotiation of the (second) Minsk agreement but also followed up on the debate on the future of EU-Russia relations, which EU Foreign Ministers had conducted in January 2015 based on a discussion paper presented by the EU High Representative for Common Foreign and Security Policy Federica Mogherini (and leaked to the *Financial Times*). In the end, this was considered too accommodating to Russia.[24] After the meeting, Mogherini underlined that 'relations can only be changed if and when the Minsk commitments are implemented'.[25] These discussions have resulted *de facto* in a shift in EU policy-making on Russia away from the High Representative towards the EU Member States, with Germany in a leading role.

In spite of doubts and complaints about the sanctions against Russia by some EU Member States, sanctions have regularly been extended ever since. Although German diplomacy has tried to encourage the parties to fully implement the Minsk agreements, especially during the German OSCE Chairmanship in 2016, suggestions for a road map of positive steps, which could lead to an eventual downscaling of sanctions,[26] have failed to produce any concrete steps forward. Russian unwillingness to take responsibility and put pressure on the separatists in Donbas to comply has resulted in a political and military stalemate. Therefore, in March 2016 the EU Foreign Ministers agreed on the five principles for the relations with Russia with the full implementation of the Minsk agreements presented as a 'key element for any substantial change in the relations'.[27] As Germany had become the chief negotiator with Russia on finding a solution to the Ukraine crisis, based on these agreements, the main

---

23 See timeline of EU sanctions, European Council and Council of the EU, available at: <https://www.consilium.europa.eu/en/policies/sanctions/ukraine-crisis/history-ukraine-crisis/> (accessed 14 March 2020).

24 See K. Liik, 'The real problem with Mogherini's Russia paper', European Council on Foreign Relations, 2015, available at: <https://www.ecfr.eu/article/commentary_the_real_problem_with_mogherinis_russia_paper402> (accessed 14 March 2020).

25 Council of the EU, Outcome of the Council Meeting, 3364th Council meeting, Brussels, 19 January 2015, available at: <https://www.consilium.europa.eu/media/21898/st05411en15.pdf> (accessed 14 March 2020).

26 Cf. 'Steinmeier formula', to which the new Ukrainian President Zelensky returned in a renewed effort to find a political solution to the conflict, available at: <https://www.rferl.org/a/what-is-the-steinmeier-formula-and-did-zelenskiy-just-capitulate-to-moscow-/30195593.html> (accessed 14 March 2020).

27 'Remarks by High Representative/Vice-President Federica Mogherini at the press conference following the Foreign Affairs Council, Brussels, 14 March 2016', available at:

role remaining for the High Representative in the EU's Russia policy seems to have been to preserve unity on the sanctions (which by itself is no small matter). Broader Russia policy became focussed on negotiations in the Normandy format and any real progress on any selective engagement with Russia on other issues of joint interest became hostage to progress on the full implementation of the Minsk agreements.

Furthermore, this crisis in the relations with Russia had led to increased Russian disinformation efforts to undermine Chancellor Merkel's political position in her own country, including by Moscow's support for the populist extreme right party, Alternative für Deutschland (AFD), and by using bilateral economic and energy links to undermine support for the sanctions within the German business community and among those *Bundesländer* (provinces) which are profiting most from business connections with Russia. Therefore, more fundamental discussions within the German political elite on a possible return to some form of the old *Ostpolitik* have re-emerged. And attempts by the new Foreign Minister Heiko Maas to produce a more balanced Eastern Policy, which would no longer prioritise constructive relations with Moscow over relations with Central and Eastern European states, have so far not been very productive. Discussions on continued German support for the construction of the Nord Stream 2 gas pipeline have increasingly undermined trust by Central and Eastern European states in Germany's ability to play the role of an honest broker in relations with Russia and also in a broader European context. EU Member States, like Poland and the Baltic states, would prefer to take sides with the United States under President Donald Trump in opposing energy dependence on Russia and imposing additional sanctions, if necessary. Therefore, whether Germany could in the future retain its leadership role in EU-Russia relations is far from certain, as a full-scale *Europeanisation* of Germany's Russia policy seems to be increasingly restrained once more by bilateral business interests.[28]

        <https://eeas.europa.eu/headquarters/headquarters-homepage/5490/remarks-by-high-representativevice-president-federica-mogherini-at-the-press-conference-following-the-foreign-affairs-council_en> (accessed 14 March 2020).

28   S. Meister, 'Nord Stream 2: the dead-end of Germany's Ostpolitik', *Berlin Policy Journal*, February 2019, available at: <https://dgap.org/en/think-tank/publications/further-publications/nord-stream-2-dead-end-germanys-ostpolitik> (accessed 14 March 2020); S. Meister, 'Searching for a new foundation in German-Russian relations', May 2018, available at: <https://dgap.org/en/think-tank/publications/further-publications/searching-new-foundation-german-russian-relations> (accessed 14 March 2020); H. Adomeit, 'A realistic German Ostpolitik is hampered by old illusions', Knowledge Platform Raam op

5   The Netherlands, EU-Russia Relations and the Ukraine Crisis

The Netherlands has had a long and often complicated relationship with Russia and the Soviet Union. Historical and cultural ties date back to the times of Czar Peter the Great, who used the Dutch experience in his efforts to modernise Russia. Furthermore, in the early 19th century Dutch King William II of Orange married a Romanov princess, binding the two royal houses together, and the Russian Czar had been an important ally in the struggle against Napoleon. The Russian Revolution led to a temporary breakdown in diplomatic relations, which were only re-established in 1942 in a joint alliance against Adolf Hitler's Germany. Relations in Soviet times can be qualified by simultaneous *mistrust* (because of the Dutch fear of the spread of communism and the Netherlands' own Atlantic security orientation) and *commitment*, especially in supporting human rights and fundamental freedoms in Eastern Europe and the Soviet Union. In the early 1990s, the Netherlands reached out to the new Russia in supporting the transition to a democratic society and a market economy. At the same time, business relations, especially in the energy sector, increased rapidly from an early start in late Soviet times: Shell and Gasunie became important players and business partners of Russian companies like Gazprom.[29]

The Netherlands has strong bilateral (economic) relations with Russia, which would leave ample room to also discuss politically more sensitive topics such as human rights and democracy. However, internal developments in Russia, especially under President Putin, have led to a situation where support for Russian civil society has diminished in practical terms and human rights (including LGBT rights) have become a bigger irritant in relations, as could already be noticed during the Netherlands-Russia bilateral year 2013.[30] At the same time, the Netherlands has tried to shift the direction of the discussion

---

Rusland, February 2019, available at: <https://raamoprusland.nl/dossiers/europa/1210-a-realistic-german-ostpolitik-is-hampered-by-old-illusions> (accessed 14 March 2020).

29   T. van der Togt, 'Wantrouwen en betrokkenheid: het verhaal van een complexe relatie. Diplomatieke betrekkingen tussen Nederland en Rusland 1942–2013' [Diplomatic relations between the Netherlands and Russia, 1942–2013], in: N. Kraft van Ermel/ J.S.A.M. van Koningsbrugge (eds.), *Nederland en Rusland, een paar apart? 400 jaar Nederlands-Russische betrekkingen* [*The Netherlands and Russia, a special couple? 400 years Dutch-Russian relations*] (Baltic Studies Groningen 2013), 66–90. For more details on energy relations, see P. Högselius, *Red gas: Russia and the origins of European energy dependence* (Palgrave Macmillan 2013).

30   A full account of the Netherlands-Russia year 2013 was sent to parliament with a letter of the Minister of Foreign Affairs: *Tweede Kamer, 2013–14, 33750 V, nr 79*, dated 11 July 2014 (in Dutch).

to reinforcing the rule of law (instead of active support for democratisation) and a focus on human rights commitments under international law, to which Russia had voluntarily subscribed. In EU-Russia relations, the Netherlands aimed for pragmatic complementarity and a division of labour, which could strengthen its position towards Russia while simultaneously reserving active trade promotion and energy relations mainly for the bilateral level.[31] In this sense, its Russia policy resembles that of Germany, albeit with a lower intensity of bilateral relations.

As business relations moved to the forefront of relations with Russia, the Netherlands was at first rather hesitant to impose economic sanctions after the annexation of Crimea and Russian destabilisation of eastern Ukraine.[32] Although the Netherlands has a strong international legal tradition and realised the challenge to the European security order, economic interests initially held The Hague back from a more proactive position on sanctions, putting the Netherlands in the same league as Germany and supporting international efforts to strive for a diplomatic and non-military solution to the crisis.

6   The Impact of MH17 on Perceptions of Russia

The downing of flight MH17 on 17 July 2014, which led to the tragic loss of life of 298 people, including 196 Dutch citizens, formed the 'watershed-moment' for the Dutch relations with Moscow. The Netherlands did not blame Russia directly, pending international investigations into the causes of the tragedy and the criminal investigations to bring those responsible to justice. But clear Russian responsibility for the ongoing crisis in Ukraine and the escalation of violence in Donbas, which had made the MH17 tragedy possible, prompted The Hague, like the other European partners, to support the EU's adoption of a number of selected sectoral sanctions against Russia.

For most of the Dutch political elite and the public at large, MH17 formed the culmination of growing concerns not only about internal developments in Russia, related to human rights and democratic freedoms, but also about Russia's external policies of turning into an aggressive and revisionist power,

---

31   A. Gerrits, 'The Netherlands, Russia and the European Union', in: A. Schout and J. Rood (eds.), *The Netherlands as an EU Member: awkward or loyal partner?* (Eleven International 2013).

32   See L. Klompenhouwer, 'Kaart: waarom de EU geen harde sancties aandurft tegen Rusland', 19 March 2014, available at: <https://www.nrc.nl/nieuws/2014/03/19/waarom-de-eu-geen-harde-sancties-aandurft-tegen-rusland-a1426414> (accessed 14 March 2020).

no longer respecting international law and fundamentally challenging the post–Cold War European security order. And like in Germany, also in the Netherlands politics finally trumped business interests.[33] The Dutch government made its position clear in an extensive letter to parliament in May 2015, that there could be no return to 'business as usual' in the relations. From now on, Dutch-Russian relations would be characterised by 'pressure' and 'dialogue', in both a bilateral and a multilateral context: the UN, EU, NATO, OSCE and Council of Europe.[34] Relations could gradually be characterised as business as unusual with serious questions about a possible return to more constructive dialogue and selective cooperation, which have been severely restricted in recent years.[35]

An important part of the policy of putting pressure on Russia to return to respect for the international legal order, including for the sovereignty and territorial integrity of Ukraine, was formed by the EU sectoral sanctions, for which the basis had been laid by the EU Foreign Affairs Council on 22 July 2014, just after then Minister of Foreign Affairs Frans Timmermans's return from New York and his vigorous appeal to the UN Security Council to bring those responsible for the MH17 tragedy to justice.[36] In practice, the EU decision on sectoral sanctions and its repeated prolongations have been fully supported by the Netherlands ever since, as well as its linkage to the full implementation of the Minsk agreements by the European Council decision in March 2015.

As MH17 became the most important issue in the relations with Russia, successive Dutch governments have basically followed two broad policy lines since 2014.[37] On the one hand, they have followed a politically neutral and more legalistic approach to the international investigations into the MH17 tragedy, combined with sustained efforts to acquire Russian cooperation in bringing

---

33 B. ter Haar, 'Dutch narratives about Russian-Western relations', in: W. Zellner (ed.), *Security narratives in Europe: A wide range of views* (Nomos Verlag 2017); T. van der Togt, 'How should Europe respond to Russia? The Dutch view', February 2015, available at: <https://www.ecfr.eu/article/commentary_how_should_europe_respond_to_russia_the_dutch_view311233> (accessed 14 March 2020).

34 Letter of Minister of Foreign Affairs to parliament on the relations with Russia: *Tweede Kamer, 2014–15, 34000 V, nr. 69, dated 13 May 2015* (in Dutch).

35 N. Eilander, 'Russian-Dutch relations: business as unusual', MA Thesis, Leiden University, May 2017, available at: <https://openaccess.leidenuniv.nl/handle/1887/49117> (accessed 14 March 2020).

36 Letter of Ministers of Foreign Affairs and Security and Justice to parliament on MH17: *Tweede Kamer, 2013–14, nr. 1, dated 24 July 2014* (in Dutch).

37 T. van der Togt, 'The impact of MH17 on Dutch-Russian relations', October 2016, available at: <https://www.clingendael.org/publication/impact-mh17-dutch-russian-relations> (accessed 14 March 2020).

those responsible to justice in accordance with UN Security Council Resolution 2166 (2014). Based on this approach, the Netherlands attempted to organise an international UN Tribunal on MH17 but these efforts were blocked by a Russian veto. Since any constructive cooperation with the investigations was not forthcoming from the Russian side and Moscow continued to publicly doubt the integrity and objectivity of the investigations, the Netherlands (and Australia) decided to hold Russia as a state responsible for actions of its citizens in bringing down MH17. On that basis, confidential talks have been started, raising the possibility of a settlement out of court. However, on the other hand, the criminal investigations by the multilateral Joint Investigation Team (JIT) have come to preliminary conclusions and have resulted in the first indictments. The trial has now started at a Dutch court in March 2020 and will probably last for years, while ongoing investigations could lead to further indictments as well. Finally, the Netherlands has decided to submit an inter-state application against Russia on MH17 before the European Court on Human Rights[38], leading to a Russian suspension of the discussions on state responsibility.

On the other hand, Dutch governments had made a continuing effort to internationalise the issue and prevent it from being turned into a purely bilateral issue between the Netherlands and Russia. This effort started by calling on the UN Security Council and following up on Security Council Resolution 2166 (2014), including during 2018 when the Netherlands was a non-permanent member of the Security Council. The Netherlands has also constantly sought support from its EU partners, resulting in a number of Council Conclusions calling on Russia to cooperate in bringing the culprits to justice. Therefore, the Netherlands deliberately 'uploaded' this issue to the level of EU-Russia relations as well.

The MH17 tragedy and the continuation of Russian disinformation and Moscow's refusal up to now to accept responsibility for the effects of its military actions in Ukraine have seriously undermined trust in cooperation with Russia. This has also continued to be a dominant factor in the re-evaluation of Dutch Russia policy, as requested by the Dutch parliament at the end of 2018.

The new policy letter on relations with Russia, which Foreign Minister Stef Blok sent to parliament by the end of 2019, basically provides a continuation of the policy of 'pressure and dialogue', as advocated by the previous government.[39] In light of recent developments and because Russia has not changed

---

38   Netherlands government announcement, available at: <https://www.government.nl/latest/news/2020/07/10/the-netherlands-brings-mh17-case-against-russia-before-european-court-of-human-rights> (accessed 30 September 2020).

39   Letter by Foreign Minister Blok to parliament on the relations with Russia: *Tweede Kamer, 2019–2020, 35373, nr 1, 22 December 2019* (in Dutch).

its position on issues of major concern, such a policy is considered to constitute a realistic way of dealing with Moscow, both bilaterally and in multilateral (including EU) contexts. Although the focus will remain on 'protecting and defending Dutch national security, investing in resilience and promoting the international legal order', the policy letter concludes that Russia remains of geostrategic importance and:

> It is therefore crucial to continue engaging in dialogue, seeking to connect and, where possible, working together on areas where we share common interests. Ultimately, dialogue is a key means of gaining insight into our mutual differences and promoting our own interests. It is also important for the broader relations between the Netherlands and Russia that we continue to encourage social ties between Dutch and Russian citizens and keep investing in Dutch knowledge of Russia, regardless of how the country develops in the years ahead.[40]

Although at present the Netherlands government remains supportive of the continuation of the pipeline project Nord Stream 2 as a 'commercial project', developments concerning the EU regulatory framework and the successful efforts by Germany and the European Commission to guarantee future gas transit through Ukraine could lead to a more balanced position, taking into account broader geopolitical considerations as well. Whereas both the Netherlands and Germany have tried to preserve energy relations with Russia as much as possible as a bilateral (commercial) issue, increased pressure from the European Commission and a number of EU Member States, supported by the United States with secondary sanctions against European companies involved in the construction of Nord Stream 2, could force The Hague and Berlin to further Europeanise energy relations as the most important part of their economic relations with Russia in the context of a wider European Energy Union.

7 Concluding Remarks

EU decision-making on relations with Russia has always been a complicated matter, as larger EU Member States (but sometimes also smaller ones like the Netherlands) have been willing to Europeanise only part of the relationship, while

---

40   See T. van der Togt, 'In search of a European Russia strategy', 9 March 2020, available at: <https://www.clingendael.org/publication/search-european-russia-strategy> (accessed 14 March 2020).

reserving especially energy relations for *bilateral* (commercial) negotiations, irrespective of the interests of other EU Member States and Eastern partners. As perspectives on Russia have changed fundamentally because of the Ukraine crisis, both the EU and its Member States have had to face some fundamental dilemmas when contemplating the future of their relationship with Russia and decision-making on EU-Russia relations has been affected accordingly.

Both for Germany and the Netherlands, the Ukraine crisis, including the annexation of Crimea and Russian military engagement in eastern Ukraine, posed the most important challenge to the post–Cold War European security order, based on international legal obligations. Although both countries had long-standing and essentially constructive bilateral economic relations with Russia, especially in the energy sphere, they ultimately came to face a situation in which political imperatives had to trump business interests. Against this background, both Berlin and The Hague concluded that real economic and financial sanctions could no longer be avoided and overruled any dissent from their respective business communities, at least for the time being. Furthermore, it became increasingly clear that the old *Ostpolitik* had failed: mutual dependence would not prevent Moscow from military intervention in Europe and would not bring about political change in Russia resulting in a more democratic society and rule of law. In the end, the Ukraine crisis (and for the Dutch the downing of MH17 and the continuing Russian disinformation about the tragedy) became a game changer in the relations: any return to business as usual was considered impossible, at least for the short to medium term.

Within the EU, Germany was initially propelled into a leadership role, as it occupied a central position in relations with Russia and was willing to act as an honest broker, even when this implied that German business interests would also suffer. The fact that the Obama administration placed trust in Berlin to manage the crisis and to strive for a negotiated solution in the Normandy format also helped, as did the close coordination in imposing mutual sanctions against Russia. In practice, the future development of EU-Russia relations came to depend on finding a diplomatic solution to the Ukraine crisis. Although the EU fully realised that sanctions could not substitute for a broader Russia policy, the five principles for the relations with Russia implied that much (if not everything) would depend on the first principle: full implementation of the Minsk agreements (to which any downscaling or lifting of the package of economic and financial sanctions had been linked). In this context, EU High Representative for Common Foreign and Security Policy Mogherini could play only a secondary role in policy-making on Russia, albeit not an unimportant one in guaranteeing continued EU unity on sanctions.

The future of EU-Russia relations has come to depend on a number of factors, affecting the complicated interplay between EU institutions and individual EU Member States in shaping a common approach towards the strategic challenge which Russia is currently posing.

As decision-making on EU-Russia relations became heavily influenced by Germany and as the German Chancellor personally became the main negotiator to find a diplomatic solution to the Ukraine crisis, the trust that other EU Member States put in German leadership and Merkel's political position at home came to be decisive elements in these complicated circumstances. German unwillingness to put a halt to the construction of the Nord Stream 2 gas pipeline has eroded trust among Central and Eastern European partners in Berlin's ability to act as an honest broker in the relations with Russia. Simultaneously, Merkel's political position at home seems to have been weakened, reopening opportunities for German business to press for closer economic engagement with Russia. Although at present no new German *Ostpolitik* seems to be forthcoming, recent incidents have reopened the debate on Germany's relations with Russia during its EU Presidency in the second half of 2020.[41] In particular, the poisoning of Russian opposition leader Alexei Navalny (who was treated in a hospital in Berlin) and the Russian role in supporting the repressive Lukashenko regime in Belarus created new tensions in EU-Russia relations. In this context, it is interesting to note that the German government has indicated its willingness to reconsider its position on Nord Stream 2 and to discuss possible new sanctions against Russia in a European framework.[42]

The Netherlands has mainly followed the German lead in EU-Russia relations over the past years. It has also remained supportive of continuing the construction of Nord Stream 2. In this sense, Dutch-Russian relations have also only partly been Europeanised, whereas the Netherlands still counts on EU partners to support its efforts to press for Russian cooperation in bringing the perpetrators of the MH17 tragedy to justice. In the new Dutch policy document on the relations with Russia, The Hague has chosen to continue its earlier policies of 'pressure and dialogue'. The Netherlands remains open to dialogue and selective cooperation on issues of common concern but this will to a large

---

41 S.Meister, 'The end of German Ostpolitik. What a change in Germany's Russia policy might look like', September 2020, available at: <https://dgap.org/sites/default/files/article_pdfs/dgap-policy_brief-2020-22-en.pdf> (accessed 30 September 2020).

42 A.Rinke, 'Merkel doesn't rule out sanctions on Russian gas pipeline, spokesman says', 7 September 2020, available at: <https://www.reuters.com/article/us-russia-politics-navalny-germany-idUSKBN25Y11R> (accessed 30 September 2020).

extent depend on Moscow's reactions and willingness to change its policies. This will also impact on the position of the Netherlands in any discussions inside the EU on a possible *reset* in the relations with Moscow, along the lines that the French President seems to be aiming for. In the meantime, Dutch perceptions and policies on Russia remain heavily affected by the MH17 tragedy and the continuing Russian disinformation efforts aimed at undermining the investigations and the trial of four suspects which has recently started.

At the same time French President Macron, as the other main EU partner participating in negotiations on solving the Ukraine crisis, has recently been attempting to reach out to Russian President Putin in an attempt to kick-start the negotiations in the Normandy format and engage the new Ukrainian President Volodymyr Zelensky in moving towards a political solution. In his view, this could pave the way for rebuilding a wider 'architecture of trust' with Russia on the European continent.[43] Although the first summit in the Normandy format in three years took place in Paris in late 2019 and some steps forward have been taken, such as an exchange of prisoners, no fundamental breakthrough has been accomplished and Moscow has thus far not reciprocated President Macron's outreach to find compromise solutions on issues of common concern.

Only time will tell whether other EU Member States would be willing to support President Macron's *Gaullist* approach and whether Russia's reactions could ultimately convince the more hard-line EU Member States, like Poland and the Baltic states, that cooperation with Moscow could lead to real results which would respect international legal obligations and fundamental values. The influence of these Member States on EU decision-making on Russia could in the future also be undermined by Brexit, as the United Kingdom has always supported a tougher position as long as Moscow does not intend to compromise. For this group of EU Member States, full implementation of the Minsk agreements remains an absolute precondition for any improvement in relations with Russia.

Furthermore, it would probably become more challenging in the coming years to keep internal unity on the Russia sanctions, as another group of EU Member States (including Greece, Hungary, Cyprus, Austria and Italy) has become more critical of sanctions and would in principle like to abolish them. Therefore, the prospect of new sanctions towards Russia could be expected only in the case of a serious (military) escalation of the present crisis. Only the

---

43 A. Robert, 'France's Macron makes Russia a top diplomatic priority', 28 August 2019, available at: <https://www.euractiv.com/section/global-europe/news/frances-macron-makes-russia-a-top-diplomatic-priority/> (accessed 14 March 2020).

fact that these EU Member States also have other, more important interests to be dealt with in the EU context has until now restrained them in blocking further renewal of the present sanctions.

Finally, a new European Commission under a German President Ursula von der Leyen has entered office and has presented itself as a 'geopolitical Commission', and the new High Representative Josep Borrell has put EU-Russia relations high on the political agenda. During the informal meeting of EU Ministers of Foreign Affairs on 5 March 2020, the future of EU-Russia relations has been discussed and ministers have agreed to revisit the five principles for the relations with Russia to develop more effective policies.[44]

Most probably, EU decision-making on relations with Russia in the next five years would be as complicated as ever before. How this will influence the future of the EU's present five principles for the relations with Russia, which has been the lowest common denominator the EU could agree on, remains very much to be seen, including whether the first principle (i.e., full implementation of the Minsk agreements) will remain a precondition for progress in any other area such as selective engagement on issues of common concern (the fourth principle). These discussions will also be influenced by debates on broader issues, including the future of the multilateral rules-based order and the EU's place in such a global order. In this context, relations with Russia can hardly be treated separately from the EU's relations with other global players such as the United States and China.

A geopolitical Commission, a weakened German leadership and a more strategically operating French President will all contribute to uncertainties in the shaping of EU decisions, including on the relations with Russia. The outcome of this process will also offer some further indications about the respective roles of EU Member States and institutions in future decision-making against the background of changing internal power configurations within the EU and their willingness to present the EU as a geopolitical actor in its own right. In this context, the EU would be served well if it could agree on a comprehensive and integrated Russia strategy which would serve the interests of all EU Member States in an equitable manner. However, for this to happen all Member States, including the bigger ones, would have to act in unity and display their willingness to make compromises in the interest of the EU as a whole.

---

44 See statement by High Representative Borrell after the informal meeting of EU Foreign Ministers, 5 March 2020, available at: <https://eeas.europa.eu/headquarters/headquarters-homepage/75608/gymnich-statement-high-representative-following-informal-meeting-eu-foreign-ministers_en> (accessed 14 March 2020).

CHAPTER 3

Two Monologues Don't Make a Dialogue
The EU's and Russia's Strategic Narratives about the Minsk Agreements and Sanctions Regime

Irina Petrova

1   Introduction

In parallel with the Minsk agreements and imposition of reciprocal sanctions, both the EU and Russia have developed coherent narratives presenting two very different stories that advocate their interpretation of these events. Arguably, these stories matter as much as the actual developments on the ground since adherence to a certain story shapes people's understandings, beliefs and, eventually, behaviour. The promotion of one's own story is therefore an important source of power in international affairs. This chapter argues that an in-depth study of the EU's and Russia's narratives about the Minsk agreements and sanctions regime as an exercise of power can help us to better understand EU-Russia relations and the prospects for overcoming the present deadlock.

This chapter uses narrative analysis as a conceptual tool to analyse strategic narratives of the two international actors. By looking at the EU's and Russia's narratives about the Minsk agreements and reciprocal sanctions as the most contentious issues of bilateral relations the chapter: (1) deconstructs the narratives and compares them; (2) compares and explains the patterns of the EU's and Russia's narrative formulation and reception; and (3) provides an insight into how the convergence of narratives could contribute to the improvement of bilateral relations between the EU and Russia. Thus, the two questions addressed here are: What are the main patterns of the EU's and Russia's strategic narrative formulation and mutual narratives' reception? What factors explain (in)effectiveness of strategic narratives?

Whereas political actors usually operate with several – sometimes competing – narratives, this chapter is interested in the main narrative which is being projected to the international arena. It therefore deals with a *strategic narrative*, defined as a 'means for political actors to construct a shared meaning of the past, present and future of international politics to shape the behaviour of domestic and international actors'.[1] Methodologically, narrative analysis implies exploration of several constitutive elements that create a coherent story. A. Miskimmon et al. suggest analysing strategic narratives based on four elements – environment, actors, problem and resolution. *Environment* consists of 'assumptions, assertions, underlying principles and rationales. These shape the range of the possible in terms of identifying issues that need resolution, and goals that might be achieved'.[2] *Actors* include the most important players involved in shaping the international system or playing major roles in a particular issue/policy. The actors have strictly assigned roles of victims, villains and heroes.[3] *Problem* presents a challenge which has to be addressed, or the issue which requires a solution. Finally, *resolution* is a combination of measures proposed or undertaken by an actor to resolve the problem.

Furthermore, a strategic narrative can be presented as a cycle that consists of three stages: formation, projection and reception. Based on these methodological considerations, this chapter analyses the EU's and Russia's strategic narrative formulation and reception using critical discourse analysis (CDA) of official documents and political speeches. For that purpose, a database was compiled from open sources comprising 158 Russian documents and 129 documents produced by the EU and its Member States in the time frame between 1 January 2014 and 31 December 2018. Specifically, the documents were produced by the Russian President, Ministry of Foreign Affairs (MFA) and the representation of the Russian Federation in the EU, as well as by the European Council, Commission, Parliament and European External Action Service (EEAS), and the EU Member States' Prime Ministers, Presidents, MFAs and party leaders. Throughout the chapter, explicit references are made to only some primary sources due to the lack of space, yet the conclusions are formulated based on a thorough analysis of all documents. The study explores the reception of the strategic narratives at the level of political elites and the general population. To account for the latter, the chapter also makes use of a wide range of established popular surveys available in English and Russian. The results from these

---

1   A. Miskimmon, B. O'Loughlin and L. Roselle, *Strategic narratives: communication power and the New World Order* (Routledge 2013), 2.
2   L. Roselle, A. Miskimmon and B. O'Loughlin, 'Strategic narrative: a new means to understand soft power', *Media, War and Conflict* 7 (1), 2014, 75.
3   E. Anker, 'Villains, victims and heroes: melodrama, media, and September 11' *Journal of Communication* 55 (1), 2005, 22–37; E. Shanahan, M. Jones, M. McBeth and R. Lane, 'An angel on the wind: how heroic policy narratives shape policy realities', *Policy Studies Journal* 41 (3), 2013, 453–483.

surveys were triangulated through comparison of different surveys to ensure data validity.

2 Strategic Narratives Formulation

This section starts by deconstructing the respective narratives into their constituent elements and evaluating their coherence. It proceeds by comparing the patterns of narrative building and sources of legitimation employed by Moscow and Brussels. Finally, an evaluation of the dynamics of the respective narratives over the five years will be developed. Ultimately, and similarly to the Cold War period, the EU and Russia have developed mirror narratives, implying that almost all elements of the strategic narratives are completely opposite to each other.

2.1 *Russia's Strategic Narrative on the Minsk Agreements*

According to the Russian strategic narrative, the civil war in Ukraine was rooted in the 'anti-constitutional *coup d'etat*'[4] largely provoked by 'the West' (primarily the United States and the EU), when President Viktor Yanukovych was ousted from Kiev on 22 February 2014 as the opposition threated his life.[5] 'The West' made Ukraine choose between the EU and Russia and advanced the 'us versus them' vision.[6] A sequence of 'unprofessional' actions by the United States and the EU led to the escalation of the internal crisis. The recurrent example of such actions in the Russian narrative is the failure of the EU to guarantee the 'Agreement on the settlement of crisis in Ukraine' (21 February 2014) signed by President Viktor Yanukovych and three Ukrainian opposition leaders witnessed by the Ministers of Foreign Affairs of Germany, France and Poland.[7]

---

4   V. Putin, 'Vladimir Putin's annual news conference', 24 December 2016, <https://russiaeu.ru/en/news/vladimir-putins-annual-news-conference-0> (accessed 13 March 2020).

5   S. Lavrov, 'Russian Foreign Minister Sergey Lavrov's interview with Bloomberg TV', 27 September 2014 <https://russiaeu.ru/en/news/russian-foreign-minister-sergey-lavrovs-interview-bloomberg-tv-27-september-2014> (accessed 13 March 2020).

6   S. Lavrov, 'Foreign Minister Sergey Lavrov's statement and answers to media questions at a joint news conference following talks with Austrian Foreign Minister Sebastian Kurz', 18 January 2017, <https://russiaeu.ru/en/news/foreign-minister-sergey-lavrovs-statement-and-answers-media-questions-joint-news-conference> (accessed 13 March 2020).

7   Agreement on the settlement of crisis in Ukraine, 21 February 2014, <https://www.auswaertiges-amt.de/blob/260130/db4f5326f21530cad8d351152feb5e26/140221-ukr-erklaerung-data.pdf> (accessed 13 March 2020).

This view is further advanced in the framing of the 'actors' in the conflict. The West and the Kiev government are presented as the main villains, Donbass as a victim and Russia as its protector. Thus, the Kiev government is presented as illegitimately usurping power in the country ignoring the protests in the Donbass region.[8] Kiev is said to have started hostilities in Donbass, including military actions, killings and an economic blockade of the region. A prominent element in portraying the central government is the emphasis on the fact that the ruling coalition included neo-Nazi forces (e.g., Oleg Tyagnibok and the Svoboda party). Another villain in the Russian strategic narrative is the West, which is presented as having consciously provoked the conflict.[9] The West is presented as an unreliable actor as, at the key moment of the crisis, it failed to guarantee the agreements reached by President Yanukovych and opposition leaders (discussed above). The United States and the EU are said to be responsible for the continuation of bloodshed in the southeast as they did not use their leverage to make Kiev stop the hostilities in Donbass. The victims of the conflict are the 'peaceful population of the South-East' and the military forces are referred to as 'self-defence fighters'.[10] The representatives of Donbass are depicted as willing to cooperate and open for dialogue.

Finally, Russia is presented as the protector of the peaceful population of Donbass and provider of humanitarian and diplomatic aid. It was also repeatedly argued that it is possible some Russian citizens are fighting in Donbass (as well as citizens of other foreign states), yet regular Russian troops are not present in the region. The Minsk agreements are considered as a major achievement of Russian diplomacy. The Normandy format and the OSCE are represented as important fora for cooperation, whereas decision-making power belongs to the states involved.

The main 'problem' in the Minsk II issue narrative is Kiev's non-compliance with the peace agreement. According to the strategic narrative, Kiev is interested in the war with the southeast until final victory and does not demonstrate willingness to maintain dialogue. The problem is rooted in the selective implementation of the Minsk agreements and its sabotage, which is exacerbated by the EU's lack of willingness to induce Kiev to comply with the agreements.

---

8 V. Putin, 'President Vladimir Putin's interview with German TV channel ARD', 17 November 2014, <https://russiaeu.ru/en/news/president-vladimir-putins-interview-german-tv-channel-ard> (accessed 13 March 2020).
9 V. Putin, 'President Vladimir Putin's interview with Il Corriere della Sera', 6 June 2014, <https://russiaeu.ru/en/news/president-vladimir-putins-interview-il-corriere-della-sera> (accessed 13 March 2020).
10 V. Putin, 'President Vladimir Putin's Interview', *op. cit.* note 8.

The 'solution' is therefore seen in the full implementation of the Minsk agreements by the Kiev government; in particular, the end of the blockade of Donbass and constitutional reform. The respective articles of Minsk II (Article 11 stipulating constitutional reform in Ukraine with 'decentralization as the key element' and Article 8 about 'resumption of socio-economic ties') have been the most frequently referred to by Russian officials. The EU holds a key to the solution of the conflict by pushing Kiev to implement the agreement and providing assistance to Ukraine.

2.2   Russia's Strategic Narrative on Sanctions

Similarly to the Minsk II narrative, the sanctions are also explained based on exogenous factors; namely, the intention of the United States and the EU to punish Russia for its independent foreign policy. In terms of 'actors', the message about the lack of consensus among the Western actors is particularly prominent. It is argued that sanctions were adopted based on a direct order from the United States and supported by an anti-Russian minority in the EU.[11] The ability of the EU to come up with a single position on sanctions is explained by the pressure of the EU bureaucracy, which effectively disregarded the position of the EU Member States and interest groups voicing their anti-sanctions positions.

The 'problem' element of the narrative points out the political nature of sanctions: 'politics should not interfere with the economy.'[12] It is argued that the sanctions were introduced to contain Russia and have little to do with the real situation in Ukraine:

> The real motives of Western decisions regarding Ukraine are highlighted by the fact that the largest package of anti-Russian economic sanctions

---

11   S. Lavrov, 'Foreign Minister Sergey Lavrov's remarks and responses to questions at the Germany-Russia Forum' 14 September 2018, <http://www.mid.ru/en/foreign_policy/news/-/asset_publisher/cKNonkJE02Bw/content/id/3344050> (accessed 13 March 2020); S. Lavrov, 'Foreign Minister Sergey Lavrov's statement and answers to media questions at a joint news conference following talks with Committee of Ministers of the Council of Europe (CMCE) Chairman, Belgian Deputy Prime Minister and Foreign and European Affairs Minister Didier Reynders', 9 April 2015, <https://russiaeu.ru/en/news/foreign-minister-sergey-lavrovs-comments-following-talks-belgian-deputy-prime-minister-and> (accessed 13 March 2020).

12   S. Lavrov, 'Foreign Minister Sergey Lavrov's remarks and answers to media questions at a joint press conference following talks with Federal Minister for Europe, Integration and Foreign Affairs of Austria Sebastian Kurz, Moscow, May 5, 2015', <https://russiaeu.ru/en/news/foreign-minister-sergey-lavrovs-remarks-following-talks-federal-minister-europe-integration> (accessed 13 March 2020).

was introduced already after the attainment of a ceasefire agreement in southeastern Ukraine.¹³

The main message, therefore, is that the Ukraine crisis was used as a pretext for containment of Russia. Another problem of the sanctions policy is that it is largely based on Kiev's implementation of the Minsk agreements:

> Everyone says that the Minsk agreements must be implemented and then the sanctions issue may be reconsidered. This is beginning to resemble the theatre of the absurd because everything essential that needs to be done with regard to implementing the Minsk agreements is the responsibility of the current Kiev authorities. You cannot demand that Moscow do something that needs to be done by Kiev.¹⁴

In terms of a 'solution', Russia's strategic narrative offers short-term and long-term measures. In the short term, sanctions must be lifted without any preconditions:

> From time to time my American interlocutors say, 'Why don't we sit down and develop some criteria?' I ask, 'What criteria?' 'Well, criteria which would be used, you know, to see when we can lift sanctions' meaning that Russia would have to do something to satisfy those criteria. We are not going to do this. And I just laughed in their faces and said, 'Guys, you did this and you decide what to do further'. We are not going to change our position. We believe it's an honest position.¹⁵

The long-term measures suggest rebuilding of bilateral relations based 'on the principles of equality, mutual respect and consideration for each other's interests'¹⁶ and development of cooperation based on the idea of integration into a common space from Lisbon to Vladivostok. The impact of sanctions on the

---

13   S. Lavrov, 'Foreign Minister Sergey Lavrov meets Association of European Businesses in Russia', 14 October 2014, <https://russiaeu.ru/en/news/foreign-minister-sergey-lavrov-meets-association-european-businesses-russia> (accessed 13 March 2020).

14   V. Putin, 'President Vladimir Putin's interview with German newspaper Bild', 11 January 2016, <https://russiaeu.ru/en/news/president-vladimir-putins-interview-german-newspaper-bild> (accessed 13 March 2020).

15   S. Lavrov, 'Foreign Minister Sergey Lavrov's remarks and responses to questions at the Germany-Russia Forum', *op. cit.* note 5.

16   S. Lavrov, 'Foreign Minister Sergey Lavrov's remarks and answers to media questions at a joint press conference following talks with Federal Minister for Europe', *op. cit.* note 12.

Russian and EU economies is presented slightly differently for the domestic and international audiences. The main message projected to both audiences is that sanctions and Russia's counter-sanctions harm the EU's economy greatly and are detrimental for European businesses. At the same time, for Russia the sanctions policy provides an opportunity for catching up and economic growth, as well as becoming more self-sufficient and exploring new markets. For the domestic audience, sanctions and counter-sanctions are mainly framed as an opportunity and positive development, while for the international audiences the narrative also refers to losses of the Russian economy.[17]

2.3 The EU's Strategic Narrative on the Minsk Agreements

The EU's strategic narrative[18] explains the reasons for the Ukraine crisis and the Minsk agreements as a result of the democratic choice of the Ukrainian people and subsequent Russian interference aimed to contain the development of democracy in Ukraine out of fear for its domestic regime:

> The Ukrainian people stood for freedom, democracy and rule of law. These are precisely the values which are at the core of the European Union. And, Europe will always stand with countries willing to engage on this path.[19]

In terms of 'actors', Russia is presented as a villain as it provoked the crisis by annexing Crimea and supporting separatist movement in Donbass. Whereas Russia's strategic narrative depicts the war in Donbass as an internal Ukrainian issue, the EU's narrative develops the idea that it is a 'conflict between Ukraine and Russia'.[20] Ukraine is therefore presented as a victim suffering from Russia's

---

17 Compare, for instance, annual 'Direct lines with Vladimir Putin' with V. Putin 'Press conference following talks between Vladimir Putin and Matteo Renzi', 10 June 2015, <https://russiaeu.ru/en/news/press-conference-following-talks-between-vladimir-putin-and-matteo-renzi> (accessed 13 March 2020).

18 The EU's strategic narrative refers here to the narrative of the major EU institutions – the European Council, European Commission and European Parliament. While their narrative is largely coherent, some slight differences are pointed out below. The variations in the narratives of the EU Member States are accounted for in the part on the narrative reception.

19 J. Barroso, 'Working together for a united Ukraine in a united continent', 12 September 2014, <http://europa.eu/rapid/press-release_SPEECH-14-598_en.htm> (accessed 13 March 2020).

20 J. Katainen, 'Introductory statement on the European Council debate at the European Parliament', 21 October 2014, <http://europa.eu/rapid/press-release_SPEECH-14-708_en.htm> (accessed 13 March 2020).

aggression. The EU is depicted as the protector of the central government and Ukraine as a whole. It demonstrates diplomatic support by constantly condemning Russian aggression and calling for a peaceful solution and the restoration of Ukraine's territorial integrity. The EU's role as a protector is supported with the 'unprecedented' financial aid allocated to Ukraine.[21]

The major 'problem' of the Minsk agreements according to the EU's narrative is that they are not complied with. The narrative contends that all parties to the conflict are obliged to comply with the Minsk agreements, yet it is 'Russia-backed separatists' and Moscow itself who are not abiding by the agreements. The 'solution' largely depends on Russia and its implementation of the Minsk agreements.[22]

2.4   EU's Strategic Narrative on Sanctions

The reasons behind sanctions are explained by the need to stop Russian aggression in Ukraine: 'if Russia continues to escalate the crisis it will come with a high cost'.[23] In terms of 'actors', the main message is about unity of the actors protecting Ukraine; that is, the unity within the EU, as well as with the United States:

> We all agreed that European unity in approaching Russia is our greatest strength. And so we will stand united.[24]
>
> A good example of a working EU-US political and economic partnership is our work in Ukraine. First of all, political alliance is working. Both the EU and the US have imposed sanctions over Russia's actions against Ukraine. Second, both support 'money for reforms' programmes in Ukraine.[25]

---

21   J. Hahn, 'Speech of Commissioner Johannes Hahn at Ukrainian Catholic University, Lviv, Ukraine', 19 November 2015, <http://europa.eu/rapid/press-release_SPEECH-15-6131_en.htm> (accessed 13 March 2020).

22   J.-C. Juncker, 'President Juncker at the St Petersburg International Economic Forum', 16 June 2016, <http://europa.eu/rapid/press-release_SPEECH-16-2234_en.htm> (accessed 13 March 2020).

23   J. Barroso, 'Statement by President Barroso following the European Council', 31 August 2014, <http://europa.eu/rapid/press-release_STATEMENT-14-266_en.htm> (accessed 13 March 2020).

24   D. Tusk, 'Report by President Donald Tusk to the European Parliament on the European Council meeting of 20–21 October 2016', <https://www.consilium.europa.eu/en/press/press-releases/2016/10/26/tusk-report-european-parliament/> (accessed 13 March 2020).

25   V. Dombrovskis, 'Speech by Vice-President Dombrovskis at the German Marshall Fund of the United States: The EU-US partnership for building strong institutions and resilient economies', 13 October 2017, <http://europa.eu/rapid/press-release_SPEECH-17-3948_en.htm> (accessed 13 March 2020).

Ultimately, the narrative also contains a strong message about unity with Ukraine:

> Our Ukrainian friends have to know that they are not alone, because the European Union stands ready to support Ukraine in more or less all the matters – mainly as far the territorial integrity of the country is concerned, the sovereignty of Ukraine, the independence of Ukraine. That is the reason why the European Union has prolonged the sanctions which are dedicated to Russia.[26]

The 'problem', according to the EU's strategic narrative, is that Russia did not change its behaviour regarding Ukraine, which required an extension and widening of sanctions. The Russian counter-sanctions are also seen as a problem, as they produced negative impacts on separate sectors of some EU Member States' economies. In terms of the 'solution', similarly to Russia's narrative, a distinction is made between short- and long-term measures. In the short term, the sanctions can be lifted under the condition of compliance with the Minsk agreements:

> The sanctions related to the destabilisation in Eastern Ukraine should be lifted once Russia has fully implemented the provisions of the Minsk agreements; whereas these sanctions should be strengthened should Russia choose to continue directly or indirectly to destabilise Ukraine and to harm its territorial integrity; whereas the sanctions related to the illegal annexation of Crimea will remain until the peninsula is returned to Ukraine.[27]

In the long term, improvement of bilateral relations, development of the new EU-Russia framework agreement and potential further integration from Lisbon to Vladivostok were mentioned as potential ways out of the crisis. Yet the short-term measures prevail in the EU's narrative.

---

26 J.-C. Juncker, 'Remarks by Jean-Claude Juncker, President of the EC, at the joint press briefing with Volodymyr Groysman, Prime Minister of Ukraine, and Johannes Hahn, Member of the EC in charge of European Neighbourhood Policy and Enlargement Negotiations', 19 July 2016, <http://europa.eu/rapid/press-release_SPEECH-16-2589_en.htm> (accessed 13 March 2020).

27 European Parliament, 'European Parliament resolution of 10 June 2015 on the state of EU-Russia relations (2015/2001(INI))', <http://www.europarl.europa.eu/sides/getDoc.do?pubRef=-//EP//TEXT+TA+P8-TA-2015-0225+0+DOC+XML+V0//EN> (accessed 13 March 2020).

2.5 Comparing the Patterns of Narratives' Formation

Both the EU's and Russia's issue narratives have been coherent and consistent. The main elements remain the same and the new events are interpreted within these existing frameworks. This can be explained by the deep embeddedness of the respective issue narratives into the other levels of international strategic narratives – that is, system and identity strategic narratives. Russia's issue narratives largely build on wider identity and its system narratives whereby Russia is presented as a re-emerging great power that was humiliated and taken advantage of by the West in the 1990s. The latter is argued to promote an exclusive, rather than inclusive, world order after the end of the Cold War and, hence, eliminating Russia from the club of equals. Russia's foreign policy today, therefore, strives for genuine – not merely declared – equality and with the West:

> Our Western colleagues sometimes say testily that there will be no 'business as usual' with Russia. I am certain that this is the case, and we agree with them on this point: indeed, there'll be no 'business as usual' when they attempted to impose on us agreements that heeded primarily the interests of either the EU or the US, and sought to persuade us that this would not harm our interests. This story is over. A story is beginning that can only develop on the basis of equality and all other principles of international law.[28]

Similarly, the EU's issue narratives also largely draw on its own identity narrative and understanding of the international system. For that reason the EU's strategic narrative sees the core of the Ukraine crisis in values:

> The situation in Ukraine is a clash of world views that touches the very heart of the European Union, its principles, its values and what it symbolises: freedom, democracy and rule of law.[29]

By the logic of mirror narratives, the EU reversed the thesis about the exclusionary vision of the world order and maintained the argument about its openness and promotion of an inclusive world order. Whereas Russia is said to

---

28   S. Lavrov, 'Sergey Lavrov's remarks and answers to media questions at a news conference on Russia's diplomacy performance in 2015, Moscow, 26 January 2016', <https://russiaeu.ru/en/news/foreign-minister-sergey-lavrovs-press-conference> (accessed 13 March 2020).

29   J. Katainen, 'Introductory statement', *op. cit.* note 20.

think in terms of 19th-century spheres of influence, it is thus portrayed as an advocate of an exclusive world order.

Similar patterns are also observed in the dynamics of the EU's and Russia's strategic narratives. It is possible to differentiate two periods of narrative formulation: in 2014–2015 the tone was utterly hostile; since 2016 these confrontational messages (in the EU this line has been promoted by the European Parliament and the Council President Donald Tusk) were complimented with more conciliatory messages stressing the need for dialogue and cooperation (prominent in the speeches by High Representative Federica Mogherini and President of the European Commission Jean-Claude Juncker).[30] This trend can be explained by several factors, including adaptation to the initial shock, substantial revision of EU foreign policy (reflected in the EU Global Strategy) and the position of the Member States interested in normalisation of bilateral relations.

2.6 Enemy Image: Old and New Frames

As shown above, by discursively building their strategic narratives, the EU and Russia effectively construct enemy images of each other. Since frames constitute mental shortcuts, they are an effective tool to create certain images and attitudes. Both actors have used the old frames that existed in public discourse for decades and were activated during periods of hostility.[31] These frames present 'the Other' as an enemy and existential threat to 'the Self' and international order.

The EU strategic narrative's prominent frame which was also widely utilised in Cold War narratives is about 'Russia as an actor seeking to undermine unity' and internal stability of the West:

> Our problem is Russia, which is undermining whatever it can undermine in Europe. ... If there is [a nation] somewhere whose main political priority is to disintegrate Europe, this certainly is Russia.[32]

---

30 For similar findings, see V. Rizhkov, 'Russia-EU relations: The current crisis and possibilities of normalisation' [Отношения России и ЕС: Текущий Кризис и Возможности Нормализации], Sovremennaya Evropa, 3, 2019, 13–24.

31 Enemy images in international relations were studied in-depth in the framework of the Image theory in the 1960s-1980s. This literature largely focused on the mutual images created by the United States and the USSR. For an overview see: R. Herrmann, 'Perceptions and image theory in international relations', in: L. Huddy, D. Sears and J. Levy (eds.), *The Oxford handbook of political psychology* (Oxford University Press 2013).

32 M. Broniatovski, 'Tusk makes scathing attack on Russian influence', 6 October 2018, <https://www.politico.eu/article/donald-tusk-poland-russia-latvia-makes-scathing-attack-on-russian-influence/> (accessed 13 March 2020).

Another frequently used frame is about 'the Russian propaganda'. Since the beginning of the crisis, this frame has been complemented with its new version – 'disinformation' coming from Russia. Connected to this, the novel frame of Russia as an actor waging 'hybrid war' on the West has become one of the most prominent in the EU's strategic narrative. As a result, the frame of 'Russia as a threat' both to the international order and the EU itself is actively promoted in the strategic narrative.

Similarly, Russia's strategic narrative makes use of the long-existing frames about the West/the EU that are widely resonant domestically. For instance, a notable frame belittles the EU through presenting it as a 'minor partner of the US'. The EU is portrayed as an actor whose foreign policy is limited by 'direct orders' from Washington: 'We are ashamed for the European Union, which after long seeking its own "unified voice" started to speak with Washington's voice'.[33]

The frame of 'the West as aiming to contain Russia' when it becomes strong and conducts independent foreign policy is also actively used to make sense of the developments regarding the Minsk agreements and sanctions. Connected to this is the frame of 'Russophobia'[34] which has been omnipresent in Russia's strategic narrative. A typical observation by a Russian official argues that 'inspired by ripples from overseas, the Russophobic forces within the EU continue to vigorously impose perception of our country as a source of 'strategic challenges'.[35]

2.7   *Sources of Legitimation*

Comparison of the patterns of narrative formulation also shows that both actors actively engage the same sources of legitimation of their narratives. The three most frequently used sources of legitimation are particularly prominent. First, both actors actively engage legislative or procedural source of legitimation. They frame their own actions as abiding by national and international law, whereas the opponent is presented as breaching the law. The EU's narrative therefore speaks of 'illegal annexation of Crimea' and 'illegal interference

---

33   The Ministry for Foreign Affairs of the Russian Federation, 'Comment by the Russian Ministry of Foreign Affairs regarding further anti-Russian sanctions agreed by the European Union', 30 July 2014, <http://www.mid.ru/en/foreign_policy/news/-/asset_publisher/cKNonkJE02Bw/content/id/676183> (accessed 13 March 2020).

34   For an in-depth analysis of the 'Russophobia' frame, see: A. Tsygankov, *Russophobia: anti-Russian lobby and American foreign policy* (Springer 2009).

35   S. Lavrov, 'Foreign Minister Sergey Lavrov's interview with DPA German press agency, Moscow, September 13, 2018', <http://www.mid.ru/en_GB/web/guest/vistupleniya_ministra/-/asset_publisher/MCZ7HQuMdqBY/content/id/3342589> (accessed 13 March 2020).

in the South-East Ukraine', whereas the Russian narrative points at 'the anti-constitutional *coup d'etat*' supported by the EU, as well as 'illegal unilateral sanctions'.[36] Law is the main source of legitimation in narratives projected internationally, as such framing emphasises that actors are playing by the internationally accepted rules and are trustworthy members of the international community.[37]

Second, strategic narratives are legitimised based on a shared identity with Ukraine. Both actors emphasised their unity with Ukraine, which makes them a legitimate actor in the Ukraine crisis. In the case of Russia, shared identity ('brotherhood nations') is presented as based on centuries of common past and, as a result, shared experiences and social structures. The EU draws its shared identity with Ukraine from adherence to common values and norms and focuses on their common future, rather than the past as in the case of Russia.[38]

Third, strategic narrative legitimation is also based on performance and consequences. Thus, sanctions are presented as illegal in Russia's narrative because they were not accepted by the international community in the framework of the United Nations, which implies that performance of international practices was undermined. In terms of consequences, it is argued that sanctions do not make any political impact on Russian foreign policy; hence, they have no sense. On the other hand, the EU refers to Russia's actions in southeast Ukraine as violating international practices; consequently, sanctions depend on Russia's compliance with the Minsk agreements.[39]

---

36   See, for instance, European Parliament, 'European Parliament resolution of 4 February 2016 on the human rights situation in Crimea, in particular of the Crimean Tatars (2016/2556(RSP))' 2016, <http://www.europarl.europa.eu/doceo/document/TA-8-2016-0043_EN.html?redirect> (accessed 13 March 2020); M. Zakharova, 'Foreign Ministry Spokesperson Maria Zakharova's answer to a media question on the decision by the EU Council to expand the list of Russian citizens under sanctions', 15 May 2018, <https://russiaeu.ru/en/news/foreign-ministry-spokesperson-maria-zakharovas-answer-media-question-decision-eu-council> (accessed 13 March 2020).

37   A. Faizullaev and J. Cornut, 'Narrative practice in international politics and diplomacy: the case of the Crimean crisis', *Journal of International Relations and Development* 20 (3), 2017, 578–604.

38   S. Lavrov, 'Foreign Minister Sergey Lavrov's remarks and answers to media questions at a joint press conference following talks with Federal Minister for Europe' *op. cit.* note 12; J. Katainen, 'Introductory statement', *op. cit.* note 20; J. Barroso, 'Working together for a united Ukraine' *op. cit.* note 19.

39   V. Chizhov, 'Ambassador Vladimir Chizhov's interview with Euractiv', 15 March 2017, <https://russiaeu.ru/en/news/ambassador-vladimir-chizhovs-interview-euractiv-3> (accessed 13 March 2020); European Parliament, *op. cit.* note 27.

3 Reception of Strategic Narratives

3.1 *Reception at the Official Level*

This section analyses the reception of the EU's narrative in Russia and vice versa. It first focusses on the reception at the level of political elites and reflects on the official response strategies. It then proceeds with discussion of variations in the reception of the opponent's narrative by general population. Out of all possible types of reception – that is, support, acquiescence, protest, appropriation, contestation, rejection[40] – both the EU and Russia's reception of each other's narratives at the official level overwhelmingly consists of contestation and rejection, which is illustrated by the response strategies employed by both actors. These strategies include disruption of opponent's narrative; delegitimising the narrative and the narrator itself; stigmatising and marginalising the narrative; and engaging with the narrative to reformulate it. These strategies are discussed in more detail below.

Disruption includes measures targeted at hindering the physical flow of narratives and preventing their penetration into the domestic information space. Since 2014, the EU has been more active in disruption of Russia's narrative. At the diplomatic level, Brussels suspended most of the channels of communication, most notably the bilateral EU-Russia summits, sectoral dialogues and parliamentary cooperation, thus preventing the capacity of Russian officials to project their strategic narrative. In 2014 the Group of 8 (G8) meeting in Sochi was cancelled and, instead, Group of 7 (G7) meetings have been organised since then. Russia, on the other hand, did not take much action in terms of disruption of the EU's strategic narrative as the domestic media space has already been largely monopolised by the state.

Another strategy of countering the opponent's strategic narrative is delegitimising this narrative. This has been done by challenging the informational content and epistemology behind the respective narratives. For instance, Russia argued that the EU's narrative is based on claims that cannot be proved (e.g., presence of Russian regular military forces in Donbass). Furthermore, the narratives have been delegitimised by pointing out the absence of causal relations between the elements of opponent's narrative, which results in the story looking irrational. For instance, Russian officials repeatedly argued that the 'problem' and 'solution' elements of the EU's sanctions narrative are disconnected (whereas the 'problem' is the presence of sanctions, the 'solution' put forward by the EU requires Russia's implementation of the Minsk agreements,

---

40 Miskimmon, O'Loughlin and Roselle, *Strategic narratives*, *op. cit.* note 1, 87.

yet the implementation depends on the Ukrainian government). The EU's narrative was therefore repeatedly labelled as 'absurd'.[41] Next to delegitimising the respective narratives, the EU and Russia have been actively involved in delegitimising the narrator itself; for example, by pointing out the discrepancies between the narratives and actions. This results in presenting the opponent as a hypocritical actor exercising double standards; hence, being unreliable and untrustworthy.

A step further from the delegitimising strategy is stigmatisation and marginalisation of the target narrative. Thus, the EU has been actively using the 'propaganda' and 'disinformation' frames when characterising Russia's narrative. By a range of measures from establishing the East StratCom Task Force in the EEAS to sponsoring NGOs aimed to uncover the 'Kremlin's disinformation' (e.g., by publishing lists of 'Russia's useful idiots'), the EU Member States not only have been fighting disinformation but also have been stigmatising Russia's entire strategic narrative by automatically equating it with fake news.

Finally, the EU and Russia have been engaging with each other's narratives to reformulate them. Mirror narratives discussed in the previous part are illustrations of this strategy of counter-narrative. In this regard, the strategy was primarily building on either rational counter-arguments or appeals to emotions (e.g., Russian officials often referred to the shocking details of the Trade Union House fire in Odessa in 2014).[42]

3.2 Reception of the EU's Strategic Narrative in Russia

The EU's strategic narrative was rejected by the Russian political elites. Yet how resonant was it among the general population? What were the patterns of reception? To answer these questions, the author used the data from several general population surveys (Levada-Center, Russian Public Opinion Research Center [VTsIOM], Foundation Public Opinion [FOM], Eurobarometer, Pew

---

41   The Ministry for Foreign Affairs of the Russian Federation, 'Comment by the Information and Press Department on the remarks by the High Representative of the European Union for Foreign Affairs and Security Policy Federica Mogherini following an EU Foreign Affairs Council meeting', 15 March 2016, <http://www.mid.ru/en/evropejskij-souz-es/-/asset_publisher/6OiYovt2s4Yc/content/id/2148856> (accessed 13 March 2020).

42   A. Lukashevich, 'Statement by Permanent Representative of Russia to the OSCE Alexander Lukashevich at the OSCE Permanent Council meeting on developments in Ukraine and the need to implement the Minsk agreements, Vienna, May 3, 2018', <https://russiaeu.ru/en/news/statement-developments-ukraine-and-need-implement-minsk-agreements> (accessed 13 March 2020).

TABLE 3.1 Attitudes towards the European Union among the Russian population[a]

	Sept. 2013	Sept. 2014	Aug. 2017
Very positive and generally positive	56	19	38
Very negative and generally negative	29	68	48

[a] Author's compilation based on Levada-Center, 'Russia-EU', 26 September 2017, <https://www.levada.ru/en/2017/09/26/russia-eu/> (accessed 13 March 2020).

Research Center) reflecting on the trust in the narrator and persuasiveness of separate narrative elements.

The resonance of narratives largely depends on trust in the narrator. The existing data shows that Russians trust local narrators and, in contrast, their distrust of the EU tended to increase until late 2018. The main mouthpieces of Russia's strategic narrative – President Vladimir Putin and Foreign Minister Sergey Lavrov – were named as the most trusted politicians.[43] Putin's approval ratings remained high especially after 2014.[44] At the same time, the attitudes towards the EU reversed as a result of the crisis (Table 3.1).

Next to trust of local narrators, the Russian population at large seems to share the elements of the official strategic narrative and, as a result, rejects the EU's narratives. Kiev was perceived as the major villain in the conflict and the overall perception of Ukraine in a negative light increased from 22% in 2013 to 55% in 2018 (Table 3.2).

The majority of the respondents also approved of Russian support to the Donbass fighters as the victims in the conflict – 69% agreed and only 17% disagreed with the idea that Russia should support them.[45] The majority of respondents also approved of the humanitarian aid to the Donbass even when

---

43   Levada-Center, 'The most trusted Russian politicians', 22 October 2018, <https://www.levada.ru/en/2018/10/22/the-most-trusted-russian-politicians/> (accessed 13 March 2020).
44   Levada-Center, 'Approval ratings', 14 January 2019, <https://www.levada.ru/en/2019/01/14/approval-ratings-6/> (accessed 13 March 2020).
45   VTsIOM, 'Sanctions against Russia: holding the Line?' [Санкции против России: держим оборону?], 17 September 2015, <https://wciom.ru/index.php?id=236&uid=115393> (accessed 13 March 2020).

TABLE 3.2 Attitudes towards Ukraine among the Russian population[a]

Attitude	Sept. 2013	Sept. 2014	Sept. 2015	Sept. 2016	Sept. 2017	Sept. 2018
Very good and generally good	69	32	33	26	32	33
Very bad and generally bad	22	55	56	56	53	55

[a] Author's compilation based on Levada-Center, 'Russia-Ukraine relations', 15 October 2018, <https://www.levada.ru/en/2018/10/15/russia-ukraine-relations-3/> (accessed 13 March 2020).

reminded that the resources are spent from the state budget.[46] When asked what policy should Russia adopt regarding the Donetsk People's Republic (DPR) and Luhansk People's Republic (LPR), 17% said it should not interfere, 23% concurred Russia should support them in obtaining autonomy within Ukraine and 22% suggested Russia should support DPR and LPR becoming independent states, whereas 21% claimed the republics should join Russia.[47] Overall, it can be concluded that all elements of the EU's strategic narrative about the Minsk agreements were largely rejected by the Russian elites and population alike.

The reception of the narrative about sanctions among the general population is more controversial. The idea that the EU's perceived objective of imposing sanctions is 'to weaken and humiliate Russia' (which goes in line with Russia's strategic narrative about sanctions as a tool for containment) was shared by 74% of respondents, while only 5% agreed that the objective of the EU was to stop the war in the eastern Ukraine.[48] When asked whether sanctions had an impact on the Russian economy, the answers were equally split between the perceived profound and minor impact (13% said they had no impact, 38% thought they had a profound impact and 39% said they had a

---

46   VTsIOM, 'Donbass: neither war, nor peace, but let humanitarian aid be!' [Донбасс: ни войны, ни мира, а гуманитарные конвои – направлять!], 9 February 2016, <https://wciom.ru/analytical-reviews/analiticheskii-obzor/donbass-ni-vojny-ni-mira-a-gumanitarnye-konvoi-napravlyat> (accessed 13 March 2020).
47   VTsIOM, *ibid*.
48   Levada-Center, 'Sanctions', 2 December 2016, <https://www.levada.ru/en/2016/12/02/sanctions-4/> (accessed 13 March 2020).

TABLE 3.3   Perceived impact of EU sanctions against Russia[a]

	Feb. 2015	Nov. 2015	June 2016	Mar. 2017	July 2017	Apr. 2018
Sanctions had a negative impact	52	47	39	27	26	28
Sanctions had a positive impact	17	21	19	35	35	30
Sanctions had no impact	22	22	32	32	29	30

[a] Author's compilation based on VTsIOM, 'Western sanctions: In the past and present, and well into the future?' [Санкции Запада: были, есть и будут?], 25 April 2018, < https://wciom.ru/analytical-reviews/analiticheskii-obzor/sankczii-zapada-byli-est-i-budut> (accessed 13 March 2020).

TABLE 3.4   Expressed concern about sanctions among the Russian population[a]

	Mar. 7–10 2014	Dec. 2014	July 2015	Aug. 2016	Dec. 2017	Nov. 2018
Very concerned	12	13	8	6	8	21
Fairly concerned	44	33	30	34	21	22
Not very concerned	30	38	40	38	44	33
Not at all concerned	9	13	18	20	22	19

[a] Author's compilation based on Levada-Center, 'Sanctions', 7 December 2018, <https://www.levada.ru/en/2018/12/07/sactions/> (accessed 13 March 2020).

minor impact).[49] Yet there was a strong variation in the opinions about what sort of impact it was (Table 3.3).

At the same time, around half of the respondents voiced concerns about sanctions (Table 3.4).

Regarding the Russian counter-sanctions, 59% of respondents believed they made an impact on the economies of the Western states, whereas the majority believed these counter-measures either had no impact or a positive impact on

---

49   FOM, 'Perceptions of sanctions and counter-sanctions' [Восприятие санкций и антисанкций], 14 February 2017, <https://fom.ru/Ekonomika/13192> (accessed 13 March 2020).

the Russian economy[50] – such framing is very much in line with the Russian strategic narrative. Finally, 60% of respondents thought the West to be more interested in lifting sanctions.

The figures therefore show that the majority of the population appeared to share the Russian narrative and reject the EU's narrative. One exception where the EU's narrative could resonate was the concern of some 30–40% of the population about the negative effects of sanctions. However, since 2018 scholars have noted a shift of public moods manifested in a growing appetite for change, diminishing hopes of state support and a switch from an external locus of control to an internal one.[51] This trend is unfolding in parallel with the decreasing approval ratings of the President and some improvement of attitudes towards the EU.[52] These processes can be explained by the decreasing energy prices, the fall in the real incomes of the population and, arguably, the international trend of declining trust in political elites (which was interrupted in Russia by the Crimea euphoria). Since it is a very recent development, it is not clear exactly how these trends will impact the narrative's reception. Yet they create conditions for a more favourable reception of the EU's strategic narrative.

3.3 *Reception of Russia's Strategic Narrative among EU Member States*

Whereas the EU's official position presenting the coordinated view of all Member States looks rather coherent, there are variations in the reception of Russia's strategic narrative among Member States, as well as different political forces in Member States. This subsection aims to empirically account for these variations.

A variation among the EU Member States is manifested in the level of trust in the narrator. The 2014 crisis resulted in a deteriorating image of Russia in the EU – a Eurobarometer survey showed that, by 2016, the perceptions of Russia in the EU amounted to 61% negative and only 32% positive attitudes.[53] The

---

50 FOM, 'Perceptions of sanctions', *op. cit.* note 49.
51 M. Dmitriev, S. Belanovskiy and A. Nikolskaya, 'Symptoms of shifting public moods and their potential consequences' [Принаки изменения общественных настроений и их возможные последствия], 11 October 2018, <https://komitetgi.ru/news/news/3902/> (accessed 13 March 2020); see also: A. Dynkin and V. Baranovsky (eds.) 'Russia and the world: 2019. Annual forecast: economy and foreign policy' [Россия и Мир: 2019. Ежегодный Прогноз: Экономика и Внешняя Политика] (Moscow, IMEMO 2018), <https://www.imemo.ru/files/File/magazines/RosMir/RosMir2019.pdf> (accessed 13 March 2020).
52 Levada-Center, 'Russia-EU', *op.cit.* note 43.
53 Eurobarometer, 'Future of Europe', 2016, 5, <https://data.europa.eu/euodp/data/dataset/S2131_86_1_451_ENG> (accessed 13 March 2020).

TABLE 3.5 How much confidence do you have in Russian President Vladimir Putin to do the right thing regarding world affairs?[a]

	No confidence	Confidence
Greece	55	45
Germany	63	35
Italy	60	31
Hungary	62	30
UK	75	22
France	79	20
Sweden	80	18
Netherlands	85	14
Spain	88	10
Poland	89	7

[a] Author's compilation based on Pew Research Center, 'Image of Putin, Russia suffers internationally', 6 December 2018, <http://www.pewglobal.org/2018/12/06/image-of-putin-russia-suffers-internationally/> (accessed 13 March 2020).

level of confidence in the Russian President as the main mouthpiece of the narrative was even lower (Table 3.5).

Yet in line with the above categorisation, in seven EU states a positive perception of Russia remained prevalent: 'Cyprus (76%), Bulgaria (72%), Greece (66%), Slovakia (61%), Romania (53%), Croatia (49% vs. 45% for a negative view) and Italy (47%)'[54] (Table 3.6).

Similar to the narrative reception patterns in Russia, there are also differences in the perception of Russia's narratives on the Minsk agreements and sanctions. The former had much less resonance among the EU Member States, while the latter, despite all states approving sanctions, had more variation in terms of domestic support.

As for the Minsk agreements strategic narrative, the EU Member States can be subdivided into two groups – states where from the beginning of the conflict in 2014 Russia's narrative was almost completely rejected by political parties and the population at large (Poland, Baltic states, Romania, the United

54   Eurobarometer, 'Future of Europe', *op.cit.* note 53, 74.

TABLE 3.6 Favourable attitudes towards Russia among the EU Member States[a]

	2013	2014	2015	2017
France	36	26	30	36
Germany	32	19	27	27
Greece	61	63	61	64
Italy	31	20	27	35
Poland	36	12	15	21
Spain	38	18	25	27

[a] Author's compilation based on Pew Research Center, 'Global Indicators Database', <http://www.pewglobal.org/database/custom-analysis/indicator/27/countries/34,58,74,81,84,98,107,126,154,175,199,205,211/> (accessed 13 March 2020).

Kingdom, Denmark, Sweden) and states where certain elements of the strategic narrative resonated among some political forces and shares of population (Germany, France, Italy, Greece, Hungary, Czech Republic, Slovakia). In this latter group, the 'environment' and the 'actor' elements of the narrative were the most controversial and divergent from the EU's official narrative. For instance, the idea that the origins of the crisis resulted not only from Russian actions but were also partially provoked by the West and the new Ukrainian government was voiced by influential political figures in Germany (leader of the left-wing Democratic Socialist Party, Gregor Gysi; former Chancellors Gerhard Schröder and Helmut Schmidt),[55] Hungary (Viktor Orban), Slovakia (Robert Fico) and the Czech Republic (Miloš Zeman). Similarly, in 2015, 43% of Germans agreed that 'both sides were responsible for the conflict'.[56] The 'environment' and 'actor' elements of the Russian narrative tended to find support either among Russia-friendly EU Member States (e.g., Greece, Bulgaria, Czech Republic, Slovakia) or among followers of some left and far-left or

---

55 T. Forsberg, 'From Ostpolitik to "Frostpolitik"? Merkel, Putin and German foreign policy towards Russia', *International Affairs* 92 (1), 2016, 21–42, 33.
56 J. Kucharczyk, A. Lada, G. Scholer and L. Wenerski, 'Closer together or far apart? Poles, Germans and Russians on the Russia-Ukraine crisis', 2015, *Bertelsmann Stiftung*, 5, <https://www.bertelsmann-stiftung.de/fileadmin/files/user_upload/Study_Close_together_or_far_apart.pdf> (accessed 13 March 2020).

extreme right political parties. For instance, the representatives of the Greek Syriza (Dimitrios Papadimoulis) and the Independent Greeks party (Panos Kammenos) shared the Russian arguments that the *coup d'etat* in Ukraine was organised by the West and the claim that the EU's Ukraine policy was guided by the United States (Euractiv 2015).[57]

Overall, however, even in the EU Member States where certain elements of Russia's narrative found support, public opinion remained rather divided and it was never the majority of population who shared Russia's narrative. Similarly, even if there were important political figures supporting Russia's narrative, there always were strong counterbalance positions among domestic political elites.

As for the sanctions narrative, whereas the official response has indeed been a unified position, separate elements of Russia's strategic narrative have found support in some EU Member States. The data show that the 'environment' and the 'actor' elements of the Russian narrative were rejected – it is a widely shared consensus among Europeans that the introduction of sanctions was caused by Russia's actions, rather than the desire to contain it as stated by the Russian narrative. The same holds true for the 'actors' element – Ukraine was perceived as having suffered from the violation of territorial integrity, and therefore is seen as a victim. Yet the 'problem' and 'solution' elements of the Russian narrative have been more controversial. It is possible to distinguish three types of responses in this regard – (1) the EU Member States arguing that Russia continues to violate Ukraine's territorial integrity and therefore further sanctions should be introduced, that is, complete rejection of Russia's narrative (Estonia, Finland, Lithuania, the Netherlands, Poland, Romania, Sweden and the United Kingdom); (2) the states having relative domestic consensus that the existing sanctions could be lifted in case of progress in the implementation of the Minsk agreements, yet no progress has been made yet (Belgium, Croatia, Denmark, France, Germany, Ireland, Latvia, Luxemburg, Malta, Portugal and Spain); and (3) the states where the latter position co-exists in political discourse with a strong belief that sanctions could be lifted even without Russia's compliance with the Minsk agreements and that sanctions must not be extended automatically (Austria, Bulgaria, Cyprus, the Czech Republic, Greece, Hungary, Italy, Slovakia and Slovenia). In this former group, the 'solution' element of the Russian narrative resonated quite strongly. The

---

57   M. Michalopoulos, 'Tsipras has first clash with EU – over Russia', 28 January 2015, <https://www.euractiv.com/section/europe-s-east/news/tsipras-has-first-clash-with-eu-over-russia/> (accessed 13 March 2020).

most convincing arguments include the ineffectiveness of sanctions, negative impacts they produce on the European economies and the idea that political problems must not be solved through economic means. This overview shows that it is mainly the 'solution' element of Russia's sanctions narrative that has found different degrees of support in around a half of the EU Member States.

4   Conclusion

This chapter argues that in the conflict unfolding between Russia and the EU, both actors exercised power by promoting their own interpretation of events. A strategic narrative approach allows for the operationalisation and accounting for how this power is translated into a foreign policy instrument (narrative formulation) and evaluation of its effects (narrative reception). Such an evaluation is especially important given the growing obsession with Russian propaganda dominating in the EU. The chapter maintains that conclusions about the influence of the Other's narrative can be made only after thorough analysis of how political elites and populations engage with foreign narratives.

Empirical analysis of strategic narratives on the Minsk agreements and sanctions shows that the formulation and reception of Brussels' and Moscow's narratives have a lot in common. In terms of formulation, the narratives are constructed based on the same patterns and the final product presents perfectly mirrored narratives. Both actors made extensive use of old frames to construct the enemy image of the opponent, whereas the EU has also started to actively use the new interconnected frames about Russia's disinformation and hybrid warfare. Importantly, both actors relied on the same sources of legitimation, legislative sources being the most frequently used.

In terms of reception, the empirical study demonstrates that in both cases the opponent's narratives are largely rejected. Only separate elements of the respective narratives have been partially resonant among some groups of the target audience. In these cases, resonance is facilitated by perceptions of shared identity, a track record of positive mutual attitudes and economic interests. This general trend towards weak resonance of the EU's narrative in Russia and vice versa can be explained by a range of factors. First, as a result of a mutually constructed enemy image, narrators are perceived as untrustworthy and manipulative. This reinforces the echo chamber effect in the EU and Russia leading to a confirmation bias manifested in polarisation of perceptions when the groups inclined towards the opponent's narrative are becoming even more reassured about elements of this narrative, whereas those prone to contest the opponent's narrative become more hostile towards it. In the case of

Russia, the rally-round-the-flag effect produced by Crimea joining Russia also contributed to this process. Second, the narratives under analysis are deeply embedded into wider narratives about the Self (identity strategic narratives) and the international order (system strategic narratives), which guaranteed coherence of the issue narratives under analysis. Another important consequence of this embeddedness is that even if anyone consciously contests the domestic issue narrative, wider identity and system narratives will still affect their perception of the issue. As an illustration, J. Szostek showed in a focus group study of Russian students that even those students who explicitly mentioned that they were aware of propaganda and sought alternative sources of information tended to reproduce elements of Russia's official issue narrative.[58] Third, as was shown above, the EU and Russia have adopted a number of strategies for countering competing narratives. These strategies undoubtedly contributed to weak resonance of foreign narratives domestically.

Beyond contributing to studies on power and narrative approaches, these conclusions yield important policy implications. Understanding how strategic narratives work and what factors explain their resonance is important for the improvement of bilateral relations between Russia and the EU. Since narratives are social practices, by altering them political elites and interest groups can also affect reality. Drawing on the analysis above, it can be concluded that EU and Russian political elites should rely on the elements of narratives they agree on and consciously aim at a greater convergence of narratives. Given their interdependence, it is important to converge narratives on the issue, identity and system levels. Therefore, both actors should aim to dismantle respective enemy images. To this end, they can draw on positive frames existing in public discourse. As discussed above, it is possible to observe a slight turn in this direction from 2016, which is a positive, if still fragile, development.

Acknowledgements

This research was generously supported by the GCRF UKRI COMPASS project (ES/P010849/1).

---

58   J. Szostek, 'News media repertoires and strategic narrative reception: a paradox of dis/belief in authoritarian Russia', *New Media and Society* 20 (1), 2018, 68–87.

CHAPTER 4

The Punitive Effect of the EU's Restrictive Measures against Russia
A Help or a Hindrance for Principled Pragmatism?

Alexandra Hofer

1   Introduction

Principled pragmatism calls for the EU to stand firm on its position on Crimea and eastern Ukraine, while leaving the door open for cooperation with Russia on issues of common interest.[1] 'Standing firm' requires the EU to assert its key values in the context of the crisis and to remain steadfast in its goal of seeking a resolution to the Ukrainian crisis. This posture is expressed, among others, through the EU's restrictive measures taken in response to the violation of international law resulting from Russia's annexation of Crimea and involvement in eastern Ukraine.[2] The EU has characterised Russia's actions in Ukraine as an aggression in breach of UN Charter Article 2(4).[3] In an effort to impose costs on Russia for its wrongful behaviour, it has adopted a series of sanctions alongside its key strategic partners, which include neighbouring states and

---

1   European Union External Action Service, 'A Global Strategy for the European Union's Foreign and Security Policy', available at: <https://eeas.europa.eu/sites/eeas/files/eugs_review_web_0.pdf> (accessed 17 March 2020); Council of the European Union, 'Outcome of the Council Meeting', available at: < https://www.consilium.europa.eu/media/22914/st07042en16.pdf> (accessed 17 March 2020), 4, setting five guiding principles for the development of the EU's relations with Russia.

2   For an overview of the EU's restrictive measures adopted in response to the crisis in Ukraine, see: <https://www.consilium.europa.eu/en/policies/sanctions/ukraine-crisis/> (accessed 17 March 2020).

3   UN General Assembly Verbatim Record (27 March 2014), UN Doc. A/68/PV.80, 5 (European Union): 'The European Union strongly condemns the clear violation of Ukrainian sovereignty and territorial integrity by acts of aggression by the Russian armed forces. The Russian actions are not only in breach of the Charter of the United Nations, they are also in clear breach of the Final Act of the Conference on Security and Cooperation in Europe and its subsequent processes and instruments within the Organization for Security and Cooperation in Europe (OSCE),. … Those actions also violate specific commitments to respect Ukraine's sovereignty and territorial integrity under the Budapest Memorandum of 1994 and the bilateral Treaty between the Russian Federation and Ukraine on Friendship, Cooperation and Partnership of 1997.'

the United States. These measures have coercive and signalling/stigmatising purposes.⁴

The EU seeks to pressure Russia into changing its behaviour towards Ukraine and into complying with the Minsk agreements and, thereby, enforce compliance with one of the most fundamental principles of international law: the prohibition of the use of force. Furthermore, at the start of the Ukrainian crisis, the President of the European Council affirmed that '[the leaders of the EU] have a special responsibility for peace, stability and prosperity on our continent, and we are ready to take that responsibility. Acts of aggression cannot be without consequences'.⁵ The EU therefore asserted its commitment to the prohibition of aggression through the adoption of restrictive measures.⁶ Accordingly, E. Moret et al. found that the primary aim of the sanctions against Russia is to signal commitment to international norms; in particular, the prohibition to violate another state's territorial and sovereign integrity.⁷ Inasmuch as signalling disproval with an actor's behaviour constitutes labelling the other as a deviant, it contributes to its stigmatisation in the international scene.⁸ Signalling sanctions thus entails stigmatisation.⁹

Moret et. al. further found that the sanctions have been successful in signalling commitment to norms but concluded that they have had less success in

---

4   F. Giumelli, *Coercing, Constraining and Signalling: Explaining UN and EU Sanctions after the Cold War* (ECPR Press 2011), the third purpose identified by Giumelli is to constrain, which is to 'impose a burden on a targets to prevent [them] from doing something'. Coercion, on the other hand, imposes a burden to affect the cost/benefit calculation to make the target adopt the behaviour desired by the sender. See *ibid.* 33, table 3.2. See also *ibid.*, 34–35.
5   European Council, the President 'Remarks by President of the European Council Herman Van Rompuy following the Extraordinary Meeting of EU Heads of State or Government on Ukraine', available at: <http://www.europarl.europa.eu/meetdocs/2009_2014/documents/d-ru/dv/dru_20140312_06_/dru_20140312_06_en.pdf > (accessed 17 March 2020).
6   European Council, 'Statement by the President of the European Council Herman Van Rompuy and the President of the European Commission in the Name of the European Union on the Agreed Additional Restrictive Measures against Russia', available at: < https://www.consilium.europa.eu/uedocs/cms_data/docs/pressdata/en/ec/144158.pdf> (accessed 17 March 2020).
7   Erica Moret et al., 'The New Deterrent? International Sanctions against Russia over the Ukrainian Crisis: Impacts, Costs and Further Actions', *Programme for the Study of International Governance*, 2016, available at: < http://g8fip1kplyr33r3krz5b97d1.wpengine.netdna-cdn.com/wp-content/uploads/2016/10/Russia_Sanctions_Final_Report_Grad_Inst_Geneva.pdf> (accessed 17 March 2020).
8   R. Adler-Nissen, 'Stigma Management in International Relations: Transgressive Identities, Norms, and Order in International Society', *International Organization* 68 (1), 2014, 143.
9   F. Giumelli, 'The Purposes of Targeted Sanctions', in: T. Biersteker et al. (eds.), *Targeted Sanctions: The Impacts and Effectiveness of United Nations Action* (CUP 2016), 47.

changing Russia's behaviour. The coercive sanctions were considered 'somewhat successful' at providing access to the MH17 crash site, at removing some weaponry from eastern Ukraine and at bringing Russia to the negotiation table during the second Minsk rounds. However, 'since the sanctions were explicitly linked to implementation of key provisions of the Minsk II process, they have proven ineffective in coercing Russia to withdraw all equipment and personnel from Eastern Ukraine'.[10] It follows that if the sanctions have enabled the EU to signal its commitment to its core values, at the time of writing it would seem they have not helped the EU reach a resolution to the crisis through the Minsk agreements.[11]

This chapter argues that the sanctions' unsuccessful coercion can be explained by their stigmatising effect. Although the sanctions' coercive and stigmatising objectives can be separated theoretically, they are inevitably intertwined in practice.[12] Feeling the effects of both objectives simultaneously, the target does not distinguish between being pressured into changing its behaviour and being stigmatised when it adopts a policy in reaction to the sanctions. It responds to the entirety of the regime. The imposition of costs in response to wrongdoing and as a means to support a general rule of society mean the sanctions become a form of punishment.[13] As already noted, the sanctions are justified as a means to enforce the prohibition of the use of force found in Article 2(4) of the UN Charter. This has been recognised as an obligation *erga omnes*, an obligation owed to the international community as a whole and where all members of the community have an interest in its performance.[14] As H. Gould writes, sanctions adopted by a non-injured party, such as the EU, to enforce a norm on behalf of the society to which it belongs are a modern form of international punishment.[15] The implication drawn here is that the

---

10 E. Moret et al., *op. cit.* note 7, 11.
11 On the state of implementation of the Minsk agreements, see the contribution by S. Van Severen (chapter 1) in this volume.
12 D. Alland, 'Countermeasures in the General Interest', *European Journal of International Law* 13(5), 2002, 1226.
13 H. Gould, *The Legacy of Punishment in International Law* (Palgrave Macmillan 2010), 35: 'Punishment is administered on behalf of the community to which the agents belong. The party inflicting the punishment ... is acting as an agent (even if self-appointed) of the community, and not as a party to the dispute'. See, further, A.F. Lang, *Punishment, Justice and International Relations* (Routledge 2008); K.R. Nossal, 'International Sanctions as International Punishment', *International Organization* 43 (2), 1989, 301.
14 International Court of Justice, Judgment of 5 February 1970, *Barcelona Traction, Light and Power Company, Limited* (Belgium v. Spain), paras. 33–34.
15 Also known as *actio popularis*, Gould, *op. cit.* note 13, 44.

restrictive measures have a punitive effect; they are perceived as punishment by the target.

Taking this into account, this chapter analyses how the EU's restrictive measures can be reconciled with its so-called 'principled pragmatism' towards the Russian Federation. Considering the sanctions' punitive effect, it is argued that if the EU's restrictive measures enable the EU to stand firm against Russia, they are a hindrance to cooperation and contribute to the existing deadlock in EU-Russia relations. This chapter aims to provide insight on how the restrictive measures contribute to the deadlock and aspires to further the discussion on how to move forward.

2 The EU as a Normative Power: The Role of Restrictive Measures

Since its conception, promoting international (legal) norms has become an integral part of the EU's identity. Article 21 of the Treaty on European Union (TEU) provides that the EU should use its external relations to promote, *inter alia*, respect for the principles of the UN Charter and international law. Article 215 of the Treaty on the Functioning of the European Union (TFEU) gives the EU the competence to use restrictive measures in case countries breach international law commitments.[16] Restrictive measures are thus one of the means through which the EU can promote its norms and values in the wider world;[17] they are also a tool through which the EU can activate its identity as a normative power;

A normative power is able to shape conceptions of the 'normal' by acting in a normative way.[18] One of the means through which the conception of normal can be shaped is through the imposition of stigma.[19] Inasmuch as the restrictive measures signal the EU's commitment to norms and have a stigmatising purpose, they enable the EU to assert what constitutes normal standards of behaviour. This, however, does not mean that the restrictive measures are an appropriate 'normative' policy tool.[20] The international community is

---

16 On this practice, see A. Hofer, 'Negotiating International Public Policy through the Adoption and Contestation of Sanctions', *Revue Belge de Droit International*, 2017, 449–457.
17 F. Martucci, 'La réaction multidimensionnelle de l'Union européenne dans la crise ukrainienne', *Journal du Droit International (Clunet)* 9 (3), 2014, 4.
18 *Ibid.*
19 Adler-Nissen, *op. cit.* note 8.
20 Consider, for example, K. Brummer, 'Imposing Sanctions: The Not so "Normative Power Europe" ', *European Foreign Affairs Review* 14 (2), 2009, 191.

divided on the legitimacy of unilateral coercive measures, including when they are adopted to uphold fundamental norms. Although the EU is acting in accordance with the expectations of its key allies (most notably, the United States), it is also acting in a non-normative manner according to other actors in the international community, including Russia.[21] Furthermore, the adoption of restrictive measures to promote its normative agenda would contradict the common definition of a normative power, which seeks to shape the thinking of other actors through non-coercive means.[22] The risk is that the EU's 'use of ... coercive economic means may impact negatively on the recognition by others of the ideas promoted by the actor in question'.[23] Notwithstanding the questions surrounding unilateral sanctions' legitimacy, the restrictive measures' stigmatising function support the EU in acting as a normative power and thereby in 'standing firm'. Similarly, the EU's principled pragmatism builds on the EU's identity as a 'normative power'.[24] This comes out in the EU's aspiration to stand firm in response to Russia's violation of international law and to contribute to a peaceful resolution to the Ukrainian crisis.

3   The EU's Response to the Ukrainian Crisis

The EU has always been wary of its Russian neighbour, unsure of whether to consider it as a friend or a foe. If after the Cold War there was some hope for peaceful relations between the two blocs, the events in Ukraine seemed to confirm Europe's worst fears. At the start of the crisis, Russia was singled out for its wrongful actions and placed in contrast to the EU and the United States, who were working to achieve a peaceful resolution. When the crisis reached its peak in Crimea, the Heads of State or Government of EU Member States issued a statement on 6 March 2014, whereby they claimed that the EU 'has a special responsibility for peace, stability and prosperity in

---

21   A. Hofer, 'The Developed/Developing Divide on Unilateral Coercive Measures: Legitimate Enforcement or Illegitimate Intervention?', *Chinese Journal of International Law* 16 (3), 2017, 57.

22   R. Bengtsson and O. Elgström, 'Conflicting Role Conceptions? The European Union in Global Politics', *Foreign Policy Analysis* 93 (1), 2012, 95.

23   *Ibid.*, 96. See also Hofer, *op. cit.* note 21, 58 and 61–62.

24   Initially coined by I. Manners, 'Normative Power Europe: A Contradiction in Terms?', *Journal of Common Market Studies* 40 (2), 2002, 235.

Europe.²⁵ They further condemned Russia's unlawful actions in Ukraine and highlighted that

> the European Union's and the Russian Federation's common objective of a relationship based on mutual interest and respect of international obligations needs to be promptly restored. It would be a matter of great regret if the Russian Federation failed to work in that direction, and in particular if it continued to refuse to participate in a productive dialogue with the Government of Ukraine. We have today decided to take actions [...]²⁶

These actions included measures that the EU Council adopted on 3 March 2014 – in response to the announcement that a referendum would take place in Crimea in 16 March – deciding to suspend bilateral talks with Russia on visa matters and on the new EU-Russia agreement. This cessation from dialogue marked a first step in the EU's separation from and discrimination of Russia. The EU further threatened to consider restrictive measures if Russia were to continue its destabilising policies.²⁷ As already mentioned, the EU stayed true to its word and imposed a series of sanctions as the crisis intensified. As the situation worsened, Russia became a threat to the international legal order that had to be countered, leading to Russia's status loss and separation from the West. A powerful symbol of this was Russia's suspension from the Group of 8 (G8) June summit to be held in Sochi and its exclusion from the group, which Russia had joined in 1997.²⁸ The EU also supported the suspension of talks over Russia joining the Organisation for Economic Co-operation and Development and the International Energy Agency.

In an effort to strengthen its role as a normative power and to further isolate Russia, the EU attempted to gain support through third-party alignment, a process through which non-EU countries join the sanction regime. This practice constitutes 'normative-boundary drawing', explained by E. Hellquist in the following manner:

---

25 European Council, 'Extraordinary Meeting of EU Heads of State or Government on Ukraine', 6 March 2014, available at: < https://www.consilium.europa.eu/media/29285/141372.pdf > (accessed 17 March 2020), para. 3.
26 *Ibid.*, para. 4.
27 See, for example, European Council, 'Remarks by Herman Van Rompuy on Ukraine ...', *op. cit.* note 6.
28 Although at the time it was the G7. S. Suzuki, "Delinquent Gangs' in the International System Hierarchy', in: A. Zarakol (ed.), *Hierarchies in World Politics* (CUP 2017), 219.

The EU uses alignment as a litmus test of neighbours' normative fidelity, in order to promote its own posture as an international actor. ... Alignment becomes intelligible as an institutionalized practice which communicates value judgments of who is 'good' and 'bad', of belonging and exclusion.[29]

Alignment is therefore 'a communicative act that sends out a message of disapproval to the target of sanctions, and a message of support to the EU as initiator'.[30] Based on Hellquist's assessment, the EU has not been as successful in gaining third-party support as it has been in other sanctions regimes, notably because of the high stakes involved in sanctioning a powerful country like Russia. Questions also surround the utility of the measures against Russia and the EU's legitimacy to 'dictate' third countries' foreign policy.[31] Divisions regarding the sanctions are also found within the EU; Italy, Greece, Austria, Hungary, Slovenia and Slovakia are reportedly the staunchest objectors.[32] This would be due to historic and cultural ties rather than economic reasons.[33] The consequences of Russia's retaliatory prohibition on agricultural imports from the sanctioning states are hard to measure, and EU Member States have been affected in varying degrees,[34] but it would seem that material loss does not correlate with opposition to sanctions.[35] The EU's internal debate has nonetheless

---

29 E. Hellquist, 'Either with Us or against Us? Third-Country Alignment with EU Sanctions against Russia/Ukraine', *Cambridge Review of International Affairs* 29 (3), 2016, 999.
30 *Ibid.*
31 *Ibid.*
32 'Italy Pushes for De-escalation as EU Moves to Renew Russia Sanctions', Reuters, 27 June 2018, available at: <https://www.reuters.com/article/us-eu-russia-sanctions-italy/italy-pushes-for-de-escalation-as-eu-moves-to-renew-russia-sanctions-idUSKBN1JN0WF> (accessed 17 March 2020); 'Opinion: Athens and Moscow's Stunning Falling-Out', *New York Times*, 23 July 2018, available at: <https://www.nytimes.com/2018/07/23/opinion/athens-moscow-greece-russia-tensions.html> (accessed 17 March 2020).
33 M. Shagina, 'Friend or Foe? Mapping the Positions of EU Member States on Russia Sanctions', European Leadership Network, 28 June 2017, available at: <https://www.europeanleadershipnetwork.org/commentary/friend-or-foe-mapping-the-positions-of-eu-member-states-on-russia-sanctions/> (accessed 17 March 2020), referencing Moret et al., *op. cit.* note 7, 12–13.
34 European Parliament, Committee on International Trade, 'Study: Russia's and the EU's Sanctions: Economic and Trade Effects, Compliance and the Way Forward', 2017, available at: <http://www.europarl.europa.eu/RegData/etudes/STUD/2017/603847/EXPO_STU(2017)603847_EN.pdf> (accessed 17 March 2020), 16–30.
35 Moret et al., *op. cit.* note 7, 5: 'While Greece and Italy rank among those experiencing the lowest decline, they are among the states most vocal in calling for the lifting of sanctions (alongside Slovakia, Hungary, Austria and Slovenia). Central and Eastern European

not prevented the sanctions from being unanimously renewed since their adoption.

Since the events in Ukraine, the EU regards Russia with suspicion, fearing that its leaders have an 'aggressive eye' towards the West and that it will take more territory. European countries fear Russian interference in their electoral processes through the spread of 'fake news' on social media. Tensions flared between Russia and the United Kingdom over the Salisbury poisoning in March 2018, leading to further diplomatic sanctions.[36] As such, Russia has become somewhat of a stereotype as it is cast in the role of the threat that lies at the Eastern border and against which the EU must defend itself.[37] As understandable as this strategy is in response to Russia's act of aggression, it contradicts the EU's need for cooperation with Russia. The next section explains why.

4 Russia's Resentment against Punishment: A Hindrance to Cooperation[38]

According to Adler-Nissen, states can respond to stigmatisation through three strategies.[39] In the first scenario, the actor accepts the collective norms and attempts to rectify its behaviour to reintegrate the group of normals (stigma recognition). In the second, the deviant accepts the distinction made between 'normal' and 'abnormal' behaviour but denies it is different from the group imposing the stigma (stigma rejection). In other words, it accepts the normative basis shared by the group but rejects that it would be responsible for wrongdoing. In the third instance, stigma is turned into

---

      Member States that have suffered the most include some of the staunchest supporters of sanctions (including Estonia, Latvia, Lithuania and Poland)'.

36   'Russia Threatens Retaliation after Britain Expels 23 Diplomats', *The Guardian*, 14 March 2018, available at: <https://www.theguardian.com/uk-news/2018/mar/14/may-expels-23-russian-diplomats-response-spy-poisoning> (accessed 17 March 2020); 'Western Allies Expel Scores of Russian Diplomats over Skripal Attack', *The Guardian*, 27 March 2018, available at: <https://www.theguardian.com/uk-news/2018/mar/26/four-eu-states-set-to-expel-russian-diplomats-over-skripal-attack> (accessed 17 March 2020).

37   See also the contribution by I. Petrova (chapter 3) in this volume on the EU's strategic narratives about the Minsk agreements and the sanctions regime.

38   On the role Russia has adopted in response to being sanctioned, see also A. Hofer, 'All the World's a Stage, and Sanctions the Merely Props: An Interactional Account of Sender-Target Dynamics in the Ukrainian Crisis', *International Peacekeeping* (published online 19 April 2020).

39   Adler-Nissen, *op. cit.*, note 8.

an emblem of pride and the transgressor attempts to stigmatise the 'audience of normals' (counter-stigmatisation). Under these circumstances, the targeted state does not share the same normative basis as the stigmatising countries.

Russia has a long history of managing stigma from Western Europe and the United States. Based on A. Zarakol's account, Russia would have adopted the strategy of stigma recognition during the post–Cold War era as it attempted to integrate 'the West' through democratisation and transitioning to a capitalist economy.[40] Circumstances have changed in the context of the current sanction regime as the Kremlin rejects the stigma imposed on its country. Recall that stigma rejection requires the stigmatised actor to share the same values as the 'audience of normals' and to reject that it is different from those imposing the stigma. Russia considers that it has the same set of values as the West but these are not always understood and put in practice in the same way.[41] Russia does not accept that its behaviour in Ukraine is wrongful, invoking Kosovo as a precedent. Russia's coping mechanism is explained by the two factors identified by Adler-Nissen.[42] First, as discussed below, Russian officials have depicted their state as being equal to (if not superior to) the EU and as more respectful of the normative order than their Western counterparts (see also chapter 3 by I. Petrova in this volume). Second, Russia is undoubtedly a powerful state and has the material and social resources to resist the sanctions. In addition to these two elements, it is argued here that Russia has adopted 'stigma rejection' because it resents[43] being sanctioned by, *inter alia*, the European

---

[40] *Ibid*, 148, reference to A. Zarakol, *After Defeat: How the East Learned to Live with the West* (CUP 2010), chapter 5.

[41] A.P. Tsygankov, 'The Frustrating Partnership: Honor, Status, and Emotions in Russia's Discourses of the West', *Communist and Post-Communist Studies* 47 (3), 2014, 351–352 (quoting Dmitry Medvedev). See also Zarakol, *op. cit.* note 40 239; and L. Mälksoo, *Russian Approaches to International Law* (OUP 2015). For illustration consider, 'The Declaration of the Russian Federation and the People's Republic of China on the Promotion of International Law', 25 June 2016, available at: < http://www.mid.ru/en/foreign_policy/position_word_order/-/asset_publisher/6S4RuXfeYlKr/content/id/2331698 > (accessed 17 March 2020).

[42] Adler-Nissen, *op. cit.* note 40, 154.

[43] According to Zarakol, during the post–Cold War era Russia would not have displayed a *ressentiment* strategy but at that time there were no sanctions against Russia, Zarakol, *op. cit.* note 40, 238–239. Although this chapter refers to *resentment*, part of it draws on the literature on *ressentiment* (both terms are sometimes used as synonyms in the literature). On the difference between resentment and ressentiment, see: B.D. Meltzer and G.R. Musolf, 'Resentment and *Ressentiment*', *Sociological Inquiry* 72 (2), 2002, 240–255; O. Malinova, 'Obsession with Status and Ressentiment: Historical Backgrounds of the Russian Discursive Identity Construction', *Communist and Post-Communist Studies* 47 (3),

Union.[44]

Wolf describes *resentment* as 'a "smoldering" sentiment elicited by the perception that another party enjoys an undeserved status position'.[45] A resentful actor feels that it is treated in an unfair manner and that 'another actor enjoys more power and/or prestige than s/he actually deserves according to established norms and values'.[46] Resentment gives rise to negative prejudices and cognitive biases that obstruct cooperation. The resenting individual or group will seek to undercut the object of resentment to 'teach it a lesson'. Usually, it will not be in a position to do so, at least not immediately, and will therefore wait for the opportune moment to correct the perceived injustice. The resentful actor will also attempt to persuade third parties of the resented's (moral) shortcomings and in this way seek support.[47] Resentment is therefore an emotion that relates to norms, social standing and recognition from others. This is relevant in the context of stigmatisation because, as explained above, such processes involve stereotyping and status loss in response to norm violation and imply a moral hierarchy between the 'audience of normals' and the deviant. Additionally, inasmuch as the restrictive measures impose costs for wrongful behaviour, they constitute a form of punishment. Sanctions' 'punitive effect' means that the target perceives the sanctions as punitive[48] and will react to the measures based on this perception. Punishment is a hierarchical practice, where the actor imposing it takes on the role of a moral authority

---

2014, 291–303; E. Brighi, 'The Globalisation of Resentment: Failure, Denial, and Violence in World Politics', *Millennium* 44 (3), 2016, 411–432.

44   Russia's reaction should be understood in the context of its relationship with the United States and the EU but, for the purpose of this chapter, we will focus on the latter.

45   R. Wolf, 'Resentment in International Relations', paper presented during an ECPR workshop on 'Status Claims, Recognition and Emotion in IR: Theoretical and Methodological Challenges', 11–13 March 2013, definition in abstract. See also R. Wolf, 'Political Emotions as Public Processes: Analyzing Transnational Ressentiments in Discourses', in: M. Clément and E. Sanger (eds.), *Researching Emotions in International Relations: Methodological Perspectives on the Emotional Turn* (Palgrave Macmillan 2018), 231–254.

46   Wolf, 2018, *op. cit.* note 45, 234.

47   *Ibid.*, 237.

48   Commenting on the sanctioning states, Medvedev stated: 'They told us we were the bad guys and had to be punished', in D. Medvedev, 'Interview with Euronews TV Channel', Munich, 14 February 2016, available at: < http://government.ru/en/news/21789/> (accessed 17 March 2020). See also President of Russia, 'Direct Line with Vladimir Putin', 7 June 2018, available at: <http://en.kremlin.ru/events/president/news/57692> (accessed 17 March 2020). In reference to the US tariffs on China, Canada and EU, Putin commented: '[the tariffs are] sanctions, in fact. ... What are they being punished for? Did they "annex Crimea" as many of our partners say? No'.

on behalf of the community.[49] Usually, the punishing actor is able to adopt this position because of its social and economic strength, further demonstrating the unequal status between the enforcer and the deviant. If punishment is believed to be undeserved, it comes across as injustice and can trigger resentment, particularly if the reprimanded actor believes the individual or group inflicting the costs is not more virtuous than itself.

Incorporating resentment has explanatory value in the study of Russian foreign policy decision-making, and particularly its response to the restrictive measures, as it is frequently considered a status-seeking power.[50] The literature is unanimous in finding that Russia sees itself as a recovering great power seeking recognition from other global powers, the United States and the EU, which have been insensitive to Moscow's attempts at integration since the end of the Cold War. R. Heller suggests that 'initial anger over Western disrespect has intruded into the consciousness of Russian decision-makers and has turned into new patterns of anti-Western resentment over the years'.[51] An important trigger for resentment is whether Russia's Western counterparts respect its sense of honour, which according to A.P. Tsygankov helps explain Russia's ambivalent attitude towards the West.[52] Moscow's sense of honour includes its concern for its geopolitical security, its quest for great-power status and the protection of its cultural allies, which are ethnic Russians and 'those who have historically gravitated toward Russia'.[53] The protection of Russia's interests and fraternal ties in its 'near abroad' is a matter of honour. If Russia feels recognised by the West, this generates hope and a willingness to cooperate. However, when the West challenges, or threatens, Russia's distinctiveness and sense of honour, this activates resentment and Russia will adopt either defensive or assertive policies.[54]

Russia's behaviour in Ukraine can be understood as assertively enhancing its honour.[55] In the context of the Ukrainian crisis, Russia's intervention in

---

49 A. Hofer, 'Creating and contesting hierarchy: the punitive effect of sanctions in a horizontal system', *Revista CIDOB d'Afers Internacionals* issue 125, 2020, 15–37.

50 Zarakol, *op. cit.* note 40; see further 'Special Issue: Status and Emotions in Russia's Foreign Policy', *Communist and Post-Communist Studies* 47 (3), 2014, 261–363.

51 R. Heller, 'More Rigor to Emotions! A Comparative, Qualitative Content Analysis of Anger in Russian Foreign Policy' in: Clément and Sanger, *op. cit.* note 45, 92–95.

52 A.P. Tsygankov, *Russia and the West from Alexander to Putin, Honor in International Relations* (CUP 2012), 5.

53 *Ibid.*, 34, table 3.1. See also *ibid.*, 37.

54 *Ibid.*, 21–22.

55 *Ibid.*, 46–48. We can draw parallels between Russia's behaviour in Georgia in 2008, *ibid.*, chapter 14, and its policy in Ukraine since 2014.

the Eastern regions and its annexation of Crimea reveals that, in its view, the West did not respect the leadership role it wishes to uphold.[56] The events that unfolded in Ukraine and the West's implications therein were interpreted as a threat to Russia's essential interests, especially the risk of NATO's expansion.[57] Furthermore, the West encroached on Russia's fraternal ties with Ukraine.[58] Vladimir Putin describes Crimea and Sevastopol as 'hav[ing] invaluable civilizational and even sacral importance for Russia, like the Temple Mount in Jerusalem for the followers of Islam and Judaism'.[59] Whereas 'Ukraine is merely a geopolitical playground for some Western politicians',[60] Russia presents itself as a nation that cares about Ukraine's well-being. From the Russian perspective, as the Ukrainian crisis unfolded the United States and the EU were not open to dialogue,[61] thereby excluding Russia. To quote Putin, under the circumstances that arose in Ukraine, it became necessary for Russia to assert itself and 'to protect [its] legitimate interests unilaterally'.[62]

By sanctioning Russia for violating international law, the EU is placing itself as morally superior to Russia.[63] However, Russia often faults the West for applying double standards and for not being committed to multilateral values, which include the UN Charter, consequently pointing to their normative shortcomings. In relation to Europe, Russia places itself as equal, if not superior to, its Western neighbour. As T. Hopf puts it, 'Russia has come to be understood as

---

56 For a foreign policy analysis of Russia's, or Putin's, decision to intervene in Ukraine, see: T. Hopf, ' "Crimea Is Ours": A Discursive History', *International Relations* 30 (2), 2016, 227. K. Roberts, 'Understanding Putin: The Politics of Identity and Geopolitics in Russian Foreign Policy Discourse', *International Affairs* 72 (1), 2017, 28; A. Tsygankov, 'Vladimir Putin's Last Stand: The Sources of Russia's Ukraine Policy', *Post-Soviet Affairs* 31 (4), 2015, 279.
57 Hopf, *op. cit.* note 56, 247. Hopf even refers to a sense of betrayal that emerged from the West's failure to respect the agreement with Russia on a negotiated solution to the Ukrainian crisis, see *ibid.*, 246.
58 *Ibid.*, 245.
59 President Putin, 'Presidential Address to the Federal Assembly', the Kremlin, Moscow, 4 December 2014, available at: <http://en.kremlin.ru/events/president/news/47173> (accessed 17 March 2020), hereafter 'Presidential Address 2014'.
60 UN Security Council Verbatim Record (3 March 2014), UN Doc. S/PV.7125, 4 (Russia).
61 'Presidential Address 2014', *op. cit.* note 59; See also: 'Full Text of Putin's speech on Crimea', *Prague Post*, 19 March 2014, available at: < http://www.praguepost.com/eu-news/37854-full-text-of-putin-s-speech-on-crimea > (accessed 17 March 2020).
62 'Presidential Address 2014', *op. cit.* note 59; see also 'Full Text of Putin's Speech on Crimea', *op. cit.* note 59.
63 After all, it takes power to stigmatise, B.G. Link and J.C. Phelan, 'Conceptualizing Stigma', *Annual Review of Sociology* 27, 2001, 375.

the True Europe, while Western Europe is a corrupted version occupied, influenced, and suborned by the United States'.[64] Being 'punished' by such an actor could trigger only negative emotions, and in particular resentment. On the surface, Russia displays the behaviour of a resentful actor: it has retaliated against the sanctions by adopting counter-sanctions as a means to teach the senders a lesson, has accused the EU of adopting unlawful and illegitimate coercive measures while denying any wrongfulness, and has sought moral support from third parties.

Russia implemented counter-sanctions in the form of travel bans in March 2014 and an embargo on agricultural products in August of the same year.[65] The latter measures were coined 'special economic measures to protect Russia's security' and were explained as part of the new Russian food security agenda,[66] an import substitution programme with both domestic and international goals.[67] In addition, Gazprom reduced its gas supplies to EU countries in September 2014.[68] Through the counter-sanctions, it demonstrates that the senders will suffer the costs of reduced cooperation. Russian policy-makers have stressed that once the EU lifts its sanctions Russia will reciprocate, suggesting that Europe first needs to learn its lesson.

Russia is careful in how it justifies coercive measures. It does not want to be portrayed as a state that adopts unilateral sanctions, which it considers unlawful, but does not shy away from adopting measures to protect its interests.[69] Whether unilateral sanctions can be legally justified as security measures is subject to debate, especially in the context of the World Trade Organisation

---

64 Hopf, *op. cit.* note 56, 235–236.
65 Ministry of Foreign Affairs, 'Statement by the Russian Ministry of Foreign Affairs on Retaliatory Sanctions with regard to Several Officials and Members of the US Congress', 20 March 2014, available at: <http://www.mid.ru/en/foreign_policy/news/-/asset_publisher/cKNonkJE02Bw/content/id/69698> (accessed 17 March 2020); President of Russia, 'Executive Order on Applying Certain Special Economic Measures to Ensure the Security of the Russian Federation', 6 August 2014, available at: <http://en.kremlin.ru/events/president/news/46404> (accessed 17 March 2020).
66 See, for example, Russian Government, 'Dmitry Medvedev Takes Part in the First National Food Security Forum', 5 June 2015, available at: < http://government.ru/en/news/18378/> (accessed 17 March 2020).
67 S. Wengle, 'The Domestic Effects of the Russian Food Embargo', *Demokratizatsiya* 24 (3), 2016, 286.
68 Moret et al., *op. cit.* note 7, 8.
69 M. Doraev, 'The "Memory Effect" of Economic Sanctions Against Russia: Opposing Approaches to the Legality of Unilateral Sanctions Clash Again', *University of Pennsylvania Journal of International Law* 37 (1), 2015, 355; Hofer, *op. cit.* note 21.

(WTO), which Russia joined in 2012.[70] Trade restrictions violate the General Agreement on Tariffs and Trade (GATT) unless they fall within one of the treaty's exceptions. In the context of the present chapter, the security exception in GATT Article XXI(b) is most relevant. Because the provision allows WTO members to take 'any action *which it considers* necessary for the protection of its essential security interests' (emphasis added), it is generally defined as self-judging and its reviewability has been disputed[71] though a WTO Panel recently provided guidance on these issues. Following a request for WTO consultations by Ukraine, which challenged certain Russian policies adopted in the context of the Ukrainian crisis, Russia invoked GATT Article XXI(b)(iii). Under subparagraph (iii), necessary measures may be 'taken in time of war or other emergency in international relations'. In its landmark report *Russia – Measures Concerning Traffic in Transit*, the Panel found it had jurisdiction to review the security exception and somewhat limited its self-judging nature. It found that it could objectively determine whether the conditions under subparagraph (iii) were met and that the exception had been raised in good faith.[72] For Russia to validly invoke Article XXI(b)(iii), there had to be a nexus between the action taken and a situation of war or other emergency in international relations. The Panel concluded that Russia had not abusively invoked Article XXI(b)(iii), as the measures were adopted within a context that fell within the scope of subparagraph (iii).[73] It was ultimately up to Russia to decide which measures were necessary.[74]

Returning to Russia's response to the restrictive measures, the Kremlin denies any wrongdoing in Crimea.[75] It argues that it is upholding one of the

---

70   R.J. Neuwirth and A. Svetlicini, 'The Economic Sanctions over the Ukraine Conflict and the WTO: "Catch-XXI" and the Revival of the Debate on the Security Exceptions', *Journal of World Trade* 49 (5), 2015, 891.

71   *Ibid.*, 904–908.

72   WTO Panel Report of 5 April 2019, *Russia, Measures Concerning Traffic in Transit*, DS512, 38–51. On the 'good faith' requirement, see *ibid.*, 56–57, paras. 7.132–7.134.

73   *Ibid.*, 54, para. 7.123.

74   *Ibid.*, 58, para. 7.146. In a separate case, Rosneft, a sanctioned Russian company, challenged the legality of the EU's restrictive measures under the EU-Russia Partnership and Cooperation Agreement (PCA). The Court of Justice found that the EU's measures were consistent with Article 99(1) PCA, which allows parties to take measures 'which it considers necessary for the protection of its essential security interests'. See Judgment of 28 March 2017, *PJSC Rosneft Oil Company v Her Majesty's Treasury and Others*, C-72/15, EU:C:2017:236, paras. 110–111. For comments, see the contributions by K. Entin (chapter 5) and C. Challet (chapter 6) in this volume.

75   President Putin, 'Interview to German newspaper *Bild*: Part 1', Sochi, 5 January 2016, available at: < http://en.kremlin.ru/events/president/news/51154> (accessed 17 March 2020). See also: 'Full Text of Putin's Speech on Crimea', *op. cit.* note 61; Doraev, *op. cit.* note 69.

international order's fundamental principles, the right to self-determination, and invokes Kosovo as a precedent to justify the Crimean people's right to self-determination.[76] In addition, the sanctioning states have linked the lifting of sanctions to Russia's fulfilment of its obligations under the Minsk agreements, which Russia is failing to adhere to. Russian officials continuously reiterate that the Ukrainian authorities are stalling the ceasefire and failing to respect their end of the deal.[77] Russia therefore contests the continuous renewal of the sanctions on the basis that the agreements are not properly respected by Ukraine. In this way, Russia denies that it carries any responsibility in the Ukrainian crisis, giving the impression that the sanctions are unreasonable. The sanctions are further explained as a policy used to 'weaken' and 'demonise' Russia. They are therefore a policy of containment that has been adopted against Russia since the Cold War. In his 2014 Presidential Address, Putin explained that even if the crisis in Ukraine had not arisen,

> [the West] would have come up with some other excuse to try to contain Russia's growing capabilities, affect our country in some way, or even take advantage of it. The policy of containment was not invented yesterday. It has been carried out against our country for many years, always, for decades, if not centuries. In short, whenever someone thinks that Russia has become too strong or independent, these tools are quickly put into use.[78]

Finally, Russia receives support from a group of states that consider unilateral sanctions to be contrary to the UN Charter and WTO rules. It has issued statements alongside China, India, and Brazil, Russia, India, China and South Africa (BRICS) declaring that unilateral coercive measures violate international law.[79]

---

76 'Full Text of Putin's Speech on Crimea', *op. cit.* note 61.
77 'Interview to German newspaper *Bild*: Part 1', *op. cit.* note 75; 'Interview with Euronews TV Channel', *op. cit.* note 48. See also A. Lukashevich, Permanent Representative of the Russian Federation to the OSCE, 'Remarks at the OSCE Permanent Council meeting', Vienna, 28 July 2016, available at: <http://www.mid.ru/en/web/guest/maps/ua/-/asset_publisher/ktnoZLTvbbS3/content/id/2375991> (accessed 17 March 2020).
78 'Presidential Address 2014', *op. cit.* note 59.
79 'The Declaration of the Russian Federation ...', *op. cit.* note 41; Joint Communiqué of the 14th Meeting of the Foreign Ministers of the Russian Federation, the Republic of India and the People's Republic of China, 19 April 2016, available at: <http://www.fmprc.gov.cn/mfa_eng/wjdt_665385/2649_665393/t1356652.shtml> (accessed 17 March 2020); 'The 6th BRICS Summit: Fortaleza Declaration, Fortaleza, Brazil', 15 July 2014, available at: <http://www.brics.utoronto.ca/docs/140715-leaders.html> (accessed 17 March 2020); See further D.V. Kuznetsov, 'China and the Ukrainian Crisis: From 'Neutrality' to 'Support' for Russia', *China Report* 52 (2), 2016, 103.

Should the Russian population suffer from the sanctions,[80] Russia could make use of the claims that sanctions violate human rights, aligning with states that have also been placed under sanctions and that condemn unilateral coercive measures such as Iran, Belarus and Myanmar, and with groups that support them such as the Group of 77 (G-77) and Non-Aligned Movement.[81] It should be noted, nevertheless, that it has failed to garner support from the members of the Eurasian Economic Union (i.e., Kazakhstan, Belarus, Armenia and Kyrgyzstan) for its counter-sanctions against the EU.[82]

As this section has demonstrated, Russia's actions in response to the sanctions demonstrate that it rejects and resents the imposition of stigma through the unilateral sanctions. The consequence is that rather than cooperate with the EU, Russia will have a tendency to remain assertive as it seeks to remedy the perceived unfair treatment. There is, however, a silver lining: a resentful actor does not seek to dissolve the social relationship with the object of resentment.[83] As long as resentment does not shift to hate, it is possible to invest in conciliatory practices that will make cooperation between the parties possible.

5 Looking Forward: A Shift Towards Compassion?

The picture painted in this chapter is focused on one variable only in the current EU-Russia relationship: the EU's restrictive measures against Russia. Although the European sanctions are not the only factor responsible for the existing deadlock (which originates from a long and complex socio-historical background), they do contribute to it. The chapter has demonstrated that sanctions must be understood within their context, which includes the social and historical interaction between the sender and the target. Sanctions are not merely the imposition of costs; they are symbolical gestures that shape the sender's identity and influence the target's identity and affective state of being.

The EU is motivated to adopt sanctions to promote its values in the wider world because it identifies itself as a normative power. If restrictive measures may not be the most effective policy tool to pressure Russia into changing its behaviour in Ukraine, their signalling function enables the EU to activate its

---

80   M.L. Schrad, 'Western Sanctions Are Shrinking Russia's Population', *Foreign Policy*, 19 October 2017, available at: <http://foreignpolicy.com/2017/10/19/western-sanctions-are-shrinking-russias-population/> (accessed 17 March 2020).
81   Hofer, *op. cit.* note 21.
82   Hellquist, *op. cit.* note 29, 1014.
83   Wolf, 2013, *op cit.* note 45, 3.

normative authority.[84] However, with regard to Russia, the EU's identity as a normative power is restricted by its dependence on Russia and the need to keep the door open to dialogue.[85] This is perceptible in the second tenant of the principled pragmatism: the need for cooperation with Russia in other areas of interest. Consequently, when put in practice, the two branches to the EU's principled pragmatism contradict each other. This contradiction clearly comes across in the EU's use of restrictive measures and their effect on the Russian Federation. Although the measures enable the EU to stand firm, they have the counterproductive effect of motivating Russia to remain assertive because they trigger resentment.

Nonetheless, behind Russian resentment may lay disappointment that the 'hope'[86] of cooperation and partnership with the EU was not fulfilled. In 2005, Hopf wrote that Russia 'understood herself as European'.[87] President Putin revealed the feeling of betrayal when he reportedly stated: 'Our biggest mistake was that we trusted you [the "West"] too much. You interpreted our trust as weakness and you exploited that'.[88] In choosing to side with the United States' more coercive approach, the EU missed an opportunity to reshape its interaction with its Eastern neighbour and to have a relationship based on cooperation, which may have had a positive influence on Russian policy decisions.[89] Ultimately, despite the tensions over Ukraine, both the EU and Russia desire cooperation and know that it is in their best interests. In his Presidential Address to the Federal Assembly in 2018, Putin reaffirmed: 'We are interested in normal and constructive cooperation with the United States and the European Union'. As Tsygankov writes, 'Russia has always been responsive to the behaviour of the West and … prepared to mend fences and pursue cooperation, rather than confrontation'.[90] The EU should be sensitive to this. Understanding the emotions that motivate Russia to act assertively in Ukraine reveals that punishing Russia for these actions (even if they contravene the international normative

---

84   Though this is debatable, recall note 20 above.
85   Bengsston and Ergström, *op cit.* note 22, 100.
86   Tsygankov, 2014, *op cit.* note 41.
87   T. Hopf, 'Identity, Legitimacy, and the Use of Military Force: Russia's Great Power Identities and Military Intervention in Abkhazia', *Review of International Studies* 31(1), 2005, 240–241.
88   'Putin Dials up Anti-U.S. Rhetoric, Keeps Mum on Re-election', Reuters, 19 October 2017, available at: <https://www.reuters.com/article/us-russia-putin-usa-energy/putin-dials-up-anti-u-s-rhetoric-keeps-mum-on-re-election-idUSKBN1CO2CX> (accessed 17 March 2020).
89   Hopf, 2005, *op. cit.* note 87, 242.
90   Tsygankov, *op. cit.* note 52, 51.

order) only increases Russian resentment, motivates it to adopt its own harmful policies and inevitably pushes cooperation further away.[91] Consequently, taking into account the affective dynamics of coercive measures can provide insight on a way out of the deadlock.[92] Although this may be controversial, rather than punish actors for wrongdoing the EU should consider having a compassionate understanding of the factors that motivated Russia to adopt its aggressive policy in Ukraine and addressing the elements that contribute to Russia's threat perception. This would contentiously require the EU, and the other actors involved in the Ukrainian crisis, to 'self-reflectively'[93] consider how their own behaviour led to an escalation in Ukraine. After all, some norms 'take the form of ideals and constitute standards almost everyone falls short some stage'.[94] This is certainly the case for international legal norms and Russia has proven more than happy to point at the EU's own shortcomings. Rather than enforce international norms and a peaceful solution in Ukraine through punitive measures, the EU should accept Russia as an equal and as a '*bona fide* contracting party' capable of satisfaction.[95] This would be a new form of principled pragmatism, one that seeks to promote norms through talk rather than '*Diktat*'.[96]

---

91 Wolf, 2018, *op cit.* note 45, 246–247.
92 S.A. Bandes and J.A. Blumenthal, 'Emotions and the Law', *Annual Review of Law and Social Sciences* 8, 2012, 170–171.
93 T. Diez, 'Constructing the Self and Changing Others: Reconsidering 'Normative Power Europe'', *Millenium* 33 (3), 2005, 613.
94 Adler-Nissen, *op cit.* note 8, 147.
95 S. Scheider, 'Pragmatism as a Path towards a Discursive and Open Theory of International Law', *European Journal of International Law* 11 (3), 2000, 696.
96 *Ibid.*; Hofer, *op cit.* note 21, 63–65.

CHAPTER 5

The EU-Russia Sanctions Regime before the Court of Justice of the EU

Kirill Entin

1   Introduction

The events in Crimea and eastern Ukraine prompted the European Union to adopt several 'packages' of restrictive measures against Russia. The first one, following the announcement of a referendum of independence in Crimea, contained only diplomatic measures such as the suspension of preparations for the G8 summit in Sochi and the freezing of bilateral talks on visa matters and a new bilateral framework agreement.[1] A second set of measures, introduced on 17 March 2014, allowed actions to be taken against persons 'responsible for actions which undermine or threaten the territorial integrity, sovereignty and independence of Ukraine, and of natural persons associated with them'. The criteria for the inclusion in the sanctions list have subsequently been considerably broadened to also include, *inter alia*, 'natural persons responsible for, actively supporting or implementing, actions or policies which undermine or threaten the territorial integrity, sovereignty and independence of Ukraine, or stability or security in Ukraine or which obstruct the work of international organisations in Ukraine, and natural or legal persons, entities or bodies associated with them'.[2] The downing of Malaysia Airlines flight MH17 prompted the EU to adopt the same month a 'third package' containing economic sanctions, including a ban on arms exports[3] and trade with regard to oil technologies, as well as restrictions on the access of Russian banks to European capital markets.[4] Finally, a separate package is specifically targeted at Crimea

---

[1] Statement of the Heads of State or Government on Ukraine, Brussels, 6 March 2014, available at: <http://www.consilium.europa.eu/media/29285/141372.pdf> (accessed 31 March 2020).

[2] See Article 1 of Council Regulation (EU) No. 811/2014 of 25 July 2014 amending Regulation (EU) No. 269/2014 concerning restrictive measures in respect of actions undermining or threatening the territorial integrity, sovereignty and independence of Ukraine, *OJ*, 2014, L 221/11.

[3] Council Decision 2014/512/CFSP, *OJ*, 2014, L 229/13.

[4] Council Regulation (EU) No. 833/2014, *OJ*, 2014, L 229/1.

and Sebastopol as it prohibits the import of goods originated there and investments or involvement in the development of its infrastructure and industry.[5]

A number of attempts have been made by natural and legal persons to challenge the validity of those measures before the General Court[6] and the Court of Justice[7] of the EU. Despite the fact that the applicants in all of these cases were unsuccessful and the judgments largely confirmed the existing case law of the Court of Justice of the European Union (CJEU), these cases deserve special attention for a number of reasons.

First, they provide an important clarification of the application of the listing criteria developed in the context of the Ukrainian crisis. In the *Rotenberg* and *Kiselev* cases, the General Court gave a restrictive reading of the notion of 'active support' used in the sanction criteria as covering only those forms of support which, by their quantitative or qualitative significance, contribute to Russia's actions and policies destabilising Ukraine. This rather restrictive reading fits well with the fifth principle guiding the EU's policy towards Russia,[8] implying that only a small group of persons will be liable to fall under this criterion and that it will not threaten people-to-people contacts at large.

Second, the Court had the opportunity to rule on the validity of different types of measures. While the *Almaz-Antey Air and Space Defence*, *Kiselev*, and *Rotenberg* cases dealt with the freezing of assets, in other cases the Court examined general economic measures such as the restriction of access to capital markets and export restrictions. *Rosneft* and *NK Rosneft and Others* present a particular interest in this regard as the Court addressed the issue of the compatibility of those measures with the provisions of the EU-Russia Partnership and Cooperation Agreement of 1994 (PCA) and World Trade Organisation (WTO) law. Those expecting an elaborate analysis were, however, quickly disappointed as the Court basically confirmed the Council's broad discretion for

---

5   Notably, Council Decision 2014/386/CFSP, *OJ*, 2014, L 183/70; and Council Regulation (EU) No. 692/2014, *OJ*, 2014, L 18/9.

6   Judgment of 30 November 2016, *Rotenberg*, T-720/14, EU:T:2016:689; judgment of 25 January 2017, *Almaz-Antey Air and Space Defence*, T-255/15, EU:T:2017:25; judgment of 15 June 2017, *Kiselev*, T-262/15, EU:T:2017:392; judgment of 13 September 2018, *NK Rosneft and Others*, T-715/14, EU:T:2018:544; judgment of 13 September 2018, *Sberbank*, T-732/14, EU:T:2018:541; judgment of 13 September 2018, *VTB Bank*, T-734/14, EU:T:2018:542; judgment of 13 September 2018, *Gazprom Neft*, T-735/14, EU:T:2018:548; judgment of 13 September 2018, *Vnesheconombank*, T-737/14, EU:T:2018:543; judgment of 13 September 2018, *Denizbank*, T-798/14, EU:T:2018:546; judgment of 13 September 2018, *Almaz-Antey*, T-515/15, EU:T:2018:545.

7   Judgment of 28 March 2017, C-72/15 *Rosneft*, EU:C:2017: 236.

8   This principle is defined as follows: 'Increasing support for Russian civil society and promoting people-to-people contacts, given that sanctions target the regime rather than Russian people'.

the adoption of political decisions. In its appraisal of the necessity of restrictive measures for the protection of EU essential security interests, it relied entirely on the Council's assessment contained in the preambles of the contested acts transforming an already limited judicial control in a pure formality. In a situation where restrictive measures are imposed by the EU on the ground of international law violations, this reluctance by the CJEU to exercise an effective control as to the respect of international law – or at least conduct its own assessment of the situation – can be seen as weakening the Court's stance as an independent non-political institution.[9]

Third, what is even more important, some of the cases brought a significant contribution to the development of the Court's jurisprudence in the area of Common Foreign and Security Policy (CFSP) as the Court was prompted to deal with several new legal issues.[10] The *Rotenberg* case, for instance, answers the question of whether persons in charge of certain businesses may be included in the sanctions list because they benefitted from the decision-makers at any point in time, or whether the EU institutions need to demonstrate the existence of such a connection at the time when the third state's illegal actions took place.[11] In the *Kiselev* case, the General Court had to ascertain the legality of restrictive measures taken against a journalist in the light of the freedom of expression.[12] In its turn in *Rosneft*, the Court of Justice ruled on the possibility to challenge the legality of autonomous restrictive measures via the preliminary reference procedure.[13]

Finally, the number and nature of the cases may also contribute to the debate on the effectiveness of the sanctions.[14] This chapter does not seek to describe the cases one by one[15] but rather analyses their contribution to the development of the CJEU case law on restrictive measures by focusing on the key issues discussed in these cases (see Table 5.1). Although the Court as a

---

9   For an analysis of the Court's political cautiousness and will to ensure the effectiveness of sanctions against Russia, see the contribution of C. Challet (chapter 6) in this volume.
10 See, more generally, C. Hillion and R. Wessel, 'The Good, the Bad and the Ugly: Three Levels of Judicial Control over the CFSP', in: S. Blockmans and P. Koutrakos (eds.), *Research Handbook on EU Common Foreign and Security Policy* (Edward Elgar 2018), 65–87.
11 Judgment of 30 November 2016, *Rotenberg*, T-720/14, EU:T:2016:689.
12 Judgment of 15 June 2017, *Kiselev*, T-262/15, EU:T:2017:392.
13 Judgment of 28 March 2017, *Rosneft*, C-72/15, EU:C:2017: 236.
14 On the question of effectiveness, see also the contribution by A. Hofer (chapter 4) in this volume.
15 For a case by case analysis of the *Rotenberg, Kiselev, Rosneft* and *Almaz-Antey* cases, see: S. Glandin, 'Evropeyskoe pravo ogranichitel'nykh mer posle pervykh rossiyskikh del v Sude Evropeyskogo Soyuza' [The European law of restrictive measures after first Russian cases before the European Court of Justice], *Mezhdunarodnoe pravosudie* 22 (2), 2017, 80–93.

non-political institution is not bound by the five guiding principles underlying the EU's policy towards Russia, the analysis of the Court's case law may provide a useful insight for the discussion of at least two of them: the first one, insisting on full implementation of the Minsk agreements before economic sanctions against Russia are lifted, as it is based on the fundamental assumption that the economic sanctions imposed by the EU are legal both under EU law and under international law; and the fifth one, as the sanction criteria need to be interpreted in such a way as not to deter people-to-people contacts.

2   The Procedure and Legal Basis for the Adoption of Restrictive Measures

The founding treaties provide different legal grounds for the adoption of restrictive measures. The initial impulse for imposing restrictive measures is most often given by the European Council, whose tasks include the definition of strategic interests and objectives of the EU in relation to a specific country or region.[16] Moreover, a statement from the European Council is sufficient for adopting diplomatic measures, such as the suspension of bilateral talks with the Russian Federation on visa matters and on a new 'strategic partnership' agreement, as they do not require implementation.[17]

Economic measures are adopted pursuant to Article 215 of the Treaty on the Functioning of the European Union (TFEU) enabling the Council to adopt measures interrupting or reducing, in part or completely, economic and financial relations with third countries or to adopt 'restrictive measures ... against natural or legal persons and groups or non-State entities'. The Council uses a 'two-tier procedure', which requires a political decision under Title 2 Chapter V of the Treaty on European Union (TEU), followed by a regulation adopted under Article 215 TFEU 'on a joint proposal from the EU High Representative and the Commission', to implement the decision. This unique and somewhat complicated mechanism is a heritage of the past EU 'pillars' system. Throughout both stages, the Council remains the sole decision-maker as the Parliament is just 'kept informed' without even being consulted. For non-economic measures, a decision under Title 2 Chapter V is enough as these measures are implemented by the Member States.

---

16 Article 22 TEU.
17 Statement of the Heads of State or Government on Ukraine, Brussels, 6 March 2014, available at: <http://www.consilium.europa.eu/media/29285/141372.pdf> (accessed 31 March 2020).

TABLE 5.1 Overview of key judgments in relation to the EU-Russia sanctions regime

	Key issues	Cases
1.	Procedure for the adoption of restrictive measures.	C-72/15 *Rosneft*
2.	Possibility to challenge the validity of restrictive measures indirectly via the preliminary reference procedure.	C-72/15 *Rosneft*
3.	*Locus standi* of individuals (possibility to challenge restrictive measures in the absence of individual concern).	T-715/14 *NK Rosneft and Others*
4.	Human rights: freedom of expression.	T-262/15 *Kiselev*
5.	Manifest error of assessment: requirement to demonstrate that the connection between the leaders and persons associated with them still existed at the time of infringement.	T-720/14 *Rotenberg*
6.	Manifest error of assessment: interpretation of the 'active support' requirement.	T-720/14 *Rotenberg*; T-262/15 *Kiselev*
7.	Compatibility of restrictive measures with the WTO General Agreement on Tariffs and Trade.	T-715/14 *NK Rosneft and Others*
8	Compatibility of restrictive measures with the Partnership and Cooperation Agreement.	C-72/15 *Rosneft*

At present, both the CFSP decision and the implementing regulation are adopted on the same day and mostly contain identical provisions,[18] which is understandable for reasons of effectiveness but in essence renders the Commission and High Representative's involvement at the second stage useless.[19] This is also due to the fact that the list of persons subject to fund-freezing measures is annexed to the initial CFSP decision. Thus, the Council is not able to really take advantage of the qualified majority rule for the adoption of the regulation, as all the important aspects have already been dealt with by consensus.

---

18 The main difference being that the implementing regulation does not include non-economic measures.

19 On the Commission's role during the initial stage, see the contribution by T. van der Togt (chapter 2) in this volume.

These inconsistencies were discussed by the Court in *Rosneft*, as the applicant in the main proceeding argued that Decision 2014/512 infringes Article 40 TEU since it defines the Union position on the restrictive measures in excessive detail, thereby encroaching on the joint power of proposal of the Commission and the High Representative. Although the Court admitted that 'the content of Decision 2014/512 is certainly detailed' and the implementing regulation was essentially reproducing the content of Decision 2014/512,[20] it pointed out that the decision was designed to introduce targeted restrictive measures concerning fields that were technical in nature. Accordingly, it came to the conclusion that it may be appropriate for the Council to use detailed wording when establishing those measures. Moreover, it found that the implementing regulation contained some definitions where clarifications were needed. Finally, the Court interpreted Articles 24 and 29 TEU as giving power to the Council, acting unanimously, to determine the persons and entities that are to be subject to the restrictive measures in the field of CFSP.

3   The Jurisdiction of the CJEU and the *Locus Standi* of Individuals

The abolishment of the pillar structure with the Treaty of Lisbon did not imply that the field of CFSP falls entirely under the Court's jurisdiction. Pursuant to Article 24 TEU, the CJEU has, in principle, no jurisdiction with respect to acts adopted under the CFSP provisions. There are, however, two exceptions: the Court has jurisdiction to monitor compliance with Article 40 TEU and to review the legality of certain restrictive measures under Article 275(2) TFEU.

The goal of the first exception is to ensure that CFSP provisions are the correct legal basis and are not used to circumvent the powers of the other institutions under the TFEU and vice versa. In *Rosneft*, the applicant unsuccessfully referred to Article 40 TEU when he argued that the Council decision imposing restrictions on the access to capital markets[21] constituted in fact a 'legislative act', whereas Articles 24 and 31 TEU preclude the adoption of such acts in the field of CFSP. The Court rejected that claim stating that Decision 2014/512 was not adopted under the TFEU and could not be considered a legislative act within the meaning of Article 289(3) TFEU. While the Court's reply may

---

20   *Rosneft*, op. cit. note 13, paras. 87, 89.
21   Council Decision 2014/512/CFSP of 31 July 2014 concerning restrictive measures in view of Russia's actions destabilising the situation in Ukraine, *OJ*, 2014, L 229/13.

appear to be formalistic, it is nevertheless consistent with the case law as the main distinction between regulatory and legislative acts is the procedure used to adopt them.[22]

The second exception concerns sanctions imposed on private individuals with the second paragraph of Article 275 TFEU allowing the Court 'to rule on proceedings, brought in accordance with the conditions laid down in the fourth paragraph of Article 263 of this Treaty, reviewing the legality of decisions providing for restrictive measures against natural or legal persons adopted by the Council'.

As the Court made it clear in a highly anticipated judgment in *Rosneft*, the reference to Article 263 TFEU merely concerns the admissibility requirements and does not rule out the possibility to challenge the validity of a CFSP decision indirectly via the preliminary reference procedure. The Court stressed that Articles 263, 267 and 277 TFEU constitute a complete system of legal remedies and procedures designed to ensure judicial review of the legality of EU acts. The right of private persons to challenge the legality of provisions contained in EU acts on which a decision or national measure adopted in respect of them is based is inherent to this system.[23] Finally, the Court invoked the principle of effective judicial protection, emphasising the need to guarantee access to judicial review of national implementing measures and to interpret any exclusion of the Court's jurisdiction strictly.[24]

By answering the preliminary questions from the British court, the ECJ essentially killed two birds with one stone: it reinforced its own competence and strengthened the judicial protection of individuals. While it could be argued that the *Rosneft* judgment did not open the 'heaven's door'[25] for additional categories of applicants as they still need to satisfy the *locus standi* criteria of Article 263(4) TFEU, this change may make a difference with regard to the duration of proceedings. Indeed, in 2018, the medium duration of proceedings for preliminary references was 16 months, while it constituted 18.8 months with regard to direct actions.[26]

However, the existence of a parallel way to challenge the validity of the Council's decision does not mean that the persons affected by the sanctions are dispensed

---

22   See order of 6 September 2011, *Inuit*, T-18/10, EU:T:2011:419, para. 60.
23   *Rosneft, op. cit.* note 13, paras. 66–67.
24   *Ibid.*, para. 74.
25   T. Tridimas, 'Knocking on Heaven's Door: Fragmentation, Efficiency and Defiance in the Preliminary Reference Procedure', *CMLR* 40 (1), 2003, 9–50.
26   CJEU Annual Report 2018. Judicial Activity, 12, available at: <https://curia.europa.eu/jcms/jcms/p1_1870421/en/> (accessed 6 April 2020).

from the necessity to bring an action for annulment within two months.[27] Failure to do so could result in the preliminary reference to be declared inadmissible.[28] Effectively, this means that individuals might have to bring an action for annulment to the General Court (GC) and to national courts at the same time, which could result in parallel cases before the GC and the European Court of Justice (ECJ) as it happened with *Rosneft*. Following the registry of the preliminary reference in *Rosneft*, the President of the GC decided to stay the proceedings not only in *NK Rosneft and Others* but also in six parallel proceedings brought by different applicants.[29]

It goes without saying that the outcome of the proceedings in *Rosneft* had a significant impact on all the applicants. The most interesting situation arose in *NK Rosneft and Others* as the pleas put forward by the applicant were essentially the same as in *Rosneft*. While the GC refused to recognise the judgment of the ECJ case as having the authority of *res judicata* because of a different procedural context and different legal basis, it admitted that it could not 'entirely disregard the reasoning set out by the Court of Justice in a case involving the same parties and raising largely the same legal issues', especially taking into account the existence of an appeal procedure and the fact that the ECJ was sitting in Grand Chamber formation.[30] As a result, on certain points the GC was merely content to reproduce the ECJ's reasoning.[31]

Thus, while the existence of parallel proceedings may not be ideal for reasons of procedural economy, it does not seem to endanger the consistency of the CJEU case law. On the contrary, it could be argued that it allows the ECJ to establish guiding principles for a whole cluster of cases. It thus bears a certain resemblance with the pilot judgment procedure used by the European Court of Human Rights (ECtHR)[32] and could, alongside the well-established practice of assigning similar cases to the same chamber and judge-rapporteur, allow the CJEU to easily deal with the caseload.

The Russian cases have also brought some interesting developments as to the interpretation of the *locus standi* criteria set in Article 263(4) TFEU. In

---

27 See judgment of 9 March 1994, *TWD*, C-188/92, EU:C:1994:90, paras. 17–18.
28 See *Rosneft, op. cit.* note 13, para. 67.
29 *VTB Bank* (T-734/14); *Sberbank* (T-732/14); *Almaz-Antey* (T-515/15); *Gazprom Neft* (T-735/14); *Vnesheconombank* (T-737/14); *DenizBank* (T-798/14).
30 Judgment of 13 September 2018, *NK Rosneft and Others*, T-715/14, EU:T:2018:544, paras. 96–100.
31 *Ibid.*, paras. 178, 189.
32 For more on this procedure, see D. Haider, *The Pilot-Judgment Procedure of the European Court of Human Rights* (Martinus Nijhoff 2013).

NK Rosneft and Others, the GC found the actions challenging certain export restrictions with regard to oil technologies to be admissible on the ground that the applicants, although not individually concerned, managed to prove direct concern and that the regulatory measures in question did not entail implementing measures. According to the Court, while the challenged measure provided for a prior authorisation system, it did not grant national authorities any margin of discretion as they were under an obligation to refuse it if they considered the transaction falling under the prohibition. It concluded that 'it would be artificial or excessive to demand that an operator request an implementing measure merely in order to be able to challenge that measure in the national courts, where it is clear that such a request will necessarily be refused and would not, therefore, have been made in the ordinary course of business'.[33]

Thus, individuals now have the possibility to bring actions for annulment against general economic measures which affect them directly and leave no discretion to the national authorities even when their names are not cited in the annex of the contested act. In theory, the measures could even be challenged by EU-based companies affected due to long-term contractual arrangements, although they are much less likely to do so due to reputational risks.

4   Autonomous Restrictive Measures: Legal Issues under EU Law

The limitation of the CJEU jurisdiction to control the legality of sanctions under Article 275 TFEU basically predetermines the legal issues that could be discussed under EU law.

The first group concerns the protection of fundamental rights. The judgments in *Kadi I and II*[34] illustrate the willingness of the Court to exercise a thorough control to ensure the compliance of the measures adopted by the EU with fundamental rights, even in cases where the EU is merely implementing UN Security Council resolutions. In this regard, the Court is heavily relying on its case law developed in connection with terrorist cases. As the Court clarified in *Bamba,*[35] the same human rights standards are applicable with regard to suspected terrorists and individuals targeted by bilateral sanctions.

---

33   *NK Rosneft and Others, op. cit.* note 30, para. 90.
34   Judgment of 3 September 2008, *Kadi I*, C-402/05 P, EU:C:2008:461, paras. 280–372; judgment of 18 July 2013, *Kadi II*, C-584/10 P, EU:C:2013:518, paras. 97–149.
35   Judgment of 16 May 2013, *Iran Transfo*, T-392/11, EU:T:2013:254, paras. 34–37.

The second group relates to the question of whether the inclusion of specific persons in the list satisfies the criteria defined by the Council. In that respect, specific case law related to targeted sanctions has developed.

4.1 Compatibility with Fundamental Rights

As a preliminary remark, it is necessary to mention that the possibility to rely on human rights is guaranteed to all applicants, even when they are, in fact, emanations of a state.[36] Most of the cases examined by the Court concern procedural rights; namely, the rights of defence and the right to effective judicial protection. They comprise, *inter alia*, the obligation to notify the persons targeted by the restrictive measures individually. As the Court established in *Sberbank,* this obligation also applies to general economic measures such as a restriction on the access to capital markets, where the names of the companies concerned appear in the annex of the decision.[37] The GC noted, however, that 'while the absence of individual communication of the contested acts has an impact on the point at which time starts to run for the purposes of the bringing of an action, it does not in itself justify the annulment of the acts at issue' if the omission did not result in a breach of the applicant's rights that could justify the annulment.

Another important aspect of the right of defence is the obligation to state reasons as it constitutes an essential principle of EU law which may be derogated from only for compelling reasons. Its primary purpose is to 'provide the person concerned with sufficient information to make it possible to determine whether the act is well founded or whether it is vitiated by an error which may permit its validity to be contested before the Community Courts'.[38] The statement of reasons must contain 'the facts and points of law on which the legal justification of the measure depend and the considerations which led it to adopt it'.[39] However, the question of whether the statement of reasons is sufficient is assessed by the Court not only with regard to its wording but also to its context. Thus, in connection with the Russian cases, the GC has repeatedly stated that it is not relevant for the reasoning to go into all the relevant facts and points of law as the general economic sanctions formed part of an international context known to the applicants.[40] The Court also took into account the fact that the stated objective of the contested acts were to increase the costs

---

36   Judgment of 5 February 2013, *Bank Saderat Iran*, T-494/10, EU:T:2013:59, para. 34.
37   Judgment of 13 September 2018, *Sberbank*, T-732/14, EU:T:2018:541 paras. 115–116.
38   Judgment of 12 December 2006, *OMPI*, T-228/02, EU:T:2006:384, para. 138.
39   *Ibid.*, para. 81.
40   See *NK Rosneft and Others, op. cit.* note 30, para. 118.

of the Russian Federation's actions to undermine Ukraine's territorial integrity, sovereignty and independence, and to promote a peaceful settlement of the crisis to conclude that it was sufficient that the contested acts 'describe the overall situation that led to their adoption and the general objectives they were intended to achieve'.[41] In *Rotenberg*, the Court held that in a situation where several criteria for listing exist, it is not necessary for the Council to explicitly mention which of the relevant criteria was used in relation to the applicant, provided it can be sufficiently clearly deduced from the statement of reasons.[42]

Apart from procedural rights, the applicants in the Russian cases also brought pleas alleging a breach of property right and freedom to conduct business, as well as the principle of proportionality. With regard to the former, the Court basically followed the approach of the ECtHR recognising that the right to property is not absolute but may be restricted in the public interest. It then checks whether the limitations of fundamental rights are provided by law, refer to an objective of general interest and are not disproportionate.[43] In relation to the latter, the Court merely reiterated its well-established position that, due to the complexity of the CFSP, the Council must be allowed a broad discretion.[44] Consequently, the standard used by the Court is one of a manifestly inappropriate measure.[45] Taking into account the general goal pursued by the Council 'to increase the costs to be borne by the Russian Federation for its actions to undermine Ukraine's territorial integrity, sovereignty and independence', the Court concluded that it was irrelevant that a Russian state-owned oil company and credit institutions did not 'play the slightest role in the actions of the Russian Federation destabilising the situation in Ukraine'.[46] It could be reminded that already in *Bosphorus*,[47] the Court accepted the possibility for restrictive measures to have adverse consequences for persons other than those responsible for the situation, which led to the adoption of sanctions – a position reiterated in *Rosneft*.[48]

The *Kiselev* case provided the GC with an opportunity to examine the compatibility of restrictive measures with the freedom of expression guaranteed by Article 10 of the European Convention on Human Rights and Fundamental

---

41   *Rosneft, op. cit.* note 13, para. 123.
42   *Rotenberg, op. cit.* note 16, para. 51.
43   *Ibid.*, paras. 170–173.
44   See, for example, *Rosneft, op. cit.* note 13, para. 146.
45   Judgment of 28 November 2013, *Kala Naft*, C-348/12 P, EU:C:2013:776, para. 120.
46   See, for example, *Sberbank, op. cit.* note 37, paras. 148–149.
47   Judgment of 30 July 1996, *Bosphorus*, Case C-84/95, EU:C:1996:312.
48   *Rosneft, op. cit.* note 13, para. 149.

Freedoms (ECHR). Both in *Mikhalchanka I and II*, the Court was dispensed from making such an assessment as it found that the Council failed to demonstrate that the Belarusian journalist fell under the listing criteria of 'persons responsible for the violations of international electoral standards in the presidential elections' or those 'responsible for the serious violations of human rights or the crackdown on civil society and democratic opposition in that country'.[49] On the contrary, the introduction of the criterion of 'active support' by the Council with regard to Russian sanctions made it necessary for the Court to proceed to an assessment of whether Kiselev's listing was lawful in the light of the case law of the ECtHR; namely, to consider whether the limitation of the applicant's rights was provided by law, pursued an objective of general interest and was necessary and proportionate to the aim sought.

In assessing the last criterion, the Court held that the Council was entitled to consider that the applicant had engaged in propaganda activities in support of the actions and policies of the Russian government destabilising Ukraine. The Court continued that in those circumstances, the adoption of restrictive measures cannot be regarded as a disproportionate restriction of the applicant's right to freedom of expression:

> If that were the case, the Council would be unable to pursue its policy of exerting pressure on the Russian Government by addressing restrictive measures not only to persons who are responsible for the actions and policies of that government as regards Ukraine or to the persons who implement those actions or policies, but also to persons providing active support to those persons.[50]

Hence, the Court accepted that, unlike the dissemination of ideas promoting racism and the Nazi ideology, and those inciting hatred and racial discrimination, propaganda as such does not automatically fall outside the scope of Article 10 ECHR. However, the qualification of the applicants' activities as propaganda will be taken into account by the Court in its analysis of proportionality.

4.2 *Checking the Absence of a Manifest Error of Assessment*

While following *Kadi* the Court, in principle, exercises full review in relation to the respect of fundamental rights, the scope of the review regarding the

---

49   Judgment of 23 September 2014, *Michalchanka I*, T-196/11, EU:T:2014:801, para. 73; judgment of 10 May 2016 *Michalchanka II*, T-693/13, EU:T:2016:283, para. 97.
50   *Kiselev, op. cit.* note 12, para. 113.

assessment of the considerations of appropriateness on which the Council based its measures appears to be more limited. This is explained by the necessity for the Council to enjoy broad discretion in applying restrictive measures that prevent the Court from substituting its assessment of the evidence, facts and circumstances justifying the adoption of restrictive measures. Consequently, the Court may assess only whether the facts are materially accurate and that there have been no manifest errors of assessment of the facts or misuse of power. The judicial review of the lawfulness of the decision in question thus extends to the assessment of the facts and circumstances relied on as justifying it, and to the evidence and information on which that assessment is based.[51]

Relating to the accuracy of the facts, it must be stressed that the burden of proof lies on the EU authorities, which may be asked to furnish information and evidence if necessary. Thus, in *Rotenberg*, one of the grounds for listing was that the applicant had been the majority shareholder of Giprotransmost, a company which was awarded the contract of a feasibility study of the construction of a bridge between Russia and Crimea. The Council failed to produce evidence supporting its claim but argued that the applicant controlled Giprotransmost via another company and produced an Interfax report. The Court remained sceptical, observing that the report merely refers to other articles, no details of which are given. It concluded that 'such indirect evidence is not a sufficient basis on which to conclude that the Council has satisfied the burden of proof it bears in accordance with the case-law'.[52]

Regarding the assessment of the facts, the Court essentially checks whether the listing of specific persons is justified with regard to the listing criteria established by the Council. The case of reference on this issue remains *Tay Za*, where the applicant successfully challenged the validity for lack of legal basis.[53] In this case, the ECJ referred to its previous case law stating that the notion of a third country for the purpose of the powers to impose sanctions 'may include the rulers of such a country and also individuals and entities associated with or controlled, directly or indirectly by them'.[54] It found that this definition could include both family members of the rulers and persons in charge of certain businesses, 'provided it is established that they are associated with the leaders of the Republic of the Union of Myanmar or that the activities

---

51 Judgment of 14 October 2009, *Bank Melli Iran v. Council*, T-390/08, EU:T:2009:401, para. 37.
52 *Rotenberg*, op. cit. note 16, paras. 75–80.
53 For a detailed analysis, see L. Pantaleo, 'Case C-376/10 P, Pye Phyo Tay Za v. Council, Judgment of the European Court of Justice (Grand Chamber) of 13 March 2012', *CMLR* 49 (5), 2012, 1769–1785.
54 Judgment of 13 March 2013, *Tay Za*, C-376/10 P, EU:C:2012:138, para. 43.

of those businesses are dependent on those leaders'[55] but not the businessmen's family members. The Court argued that it is 'not easy to establish even an indirect link between the absence of progress towards the democratization and the continuing violation of human rights in Myanmar and the conduct of the family members of those in charge of businesses, which, in itself, has not been criticised'.[56]

As can be seen from the *Rotenberg* case, another element that needs to be taken into account when targeting persons associated with the leaders of a state is the issue of time frame. In the situation where EU restrictive measures are taken against a third country in response to specific actions or policies, as opposed to the conduct of the country's authorities in general, it is no longer sufficient for the Council to demonstrate that the persons targeted benefitted from the decision-makers – such a connection must still exist at the time where the alleged actions or policies have either taken place or were at least under preparation. Otherwise, the principle of legal certainty would be compromised as the persons targeted would have been unaware of the decision-makers' involvement in the illegal actions and could not have expected their resources to be targeted with the aim of preventing them from being able to support these decision-makers. As the Court noted in relation to Mr. Rotenberg, the evidence submitted by the Council relates to an earlier period than that during which Russian decision-makers had started to threaten Ukraine; namely, the organisation of the Olympic games in Sochi in 2014. As a result, the Court held that the Council failed to prove that the applicant had been favoured by President Vladimir Putin at the time when the latter took action in relation to Ukraine and upheld the applicant's plea of a manifest error of assessment in relation to the measures taken in July 2014.[57]

The Treaty of Lisbon substantially modified the legal basis for the adoption of restrictive measures. As the Court noted in *Parliament v Council*, 'Article 215(2) TFEU allows the Council to adopt restrictive measures against natural or legal persons and groups or non-State entities, namely, measures that, before the Treaty of Lisbon entered into force, required Article 308 EC also to be included in their legal basis if their addressees were not linked to the governing regime of a third country'.[58] These measures necessitate either a separate act of the Council or, at least, the inclusion of separate listing criteria in order not to be confounded with those targeting rulers and persons associated with

---

55   *Ibid.*, para. 55.
56   *Ibid.*, para. 67.
57   *Rotenberg, op. cit.* note 16, paras. 87–95.
58   Judgment of 19 July 2012, *Parliament v Council*, C-130/10, EU:C:2012:472, para. 53.

them. Thus, in *Tomana*, the Court established that the Council has not made use of these powers as Regulation No. 314/2004 concerning restrictive measures against Zimbabwe because it continued to refer to 'individual members of the Government of Zimbabwe and to any natural or legal persons, entities or bodies associated with them'.[59]

Nevertheless, the Council is able to circumvent or at least to significantly reduce the implication of the *Tay Za* case law by formulating broader listing criteria. With regard to Russia, the second 'package' of measures adopted by the Council contained travel restrictions and the freezing of assets of 'persons responsible for actions which undermine or threaten the territorial integrity, sovereignty and independence of Ukraine, including actions on the future status of any part of the territory which are contrary to the Ukrainian Constitution, and persons, entities or bodies associated with them'.[60] The definition thus included both the decision-makers and persons associated with them, while taking into account the necessity of a link between the persons and illegal actions in Crimea or eastern Ukraine. However, the listing criteria have been subsequently amended several times.[61] The formulation adopted on 18 July 2014 included 'natural persons responsible for, actively supporting or implementing, actions or policies which undermine or threaten the territorial integrity, sovereignty and independence of Ukraine, or stability or security in Ukraine, or which obstruct the work of international organisations in Ukraine, and natural or legal persons, entities or bodies associated with them'.[62] The inclusion, aside from decision-makers, of persons in charge of implementing the policy has already been applied by the Council on a number of occasions, most recently with regard to Syria. The most interesting feature, however, has been the introduction of the 'active support' criterion, giving the Council substantial flexibility as this notion could cover a broad range of activities.

A certain indication as to the interpretation of this criterion has been given in the *Kiselev* case. Referring to the *National Iranian Oil Company* case,[63] where it had the opportunity to define 'support', the GC stated that 'the criterion at issue does not cover all forms of support for the Russian Government, but rather concerns forms of support which, by their quantitative or qualitative

---

59　Judgment of 22 April 2015, *Tomana*, T-190/12, EU:T:2015:222, para. 123.
60　Council Decision 2014/145/CFSP, *OJ*, 2014, L 78/16.
61　The criteria for listing were amended by Council Decision 2014/265/CFSP, *OJ*, 2014, L 137/9; Council Decision 2014/475/CFSP, *OJ*, 2014, L 214/28; Council Decision 2014/499/CFSP, *OJ*, 2014, L 221/15.
62　See Article 1 of Council Decision 2014/475/CFSP, *OJ*, 2014, L 214/28.
63　Judgment of 16 July 2014, *National Iranian Oil Company*, T-578/12, EU:T:2014:678.

significance, contribute to the continuance of its actions and policies destabilising Ukraine'.[64] While the Court did not give an extensive definition of the notion of 'active support' leaving, thus, some room for ambiguity, it clearly endorsed a restrictive reading of the sanction criterion and showed its readiness to effectively control its application. In that instance, the relevant factor for Kiselev not only was that he engaged in propaganda activities promoting war but also that he enjoyed a special position and resources as head of the news agency RS and was hosting popular television programmes. The restrictive interpretation given by the Court also appears to be fully consistent with the fifth guiding principle of EU policy towards Russia; namely, the fact that sanctions are imposed on Russia but not on its citizens, and that these measures shall not have a deterrent effect for people-to-people contacts.

Another practical example of the application of the 'active support' criterion is the *Rotenberg* case.[65] The measures adopted in relation to the applicant in March 2015 contained two separate grounds of listing: the fact that the applicant was the owner of the company *Stroygazmontazh* which has been awarded a state contract for the construction of a bridge from Russia to Crimea and the fact that he was the chairman of the board of directors of publishing house Prosvescheniye, which has notably implemented the project 'To the Children of Russia: Address – Crimea', a public relations campaign that was designed to persuade Crimean children that they are now Russian citizens living in Russia and thereby supporting the Russian government's policy to integrate Crimea into Russia. While it was clear from the outset that the construction of a bridge reinforces the integration of Crimea into the Russian Federation and thus undermines the territorial integrity of Ukraine, the launch of a public relations campaign provided a more interesting example of 'active support'. In that regard, the Court noted the massive character of the campaign and the quantity of printed books while noting that as the board of directors' chairman, the applicant 'could not reasonably have been unaware of the editorial line in publications of the publishing house which he headed'.[66] This, in its turn, demonstrates the importance of interpreting the sanction criteria in the light of the goals and aims of the sanction policy.

With regard to general economic sanctions such as export restrictions or restrictions on the access to capital market, the attempts of various

---

64   *Kiselev, op. cit.* note 12, paras. 74–75.
65   *Rotenberg, op. cit.* note 16.
66   *Rotenberg, op. cit.* note 16, para. 131.

applicants to prove that, although owned by the Russian Federation, they were in fact independent entities vis-à-vis the Russian Federation with regard to their daily activities and, therefore, had no connection to the events in Donbass proved to be useless. In *Rosneft* and *Sberbank,* the Court noted that there is a reasonable relationship between the restrictive measures and the objective pursued by the Council in adopting them. Taken into account that the aim pursued was to increase the costs to be borne by the Russian Federation for its actions to undermine Ukraine's territorial integrity, sovereignty and independence, the Court found the approach of targeting Russian state-owned banks and the Russian oil sector to be consistent with this objective.[67]

5 Legal Issues under International Law

Russian cases have also been the occasion for the CJEU to address a number of issues raised by the applicants as to the compatibility of the restrictive measures with international law. As a preliminary remark, it must be recalled that, as the CJEU has consistently held, the EU has an obligation to respect international law.[68] Being a subject of international law, the EU not only is bound by the agreements it concludes with third states or international organisations but also by international customary law.[69] As has been noted, "It is plain that the EU cannot take part in international treaty-making without respecting and applying general international law."[70]

In this context it was not surprising to see *Rosneft* bring, both before the GC and the ECJ, several arguments based on public international law. Some of them deserve little attention, such as the general claims relating to the impossibility for the EU to adopt restrictive measures outside those endorsed by the UN Security Council,[71] as they are automatically dismissed by the Court due to the existence of specific treaty provisions authorising the adoption of such measures.[72] Their inclusion could be thus regarded more as a tribute to the

---

67 See *Rosneft, op. cit.* note 13, para. 147; and *Sberbank, op. cit.* note 37, para. 152.
68 See Judgment of 21 December 2011, *Air Transport Association of America,* C-366/10, EU:C:2011:864., para. 101.
69 See Judgment of 24 November 1992, *Poulsen,* C-286/90, EU:C:1992:453, para. 9; Judgment of 16 June 1998, *Racke,* C-162/96, EU:C:1998:293, paras. 45–46.
70 P. Eeckhout, *EU External Relations Law,* 2nd ed. (Oxford University Press 2012), 383.
71 *NK Rosneft and Others, op. cit.* note 30, para. 159.
72 See *Bank Melli, op. cit.* note 51, para. 51.

official Russian discourse on the illegality of sanctions,[73] rather than part of a coherent legal strategy. Others, relating to the incompatibility of general economic restrictive measures with the provisions of the WTO General Agreement on Tariffs and Trade (GATT) and the EU-Russia PCA, are much more interesting.

Indeed, WTO members are not allowed to impose 'new burdens or prohibitions on imports from another Member; change domestic laws regarding intellectual property; or, in a few situations, impose new limits on foreign investment'.[74] Article XXI, however, contains two major exceptions. One authorises the members to derogate from WTO rules 'taking any action in pursuance of its obligations under the United Nations Charter for the maintenance of international peace and security'. The other provides that nothing in the GATT agreement shall be construed 'to prevent any contracting party from taking any action which it considers necessary for the protection of its essential security interests'. It must be noted that actions necessary for the protection of essential security interests have to either be related to fissionable materials or to the traffic in arms, ammunition and implements of war or related goods and materials, or be taken in time of war or other emergency in international relations.

As these conditions are not cumulative, it becomes apparent that an arms embargo or restriction on the export of dual-use goods is not contrary to WTO rules as it falls under paragraph (b)(ii) of Article XXI. Purely economic restrictions, on the other side, may be adopted only in times of 'war or in case of emergency'. This means that in other situations 'the GATT does not allow tariffs or other measures that would discriminate against a Member on foreign policy grounds, such as human rights, the form of government, or proliferation policies'.[75]

At the time of the *NK Rosneft and Others* case, the precise scope of the notions of 'essential security interests' and 'times of war or in case of emergency' remained unclear due to the absence of relevant WTO case law.[76] The General Court's judgment, while certainly not conclusive, provided an interesting example of the interpretation of these terms. It must be recalled that according to a well-established case law of the CJEU, GATT provisions are not

---

73   See J. Alexandre, 'Russia's Sanctions Narrative in the Ukrainian Crisis: Implications for the West', *Revista UNISCI* 89 (43), 2017, 89–104. See also the contributions of I. Petrova (chapter 3) and A. Hofer (chapter 4) in this volume.
74   B. E. Carter, 'Economic Sanctions', in: R. Wolfrum (ed.), *the Max Planck Encyclopedia of Public International Law: volume iii* (Oxford University Press 2012), 323–329.
75   *Ibid.*, 327.
76   For a discussion of whether the WTO security exceptions are self-judging, see G.-D. Bian, 'On Fissionable Cows and the Limits to the WTO Security Exceptions', *Global Trade and Customs Journal* 14 (1), 2019, 2–10.

capable of having direct effect[77] and, thus, may not be relied on by individuals unless the EU measure at stake expressly refers to a specific GATT provision[78] or aims to implement a particular obligation entered into within the framework of GATT.[79] In *NK Rosneft and Others,* however, the GC decided to address the substance of the arguments put forward by the plaintiff. It stated that even if GATT provisions were directly applicable and could usefully be relied on by the applicants in the present case, that agreement contains a provision relating to 'security exceptions'. Consequently, the Council 'was entitled to consider that the actions of the Russian Federation undermining or threatening Ukraine's territorial integrity, sovereignty and independence could amount to a case of an "other emergency in international relations" and that the restrictive measures at issue were "necessary for the protection of [the] essential security interests [of the Member States of the European Union]", within the meaning of Article XXI of GATT.'[80] These findings have been indirectly confirmed by the WTO Dispute Settlement Body (DSB) in the *Russian Traffic in Transit* case.[81] The DSB Panel established in its Report that 'the specific interests that are considered directly relevant to the protection of a state from such external or internal threats will depend on the particular situation and perceptions of the state', and held that 'it is left, in general, to every Member to define what it considers to be its essential security interests'.[82] The Panel Report also suggests that while it is incumbent on the invoking member to articulate the essential security interests said to arise from the emergency in international relations to demonstrate that the designation was made in good faith, a minimal level of articulation is sufficient when the emergency in international relations is very close to the 'hard core' of war or armed conflict.[83]

Contrary to the WTO, the PCA has been recognised by the CJEU as capable of having direct effect.[84] While the negotiations of a new strategic agreement with Russia have been frozen by the EU as part of the first package of sanctions, the application of the PCA has not been suspended and it is still part of the EU-Russia relations' legal framework. In *Rosneft* the Court noted, however, that according to Article 99(1)(d) of the PCA, 'nothing in that agreement is to

---

77   Judgment of 5 October 1994, *Germany v Council,* C-280/93, EU:C:1994:367, paras. 103–112.
78   Judgment of 22 June 1989, *Fediol v Commission.* C-70/87, EU:C:1989:254, paras. 19–22.
79   Judgment of 7 May 1991, *Nakajima v Council,* C-69/89, EU:C:1991:186, para. 31.
80   *NK Rosneft and Others, op. cit.* note 30, paras. 180–182.
81   Panel report of 29 April 2019, *Russia – Measures Concerning Traffic in Transit,* DS512.
82   *Ibid.,* 7.131.
83   *Ibid.,* 7.132–7.137.
84   See judgment of 12 April 2005, *Simutenkov,* C-265/03, EU:C:2005:213.

prevent a party from taking measures that it considers necessary for the protection of its essential security interests, particularly in time of war or serious international tension constituting a threat of war or in order to carry out obligations it has accepted for the purpose of maintaining peace and international security'. The Court proceeded to interpret the wording of that provision as not requiring that the 'war' or 'serious international tension constituting a threat of war' refer to actions directly affecting the territory of the European Union. It thus confirmed that the events that took place in Ukraine were capable of justifying 'measures designed to protect essential European Union security interests and to maintain peace and international security' in accordance with the EU Treaty. While recognising a broad discretion of the Council, the Court nevertheless proceeded to examine whether the adoption of the restrictive measures involved the protection of essential EU security interests and the maintenance of peace and international security. Analysing the statements of the Council and Heads of State or Government of the Member States, the Court concluded that it was apparent that the aim of the restrictive measures was to promote a peaceful settlement of the crisis in Ukraine, a goal 'consistent with the objective of maintaining peace and international security' under Article 21 TEU.[85]

While it would have been hard to imagine the Court coming to a different conclusion given the factual circumstances, the reasoning developed by the Court leaves a mitigated impression. On the one hand, the CJEU essentially agreed with the necessity to exercise a limited control of whether the measures imposed were necessary to protect essential security interests, thus encouraging applicants to put forward pleas based on international agreements. On the other hand, the control appears to be purely formal at best as the Court consistently refuses to give its own assessment relying, instead, on the preambles of the contested measures. Although it could be argued that such an approach is the direct result of the broad discretion of the Council, it appears to be problematic for two main reasons. First, the reputation of the Court as an independent non-political institution is directly linked to its ability to conduct an independent assessment of the compatibility of the restrictive measures with the treaties and general principles of EU law such as the respect of fundamental rights and international treaties. Second, on a broader scale the first guiding principle as a cornerstone of the EU policy towards Russia is based on the fundamental assumption that the restrictive measures imposed by the EU are legal from the perspective not only of EU law but also of public international law.

---

85   *Rosneft, op. cit.* note 13, paras. 108–116.

6   Concluding Remarks

In conclusion, despite their obvious outcome, the judgments in the Russian cases represent a significant step forward in the development of the CJEU case law on restrictive measures. The CJEU managed to establish its jurisdiction regarding preliminary references concerning the validity of restrictive measures, clarify the *locus standi* of individuals in actions for annulment and provide criteria for examining the compatibility of restrictive measures with the freedom of expression. It also gave a restrictive interpretation of the notion of 'active support', thus implicitly underlying the importance to respect the fifth guiding principle of EU policy towards Russia and making sure that restrictive measures are directed against the state and not its citizens. On the other hand, the CJEU's reluctance to conduct an in-depth assessment of the compatibility of restrictive measures with international agreements still reflects a somewhat careful approach towards the exercise of its jurisdiction in the field of CFSP, to the detriment of its role of providing effective judicial control over the EU's sanction policy.

CHAPTER 6

The Impact of the Adjudication of Sanctions against Russia before the Court of Justice of the EU

Celia Challet

1 Introduction

The imposition of sanctions against Russia by the European Union has led to the listing of numerous persons and entities. The EU has adopted various asset freezes and/or imposed travel restrictions on legal and natural persons in respect of Russia's actions undermining or threatening the territorial integrity, sovereignty and independence of Ukraine.[1] Numerous Russian legal persons also remain subject to economic sanctions targeting, *inter alia*, the banking, energy and defence sectors.[2] At the beginning of 2021, litigation on these sanctions has led to 16 judgments of the Court of Justice of the European Union (CJEU). Since some sanctions have been renewed by the EU, it is likely that more actions for annulment might be brought before the CJEU.

Several observations with respect to the case law on sanctions against Russian natural and legal persons can be highlighted. First, the outcome of the adjudication of such sanctions could be considered as 'obvious': with the exception of the *Rotenberg*[3] case, all the actions challenging the sanctions against Russia have been dismissed by the CJEU. The fact that such judicial outcomes seem to be predictable might reveal legal issues regarding the features of the sanctions (which keep being challenged despite their similar outcome) and the way the Court adjudicates them. Second, the sanctions against Russia were adopted in the context of the Ukrainian crisis and the EU's attempt to both restore the rule of law in Ukraine and pressure Russia into ceasing its actions of destabilising that country. The analysis of these sanctions and their judicial review should

---

1   See, for instance, Council Decision (CFSP) 2020/399 of 13 March 2020 amending Decision 2014/145/CFSP concerning restrictive measures in respect of actions undermining or threatening the territorial integrity, sovereignty and independence of Ukraine, *OJ*, 2020, L 78/44.
2   See, for instance, Council Decision (CFSP) 2019/2192 of 19 December 2019 amending Decision 2014/512/CFSP concerning restrictive measures in view of Russia's actions destabilising the situation in Ukraine, *OJ*, 2020, L 330/71.
3   General Court, 30 November 2016, *Rotenberg*, T-720/14, EU:T:2016:689.

also take into account those imposed on Ukrainian persons in view of the situation in Ukraine.[4] Indeed, these two sets of sanctions, although very distinct and pursuing different purposes, are complementary and can provide an interesting basis for comparison.[5] Finally, although some of the CJEU judgments, such as *Rosneft*,[6] laid down various developments, which might improve the judicial protection of the persons targeted by EU sanctions, certain reasonings of the Court can still be questioned.

While the previous chapter in this volume analysed the contribution of these cases to the development of the CJEU case law on restrictive measures,[7] this contribution adopts a complementary and transversal approach. Indeed, the CJEU judgments on sanctions against Russia reveal certain common features and highlight the position of the Court with respect to the legality of the EU's actions towards Russia. This contributes to the analysis of the implementation of the five guiding principles for EU-Russia relations and, in particular, the full implementation of the Minsk agreements and the support for people-to-people contacts.

2 The Court's Political Cautiousness and the Effectiveness of Sanctions against Russia

The Court has, throughout its case law on restrictive measures, progressively introduced a more substantive judicial review over the Council's decisions and reinforced the targeted person's individual rights. However, the case law on sanctions against Russia is a reminder that the Court is still highly aware of the intergovernmental dimension of the Common Foreign and Security Policy (CFSP), and remains particularly cautious when adjudicating the measures concerned.

The first example of this cautiousness concerns the Court's scope of review of the sanctions, which remains, to a large extent, limited to the Council's compliance with the procedural rules and with the obligation to state reasons as

---

[4] The first legal bases were Council Decision 2014/119/CFSP of 5 March 2014 concerning restrictive measures directed against certain persons, entities and bodies in view of the situation in Ukraine, *OJ*, L/66; Council Regulation (EU) 208/2014 of 5 March 2014. concerning restrictive measures directed against certain persons, entities and bodies in view of the situation in Ukraine, *OJ*, 2014, L 66/26.
[5] See Section 4 of this chapter.
[6] ECJ, 28 March 2017, *PJSC Rosneft Oil Company v. Her Majesty's Treasury*, C-72/15, EU:C:2017:236.
[7] See the contribution by K. Entin (chapter 5) in this volume.

laid down by Article 296 of the Treaty on the Functioning of the European Union (TFEU). The preoccupation of the Court to maintain the Council's broad margin of appreciation, as well as its refusal to conduct a substantive assessment of the sanctions, is particularly obvious in the case law on sanctions against Russia. This is clearly illustrated in the Court's reasoning, in *Rosneft* and subsequent cases,[8] with respect to the legality of the sanctions in light of the Partnership and Cooperation Agreement (PCA) concluded between the EU and Russia. The Court first asserted that the contested sanctions were compliant with Article 99(1)(d) of the PCA and also stressed that under this agreement, a party that wishes to adopt measures on the basis of such provision is not required to provide the other party with the reasons for its actions, nor to inform it beforehand.[9] More generally, the Court has declared that since the objective of the contested measures is to exert pressure on the Russian decision-makers and to increase the costs of Russia's action in Ukraine, the Council enjoys a broad discretion as to the type and scope of the measures adopted.[10]

Moreover, beyond a mere confirmation of the Council's wide margin of appreciation, the Court also showed its willingness to ensure the effectiveness of the challenged sanctions, leading to debatable developments. This is particularly true regarding the assessment of claims based on fundamental rights as guaranteed by the Charter of Fundamental Rights (the Charter). The Court has always dismissed the claims based on the infringement of the right to property, privacy and the freedom to conduct a business,[11] stressing that the challenged sanctions were not supposed to deprive the persons concerned of such rights.[12] They were not penalties but 'prospective precautionary measures'.[13] In other words, 'the mere existence of a risk that an entity may act reprehensibly may be sufficient to impose restrictive measures on [it]'.[14] The same reasoning

---

8   General Court, 15 June 2017, *Kiselev v. Council*, T-262/15, EU:T:2017:392; General Court, 13 September 2018, *Rosneft and Others*, T-715/14, EU:T:2018:544.

9   See, for example, *Kiselev, op. cit.* note 8, para. 32. Article 99 PCA concerns the 'security exception' of the agreement, allowing the parties to take any measures needed to protect their essential security interests. For a more detailed analysis of this provision, see the contribution by K. Entin (chapter 5) in this volume.

10 See, for instance, General Court, 13 September 2018, *VTB Bank PAO v. Council*, T-734/14, EU:T:2018:542, paras. 149–151.

11 Based, respectively, on Articles 17, 7 and 16 of the Charter.

12 *Rotenberg, op. cit.* note 3, para. 167.

13 General Court, 25 January 2017, *Almaz-Antey*, T-255/15, EU:T:2017:25, para. 110.

14 *Ibid.*

was applied to the claim based on freedom of expression in *Kiselev*: restrictive measures are 'by nature temporary and reversible'.[15]

The balance that was struck between the protection of fundamental rights and the achievement of CFSP purposes is not surprising. However, the arguments underpinning it seem highly debatable: some sanctions have been renewed since 2014, and the economic impact of asset freezes and export restrictions on the targeted persons is both undeniable and irreversible.[16] Similar questions can be raised concerning the way the Court rejected claims based on the rights of defence and effective judicial protection. Indeed, neither the absence of individual communication of the disputed acts,[17] nor the fact that an applicant had access to its file only days before the expiry of the time limit to challenge the restrictive measures, have been considered as a sufficient ground for annulment.[18] Another example of the willingness of the Court to ensure the effectiveness of sanctions is its assertion that the Council could target persons that had no connection with the Ukrainian conflict, without departing from the requirement that sanctions adopted on the basis of Article 215(1) TFEU be sufficiently targeted.[19] The Court considered that since the sanctions were adopted to increase the costs of Russia's actions in Ukraine, and targeted crucial sectors of the Russian economy, they met the criteria laid down in Article 215 TFEU.[20]

This strong tendency of the Court to confirm the sanctions imposed on Russian persons, in an area governed by intergovernmentalism, is not particularly surprising. It might also reveal the Court's awareness of the complexity of the implementation of CFSP sanctions. The identification of the targeted persons requires detailed knowledge that is difficult to obtain,[21] while the effectiveness of measures such as asset freezes requires the EU to act fast. Thus, setting an excessively high standard of review of the sanctions could potentially deprive them of any concrete effect. It seems fair to assume that the Court took those factual elements into consideration when adjudicating the

---

15 *Kiselev, op. cit.* note 8, para. 124.
16 H. Over de Linden, 'The Court of Justice's Difficulty with Reviewing Smart Sanctions as Illustrated by Rosneft', *European Foreign Affairs Review* 24 (1), 2019, 39–40.
17 General Court, 13 September 2018, *Sberbank of Russia v. Council*, T-732/14, EU:T:2018:541, para. 124.
18 General Court, 13 September 2018, *Vnesheconombank v. Council*, T-737/14, EU:T:2018:543, para. 124.
19 *Rosneft and Others, op. cit.* note 6, para. 152.
20 *Ibid.*, paras. 155–163.
21 F. Giumelli, 'Winning without Killing: The Case for Targeted Sanctions', in: P. Ducheine and F. Osinga (eds.), *Netherlands Annual Review of Military Studies* (Asser Press 2017), 93.

sanctions against Russia. However, this might have been done at the expense of legal certainty: given the increasing use of autonomous sanctions by the EU, as well as the confirmed Council's broad discretion in the listing of persons, it might become more difficult for the latter to determine whether they will be targeted, and on which grounds. Moreover, the Court's dismissal of almost all the actions for annulment against Russian sanctions might lead them to consider the judgments as being politically motivated.[22]

3 A Difference of Treatment between Russian Natural and Legal Persons

The CJEU case law on sanctions against Russia presents significant differences depending on whether the applicant is a natural or a legal person. First, the Court tends to develop a more substantiated motivation when ruling on actions for annulment brought by natural persons, whatever the outcome of the cases. In *Rotenberg*, the Court carried out an in-depth assessment of the evidence relied on by the Council, to consider that there was only indirect evidence of the applicant's control over *Giprotransmost*,[23] and that the additional listing criterion of having benefitted from 'Russian decision-makers' was too vague.[24] In *Kiselev*, before dismissing the case, the Court developed an extensive analysis of the applicant's factual and legal situation. In particular, when answering the applicant's claim based on the infringement of his freedom of expression protected by Article 11 of the Charter, the Court assessed the possibility to apply the principles deriving from the corresponding provisions on freedom of expression laid down in Article 10 of the European Convention on Human Rights and Fundamental Freedoms (ECHR). In that regard, it stressed that the core principles of the freedom of expression, as set out in the case law of the European Court of Human Rights (ECtHR), were established in view of situations that were different from the one in the main proceedings.[25] In those cases, restrictive measures had been imposed on a person who had made statements or actions considered inacceptable by a state which had acceded the ECHR, and that person invoked the freedom of expression as a defence against that same state.[26]

---

22 H. Over de Linden, *op. cit.* note 16, 41.
23 *Rotenberg, op. cit.* note 3, paras. 84–85.
24 *Ibid.*, para. 90.
25 *Kiselev, op. cit.* note 8, para. 93.
26 *Ibid.*, para. 94.

However, in *Kiselev* the applicant was a Russian citizen, appointed by the Russian President as Head of a Russian news agency who did not rely on Article 10 ECHR to defend himself against the Russian state.[27] Moreover, the Court took into account a resolution of the Russian Public Collegium for Press Complaints, which considered that the applicant's disputed programme contained propaganda on the events occurring in Ukraine. The Court stressed extensively that such propaganda had been confirmed by radio commissions and authorities of neighbouring countries.[28] These elements led the Court to dismiss the action.

This effort of motivation and review in cases involving natural persons stands in sharp contrast with the one carried out for actions brought by legal persons. In its 2017 *Almaz-Antey* judgment, the Court ruled that the criterion of active support to Russia's actions undermining Ukraine was fulfilled, even though uncertainties remained about whether or not the applicant's manufactured weapons had been used by the Ukrainian separatists for the downing of the MH17 flight. The Court stressed that by merely selling arms to Russia, which itself supplies weapons to the eastern Ukraine separatists, the applicant materially supported Russia's actions against Ukraine.[29] It also upheld the challenged Council's evidence based on press articles showing Russian weapons being used by separatists, stressing that it would be excessive and disproportionate to require the Council to investigate on the ground the accuracy of facts which are described by numerous media.[30] Moreover, the Court explicitly admitted that, even if those press articles were to be partially biased, 'genuine objectivity is impossible'.[31] It concluded that the imposition of the challenged asset freezes on the applicant was lawful.

A similar, if not even lower, standard of review and motivation of the Court has been applied in cases of restrictions on access to capital markets and certain technologies. In its 2018 *Almaz-Antey* ruling, the Court recalled that an undertaking could be listed on the sole basis that it was a Russian entity operating in a crucial sector of the Russian economy: the questions of whether it had links with the Russian government (for instance, through state ownership) or had supported Russia's actions of undermining Ukraine were irrelevant.[32]

---

27   *Ibid.*, paras. 95–97.
28   *Ibid.*, paras. 106–107.
29   *Almaz-Antey*, T-255/15, *op. cit.* note 13, para. 137.
30   *Ibid.*, para. 148.
31   *Ibid.*
32   General Court, 13 September 2018, *Almaz-Antey v. Council*, T-515/15, EU:T:2018:545, para. 124.

Although the Court recalled that those economic sanctions were adopted in a specific context (i.e., the worsening of the situation in Ukraine) that led the Council to take further restrictive measures against Russia,[33] the standard of motivation of the relevant judgments is questionable. This concern was raised by Gazprom, which challenged the restrictions on access to capital markets and certain export restrictions to which it was subject.[34] According to the applicant, there was a lack of reasoning regarding its required connection with the Russian government or the proportionality of the measures, which made it harder for it to contest their legality.[35] This lack of reasoning stood 'in sharp contrast to the reasoning provided to the individual and entities targeted by the other restrictive measures, such as [asset freezes]'.[36] The Court dismissed this argument by explaining that provisions of general applications such as export restrictions did not require an extensive statement of reasons, and that the Council's motivation regarding restrictions on capital market (i.e., restrictive measures of individual application) was sufficient.[37] Nevertheless, the applicant's argument raises an interesting point. Since asset freezes are statistically more imposed on natural persons than on legal persons, who can also be subject to other economic sanctions, a higher standard of reasoning applied by the Court to asset freezes would inevitably lead to a *de facto* difference of treatment between natural and legal persons.

Second, the Court seems to have set a higher standard of admissibility for claims based on the infringement of the rights of defence of legal persons. A particular issue is the question of individuals' access to their file, especially if it has not been communicated by the Council. It is settled case law that for an infringement of the rights of defence to result in the annulment of an EU act, the applicant must demonstrate that, had it not been for that irregularity, the outcome of the procedure would have been different.[38] However, it appears that the Court has been stricter on compliance with that principle in cases involving natural persons. In *Kiselev*, the applicant argued that when maintaining his name on the list of sanctioned persons, the Council did not grant him access to his file, thereby breaching his right to effective judicial

---

33 *Almaz-Antey*, T-255/15, *op. cit.* note 14, para. 104; *Almaz-Antey*, T-515/15, *op. cit.* note 32, para. 94.
34 General Court, 13 September 2018, *Gazprom v. Council*, T-735/14 and T-799/14, EU:T:2018:548.
35 *Ibid.*, para. 109.
36 *Ibid.*
37 *Ibid.*, paras. 114–119.
38 General Court, 18 September 2014, *Georgias and Others v. Council and Commission*, T-168/12, EU:T:2014:781, para. 106.

protection as laid down in Article 41(2)(a) of the Charter. The Court dismissed this argument, recalling that the applicant did not challenge its initial listing and, therefore, had waited almost a year before requesting access to his file.[39] While the outcome of the applicant's arguments could be expected in the *Kiselev* case, the Court has proved to be much more severe towards the procedural behaviour of legal persons. In cases such as *VTB Bank* and *Sberbank*, the Court recalled that even if the Council failed to publish a notice in the *Official Journal* and to send an individual notification letter to the applicant, there was no evidence that his rights of defence or judicial protection may have been affected.[40] Therefore, these were not sufficient grounds to annul the sanctions.[41] In *Vnesheconombank*, as stated above, the Court stressed that the fact that the applicant had access to the file only days before the expiry of the time limit to lodge an appeal against the restrictive measures concerned was not sufficient to conclude that there had been a breach of the rights of defence. In support of this assertion, the Court noted that the applicant waited a month and a half to make a request of access to the file after having being notified of the contested acts, even though some EU banks had already refused to carry out transactions prohibited by the restrictive measures.[42] Thus, the applicant did not sufficiently demonstrate the alleged infringement of its rights of defence. Although these developments can obviously be explained by the Court's interest in setting a certain threshold of admissibility for procedural claims, they seem to put an increasingly heavy burden on the entities targeted by EU sanctions: failure to request access to the file within a short period of time will be taken into consideration by the Court when reviewing their claims.

4 A Difference of Treatment between Russian and Ukrainian Nationals?

The impact and the main features of the adjudication of sanctions against Russia need to be analysed in the broader context of EU measures adopted in response to the Ukrainian crisis. Indeed, simultaneously to the imposition of sanctions against Russia, the EU adopted a complementary set of restrictive measures to consolidate and support democracy and the rule of law in

---

39   *Kiselev, op. cit.* note 8, paras. 143–152.
40   *VTB Bank, op. cit.* note 10, para. 119; *Sberbank, op. cit.* note 17, para. 124.
41   Ibid.
42   *Vnesheconombank, op. cit.* note 18, para. 124.

Ukraine, and maintain its territorial integrity. These measures, adopted from 2014 onwards, targeted certain natural and legal persons with regard to the situation in Ukraine.[43] In particular, the EU imposed restrictions on natural persons that were subject to criminal proceedings in Ukraine in connection with misappropriations of public funds. For the purpose of supporting Ukraine and its judiciary in the investigations and judicial proceedings, the EU froze the assets of the persons concerned. These measures mostly targeted Ukrainian leaders that had strong connections with Russian intelligentsia. They were imposed on former President Viktor Yanukovych[44] and former members of his administration such as Mykola Azarov,[45] Sergej Arbuzov,[46] Andriy Portnov,[47] Edward Stavytskyi[48] and Andrii Klyuyev.[49] Family members of the Ukrainian leaders, such as Oleksii Azarov[50] and Oleksandr Yanukovych,[51] were included in the sanctions list. The EU also imposed restrictive measures on Ukrainian undertakings, such as Prominvestbank,[52] which were considered as being controlled by Russian entities close to the Russian power. The restrictive measures adopted against Ukrainian legal and natural persons resulted in a caseload that is more extensive than the one related to sanctions against Russian entities and persons: the CJEU has issued more than 40 judgments, and 6 cases were

---

43 The first legal bases for the impositions of these sanctions were Council Decision (CFSP) 2014/119 and Council Regulation (EU) 208/2014 of 5 March 2014, *op. cit.* note 4.
44 General Court, 15 September 2016, *Viktor Yanukovych v. Council*, T-346/14, EU:T:2016:497; ECJ, 19 October 2017, *Viktor Yanukovych v. Council*, C-598/16 P, EU:C:2017:786; General Court, 11 July 2019, *Viktor Yanukovych v. Council*, T-244/16 and T-285/17, EU:T:2019:502.
45 See, *inter alia*, General Court, 28 January 2016, *Mykola Azarov v. Council*, T-331/14, EU:T:2016:49; General Court, 7 July 2017, *Mykola Azarov v. Council*, T-215/15, ECLI:EU:T:2017:479; General Court, 26 April 2018, *Mykola Azarov v. Council*, T-190/16, EU:T:2018:232; ECJ, 11 July 2019, *Mykola Azarov v. Council*, C-416/18 P, EU:C:2019:602.
46 See, *inter alia*, General Court, 28 January 2016, *Sergej Arbuzov v. Council*, T-434/14, EU:T:2016:46; General Court, 7 July 2017, *Sergej Arbuzov v. Council*, T-221/15, EU:T:2017:478; General Court, 11 July 2019, *Sergej Arbuzov v. Council*, T-284/18, EU:T:2019:511.
47 General Court, 26 October 2015, *Portnov v. Council*, T-290/14, EU:T:2015:806.
48 See, *inter alia*, General Court, 22 March 2018, *Edward Stavytskyi v. Council*, T-242/16, EU:T:2018:166; General Court, 30 January 2019, *Edward Stavytskyi v. Council*, T-290/17, EU:T:2019:37.
49 See, in particular, General Court, 15 September 2016, *Klyuyev v. Council*, T-340/15, EU:T:2016:496.
50 General Court, 28 January 2016, *Oleksii Mykolayovych Azaro v. Council*, T-332/14, EU:T:2016:48.
51 See, *inter alia*, General Court, 15 September 2016, *Oleksandr Viktorovych Yanukovych v. Council*, T-348/14, EU:T:2016:508; ECJ, 19 October 2017, *Oleksandr Viktorovych Yanukovych v. Council*, C-599/16 P, EU:C:2017:785.
52 General Court, 13 September 2018, *PSC Prominvestbank v. Council*, T-739/14, EU:T:2018:547.

still pending at the beginning of 2021.[53] Such litigation can therefore provide a substantial basis of comparison for the assessment of the adjudication of sanctions against Russia.

In that regard, significant differences can be underlined regarding the way the Court has been adjudicating these two sets of sanctions. As explained above, in the case of sanctions against Russia, almost all actions for annulment were dismissed by the Court. By contrast, the Court seems to have progressively raised the standard of validity of restrictive measures imposed on Ukrainians, leading to their annulment in first instance or in appeal in more than 90% of the cases.[54]

Indeed, substantial evolutions can be pointed out between the first CJEU judgments on Ukrainian sanctions and the most recent ones, particularly when it comes to the margin of appreciation of the Council. Since the majority of the relevant cases concerned asset freezes for the misappropriation of public funds, the core question was the extent of the Council's ability to rely on the prosecutions of individuals by the current Ukrainian authorities for the purpose of the imposition of the sanctions. Indeed, it was quickly suspected that the prosecution of former leaders by the new Ukrainian political and judicial authorities was intended to target political opponents, rather than actually fighting against corruption and rule of law challenges.[55] This led some applicants to criticise their inclusion in the sanctions list, without prior assessment by the Council of the allegations made against them by the Ukrainian government and judiciary, in a context of alleged violations of the rule of law and human rights by the latter.[56] In its earliest case law on restrictive measures targeting Ukrainians, the Court confirmed the wide margin of appreciation of the Council when imposing asset freezes in connection with prosecutions for the misappropriation of public funds. It stressed that the rule of law and the institutional foundations of Ukraine were threatened by the fact that 'a significant part of the former Ukrainian leadership [was] suspected of having committed serious crimes in the management of public resources'.[57] The restrictive

---

53 Cases *Klymenko v. Council* (T-258/20), *Arbuzov v. Council* (T-267/20), *Artem Pshonka v. Council* (T-268/20), *Viktor Pshonka v. Council* (T-269/20), *Viktor Yanukovych v. Council* (T-291/20) and *Oleksandr Yanukovych v. Council* (T-292/20) were still pending before the General Court at the time of this writing.

54 Out of 40 closed cases that led to a CJEU judgment, 33 led to a total or partial annulment of the sanctions in first instance. 4 led to an annulment in appeal.

55 House of Lords, *The Legality of EU Sanctions*, European Union Committee 11th Report of Session 2016–2017 HL 102, 2017, para. 43.

56 *Viktor Yanukovych* (T-346/14), *op. cit.* note 44, paras. 105–110; *Viktor Yanukovych* (C-598/16 P), *op. cit.* note 44, paras. 39–41; *Klyuyev* (T-340/15), *op. cit.* note 49, para. 74.

57 *Ibid.*, para. 117.

measures contributed to facilitating the prosecution of such crimes, and thus to fighting corruption and re-establishing the rule of law in Ukraine.[58] This was consistent with the objectives of the external action of the EU[59] as laid down in Article 21 in the Treaty on European Union (TEU). Moreover, the Court dismissed claims based on a dysfunctioning of the Ukrainian judicial and political system. In particular, the freedom of the Council to rely on evidence provided by Ukrainian prosecutors was justified by Ukraine's membership in the Council of Europe, and by the fact that the new Ukrainian regime was recognised as lawful by the EU and the international community.[60] The Court stressed that the Council's decision to support these new authorities in the consolidation of the rule of law was political. If such decisions were subject to the condition that Ukraine guarantees, immediately after the regime change, a level of fundamental rights protection similar to the one guaranteed by the EU, the Council's broad margin of appreciation would be undermined.[61] These developments led the Court to assert that when imposing restrictive measures on Ukrainian persons, the Council could rely on evidence supplied by Ukrainian authorities and was not required to conduct its own investigations or to carry out checks to obtain additional details.[62]

In its subsequent case law, however, the Court substantially changed its approach towards the Ukrainian sanctions and significantly reduced the Council's discretion when adopting them. It is now clear that before acting on the basis of a decision of a third-state authority, the Council must verify whether it was adopted in accordance with the rights of defence and the right to effective judicial protection.[63] This entails a double obligation: the Council must prove not only that there has not been any infringement of fundamental rights by the third-state authority but also that the latter's decision positively respected those rights when it was adopted.[64] The Court also changed its position regarding Ukraine's membership in the Council of Europe as a valid justification for the Council's broad discretion: although such membership entails review, by the ECtHR, of fundamental rights which form part of the general principles of EU law, it 'cannot render superfluous the verification

---

58 *Mykola Azarov* (T-215/15), *op. cit.* note 45, para. 155.
59 *Ibid.*
60 *Sergej Arbuzov* (T-221/15), *op. cit.* note 46, para. 146.
61 *Mykola Azarov* (T-215/15), *op. cit.* note 45, para. 173.
62 *Ibid.*, para. 120.
63 ECJ, 19 December 2018, *Mykola Azarov v. Council*, C-530/17, EU:C:2018:1031, paras. 35–42; ECJ, 26 September 2019, *Klymenko v. Council*, C-11/18 P, EU:C:2019:786, para. 21.
64 General Court, 11 July 2019, *Klyuyev v. Council*, T-305/18, EU:T:2019:506, paras. 62–65.

requirement'.⁶⁵ Even more interestingly, the Court declared that where a person has been subject to restrictive measures for several years, on account of the same preliminary investigations conducted by the prosecutor, the Council must 'explore in greater detail the question of a possible infringement of the fundamental rights of [the person concerned] by the Ukrainian authorities'.⁶⁶

By contrast, the adjudication by the Court of sanctions against Russia has not led to a similar control over the Council's discretion. The Court has repeatedly asserted that, for the purpose of pressuring Russia into ceasing its actions of destabilisation of Ukraine, and in view of the ineffectiveness of the first waves of sanctions, the Council remains free to exert additional pressure by targeting certain Russian legal persons that were not involved in or supportive of the Russian's actions of destabilisation.⁶⁷ If put in perspective with the Court's developments in the case law regarding Ukraine, such a reasoning could be called into question: there has been no evidence of an improvement of the rule of law in Ukraine as a result of the restrictive measures, yet the Court raised the standard of validity of the measures imposed. Another example of this difference of adjudication between sanctions against Russians and Ukrainians could be seen in the standard of evidence on which the Council can rely to impose sanctions. There is a clear difference between the Council's ability to rely on potentially biased press articles to target a Russian natural or legal person, and the requirement to verify decisions adopted by judicial authorities of a third state to sanction Ukrainian persons.

Undeniably, these differences of adjudication might be explained by the Court's awareness of the distinct features of these two sets of measures: pressuring Russia to stop threatening and undermining the independence and territorial integrity of Ukraine might indeed require more intense measures than supporting and consolidating the rule of law in Ukraine. What is more, most of the actions for annulment against Ukrainian sanctions were brought by natural persons. The Court's tendency to exercise a stronger judicial review over these sanctions might have been motivated by an assumption that consequences of restrictive measures can potentially be more damaging for individuals than for legal persons. Finally, the imposition of restrictive measures against Ukrainians has met such a high degree of criticism from the applicants⁶⁸ that the Court might have wished to reinforce the legitimacy of the EU measures through a

---

65   *Ibid.*, para. 63.
66   *Stavytskyi, op. cit.* note 48, para. 132.
67   *Vnesheconombank, op. cit.* note 18, paras. 96–97 and 152–153.
68   See, for instance, *Oleksandr Viktorovych Yanukovych v. Council* (T-348/14), *op. cit.* note 44, para. 120; *Viktor Yanukovych* (T-346/14), *op. cit.* note 44.

more extensive judicial review. However, the difference of treatment between Russian and Ukrainian nationals might also be another indicator of the political considerations that characterise the CJEU adjudication of CFSP measures.

5 The Impact of the Adjudication of Sanctions on the Situation of the Targeted Russian Persons

As a general comment, the impact of the CJEU adjudication of sanctions against Russia can first be seen in the dismissal of almost all cases. Moreover, a quantitative analysis of the cases shows the low number of sanctions that were subject to an action for annulment: at the beginning of 2021 there had been only 13 judgments of the General Court (against more than 40 regarding restrictive measures imposed on Ukrainians), and 3 judgments of the Court of Justice on the basis of Article 263 TFEU. The low proportion of sanctions challenged might indicate a reluctance of the Russian targeted persons to file actions for annulment, which itself could be linked to the way the Court addressed the litigation over those measures. The various developments laid down by the Court in support of the Council's choice to add and maintain the targeted persons on the sanctions lists, as well as the undeniably heavy burden imposed on them in terms of procedural behaviour, might have the effect of deterring a wide number of potential applicants to engage in costly and further reputational damaging procedures whose chances of success are particularly low.

In addition, the CJEU judgments on sanctions against Russia do not seem to have provided more clarity about the process leading to the adoption of the restrictive measures. Uncertainties also remain with regard to the scope of the sanctions. In the course of the latest litigation against these measures, applicants have insisted on the fact that the wording of many sanctions provisions remains unclear. In *Rosneft and Others,* the applicants argued that the provisions imposing restrictions on access to technologies in the field of oil exploration and production used a 'variety of key terms which remain[ed] undefined both in the contested decision and in the contested regulation'.[69] As a result, they were considered as 'ambiguous or vague'.[70] The applicants also underlined contradictions between the contested decisions and implementing regulations with regard to the authorisation framework of access to these technologies that was to be implemented within the EU Member States.[71] These

---

69 *Rosneft and Others, op. cit.* note 6, para. 220.
70 *Ibid.,* para. 221.
71 *Ibid.,* para. 188.

elements resulted both in uncertainties on the scope of the sanctions on the applicant's side, and in divergent interpretations by the national authorities of the key terms of the contested acts.[72]

The fact that the Council sought to clarify some of these terms in subsequent acts was yet another indicator of the need for a clarification of the measures.[73] The Court dismissed this series of arguments, stressing that the wording of measures of general application, such as the one at stake in the main proceedings, could not be absolutely precise.[74] Moreover, although 'the use of the legislative technique of referring to general categories [of targeted technologies], rather than to exhaustive lists, often leaves grey areas at the fringes of a definition',[75] this was not a sufficient ground to consider that the Council had breached the principle of legal certainty.[76] This reasoning seems debatable, in particular since the Court has repeatedly insisted on the responsibility of the targeted legal persons to be aware of the sanctions imposed and to conduct their own self-assessment of the latter; for instance, by seeking appropriate legal advice.[77] Such an assessment, by Russian legal persons, of the consequences that given actions may entail, seems to remain difficult to achieve. For EU companies, complying with the prohibition to export certain services and technologies to Russia is already 'one of the most challenging tasks'.[78] It is likely to be even more so for third-country operators when dealing with CFSP measures whose legal framework shows 'unique features that no other legal system in the world foresees'.[79]

Given the increasing chances for non-state actors in third countries of being targeted by EU sanctions,[80] the economic impact of these measures and the almost inexistent probabilities for the targeted Russians to obtain their annulment, more emphasis should be put by both the Council and the Court on ensuring a higher degree of legal certainty with regard to the sanctions. This is

---

72   Ibid., para. 220.
73   Ibid.
74   Ibid., para. 227.
75   Ibid., para. 228.
76   Ibid.
77   Ibid., para. 230.
78   D. Rovetta and L.C. Beretta, 'EU Economic Sanctions Law against Russia after the 'Rosneft' Judgment by the Grand Chamber of the Court of Justice of the European Union: Get Me a Lawyer!', *Global Trade and Customs Journal* 12 (6), 2017, 244.
79   Ibid., 246.
80   S. Poli, 'Effective Judicial Protection and Its Limits in the Case Law concerning Individual Restrictive Measures in the European Union', in: E. Neframi and M. Gatti (eds.), *Constitutional Issues of EU External Relations Law* (Nomos 2018), 288.

all the more true since the legal process for the imposition of CFSP sanctions in itself makes it harder for the applicants to challenge them. The majority of sanctions imposed on Russian natural and legal persons are usually adopted for a period of six months, and are then renewed every six months until they are lifted. Thus, by the time an action for annulment is assessed by the General Court, the sanctions concerned have ceased to be in force and have been renewed by the Council on the basis of new decisions and implementing regulations. This inevitably further complicates the process of judicial review of those sanctions. To quote the applicants in the *Rosneft and Others* case, 'the proceedings are undeniably lopsided, in that the applicants [have] to challenge the sanctions very swiftly, under difficult, time-sensitive conditions, while the sanctions will continue to apply throughout the duration of the proceedings before the General Court'.[81]

6   Concluding Remarks

To conclude, common features and specific trends in the reasoning of the Court can be identified. It appears that the outcome of an action for annulment depends on the sensitivity and on the type of sanction imposed, with inevitable differences between Russian and Ukrainian applicants and between legal or natural persons.

In addition, the adjudication of Russian cases by the Court has, so far, been a clear example of the Court's difficult position when reviewing CFSP acts: caught between, on the one hand, the imperative of preserving the intergovernmental dimension of this policy and, on the other, the need to ensure the protection of the applicants' fundamental rights, the Court struck a balance in favour of the effectiveness of the CFSP measures. Moreover, the sensitivity of the current EU-Russia relations and of the imposition of economic sanctions on the latter might explain the significantly more marginal judicial review exercised over the Council's action, as compared to the one exercised in Ukrainian cases. However, this obvious willingness of the Court to confirm the sanctions imposed by the EU, sometimes at the expense of a consistent and clear legal reasoning, bears the risk of undermining the credibility and legitimacy of the EU as a global actor. Indeed, on the one hand, the EU seeks to restore or foster the rule of law in some of the countries subject to CFSP sanctions. On the other hand, the adoption of the sanctions against Russia,

---

81   *Rosneft and Others*, op. cit. note 6, para. 105.

and their marginal judicial review by the Court, questions the EU's compliance with the main rule of law principles (i.e., legal certainty and the protection of fundamental rights).

To summarise, the adjudication of sanctions against Russia before the CJEU has had an impact on the individual situation of the targeted Russian persons: most of their actions for annulment have been dismissed, and they might increasingly be deterred from challenging the sanctions imposed on them. It might have also had an impact on EU-Russia relations in general: since the EU sanctions were not adopted on the basis of a UN resolution, Russia has contested their legality already since the time of their adoption.[82] The CJEU's approach to the adjudication of sanctions against Russia might encourage the latter to increasingly challenge the legitimacy and legality of the EU's responses to the Ukrainian crisis.

---

82   On the contestation of the EU's sanctions regime from a Russian perspective, see also the contribution by A. Hofer (chapter 4) in this volume.

PART 2

EU-Russia Relations and the Shared Neighbourhood

CHAPTER 7

Armenia

A Precarious Navigation between Eurasian Integration and the European Union

Laure Delcour and Narine Ghazaryan

1   Introduction

In 2013, Armenia's backtracking from an Association Agreement (AA) with the European Union was the first strong signal of a clash between the EU's and Russia's policies in their 'contested neighbourhood'. Since turning down the prospect of an AA, Armenia has acted carefully between its constrained Eurasian integration membership and advancing its cooperation with the EU. Having become a member of the Eurasian Economic Union (EAEU) in 2015,[1] the country succeeded in concluding a Comprehensive and Enhanced Partnership Agreement (CEPA) with the EU in 2017.[2] However, Armenia's position between two integration projects remains highly precarious, and the implementation of the CEPA is a key exercise in testing the parameters of engagement permitted not only by its EAEU membership *per se*, but also by Russia's political agenda.[3] Therefore, the political and legal trajectory of Armenia's relations with the EU remains strongly sensitive to the general state of affairs in EU-Russia relations.

Remarkably, the conclusion of the CEPA did not lead to the same reaction by Russia (such as trade bans, security threats and military intervention) as did the AAs with Ukraine, Moldova and (to a lesser extent) Georgia. Nevertheless, the developments following Armenia's 2018 'Velvet Revolution' may change both the regional dynamics and Russia's perception of the CEPA.[4] Crucially,

---

1   Treaty on the Accession of the Republic of Armenia to the Treaty on Eurasian Economic Union, 29 May 2014.
2   Comprehensive and Enhanced Partnership Agreement between the European Union and the European Atomic Energy Community and Their Member States, of the one part, and the Republic of Armenia, of the other part, *OJ*, 2018, L 23.
3   N. Ghazaryan and L. Delcour, 'From EU Integration Process to the Eurasian Economic Union', in: R. Petrov and P. van Elsuwege (eds.), *Post-Soviet Constitutions and Challenges of Regional Integration: Adapting to European and Eurasian Integration Projects* (Routledge 2017), 146.
4   The 2014 Astana Treaty on the EAEU permits its members to conclude international agreements with third parties on the condition that they 'do not contradict the objectives and principles of the Treaty' (Art. 114, The Treaty on Eurasian Union, Astana, May 2014 (hereinafter Astana Treaty)). The EAEU legal framework has been viewed as incomplete, leaving

the CEPA signals the EU's ability to adjust its offer to the sheer diversity of partner countries' contexts and constraints. It is a manifest expression of the principle of differentiation of the European Neighbourhood Policy (ENP) and the Eastern Partnership (EaP),[5] emphasised in Article 8 of the Treaty on European Union (TEU) more generally.[6] Although the EU's application of the principle of differentiation was criticised in the past,[7] the CEPA marks a departure from the previous approach by recognising Armenia's needs and political circumstances.[8] At the same time, the CEPA offers a blatant illustration of the EU's second guiding principle in its relations with Russia; namely, the strengthening of ties with Eastern partners.[9] The agreement is the most far-reaching treaty signed with an EAEU Member State, and goes further than the Enhanced Partnership and Cooperation Agreement (EPCA) with Kazakhstan.[10] It is also the most advanced – falling short of association – agreement in the EU neighbourhood. Its implementation is to be facilitated *inter alia* through the Partnership Priorities, a soft law document signed in February 2018 in line with the priorities of the revised ENP.[11]

'much room for inter-state bargaining' to define the terms of integration, characterised by blurred lines of competence division and weak enforcement mechanisms; R. Dragneva, L. Delcour and L. Jonavicius. 'Assessing Legal and Political Compatibility between the European Union Engagement Strategies and Membership of the Eurasian Economic Union', EU-STRAT Working Paper No. 07, 2017, 11, available at: <http://eu-strat.eu/wp-content/uploads/2016/05/EU-STRAT-Working-Paper-No.7.pdf> (accessed 9 March 2020).

5   See P. Van Elsuwege, 'Variable Geometry in the European Neighbourhood Policy: The Principle of Differentiation and its Consequences', in: E. Lannon (ed.), *The European Neighbourhood Policy's Challenge* (Peter Lang 2012), 59–84; N. Ghazaryan, 'The Evolution of the European Neighbourhood Policy and the Consistent Evolvement of Its Inconsistencies', *Russian and European Affairs Review* (7) 1, 2013, 1–13.

6   C. Hillion, 'Anatomy of EU Norm Export towards the Neighbourhood: The Impact of Article 8 TEU', in: R. Petrov and P. van Elsuwege (eds.), *Legislative Approximation and Application of EU Law in the Eastern Neighbourhood of the European Union* (Routledge 2014), 19.

7   E. Korosteleva, 'Eastern Partnership: Bringing "The Political" Back in', *East European Politics* 321 (33), 2017, 329.

8   L. Alieva, L. Delcour and H. Kostanyan, 'EU Relations with Armenia and Azerbaijan', European Parliament, AFET, 2017, 7, available at: <https://www.europarl.europa.eu/RegData/etudes/IDAN/2017/603846/EXPO_IDA(2017)603846_EN.pdf> (accessed 9 March 2020).

9   European Parliament, 'The EU's Russia Policy: Five Guiding Principles', Briefing, February 2018, available at: <http://www.europarl.europa.eu/RegData/etudes/BRIE/2018/614698/EPRS_BRI(2018)614698_EN.pdf> (accessed 2 March 2020).

10 Enhanced Partnership and Cooperation Agreement between the European Union and Its Member States, of the one part, and the Republic of Kazakhstan, of the other part, *OJ*, 2016, L 29.

11 'Partnership Priorities between the EU and Armenia', 21 February 2018; available at: < https://eeas.europa.eu/headquarters/headquarters-homepage/40175/partnership-priorities-between-european-union-and-armenia_en> (accessed 29 March 2019).

The analysis of the CEPA provided in this chapter is necessary to understand the parameters of the EU's differentiated engagement with Armenia in the shadow of the EAEU. First of all, the aims and goals of the new era of bilateral cooperation are considered in light of the Russian-dominated regional geopolitics. Second, the legal scope of EU-Armenia cooperation is analysed with reference to the political and trade cooperation, as well as *acquis* approximation obligations set in the CEPA. Subsequently, the fast-changing and challenging political context of EU-Armenia cooperation is discussed. Finally, the chapter is summarised with brief conclusions, which offer reflections about future EU-Russia relations and Armenia's role therein.

2 The Objectives of EU-Armenia Relations in the Context of Armenia's EAEU Membership: Stretching Opportunities for Cooperation

Over the past five years, the objectives of EU-Armenia relations have been extensively remodelled to take into account the changing regional context in which bilateral cooperation unfolds. Clearly, Armenia's unexpected accession to the Russia-driven EAEU has severely constrained the scope and depth of cooperation. Within the limitations set forth by EAEU membership, however, both Armenia and the EU have sought to deepen their links to the greatest possible extent, *inter alia*, through negotiating a new comprehensive contractual framework.[12] For the EU, this entailed flexibility in adjusting its offer to Armenia's new circumstances; for Armenia, this involved carefully weighing the implications of its commitments as part of the EAEU.

Armenia's former President Serzh Sargsyan's decision not to sign the AA (announced on 3 September 2013) put the EU's foreign policy to a severe test. For the first time in the history of EU external relations, a country with a highly asymmetrical political and economic interdependence with the EU renounced an agreement offering a deeper degree of integration with the Union. What is more, it did so after launching substantial reforms in view of complying with EU strict *ex ante* conditionality and successfully completing demanding negotiations.[13] Sargsyan's move (even if strongly influenced

---

12   H. Kostanyan and R. Giragosian, 'EU-Armenia Relations: Charting a Fresh Course', CEPS Research Report No. 2017/14, 2017, 23–25.

13   L. Delcour and K. Wolczuk, 'The EU's Unexpected "Ideal Neighbour"? The Perplexing Case of Armenia's Europeanisation', *Journal of European Integration* 37 (4), 2015, 491.

by the Russian pressure)[14] had important implications for the EU's Eastern policy. Despite the attractiveness of the EU's model in Armenia, it signalled the limitations of the EU's influence in a region dominated by Russia. It compelled the EU to design an alternative offer for Armenia. This is due to the fact that the decision to join the EAEU precluded the establishment of a Deep and Comprehensive Free Trade Area (DCFTA), an inalienable part of the AAs,[15] which was the gist of the new level of integration promised through the EaP.

Thus, Armenia emerged as a litmus test for both the EU's new strategy in its neighbourhood following the ENP review of 2015 and its ability to tailor its offer to specific country circumstances.[16] The 'scoping exercise' undertaken to identify possible areas for a new agreement after Armenia's accession to the EAEU roughly coincided with a major paradigm shift in the EU's approach to its neighbourhood. The 2015 ENP review acknowledged the heterogeneity of partners' aspirations and the resulting diversity in patterns of relations.[17] Thus, the revised neighbourhood policy was expected to start not from the EU's offer and experience, but from partner countries' needs and expectations vis-à-vis the EU.

Armenia was especially challenging for the EU's ability to adjust its policy as it combined two specificities: a desire for closer ties with the Union and limitations stemming from its forthcoming EAEU membership. For the EU, Armenia's decision to delegate its sovereignty on tariff-related issues to the EAEU entailed a shift away from the focus on trade-related legal approximation prioritised during AA negotiations with the EaP partners.[18] At the same time, the Armenian authorities sought to deepen links with the EU in all other possible areas, such as political reforms, socio-economic development, sectoral cooperation and mobility, which *de facto* gained prominence in the relations with the EU after Armenia decided to join the EAEU.[19]

---

14 A. Grigoryan, 'Armenia: Joining under the Gun', in: S. F. Starr and S. Cornell (eds.), *Putin's Grand Strategy: The Eurasian Union and its Discontents* (Washington, DC: Central Asia-Caucasus Institute and Silk Road Studies Program 2014), 98–108.

15 L. Delcour, H. Kostanyan, B. Vandecasteele and P. van Elsuwege, 'The Implications of Eurasian Integration for the EU's Relations with the Countries in the Post-Soviet Space', *Studia Diplomatica* 68 (1), 2015, 5–33; P. de Micco, 'When Choosing Means Losing: The Eastern Partners, the EU, and the Eurasian Economic Union', European Parliament, DG EXPO, 2015, 7–8.

16 Alieva et al., *op. cit.* note 8.

17 Joint Communication, 'The Review of the European Neighbourhood Policy', JOIN (2015) 50 final, 2015, 4.

18 L. Delcour and K. Wolczuk, 'Spoiler or Facilitator of Democratization? Russia's Role in Georgia and Ukraine', *Democratization* 22 (3), 2015, 462.

19 Authors' interview, EU official, EU delegation to Yerevan, February 2015.

For Armenia, the accession to the EAEU put an end to any hope of combining Russia's security umbrella with adherence to the EU's economic model.[20] However, it made the search for complementarity more relevant, even if only to hedge against an overwhelming dependence on Russia.[21] Since the early 2000s, Armenia had sought to complement its strategic alliance with Russia with new economic, political and security partnerships; for instance, with the EU and NATO. Despite these attempts, the country's dependence on Russia remains strong and multifaceted. In 2010, the Armenian authorities agreed to extend until 2044 the lease on the Gyumri base, where approximately 3,000 Russian soldiers are stationed. Armenia's economic dependence on Russia is equally important. Even though the EU is still Armenia's major trading partner, its share in the latter's total trade is decreasing.[22] Russia's stranglehold over the Armenian economy is primarily based on energy supply and remittances; in addition, Russian companies own Armenia's few strategic assets. Accession to the EAEU has allegedly protected Armenia from the retaliatory measures that Russia would have introduced if the AA/DCFTA had been initialled and signed (as was the case in Moldova and Ukraine).[23] However, the so-called 'benefits associated with EAEU accession' (in fact, the mere possibility of maintaining economic links with Russia) perpetuate and even increase the dependence on Russia. In fact, Russia's grip over the Armenian economy has only grown in recent years.

The steps taken by Moscow allegedly to ensure Armenia's energy security[24] came at a price: a 2013 deal granted Gazprom a monopoly in operating pipelines that prevents the country from making regulatory changes until 31 December 2043.[25] Furthermore, EAEU membership raised the country's vulnerability to developments in Russia and Russia's policies. For instance, accession to the EAEU came together with freedom of movement within the Union, thereby making it easier for Armenian citizens to work in Russia at a time when Russia significantly harshened migration rules for non-EAEU countries. However, this also coincided with the economic crisis in Russia, which resulted in a decrease

---

20   L. Delcour and K. Wolczuk, 'The EU's Unexpected "Ideal Neighbour"?', *op. cit.* note 13.
21   L. Delcour, 'Regionalism as You Like It? Armenia and the Eurasian Integration Process', *The International Spectator* 53 (3), 2018, 55–69.
22   Dragneva, Delcour and Jonavicius, *op. cit.* note 4.
23   *Ibid.*
24   These include an agreement on duty-free supplies of gas and petrochemicals, a proposal to extend the operation of Armenia's nuclear power plant until 2026 and offer of a loan of US$270 million.
25   Kostanyan and Giragosian, *op. cit.* note 12, 14.

in remittances from Armenian workers in Russia.²⁶ In a similar vein, accession to the EAEU boosted trade with Russia (an increase by 24% during the first half of 2017) and, thereby, raised concerns about an increasing trade dependence with Russia.²⁷ In this context, the Armenian authorities were interested in preserving as broad a scope of cooperation with the EU as possible, which entailed using the draft AA (minus the deep and free trade part) as a basis for negotiations for a new agreement.

Importantly, the Armenian authorities also framed their desire for deeper links with the EU in terms of identity. This is because the EU is associated with values (individual freedoms, democracy, the rule of law) widely shared in the Armenian society.²⁸ As stressed by former president Serzh Sargsyan during the Eastern Partnership Vilnius Summit:

> [The Eastern Partnership] provides with an opportunity to build qualitatively new, closer and expanded relationship upon the basis of shared European values. Developing such a relationship stems from Armenia's and Armenian people's spiritual-cultural and historical-political heritage, and it is the conscious demand of our society.²⁹

Therefore, despite Armenia's backtracking from the AA/DCFTA, both the EU and the Armenian authorities agreed on an ambitious agenda for cooperation. The CEPA was negotiated with these objectives in mind. It covers a wide range of areas to become a 'comprehensive' agreement.

3   The CEPA and the Legal Scope of EU-Armenia Cooperation

The CEPA is a significant step forward in intensifying EU-Armenia cooperation in a large number of areas while accommodating the country's membership to the EAEU. The advanced nature of the agreement lies in the fact that, in

---

26   M. Grigoryan, 'Armenia Faces Cash-Crunch as Russian Remittances Slump', 9 April 2015, available at: <https://eurasianet.org/armenia-faces-cash-crunch-as-russian-remittances-slump> (accessed 15 January 2019); N. Konarzewska, 'Armenia's Economic Woes', Central Asia-Caucasus Analyst, 15 September 2015.

27   Kostanyan and Giragosian, *op. cit.* note 12, 17.

28   Authors' interview, Armenian official, Ministry of Foreign Affairs, Yerevan, February 2015.

29   Statement by Serzh Sargsyan, President of the Republic of Armenia at the Third Eastern Partnership Summit, 29 November 2012, available at: <http://www.president.am/en/statements-and-messages/item/2013/11/29/President-Serzh-Sargsyan-at-the-third-Eastern-Partnership-summit-speech/> (accessed 15 January 2019).

the majority of areas of cooperation, the commitments remain the same as in the previously negotiated AA.[30] The main difference obviously stems from the absence of the DCFTA and in fact any free trade agreement, now replaced by a new trade title.[31] With some noteworthy differences, pertaining to the absence of gradual convergence in foreign and security policy, the title on political cooperation in CEPA resembles that of the AAs with Ukraine, Moldova and Georgia.

3.1 Political Dialogue, Reform and Cooperation

The CEPA puts political cooperation at the centre stage by including the enhancement of political partnership and cooperation among its main objectives.[32] It represents an upgrade from the Partnership and Cooperation Agreement (PCA) by including a separate title on political dialogue and reform, and cooperation in the field of foreign and security policy.[33] Unlike the EPCA with Kazakhstan,[34] Title II includes 'reform' in its title, which is reflected in the obligations set therein. In terms of the scope of political dialogue and cooperation, the CEPA is much closer to the Eastern AAs than it is to the EPCA. The CEPA in Article 3 specifies the aims of the political dialogue in a long ambitious list (exceeding the one in the EU-Ukraine AA),[35] with the main emphasis on partnership and cooperation instead of association.

The provisions on political reform should be placed under the umbrella of the so-called 'human rights clause' mostly comparable in scope to its counterparts in the Eastern AAs with certain variation.[36] Thus, respect for democratic principles, rule of law, human rights and fundamental freedoms constitute *essential elements* similar to the Eastern AAs. The fight against the proliferation of weapons of mass destruction alongside other elements is referred to under the 'General principles' without being an essential element as is the case of the

---

30   Alieva et al., *op. cit.* note 8, 9.
31   Title VI, CEPA.
32   Art. 1(a) CEPA.
33   Partnership and Cooperation Agreement between the European Communities and Their Member States, of the one part, and the Republic of Armenia, of the other, *OJ*, 1999, L 239/3.
34   Title II in the EU-Kazakhstan EPCA is entitled 'Political Dialogue; Cooperation in the Field of Foreign and Security Policy'.
35   Art. 4, Association Agreement between the European Union and Its Member States, of the one part, and Ukraine, of the other part, *OJ*, 2014, L 161.
36   Art. 2 CEPA; N. Ghazaryan, 'A New Generation of Human Rights Clauses? The Case of Association Agreements in the Eastern Neighbourhood European Law Review', *European Law Review* (40), 2015, 391.

EU-Georgia AA, for instance. The breach of the essential elements might lead to restrictive measures, including the suspension of the trade cooperation.[37] While this resembles the Eastern AAs, where the breach of essential elements might lead to the suspension of the DCFTA,[38] the trade cooperation established in the CEPA is of lower intensity as discussed below. A closer look also at the EPCA with Kazakhstan suggests a wider tendency by the EU to envisage the possibility of disruption of trade and business in case of a breach of essential elements.[39] It would appear, thus, that the EU is willing to flex its trade muscles to uphold its values, at least on paper. The EU's past record demonstrates limited reliance on the suspension mechanism.[40] Instead, the main function of this provision is the setting of a normative framework for positive engagement in all areas of cooperation.[41] It is within this normative framework that the parties will pursue their broadly themed political cooperation. The CEPA lists a number of areas pertaining to domestic political reform where the parties 'shall cooperate' similar to the Eastern AAs.[42] This provision resembles Article 68 of the PCA, which is similarly worded but more limited in scope. These obligations are reinforced further in the area of Justice, Freedom and Security.[43] Although it can be argued that the need for political reform has been rendered more visible in the CEPA, the latter does not contain an implementation mechanism. Hence, it is not granted that this would lead to a departure from the EU's practice of favouring engagement despite Armenia's poor political record in the past.[44] It can be argued that a somewhat firmer stance on political reform can be traced in targeted financial assistance allocated for the period ending in 2020 as part of the support for the implementation of Partnership Priorities.[45]

---

37   The suspension mechanism is found in the non-execution clause which constitutes another element of the standard human rights clause, Art. 379 CEPA.
38   See, for instance, Art. 478 EU-Ukraine AA.
39   Art. 279 EPCA.
40   European Commission, 'Using EU Trade Policy to Promote Fundamental Human Rights: Current Policies and Practices', Non-Paper, February 2012, available at: <http://trade.ec.europa.eu/doclib/docs/2012/february/tradoc_149064.pdf> (accessed 15 January 2019); L. Bartels, 'The Application of Human Rights Conditionality in the EU's Bilateral Trade Agreements and Other Trade Arrangements with Third Countries', Policy Department External Policies, European Parliament, 2008, 14.
41   Ghazaryan, 'A New Generation of Human Rights Clauses', *op. cit.* note 36.
42   Art. 4 CEPA.
43   Art. 12 CEPA.
44   N. Ghazaryan, *The European Neighbourhood Policy and the Democratic Values of the EU: A Legal Analysis* (Hart 2014), 172–175.
45   These include democratic governance, rule of law, human rights, anti-discrimination through Human Rights Budget Support based on strict conditions, reform of electoral legislation, fight against corruption, civil society initiatives and justice sector reforms.

The EU's stance on advancing political reform is also expressed in the role accorded to the civil society not only within the implementation of the agreement but more widely. As part of an elaborate institutional framework,[46] a Civil Society Platform is established where EU civil society organisations can meet their Armenian counterparts stimulating socialisation and transfer of experience.[47] Most importantly, the Platform shall be informed of the decisions of the Partnership Council, and it can make recommendations to the Partnership Council, the Partnership Committee and the Parliamentary Committee. Furthermore, the role of the civil society is reinforced through a separate chapter on civil society cooperation.[48] Depending on the ability of the civil society to capitalise on this development, it might become the answer to the past criticism on the lack of a meaningful role for civil society in the EU's policies in Armenia.[49] A more proactive role for civil society is also envisaged in the Roadmap for Engaging with Civil Society in Armenia 2018–2020. The combination of the CEPA's provisions on political reform with an enhanced role for the civil society places it on par with the AAs as opposed to the EPCA with Kazakhstan. Armenia's internal transformation and apparent intention of the current authorities to advance political reform are expected by some to 'facilitate the proper implementation of CEPA' including in the area of political reform.[50] However, the EU's support for such developments can attract Russia's wrath in view of its preference for nominally democratic states allowing for tight control by, and cooperation with Russia.

At the same time, Armenia's precarious position is acknowledged in provisions on foreign and security policy cooperation. Even though the cooperation is to be based on 'common values and mutual interests',[51] unlike the AAs[52] the CEPA does not require 'gradual convergence' in the area of CFSP, instead settling for 'developing and strengthening' the political dialogue, which will

---

EEAS, 'EU and Armenia Sign Cooperation Priorities Until 2020', 21 February 2018, available at: <https://eeas.europa.eu/headquarters/headquarters-homepage/40231/eu-and-armenia-sign-cooperation-priorities-until-2020_en>.

46 See Arts. 362–366 CEPA; see further A. Khvorostiankina, 'Europeanization through EU External Agreements and the Issue of "Constitutional Identity": The Case of the EU-Armenia CEPA', *Kyiv-Mohyla Law and Politics Journal* 15 (4), 2018, 40–41; A. Khvorostiankina, 'EU-Armenia Comprehensive and Enhanced Partnership Agreement: What Does It Mean for Armenian Legal System?', *Armenian Journal of Political Science* 2 (7), 2017, 5–30.
47 Art. 366 CEPA.
48 Chapter 21, Title V CEPA.
49 Ghazaryan, *The European Neighbourhood Policy*, op. cit. note 566, 144–145.
50 Khvorostiankina, 'Europeanization through EU External Agreements', op. cit. note 568, 30.
51 Art. 5 CEPA.
52 See, for instance, Art. 7, EU-Ukraine AA.

'increase the effectiveness of political cooperation', *inter alia*, in international organisations.[53] It also recognises 'the importance [Armenia] attaches to its participation in international organisations and cooperation formats and its existing obligations arising therefrom', which undoubtedly implies the EAEU membership.

Another central matter for political cooperation is conflict prevention and resolution – an area dominated by Russia.[54] While Article 7 provides for practical cooperation in conflict prevention and crisis management in international fora, Article 8 focuses on regional stability and peaceful resolution of conflicts. Without naming the Nagorno-Karabakh conflict as such, it obliges the parties to undertake joint efforts towards establishing regional cooperation and peaceful resolution of conflicts within existing formats, presumably alluding to the Organisation for Security and Co-operation in Europe (OSCE) Minsk Group – the main forum for negotiating a resolution to the conflict. A direct reference to the Nagorno-Karabakh conflict and its peaceful resolution is found in the preamble, but crucially it claims no special role for the EU in this process. Instead, in line with its previous position,[55] the EU reinstates its commitment to 'support [the] settlement process'.

3.2 *Trade Cooperation in the Shadow of the EAEU*

Armenia's EAEU membership had the most drastic impact on its prospects of trade cooperation with the EU as the originally envisaged DCFTA had to be abandoned due to its incompatibility with EAEU membership. The CEPA's amended trade chapter has, therefore, been significantly watered down in comparison with the DCFTA.

In terms of the scope of trade cooperation, the CEPA covers the same issues as under the DCFTA, although now the depth and intensity of the cooperation differ significantly.[56] The main gap in the trade title is the investment chapter, which is to be reviewed within three years from the date of the CEPA's entry into force to supplement the agreement with provisions on investment and investment protection.[57] This gap has been explained by the lack of clarity that surrounded the competence division between the EU and its Member States

---

53   Art. 3 CEPA.
54   Ghazaryan and Delcour, *op. cit.* note 3, 145.
55   N. Ghazaryan, ' "Good Neighbourliness" and Conflict Resolution: A Rhetoric or Part of the Legal Method of the European Neighbourhood Policy', in: D. Kochenov and E. Basheska (eds.), *Good Neighbourliness in the European Legal Context* (Brill 2015), 306–333.
56   Alieva et al., *op. cit.* note 8, 14.
57   Art. 203 CEPA.

over the matter of investment, resolved meanwhile in *Opinion 2/15*.[58] While the Commission currently prefers to split its trade deals to avoid the complexities around competence matters,[59] the CEPA being mixed in nature did not present such an issue which casts doubts on the above explanation. The rest of this section addresses only those areas of trade cooperation which overlap with the EAEU legal framework.

Trade in goods is one of the most important aspects of EU-Armenia trade relations, as it amounts to over a quarter of Armenian trade.[60] In view of the EAEU, the trade tariffs between the two parties will not be eliminated. Armenia, however, will maintain its preferential tariff arrangements with the EU under the Generalised Scheme of Preferences + (GSP +) enacted prior to the CEPA and allowing for tariff abolition on more than 66% of tariff lines.[61] The GSP + is conditional on the ratification of 27 core international conventions on human rights and labour standards, good governance and environmental protection subject to monitoring by the Commission.[62] Despite recording various shortfalls in Armenia's performance of its obligations under respective international agreements,[63] the EU did not resort to the withdrawal of the GSP +, which is a rare occurrence. Instead, the positive conditionality embedded in the incentive element of the GSP + is more attuned to the EU's preference for continuous engagement.

A further downgrade from the DCFTA is noticeable in relation to the chapters on technical barriers to trade (TBT) and sanitary and phytosanitary standards (SPS). The cooperation framework on the elimination of TBT is based on the Agreement on Technical Barriers to Trade forming part of the World Trade Organisation (WTO) Agreement without the imposition of strict approximation obligations, as discussed below.[64] This eschews any possible conflict with the EAEU member status by allowing for future accommodation.[65] Experts are

---

58 Alieva et al., *op. cit.* note 8, 16.
59 'EU Commission Tends to Split up Trade Deals', Euranet, 23 April 2018.
60 European Union, 'Trade in Goods with Armenia', available at: <http://trade.ec.europa.eu/doclib/docs/2006/september/tradoc_113345.pdf> (accessed 20 September 2018).
61 'The EU Special Incentive Arrangement for Sustainable Development and Good Governance ("GSP+") assessment of Armenia Covering the Period 2016–2017', Joint Staff Working Document, SWD (2018) 23 final, 19 January 2018.
62 Regulation No. 978/2012 of the European Parliament and of the Council of 25 October 2012 applying a scheme of generalised tariff preferences and repealing Council Regulation (EC) No. 732/2008, *OJ*, 2012, L 303.
63 SWD (2018), *op. cit.* note 62, 2–5, 7–9, 10–11, 14–15.
64 Art. 127 CEPA.
65 Dragneva et al., 'Assessing Legal and Political Compatibility', *op. cit.* note 4, 14.

also sceptical about the possibility of concluding an Agreement on Conformity Assessment and Acceptance of Industrial Products in the future.[66] The chapter on the SPS similarly falls back on the WTO SPS Agreement as a framework for cooperation without approximation obligations.[67] This downgrade was needed to accommodate Article 56 of the Astana Treaty providing for integration in this area. Importing the Armenian products would be possible under the previously existing regime of granting the Commission's permission under Regulation No. 853/2004.[68]

The most impressive and considerable part of the trade title is found in the services and establishment chapter,[69] despite the low level of trade flows in services. Although the cooperation here is based on the General Agreement on Trade in Services (GATS), it promises to go further and include mutual access in the services markets.[70] The CEPA sets national treatment for cross-border supply of services for which market access is prescribed, and most favourable nation treatment for the establishment of subsidiaries, branches and representative offices by EU natural or legal persons.[71] The chapter branches out to sectoral services with certain approximation obligations discussed in the next subsection. While the EAEU Treaty provides for a scope for integration in the area of services liberalisation,[72] it is seen as 'more akin to a blueprint for integration rather than a framework for specific and immediate commitments',[73] thus leaving a scope for developing trade in services with the EU.

Armenia also assumed extensive obligations in the area of intellectual property (IP) based on the Trade-Related Aspects of Intellectual Property Rights (TRIPS) agreement,[74] but reaching further with its obligations.[75] The most problematic aspect of Chapter 7 on Intellectual Property concerned the labelling of Armenian brandy 'cognac' familiar in the post-Soviet territory.[76] While the prior trademarks will be phased out within 14 years for cognac and

---

66 Alieva et al., *op. cit.*. 8, 15.
67 Art. 134 CEPA.
68 Regulation No. 853/2004 of the European Parliament and of the Council of 29 April 2004 laying down specific hygiene rules for on the hygiene of foodstuffs, *OJ*, 2004, L 139/55.
69 Chapter 5, Title VI CEPA.
70 Art. 149 CEPA.
71 Art. 144 CEPA.
72 Art. 66, Annex 16, Astana Agreement.
73 Dragneva et al., 'Assessing Legal and Political Compatibility', *op. cit.* note 4, 11.
74 Art. 210 CEPA.
75 Alieva et al., *op. cit.* note 8, 16.
76 *Ibid.*

2 years for champagne, the products themselves can be exported to their traditional markets with non-Latin labelling for 25 years for cognac and 3 years for champagne after the CEPA's entry into force.[77] Armenia could assume such IP-related obligations under the CEPA as the EAEU established only a loose cooperation in this field with a view of harmonisation in accordance with international instruments.[78] A coverage beyond the WTO parameters is also recorded in relation to the procurement chapter.[79]

A significant downgrade from the AA is notable also in the provisions on competition and state aid, which are lacking approximation obligations. At the same time, the basic obligations resemble those found in EU law; namely, measures addressing anti-competitive agreements and concerted practice, abuses of dominant position and concentrations and mergers.[80] No conflict is recorded in this area as the EAEU Treaty, despite covering competition issues, leaves much flexibility and avoids imposing prescriptive laws.[81] The next subsection considers the scope of approximation under the trade title as well as in the areas of sectoral cooperation.

3.3   *Fifty Shades of Approximation*

The CEPA includes a long list of areas where sectoral cooperation is established to reflect the 'comprehensive' nature of the agreement. It is in these areas, mentioned below, that more substantive approximation obligations are encountered. First, the nature of Armenia's obligations in relation to approximation and regulatory convergence under the trade title is discussed.

The approximation-related commitments in the CEPA's trade chapter are soft in nature to allow for flexibility in determining the pace of closer cooperation with the EU. A range of formulations for these soft obligations has been used in such areas as customs cooperation, technical regulations, postal services, electronic communications and transport services.[82] For instance, under the chapter on TBT and SPS, the parties 'shall endeavour to establish and maintain a process through which gradual approximation ... can be achieved', shall work 'towards the possibility of converging or aligning technical regulations and conformity assessment procedures' and seek to 'reduce the differences'.[83]

---

77   Arts. 235, 237 CEPA.
78   Art. 89, CEPA.
79   Chapter 8, Title VI CEPA.
80   Arts. 287–287 CEPA.
81   Arts. 74–77 Astana Treaty.
82   Art. 123(2)(a), Art. 130, Art. 169, Art. 180, Art. 189, Art. 192 CEPA.
83   Art. 130(1)(b), 2(a),(3) CEPA.

Other formulations include 'recognis[ing] the importance of gradual approximation' of Armenia legislation to that of the EU.[84]

Obligations of this nature should be categorised alongside the 'endeavour' obligation in Article 43 of the PCA as they do not establish an unequivocal legal obligation: Armenia *is not obliged* per se *to* approximate or converge its legislation in these areas. This approach has been interpreted as one which 'demonstrates complex balancing',[85] creating an intentional grey area. On the one hand, this can be seen as a successful manoeuvring by Armenia in areas where the EAEU legal regime is characterised by underdevelopment or lack of clarity. On the other hand, this can be open to manipulation by Russia, which in theory can foster integration in these areas covered by both legal frameworks.[86] While a carve-out clause was not allowed during the negotiations of the CEPA,[87] the formulation of the relevant obligations under the CEPA would accommodate for such eventualities, as Armenia can still continue 'recognising the importance' of gradual approximation or 'endeavour' towards it, which was not too onerous as demonstrated by the PCA practice.[88]

Hard legal obligations, most ambitious in terms of the approximation agenda, are found in such areas as transport, energy, environment, climate action, consumer protection and employment.[89] Here, the approximation obligations are unequivocal and imperative, substantiated by Annexes listing the relevant EU *acquis*. Article 370 states that Armenia '*shall carry* out gradual approximation of its legislation to EU law as referred to in the Annexes' in the relevant areas subject to monitoring comparable to that undertaken under the Eastern AAs.[90] Crucially, the approximation in these areas 'shall be without prejudice to any specific provisions' under the Trade Title.[91] These substantive approximation obligations are also qualified as 'dynamic' because the Partnership Council can update the Annexes through a periodical review to reflect developments in EU law.[92] Such stipulations have been viewed as

---

84 For instance, Art. 169 CEPA.
85 Dragneva et al., 'Assessing Legal and Political Compatibility', *op. cit.* note 4, 15.
86 *Ibid.*, 16–17.
87 Kostanyan and Giragosian, *op. cit.* note 12, 7.
88 See further, N. Ghazaryan and A. Hakobyan, 'Legislative Approximation and Application of EU Law in Armenia', in: R. Petrov and P. van Elsuwege (eds.), *Legislative Approximation and Application of EU Law in the Eastern Neighbourhood of the European Union* (Routledge 2014), 192–203.
89 Arts. 41, 44, 50, 56, 65, 83, 90 CEPA.
90 Art. 372 CEPA.
91 Art. 30 CEPA.
92 Art. 371 CEPA.

attempts by Armenia to secure the deepest possible integration while still complying with the EAEU legal framework.[93]

Most importantly, the ability to undertake such approximation obligations was determined by the lacunae in the legal framework of the EAEU regarding some sectors (e.g., environment), or the programmatic nature of the cooperation in others (e.g., energy). In case of conflicting obligations which would result from the evolution of the EAEU's legal framework, perhaps a way out can be found through the above-mentioned procedure in the Partnership Council. The updating of the lists contained in the Annexes can reflect not only developments in EU law but also *inter alia* 'applicable standards set out in international instruments deemed relevant by the Parties'. Ultimately, the CEPA's success and the effective fulfilment of Armenia's obligations cannot be detached from the country's internal and external political context.

4   EU-Armenia Relations in a Fast-Changing and Challenging Political Context

While the negotiations and the conclusion of the CEPA have been a relatively smooth process, further progress in EU-Armenia relations is highly sensitive to both domestic and regional developments. This sensitivity is exacerbated by a rapidly changing context, where domestic shifts and reactions of regional players are in fact closely intertwined. Even though it reflects a home-grown process, the shift of power in Armenia, which took place in the spring of 2018, undoubtedly offers a window of opportunity for closer links with the EU. However, whether such an opportunity will materialise hinges crucially on the new authorities' ability to deliver on reforms (among others, the fight against corruption) and, especially Russia's readiness to accept a drastically new course in Armenia's domestic politics.

In late April 2018, Armenia went through the most substantial political change of its post-Soviet existence. Constitutional amendments adopted in late 2015 changed the country's political system into a parliamentary regime, with the Prime Minister now being elected by the National Assembly and being granted extended powers. The appointment of Serzh Sargsyan (then serving his last term as a President) to the position of Prime Minister triggered mass protests uniting various groups under the leadership of Nikol Pashinyan, Head of the Civil Contract party. Sargsyan's unexpected resignation on 23 April paved

---

93   Dragneva et al., 'Assessing Legal and Political Compatibility', *op. cit.* note 4, 15.

the way for the election of Pashinyan as Prime Minister. Early parliamentary elections were held in December 2018, resulting in Pashinyan's re-election as a Prime Minister after his party won an astounding majority.[94]

From the outset of the protests, their leaders emphasised their domestic nature. They stressed that demonstrations were an internal affair, driven by the need to change the country's governance practices and neatly disconnected from Armenia's foreign policy. This is in sharp contrast to the so-called 'colour revolutions' in Georgia (2003) and Ukraine (2004), where the shift of power was associated with a drastic reorientation of the countries' diplomacies – a process which had triggered Russia's concern over a loss of influence in the post-Soviet space and fury over the perceived role of 'Western agents'.[95] By contrast, the new Armenian authorities made it clear that continuity would prevail in Armenia's foreign policy. On meeting President Vladimir Putin in his first visit abroad, the new Prime Minister Nikol Pashinyan confirmed that Russia would remain Armenia's strategic ally (even if on a more equal footing):

> We have things to discuss, but there are also things that do not need any discussion. That is the strategic relationship of allies between Armenia and Russia.[96]

The key reason behind Armenia's continuous engagement with Russia is the latter's role as a security provider as noted by the new Foreign Minister Zohrab Mnatsakanyan during his first visit to Brussels:

> Look at Azerbaijan. Look at Turkey. We're a country that has been blockaded for 27 years by these two states, a country which has existential security threats. ... We can't afford a security vacuum for ten minutes. ... Russia today is playing the role which provides hard security [for Armenia]. Is there anyone else standing there ready to help?[97]

---

94 'Pashinian Alliance Scores "Revolutionary Majority" in Landslide Armenian Win', 10 December 2018, available at: <https://www.rferl.org/a/armenian-elections-pashinian-my-step-sarkisian-hhk/29645721.html> (accessed 15 January 2019).

95 Delcour and Wolczuk, 'Spoiler or Facilitator of Democratization?' *op. cit.* note 18, 460.

96 Quoted in Reuters, 'New Armenian PM Tells Putin He Wants Closer Ties with Russia', 14 May 2018, available at: <https://www.reuters.com/article/us-russia-armenia-putin-pashinyan/new-armenian-pm-tells-putin-he-wants-closer-ties-with-russia-idUSKCN1IF1A3> (accessed 17 September 2018).

97 A. Rettman, 'No Change in EU Relations after Armenia's Revolution', 2 July 2018, available at: <https://euobserver.com/foreign/142245> (accessed 7 July 2018).

Therefore, at least initially the Velvet Revolution did not seem to bear any substantial implications on Armenia's relations with key regional players. In contrast to the political changes in Ukraine and Georgia, the Russian authorities approached the April demonstrations with restraint and caution.[98] They reiterated that Armenia was a sovereign country and (even if reportedly surprised by President Sargsyan's resignation)[99] acknowledged political change there, especially as it was combined with reassurances of a tight relation with Russia. This is because the initial signals sent by the new Armenian authorities (among others, regarding Armenia's EAEU membership) were regarded as sufficient guarantees of loyalty. Russia's attitude to the shift of power in Armenia was shaped, therefore, by the foreign policy status quo rather than the change of elites.[100]

The imperviousness of the Velvet Revolution to external actors and factors is nonetheless delusive. This is because Pashinyan's domestic agenda for reforms dovetails (even if for opposite reasons) with both the EU's and Russia's policies and interests. Despite the affirmation that no reorientation toward the West was to be expected, political change in Armenia coincided with a new momentum in EU-Armenia relations. Together with the expected entry into force of the CEPA, the congruence between the reform agenda of the new government and EU priorities opens new opportunities for strengthening the EU-Armenia partnership. Importantly, the Velvet Revolution has taken place at a time when the EU seems prepared to support democratisation and political reform more actively,[101] whether as part of its dialogue with the authorities, assistance programmes or the forthcoming visa liberalisation process. Thus, as reflected in the first meeting of the CEPA's Partnership Council, the EU is expected to contribute more actively (even if indirectly and in the longer term) to changing the political environment in the country.[102]

---

98   Cf., for instance, Ministry of Foreign Affairs of the Russian Federation, 'Comment by the Information and Press Department on the Situation in Armenia', Moscow, 25 April 2018, available at: <http://www.mid.ru/en/maps/am/-/asset_publisher/OO85pcnduakp/content/id/3193492> (accessed 12 September 2018); P.K. Baev, 'What Made Russia Indifferent to the Revolution in Armenia', *Caucasus Analytical Digest*, No. 104, 2018, 22.
99   *Ibid.*
100 L.A. Way, 'Why Didn't Putin Interfere in Armenia's Velvet Revolution?', *Foreign Affairs*, 2018, available at: < https://www.foreignaffairs.com/articles/armenia/2018-05-17/why-didnt-putin-interfere-armenias-velvet-revolution> (accessed 2 March 2020).
101 L. Delcour, 'Political Changes in Armenia: A Litmus Test for the European Union', *Caucasus Analytical Digest*, No. 104, 23 July 2018, 19.
102 For instance, the EU welcomed the new authorities' commitment to fight against corruption and stressed the importance of changing the electoral code; EEAS, 'Joint Press Statement following the first Partnership Council Meeting between the European Union and Armenia', 21 June 2018.

The new reform agenda has also potential (detrimental) effects on the relationship with Russia. Some of Pashinyan's domestic measures have stood out as growing irritants for the Russian authorities. Investigations into instances of corruption have not spared Russian interests. For instance, the Armenian government cancelled the contract transferring electricity networks to the Tashir Group (whose Armenian branch is owned by a Russo-Armenian oligarch connected to former President Sargsyan's Republican Party) and left them under state control. Importantly, the charges filed against General Yuri Khachaturov (the Secretary-General of the Collective Security Treaty Organisation) and, especially, former President Robert Kocharyan (both in relation to the crackdown on protesters in the wake of 2008 presidential elections) triggered Russia's concern and provoked the first irritated statements against the new authorities.[103] Putin's personal birthday and festive congratulations to Kocharyan, together with messages of support following charges being brought against him, could not have passed unnoticed in Armenia.[104] Russia's decision to increase gas prices for Armenia is a major signal of the Kremlin's growing irritation vis-à-vis the new Armenian authorities.[105] Therefore, political upheavals in Armenia put the CEPA (and Russia's apparent acceptance thereof) in a new light.

Admittedly, both the Russian authorities and EAEU officials have so far welcomed the CEPA, which is however regarded as subordinated to Armenia's deep integration as part of the EAEU.[106] According to Foreign Minister Sergey Lavrov:

> Post-Soviet countries must not accept this false choice between Russia and the West. I believe the fact that Armenia insisted on such relations

---

[103] 'Russia Claims Political Motives in Armenian Charges against Ex-Leaders', 1 August 2018, available at: <https://www.rferl.org/a/lavrov-russia-concerned-armenian-arrest-former-pro-moscow-leaders-kocharian-khachaturov-pashinian/29402249.html> (accessed 15 January 2019).

[104] 'Putin Congratulates Kocharyan on Birthday', ArmRadio, 31 August 2018; 'Putin Congratulates Kocharyan on New Year and Christmas Holidays', 28 December 2018, available at: <https://www.panorama.am/en/news/2018/12/28/Putin-Kocharyan/2053902> (accessed 15 January 2019).

[105] J. Kucera, 'Russia Raises Gas Prices for Armenia in the New Year', 3 January 2019, available at: <https://eurasianet.org/russia-raises-gas-prices-for-armenia-in-the-new-year> (accessed 13 January 2019).

[106] EurAsia Daily, 'Валовая: в ЕАЭС не возражают против соглашения между Арменией и Евросоюзом' [Valovaya : The EAEU Has No Objections to the Agreement between Armenia and the EU], 7 July 2017, available at: <https://eadaily.com/ru/news/2017/07/07/valovaya-v-eaes-ne-vozrazhayut-protiv-soglasheniya-mezhdu-armeniey-i-evrosoyuzom> (accessed 1 November 2017).

with the EU – with Armenia's rights and responsibilities in other integration processes recognised in approved documents – is a step in the right direction.[107]

Nevertheless, in view of the developing nature of the EAEU agenda, the exact scope of 'Armenia's rights and responsibilities in other integration processes' is yet to be determined. Existing overlaps between the EAEU and the CEPA provide Russia with a major leverage (i.e., a push in Eurasian integration in those policy areas) to prevent deepening of EU-Armenia relations. Crucially, the Russian authorities may also resort to a broad array of tools in the bilateral relationship with Armenia should they wish to undermine the country's links with the EU. Armenia's ability to pursue domestic change and deeply engage with the EU remains subordinate, therefore, to Russia's tolerance for some degree of autonomy in EAEU members' (domestic and foreign) policy. This leaves the country in a continuously precarious position.

5 Conclusion

The signature of the CEPA seemingly put an end to the period of uncertainty in EU-Armenia relations following the country's withdrawal from the AA/DCFTA project. While recognising the limitations stemming from Armenia's EAEU membership (and thereby falling short of offering a DCFTA), the CEPA envisages as comprehensive a cooperation as possible. Arguably, the expanded scope of EU-Armenia cooperation results from a combination of two factors: Armenia's continuous quest for deep links with the EU and the EU's flexibility in tailoring its policy to the country's context.

However, the CEPA should be regarded as a basis (and not an end state) for renewed cooperation. The agreement itself reflects a dynamic understanding of legal approximation obligations, thereby suggesting an ability to adjust to changing circumstances. This is crucial as EU-Armenia relations, the CEPA and its implementation cannot be detached from the internal and external political context of Armenia. EU-Armenia relations remain essentially in a state of flux and may considerably vary subject to two interwoven factors; namely, the domestic change within Armenia and the Russian policies and reactions. While

---

107 Ministry of Foreign Affairs of the Russian Federation, 'Foreign Minister Sergey Lavrov's Answers to Questions from the Armenian Media', 8 April 2018, available at: <http://www.mid.ru/en/maps/am/-/asset_publisher/OO85pcnduakp/content/id/3155600> (accessed 12 September 2018).

Armenia's political transformation triggered by the Velvet Revolution did not lead to an immediate Russian reaction, the new trends in Armenia and the EU's support for democratic reform can change perceptions, including of the CEPA, in Russia. It is, therefore, understandable why Prime Minister Pashinyan keeps reiterating the 'no-change in foreign policy' mantra,[108] in addition to confirming the country's commitment to further integration within the EAEU.[109] Dealing with Armenia's precarious position in these circumstances will be one of the major challenges of the new authorities.

The CEPA for now serves as a major indicator of the EU's policy towards a Russian-dominated neighbouring country constrained by its EAEU membership, yet willing to pursue an integration agenda with the EU. In the years to come, Armenia will thus be a litmus test for both the EU's ability to strengthen ties with its Eastern partners (as indicated in its second guiding principle of EU-Russia relations) and Russia's acceptance thereof. In this context, the effective scope and depth of domestic reforms conducted by the new authorities will emerge as a decisive factor.

108 'Prime Minister Nikol Pashinyan Delivers Speech at UN General Assembly,' Press Release, The Prime Minister of the Republic of Armenia, 26 September 2018.
109 'Armenia "Committed to Further Integration" within Eurasian Union', 27 December 2018, available at: <https://www.rferl.org/a/armenia-committed-to-further-integration-within-eurasian-union/29680038.html> (accessed 15 January 2019).

CHAPTER 8

The EU and the *De Facto* States of the East European Periphery

Constraints in International and European Law

Benedikt Harzl

1 Introduction

The unresolved territorial disputes at the Eastern periphery of the EU represent a haunting reminder of humanitarian tragedies, which the EU had also formally identified as security threat on the eve of the eastward enlargement round.[1] As of today, most of the Eastern Partnership (EaP) countries are actively or passively involved in and affected by the existence of *de facto* states. While isolated by the international community and treated as bizarre anomalies, they have all defied their metropolitan states' jurisdiction for more than 25 years and, as it seems, are set to stay indefinitely. That raises a pivotal question, which lies at the core of this chapter: to what extent has the Europeanisation[2] of these metropolitan states[3] contributed to the resolution of these conflicts? This question also arises indirectly in relation to the EU's five guiding principles vis-à-vis Russia, in particular the one on strengthening relations with the Eastern partners and other neighbours. As these principles have been formulated relatively recently, it would be premature to conclusively assess their effect on conflict

---

1 Council of the EU, *European Security Strategy*, Doc. 15895/03, 12 December 2003.
2 The term *Europeanisation* is understood in this work as an amalgam of different policies and processes that are aimed to draw the countries of the Eastern periphery of the EU closer to the latter's legal space after the collapse of the Soviet Union and to encourage them to adopt EU rules. (See a largely congruent definition at: F. Schimmelfennig and U. Sedelmeier (eds.), *The Europeanization of Central and Eastern Europe* (Cornell University Press 2005)). It, therefore, encompasses not only legal approximation through Association Agreements (AAs) but also includes prior policies with a lower approximation intensity such as Partnership and Cooperation Agreements (PCAs).
3 The author of this work chooses to use the term *metropolitan state* when discussing such states as Georgia or Azerbaijan and their relationship vis-à-vis the disputed territories, rather than *mother state* or *parent state* to avoid a biased or emotional undertone which is presented when a term such as '*mother*' or '*parent*' is used. The term *metropolitan state* was first used by Dov Lynch. See: D. Lynch, *Engaging Eurasia's Separatist States: Unresolved Conflicts and De Facto States* (United States Institute of Peace 2004).

resolution. Yet their very formulation also suggests to look closer into the issue of whether the EU has succeeded in designing a creative approach towards the various *de facto* states in the region.

These related questions will be addressed by looking into existing repositories in public international and EU law and the way they were implemented. The chapter is structured as follows. After a brief overview of the conflicts in the Eastern periphery of the EU, the EU's engagement with the unrecognised states in this region is examined. The analysis zooms in on the interplay between the EU Common Foreign and Security Policy (CFSP) and the national competences of the Member States. In addition, the impact of the bilateral EU Association Agreements (AAs) with Ukraine, Moldova and Georgia on the disputed states is scrutinised. It is concluded that while the conflicts in the Eastern periphery were generally seen as major obstacles for the area and the states' rapprochement with the EU,[4] paradoxically they did not represent a significant impediment to the Europeanisation of the countries concerned. Nevertheless, there remains a clear need for designing a creative engagement strategy regarding the unrecognised states to improve the security situation in the region. This chapter argues that, so far, the EU has failed to make use of its potential to help resolving these conflicts.

2 A Glance at the Conflicts

2.1 Brief Overview of the Conflicts

Since 2014, most of the EaP countries are to varying degrees involved in or affected by separatist conflicts. This situation also applies to Ukraine, after the Russian Federation annexed the Crimean Peninsula and supported rebels in the Lugansk and Donetsk Oblasts, leading to the self-proclaimed Donetsk and Lugansk People's Republics (DPR and LPR). While Russia formally adopts a neutral position in the conflicts over the DPR and LPR and rejects accountability for their acts, it leaves no doubt whatsoever about acquiring jurisdiction over the Crimean Peninsula.[5] In fact, the annexation of Crimea into the

---

4   See the European Neighbourhood Policy (ENP) review of 2015: 'Protracted Conflicts Continue to Hamper Development in the Region'. European Commission, 'Joint Communication to the European Parliament, the Council, the European Economic and Social Committee and the Committee of the Regions, Review of the European Neighbourhood Policy', Joint (2015) 50 final, 2.

5   With regard to Crimea, the official legal narrative of the Russian Federation is that the people of Crimea lawfully executed their right to independence. This narrative is based, in particular, on the case of Kosovo and the Advisory Opinion of the International Court

Russian Federation in March 2014 was formally conducted through a Federal Constitutional Law Act of the Russian Federation[6] and leaves little, if any, doubt about Russia's accountability.[7]

The other conflicts, which concern Abkhazia, Nagorno-Karabakh, Transnistria and South Ossetia, are considerably older and lean back to the ethnopolitical upheavals shortly before and after the collapse of the Soviet Union.[8] Even if all of those conflicts differed significantly from one another,[9] they shared qualities that proved conducive to the creation of a security dilemma, which was ignited by mutually hostile narratives and imagined histories of ethnic domination. As M. Beissinger aptly argues, the rise of nationalism as the most dominant force of *glasnost* triggered a mobilisation cycle, which – by easing institutional constraints of the rapidly declining cohesive power of the Communist Party of the Soviet Union (CPSU) – relied on structural conditions and event-specific processes.[10] It was this particular interplay between structural conditions and specific events that proved to be toxic and quickly led to the escalation of the conflicts such as the violent crackdown of mass demonstrations in Tbilisi on 9 April 1989 by Soviet interior ministry troops, which was a transformative event in the sense that it strengthened the perception and narrative among Georgians that Russia stands behind the separatist ideology of the Abkhaz and the Ossetians. Likewise, the Moldovan

---

of Justice (ICJ). Yet even if one assumes that a right to secession exists under public international law, the Russian Federation has violated the prohibition of force by deploying military force to secure the referendum and to prevent Ukrainian authorities to intervene. See: S. van den Driest, 'Crimea's Separation from Ukraine: An Analysis of the Right to Self-Determination and (Remedial) Secession in International Law', *Netherlands International Law Review* 62, 2015, 361.

6   See the enumeration of legal domestic acts of the Russian Federation leading to the annexation in: T. D. Grant, 'Annexation of Crimea', *American Journal of International Law* 109, 2015, 71.

7   Therefore, a meticulous analysis of why a state can be held responsible where there has not been an open military invasion as provided in *Ilascu and Others* or *Louizidou* by the European Court of Human Rights (ECtHR) does not need to be undertaken to establish the applicability of Article 1 European Convention on Human Rights and Fundamental Freedoms (ECHR) in the case of Crimea.

8   This topic has received significant scholarly attention. Just to name one important monograph: C. Zürcher, *The Post-Soviet Wars: Rebellion, Ethnic Conflict, and Nationhood in the Caucasus* (NYU Press 2007).

9   While interethnic violence was epidemic in the wider conflict history over Nagorno-Karabakh, the conflict over Transnistria was rather elite driven, and massive ethnic violence was averted.

10 M. Beissinger, *Nationalist Mobilization and the Collapse of the Soviet State* (Cambridge University Press 2002), 49.

language law, which was adopted in 1989, intensified the resentments of the Russophones as its implementing regulations required testing nearly all workers in the country for Moldovan language proficiency within a period of four years.[11]

The aim of this subsection is not to retrace the conflict history in all of these cases. It suffices to state that in each confrontation, a spiral to violence was deliberately chosen over compromise, which quickly escalated to war. In the case of Nagorno-Karabakh, the period between 1992 and 1994 saw a full-scale war between Armenia and Azerbaijan, whereby Armenia pushed the Azerbaijani forces beyond today's demarcation line and, additionally, occupied adjacent territories to secure access to the otherwise landlocked Nagorno-Karabakh and conducted expulsions of the Azerbaijani population of the former autonomous oblast. In Georgia the armed conflict over South Ossetia lasted from January 1991 until June 1992, while in Abkhazia the ultimate escalation took place in August 1992, when Georgian troops entered this former autonomous republic – under the pretext of securing the railway lines – and thereby gradually triggered a conflict that turned into a fully fledged war.

This intervention, however, failed miserably. With some limited support by the Russian Federation and volunteer fighters from the North Caucasus, the Abkhaz militia managed to oust the Georgian troops from Abkhazia in the autumn of 1993. The humanitarian costs were tremendous: almost 250,000 ethnic Georgians became internally displaced persons and were forced to leave Abkhazia, while only some 50,000 would return to the eastern Gali district in the years to come. Furthermore, the conflict's overall death toll of about 10,000 to 15,000[12] also demonstrated the severity of these battles. Still, it needs to be noted that some areas of South Ossetia and Abkhazia – for example, the Kodori Gorge – continued to remain under Georgian control. In 2008, the region fell back to full-scale violence, which changed the picture completely with the swift and completely unexpected Russian diplomatic recognition of both entities.[13] The shortest and – in comparison – the least bloody armed conflict over Transnistria lasted between March and July 1992. In this brief

---

11 That was a problematic provision, as it constituted an existential threat to the social and economic well-being of virtually all non-Moldovan speakers in the country. See: S. Kaufmann, *Modern Hatreds: The Symbolic Politics of Ethnic War* (Cornell University Press 2001), 142.

12 J.A. George, *The Politics of Ethnic Separatism in Russia and Georgia* (Palgrave Macmillan 2009), 120.

13 Interestingly, then President Dmitry Medvedev made use of the 'Kosovo precedent' when justifying the decision to recognise South Ossetia and Abkhazia. Evidently, he meant the word 'precedent' only as a factual element, rather than a precedent in a legal sense.

conflict episode, the Russian 14th Army, which was based in Moldova at that time, openly sided with the ethnic Russians of Transnistria who had initiated a secessionist campaign and finally succeeded proclaiming the Transnistrian Republic.[14]

All of these conflicts share significant traits. In each case, the EU seems to have been absent as potential conflict manager in the initial phases of the conflict. Furthermore, in all cases, an ethnic minority community successfully defied the metropolitan state in an armed confrontation concerning the jurisdiction over those territories. These decisive military victories were all achieved in the first half of the 1990s, and in practically all cases these outcomes would have been impossible had it not been for significant external support provided by third states such as Russia, kin states such as Armenia or through assistance conveyed through other sources.[15] This factor is essential and particularly contentious as it relates to the very underlying legal qualification of the outcomes of these wars: the creation of *de facto* states. The governments of the metropolitan states argue that – even provided that those entities meet factual criteria of statehood – those very facts were produced in violation of norms of international law, whereby this violation is attributed to those third states.[16] The entire turnaround of the ethnic composition, thus the argument, could not have happened without ethnic cleansing. Evidently, this position is rejected by the authorities of the *de facto* states, which point to additional political extralegal factors such as legitimacy among its citizens, their democratic political systems and even, occasionally, their wish to integrate into the EU.[17]

Hence, all sides tend to perpetuate their pre-existing positions rather than to lower their maximalist demands. That is the main reason why there is

---

14   P. Baev, *The Russian Army in a Time of Troubles* (SAGE 1996), 105.
15   B. Harzl, *The Law and Politics of Engaging De Facto States: Injecting New Ideas for an Enhanced EU Role* (Brookings Institution Press 2018), 14.
16   The principle of *ex iniuria ius non oritur* plays an important role in the theory and practice of international law and is accordingly invoked in these cases. By this token, Article 41(2) of the Articles on Responsibility of States for Internationally Wrongful Acts of 2001 recognises the obligation of states to not recognise as lawful a situation created by a serious breach of an obligation arising under a peremptory norm of general international law. Even if one assumes that diplomatic recognition of those entities is of merely declaratory nature, it may be argued that this very recognition has the effect to bolster the independence of the recognised state.
17   With regard to Nagorno-Karabakh, this desire to integrate together with Armenia into the EU has often been mentioned in the political discourse. See: E. Berg and M. Möller, 'Who Is Entitled to "Earn Sovereignty"? Legitimacy and Regime Support in Abkhazia and Nagorno-Karabakh', *Nations and Nationalism* 18, 2012, 539.

no mutually accepted definition that reflects the legal nature of those entities.[18] What can, however, be agreed on is one central feature, which helps to approach the general underlying dilemma: 'A *de facto* state is internationally unrecognised because it is part of an unresolved conflict where sovereignty is the main stake'.[19]

2.2 Controversial Legal Claims and Politics

The normative discourses surrounding these so-called 'frozen conflicts'[20] of the EU's Eastern neighbourhood also touch on core issues in international law. That becomes apparent if one considers the key legal arguments on which the political elites of both the separatist entities and the governments of metropolitan states rely when justifying their opposing claims. These arguments persistently lack a comprehensive definition: Who precisely is eligible for the principle of self-determination of peoples, what exactly does this right entail and how does this principle relate to the obligation of states to refrain from 'the unlawful use of force or other egregious violations of norms of general international law'?[21]

As if that normative conundrum were not sufficiently complex as it is, collective narratives further intermingle with these questions and feed into the respective legal discourse. The Abkhaz highlight the fact that only the ethnic Georgian Joseph Stalin downgraded Abkhazia into an autonomous republic

---

18   Admittedly, there is much ECtHR case law concerning the establishment of jurisdiction pursuant to Article 1 ECHR. Also the European Court of Justice (ECJ) handed down judgments in the *Anastasiou* saga concerning the issue of Northern Cyprus. Since the authorities in Northern Cyprus are not under the effective control of the Republic of Cyprus, they cannot issue valid customs certificates and, as a consequence, Northern Cypriote products could not be treated as goods originating from a country associated with the EU. See: *Anastasiou and Others*, C-140/02, Judgment of 30 September 2003, EU:C:2003:520.

19   R. Bryant, 'Living with Liminality: De Facto States on the Threshold of the Global', *Brown Journal of World Affairs* 20, 2014, 127. Many helpful definitions of a *de facto* state have been brought forward such as five criteria elaborated by Nina Caspersen: (1) *de facto* independence after secessionist struggle; (2) the building of state institutions; (3) a formal declaration of independence; (4) no or hardly any outside diplomatic recognition; (5) existence for at least two years. See: N. Caspersen, *Unrecognized States* (Polity Press 2012), 11.

20   The term *frozen conflict* applies to those post-war situations of separatist conflicts in the post-Soviet space, that – while ongoing armed skirmishes do not occur – have not seen any sustainable peace process, let alone reintegration into their metropolitan states. See: D. Lynch, 'Separatist States and Post-Soviet Conflicts', *International Affairs* 4, 2002, 831–848.

21   *Accordance with International Law of the Unilateral Declaration of Independence in Respect of Kosovo*, Advisory Opinion, ICJ Rep. 2010, 18, para. 81.

in 1931,[22] while the Armenians of Nagorno-Karabakh argue – both with considerable grain of legitimacy – that their incorporation into Azerbaijan in the 1920s was arbitrary and undemocratic.[23] The metropolitan states voice their grievances, too, and are equally willing to position historical narratives as constitutive landmarks for their normative claims.[24] Obviously, turning these narratives into ontological actualities for creating legal positions has a strategic component. The domestic aspect of conflict is omitted while the external dimension of portraying an interstate conflict with Russia becomes the desired legal conceptualisation, whereby more legal remedies are available.[25]

Correspondingly, the lack of a mutually agreeable framework for these conflicts makes it difficult to operate with legal terminologies and, at the same time, constitutes a principal challenge for the EU to approach these troubled spots. The governments of the metropolitan states repudiate the term *de facto states* and argue that those entities had not the sufficient capabilities at their own autonomous discretion to succeed in the creation of factual independence.[26] Instead, these disputed territories are depicted as unlawfully occupied territories, while legislation to that purpose also has been enacted[27] and

---

22   This grievance is central to the interpretation of the *uti possidetis* principle governing the establishment of new borders. See: B. Coppieters, 'A Moral Analysis of the Georgian-Abkhaz Conflict', in: B. Coppieters and R. Sakwa (eds.), *Contextualizing Secession: Normative Studies in a Comparative Perspective* (Oxford University Press 2003), 190.

23   After the victorious Soviet military operation against the anti-Soviet Armenian uprising in Zangezur and, supposedly, personal intervention by Joseph Stalin himself, the *Kavburo* border commission decided to place Nagorno-Karabakh as autonomous oblast within the territory of Soviet Azerbaijan. Hence, to win hearts and minds of the Armenians by transfering Nagorno-Karabakh to the Armenian Soviet Socialist Republic did not seem any longer worthwhile. See: A. Saparov, 'Why Autonomy? The Making of Nagorno-Karabakh Autonomous Region 1918–1925', *Europe-Asia Studies* 2, 2012, 312.

24   Kaufmann, *op. cit.* note 11, 92.

25   Public international law does not prohibit secession. It only obliges third states to refrain from intervening on behalf of a secessionist party.

26   Evidently, they accuse third states for having violated the prohibition of force and also claim that the *de facto* state could not have emerged had not ethnic cleansing occurred. See: Harzl, *op. cit.* note 15, 21.

27   In January 2018, the Ukrainian Parliament adopted the Law on Certain Aspects of State Policy on Securing State Sovereignty over the Temporarily Occupied Territories of the Donetsk and Luhansk Oblasts, complementing the 2014 Law of Ukraine on Securing the Rights and Freedoms of Citizens and the Legal Regime on the Temporarily Occupied Territory of Ukraine concerning the Crimea. Likewise, the Georgian government adopted the 2008 Law on Occupied Territories. These laws not only recognise Russia as military occupant under international law but they, furthermore, establish a special regime in these territories and restrict entry and exit into those territories. For an overview on Donbas, see: The Polish Institute of International Affairs, 'Ukraine's Law on the Occupied

is consistently implemented, no matter how politically questionable.[28] They also reject the conclusion of non-use-of-force treaties with these entities.[29] The EU, which had complemented the presence in this area of other international organisations working on conflict resolution such as the UN or the Organisation for Security and Co-operation in Europe (OSCE), has chosen to operate with the EaP countries on a bilateral level while simultaneously employing a policy of strict non-recognition towards *de facto* states as a centrepiece of the EU's engagement in the region.

3 EU Foreign Policy and *De Facto* States

3.1 *Between CFSP and National Competences: Hybrid Approaches*

How did the EU approach the frozen conflicts? In general, the EU is structurally biased to tip the scales in favour of the doctrine of territorial integrity over the concept of self-determination, if the latter concept entails the right to secede from an existing state. Moreover, public international law as well as the 'international normative regime'[30] is tendentiously set against ethnonationalist ideology as a basis for the attainment of statehood. That explains why the EU and its Member States have been pursuing a firm line of non-recognition of these entities and have, occasionally, provided only limited engagement.[31]

Territories in Donbas', 24 January 2018, available at: <https://www.pism.pl/publications/bulletin/no-12-1083 > (accessed 1 March 2020).

28   Also EU engagement is seriously hampered by these domestic legal provisions, and this can be best illustrated by the fact that even Peter Semneby, former EU Special Representative for the South Caucasus, temporarily found his name on a list of *personae non gratae* in Azerbaijan for visiting Nagorno-Karabakh in 2012. See: 'Azerbaijani Foreign Ministry publishes a list of personas non grata', *Trend*, 2 August 2013, available at: <https://en.trend.az/azerbaijan/politics/2176569.html> (accessed 1 March 2020).

29   In fact, a number of agreements has been concluded that not only contained the signatures of recognised states (such as the metropolitan state Azerbaijan and the kin state Armenia) but also of the non-recognised separatist entity (Nagorno-Karabakh). These agreements include the Bishkek Protocol of 5 May 1994 and the ceasefire agreement of 12 May 1994, each signed by representatives of Armenia, Azerbaijan and Russia as well as the unrecognised Republic of Nagorno-Karabakh. Those agreements have the same legal value as other treaties pursuant to Article 12 of the Vienna Convention of the Law of Treaties.

30   One could argue that this term also encompasses, aside from public international law, principles of behaviour within the international system governing interstate relations. See: R. Taras and R. Ganguly, *Understanding Ethnic Conflict* (Routledge 2016), 34.

31   This has been done mostly through donor activities such as the funding of humanitarian projects. But these efforts have also been quite limited.

Besides, this stance seems to be politically consistent insofar as it reflects the decision of the Member States of the European Community to recognise the post-Soviet republics along their Soviet administrative boundaries in 1991 and 1992.[32]

Hence, from the outset, the EU dealt with those countries on an exclusively bilateral level. Nevertheless, this structural bias was complemented by hybrid approaches towards the post-Soviet space that crystallised in two different, yet intertwined, ways. On the one hand, the EU pursued by default a binary concept, mixing hard and soft law in dealing with the region. The first hard law instrument in this context was the Partnership and Cooperation Agreements (PCAs), which were concluded with the successor states of the Soviet Union in the course of the 1990s, including Russia, and may be regarded as less far-reaching alternatives to the Association Agreements concluded with the countries of Central and Eastern Europe in the same period. Significantly, the PCAs did not specifically target or address the frozen conflicts, which – with the exception of Ukraine – already existed at the time of their adoption in Moldova and Georgia.[33] If anything, only the chapter on political dialogue referred to a contribution 'towards the resolution of regional conflicts and tensions'.[34] Arguably, the PCAs could have been used to deal with certain troublesome issues only indirectly, through the employment of negative conditionality.[35]

The launch of the European Neighbourhood Policy (ENP) in 2003–2004 did not entirely transform the EU's reluctance to engage more directly in the frozen conflicts. At least, it explicitly recognised for the first time the necessity to

---

32 While the European Community Member States recognised Armenia, Azerbaijan and Ukraine on 31 December 1991, Georgia was recognised on 23 March 1992. All of these republics pledged to abide by the *Guidelines on the Recognition of New States in Eastern Europe and the Soviet Union* (See: Statement concerning the Future of Russia and Other Former Soviet Republics, December 23, 1991, EFPB, Document 91/469). Besides, this position seems to be in line with numerous General Assembly resolutions, confirming the territorial integrity of those countries.

33 The PCA with Georgia merely reads in the preamble that the EU Member States 'support the independence, sovereignty and territorial integrity of Georgia'. The same formulation can be found in the Azerbaijani version of the PCA as well as in the Armenian PCA.

34 See: Article 5 of the EU-Armenia PCA.

35 For instance, Article 95(2) of the Armenian PCA allows the termination of the agreement if 'either party has failed to fulfil an obligation'. These obligations encompass also the 'respect for principles of international law' (see Article 2 of the EU-Armenia PCA). Theoretically, this could serve as an instrument of negative conditionality if a country involved in a separatist conflict violates international law. However, given the fact that even after the unlawful annexation of Crimea the EU did not suspend the EU-Russia PCA, one can see the limited substance of this provision. The EU has been hesitant to make full use of the negative conditionality mechanisms in bilateral agreements.

increase efforts to promote the resolution of the conflicts in its periphery as a precondition to the fulfilment of EU objectives.[36] As to the legal and political nature of the ENP, again a rather mixed image emerges. Prior to the adoption of the Lisbon Treaty, the ENP was little more than a hybrid and not explicitly standardised political field, which was partly rooted in the EU Trade and Development Policy and partly based on the CFSP.[37] The main leitmotif behind ENP was based on the operation of non-binding soft law instruments such as the so-called 'Action Plans' (AP) enacted in 2005 and 2006. Procedurally, the EU negotiated with its Eastern neighbours a package of legislative and administrative acts that the respective country pledged to undertake. The results of these negotiations were subsequently laid down in the APs and became subject to joint monitoring. These APs became a basic tool for the implementation of the PCAs' objectives and precisely defined priority areas for each country.[38]

Indeed, those instruments contained rather specific commitments vis-à-vis the frozen conflicts. For instance, the Georgia AP explicitly addressed the separatist conflicts as the sixth priority area and obliged Georgia to enhance its confidence-building efforts, while it required the EU to step up support to the UN in the Geneva process and to the OSCE in the Joint Control Commission (JCC) framework.[39] These APs were also simultaneously negotiated with Armenia and Azerbaijan, and it seems that this momentum could have been used to bring those conflict parties together and have them agree over some basic features. Instead, while the Azerbaijan AP contains strong language on territorial integrity,[40] the EU-Armenia AP only lists the contribution to conflict solution in Nagorno-Karabakh as Priority Area 7 and – in contrast to the

---

36 See: European Neighbourhood Strategy Paper, COM(2004) 373 final, 12 May 2004, 4.
37 Arguably, since the adoption of the Lisbon Treaty, Article 8 TEU provides for a legal basis for the ENP, even if this provision still represents 'uncharted territory'. See: K. Schmalenbach, 'Schwierige Nachbarn: Ukraine, Russland und die Europäische Union' in: S. Kadelbach (ed.), *Die Welt und Wir: Die Außenbeziehungen der Europäischen Union* (Nomos 2017), 231.
38 Legally speaking, the APs are merely 'bilateral declarations of intent'. They did not need to undergo any ratification procedure whatsoever. See: D. Thürer and R. Bretschger, 'Article 8: Relations with Neighboring Countries', in: H. Blanke and S. Mangiameli (eds.), *The Treaty on European Union (TEU): A Commentary* (Springer 2013), 382.
39 See point 4.2 of the EU-Georgia AP, 14 November 2006. Interestingly, the Georgian side seems to have succeeded in characterizing their territorial conflicts in the AP as a dispute with Russia as the EU is also required to 'Include the issue of settlement of internal conflict in Abkhazia, Georgia in EU-Russia political dialogue meetings'.
40 See point 1 of the EU-Azerbaijan AP, at <https://eeas.europa.eu/sites/eeas/files/au-az_action_plan_azerbaijan.pdf> (accessed 1 March 2020). Besides, the contribution to a peaceful solution of the Nagorno-Karabakh conflict is listed as Priority Area 1.

Azerbaijani AP – does not mention territorial integrity.[41] This inconsistency indicates that the EU seems to have been satisfied with settling for the lowest common denominator.[42]

By 2009, after the adoption of the EaP, the ENP underwent a long-awaited regionalisation. Since its very goal was to 'create the necessary conditions to accelerate political *association*'[43] this policy culminated in the adoption of Association Agreements, including the Deep and Comprehensive Free Trade Areas (DCFTAs) with Moldova, Ukraine and Georgia in 2014. Hence, that also meant a qualitative shift and a return to hard law, leading to massive legal approximation commitments on the part of the associated countries.[44] At the same time, this also meant that efforts concerning the resolution of existing territorial disputes gradually lost their prominent place in EU hard law instruments.[45] AAs are very ambitious agreements, which go beyond the PCAs of the 1990s and are liable to perform a 'stress test on the sovereignty of these states'.[46] They require these countries to adopt a significant part of the EU *acquis* and to have their results monitored and periodically examined. With Armenia and Azerbaijan outside of the AA realm, a situation was created with *haves* and *have-nots* in the Eastern periphery, thereby further complicating the picture of the EU's strategy in the fields of both norm diffusion and conflict resolution.

The other hybrid formula was the mix between CFSP instruments and selective initiatives of Member States in foreign affairs. It seems that the EU has preferred to act vis-à-vis the frozen conflicts through the mostly intergovernmental CFSP. Indeed, an enhanced engagement can be seen with the establishment of the offices of EU Special Representatives (EUSR) in Moldova and the South Caucasus. In particular, the mandate for the EUSR on the South Caucasus epitomised a regional approach that allowed for drawing the governments of *de facto* states into informal discussions, so that dialogue for the

---

41 Moreover, it reads: 'Increase political support to the OSCE Minsk Group conflict settlement efforts on the basis of international norms and principles, including the *principle of self-determination of peoples*'. See point 4.2. of the EU-Armenia AP, 14 November 2006.

42 B. Harzl, 'Potentials and Shortcomings for Conflict Resolution in the Caucasus', in: T. Kruessmann (ed.), *Moving Beyond the Kosovo Precedent: EU Integration for Moldova and the South Caucasus* (LIT 2015), 33.

43 Council of the EU, Joint Declaration of the Prague Eastern Partnership Summit, Doc. 8435/09, 7 May 2009.

44 L. Delcour, 'Between the Eastern Partnership and Eurasian Integration: Explaining Post-Soviet Countries' Engagement in (Competing) Region-Building Projects', *Problems of Post-Communism* 62, 2015, 317.

45 Abkhazia and South Ossetia are mentioned only in Article 429 of the EU-Georgia AA, clarifying that both territories are presently outside of the scope of territorial application.

46 Schmalenbach, *op. cit.* note 37, 232.

sake of dialogue never came to a halt.[47] As of today, the mandate of the EUSR has been extended and includes an express reference to the crisis in Georgia in its name.[48] The August war of 2008 further accelerated the role of the EU in different ways.[49] The EU has 'bought' itself into informal mechanisms by co-chairing the Geneva talks.[50] Furthermore, the Council established a non-armed EU Monitoring Mission (EUMM) in Georgia, whose mandate includes[51] not only generating knowledge but also monitoring whether the parties comply with the six-points plan.[52]

While some level of engagement is, hence, quite evident, the character of the EU's policy devices proved a highly problematic fit in those conflicts in which sovereignty is the main stake. This is obviously the case in Georgia as well as in the other countries affected by separatist disputes. The fundamental problem of EUMM remains its claim to access and move freely on the territories of the *de facto* states on the basis of a mandate, which was not agreed with the governments of the *de facto* states but with Georgia.[53]

Yet a lack of cohesion between EU foreign policy and national initiatives cannot be concealed. A number of EU Member States, among them Lithuania and Poland, adopted parliamentary resolutions in which they condemned the military occupation of Abkhazia and South Ossetia by the Russian Federation.[54]

---

47 The Abkhazian government has continuously refused the entry of Tbilisi-based Ambassadors of EU Member States. The regional mandate provided the EU Special Representative (EUSR) with easier access to interlocutors in Sukhumi. A status neutral formulation was agreed in Article 3(e) of the Council Joint Action. Accordingly, the EUSR shall 'intensify EU dialogue with the *main interested actors*'. See: Council Joint Action 2003/496/CFSP, *OJ*, 2003, 7 July 2003, L 169/74.

48 Not only by the very name but also by the substantive contents, the EUSR's mandate is 'to help prepare for the international talks' within the framework of the Geneva discussions. See: Council Decision (CFSP) 2015/2118, *OJ*, 2015, L 306/26.

49 For instance, Georgia and Russia agreed on a ceasefire plan brokered by the French EU Presidency.

50 These talks started as an informal mechanism in the format 3 + 3 (EU, OSCE, UN + USA, Russia, Georgia).

51 Council Joint Action 2008/736/CFSP, *OJ*, 2008, L 248/26.

52 *Ibid.*, Article 3.

53 At least the establishment of the Incident Prevention and Response Mechanism (IPRM) was one of the few successful initiatives, through which the EUMM gained legitimacy for all conflict sides. In the framework of this mechanism, Georgians, South Ossetians and Abkhaz can address the EUMM in the case of security breaches and meet along the administrative borders. See: D. Philipps, *Implementation Review: Six-Point Ceasefire Agreement Between Russia and Georgia* (The National Committee on American Foreign Policy 2011), 12.

54 The Baltic Course, 'Lithuanian Seimas Passes Resolution on Support to Georgia', available at: <http://www.baltic-course.com/eng/legislation/?doc=27677> (accessed 1 March 2020).

In other words, the EU provides an unclearly arranged mixture of hard EU law and non-binding declarations, and at the same time pursues the parallel structure of CFSP and national foreign policy with regard to the frozen conflicts. The underlying philosophy of Europeanisation is primarily focused on economic integration of these countries. This provided, indeed, some limited moments of engagement, yet one can argue that the EU did not – and still does not – see itself as having or intending to have a more robust role in conflict resolution mechanisms as everything that would clearly show support for these entities is off the table.[55] The only viable and potentially positive contribution could be found in an approach that does not abandon the strict non-recognition policy but, otherwise, actively seeks engagement and reaches out to these entities. However, practice augurs poorly. These initial engagement ideas have not been consistently followed up with policy proposals and the single-handed initiatives of some EU Member States have not proved effective either.

3.2 *Association Agreements and* De Facto *States*

The limitations of EU engagement can be best illustrated by the way how the *de facto* entities are addressed in the AAs concluded with Ukraine, Moldova and Georgia. While the EU-Ukraine AA was initialled *before* the annexation of Crimea and the outbreak of clashes in eastern Ukraine, those territories would still be legally considered to fall under the territorial scope of the EU-Ukraine AA. However, these territories are no longer under effective Ukrainian jurisdiction, making it impossible for Ukrainian authorities to issue Ukrainian custom certificates that would enable the sale of products originating from Crimea or the contested areas in eastern Ukraine under the preferential treatment of the DCFTA.

In this context, there is well-established case law of the European Court of Justice (ECJ),[56] according to which certifications of origin of goods are necessary for the functioning of free trade agreements as they are founded on the principle of mutual trust and cooperation between the competent authorities

---

55 Indeed, the EU has concluded a number of international agreements with non-recognised entities but those were either very specific or of transitional nature. See: P. Van Elsuwege, 'Legal Creativity in EU External Relations: The Stabilization and Association Agreement Between the EU and Kosovo', *European Foreign Affairs Review* 22, 2017, 394. Equally important, Taiwan and the Palestine Liberation Organisation do not feature as good examples since both have not broken off from their metropolitan states.

56 See, in particular, ECJ, Case C-432/92 *Anastasiou (Pissouri)*, Judgment of 5 July 1994, EU:C:1994:277 concerning Northern Cyprus and Case C-386/08, *Brita GmbH*, Judgment of 25 February 2010, ECLI:EU:C:2010:91 concerning Israeli settlements in the West Bank.

of the exporting state and of the importing state.⁵⁷ Since the conflicts in Georgia and Moldova date back to the early 1990s, the territorial scope of their AA has been adopted accordingly. Both agreements include provisions that allow the application of these agreements only on the territory on which both states exercise effective control.⁵⁸ Only a decision by the Association Council could, in both the case of Georgia and Moldova, extend the application of the AA (in particular, the DCFTA) to those disputed territories.

This is precisely what has been done with regard to Transnistria. An informal agreement between the authorities of Transnistria and the government of Moldova made it possible for the Association Council to approve Transnistria's coverage under the umbrella of the DCFTA.⁵⁹ Ironically, this will require the Association Council to periodically monitor the implementation of the DCFTA in Transnistria.⁶⁰ One might argue that also in Georgia's case, the AA and DCFTA could informally apply to Abkhazia and South Ossetia. Yet it is highly unlikely that the potential economic incentives under the EU-Georgia AA and DCFTA would be sufficiently convincing for Abkhaz and South Ossetian authorities to seek rapprochement with their Georgian counterparts. The deeply entrenched dispute is not primarily about economic issues, thus the potential of economic advantages drawing from the AA/DCFTA does not appear to be a suitable instrument for bringing the breakaway regions closer to Georgia. Even apart from this, the EU finds itself in a problematic situation. It is, on the one hand, unable to conclude agreements with the *de facto* states analogously to the one with Kosovo,⁶¹ as this amounts to an unlawful interference with the domestic

---

57 See: ECJ, Case C-432/92 *Anastasiou I*, Judgment of 5 July 1994, EU:C:1994:277, para. 201. Yet even apart from this, the Council has adopted in addition Regulation No. 692/2014 of 23 June 2014 'Concerning Restrictions on the Import into the Union of Goods Originating in Crimea or Sevastopol, in Response to the Illegal Annexation of Crimea and Sevastopol', *OJ*, 2014, L 183/9.

58 See Article 429(2) EU-Georgia AA or Article 462(4) EU-Moldova AA.

59 It must be noted that about 30 to 40 % of Transnistria's exports are destined for the EU, making the application of the DCFTA a matter of economic survival. See: B. Harzl, *Keeping the Transnistrian Conflict on the Radar of the EU*, ÖGfE Policy Brief, 2016, 24.

60 See Decision No. 1/2015 of the EU-Moldova Association Council of 18 December 2015, *OJ*, 2015, L 336/93.

61 Also Kosovo is not recognised by all EU Member States but it concluded a Stabilisation and Association Agreement with the EU pursuant to Article 217 TFEU in conjunction with Articles 31(1) and 37 TEU. This agreement is remarkable because, in contrast to similar agreements with other Western Balkan countries, it was not concluded by the EU *and* its Member States but by the EU alone, with the explicit provision that this is not to be considered as a recognition of Kosovo's independence. See: P. Van Elsuwege, *op. cit.* note 55, 394.

affairs of the metropolitan states given the position that the *de facto* states are not to be treated as states. On the other hand, an interpretation of the AAs in conformity with international law[62] will compel the EU to apply these agreements in a territorially limited manner excluding these entities if the governments of these *de facto* states are seen as pro-Russian puppets.

4 Conclusion

Quid multa? On closer inspection, it seems that the principle of strengthening relations with the Eastern partners fails to include a firm strategy on how to deal with the *de facto* states short of strict non-recognition. While economic integration and free trade became the centrepiece of the EU's approach to its Eastern neighbours, the EU seems to contribute only indirectly to conflict transformation as a side product, planting the seeds through which meaningful discussions could theoretically start. The limited engagement of the EU in the issue of conflict resolution reflects the Union's competences, as delineated according to the principle of conferral under Article 5(1) and (2) of the Treaty on European Union (TEU).[63] These competences, closely tied to the Treaty objectives, permit action relating to economic integration to a much larger degree than that relating to conflict resolution outside the EU.

Indeed, economy played some part in these conflicts but it was not the main reason why confrontation was chosen over cooperation and why the conflict parties resorted to violence.[64] The frozen conflicts are essentially self-determination conflicts involving opposing collective grievances that make the application of international law futile. One side to the conflict claims its practices are lawful, while the other disputes them as unlawful. The nature of

---

62   See, analogously, Case C-104/16 P *Council v. Front Polisario*, Judgment of 21 December 2016, EU:C:2016:973, in which the ECJ concluded that the *erga omnes* nature of the right to self-determination by peoples of a former colony must not be interfered with by an Association Agreement with Morocco.

63   Article 5(1) and (2) TEU lay down that the EU may act only within the limits of its competences, as conferred to it by the Member States, with the aim to achieve the objectives of the Treaties. All competences not conferred on it remain within the Member States.

64   That was nicely captured in a televised conversation between a Georgian and an Abkhaz as part of a reconciliation project. While the Georgian pointed to the positive economic prospects for Abkhazia in a reintegrated Georgia, the Abkhaz said: 'I want you to live well in Tbilisi rather than to live bad in Sukhum/i. Let us better be separate'. See: 'Vmeste i Vroz', 23 April 2011 <https://www.youtube.com/watch?v=Hk5mGgSKrnM> (accessed 1 March 2020).

these conflicts elevates legal indeterminacy to the basic rule. As demonstrated, existing EU law also is not very helpful in bringing an end to these conflicts. These are essentially power-sharing conflicts that can be dealt with only by creative institutional design, which can function only if all sides are prepared to move away from maximalist goals and to allow significant concessions. That is precisely the question which Ukraine, Moldova, Georgia and Azerbaijan need to answer for themselves. What are they willing to sacrifice politically for reintegration of their breakaway territories? As of today, Article 1 of the Constitution of Georgia refers to Abkhazia as 'Autonomous Soviet Socialist Republic of Abkhazia', an entity that ceased to exist decades ago. The painful question is: Are those countries prepared, for instance, to agree on a bicommunal and bizonal federation as is currently discussed in Cyprus?

Ironically, this stalemate has not hindered the countries' Europeanisation. States with complex power-sharing concepts and problematic institutional designs are not for the impatient. Arguably, dysfunctional states in which power is asymmetrically, horizontally and vertically shared are not the best candidates for the enormous obligations under an AA and DCFTA.[65] In this context, Europeanisation presupposes and requires quick and swift decision-making, and cannot tolerate political setbacks. In all conflict cases, there has been no shortage of proposals on whether federalisation or confederate features can stitch the countries together. Yet it may be argued that the political costs of reintegration outweigh the benefits of Europeanisation. This highlights a significant downside of the Europeanisation process: states can aspire Europeanisation without needing to find complex power-sharing mechanisms. The EU is unable to prescribe, let alone impose, a particular solution.

Russia has ceased to be a neutral broker, at least in Ukraine, Georgia and Moldova. Yet Eurasian integration will make things more difficult and one will need to ask how these integration processes will resonate with the *de facto* states in the future, as the outlook for reunification of these states is more than bleak. That makes a good argument for principled pragmatism in the EU's relations with Russia, allowing them to compartmentalise issues of shared concern from issues of disagreement. Furthermore, it should motivate the EU to design a policy that allows for cooperation with the *de facto* states under the threshold of recognition and to devise a smart strategy of engagement without recognition. Evidently, this engagement strategy will require a sophisticated and tailor-made approach based on the differences of each *de facto* state and its

---

65   Consider, in this regard, also the failure of the EU's conditionality strategy in the highly decentralized Bosnia and Herzegovina. See, *inter alia*, S. Sebastian, 'The Role of the EU in the Reform of Dayton in Bosnia-Herzegovina', *Ethnopolitics* 8, 2009, 341–354.

specific circumstances. Yet engagement, for instance in the fields of healthcare and higher education, can help these entities' modernisation through alignment with Brussels rather than Moscow, theoretically creating more spaces for convergence with their metropolitan states.

CHAPTER 9

The EU's and Russia's Visa Diplomacy in a Contested Neighbourhood

Igor Merheim-Eyre

1   Introduction

At the 2003 St. Petersburg Summit, the EU and Russia proposed creating a 'common space of freedom, security and justice', which was expected to serve the objective of 'building a new Europe without dividing lines, thus facilitating travel and contacts between all Europeans'.[1] This goal has not materialised and, today instead, European security architecture is broken:[2] from the Russian annexation of Crimea and conflict in the Donbas to the unresolved conflicts in Nagorno-Karabakh, Abkhazia, South Ossetia and Transnistria; the downing of Malaysian Airlines flight MH17; the Russian military posturing and the continuous extension of economic sanctions and visa bans between the EU, the United States and Russia.[3] Instead of a common space from Lisbon to Vladivostok, Europe has become once again a contested space, while the countries of Eastern Europe and the South Caucasus[4] are faced with two simultaneous region-building projects, the Eastern Partnership (EaP) and the Eurasian Economic Union (EAEU).[5]

---

1   Council of the European Union, 'EU-Russia Summit St. Petersburg Joint Statement', 9937/03 Presse 154 2003.
2   I. Merheim-Eyre, 'The West-Russia Confrontation and Limits to a Cooperative World Order' in: P. Kalra and E. Van Gils (eds.), *Governance & Resilience in Wider Eurasia: Are Cooperative World Orders Possible?*, GCRF COMPASS Signature Conference Proceedings 2019, available at: <https://research.kent.ac.uk/gcrf-compass/wp-content/uploads/sites/1767/2019/10/COMPASS-Signature-Conference-Proceedings-2019-Updated-4-Oct-2019.pdf> (accessed 15 March 2020).
3   For a more comprehensive discussion, see the contributions by S. Van Severen (chapter 1), T. van der Togt (chapter 2), A. Hofer (chapter 4) and B. Harzl (chapter 8) in this volume.
4   Although this chapter largely deals with the six countries of Armenia, Azerbaijan, Belarus, Georgia, Moldova and Ukraine (hereby referred to as the 'common neighbourhood' or simply as 'neighbours'), due to both the EU's and Russia's interaction with countries of Central Asia, there are also occasional references to the wider post-Soviet space.
5   L. Delcour, *The EU and Russia in Their 'Contested Neighbourhood* (Routledge 2017).

Despite this context, people-to-people contact is one of five areas currently prioritised by the EU in the development of EU-Russia relations, while the EU also pledges to develop closer relations with its common neighbours.[6] The EU has further acknowledged the growing confrontation, particularly in the neighbourhood countries. Consequently, this chapter seeks to address this contestation by focusing on the EU's and Russia's visa diplomacy[7] in the neighbourhood. The chapter intends to show that visa diplomacy (be it the denial or the facilitation of travel) is used by both the EU and Russia not merely to manage cross-border mobility *per se* but also to shape the neighbourhood countries in their own image.[8] It argues that visa diplomacy is not simply about 'imposing constraints' but also a means to govern the external space through a narrowly defined set of conditions attached to the simplification or full removal of the visa regime on the citizens of third countries.[9]

This chapter further seeks to offer a contribution to the understanding of how today's contestation between the EU and Russia play out on a sectoral level and in the neighbourhood countries.

The significance of visa and migration-related issues in the ties between the EU, Russia and the countries of the neighbourhood is not exaggerated. For example, in 2013 alone (in one of the busiest years for Schengen visa applications in the EaP, and also a year before the visa liberalisation with Moldova – the first with an EaP country – came into effect), Schengen countries issued 16.1 million short stay visas and a further 176,948 Limited Territorial Validity (LTV) visas worldwide. Of these more than 2.5 million short stay visas and 27,338 LTVs were issued for EaP countries' nationals, making the common neighbourhood, aside from Russia, the busiest area for Schengen visa applications anywhere in the world. On the other hand, it is believed that up to

---

6 See European Parliament, 'EU's Russia Policy: Five Guiding Principles' Briefing 2018, available at: <http://www.europarl.europa.eu/thinktank/en/document.html?reference=EPRS_BRI(2018)614698> (accessed 14 March 2020).

7 K. Stringer, 'The Visa Dimension of Diplomacy', *Discussion Papers in Diplomacy* (Netherlands Institute of International Relations 'Clingendael' 2004).

8 This contribution seeks to distinguish *visa diplomacy* from *passportisation*, which is defined as the issuance of passports to achieve foreign policy goals. As shown below, Russia has used passportisation in Georgia's breakaway regions of Abkhazia and South Ossetia, as well as in the Donbas.

9 I. Merheim-Eyre, 'Protecting Citizens, Securitising Outsiders? Consular Affairs and the Externalisation of EU's Internal Security', in: R. Bossong and H. Carrapico (eds.), *EU Borders and Shifting Internal Security: Technology, Externalisation and Accountability* (Springer 2016), 112.

10 million people from the other former Soviet countries reside and work in Russia.[10]

More broadly, visas are employed by states as microdevices through which it is possible to confirm or deny citizens of third countries to enter the territory of another polity, be it for political, economic, leisure or any other reason. As such, for example, the visa application process helps to manage the legal flow of third countries' nationals to a polity, through a process of interviews, security checks and surveillance methods to prevent any insecurities from affecting the internal space.[11] In the context of the common neighbourhood countries, however, visa diplomacy is also employed for broader foreign policy ends; for example, region-building (as in the case of the EAEU or the EaP), to shape the outside according to one's own image or to show disapproval with a particular state's or individual's actions.

In this regard, visa diplomacy is not always coercive. In fact, the ability to simplify or fully remove visa regime has proved far more effective in the neighbourhood than coercive measures such as visa bans. This has particularly been the case with the EU, which has been using the process of visa facilitation to manage cross-border mobility borders to secure the internal space (by way of linking visa facilitation agreements with readmission agreements), as well as using the visa liberalisation process to stimulate reforms (according to EU rules and regulations).

Moreover, it is not merely the EU that seeks to offer market and visa-free access to citizens of the neighbourhood countries through the EaP. Russia's own region-building project, the Eurasian Economic Union, has also been created on the basis of facilitating free movement of goods, capital, services and people.[12] Russia has sought to retain a visa-free access for labour migrants from post-Soviet countries that rely heavily on remittances from abroad (especially, in the case of Tajikistan, Armenia and Moldova), and continues to use it as noncoercive means of keeping the post-Soviet countries closer to Russia.

Following this introduction, the main body of the chapter is divided into three subsections. The first subsection focuses on the EU's and Russia's use of visa bans or tightening of visa regimes not only against one another but also

---

10 M. Pluim, M. Hofman, R. Zak and A. Bara, 'Changing Migration Realities: Why Migration between the EU and the Eastern Neighbourhood Will Change', Working Paper No. 7 (International Centre for Migration Policy Development 2014).

11 E. Zureik and M. Salter, *Global Surveillance and Policing: Borders, Security, Identity* (Willan 2005).

12 T. Romanova, 'Russia and Europe: Somewhat Different, Somewhat the Same?', Policy Brief No. 5 (Russian International Affairs Council 2016).

against the neighbours. The next subsection then further deals with visa facilitation and liberalisation for up to 90 days, and the third subsection focuses on the growing role played by labour migration in the relations between the neighbourhood countries, the EU and Russia to highlight that, despite demographic problems across wider Europe and Eurasia, the changing migratory patterns across this space and the possibility to facilitate free movement of labour may prove to be additional sources of contestation between the EU and Russia in the future.

As the conclusion seeks to highlight, despite the calls over the past decade to create a Europe without dividing lines, areas such as cross-border mobility are now also increasingly providing a space for sectoral competition in the neighbourhood countries. The study of both EU and Russian visa diplomacy, therefore, offers a relevant analysis at a time when the European space is once again becoming contested, and the mobility of people used for geopolitical ends.

2 Forms of Visa Diplomacy

2.1 *Widening Alienation: Coercive Visa Bans and Restrictions*

Despite worries that the 2004 enlargement and the consequent expansion of the Schengen zone eastwards would create new dividing lines on the European continent, the 2000s actually witnessed a multitude of cooperative measures to mitigate its potential impact on the countries of the common neighbourhood.[13] On top of signing visa facilitation agreements with its neighbours, launching dialogues leading towards visa liberalisation and introducing the Local Border Traffic (LBT) Agreements, the EU (and also individual Member States such as Poland and Latvia) sought multiple measures to continue cross-border mobility (see below). At the same time, Russia also introduced new measures, including the Union of Russia and Belarus, that sought to preserve mobility across the post-Soviet space, and manage alienation within this space.

Crucially, there was also bourgeoning cooperation between the EU and Russia in the sphere of migration not only in shared border areas but, as O. Korneev shows,[14] also as far as Central Asia.[15] By 2007, the EU and Russia

---

13 I. Merheim-Eyre, 'The Visegrad Countries and Visa Liberalisation in the Eastern Neighbourhood', *Journal of East European Politics and Societies* 31 (1), 2017, 93–114.

14 See O. Korneev, 'Deeper and Wider than a Common Space: European Union-Russia Cooperation on Migration Management', *European Foreign Affairs Review* 17 (4), 2012, 605–624; O. Korneev, 'EU Migration Governance in Central Asia: Everybody's Business – Nobody's Business', *European Journal of Migration and Law* 15, 2013, 301–318.

15 For example, this included joint trainings for border guards of the Central Asian Republics.

signed a Visa Facilitation Agreement (VFA), with the aim of simplifying visa procedures for Russians travelling to the EU, although discussions about visa-free travel as a long-term goal between the EU and Russia already had begun at the aforementioned 2003 St. Petersburg Summit, where both sides committed to the creation of a 'common space' of freedom, security and justice[16] that would manage alienation across wider Europe.

By 2011, the two sides published Common Steps towards visa liberalisation, and the Readmission Agreement (RA) was implemented by Russia, who consequently began to use the document to sign such agreements with its respective neighbours. Moreover, important local agreements were implemented in the case of the Kaliningrad enclave, especially as the countries around it began joining Schengen and, thus, stricter border measures began to be implemented. Thus, in 2011, Poland and Russia signed an LBT which allowed citizens of bordering Polish regions and Kaliningrad to travel visa-free (subject to an obtained permit). However, unlike in other cases where the LBT is normally restricted to 50 kilometres of the border, the arrangements included the whole of Kaliningrad and in Poland extended to Olsztyn, Elblang and Gdansk.[17]

Additional LBTs have been signed with Kaliningrad and Latvia, and Norway and the Murmansk Oblast, although Finland found no need to sign such agreement, while increasing border disagreements between Russia and Estonia prevented the consideration of such agreements between the two states.[18] By 2013, however, technical disagreements between the EU and Russia also arose around upgrades to the VFA, especially with regards to service passports.[19] While Russia wanted all service passport holders exempt from the visa regime, at the 2013 Yekaterinburg Summit the EU side argued that such passports are too widespread in the Russian administration to be granted the same privileges as for holders of the diplomatic passports.

The road towards a visa-free regime also became complicated as the EU increasingly linked the issue of human rights violations in Russia with visa

---

16   Council of the European Union, *op. cit.* note 1.
17   The only other such agreement to go beyond the 50-km radius is the LBT between Moldova and Romania. See: P. Van Elsuwege et al., 'EU-Russia Visa Facilitation and Liberalisation: State of Play and Prospects for the Future' (EU-Russia Civil Society Forum 2013), 18.
18   A. Yeliseyeu, 'Belarus-EU: The Likely Consequences of a Readmission Agreement' (Belarusian Institute for Strategic Studies 2013).
19   S. Utkin, 'Overcoming the Stalemate in EU-Russia Relations: Start with the Visa Dialogue' (European Leadership Network 2019), available at: <https://www.europeanleadershipnetwork.org/commentary/overcoming-the-stalemate-in-eu-russia-relations-start-with-the-visa-dialogue/> (accessed 14 March 2020).

liberalisation, an attempt to put pressure on the Kremlin in light of high-profile cases such as that of Fyodor Khodorkovsky and the Pussy Riot punk band. Interestingly, however, unlike in the case of the neighbourhood countries where human rights are a specific condition under Block 4 of the Visa Liberalisation Action Plans (VLAPs), human rights were never an explicit point in the visa dialogue between the EU and Russia.[20]

In the case of Belarus, as with the other neighbourhood countries, human rights were always regarded by the EU as a precondition to any dialogue on visa liberalisation. However, in relations with Belarus, visa bans actually have a longer history. In fact, visa bans targeting President Alexander Lukashenko, members of the Council of Ministers and their administrators have been in place since 1998 following a series of incidents in Drozdy, a diplomatic district of Minsk. According to the EU, intrusions on the territory of the residencies, unannounced maintenance works and welding of the gate of the US Ambassador's residence infringed the Vienna Convention on diplomatic relations, leading to the departure of both the EU and US ambassadors, suspension of development projects and visa bans.[21]

Visa bans, accompanied by economic sanctions, became a permanent feature of EU-Belarus relations due to the deterioration of human rights in the country and the lack of free and fair elections. It was only a thaw in relations in the context of Russian aggression in Ukraine that has led to the EU abolishing visa bans against 170 members of the Belarusian government,[22] although no progress has been made by the Belarusian regime on human rights. The failure of this thaw to stimulate meaningful political and economic reforms in Belarus have been highlighted by the brutal repressions in the context of the 2020 presidential elections, and the (re)-imposition of targeted sanctions against those responsible for human rights abuses.

The aforementioned conflict in Ukraine had a major impact on the future of mobility between the EU and Russia. Despite technical disagreements even before the crisis, it was the annexation of Crimea and conflict in the Donbas that led to the worsening of relations between the EU and Russia and, on the sectoral level, led to the freezing of the visa liberalisation dialogue. Moreover, both sides engaged in a war of visa bans, coupled with economic sanctions. On top of the financial restrictions and arms embargo connected to the shooting

---

20   On the visa liberalisation dialogue between the EU and Russia, see also the contribution by O. Potemkina (chapter 13) in this volume.
21   Stringer, *op. cit.* note 7, 21–22.
22   Council of the European Union, 'Outcome of the 3447th Council Meeting: Foreign Affairs', 6122/16 PRESSE 6 PR CO 6 2016.

down of the MH17 flight,[23] the EU placed asset freezes on 37 Russian entities and banned 152 people from entering the EU as a response to the annexation of Crimea.[24]

In response, Russia banned some 89 European political and military figures from entering the Federation, including the former Polish Foreign Minister Radek Sikorski, former UK Foreign Secretary Sir Malcolm Rifkind and several Members of the European Parliament. According to German President Frank-Walter Steinmeier, 'At a time in which we are trying to defuse a persistent and dangerous conflict, this does not contribute towards that'.[25] As in the case of Belarus, neither the EU visa bans nor Russia's response changed the attitudes or actions of the other side. Instead, however, they perpetuated the stand-off and, mixed with the effective freezing of dialogue on visa liberalisation, limited the prospects for simpler cross-border mobility for ordinary Russians and citizens of the EU, or the possibility for strengthening civil society cooperation, as shown in Chapter 16 by Elena Belokurova and Andrey Demidov in this volume.

At the same time, however, it is also interesting to note that, unlike the EU, Russia has not engaged in formally imposing either visa regimes (with the exception of Georgia in 2000) or visa bans on citizens of the neighbourhood countries. For example, even when applying pressure on Moldova around the signing of the Association Agreement with the EU, Russia chose to target Moldova economically by restricting access for its wine on the Russian market, citing health concerns,[26] while no official bans or visa impositions were placed on Moldovan citizens working in Russia. Instead, they were targeted under 'new' stricter administrative rules that Russia attributed to the EU. According to Korneev,

---

23 See the contribution by T. van der Togt (chapter 2) in this volume.

24 These included people identified as involved in the annexation, including Denis Berezovskyi, former Commander of the Ukrainian navy, Victor Ozerov, Chairman of the Security and Defence Committee of the Federation Council and Dmitry Rogozin, Deputy Prime Minister of Russia. See Council of the European Union, Council Decision 2014/145/CFSP concerning Restrictive Measures in Respect of Actions Undermining or Threatening the Territorial Integrity, Sovereignty and Independence of Ukraine, *Official Journal of the European Union OJ*, L 78, 2014.

25 *The Guardian*, '89 European Politicians and Military Leaders Banned from Russia', 30 May 2015, available at: <https://www.theguardian.com/world/2015/may/30/russia-entry-ban-european-politicians-eu-moscow> (accessed 30 May 2019).

26 *BBC News*, 'Why Russian Wine Ban Is Putting Pressure on Moldova', 21 November 2013, available at: <https://www.bbc.com/news/world-europe-24992076> (accessed 21 June 2019).

Russian officials trying to keep the image of an open and welcoming neighbour, necessary for Russia's efforts aimed at fostering integrationist dynamics in the region, often justify restrictiveness of Russian immigration policies by pressure from the EU.[27]

In other words, Russian visa diplomacy is actually more cunning than that of the EU; instead of formal visa restrictions, it blames EU norms and standards for imposition of tougher administrative rules on citizens of the post-Soviet states (see below), as well as complicating mobility across wider Europe as a whole. From searching for a 'common space' of freedom, security and justice, it now uses EU-ropean norms (and rhetoric) to justify its own policies.

2.2 Managing Alienation: Visa Facilitation and Liberalisation

A simplified or a visa-free regime (or, at least, the process of attaining it) has proved to be the most widespread use of visa diplomacy by the EU and Russia in the neighbourhood for their own policy goals. For example, Russia has been using such techniques since the break-up of the Soviet Union to manage alienation and keep the former Soviet republics more closely integrated with Russia, as the successor state, at its centre. The EU, on the other hand, has initially (in the wake of the 2004 enlargement) widened alienation by imposing stricter visa rules than those that have existed between countries such as Slovakia and Ukraine, or Poland and Belarus beforehand. In the post-enlargement period and the EU's eventual region-building (in the shape of the EaP initiative), the Union's restrictive policies took on a more inclusive but managed form of visa diplomacy.[28] In other words, while Russia uses inclusive forms of visa diplomacy to prevent further disintegration of the post-Soviet space, the EU has succinctly created divisions between itself and the neighbours, and is now using this form of visa diplomacy to highlight its inclusive nature by gradually removing those barriers, albeit subject to narrowly defined conditions.

Thus, while in the case of the Western Balkans the EU used visa liberalisation as a tool for stabilisation and transformation of the region, in the Eastern neighbourhood visa diplomacy has been a crucial element in seeking to manage potential (in)security beyond the borders of the EU by way of: (1) extending its rules and regulations through conditionality, (2) external migration management and (3) region-building. Moreover, while simplification of the visa application process became increasingly conditioned on the return of

---

27   Korneev, *op. cit.* note 14, 624.
28   Merheim-Eyre, *op. cit.* note 13.

illegal migrants and overstayers, the process of visa liberalisation sought to create a form of extraterritorial border control in the form of democratic reforms and increased governance capacity of the EU's neighbours. This became clear when visa liberalisation with the countries of the Western Balkans led to a 76% rise in asylum applications from Serbia alone,[29] and further illegal migration and asylum claims were feared from the Eastern neighbours.[30] Consequently, the EU's visa diplomacy (while appearing inclusive) became increasingly more controlling, and used to shape the neighbourhood countries in the EU's image through a focus on wider governance. It is made up of two tiers of benchmarks, including both the planning and legislative alignment, and the consequent implementation of predetermined EU norms and regulations.[31] In this respect, the EU presents set conditions but discussions on specific issues range only to the extent of whether particular rules or regulations are already being implemented or not.

Moreover, despite EU declarations of inclusivity and desire for increased people-to-people contact, its achievements remain sketchy at best. The EU tends to look at the glass as half full, pointing to the fact that in the first year (May 2014-May 2015) of the visa-free regime with Moldova, some 500,000 citizens made use of new travel possibilities to the EU. However, the remainder of the glass remains a more complex mixture. Visa liberalisation with Moldova was partly a response to a widespread application for Romanian passports, and increasing migration of Moldovans to the EU through this possibility.

In fact, since Moldova's independence, around a million (out of a population of circa 3.5 million) of its citizens have applied for Romanian passports,[32] making this both an economic drain on the country and an unresolved migration issue that required a better management system. In the case of Ukraine and Georgia, though eventually attaining a visa-free regime in 2017, the visa

---

29   F. Trauner and E. Manigrassi, 'When Visa-Free Travel Becomes Difficult to Achieve and Easy to Lose: The EU Visa Free Dialogue after the EU's Experience with the Western Balkans', *European Journal of Migration and Law* 16, 2014, 125.

30   I. Merheim-Eyre, 'The EU and the European Other: The Janus Face of EU Migration and Visa Policies in the Neighbourhood', in: Paul Flenley and Mike Mannin (eds.), *The European Union and the Eastern Neighbourhood: Europeanisation and Its 21st Century Contradictions* (Manchester University Press 2017).

31   Trauner and Manigrassi, *op. cit.* note 29, 130.

32   Publika, 'Almost One Million Moldovans Acquired Romanian Citizenship in the Past Years', 27 March 2018, available at: <https://en.publika.md/around-1-million-moldovans-acquire-romanian-citizenship-in-past-years-_2647124.html> (accessed 27 September 2018).

liberalisation process was taken hostage and delayed by the political fallout from the migration crisis.

At the same time, progress on visa issues with Belarus and Azerbaijan has been made awkward by the EU's insistence on the improvement of human rights as a precondition, though arguably visa liberalisation would benefit the civil society, especially in Belarus, which (after Russia) is the second-busiest country for Schengen visa applications in the world. After a long process protracted by both sides, the EU and Belarus finally agreed on visa facilitation and readmission agreements in 2020.[33] Given that out of the 16 million Schengen visas issued in 2018 globally almost 700,000 were for citizens of Belarus, and that Belarusian citizens are of low risk (only 0.3% of visas applications were denied), this is a positive but much overdue step.[34]

The trouble, however, is that with no overall improvement in the human rights situation in Belarus, the question remains of why the EU does not amend its methodology, and use visa liberalisation instead to engage with Belarusian citizens and foster democratisation from below, rather than hold citizens' ability to travel visa-free hostage to the authoritarian practices of Lukashenko's regime. Given the regime-orchestrated repressions and mass protests in the context of the 2020 presidential elections, the case for allowing Belarusian citizens visa-free travel to the EU has become all the more timely.

Overall, the visa liberalisation process has become increasingly more controlling, as it is being used more specifically to shape the neighbourhood in the EU's image and extend extraterritorial migration control as a price for (eventual) removal of barriers people-to-people contact. In the Russian case, however, an inclusive form of visa diplomacy has been at the heart of its policies towards the post-Soviet republics since the break-up of the Soviet Union, although also increasingly more regulative and controlling.[35] Generally, travel between Russia and the other post-Soviet countries (notably excluding the three EU Member States – Estonia, Latvia and Lithuania) is guided by a 1992 multilateral agreement on visa-free travel, which allows for visa-free travel of up to 90 days (as in the case of the Schengen visa-free travel).[36]

---

33   At the time of this writing, however, these agreements were yet to come into effect.
34   European Commission, 'Complete statistics on short-stay visas issued by the Schengen states 2018', available at: <https://ec.europa.eu/home-affairs/what-we-do/policies/borders-and-visas/visa-policy_en#stats> (accessed 20 February 2020).
35   Korneev, op. cit. note 14, 609.
36   'Agreement on Visa-Free Movement of Citizens of the States of the Commonwealth of Independent States on the Territory of His Participants', 9 October 1992, available at: <https://cis-legislation.com/document.fwx?rgn=25681> (accessed 20 November 2019).

For Russia, the policies were aimed at reintegration (or, at best, to prevent further disintegration) of the post-Soviet space. Consequently, it is also a means of retaining some form of influence as other regional actors, such as the EU, China, Iran and Turkey, become increasingly present in the post-Soviet space,[37] or seek to conduct their own region-building, as in the case of the EU's EaP. That these ties remain important has been highlighted in the case of Russo-Ukrainian relations. Despite Russian annexation of Crimea and involvement in the conflict in Donbas, visa-free travel remains in place. In October 2016, despite calls for imposition of visa restrictions on Russian citizens, there was limited support for such move from the *Verkhovna Rada*. In fact, it was also opposed by President Petro Poroshenko's bloc, arguing that such measures would be counterproductive, especially impacting Ukrainian labour migrants in Russia.[38]

The Russian government, in fact, increased visa-free travel privileges to Ukrainian citizens beyond the usual 90 days,[39] and Ukrainians entering the Russia can still enter with only internal documents – by contrast, Russian citizens entering Ukraine must now show passports. In particular, this form of visa diplomacy sought to target Ukrainians of draft age who wish to 'sit out' conscription into the Ukrainian military.[40] Although how many Ukrainian men took the offer is unknown, combined together with an official welcoming rhetoric towards the refugees from the Donbas, the narrative sought to portray Russia as an inclusive society wishing peaceful coexistence, while presenting the image of Kyiv's intolerant post-Maidan government waging war on its own people. Moreover, Russia has also engaged in passportisation, offering passports in Georgia's breakaway territories of South Ossetia and Abkhazia, as well as in the Donbas.[41] In the case of the Donbas, Russia used passportisation to

---

37 T. Bordachev and A. Skriba, 'Russia's Eurasian Integration Policies', in: D. Cadier (ed.), *The Geopolitics of Eurasian Economic Integration*, Special Report No. 21 (LSE IDEAS 2015).

38 UA Today, 'Ukrainian Parliament in Session on Visa Regime with Russia', 6 October 2016, available at: <http://uatoday.tv/politics/ukrainian-parliament-in-session-on-visa-regime-with-russia-780859.html> (accessed 6 December 2019).

39 Pravda.com.ua, Росіяни зможуть в'їжджати в Україну лише за закордонними паспортами, 3 February 2015, available at: <http://www.pravda.com.ua/news/2015/02/3/7057314/?attempt=2> (accessed 5 July 2019).

40 *Ibid.*

41 *Moscow Times*, 'Putin's "Passportisation" Move Aimed at Keeping the Donbas Conflict on Moscow's Terms', 26 April 2019, available at: <https://www.themoscowtimes.com/2019/04/26/putins-passportization-move-aimed-at-keeping-the-donbass-conflict-on-moscows-terms-a65405> (accessed 27 April 2019).

increase pressure on the Ukrainian government, and as further steps to its employment of 'visa diplomacy'.

It is nevertheless noteworthy that, given ongoing confrontation and attempts to shape the neighbourhood, citizens of Moldova and Ukraine enjoy the most privileges in terms of cross-border mobility – currently, they are the only countries in Europe whose citizens enjoy visa-free travel from Lisbon to Vladivostok.

It is possible that Georgia may soon follow suit as there are also ongoing discussions about the simplification of visa procedures for Georgians entering Russia. Russia imposed a visa regime on Georgia in 2000,[42] with Georgia retaliating in suit although unilaterally simplifying visa requirements for Russians in 2004. Moreover, Georgia also used visa diplomacy towards Russia in the context of the 2008 conflict, granting Russian citizens visa-free travel in 2012. As the Georgian President Mikheil Saakashvili noted in an evident public relations stunt: 'Let every citizen of the Russian Federation know that he can come to Georgia without visa to do business, spend vacations on our resorts, visit relatives and friends'.[43] Responding to overtures of the Georgian government towards a normalisation of relations, Russia simplified visa procedures for Georgians, removing the requirement of a host invite.[44]

In this sense, rhetoric by the EU and Russia note the inclusiveness of both sides in promoting cross-border mobility with the neighbourhood countries. In each case, however, the degree of inclusiveness remains sketchy as the EU and Russia pursue their respective goals. Nevertheless, with ongoing trends towards the pursuit of a visa-free or a simplified visa regime by both the EU and Russia, increasingly more and more citizens of the neighbourhood countries may enjoy the possibility of travelling freely from Lisbon to Vladivostok, ironically thanks to the on-going confrontation between the EU and Russia.

2.3 *Labour Migration*
Despite the use of visa bans and facilitation of short-term visas, labour migration is continuously showing an important dynamic, highlighting its important

---

42 The official reason given by Russia was that Georgia became a safe haven for Chechen terrorists. See NewsRU.com, Россия ввела визовый режим с Грузией в наказание за ее лояльность к чеченским боевикам, 5 December 2000, available at: <https://www.newsru.com/russia/05dec2000/visa_deal.html> (accessed 10 December 2019).

43 Russkyi Mir Foundation, 'Georgia Introduces Visa-Free Travel for Russians', 1 March 2012, available at: <https://russkiymir.ru/en/news/128157/> (accessed 10 July 2019).

44 *Eurasian Review*, 'Russia Eases Visa Rules for Georgia', 23 December 2015, available at: <http://www.eurasiareview.com/23122015-russia-eases-visa-rules-for-georgia/> (accessed 15 August 2019).

role in both the EU's and Russia's visa diplomacy. In the case of the EU, net migration contributed almost 0.9 million of people, or 62% of the total population growth in 2010.[45] According to the European Commission, 'Despite the current economic crisis and unemployment rates, European countries are facing labour market shortages and vacancies that cannot be filled by the domestic workforce in specific sectors, e.g. in health, science and technology.'[46] Moreover, by the Commission's admission, 'All indicators show that some of the additional and specific skills needed in the future can be found only outside the EU.'[47]

In the case of Russia, the most negative projections show that Russia's population is projected to decrease by 16% from 146 million by 2050,[48] all despite the fact that an estimated 9 million people arrived in Russia between 1990 and 2014 and there was some modest growth in the past two years.[49] In fact, while in 2013 2.4 million foreign nationals from the post-Soviet countries and beyond were legally registered to work in Russia, the numbers can be even higher, with circa 16–18 million illegal migrants currently living and working in Russia.[50] Thus, both the EU and Russia are not only facing declining demographics but, crucially, also declining populations in traditional countries of emigration in the neighbourhood.[51]

Admittedly, Russia remains the key country of destination for migrants from the post-Soviet space. As of 1 January 2015, there were 2.4 million Ukrainians, 579,493 Azeris, 561,033 Moldovans, 517,828 Belarusians and 480,017 Armenians residing on the territory of Russia,[52] as well as over 1 million Georgians.[53] In the case of the EU, the migration numbers from the common neighbourhood remain significantly lower. For example, with 60.4% of the total, in 2013 the

---

45 European Commission, 'The Global Approach to Migration and Mobility', COM (2011) 743 final, 3.
46 *Ibid.*
47 *Ibid.*
48 Pew Research Centre, *Attitudes About Ageing: A Global Perspective* (2014).
49 S. Aleksashenko, 'The Russian Economy in 2050: Heading for Labour-based Stagnation' (Brookings Institution 2015).
50 Pluim et al., *op. cit.* note 10, 10–11.
51 In the neighbourhood countries, the trends are even more worrying. According to the International Centre for Migration Policy Development's projections, by 2025 the population of Georgia is expected to decrease by 17% and that of Belarus by 14% due to fertility rates, excluding the possibilities of emigration. See Pluim et al., *op. cit.* note 10, 12.
52 Aleksashenko, *op. cit.* note 49.
53 Over a million Georgians reside in Russia. See FactCheck.ge, 13 February 2014, at: <https://factcheck.ge/en/story/11757-over-a-million-georgians-reside-in-russia> (accessed 12 December 2019).

666,000 Ukrainians represented the highest (official) number of migrants from the common neighbourhood. This also includes 210,000 Moldovans, 78,000 Belarusians, 69,000 Armenians, 55,000 Georgians and 24,000 Azeris.[54]

As in the case of Russia, the unofficial numbers are much higher. For example, while the Italian Ministry of Labour estimated that there are 141,305 Moldovans residing in Italy, the unofficial number is unknown given overstays, people taking advantage of the visa-free regime and those residing on Romanian passports.[55] Similarly, while official government surveys suggest that 1.5 million Ukrainian worked abroad between 2005 and 2008 (5.1% of the working age population),[56] the EU Neighbourhood Migration Report estimates the number of Ukrainians in the EU to be over 1 million in 2012.[57] Between 2014 and 2019, it is estimated that some 2 million Ukrainians moved to Poland alone.[58]

However, the growth trends are arguably a more important phenomena than the official figures *per se*. According to M. Jaroszewicz and M. Kindler, despite the large numbers the number of Ukrainian migrants in Russia actually decreased 48% between 2007 and 2008 and 43% between 2010 and 2012,[59] although in real terms the annexation of Crimea and the war in the Donbas have actually increased the mobility of Ukrainians (or, at least, those now living under a Russian or Russian-backed regime) and the Federal Migration Service of Russia estimates that further 500,000 Ukrainians arrived in Russia between January 2014 and July 2015.[60]

---

54 Pluim et al., *op. cit.* note 10, 6.
55 Italian Ministry of Labour and Social Policy, *The Moldovan Community: Annual Report on the Presence of Migrants in Italy*, <http://www.integrazionemigranti.gov.it/Areetematiche/PaesiComunitari-e-associazioniMigranti/Documents/ES_MOLDOVA_en.pdf> (accessed 22 November 2019).
56 M. Jaroszewicz and M. Kindler, 'Irregular Migration from Ukraine and Belarus to the EU: A Risk Analysis Study', CMR Working Papers 80/138- (Centre of Migration Research University of Warsaw 2015), 12.
57 A. Bara, A. Di Bartolomeo, A. Brunarska, S. Makaryan, S. Mananashvili and A. Weinar, 'Regional Migration Report: Eastern Europe' (Migration Policy Centre, European University Institute 2013), 7.
58 *Wall Street Journal*, 'Turning Muslims Away, Poland Welcomes Ukrainians', 26 March 2019, available at: <https://www.wsj.com/articles/turning-muslims-away-poland-welcomes-ukrainians-11553598000> (accessed 26 June 2019).
59 Jaroszewicz and Kindler, *op. cit.* note 56, 13.
60 This includes those coming as temporary refugees, those on residency permits and those on voluntary resettlement scheme for ethnic minorities. Such numbers are overestimated, although independent estimates have not been made. See M. Jaroszewicz, 'The Migration of Ukrainians in Times of Crisis', Commentary No. 187 (Centre for Eastern Studies OSW 2015).

Nevertheless, it is possible to observe that between 2002 and 2013, the number of recorded migrants from the neighbourhood within the Union tripled from 370,000 to circa 1.1 million. According to the International Centre for Migration Policy Development, this represented a 500% increase of migrants coming from Moldova, 237% from Belarus, 183% from Ukraine, 134% from Armenia, 89% from Georgia and 69% from Azerbaijan.[61] In other words, despite the ongoing attraction of the Russian labour market whether it be for language or cultural reasons, the EU is increasingly becoming an important source of employment. However, it should be pointed out that these rising numbers are not evenly spread throughout the Union. For example, despite the presence of Ukrainian and Belarusian diaspora, the Baltic states retain a mainly restrictive policy towards migration from the neighbourhood because of ongoing pressures to integrate existing Russian-speaking minorities.[62] Nevertheless, it is estimated that circa 285,187 Belarusians resided in the EU in 2012, most of them in Poland, Latvia and Lithuania, including labour migrants and political exiles.[63] Ukrainians, however, represent a much higher increase. In 2013, 191,000 Ukrainian migrants were registered in Italy, a figure increasing to 233,000 in 2014. In the case of the Czech Republic, 104,000 Ukrainian are now officially registered, forming the largest migrant group (after Slovaks).[64] Although the numbers remain similar as those in Germany, they are statistically significant as Ukrainians now represent 30% of all foreign nationals in a country of 10.5 million.

In Poland, the numbers are even higher. In fact, in 2015 52,000 Ukrainians held residency permits in Poland, while an estimated 400,000 were registered on temporary contracts. As M. Jaroszewicz points out, this represents a twofold increase in the issuance of temporary permits to Ukrainians between 2014 and 2015, a phenomenon further spurred by the war in the Donbas, economic problems in Ukraine and stagnation in the Russian economy.[65] Nevertheless, while the EU's rhetoric is still largely concerned with visa liberalisation for a 90-day visa (rather than addressing the above-mentioned labour migration trends), owing to the political impact of the migration crisis Russia has been more proactive in using labour migration as a form of visa diplomacy while, as noted earlier, using EU rules and regulations as a *raison d'etre* for tightening administrative procedures that guide cross-border mobility.[66]

---

61 Pluim *et al.*, *op. cit.* note 10, 6.
62 Jaroszewicz and Kindler, *op. cit.* note 56, 27.
63 *Ibid.*, 15.
64 Jaroszewicz, *op. cit.* note 60.
65 *Ibid.*
66 Korneev, *op. cit.* note 14, 609.

Even more interestingly, Russia has copied the EU's four freedoms of movement (goods, capital, services and people) as the basis for its own integrationist project (the Eurasian Economic Union) in the wider post-Soviet space and, consequently, as an alternative to the Eastern Partnership. For Russia, this is a significant step because, thus far, labour migration has been regulated through bilateral agreements rather than multilateral ones.[67]

Thus, while citizens of all Commonwealth of Independent States (CIS) (with the exception of Turkmenistan but inclusive of the departed Ukraine) can stay in Russia without a job contract up to 90 days and on one-year renewable work permits, citizens of those states that are members of the EAEU may stay in the territory of any Member State indefinitely as long as they have a work contract.[68] Moreover, migration cards no longer need to be filled when travelling between the EAEU Member States, while neither the workers nor their families are required to register with law enforcement authorities if staying for less than 30 days.[69] In other words, labour migration is and will continue to be a major source of relations between the EU, Russia and the neighbourhood. However, while trends are increasingly showing growing migration to the EU, the Union has so far made little use of this form of visa diplomacy given its limited competencies in this issue and also the continued political fallout from the migration crisis. Russia, on the other hand, has been responding, recognising the importance labour migration plays in its relations with the neighbouring countries not only in terms of shaping the neighbours but also in how it is used to address Russia's own demographic issues. However, with ongoing attempts at region-building in the neighbourhood by both the EU and Russia, labour migration may prove to be an additional source of sectoral competition between the EU and Russia, and an important aspect of their respective visa diplomacy vis-à-vis the neighbourhood countries.

3   Concluding Remarks

Visas remain obstacles to social, political and economic development of wider Europe and beyond, contributing to the gap of separateness within this

---

67   C. Schenk, 'Labour Migration in the Eurasian Union: Will Freedom of Movement Trump Domestic Controls?', Policy Memo No. 378 (PONARS Eurasia 2015), 2.
68   Armenia, Belarus, Kazakhstan and Kyrgyzstan.
69   Eurasian Economic Commission, 'The Treaty on the Eurasian Economic Union Is Effective',, 1 January 2015, available at: <http://www.eurasiancommission.org/en/nae/news/Pages/01-01-2015-1.aspx> (accessed 14 March 2020).

space. According to the German Committee on Eastern European Economic Relations, slow visa application procedures cost the Germans and Russians alone an estimated €162 million annually.[70]

As this chapter has intended to show, both the EU and Russia use various forms of visa diplomacy to pursue their respective region-building and other foreign policy goals in the increasingly contested neighbourhood of Eastern Europe and the South Caucasus. Despite some use of visa bans, sanctioning coercive tools have seen limited use. Inclusive forms of visa diplomacy, on the other hand, remain the most widespread use by both EU and Russia to shape the neighbourhood in their image. However, while the EU uses the process of visa liberalisation to extend its norms and regulations, Russia has increasingly resulted to using tighter administrative controls as a way of coercing its neighbours but without abandoning established visa-free regimes. While the EU's visa diplomacy has sought to contribute to the EaP region-building project and external border management by strengthening the governance capacity of its neighbours, Russia on the other hand has instead tried to keep the post-Soviet space closer to Russia (by copying the EU's four freedoms of movement) or, at best, to prevent further disintegration in relations. Thus, even in the context of the conflict in the Donbas and Russian annexation of Ukraine, neither Russia nor Ukraine have imposed visa regimes on the other side. However, to what extent Russian aggression may contribute to more long-term alienation between the two countries and their citizens remains to be seen.

Furthermore, migration trends increasingly show that, while Russia remains the most important destination for labour migrants from the post-Soviet space as a whole, citizens of the neighbourhood countries are increasingly seeking work in the EU. Thus, one may speculate that, with demographic changes and shifting migration patterns, labour migration may become yet another sectoral source of contestation between the EU and Russia as they continue their region-building. At the same time, the competition that we have witnessed in the case of short-term visas is also having unintended consequences on the neighbours, facilitating the possibility for their citizens to increasingly travel freely from Lisbon to Vladivostok – a privilege that neither EU nor Russian citizens enjoy. Nevertheless, with ongoing contestation, the possibility of creating a common European space of freedom, security and justice remains a distant (im)possibility. The neighbourhood countries' citizens may reap some benefit but, overall, Europe

---

70   Van Elsuwege et al., *op. cit.* note 17, 31.

remains a divided space where alienation between the two sides and their respective region-building projects is in fact increasing. However, whether visa diplomacy has the potential to limit the impact of that alienation (or, in fact, widen it even further) remains to be seen.

PART 3

EU Resilience to Russian Threats

CHAPTER 10

The EU's Concept of Resilience in the Context of EU-Russia Relations

Elena Pavlova and Tatiana Romanova

1 Introduction[1]

The concept of *resilience* initially appeared in the EU's development policy and the Commission first clarified its meaning in 2012, using food crises as a case.[2] In 2015–2016, the EU further developed the concept of resilience with the view toward applying it to the relations with all its partners, including Russia. Today, the concept is omnipresent in various documents on the European Neighbourhood Policy (ENP) and development activities, as well as in the five guiding principles on the relations with Russia.[3] Most importantly, it dominates the 2016 EU's Global Strategy,[4] in which it is mentioned over 40 times. This policy document describes the present and future of EU external relations with various partners around the world, including Russia. However, the meaning, significance and applicability of the resilience concept remain a matter of contention in both political and academic circles.[5] Although many in Brussels would argue that it is just a buzzword, the reality is that resilience

---

1 This work was supported by the grant of the Russian Science Foundation (Project No. 17-18-01110).
2 European Commission, 'Communication from the Commission to the European Parliament and the Council: The EU Approach to Resilience: Learning from Food Security Crises', COM(2012) 586 final, 3 October 2012, available at: <http://ec.europa.eu/transparency/regdoc/rep/1/2012/EN/1-2012-586-EN-F1-1.Pdf> (accessed 12 February 2019).
3 F. Mogherini, 'Remarks by High Representative/Vice-President Federica Mogherini at the Press Conference following the Foreign Affairs Council', Brussels, 14 March 2016, available at: <https://eeas.europa.eu/headquarters/headquarters-homepage/5490/remarks-by-high-representativevice-president-federica-mogherini-at-the-press-conference-following-the-foreign-affairs-council_en> (accessed 12 February 2019).
4 European Union, 'Shared Vision, Common Action: A Stronger Europe. A Global Strategy for the European Union's Foreign and Security Policy', Brussels, June 2016, available at: <https://eeas.europa.eu/sites/eeas/files/eugs_review_web.pdf> (accessed 12 February 2019).
5 See, for example, W. Wagner and R. Anholt, 'Resilience as the EU Global Strategy's New Leitmotif: Pragmatic, Problematic or Promising?', *Contemporary Security Policy* 37 (3), 2016, 414–430.

dominates many EU documents (including a special communication and texts on the relations with Russia). Therefore, it deserves closer examination.

Crimean events, defined as annexation in the EU and in the West at large and as reunification in Russia, brought dramatic changes in the EU-Russian relationship. However, the preconditions for these changes existed long before. EU-Russian relations had worsened already since 2004, following the EU's big bang enlargement. Vladimir Putin's infamous Munich speech[6] sent a powerful signal of this change as it clarified that Russia was not happy with the place that the EU and the United States accorded to it. More specifically, the President of Russia stressed that the place of Russia in world politics allows it to demand equality whereas this is not granted in reality, and many important decisions are still made without Russia's participation or without its opinion being properly taken into account. The Munich speech had a rather negative effect on most Western politicians and analysts; they interpreted it as being too aggressive and, hence, adopted a more cautious wait-and-see attitude towards Russia.

The 2008 events in South Ossetia and Abkhazia (where Russia supported the authorities of these break-away entities) deepened the divide. Negotiations on a new agreement to substitute the outdated 1994 Partnership and Cooperation Agreement (PCA) stalled because the views of the EU and Russia were so different – Russia wished to just reiterate the World Trade Organisation (WTO) provisions whereas the EU insisted on deeper liberalisation. The Partnership for Modernisation failed to stand up to the expectations of both sides: the EU looked first and foremost for liberal reforms, while Russia mostly searched for innovations and legitimation of its own policy course.[7] Initiatives, such as visa-free travel or a comprehensive free trade area, were less and less realistic. Analysts on both sides emphasised growing alienation of the EU and Russia.[8]

In sum, by 2013, EU-Russian relations were already frosty. The 2014 Ukrainian events resulted in the imposition of sanctions against Russia, which included the suspension of many activities and diplomatic initiatives that had stalled before. The year 2014 thus signified a new stage in EU-Russia relations when

---

6 V. Putin, 'Speech and the Following Discussion at the Munich Conference on Security Policy', 10 February 2007, available at: <http://kremlin.ru/events/president/transcripts/24034> (accessed 12 February 2019).

7 T. Romanova and E. Pavlova, 'What Modernisation? The Case of Russian Partnerships for Modernisation with the European Union and Its Member States', *Journal of Contemporary European Studies* 22 (4), 2014, 499–517.

8 O. Potiomkina and N. Kaveshnikov, 'Russia and EU: "Cold Summer" of 2007', *Contemporary Europe [Sovremennaya Evropa]*, 3, 2007, 24–39; T. Casier and J. DeBardeleben (eds.), *EU-Russia Relations in Crisis: Understanding Diverging Perceptions* (Routledge 2018).

the logics of confrontation and competition nearly completely supplemented notions of partnership and cooperation. This new logic of EU-Russia relations was one of the reasons (together with various other crises that the EU faced) for the concepts of principled pragmatism and resilience to be introduced in the EU's Global Strategy. However, resilience rather than principled pragmatism became the focus of the EU's Global Strategy. Being referred to only a few times, principled pragmatism ultimately became a justification for resilience because the latter is built on the basis of the EU's principles (norms and values) and the past experience of their promotion.

This chapter aims at identifying the specificity of the EU's policy towards Russia today as it comes out in Brussels's interpretation of resilience. To achieve this goal, this chapter uses contemporary academic debates on the concept of resilience and on pragmatism. The chapter then identifies with the help of critical discourse analysis[9] the most important connotations of the resilience concept in EU foreign policy documents as well as in the commentaries which clarify how these documents were developed. The section that follows is devoted to the normative dimension of the EU's concept of resilience while the third section describes Russian activities in the international arena as a threat to the EU's resilience and looks at how this conceptualisation of resilience leads to the perpetuation of geopolitical competition in the shared neighbourhood. The chapter concludes by reflecting on how future EU-Russia relations might develop on the basis of the concept of resilience.

2 The Concept of Resilience in the EU's Official Discourse: A Defensive Normative Power Europe?

'Resilience' is not a new word in either political or academic discourse. It is mentioned in numerous documents on natural disasters, humanitarian crises and development, developed by the UN and its bodies,[10] as well as in various discussions of the Organisation for Economic Co-operation and Development (OECD)[11] and some other international organisations. Resilience is also part

---

9   N. Fairclough, *Critical Discourse Analysis* (Addison Wesley 1995).
10 'Transforming Our World: The 2030 Agenda for Sustainable Development. Resolution adopted by the General Assembly on 25 September 2015', available at: <http://www.un.org/ga/search/view_doc.asp?symbol=A/RES/70/1&Lang=E> (accessed 12 February 2019).
11 'OECD 2014. Guidelines for Resilience Systems Analysis, OECD Publishing', 15 December 2014, available at: <https://www.oecd.org/dac/conflict-fragilityresilience/Resilience%20Systems%20Analysis%20FINAL.pdf> (accessed 12 February 2019).

and parcel of the security concept (including prevention of terrorist activities) in some states, the UK being the most evident and widely cited example. The EU's initial application of the term *resilience* was consistent with the general academic and political discussion on this topic. However, the preparation of the Global Strategy brought a serious change in the EU's understanding and articulation of the concept of resilience. In fact, the Strategy signified that resilience became a new norm of European integration.

The origin of the contemporary academic concept of *resilience* is usually traced to the 1973 article by Crawford Holling, who defined it as 'a measure of the persistence of systems and of their ability to absorb change and disturbance and still maintain the same relationships between populations or state variables'.[12] The first important conclusion from this definition is that resilience is a systemic feature which allows the system to survive. Resilience is therefore immanent and does not need any additional articulation or formulation; it allows any system to survive. The *system* – when researching political international phenomena – can be understood as a community, a state or the world in its entirety. In this particular case, this is the international neoliberal system of governance. Yet resilience is the quality of any system.

Second, the key elements of resilience are (1) resources, which are in direct relations with (2) the challenges and threats to the system; both are internal to the system. As David Chandler argues, 'The dichotomy between the subject and the object is disappearing here'.[13] This feature represents the key difference between the concept of resilience and the theory of securitisation. The latter is focused on the study of how the threat to a reference object is articulated whereas the concept of resilience studies grass-rooted practices of a system, which can be transformed into resources to counter challenges or threats.

Third, and logically resulting from the previous point, because both threats/challenges and resources are internal to the system, efforts to bring resilience from outside have been criticised on many occasions.[14]

Finally, ethical connotations are not important in the academic concept of resilience. Resilience is a norm of the system but not a moral societal norm. Resilience becomes a positive feature if the system, which has it, is worth

---

12 C.S. Holling, 'Resilience and Stability of Ecological Systems', *Annual Review of Ecology and Systematics* 4 (1), 1973, 14.

13 D. Chandler, *Resilience: The Governance of Complexity* (Routledge 2014), 8.

14 P. Rogers, 'The Etymology and Genealogy of a Contested Concept', in: D. Chandler, J. Coaffee (eds.), *The Routledge Handbook of International Resilience* (Routledge 2017), 13–25; S. Bracke, 'Is the Subaltern Resilient? Notes on Agency and Neoliberal Subjects', *Cultural Studies* 30 (5), 2016, 839–855.

existing, and negative if the system in question should not exist or is harmful in its present form. For example, resilience of an authoritarian system is viewed in a negative way, whereas resilience of a democratic system is welcomed. But by itself, resilience is neither good nor bad.

The EU's academic, bureaucratic and political elites departed from the above-described aspects of the resilience concept in several ways. First, having proclaimed resilience a new normative trend of European integration, and having focused on its achievement, Brussels declared its readiness to support both its own resilience and that of the neighbouring countries as well as of neighbours of the neighbours, all the way to Central Asia and Central Africa. Second, while resilience presupposes that both a threat/challenge and relevant resources make up the same system (i.e., the multilateral system in this case),[15] the EU's Global Strategy stresses external threats to its *resilience* and defines the latter as 'the ability of states and societies to reform, thus withstanding and recovering from internal and external crises'.[16]

Third, unlike in the academic discussion, distinctive ethical connotations emerge in the EU's discussion of resilience. The EU articulates resilience in a normative way and the very discussion on enhancing resilience is transformed from an operational and analytical level to the ideological level. The EU's concept of resilience is therefore linked to the values that the EU has been promoting since the 1970s and that led to the EU being conceptualised as a normative power Europe.[17] However, the articulation of the EU's concept of resilience is different from the previous debates about European (and, hence, global) norms. Values like democracy or human rights have been debated for centuries, whereas resilience is imported in the EU's discourse mostly from the academic debates (and before that from technical and environmental disciplines) with no societal discussion.

The EU only states that a 'resilient state is a secure state, and security is key for prosperity and democracy',[18] declaring that democracy is resilient by definition. At the same time, the EU specifies that a 'resilient society featuring democracy, trust in institutions, and sustainable development lies at the heart of a resilient state',[19] thus concluding that resilience leads to democracy.

---

15   N. Tocci, 'Resilience and the Role of the European Union in the World', *Contemporary Security Policy*, 2019, 41 (2), 2020, 176–194.
16   European Union, *op. cit.* note 4.
17   I. Manners, 'Normative Power Europe: A Contradiction in Terms?', *Journal of Common Market Studies* 40 (2), 2002, 235–258.
18   European Union, *op. cit.* note 4.
19   *Ibid.*

Hence, the EU brings in a normative trend, which on the one hand is new compared to the previously promoted values, and on the other hand will be instrumental to reinforce the already articulated values. As a result, from the theoretical point of view, resilience transforms the normative power Europe concept from the mechanism to promote the norms and their dissemination to an instrument of their protection. The resulting mechanism can be called a 'defensive normative power Europe'.

This evolution is important in relation to Russia because its international agenda is sometimes implicitly,[20] and sometimes explicitly,[21] referred to as an external challenge. Hence, resilience as a norm has to protect the EU and its neighbours (particularly in the East) from Russia. This articulation means that the EU can use resilience in a wider way compared to the academic reading of the concept. It becomes an instrument for a new stage of Russia's exclusion as the Other in the context of the idea about European identity. As a result, the EU acquires a possibility to strengthen its internal policies and cohesion through the construction of a new external policy towards Russia, similar to previously established patterns, as thoroughly analysed by Iver Neumann.[22] In the context of the overall EU crisis, resilience as an essential feature of the European integration allows the EU to reassess the image of the Other in its identification discourse and to strengthen the European unity in the face of an external threat. Russia in this EU articulation stays outside of any potential solution, and outside of the discussion on any potential reconciliation.

These conditions leave all the Russian elite – those who are pro-Kremlin, those maintaining neutrality or those who are liberal – perplexed. For example, Andrey Kortunov writes that 'both Russian and foreign Western-oriented scholars make some believe that Russia could simply return to the European world and order that existed 15, 20 or even 30 years ago. That European world, which existed twenty or thirty years ago, does not exist any longer'.[23] Hence, the problem of 'Russia's return to Europe' remains open and the target is

---

20   *Ibid.*
21   Mogherini, *op. cit.* note 3; European Commission and European External Action Service, 'Joint Communication to the European Parliament and the Council: A Strategic Approach to Resilience in the EU's External Action', JOIN(2017) 21 final, 7 June 2017, available at: <https://eeas.europa.eu/sites/eeas/files/join_2017_21_f1_communication_from_commission_to_inst_en_v7_p1_916039.pdf> (accessed 12 February 2019).
22   I.B. Neumann, *Russia and the Idea of Europe: A Study in Identity and International Relations* (Routledge 2017).
23   A. Kortunov, 'Will Russia Return to Europe?', 17 August 2018, available at: <http://russiancouncil.ru/analytics-and-comments/analytics/vernetsya-li-rossiya-v-evropu/> (accessed 12 February 2019).

vague. The question of further cooperation between the EU and Russia also remains unanswered. Evgeny Gontmakher, a Russian public figure and scholar, stresses that the classical question of 'what to do' remained unanswered by his European colleagues, the only exception being Russia's implementation of the Minsk agreements.[24] In other words, what politics has to follow after this implementation is not clear even for Russian liberals. Our interviews in various EU bodies, conducted in 2017 and 2018, also demonstrate that the question about the long-term future of EU-Russian relations remains an enigma for EU politicians and bureaucrats.[25]

This situation complicates the position of the Russian political elite, which is used to following the course of the European Union. Most structures, documents and instruments that exist in EU-Russian relations have been put forward by Brussels. This is not to say that the Kremlin ever ignored its own interests but rather to describe the pattern that was formed in EU-Russian relations already in the early 1990s. Today, when Russia is openly and officially announced as the Other, Russian pro-Western elites are in dismay. On the one hand, they believe that Russia has to make the first move to demonstrate its good intentions. On the other hand, it is obvious that the EU does not trust Russia and rejects most of its initiatives (be it trade or investments, cooperation on terrorism, Syria or cyber security). It looks like an initiative for any selective engagement should come from the EU to be accepted for the latter. And Russian diplomats confirm this, repeating on various occasions that they are ready to engage on any issue which the EU will be ready to engage.

The Global Strategy further deteriorates this situation because it draws a clear line between the EU's resilience, other countries which either have or can develop resilience and the Other (in this case, official Russia and its foreign policy) which is perceived to be the challenge to this resilience and from which the EU and its partners have to defend themselves. Normative power Europe focused on the promotion of neoliberal norms and a priori presupposed the inclusion of new members that have recognised these values as agents of these norms.[26] Therefore, Russia had a chance to be included in these discussions on norms (maybe not as an equal player but at least as a significant one, with a place at the table). Now, the EU discourse locates Russia either outside of

---

24   E. Gontmakher, 'How to Overcome Alienation from Europe', 22 October 2018, available at: <https://snob.ru/entry/167148> (accessed 12 February 2019).
25   For more details, see T. Romanova, 'The Concept of 'Resilience' in EU External Relations: A Critical Assessment', *European Foreign Affairs Review* 24 (3), 2019, 349–366.
26   E. Pavlova and T. Romanova, 'Normative Power: Some Theory Aspects and Contemporary Practice of Russia and the EU' [in Russian], *Polis. Political Studies* 1, 2017, 162–176.

this system or alternatively as a follower of the EU, as a recipient of what it will suggest if Moscow chooses to harness its ambitions.

In sum, the EU's political and bureaucratic elites, on the one hand, make active use of the term *resilience* in the official discourse. On the other hand, key theoretical studies on resilience are ignored. Resilience comes out in the EU's discourse as an empty signifier that is linked to the evolution of the EU's mechanisms of normative influence. This approach has so far brought more problems than solutions, including in the EU's relations with Russia which are at a dead end.

The call to increase resilience of both the EU and its partner countries is linked to threats, many of which (energy supply, strategic communication, cyber security) are linked to Russia. As a result, the logics of confrontation with the Kremlin as the normative Other emerges. Among other things, it manifests itself in the confrontation over the post-Soviet space (or shared/contested neighbourhood). This logics of confrontation is examined in more detail in the next section of this chapter.

3 Russia as a Source of Threat to the Resilience of the EU and Its Neighbours and the Logic of Confrontation in the EU's External Activities

The most important element of the Global Strategy is the readiness of the EU to support the resilience of the Union and to promote the resilience externally. The Strategy openly declared that the EU 'will therefore promote resilience in its surrounding regions',[27] first and foremost in the ENP countries, Turkey and the Western Balkans. Moreover, the EU states the interests of EU citizens 'to invest in the resilience of states and societies to the east stretching into Central Asia, and to the south down to Central Africa'.[28] In fact, the EU openly declares its intention to actively participate in the internal affairs of other countries to achieve democratic resilience, as well as the resilience of human rights and of the rule of law.

Consequently, not only do norms make up the object that the EU's concept of resilience defends but resilience is also meant to preserve the EU's position of the normative leader. The Global Strategy is not explicit about it. Yet, its main author, Nathalie Tocci, in a 2016 article discusses the 'deepest existential

---

27 European Union, *op. cit.* note 4.
28 *Ibid.*

crisis' and the wish of the Europeans 'to see a stronger EU role in the world'.[29] At the same time, she refers to the concept of soft power.[30] The Global Strategy also mentions it, saying that the EU 'has always prided itself on its soft power – and it will keep doing so, because we are the best in this field'.[31] The text is ambiguous because on the one hand it implies that the concept is irrelevant now, yet on the other hand it remains a valid instrument for the EU to enhance its influence in international relations through being attractive to the others. In particular, the Global Strategy argues that today's politics has to be more realistic but should not depart from the norms and principles that were its foundation in the years before.

The logical connection between principled pragmatism and resilience was made before the Global Strategy. Jessica Schmidt, referring to the work of John Dewey, underlined that being less ideologised, principled pragmatism explains existing practices of resilience better than neoliberalism. Its key element is the process of constant self-learning, which is based on one's own experience. This approach allows for focusing on consequences rather than reasons for actions.[32] In this case, the EU revises the logics of its foreign policy, focusing not so much on the reasons but rather on the consequences of its potential activities.

The concept of principled pragmatism introduced by John Ruggie, on the other hand, emphasises norms. According to him, *principled pragmatism* is defined as 'an unflinching commitment to the principle of strengthening the promotion and protection of human rights as it relates to businesses, coupled with a pragmatic attachment to what works best in creating change where it matters most – in the daily lives of people'.[33]

The principled pragmatism of the Global Strategy is a symbiosis of both approaches. On the one hand, principles are declared as stemming 'as much from a realistic assessment of the strategic environment as from an idealistic aspiration to advance a better world'.[34] On the other hand, following the

---

29 N. Tocci, 'The Making of the EU Global Strategy', *Contemporary Security Policy* 37 (3), 2016, 462.
30 *Ibid.*
31 European Union, *op. cit.* note 4.
32 J. Schmidt, 'Intuitively Neoliberal? Towards a Critical Understanding of Resilience Governance', *European Journal of International Relations* 21 (2) 2015, 402–426.
33 J. Ruggie, 'Principled Pragmatism – The Way Forward for Business and Human Rights', United Nations Human Rights, Office of the High Commissioner for Human Rights, 2010, available at: <http://www.ohchr.org/EN/NewsEvents/Pages/PrincipledpragmatismBusinessHR.aspx. > (accessed 12 February 2019).
34 European Union, *op. cit.* note 4.

theoretical discussion of pragmatism, the Global Strategy stresses the importance of the past experience as a source for the future course. *Pragmatism* in the promotion of norms here refers to the reassessment of the role of the EU where normative power Europe led to the decline of the EU's influence as a result of the gradual inclusion of other players in the discussion on norms.

Pragmatism, according to Richard Rorty can be understood only 'within a certain kind of polity with a certain kind of history'.[35] At first sight, Tocci fully embraces this point of view. She argues that

> the pragmatism comes in the diagnosis of the geopolitical predicament the EU finds itself in. It echoes a rediscovery of pragmatism philosophy that entails a rejection of universal truths, an emphasis on the practical consequences of acts, and a focus on local practices and dynamics.[36]

Yet in the following paragraph she writes that

> while different pathways, recipes and models are to be embraced, international law and its underlying norms should be the benchmark of what is acceptable for the EU and what is not.[37]

In other words, the universality of norms, undermined in the preceding paragraph, disappears, while the idea of the EU's leadership is maintained. The EU's experience (as a coalition of European states) in the norms' promotion comes out as the maintenance of its leadership in the formation of global normative trends. This leadership is no less significant than the promotion of norms *per se*.

This aspect became so clear-cut as a result of both the EU's internal developments and the Russian activities in Ukraine; it also defined a new EU agenda in its policy towards Russia. This new logics of the EU towards Russia was formulated in several EU texts. The first one is the speech of Federica Mogherini, devoted to the five guiding principles of the relations with Russia as developed by the EU.[38] When it comes to resilience, it says the EU will strengthen its internal resilience 'in particular on energy security, hybrid threats and strategic

---

35 R. Rorty, *Objectivity, Relativism, and Truth: Philosophical Papers* (Cambridge University Press 1991), 76.
36 N. Tocci, *Framing the EU Global Strategy: A Stronger Europe in a Fragile World* (Palgrave Macmillan 2017), 64.
37 *Ibid.* 65.
38 Mogherini, *op. cit.* note 3.

communication'.³⁹ The EU's dependence on the import of Russian oil and natural gas is not new but the EU visibly tones down the rhetoric about market integration and interdependence and emphasises the EU's vulnerability. Strategic communication and cyber threats are relatively new. They form the part of the so-called 'hybrid threats', which the EU defines as follows:

> The concept aims to capture the mixture of coercive and subversive activity, conventional and unconventional methods (i.e. diplomatic, military, economic, technological), which can be used in a coordinated manner by state or non-state actors to achieve specific objectives while remaining below the threshold of formally declared warfare.⁴⁰

The Global Strategy embraces these concerns while putting them into a global perspective. Russia and its present foreign policy is portrayed as a strategic challenge to the EU because of its 'illegal annexation of Crimea' and 'destabilisation of eastern Ukraine'.⁴¹ Although the Global Strategy does not link Russia with threats to the resilience of the EU and its neighbours, today's Brussels firmly associates the threats in question with Russia. Moreover, while the five principles include the development of the relations with the Eastern neighbours, the Global Strategy already talks about enhancing their resilience – hence, extending the EU's concept to them. The third document, which is relevant in this case, is the 2017 Communication on resilience, which explicitly makes a link between the resilience of the EU and its neighbours, and threats coming from Russia. Moreover, the document says that resilience is essential for their security, in particular in countering these threats.⁴²

For both long-known (energy) and new (hybrid) threats, the EU first and foremost mobilises its internal resources. For example, in the case of energy supply these are crisis stocks, development of internal resources (e.g. renewables), energy efficiency and decreased consumption as well as creation of alternative transportation routes.⁴³ In the case of fake news and strategic

---

39 European Commission and European External Action Service, *op. cit.* note 21.
40 European Commission and European External Action Service, 'Joint Communication to the European Parliament and the Council. Joint Framework on Countering Hybrid Threats a European Union Response', Brussels, 6 April, JOIN(2016) 18 final, available at: <https://eur-lex.europa.eu/legal-content/en/TXT/?uri=CELEX%3A52016JC0018> (accessed 12 February 2019). See also the contribution by A. Marazis (chapter 12) in this volume.
41 European Union, *op. cit.* note 4.
42 European Commission and European External Action Service, *op. cit.* note 21.
43 European Commission, 'Communication to the European Parliament, the Council, the European Economic and Social Committee, the Committee of the Regions and the

communication, the EU promotes fact-checking groups and disinformation codes but also education of citizens.[44] The EU also plans to develop various schemes and minimum security rules and codes of conduct for cyber space.[45]

As a result, the EU tries with these activities to change grass-rooted practices and to include the maximum number of its residents to the conscious resilience against Russia-related threats. Moreover, the EU also passes to citizens a responsibility for their security. All these aspects are in line with the academic concept of resilience. At the same time, the attention of citizens is focused on threats coming from Russia, which reinforces the EU's and Russia's drift away from each other.

According to the EU's documents, Russia-related threats are directed not only against the EU but also against neighbouring countries; and the EU has to assist them through the promotion of their resilience and through the export of its practices. At first sight, the notion of resilience, which is focused on internal resources and grass-rooted practices, gives the EU an excellent chance to avoid accusations in neocolonialism. However, as Ana Juncos points out, Brussels cannot dodge these accusations because the EU shifts the responsibility on the civil society of the countries only where it promotes resilience.[46] Such EU promotion of resilience, as indicated above, is not in line with the contemporary discussion on resilience.

A shared definition of Russia-related threats becomes an important resource for the cooperation between the EU and neighbouring countries.[47] The resulting export of Brussels' understanding of resilience creates one more field of

---

European Investment Bank: A Framework Strategy for a Resilient Energy Union with a Forward-looking Climate Change Policy', COM(2015) 80 final, 25 May 2015, available at: <https://eur-lex.europa.eu/resource.html?uri=cellar:1bd46c90-bdd4-11e4-bbe1-01aa75ed71a1.0001.03/DOC_1&format=PDF > (accessed 12 February 2019).

44   High Level Expert Group, 'A Multi-dimensional Approach to Disinformation: Report of the Independent High Level Group on Fake News and Online Disinformation', 12 March 2018, available at: <https://ec.europa.eu/digital-single-market/en/news/final-report-high-level-expert-group-fake-news-and-online-disinformation> (accessed 12 February 2019).

45   'Resilience, Deterrence and Defence: Building Strong Cybersecurity for the EU', 11 December 2018, available at: <https://ec.europa.eu/digital-single-market/en/news/resilience-deterrence-and-defence-building-strong-cybersecurity-europe> (accessed 12 February 2019); European Commission and European External Action Service, 'Joint Communication to the European Parliament and the Council: Resilience, Deterrence and Defence: Building Strong Cybersecurity for the EU', JOIN(2017) 450 final, 13 September 2017. See also the contribution by A. Marazis (chapter 12) in this volume.

46   A.E. Juncos, 'Resilience as the New EU Foreign Policy Paradigm: A Pragmatist Turn?', *European Security* 26 (1), 2016, 1–18.

47   Interview, EEAS official, 22 October 2018, Brussels.

confrontation between Moscow and Brussels. This is a new confrontation for normative influence, or a new turn in this spiral.

In sum, the EU applies its resilience concept to Russia with a good deal of ambiguity. It formulates resilience as a norm and draws a line between Europe (which potentially includes neighbouring countries) and Russia. This articulation of external policy through Othering leads to the construction of a new external relations' logics; that of confrontation over normative influence. On the other hand, resilience is represented as a potentially universal norm because it is linked to democracy, rule of law and good governance. Hence, Russia is excluded as a potential agent of normative discussions but remains a potential recipient of the results of these discussions. Similarly, the EU reserves the right to define which practices constitute a (universal) threat to resilience (in this case, those coming from Russia), which stresses the existence of a shared security system in wider Europe – the system in which Russia is an integral part. This EU agenda corresponds to the logic of the theory of resilience, which is rooted in the idea of systemic origin of threats. Defining Russian foreign policy as a threat, Brussels includes Russia in the same system.

4 Conclusion: The EU's Discourse on Resilience and the Future of EU-Russian Relations

The EU's Global Strategy mentions Russia only a few times, mostly negatively. Probably, the only positive thing is the phrase that 'the EU and Russia are interdependent'. However, even in this context, the document adds that the EU 'will therefore engage Russia to discuss disagreements and cooperate if and when our interests overlap'.[48] This wording stresses that there are no overlaps today and that they are possible only in the future. This situation is extremely dangerous for both the EU and Russia. The reasons for the frosty relations are serious but the problem is that both parties are adopting a wait-and-see attitude and neither is looking for a solution.

The EU's resilience concept provokes more questions than answers. The peculiar use of the academic concept of resilience complicates the analysis of the EU's new foreign policy course. Resilience as a new norm of European integration remains difficult for any day-to-day decision-making. The case of Russia is not exceptional but rather vividly illustrates this feature of the EU's resilience concept.

---

48   European Union, *op. cit.* note 4.

First and foremost, the concept of resilience allows the EU to bring its policy and norms in opposition to those of Russia. As a result, a new cycle of Otherness emerges in the identification discourse of the EU. From a potential partner Russia turns into an Other, whose behaviour leads the EU to emphasise the norms that are core in the articulation of the European identity. Moreover, the EU formulates a new normative trend, that of resilience, which is closely linked to the set of previous values and allows for drawing a border between the EU and its members on the one hand, and Russia, which challenges the norms, on the other hand. From the theoretical point of view, a defensive normative power emerges because resilience is targeted at defending the norms that form the core of the EU identity (rather than promoting them as in previous years). The EU's internal resilience should be therefore strengthened. Russia, for its part, turns into a non-democratic state with which a productive dialogue is highly unlikely but yet it preserves the status of a potential recipient of the norms.

Second, the problem is exacerbated by the fact that Russia recognises the EU's authority (as a successor of European states) and still expects the EU to show the initiative towards reconciliation.

Third, the EU either consciously or not reinforces its own authority as the agent of norms through resilience. In doing so, it draws on pragmatism and its experience in promotion of values in previous years. It is in this light that one has to interpret principled pragmatism. Brussels counters any threat from Russia with the help of historical practice of creating a new norm.

Fourth, the EU describes with the concept of resilience its internal achievements. However, the key problem of this tactic is its artificiality: while the norms of democracy or human rights took ages to form through endless discussions, resilience is only borrowed from academic studies and filled with normative content. As a result, the number of articles which question the way the EU's resilience can be implemented constantly grows.[49] This fuzziness, however, does not do any good for Russia or its relations with Brussels because the concept just reinforces the opposition between the EU and Russia, with the latter being the threat to the resilience of the former and their neighbours.

Fifth, the concept of resilience becomes an instrument of the EU's competition with Russia in the post-Soviet space. Declaring a common for democracies' understanding of resilience and a shared set of threats coming from Russia, the EU declares its readiness to support the resilience of neighbouring

---

49 E. Korosteleva, 'Paradigmatic or Critical? Resilience as a New Turn in EU Governance for the Neighbourhood', *Journal of International Relations and Development* 23 (3), 2018, 682–700.

countries, extrapolating its practices to this region. Hence, the EU stresses its commonality with post-Soviet states through opposition to Russia. Moscow takes this agenda as a serious challenge, which it has difficulty in accepting.

Therefore, the articulation of Russian foreign policy as a threat, the articulation of the EU's external strategy through the opposition of the EU and Russia, leaves Moscow at a dead end. Being used to following Brussels' initiatives, Moscow is not ready to demonstrate any new type of behaviour or suggest a solution. Moreover, it is highly unlikely that the EU is ready to accept any initiative coming from the Kremlin. As a result, the only way that Russia can change the existing EU-Russian relationship is to reverse its present foreign policy course. This change is difficult to envisage for the time being. Moreover, Russian political, bureaucratic and academic elites (both conservative and Western oriented) have no clue as to what pattern of relations the EU can offer if that change in the Russian foreign policy course happens.

CHAPTER 11

The EU's Energy Relationship with Russia

Between Resilience and Engagement

Marco Siddi

1   Introduction

Energy security is one of the key policy fields mentioned in the five principles guiding the EU's approach to Russia, which were outlined by High Representative for Foreign Affairs and Security Policy Federica Mogherini and endorsed by the EU's Foreign Affairs Council in March 2016. Energy security is included under the third principle, which concerns strengthening the EU's internal resilience, next to hybrid threats and strategic communication.[1] However, due to their largely transactional and cooperative nature, EU-Russia energy relations can be seen as falling under the fourth principle too, which focuses on selective engagement with Russia in areas 'where there is a clear European Union's interest'.[2] As Russia is the main external supplier of fossil fuels to the EU, and as it is in the EU's economic interest to maintain this trade with Moscow, energy can be considered an area where engagement with Russia is necessary.

The pertinence of both the third and the fourth principles to the energy relationship reveals a crucial duality in the EU's approach to Russia after the Ukraine crisis. From a political perspective, EU Member States such as Poland and the Baltics consider dependence on Russian energy supplies as a security issue. This contributes to explaining why energy was included under the third principle. To tackle energy security concerns, the EU also adopted an Energy Security Strategy (in May 2014) and the Energy Union framework (in February 2015), which included among their goals the diversification of energy suppliers and strengthening resilience against supply shock–induced energy crises.[3]

---

1   See Remarks by High Representative/Vice-President Federica Mogherini at the press conference following the Foreign Affairs Council, 14 March 2016, available at: <https://eeas.europa.eu/headquarters/headquarters-homepage/5490_en> (accessed 15 January 2019).
2   *Ibid.*
3   European Commission, 'European Energy Security Strategy', COM (2014) 330 final, 28 May 2014; European Commission; 'A Framework Strategy for a Resilient Energy Union with a Forward-looking Climate Change Policy', COM (2015) 80 final, 25 February 2015.

Despite the persistence of serious disagreements between Brussels and Moscow especially in the security, legal and normative arenas, EU-Russia energy trade has experienced a considerable increase since 2016, particularly with regard to gas.[4] This development reflects the other aspect of the EU's dual approach: from an economic perspective, the EU finds it beneficial to cooperate with Russia in the energy domain. The EU and Russia remain interdependent in the sphere of energy, which is thus one of the few sectors where a substantial level of cooperation has continued after the Ukraine crisis.[5]

This chapter explores the duality in the EU's approach to energy relations with Russia. The analysis proceeds as follows. It begins by outlining the implications of the Ukraine crisis for EU energy relations with Russia. The five principles are put into the context of the crisis and of relevant EU policy responses (such as the Energy Union), as well as of the market developments that impinge on political choices. Subsequently, the chapter discusses the measures undertaken to strengthen the EU's resilience in the energy domain. It argues that energy policy is a complex field where numerous factors matter. Within the EU, it is an area of shared competence between the Union and its Member States – as specified in Article 194 of the Treaty on the Functioning of the European Union (TFEU) – many of which have very different national energy portfolios and diverging attitudes towards Russian energy imports.[6] EU and national legal frameworks exist, which are generally oriented towards the competitiveness and liberalisation of energy markets and thus towards curbing political interference in them.

Moreover, commercial actors contribute to shaping European energy policy and *de facto* 'do the business on the ground'; that is, they carry out energy trade. When doing so, their choices are shaped by economic considerations (such as the cost and reliability of energy supplies) and generally less by political or ideological ones. Hence, in the context of energy policy, the five principles can function only as broad and general political guidelines, leaving plenty of discretion to EU Member States and commercial actors on how to interpret them and do energy policy in practice. This is particularly true as, in the spirit

---

4　J. Henderson and J. Sharples, 'Gazprom in Europe – Two "Anni Mirabiles", but Can It continue?' (Oxford Institute for Energy Studies March 2018), available at: <https://www.oxfordenergy.org/publications/gazprom-europe-two-anni-mirabiles-can-continue/> (accessed 20 January 2020).

5　M. Siddi, 'The Role of Power in EU-Russia Energy Relations: The Interplay between Markets and Geopolitics', *Europe-Asia Studies* 70 (10), 2018, 1560.

6　For an overview of the complexities of EU energy policy, see S. Schubert, J. Pollak and M. Kreutler, *Energy Policy of the European Union* (Palgrave 2016), 127–147.

of the five principles, energy policy can be seen as an area where the EU should strengthen its resilience vis-à-vis Russia and as a field of selective engagement with Moscow.

2 EU Energy Policy Responses to the Ukraine Crisis

When the Ukraine crisis escalated in early 2014 and the EU imposed sanctions on Russia, energy security was one of the main concerns among policy-makers in Brussels. Russian energy supplies covered approximately 40% of the gas, 33% of the crude oil and 29% of the solid fuels imported by the EU.[7] Gas was seen as the most politically sensitive commodity because gas transportation is technically more difficult and diversifying suppliers requires large, long-term investments into pipelines or liquefied natural gas (LNG) terminals. Since approximately half of the EU's imports of Russian gas were channelled via Ukraine, it was feared that EU energy security would fall victim to the political crisis, and that Europe would experience gas shortages such as those caused by the Russian-Ukrainian gas transit crisis of January 2009.[8] This concern was particularly strong in Eastern European countries that were more dependent on Russian gas supplies such as Latvia, Bulgaria and Slovakia.

In this context, the EU and its Member States agreed to draft the 2014 European Energy Security Strategy and the 2015 Energy Union framework. The implementation of the Energy Union was made a priority of the newly appointed European Commission presided by Jean-Claude Juncker. The Energy Union focused on increasing energy security and solidarity, creating an integrated EU energy market, improving energy efficiency, decarbonising the economy and supporting innovation and competitiveness. To strengthen energy security, the Energy Union envisaged the construction of new pipelines – most notably, the Southern Gas Corridor[9] – and of LNG terminals to import non-Russian gas. With regard to Russia, the Energy Union framework

---

7   Eurostat, 'Main Origin of Primary Energy Imports, EU-28', 9 August 2018, available at: <https://ec.europa.eu/eurostat/statistics-explained/index.php?title=File:Main_origin_of_primary_energy_imports,_EU-28,_2006-2016_(%25_of_extra_EU-28_imports).png&oldid=398029> (accessed 15 January 2019).

8   See S. Pirani, J. Stern and K. Yafimava, 'The Russo-Ukrainian Gas Dispute of January 2009: A Comprehensive Assessment' (Oxford Institute for Energy Studies 2008), available at: <https://www.oxfordenergy.org/publications/the-russo-ukrainian-gas-dispute-of-january-2009-a-comprehensive-assessment> (accessed 20 January 2020).

9   M. Siddi, 'The EU's Botched Geopolitical Approach to External Energy Policy: The Case of the Southern Gas Corridor', *Geopolitics* 24 (1), 2019, 124–144.

adopted a cold and wary approach, arguing that 'when the conditions are right, the EU will consider reframing the energy relationship with Russia based on a level playing field in terms of market opening, fair competition, environmental protection and safety, for the mutual benefit of both sides'.[10]

Eventually, in 2014–2015, a Russian-Ukrainian gas transit crisis comparable to that of 2009 was avoided thanks to successful trilateral negotiations between the EU, Russia and Ukraine, as well as to Russian and Ukrainian willingness to shelter their lucrative gas trade from the political crisis.[11] As during the Cold War, EU-Russia gas trade continued and even intensified amidst political tensions.[12] Part of the reason why trade continued is that Russia is at least as dependent as the EU is on this energy relationship. Most of Russian oil and gas exports, which are vital to the Russian state budget, are sold in the EU market and cannot easily be reoriented towards other markets.[13] During the summer of 2015, Western European companies and the Russian state company Gazprom even developed a new large-scale project to export Russian gas to the EU, Nord Stream 2.

Nevertheless, the political climate around energy cooperation remained difficult. Eastern EU members such as Poland and the Baltic States remained fiercely critical of further energy trade with Russia and attempted to shape EU policy accordingly.[14] In 2015, the European Commission proceeded with an antitrust investigation against Gazprom, which it had launched in 2012 on Lithuania's request and claims that Gazprom was abusing its monopolistic position in East-Central European markets.[15] Moreover, in late 2013, the Commission stated that the intergovernmental agreements signed by Russia and EU Member States to build the South Stream pipeline (another large-scale project to export Russian gas to the EU) did not conform to EU law. Together

---

10   European Commission, 'A Framework Strategy for a Resilient Energy Union', COM(2015) 80 final. For a critical analysis, see M. Siddi, 'The EU's Energy Union: A Sustainable Path to Energy Security?', *The International Spectator* 51 (1), 2016, 131–144.
11   A. Stulberg, 'Out of Gas? Russia, Ukraine, Europe, and the Changing Geopolitics of Natural Gas', *Problems of Post-Communism* 62 (2), 2015, 112–130.
12   P. Högselius, *Red Gas* (Palgrave 2013), 197–216.
13   J. Sharples, 'The Shifting Geopolitics of Russia's Natural Gas Exports and Their Impact on EU-Russia Gas Relations', *Geopolitics* 21 (4), 2016, 885–886.
14   M. Siddi, 'Identities and Vulnerabilities: The Ukraine Crisis and the Securitisation of the EU-Russia Gas Trade', in: K. Szulecki (ed.), *Energy Security in Europe: Divergent Perceptions and Policy Challenges* (Palgrave Macmillan 2018), 265–266.
15   J. Stern and K. Yafimava, 'The EU Competition Investigation of Gazprom's Sales in Central and Eastern Europe: A Detailed Analysis of the Commitments and the Way Forward', OIES Paper No. NG 121 (Oxford Institute for Energy Studies 2017), 30.

with the escalating tensions in Ukraine, this led Russia to cancel the South Stream project in late 2014.[16]

In the months preceding Mogherini's announcement of the five principles, EU-Russia relations were negatively affected by the lack of implementation of the Minsk 2 agreement, allegations of Russian disinformation campaigns in the EU and Russia's military intervention in the Syrian civil war. The five principles were a response to this tense climate and sought to combine a firm and critical stance with selective engagement. Tensions affected the way energy relations were conceived in the five principles. The inclusion of energy under the third principle highlighted concerns about the security of supply, and reflected the political aspect of the EU's dual approach to energy relations with Russia. According to the third principle, strengthening the EU's energy resilience vis-à-vis dependence on Russian energy supplies is a key goal of EU energy policy.

In the past five years, the EU made considerable progress in reducing its vulnerability to disruptions in Russian gas supplies, while at the same time continuing energy trade with Russia. Some of the most dependent countries have developed alternative routes. Lithuania opened an LNG terminal in late 2014; Latvia expanded its gas storage capacity; Slovakia, Hungary and Poland have built interconnecting pipelines, and further interconnections have been planned. The possibility of reverse flows of gas from West to East strengthened the energy security of Eastern members; Ukraine benefitted from this technology too. As the Energy Union framework has been implemented, interconnections between the energy systems of Member States have improved and the possibility of external supply shocks affecting one or a group of countries has diminished.[17]

At the same time, the EU-Russia gas relationship has been rendered more predictable by the resolution of long-standing disputes, most notably the European Commission's antitrust investigation concerning Gazprom and Russia's complaint at the World Trade Organisation (WTO) against some key EU market regulations (the third energy package). As shown below, the settlement of the antitrust case between the European Commission and Gazprom has reduced the potential for legal conflict in EU-Russia gas trade and contributed to the integration of the EU gas market. However, disagreements persist among EU Member States regarding the desirable EU stance vis-à-vis

---

16   M. Siddi, 'EU-Russia Gas Trade: New Projects, New Disputes?', Briefing Paper No. 183 (Finnish Institute of International Affairs October 2015).

17   See M. Russell, 'The EU's Russia Policy: Five Guiding Principles', European Parliament, February 2018, 5, available at: <http://www.europarl.europa.eu/RegData/etudes/BRIE/2018/614698/EPRS_BRI(2018)614698_EN.pdf> (accessed 15 January 2019).

Russian energy exports, and particularly new infrastructural projects such as Nord Stream 2. The project has ignited heated debates within the EU, where some East-Central Member States staunchly oppose the project. Conversely, Russia's main import partners in Western Europe seem happy to continue and even increase their energy purchases from Russia. The United States has intervened in the debate, too, by threatening to sanction European companies that are involved in the project and advocating its prospective LNG exports as an alternative.

3 Main Developments in EU-Russia Energy Trade after the Five Principles[18]

Russian gas exports to Europe rose to unprecedented records from 2016 to 2018. According to Gazprom's data, around 201 billion cubic metres (bcm) of gas were exported to Europe and Turkey in 2018, compared to 192.2 bcm in 2017 and 158.6 in 2015.[19] This performance may appear surprising, given the context of political crises and reciprocal sanctions between the EU and Russia (which have nonetheless left the energy sector largely unscathed). The rise in Russian gas supplies to Europe is due to commercial and contextual factors that have little to do with politics. In other words, growing gas flows reflect the economic component of the EU's dual approach to energy relations with Russia. From 2015 to 2017, the EU saw considerable growth in gas demand, which reached 548 bcm/year in 2017. This is 76 bcm higher than in 2014 (even though it is still below the peak of 585 bcm reached in 2010).[20] The economic recovery in Europe, decreasing gas production in the EU, lower Russian gas prices and the limited availability of non-Russian LNG in the European market were among

---

18   This section and the following ones in this chapter are based on and develop further the analysis in M. Siddi, 'Russia's Evolving Gas Relationship with the European Union: Trade Surges despite Political Crises', Briefing Paper No. 246 (Finnish Institute of International Affairs September 2018).
19   Gazprom Export, Delivery Statistics 2018, available at: <http://www.gazpromexport.ru/en/statistics/> (accessed 15 January 2019); 'Gazprom Expects 2018 Natural Gas Exports to Europe, Turkey to Total 201 bcm: CEO', Platts, 28 December 2018, available at: <https://www.spglobal.com/platts/en/market-insights/latest-news/natural-gas/122818-gazprom-expects-2018-natural-gas-exports-to-europe-turkey-to-total-201-bcm-ceo> (accessed 15 January 2019).
20   A. Honoré, 'Natural Gas Demand in Europe in 2017 and Short Term Expectations', *Oxford Energy Insight,* No. 35 (Oxford Institute for Energy Studies, April 2018), 1.

the main commercial reasons. Cold winter temperatures and increased coal to gas switching in some European countries also boosted gas demand.

Growing demand has been accompanied by decreasing indigenous production in the EU, from 300 bcm in 2010 to 250 bcm in 2016. This was mostly due to the progressive depletion of North Sea resources and cuts in production in Groningen, the Netherlands, because of related seismic activity. Hence, Europe's growing demand for external gas supplies has been satisfied primarily by Russian gas. Following pressure from the European Commission and its customers, Gazprom has partly renegotiated the terms of its supply contracts by adopting market-based pricing in place of oil-linked prices. Together with the rouble's weakness (which reduces the domestic cost base for Gazprom in US dollar terms), this has made Russian gas more competitive.[21]

The availability of sufficient reserves and spare infrastructural capacity have also played an important role. While Gazprom was able to sustain increased supplies of gas to the EU, other exporters such as Algeria (the third-largest external supplier of gas to the EU after Russia and Norway) saw a 14% decline in pipeline exports in 2017. Not only did Gazprom use the Nord Stream and Yamal-Europe (via Poland/Belarus) pipelines at near full capacity, it also increased the gas it exported via Ukraine by 13.7%, reaching a total volume of 93.5 bcm in 2017, the highest figure since 2011.[22] Despite the continuation of political tensions with the EU, Russian companies felt confident enough to implement new infrastructural projects for the export of gas to Europe and beyond. This included the launch of the Yamal LNG project in December 2017 and the ongoing construction of the TurkStream and Nord Stream 2 pipelines.

On the other hand, LNG's competition with Russian gas has been weaker than expected. This was the result of delays in some LNG projects and especially of higher LNG demand in Asia (particularly China), which remains the primary market for LNG due to higher demand and prices. The availability of LNG in the European market began to increase in 2017 and may continue to do so in the next five years depending on demand in Asia. In a scenario of lower Asian demand, LNG from the United States (the closest prospective large supplier to Europe) could compete with Gazprom and other pipeline suppliers for some shares of the European market.[23] The availability of LNG from the United States or Qatar contributes to the resilience of the European energy

---

21 Henderson and Sharples, 'Gazprom in Europe', *op. cit.* note 4, 3–5.
22 'Ukraine sees 13.7% rise in gas transit in 2017', Interfax Ukraine, 2 January 2018, available at: <https://en.interfax.com.ua/news/economic/474366.html> (accessed 15 January 2019).
23 For a detailed discussion, see Henderson and Sharples, 'Gazprom in Europe', *op. cit.* note 4, 1–16.

market by providing an alternative to pipeline gas. Russian gas shipped via pipeline tends to be cheaper than LNG, which explains why European commercial actors have preferred and may continue to prefer additional imports of Russian gas. Growing EU imports of Russian gas do not necessarily have a negative impact on European energy security thanks to the possibility of using the large spare capacity in LNG terminals to switch to LNG imports from other countries, depending on the commercial or political circumstances.

4 Settling EU-Russia Energy Disputes: The Antitrust and WTO Cases

While developing alternative supply options strengthens the EU's resilience, agreement with suppliers on the rules regulating energy trade is no less important. This is particularly true of EU-Russia energy relations, where the two sides have sometimes held different views. The EU has focused on the liberalisation of its energy market, promoting competition between energy importers to achieve security of supply and cheaper prices for domestic consumers. On the other hand, as a major energy exporter Russia has focused on the security of demand by minimising price volatility, countering the competition of other suppliers and concluding long-term contracts with its customers, which help cover the costs of building and maintaining the necessary export infrastructure.[24]

The different priorities of the EU and Russia regarding energy trade has complicated the pursuit of shared practices and norms. In East-Central Europe, Gazprom has been accused of monopolistic behaviour, which led the European Commission to investigate the company's practices. In 2011, the Commission launched an antitrust investigation and, subsequently, accused Gazprom of abusing its dominant market position in Eastern Europe. According to the Commission, Gazprom's contracts in the region hindered the cross-border flow of gas, which resulted in the fragmentation of the regional market and different prices from country to country.[25]

However, in the ensuing negotiations, Gazprom committed to removing contractual barriers to the cross-border flow of gas. It also linked gas prices in Eastern EU members to benchmark prices in Western European hubs. Gazprom's commitments will adjust prices in Eastern European markets that

---

24 See Siddi, 'The Role of Power in EU–Russia Energy Relations', *op. cit.* note 5, 1556–1157.

25 See M. Siddi, 'The Antitrust Dispute between the European Commission and Gazprom: Towards an Amicable Deal', FIIA Comment, 25 April 2017.

are isolated due to the lack of infrastructure to market-based prices in Western Europe. They are thus conducive to the further integration of the EU energy market. As a result, in May 2018 the European Commission ended its antitrust case against Gazprom, arguing that it had secured substantial commitments from the Russian company on more competitive prices and greater market integration for Eastern European Member States.

By making these commitments, Gazprom has avoided a fine being imposed by the European Commission. However, the Russian company had to make important concessions, and essentially change its marketing strategy from oil-linked contracts to more market-based and, at present, lower prices. Failure to honour the commitments could still lead to Gazprom being fined over the next eight years.[26] The resolution of the antitrust investigation on terms that are favourable to the EU, and are also accepted by Russia, has contributed to the EU's energy security. The EU's competition policy has helped correct Gazprom's *modus operandi* in the European market in a way that is functional to market integration and competition, thereby also strengthening the Union's resilience to energy supply shocks.

Moreover, in mid-August 2018 the WTO published its ruling on Russia's complaint against the EU concerning certain provisions of the third energy package, duly ending the other main dispute concerning EU-Russia gas relations. The European Commission had introduced the third energy package in 2009 with the aim of integrating the EU's energy market and increasing competition. One of its central requirements is unbundling the ownership of energy production and supply from that of energy transportation.

In April 2014, Russia had filed a complaint with the WTO about this legislation, arguing that it treated Russian gas and gas transportation services unfairly. However, the WTO ruled that the main principles of the third energy package are lawful. On the other hand, it also stated that some of its aspects were not in line with WTO norms. Most notably, this concerned a 50% cap imposed by the EU on the utilisation capacity of the OPAL pipeline, a land-based continuation of the Nord Stream pipeline, which *de facto* artificially constrained the use of the latter. The WTO ruling also stated that the EU's Trans-European Networks for Energy (TEN-E) strategy, which aims at linking the infrastructure of EU members, is inconsistent with WTO law because it provides most

---

26 F. Chee and A. de Carbonnel, 'EU Ends Antitrust Case against Gazprom without Fines', *Reuters,* 24 May 2018, available at: <https://www.reuters.com/article/us-eu-gazprom-antitrust/eu-ends-antitrust-case-against-gazprom-without-fines-idUSKCN1IP1IV> (accessed 10 September 2020).

favourable conditions for the transportation of natural gas of any origin other than Russian (thus discriminating against the latter).[27]

Both the EU and Russia issued positive comments about the WTO ruling, despite their decision to appeal certain issues of law and legal interpretations in the panel report. The EU was satisfied with the overall WTO assessment of the third energy package. In the years after Russia filed the complaint, Gazprom had largely adjusted its strategy to this new legislation. For the Russian company, the WTO pronouncement on the TEN-E strategy and the OPAL pipeline are seen as the main achievements. The WTO's view on OPAL strengthens the case for fuller utilisation of the Nord Stream pipeline and can constitute a precedent for the Nord Stream 2 project. Overall, while the two sides may not be entirely satisfied with some of its aspects, the WTO ruling has helped clarify the rules of EU-Russia gas trade. The clarification of regulatory aspects catalyses trade and is thus functional to the economic component of the EU's dual approach to Russia in the field of energy.

5   Russia's New Projects: LNG, TurkStream and Nord Stream 2

While market developments and the resolution of commercial disputes with Gazprom strengthened EU-Russia energy relations, new large-scale energy projects led by Russian companies have generated controversy and even acrimony within the EU. All too often, the internal EU discussion is shaped by (and becomes acrimonious because of) political considerations that are at best marginally related to achieving energy security and resilience.[28] The broader political crisis in EU-Russia relations has influenced discussions on new energy projects, sometimes overshadowing more important (for the purposes of energy security) considerations on the functioning of energy markets and trade. While some politicians and commentators continue to fear the deployment of a hypothetical Russian 'energy weapon', the availability of different suppliers, the integration of the EU's internal energy market and Russia's

---

27   See 'European Union and its Member States – Certain Measures Relating to the Energy Sector', World Trade Organization, 21 November 2018, available at: <https://www.wto.org/english/tratop_e/dispu_e/cases_e/ds476_e.htm> (accessed 15 January 2019); R. Griffin, 'WTO Court Rules in Favor of Key Principles of EU Third Energy Package', Platts, 10 August 2018, available at: <https://www.spglobal.com/platts/en/market-insights/latest-news/natural-gas/081018-wto-court-rules-in-favor-of-key-principles-of-eu-third-energy-package> (accessed 10 September 2020).

28   M. Siddi, 'Identities and Vulnerabilities', *op. cit.* note14, 256–263.

dependence on this market for its national budget have strengthened considerably the EU's resilience and decreased its exposure to 'energy blackmail'.[29]

Against this background, the new projects of Russian energy companies should be seen primarily as attempts to retain their shares in the European market in the face of growing competition, as well as ways of bypassing political issues (such as conflicts over Ukrainian gas transit) that have been exacerbated by Putin's foreign policy. It is highly unlikely that these new projects will play a decisive role in terms of possible foreign policy goals (such as coercing Ukraine into a Russian sphere of influence) or undermine the EU's energy security. The main risk for the EU is that if Member States take intransigent stances towards each other, and some even see the new projects as 'hybrid weapons', the EU's internal coherence will be undermined.

In 2018, the first large project that can export Russian LNG to the European market was launched – even though most of its gas might, in fact, go to Asia. Yamal LNG is expected to produce 16.5 million tons of LNG per year from 2019. The project was developed by a consortium including Russia's Novatek, France's Total, the China National Petroleum Corporation and the Silk Road Fund. Yamal LNG is also significant because Novatek, the Russian consortium leader, is a private company, unlike state giant Gazprom. The project was completed on time and within budget despite being targeted by US sanctions. This was possible thanks to Chinese lenders, who swiftly replaced Western investment, and the switching of financing from dollars to euros.[30]

The TurkStream project has also been completed. Together with the Nord Stream pipelines, TurkStream is part of Gazprom's strategy to reduce drastically gas transit in Ukraine. It can transport 31.5 bcm/year of gas to Turkey and the EU along a route that goes from Russia's Black Sea coast to European Turkey under the Black Sea. Gas started flowing through the pipeline in January 2020. The first string of TurkStream (with half the total capacity) will replace Russian gas exports to Turkey that were previously transported via Ukraine and the Balkans. The second string of the project is mostly intended for exports to Southeast and Southern Europe. This section of the project will end at the Turkish-EU border, where it will be linked to EU interconnectors.[31]

---

29 T. Boersma, 'The End of the Russian Energy Weapon (that Arguably Was Never There)', Brookings Institution, 5 March 2015, available at: <https://www.brookings.edu/blog/order-from-chaos/2015/03/05/the-end-of-the-russian-energy-weapon-that-arguably-was-never-there/> (accessed 15 January 2019).

30 M. Siddi, 'The Arctic Route for Russian LNG Opens', WE – World Energy, 9 May 2018, available at: <https://www.aboutenergy.com/en_IT/topics/arctic-route-for-russian-lng-opens.shtml> (accessed 15 January 2019).

31 Henderson and Sharples, 'Gazprom in Europe', *op. cit.* note 4, 23.

Nord Stream 2 is the new Gazprom-led project that has aroused more controversy in the EU. With a capacity of 55 bcm/year, it will carry gas from the Russian Baltic Sea coast to Germany via an offshore route running parallel to the already existing Nord Stream pipeline. Following its completion, the total capacity of the Nord Stream route will rise to 110 bcm/year, making it the main export corridor for Russian gas to Europe.[32] The project was announced in the summer of 2015 by a consortium including Gazprom, German companies Uniper and Wintershall, France's Engie, Austria's ÖMV and Dutch/British Shell. Its proponents argued that Nord Stream 2 will connect Gazprom's newer gas fields in the Yamal Peninsula to its bigger customers in Western Europe through a shorter route without transit-related risks and fees. However, the project soon attracted criticism, with opponents arguing that it will consolidate Gazprom's position in the European energy market, weakening Ukraine's role as a gas transit country and thus its strategic leverage vis-à-vis Moscow in the ongoing political crisis.

Poland, the Baltic states, Romania and Slovakia have consistently opposed the project. Their opposition tends to be explained by a number of factors including strategic reasons (notably the loss of their current strategic importance as transit countries), the intention to diversify energy imports away from Russia and concerns about being bypassed by the main flows of East-West energy trade. Long-standing fear of Russia and of German-Russian cooperation also play a role in Poland and the Baltic states. Slovakia also sees its substantial revenues from transit fees (€355 million in 2015) as being endangered.[33] On the other hand, Germany and Austria have emerged as the main advocates of the project. France and the Netherlands appear amenable to it as well due to the involvement of domestic corporate interests. The main argument that has been put forward to support the project is that it follows commercial logic by linking suppliers and customers with competitively priced gas. It has been argued that Nord Stream 2 can provide cheap gas to compensate for dwindling North Sea gas production. It will also meet further demand that will stem from the closure of nuclear power plants in Germany and the need

---

32 For a full analysis of the project, see A. Goldthau, 'Assessing Nord Stream 2: Regulation, Geopolitics and Energy Security in the EU, Central Eastern Europe and the UK', European Centre for Climate, Energy and Resource Security (EUCERS) Strategy Paper No. 10 (King's College London, 2016); K. Lang and K. Westphal, 'Nord Stream 2 – A Political and Economic Contextualisation', SWP Research Paper (Stiftung Wissenschaft und Politik, March 2017).

33 For a discussion of opponents' arguments, see Lang and Westphal, 'Nord Stream 2', op. cit. note 32, 28–34; A. Loskot-Strachota, 'The Case against Nord Stream 2', Energy Post, 23 November 2015.

to switch energy consumption from more polluting coal and oil to gas. The controversy around Nord Stream 2 reflects the tension inherent in the EU's dual approach to energy relations with Russia. On the one hand, the economic drivers of the relationship advocate the construction of the pipeline, citing commercial reasons. On the other hand, opponents argue against the project by focusing on political arguments such as solidarity with Ukraine and Russia's aggressive foreign policy.

Caught between opposing views at the Member State level, EU institutions have taken different stances towards Nord Stream 2. The European Commission opposed the project. In June 2017, it requested a mandate from the Council of the EU to negotiate an agreement with Russia concerning the operation of Nord Stream 2, arguing that it was necessary to define a legal framework. The request seemed to respond to pressure by Member States opposing Nord Stream 2 and had the apparent goal of limiting Gazprom's ability to use the pipeline's capacity. However, the Legal Service of the Council concluded that there was no legal basis for an EU-Russia agreement concerning the project. It also stated that the third energy package does not apply to the Nord Stream 2 pipeline.[34] The reasoning of the Legal Service of the Council reflects existing precedents: pipelines from non-EU countries have been built in accordance with the United Nations Convention on the Law of the Sea, whereas the third energy package applies to pipelines within EU territory. In the case of Nord Stream 2, the package would apply to adjoining, land-based pipelines in the EU. Moreover, the EU energy market has been built around the principles of liberalisation and competition, and political attempts to block new projects run counter to this logic.

Following the Council's response, the Commission proposed amending the third energy package to create a legal rationale for requesting the negotiating mandate. To become law, the amendment of the Gas Directive required the support of a qualified majority of Member States (that is, 55% of Member States voting in favour, and representing at least 65% of the total EU population). In 2017 and 2018, this seemed highly unlikely, as the opposition of Germany, France and several other smaller EU members ensured the existence of a blocking minority. A turning point occurred in February 2019, when France suddenly voiced its support for amending the Gas Directive. The French stance urged Germany to seek bilateral negotiations with France to achieve a compromise. Eventually, a common text was agreed that made the Gas Directive

---

34 For an in-depth discussion, see K. Yafimava, 'The Council Legal Service's Assessment of the European Commission's Negotiating Mandate and What It Means for Nord Stream 2', *Energy Insight 19* (Oxford Institute for Energy Studies October 2017).

applicable to EU territorial waters but left the Member State where the pipeline first lands in charge of implementation and of authorising exemptions (which, however, have to be agreed on by the European Commission). The Franco-German compromise was then endorsed by EU institutions.[35]

To complicate matters further, the United States has intervened in the Nord Stream 2 debate through both congressional legislation and President Donald Trump's fiery rhetoric. Legislation passed by Congress in the summer of 2017 threatened to sanction European companies involved in Nord Stream 2 and in other energy projects with Russian involvement. This led to a diplomatic argument with the German and Austrian governments. Berlin and Vienna argued that the US extraterritorial sanctions were illegal and that 'Europe's energy supply network is Europe's affair, not that of the United States of America'.[36] Following negotiations with European diplomatic envoys, the 2017 legislation was softened with the addendum that sanctions would be imposed at the US President's discretion in coordination with US allies.[37] In 2018, however, Congress passed a new draft law that could make the sanctions mandatory without requiring the approval of the US President or other coordination. Opponents of Nord Stream 2 see it as the last tool for attempting to stop the project. Conversely, supporters of the pipeline see the proposed extraterritorial sanctions as an illegal attempt to interfere in EU energy policy and promote US LNG exports as an alternative, regardless of their potentially higher cost for the EU and uncertainty about available volumes.

Despite the risk of US sanctions, construction of the Nord Stream 2 pipelines started during the summer of 2018 and proceeded in the following months.[38] However, in December 2019 Congress approved sanctions against Nord Stream 2, leading the Swiss constructor Allseas to suspend the laying of the pipeline in the Baltic Sea, when nearly all the work had been completed. US sanctions will probably fall short of the objective of cancelling the project but will delay it by several months because Gazprom was forced to find another vessel with the

---

35 A. Gurzu, 'Nord Stream 2: Who Fared Best', Politico, 13 February 2019, available at: <https://www.politico.eu/article/the-winners-and-losers/> (accessed 20 January 2019).
36 German Foreign Office, Press Release 15 June 2017, available at: <https://www.auswaertiges-amt.de/en/newsroom/news/170615-kern-russland/290666> (accessed 15 January 2019).
37 See 'Countering America's Adversaries through Sanctions Act', 2017, https://www.treasury.gov/resource-center/sanctions/Programs/Pages/caatsa.aspx (accessed 15 January 2019).
38 O. Astakhova and V. Eckert, 'Nord Stream 2 Pipeline on Track despite Sanction Risk', Reuters, 31 August 2018, available at: <https://br.reuters.com/article/russia-gazprom-nordstream-idAFL8N1VM1W9> (accessed 10 September 2020).

capability of laying pipes in deep sea waters.[39] This means that Gazprom will have to continue to export large volumes of gas via Ukraine in the early 2020s.

6 Ukraine's Role in EU-Russia Energy Trade

Many EU politicians consider the preservation of Ukraine's gas transit role as the most politically pressing issue in the light of Gazprom's new projects. Preserving gas transit through Ukraine would contribute to EU energy security because Russian gas would continue to be channelled to the EU via three pipeline routes (Nord Stream, Belarus-Poland and Ukraine) rather than just two.[40] However, due to the ongoing conflict between Moscow and Kiev and the risk of spillovers to the energy sphere, the Ukrainian route appears as the least secure. Hence, the EU's position seems to be guided primarily by political factors, most notably solidarity with Ukraine. Ukraine has earned $2–3 billion a year from transit revenues, which are important to its economy. The construction of alternative pipelines could deprive Ukraine of this income, weakening it both financially and strategically vis-à-vis Russia. The main question is whether Ukraine will be able to preserve its transit role in coming years.

Ukrainian concerns increased in February 2018 when Gazprom stated that it would start a termination procedure for its supply and transit contracts with Ukraine.[41] Gazprom's statement was made in response to the outcome of a long-standing arbitration process concerning contracts with Ukraine's state company, Naftogaz. After 2014, Gazprom and Naftogaz had filed claims against each other at the Arbitration Institute of the Stockholm Chamber of Commerce. The claims concerned the implementation of supply and transit contracts. A series of pronouncements left Gazprom with a net debt of $2.56 billion – a considerable sum but only a fraction of what the two companies were claiming from each other.[42] Gazprom stated that it wished to terminate

---

39 Platts, 'Russia Expects to Delay Nord Stream 2 Launch to mid-2020: Report', 21 November 2019, available at: https://www.spglobal.com/platts/en/market-insights/latest-news/natural-gas/112119-russia-expects-to-delay-nord-stream-2-launch-to-mid-2020-report (accessed 20 February 2020).

40 When finalised, Turkish Stream will constitute an additional southern route.

41 V. Soldatkin and N. Zinets, 'Gazprom Seeks to halt Ukraine Gas Contracts as Dispute Escalates', Reuters, 2 March 2018, <https://www.reuters.com/article/us-russia-ukraine-gas/gazprom-seeks-to-halt-ukraine-gas-contracts-as-dispute-escalates-idUSKCN1GE2DW> (accessed 15 January 2019).

42 Gazprom claimed $56 billion from Naftogaz for the alleged breach of take-or pay contracts, whereas Naftogaz demanded $16 billion for Gazprom's failure to deliver agreed transit volumes of gas.

the current gas transit agreement with Ukraine in this context, before arguing that it would use all legal means to challenge the outcome of the arbitration.[43]

On closer inspection, Gazprom's statement appeared unlikely to have any concrete effects. As indicated above, in 2017 the company exported over 93 bcm of gas via Ukraine; similar volumes transited Ukraine in 2018 and 2019. To maintain these export volumes, Gazprom cannot manage without Ukrainian transit pipelines at present. In fact, this will hold true even if both Nord Stream 2 and TurkStream are built. Certainly, when these projects become operational, gas volumes via Ukraine will diminish markedly but they will not disappear. In December 2019, Gazprom and Naftogaz signed a five-year transit contract, in which the Russian company agreed to ship a minimum of 65 bcm of gas in 2020 and a minimum of 40 bcm/year in 2021–2024, including a ship-or-pay clause (meaning that Gazprom would have to pay for the minimum contracted volumes even if it ships less). As part of these negotiations, Gazprom also agreed to pay the net debt resulting from the Stockholm arbitration.[44]

Hence, gas transit via Ukraine will continue in the 2020s but with smaller volumes than in the 2000s and 2010s. While transit volumes will diminish, it is also important to note that Ukraine is no longer as exposed to disruptions in gas supplies from Russia as it was in the past. Ukraine's gas demand fell from around 65 bcm in 2011 to approximately 35 bcm in 2017. Most of the current demand is covered by domestic gas production and imports from the EU (even though the latter include reverse flows of Russian gas).[45] This means that while Ukraine will probably lose most of its leverage as a key transit country, Russia has also lost much of its leverage over Ukraine's energy security.

From the perspective of the EU's energy security and resilience, Ukrainian gas transit is a more complex and multifaceted matter than may appear from mainstream political debates. On the one hand, the EU feels obliged to show solidarity with Ukraine, which is also a fellow member of the Energy Community, an international organisation that aims at extending the EU's energy *acquis*.[46] As argued, maintaining Ukrainian transit will contribute to the diversification

---

43 See Marc-Antoine Eyl_Mazzega, 'The *Gazprom-Naftogaz* Stockholm Arbitration Awards: Time for Settlements and Responsible Behaviour' (IFRI, Paris 13 March 2018); S. Pirani, 'Russian Gas Transit through Ukraine after 2019: The Options', *Oxford Energy Insight*, No. 41 (Oxford Institute for Energy Studies November 2018), 6.
44 A. Isachenkov, 'Russia, Ukraine Finalize Deals for Gas Transit to Europe', AP, 31 December 2019, available at: <https://apnews.com/4615057928c343afb421a24cddobedfi> (accessed 20 February 2020).
45 See E. Mazneva, 'Russian Gas Return to Ukraine to Cost EU Traders $1 Billion', Bloomberg, 10 January 2018.
46 Schubert, Pollak and Kreutler, *Energy Policy of the European Union, op. cit.* note6, 220–222.

of import routes. On the other hand, several technical factors should discourage excessive political interference in the matter. The Ukrainian pipeline network is old, with large parts of it dating back to Soviet times, and requires extensive investments. The new Russian gas fields are located further north than the West Siberian fields that have traditionally supplied gas to Europe and where production is now declining. These factors make the Nord Stream route to the large Northwestern European markets shorter, and thus more competitive in terms of transportation costs.[47] Furthermore, for the EU, maintaining reliance on Ukrainian transit means remaining hostage to the heated Russian-Ukrainian relationship for its gas supplies, which is hardly a sensible strategy. The EU could show solidarity with Ukraine and support it financially in different ways, without putting its own energy supplies at risk.

7 Conclusion

Currently, the EU has a dual approach to energy relations with Russia, which responds to both a political and a commercial logic. This dual approach is reflected in the five principles currently guiding the EU's policy towards Russia. The third principle identifies energy security as an area where the Union should strengthen its internal resilience, mostly due to political concerns related to excessive dependence on Russian energy supplies. This is particularly relevant to gas supplies, as gas is arguably the most sensitive energy source for the EU due to transportation complexities and high import needs. The EU has made good progress in this regard. It has developed both legislation (such as the third energy package) and a policy framework, the Energy Union, which are functional to strengthening its internal resilience. Most significantly, the EU has strengthened interconnections between national energy markets, and supported the construction of new infrastructure in Member States that were dependent on a single supplier.

As Russia is an important supplier of energy at relatively low cost, Brussels also faced the daunting task of managing the energy relationship with Moscow amidst an unprecedented political crisis and reciprocal sanctions. Also in this respect, the EU has been remarkably successful. Following a commercial logic, and according to the wishes of the Member States that value energy trade with Russia (such as Germany, Italy and France), the EU has largely preserved the energy relationship with Moscow. Hence, energy can now be seen as an area of

---

47   Pirani, 'Russian Gas Transit', *op. cit.* note 43, 8–16.

selective engagement with Russia, in accordance with the fourth principle. The European Commission successfully negotiated transit and supply agreements between Russia and Ukraine in 2014–2015. Despite the political crisis, EU-Russia energy trade was maintained and even reached new record volumes in 2017 and 2018. At the same time, the European Commission managed to settle an antitrust dispute with Gazprom through negotiations, thereby enforcing EU rules for commercial operations in the internal market. The fact that Gazprom has an interest in preserving its lucrative exports to the EU, and that it was put under pressure by other potential suppliers (such as LNG producers), contributed to the EU's cause.

The main outstanding issue regarding EU-Russia energy relations concerns the routes through which Russian gas will be exported to the EU in the future, particularly the fate of Ukrainian transit pipelines. Arguably, this is an issue that relates more to the EU's political stance than to its resilience or energy security. The EU has supported Ukraine politically and financially since Russia's annexation of Crimea in 2014, and preserving imports via Ukraine would be consistent with the strategy adopted thus far. Ukrainian transit pipelines constitute an important, and currently indispensable, corridor for EU gas imports from Russia. However, they are in need of renovation and their commercial use is exposed to political crises between Kiev and Moscow. The completion of Nord Stream 2 and Turkish Stream, which are potentially more efficient and less exposed to political controversies, could make them largely (but not completely) redundant within a few years. For the EU, the best long-term strategy appears to be allowing the development of new, privately funded and commercially viable routes, while simultaneously ensuring that Ukraine's energy security is also guaranteed.

CHAPTER 12

Addressing Cyber Security Threats from Russia in the EU

Andreas Marazis

> We face a dangerous, unpredictable, and fluid security environment, with enduring challenges and threats from all strategic directions; from state and non-state actors; from military forces; and from terrorist, cyber, and hybrid attacks.
>
> Brussels NATO Summit Declaration, 11 July 2018

∴

1   Introduction

Cyber operations are not a new phenomenon. In 1960 Evgeny Messner, a Russian military theorist, spoke about a new form of warfare called *myatezhevoyna* (subversion war). During the 1990s, many theorists used the term *fourth-generation warfare*. They all agree with the fact that it is a long-term psychological strategy aiming to wane the adversary by demoralising the spirit of citizens and, thus, undermining the legitimacy of the authorities.

This form of operations has become the norm and a daily headache for several Member States of the European Union. It can be conducted by states and non-state actors and involves a range of different modes of operations.[1] Numerous EU Member States have been targeted by Russian cyber espionage campaigns that infiltrated the networks of their critical infrastructure, and the same malware that was used, for example, in Ukraine was found in Swedish industrial control system networks.[2] Hybrid and cyber activities such as

---

1   F.G. Hoffman, *Conflict in the 21st Century: The Rise of Hybrid Wars* (Potomac Institute for Policy Studies 2007), available at: <https://www.potomacinstitute.org/images/stories/publications/potomac_hybridwar_0108.pdf> (accessed 8 August 2018).
2   O. Williams, 'Russia Is Targeting UK Infrastructure through Supply Chains, NCSC Warns', 6 April 2018, available at: <https://tech.newstatesman.com/business/russia-uk-critical-infrastructure> (accessed 8 August 2018).

state-sponsored cyber sabotage are increasing year by year and could become a common occurrence in the future.

In focusing on the third principle that currently guides the EU's policy towards Russia – namely, strengthening the resilience of the EU to Russian threats – this chapter outlines how the EU has attempted to boost its resilience to Russian cyber threats, especially since the annexation of Crimea. The main goal of the chapter is to assess to what extent the EU is following up on this principle with respect to Russian cyber security threats, and what challenges the EU is facing in strengthening its resilience to these threats.

The chapter is divided in two parts. The first part briefly introduces the reader to the Russian cyber operations approach, identifies the main targets and provides a list of reported Russian cyber operations in the EU since 2014. The second part is dedicated to the EU's cyber security strategy, the legal framework and the instruments – financial and deterrent – which were developed especially after the annexation of Crimea. Due to space constraints and the primary focus of the study, this chapter covers to some extent only the types of cyber operations and the types of targets. The study is based on primary sources (EU official documents) and secondary literature.

2   Understanding the Russian Cyber Threat

2.1   *Russian Cyber Approaches*

Russia is considered a pro in the cyber warfare arena, an actor with sophisticated cyber mechanisms ready to be used as foreign or security tools at any moment against any adversary.[3] To understand the methodology and the aim of Russian cyber attacks towards the EU it is necessary to deconstruct the Russian cyber threat, which encompasses three types of interlinked operations. The first type is *information operations*, which can be defined as actions that aim to achieve information superiority over adversaries that can be exploited for the benefit of the actor utilising information warfare.[4] The second type is *hybrid operations*, which is defined as 'the combination of conventional and unconventional, military and non-military, overt and covert actions with the aim of

---

3   N. Popescu and S. Secrieru, *Hacks, Leaks and Disruptions Russian Cyber Strategies*, Institute for Security Studies, 23 October 2018, available at: <https://www.iss.europa.eu/content/hacks-leaks-and-disruptions-%E2%80%93-russian-cyber-strategies> (accessed 28 March 2020).

4   'Glossary of Cyber Terms and Definitions Substantially Updated', available at: <https://ccdcoe.org/news/2015/glossary-of-cyber-terms-and-definitions-substantially-updated/> (accessed 29 March 2020).

creating ambiguity and confusion on the nature, the origin and the objective of the threat'.[5] It has the ability 'to identify and exploit vulnerabilities of the targets with the capacity to keep the level of hostility below the "threshold" of conventional war'.[6] The third type is cyber operations. These are 'cyber-attacks that are authorised by (non-)state actors against cyber infrastructure'.[7]

Russian cyber operations are thus part of the Kremlin's wider approach to information and hybrid operations that supplements their conventional military efforts, as well as providing the ability to maintain leverage over its adversaries in peacetime.[8] As explained by Sergey G. Chekinov and Sergey A. Bogdanov, information operations are designed to destabilise a country by fuelling anti-government protests and provoke negative sentiments among citizens towards the authorities, among other things.[9]

Chekinov and Bogdanov went to emphasise the importance of good timing by highlighting that information operations should precede any traditional military operations. Therefore, the Russian cyber threat can be understood as a pivotal facet of their information operations within the EU. Moreover, the Russian cyber threat is also a subgroup of the Russian hybrid operations campaigns throughout the EU. As defined above, a hybrid threat is a conglomerate of conventional and non-conventional military tactics, as well as other subversive and exploitative tactics. Russian cyber operations are equally influenced from information operations and hybrid operations. To help further understand Russian hybrid operations, a recent RAND report[10] has categorised this phenomenon succinctly, distinguishing between the key characteristics, objectives and toolkit (see Table 12.1).

---

5   J.J. Andersson and T. Tardy, *Hybrid: What's in a Name?*, Institute for Security Studies, 28 October 2015, available at: <http://dx.publications.europa.eu/10.2815/422877> (accessed 29 March 2020).
6   *Ibid.*
7   J.B. Godwin III et al., 'Critical Terminology Foundations 2: Russia-U.S. Bilateral on Cybersecurity' (EastWest Institute 2014), 82.
8   J. Weedon, 'Beyond "Cyber War": Russia's Use of Strategic Cyber Espionage and Information Operations in Ukraine', in: K. Geers (ed.), *Cyber War in Perspective: Russian Aggression against Ukraine* (NATO Cooperative Cyber Defence Centre of Excellence 2015), 67–77.
9   M. Jaitner, 'Russian Information Warfare: Lessons from Ukraine', in: K. Geers (ed.), *Cyber War in Perspective: Russian Aggression against Ukraine* (NATO Cooperative Cyber Defence Centre of Excellence 2015), 89; The Military Doctrine of the Russian Federation, approved by Russian Federation Presidential Edict on 5 February 2010, 4.
10 C. Chivvis, *Understanding Russian 'Hybrid Warfare': And What Can Be Done about It* (RAND Corporation 22 March 2017), available at: <http://www.rand.org/pubs/testimonies/CT468.html> (accessed 29 March 2020).

TABLE 12.1 Russian hybrid operations: characteristics, objectives and toolkit[a]

Key characteristics of Russian hybrid operations	1. It economizes the use of force; allowing Russia to conduct operations without formal military confrontation. 2. It is persistent; it is a constant but may become more acute and intense as it moves toward conventional warfare. 3. It is population centric; seeks to influence precise populations to work within existing socio-political frameworks.
Typical objectives of Russian hybrid operations	1. Capturing territory without resorting to overt or conventional military force; shown by creation of frozen conflicts and support for separatism. 2. Creating a pretext for overt, conventional military action; creates narrative that justifies action 3. Using hybrid measures to influence the politics and policies of countries in the West and elsewhere; to gain influence or gain strategic geopolitical advantage.
Russian hybrid operations toolkit	1. Information operations; Russia's pervasive Dis & Prop campaigns 2. Cyber; allowing various operations discussed in this report. 3. Proxies; through support of far-right parties/pro-Russian in other countries and lobbying groups. 4. Economic influence; utilizing Russian energy for strategic gain. 5. Clandestine measures; utilizing traditional Cold War espionage. 6. Political influence; use of Russian soft power.

[a] ECSO, *op. cit.* note 61.

2.2 *Types of Targets*

The most susceptible and vulnerable targets for cyber attacks include critical infrastructure, political institutions and confidential information. Russian cyber attacks on critical infrastructure have been reported on only four occasions since 2014. The first attack in 2015 left more than 200,000 Ukrainians without power for up to six hours. APT28[11] deployed an advanced malware, called Black Energy, after daily phishing campaigns and flooded the power distribution centres with a distributed denial-of-service attack.[12] A year later, another cyber sabotage operation targeted Ukraine but disabled only one transmission substation.[13] In 2017, a new malware, called VPNFilter, targeted Ukrainian critical water systems which provided chlorination and filtering. Ukraine's Secret Service was able to detect and deter the attack but VPNFilter has been discovered in 500,000 networking devices across 54 countries.[14] Targeting critical infrastructure is of serious concern not only for the EU Member States. Black Energy has been detected in numerous energy utilities in the United States. The proliferation of dangerous malware like Black Energy and VPNFilter displays Russia's comprehensive cyber sabotage capabilities and can be said to be a foreshadowing of the future of cyber warfare. Disabling critical infrastructure is not the objective of cyber warfare and cyber sabotage; the effect that such an attack can have on a society is.[15] Cyber sabotage attacks of this type are a dangerous part of Russia's cyber and hybrid warfare capabilities, regardless of their frequency.[16]

When it comes to targets linked to political institutions included, among others, are political campaigns, political parties, elections and government bodies (Ministries of Foreign Affairs, Internal Affairs, and Transportation,

---

11 Advanced Persistent Threat 28 (APT28) is a skilled team of developers and operators collecting intelligence on defence and geopolitical issues – intelligence that would be useful only to a government.

12 A distributed denial-of-service (DDoS) attack is a malicious attempt to disrupt normal traffic of a targeted server, service or network by overwhelming the target or its surrounding infrastructure with a flood of Internet traffic.

13 'Cyberattack on Critical Infrastructure: Russia and the Ukrainian Power Grid Attacks' (The Henry M. Jackson School of International Studies, 11 October 2017), available at: <https://jsis.washington.edu/news/cyberattack-critical-infrastructure-russia-ukrainian-power-grid-attacks/> (accessed 31 March 2020).

14 C. Osborne, 'Ukraine Blocks VPNFilter Attack against Core Country Water System', 13 July 2018, available at: <https://www.zdnet.com/article/ukraine-blocks-vpnfilter-attack-against-core-country-water-system/> (accessed 31 March 2020).

15 Kyiv Post, 'How an Entire Nation Became Russia's Test Lab for Cyberwar', 21 June 2017, available at: <https://www.kyivpost.com/ukraine-politics/wired-entire-nation-became-russias-test-lab-cyberwar.html> (accessed 31 March 2020).

16 Some of the main critical infrastructure targets are the following: operators of essential services: energy sector – electricity, oil and gas; transport – air, rail, water and road; banking – credit institutions; financial market infrastructures – trading venues, central counterparties; health – healthcare providers (including hospitals and private clinics); water – drinking water supply and distribution.

etc.). Russian disclosure operations[17] facilitate existing disinformation and propaganda campaigns against EU Member States by providing acutely timed leakage of damaging information with the purpose of swaying an election in favour of Russian interests. Prominent examples include the cyber operation conducted on the campaign of Emmanuel Macron in the 2017 French presidential election and the intense disinformation and propaganda campaigns targeting the German federal elections in September 2017.[18]

Last but certainly not least, confidential information is the target of any cyber espionage and disclosure operation. Government ministries, offices and networks have been targeted across the EU. Cyber espionage operations are often the first step in gathering the necessary intelligence to conduct a more malicious cyber operation. Table 12.2 provides a detailed list of reported Russian cyber operations targeting different EU Member States and the EU institutions/agencies between 2016 and 2018, with information about the type of cyber operation, the objective, the threat agent and the target.

3 The European Union's Response to the Russian Cyber Threat

3.1 *The EU's Strategies, Actors and Resources*

While the EU and its Member States underinvested in cyber defence, they have recently started to catch up. As a result of Russia's increasingly assertive cyber operations, the EU has been developing a common response and approach to deal with the cyber threats from Russia and boost the cyber resilience of the EU institutions and Member States. In 2017, the EU released a comprehensive report which expanded on the Union's 2013 Cybersecurity Strategy, titled 'Resilience, Deterrence, and Defence: Building Strong Cybersecurity for the EU'.[19] The report's recommendations provide an outline for the EU's response to cyber threats, which focus on developing cyber resilience, deterrence and defence across EU Member States and their institutions.

---

17   *Disclosure* is a form of Russian information warfare and hacktivism defined by unauthorized access and leakage of information to damage the politics of an adversary, by disclosing information that is damaging to the target so that the population's trust in the target erodes or to pursue a political message.

18   E. Brattberg and Tim Maurer, 'Russian Election Interference: Europe's Counter to Fake News and Cyber Attacks', Carnegie Endowment for International Peace, 23 May 2018, available at: <https://carnegieendowment.org/2018/05/23/russian-election-interference-europe-s-counter-to-fake-news-and-cyber-attacks-pub-76435> (accessed 31 March 2020).

19   European Commission, 'Cybersecurity Package "Resilience, Deterrence and Defence: Building Strong Cybersecurity for the EU"', 19 September 2017, available at: <https://ec.europa.eu/digital-single-market/en/news/cybersecurity-package-resilience-deterrence-and-defence-building-strong-cybersecurity-eu> (accessed 31 March 2020).

TABLE 12.2 List of reported Russian cyber operations targeting different EU Member States from 2016 until 2018

Date	Cyber operation	Objective of cyber threat	Threat agent	Primary attack vector	Target type	Victim
March 2018[a]	Cyber espionage	Malware	APT28	Phishing/spear phishing	Defence	European Defence Agency
February 2018[b]	Cyber espionage	Malware	APT28	Unknown	Government	German government departments
February 2018[c]	Cyber espionage	Malware	APT28	Phishing	Government	Numerous European Ministries of Foreign Affairs
January 2018[d]	Cyber espionage	Web browser attack	Turla	Unknown	Government	Consulates and embassies in Eastern Europe
January 2018[e]	Disruption	DDoS	Nation state	Botnets	Finance sector	Netherlands: banks
November 2017[f]	Cyber espionage	Web browser attack	APT28	Spear phishing	Private organisation	Bellingcat

[a] Unit42, 'Sofacy Uses DealersChoice to Target European Government Agency', 15 March 2018, available at: <https://unit42.paloaltonetworks.com/unit42-sofacy-uses-dealerschoice-target-european-government-agency/> (accessed 31 March 2020).

[b] BBC News, 'Hacking of German Ministries "Ongoing"', 1 March 2018, available at: <https://www.bbc.com/news/world-europe-43248201> (accessed 31 March 2020).

[c] Ibid.

[d] ESET, 'Diplomats in Eastern Europe Bitten by a Turla Mosquito', 10 January 2018, available at: <https://www.eset.com/me/whitepapers/eset-turla-mosquito/> (accessed 31 March 2020).

[e] NL Times, 'Russian Servers Linked to DDoS Attack on Netherlands Financial Network: Report', 29 January 2018, available at: <https://nltimes.nl/2018/01/29/russian-servers-linked-ddos-attack-netherlands-financial-network-report> (accessed 31 March 2020).

[f] 'Fancy Bear Pens the Worst Blog Posts Ever' (ThreatConnect | Intelligence-Driven Security Operations, 2 November 2017), available at: <https://threatconnect.com/blog/fancy-bear-leverages-blogspot/> accessed 31 March 2020.

TABLE 12.2 List of reported Russian cyber operations targeting different EU Member States from 2016 until 2018 (cont.)

Date	Cyber operation	Objective of cyber threat	Threat agent	Primary attack vector	Target type	Victim
October 2017[g]	Cyber espionage	Malware	Group 74	Phishing	Individuals	NATO CCE CoE attendees
October 2017[h]	Cyber espionage	Involuntary insider threat	Nation state	Vulnerability	Military	NATO troops in Poland
July 2017	Destruction	Malware: NotPetya	APT28	Unknown	Businesses	Worldwide, including EU
April 2017[i]	Cyber espionage	Not reported	APT28 and APT29	Phishing	Government, military, defence	Denmark: Ministry of Defence and Ministry of Foreign Affairs
April 2017[j]	Disclosure	Information leakage	APT29, APT28	Phishing	Campaign	France: Macron's campaign
April 2017[k]	Cyber espionage	Web application attack	APT28	Phishing	Organisation: NGOS	Germany: think tanks tied to CDU and SPD
February 2017[l]	Cyber espionage	Not reported	APT29	Phishing	Government	Norway: government branches

[g] Executive Gov, 'Foreign Hacking Group Targets Cybersecurity Conference Attendees with Phishing Campaign', 25 October 2017, available at: <https://www.executivegov.com/2017/10/foreign-hacking-group-targets-cybersecurity-conference-attendees-with-phishing-campaign/> (accessed 31 March 2020).

[h] WSJ, 'Russia Targets NATO Soldier Smartphones, Western Officials Say', 4 October 2017, available at: <https://www.wsj.com/articles/russia-targets-soldier-smartphones-western-officials-say-1507109402> (accessed 31 March 2020).

[i] Reuters, 'Russia Hacked Danish Defense for Two Years, Minister Tells Newspaper', 23 April 2017, available at: <https://www.reuters.com/article/us-denmark-security-russia-idUSKBN17P0NR> (accessed 31 March 2020).

[j] Ibid.

[k] Reuters, 'Cyber Spies Target German Party Think-Tanks Ahead of Election', 25 April 2017, available at: <https://www.reuters.com/article/us-germany-election-cyber-idUSKBN17R273> (accessed 31 March 2020).

[l] Ibid.

TABLE 12.2 List of reported Russian cyber operations targeting different EU Member States from 2016 until 2018 (cont.)

Date	Cyber operation	Objective of cyber threat	Threat agent	Primary attack vector	Target type	Victim
February 2017[m]	Cyber espionage	Malware	Nation state	Phishing	Government	Italy: Ministry of Foreign Affairs
January 2017[n]	Cyber espionage	Malware	Nation state	Phishing	Government, defence	Czech Republic: Ministry of Foreign Affairs
May 2016[o]	Cyber espionage, disclosure	Data breach	APT28	Phishing	Government, political party	Germany: CDU
April 2016[p]	Cyber espionage, disclosure	Data breach	APT28	Phishing	Government, campaign, political party	Germany: CDU

[m] S. Kirchgaessner, 'Russia Suspected over Hacking Attack on Italian Foreign Ministry', 10 February 2017, available at: <https://www.theguardian.com/world/2017/feb/10/russia-suspected-over-hacking-attack-on-italian-foreign-ministry> (accessed 31 March 2020).

[n] H. de Goeij, 'Czech Government Suspects Foreign Power in Hacking of Its Email', 31 January 2017, available at: <https://www.nytimes.com/2017/01/31/world/europe/czech-government-suspects-foreign-power-in-hacking-of-its-email.html> (accessed 31 March 2020).

[o] P. Beuth et al., 'Cyberattack on the Bundestag: Merkel and the Fancy Bear', 12 May 2017, available at: <https://www.zeit.de/digital/2017-05/cyberattack-bundestag-angela-merkel-fancy-bear-hacker-russia-komplettansicht> (accessed 31 March 2020).

[p] P. Paganini, 'Pawn Storm Hackers Hit the German Christian Democratic Union Party', 13 May 2016, available at: <https://securityaffairs.co/wordpress/47261/cyber-crime/pawn-storm-cdu.html> (accessed 31 March 2020).

The legislative framework and several instruments are already in place at the EU as well as at the Member State level. The Network and Information Security (NIS) Directive[20] and the 'NIS Toolkit',[21] since 2016 and 2017

20 European Commission, 'The Directive on Security of Network and Information Systems (NIS Directive)', 5 July 2016, available at: <https://ec.europa.eu/digital-single-market/en/network-and-information-security-nis-directive> (accessed 31 March 2020).

21 Ibid.

respectively, implemented new policies which develop the EU's capacity to withstand and prevent cyber threats across the whole EU. The latter provided practical information to Member States on how the Directive should work in practice, thus speeding up the transposition process. The main instrument that oversees and helps Member States in the implementation of the NIS Directive policies as well as fosters cooperation among their Computer Security Incident Response Teams (CSIRTs) is the European Union Agency for Network and Information Security (ENISA). The Digital Single Market Strategy[22] – another legal document – aims to bring trust and security to private and public sectors that are targeted in cyber attacks through the creation of contractual public-private partnerships (cPPPs)[23] on cyber security and funding drawn from Horizon 2020 and later on from the next research and innovation framework programme Horizon Europe. To develop cyber deterrence, the EU is focusing on the following tasks: identifying malicious actors, stepping up law enforcement response to cyber crime, fostering public and private cooperation on private crime, stepping up political pressure on states carry out cyber operations through soft power, and increasing Member States' defence capability. The agencies that have been tasked with cyber deterrence development are Europol/EC3, Eurojust, and the European External Action Service (EEAS).[24] The EU's cyber defence development focuses on three tasks: developing a dialogue and international cooperation on cyber security through foreign relations, building cyber security capacity and cooperating with defence organisations such as NATO and other states. The Common Security and Defence Policy (CSDP) has recently added cyber security to its framework. The introduction of the European Cybersecurity Coordination Platform, which has been proposed by the European Commission, would place a priority on detection, prevention, cooperation, protection and prosecution to ensure the Member States' cyber security.[25]

---

22   European Commission, 'Shaping the Digital Single Market', 25 March 2015, available at: <https://ec.europa.eu/digital-single-market/en/policies/shaping-digital-single-market> (accessed 31 March 2020).
23   European Commission, 'Cybersecurity Industry', 18 December 2015, available at: <https://ec.europa.eu/digital-single-market/en/cybersecurity-industry> (accessed 31 March 2020).
24   EEAS, 'A Stronger EU on Security and Defence', 19 November 2018, available at: <https://eeas.europa.eu/headquarters/headquarters-homepage/35285/stronger-eu-security-and-defence_en> (accessed 31 March 2020).
25   *Ibid.*

3.2 Network and Information Security Directive – NIS and CSIRTS

The proposal for the NIS Directive was first introduced in the EU Cybersecurity Strategy in 2013 and came into effect in July 2016.[26] It aims to improve the EU's ability to respond and prevent cyber threats by harmonizing Member State cooperation in cyber security. The NIS Directive's obligations and recommendations aim to achieve the following: ensure Member States' preparedness by requiring them to have a CSIRT and a national NIS authority; ensure cooperation between Member States' CSIRTs in a unionwide Cooperation Group which offers a platform for cooperation, support and exchange of information on cyber security incidents and risks; and ensure a culture of security by requiring Member States to protect and cooperate with operators of essential services and digital service providers.[27] A framework for implementation was created by the European Commission, called the NIS Toolbox,[28] which lays out practical information for the speedy transposition of the NIS Directive.

Member States had until 9 May 2018 to implement the Directive's recommendations and mandates into their national laws and had six more months to identify the sectors and members of their essential services. Despite the risk of penalties, some Member States have not completed the transposition of the NIS Directive.

The NIS Cooperation Group meets to discuss the development of the Directive's transposition every three to four months, ensuring that the states continue to be held accountable for their rate of transposition.[29] The NIS applies to entities, which are necessities for society to function.[30] Technical requirements placed on CSIRTS, which aim to protect critical infrastructure

---

26   European Commission, *op. cit.* note 20.

27   European Commission, 'EU Cybersecurity Initiatives: Working towards a More Secure Online Environment', 18 January 2017, available at: <https://ec.europa.eu/information_society/newsroom/image/document/2017-3/factsheet_cybersecurity_update_january_2017_41543.pdf>.

28   In the NIS Toolkit, the Member States are given a strategy for the implementation of the NIS Directive's obligations. The obligations include the following: (1) a National Cybersecurity Strategy of network and information systems; (2) national competent authorities, Member States must designate one national governance structure to ensure that the Directive will be fulfilled which link the authorities to the entities included in the cyber security strategy; (3) single contact points, must designate a single point of contact to ensure cross-border cooperation with authorities in other Member States, the Cooperation Group, and the CSIRT network by 9 August 2018; (4) Computer Security Incident Response Teams (CSIRTS).

29   'NIS Cooperation Group', available at: <https://ec.europa.eu/digital-single-market/en/nis-cooperation-group> (accessed 1 April 2020).

30   European Commission, *op. cit.* note 20.

and ensure a stable digital market, include: an understanding of their sector's assets and a mechanism to identify unknown devices; a mature vulnerability management programme; mature threat detection systems: effective incident reporting mechanisms that can record and report incidents within 72 hours of detection; and response and recovery plans that can be employed following an incident.[31] The NIS also places organisational requirements on the various actors facilitating EU cyber security in terms of the governance, risk management process, supply chain and staff awareness and training to ensure that Directive is appropriately instituted.[32]

The NIS Directive's obligations and recommendations enable each Member State to respond to and prepare for future cyber attacks. In that sense CSIRTs are the first-line responders to cyber attacks, who have access to unionwide information on current and emerging cyber threats. Critical infrastructure has been targeted in four separate attacks in Ukraine since 2014 and in one attack on Dutch banks in January 2018.[33] The NIS Directive makes it mandatory for CSIRTs to protect and cooperate with the operators of essential services and digital service providers. CSIRTs protect and cooperate with key sectors and services within their Member States, which are: energy, including electricity, oil and gas; transport, including road, rail, water and air; banking; financial market infrastructures; the health sector, including hospitals and private clinics; drinking water and supply distribution; digital infrastructure, including exchange points, domain name system service providers and top-level domain name registries. CSIRTs are a key part of the EU's ability to respond and counter Russian cyber threats to critical infrastructure.

Member States' CSIRTs collectively belong to the CSIRT Network 'to contribute to developing confidence and trust between the member states and to promote swift and effective operational cooperation'. It is composed of the representatives from the Member States' CSIRTs and the EU's own CSIRT – that is, the Computer Response Team for the EU (CERT-EU). The CSIRT Network provides a platform for cooperation and trust development on cyber security and for information exchange on new cyber security strategies and threats.

---

31 VentureBeat, 'While Everyone Was Focused on GDPR, the NIS Directive Snuck in through the Back Door', 7 July 2018, available at: <https://venturebeat.com/2018/07/07/while-everyone-was-focused-on-gdpr-the-nis-directive-snuck-in-through-the-back-door/> (accessed 1 April 2020).
32 *Ibid.*
33 Reuters, 'Dutch Tax Office, Banks Hit by DDoS Cyber Attacks', 29 January 2018, available at: <https://www.reuters.com/article/us-netherlands-cyber-idUSKBN1FI1LM> (accessed 1 April 2020).

Some Member States have gone beyond the obligations outlined in the NIS Directive to further protect themselves from cyber attacks. Germany recently created its own cyber troops that are composed of 13,500 military and civilian personal as part of its army.[34] It has also boosted its cyber security budget by €200 million over a period of five years and created new institutions and special structures to combat cyber threats such as the Cyber Innovation Agency.[35] Finland has taken the lead in combatting cyber threats and hybrid warfare by prompting the establishment of the EU-NATO European Centre of Excellence for Countering Hybrid Threats in Helsinki. Estonia is considered one of Europe's cyber security leaders, which is exemplified by the Estonian Presidency of the Council of the EU's focus on cyber security.[36] Tallinn is the location of an important cyber research centre: NATO's Cooperative Cyber Defence Centres of Excellence. Lithuania established a Centre for Cyber Security that focuses on the protection of the nation's critical information technology (IT) infrastructure. Latvia has criminalized hybrid and information warfare. These are just a few examples of EU Member States taking specific measures to combat Russian cyber threats which complement the reforms and strategies in the EU.[37]

3.3 *The European Union Agency for Network and Information Security – ENISA*

Although ENISA was established in 2004, the agency has evolved several times in accordance with the rapidly increasing and changing cyber threats. ENISA was strengthened following the 2013 Cybersecurity Strategy of the European Union with new tasks laid out in the 2016 NIS Directive and the proposal for the Cybersecurity Act in 2017.[38]

---

34 Deutsche Welle, 'German Army Launches New Cyber Command', 1 April 2017, available at: <https://www.dw.com/en/german-army-launches-new-cyber-command/a-38246517> (accessed 1 April 2020).

35 M. Schulze and S. Herpig, 'Germany Develops Offensive Cyber Capabilities without a Coherent Strategy of What to Do with Them', 3 December 2018, available at: <https://www.cfr.org/blog/germany-develops-offensive-cyber-capabilities-without-coherent-strategy-whatdo-them> (accessed 1 April 2020).

36 'Cybersecurity and the Estonian EU Presidency', 1 August 2017, available at: <https://investinestonia.com/cybersecurity-and-the-estonian-presidency/> (accessed 1 April 2020).

37 S. Sukhankin, 'European Response to Russia's Disinformation and Cyber Aggression: Reaction or Strategy?', 20 June 2017, available at: <https://jamestown.org/program/european-response-russias-disinformation-cyber-aggression-reaction-strategy/> (accessed 1 April 2020).

38 European Commission, 'Communication on a Cybersecurity Strategy of the European Union – An Open, Safe and Secure Cyberspace', 7 February 2013, available at: <https://ec.europa.eu/digital-single-market/en/news/communication-cybersecurity-strategy-european-union-%E2%80%93-open-safe-and-secure-cyberspace> (accessed 1 April 2020).

Currently, ENISA is dealing with policy development and implementation tasks that focus on supporting the European Commission and Member States in their development, implementation and review of their cyber security policies in key sectors making up necessary services. ENISA's task of operational cooperation revolves around the cooperation between EU-level CSIRTs and Member States to handle cyber incidents. ENISA's capacity-building tasks aim to ensure that Member States develop the cyber capabilities required by the NIS Directive, including: their own national cyber security strategy to develop cyber defence policies and capabilities; achieve cyber resilience; reduce cyber crime; support industry on cyber security; and secure critical information infrastructures. It also encourages the mutual financial and developmental aid of private sector industries outlined by the NIS Directive.[39]

Critical infrastructure is also a major focus for ENISA. ENISA has an information sharing group, the ENISA ICS Security Stakeholder Group, set up specifically to facilitate cooperation and dialogue on energy sector threats and cyber security options to deter them.[40] ENISA also has expanded its existing training programmes since 2013 and now conducts pan-European cyber exercises with participants from CSIRTs, NATO and members of the information and communication technologies community.[41] For example, ENISA's Cyber Security Training programmes[42] – online and offline – focus on CSIRT training in four areas: 'Technical, Operational, Setting up a CSIRT and Legal and Cooperation'.[43] The TRANSITS,[44] another training programme, allows new CSIRT personnel to develop a practical understanding of working within a CSIRT team initially, and then develop their capabilities in incident handling and response operations. Cyber Europe is a biyearly EU cyber security exercise conducted over three stages, which includes a two-day main exercise. ENISA also provides extensive resources on their websites, including CSIRT training resources, a handbook for teachers and a toolset for students. This allows

---

39   D. Healey et al., 'Cyber Security Strategy for the Energy Sector', Study for the ITRE Committee, European Parliament, 4 October 2016, 40, available at: <http://publications.europa.eu/resource/cellar/8cf0f709-fcb9-11e6-8a35-01aa75ed71a1.0001.01/DOC_1 > (accessed 1 April 2020).
40   Ibid.
41   'Cyber Europe 2016: The Pan-European Exercise to Protect EU Infrastructures against Coordinated Cyber-Attack', 20 October 2016, available at: <https://www.enisa.europa.eu/news/enisa-news/cyber-europe-2016> (accessed 1 April 2020).
42   'Trainings for Cybersecurity Specialists', available at: <https://www.enisa.europa.eu/topics/trainings-for-cybersecurity-specialists> (accessed 1 April 2020).
43   Ibid.
44   'TRANSITS Training – GÉANT', available at: <https://www.geant.org:443/Services/Trust_identity_and_security/Pages/TRANSITS_Training.aspx> (accessed 1 April 2020).

Member States to implement ENISA's CSIRT strategies and develop effective responses against potential Russian cyber threat situations.

3.4 Research and Collaboration with Centres of Excellence

To achieve cyber resilience, the EU has invested in research programmes such as Horizon 2020 and cooperated with Centres of Excellence to train Member State cyber security staff, establish platforms for cyber security dialogue and conduct situational exercises.

The EU currently cooperates with numerous Centres of Excellence across Europe on issues of cyber security, cyber resilience and cyber defence. The most prominent centre that the EU works with is the NATO Cooperative Cyber Defence Centre of Excellency in Tallinn. Twenty-five EU Member States are part of this centre, which conducts research and offers training, exercises and workshops in the fields of cyber security and defence. NATO and the EU have also opened their own Centre of Excellence 'dedicated to furthering a common understanding of hybrid threats and promoting the development of comprehensive, whole-of-government response at national levels and of coordinated response at EU and NATO levels in countering hybrid threats'.[45] The European Centre of Excellence for Countering Hybrid Threats in Helsinki conducts research and training exercises and facilitates dialogue between governments, non-governmental experts and practitioners. This centre was established by the EU and NATO in 2016. SENTER is a EU-funded network of European Centres of Excellence that focus on cyber crime research, training and education. The network is a joint effort between European Centres of Excellence, such as the Lithuanian Cyber Crime Centre of Excellence for Training, the French Cybercrime Centre of Excellency and various European universities, which have consolidated their resources to further study and develop methods to combat cyber crime.[46]

In addition, the European Commission Vice-President and Commissioner for Digital Single Market, Andre Ansip, announced in 2017 plans for the EU to create its own Centre of Excellence that would promote cyber security technology and technical skills.[47] Despite the fact that the legislative framework is

---

45 'What Is Hybrid CoE?' (Hybrid CoE), available at: <https://www.hybridcoe.fi/what-is-hybridcoe/> (accessed 1 April 2020).

46 'SENTER: A Network of the European Centres of Excellence in Cyber Crime Research, Training, and Education', 11 July 2016, available at: <https://ercim-news.ercim.eu/en106/special/senter-a-network-of-the-european-centres-of-excellence-in-cyber-crime-research-training-and-education> (accessed 1 April 2020).

47 C. Stupp, 'Ansip Plans New EU Cybersecurity Centre', 20 July 2017, available at: <https://www.euractiv.com/section/cybersecurity/news/ansip-plans-new-eu-cybersecurity-centre/> (accessed 1 April 2020).

still at the work-in-progress level, the expected new European Cyber Security Competence Centre and Network will – once operational – 'foster regular dialogue with the private sector, consumer organisations and other relevant stakeholders, enabled by the set-up of an industrial and scientific advisory board that would build on and scale up the effect of the existing cPPP on cyber security'.[48] More importantly, it will boost synergies between the civilian and defence components of cyber security emphasizing on research and it will – hopefully – address the skills gap in cyber security[49] by supporting skills development and training and educational programmes in cooperation with respected academic institutions such as the IT University of Copenhagen and Tallinn University of Technology, to name but a few.

It is worth mentioning that the European Security and Defence College launched its own cyber security and defence platform in September 2018 with the purpose of providing an online space for coordinating cyber security/cyber defence education, training, evaluation and exercises.[50]

The EU is also developing its cyber capabilities through its comprehensive research and innovation programme, Horizon 2020. Horizon 2020's cyber security research and innovation projects had a budget of €160 million from 2014 to 2016.[51] From 2017 to 2020, the EU is investing €450 million into the programme's cyber security research and innovation projects due to a contractual public-private partnership on cyber security.[52] Each Member State's CSIRT will be able to benefit from cPPP research, an example of the harmonizing effect that the NIS Directive hopes to achieve. The expected impact of this programme includes important developments in EU cyber security that will increase the resilience and deterrence capabilities of EU Member States, their cyber security professionals, and the information and communication technologies systems/infrastructures.[53] Horizon 2020 – and later on its successor, Horizon Europe – and the cPPP are only two of the EU programmes with cyber

---

48 N. Mar and B. Alessia, 'The New Cybersecurity Competence Centre and Network', 11.
49 *Ibid.*
50 'EAB.Cyber', available at: <https://esdc.europa.eu/eab-cyber/> (accessed 1 April 2020).
51 European Commission, 'EU Cybersecurity Initiatives: Working towards a More Secure Online Environment', 18 January 2017, available at: <https://ec.europa.eu/digital-single-market/en/news/eu-cybersecurity-initiatives-working-towards-more-secure-online-environment> (accessed 1 April 2020).
52 *Ibid.*, 6.
53 European Commission, Horizon 2020, 'Secure Societies – Protecting Freedom and Security of Europe and Its Citizens', 22 October 2013, available at: <https://ec.europa.eu/programmes/horizon2020/en/h2020-section/secure-societies-%E2%80%93-protecting-freedom-and-security-europe-and-its-citizens> (accessed 1 April 2020).

security components to them that are receiving drastic budget increases; the Digital Europe programme will increase the cyber budget from around €1 billion to €9.2 billion, while the Connecting Europe Facility intended to finance digital connectivity infrastructure will have a budget of €3 billion from 2021 to 2027.[54]

3.5 The European Defence Agency – EDA

At the frontline of European defence measures is the European Defence Agency (EDA), which perceives cyber space as the fifth domain of warfare on which military operations are increasingly dependent. The European Defence Fund, which finances the agencies capability development and defence research, will be seeing a dramatic increase in its total funds. Allocation of at least €1.5 billion Every year will occur from 2021 onwards.[55] Capability development and defence research will have their budgets almost doubled during this period.[56] The EDA made cyber security one of its five priority actions and as it is depicted in the Cyber Defence Policy Framework[57] – drafted in 2014 and updated in 2018 – several priorities on cyber security are related to EDA:

– Supporting the development of Member States' cyber defence capabilities related to CSDP;
– Enhancing the protection of CSDP communication networks used by EU entities;
– Promotion of civil-military cooperation and synergies with wider EU cyber policies, relevant EU institutions and agencies as well as with the private sector;
– Improve training, education and exercises opportunities;
– Enhancing cooperation with relevant international partners.

The EDA is supporting the development of Member States' skilled military cyber defence workplace, as well as ensuring proactive and reactive cyber

---

54   European Commission, 'EU Budget for the Future – Digital Transformation', 2 May 2018, available at: <https://ec.europa.eu/digital-single-market/en/news/eu-budget-future-digital-transformation> (accessed 1 April 2020).
55   European Commission, 'The European Defence Fund: Questions and Answers', available at: <https://ec.europa.eu/commission/presscorner/detail/en/memo_17_1476> (accessed 1 April 2020).
56   Council of the EU, 'European Defence Fund: Council Adopts Its Position', 19 November 2018, available at: <http://www.consilium.europa.eu/en/press/press-releases/2018/11/19/european-defence-fund-council-adopts-its-position/> (accessed 1 April 2020).
57   'EU Cyber Defence Policy Framework', 5 October 2019, available at: <https://eucyberdirect.eu/content_knowledge_hu/eu-cyber-defence-policy-framework/> (accessed 1 April 2020).

defence technology availability. Training courses and exercises on various topics soon will be taking place under EDA's collaborative platform, the Cyber Defence Training and Exercises Coordination Platform. This platform aims to increase access to cyber ranges and their occupation rate and efficiency, as well improve cyber defence training and exercises such as the Cyber Phalanx.

Cyber situation awareness is being developed through the cooperation between the EU Military Staff and the EDA with the help of the Cyber Situation Awareness Package. This project aims to give Cyber Defence Commanders and their staff a standardization of cyber defence planning and management in a practical manner.

3.6 The EU's Cyber Resilience Agenda: Current State of Play and Remaining Challenges

Undoubtedly, the EU has gone to great lengths to address the challenges that Member States face in the cyber dimension, especially since the annexation of Crimea in 2014. One could argue that the EU's hybrid threat management has been institutionalised to a degree that the unknown becomes understood and easier to digest and entered the routine sphere in terms of dealing with it.[58] A first step was to update the existing legal framework to boost cooperation among Member States. Several legal documents were updated during the past five years, including the 2013 EU's Cybersecurity Strategy, while others came into force during the same periods such as the Digital Single Market (2015) and the Cybersecurity Act (2019). Once the legal framework was in place, the next step was the harmonisation of legislation in each Member State and the setting up of national CSIRTs. Interinstitutional cooperation and shared understanding of security is at the core of the EU's approach towards hybrid warfare threats with the step-by-step development of a common approach to cyber security among Member States and by strengthening cooperation among national states, instruments and policies.[59] This gave birth to the NIS Directive in 2016 and to the NIS Toolkit (2017) providing Member States with guidelines to make sure that the transposition process runs smoothly. To keep Member States on the right track, the EU set deadlines and penalties – for those not delivering on time – and set up the NIS Cooperation Group to meet every three to four months for status reports.

---

58   M. Mälksoo, 'Countering Hybrid Warfare as Ontological Security Management: The Emerging Practices of the EU and NATO', *European Security* 27 (3), 2018, 374–392.

59   H. Carrapico and A. Barrinha, 'The EU as a Coherent (Cyber)Security Actor?', *Journal of Common Market Studies* 55 (6), 2017, 1254–1272.

However, most EU Member States missed the deadline for transposing the NIS Directive into their national legislation.[60] Coordinating 28 Member States and building trust among them is easier said than done. ENISA – as of 27 June 2019 known as the EU Agency for Cybersecurity – significantly strengthened with its new permanent mandate and increased personnel and budget, became the focal point and the institution tasked with supporting Member States in their transposition phase and enhancing CSIRT cooperation. The latter is also boosted by the establishment of the CSIRTs Network, which provides a forum where members can cooperate, exchange information and build trust, as well as improve the handling of cross-border cyber incidents.

In an effort to build trust and boost cooperation among private and public sector, the EU through its Digital Single Market strategy actively promotes cPPPs such the one with the European Cyber Security Organisation signed on July 2016 which aims to foster cooperation between public and private actors at early stages of the research and innovation process.[61]

The slow process of harmonisation at the level of Member States and the fact that some countries are well ahead compared to others and have gone beyond the 2016 NIS Directive (especially Germany, Estonia and Latvia) clearly indicate that it is a 'two-speed' implementation. On top of that, there are several – relatively new – instruments available, such as the EU-NATO Enhanced Cooperation and the Permanent Structured Cooperation (PESCO) both with clear focus on cyber security among other things, which have not yet been fully utilised. For example, the new EU Cyber Rapid Response Force, one of the 17 projects under PESCO's umbrella which will be on standby in the case of a cyber event to neutralize and investigate the threat, is currently composed of representatives from only six EU Member States: Croatia, Estonia, the Netherlands, Romania, Lithuania and Spain.[62]

Another challenge is the lack of understanding among policy-makers, IT and cyber security experts from the private sector and academia, and the general population. It seems that the policy-makers are detached from what are the latest IT developments in cyber security field, and the public is unaware of the cyber threats and the impact to their privacy. To that end, cPPPs are a good

---

60 EUObserver, 'EU Countries Miss Cybersecurity Deadline', 30 July 2018, available at: <https://euobserver.com/digital/142493> (accessed 1 April 2020).
61 ECSO, 'ECSO – European Cyber Security Organisation', available at: <https://ecs-org.eu/cppp> (accessed 1 April 2020).
62 'Cyber Rapid Response Teams and Mutual Assistance in Cyber Security', available at: <https://pesco.europa.eu/project/cyber-rapid-response-teams-and-mutual-assistance-in-cyber-security/>, (accessed 1 April 2020).

starting point in an effort to bring together think tanks, academic institutions, policy-makers and IT experts from the private sector.

4 Conclusions

To boost the resilience of its institutions and Member States against Russia's cyber security threats, in the past few years and especially after the annexation of Crimea in 2014, the EU has worked diligently on updating its legal framework and tried to harmonise the legislation in all 28 Member States to boost cooperation and build trust among national CSIRTs through various platforms. It also has strengthened the newly renamed EU Agency for Cybersecurity with a permanent mandate and increased the budget to make it the main focal point on cyber security issues. Given the level of coordination it required, the lengthy negotiations and the fact that trust was – and still is to a certain extent – in short supply among Member States in terms of sharing information, one might say that the EU responded quite rapidly to the growing cyber security threats stemming from Russia. Adhering to one of the five main principles that dictates EU's relations with Russia – strengthening the resilience of the EU to Russian threats – the former stepped into the practical implementation realm by siphoning hundreds of millions of euros for research purposes through various instruments such as the Horizon 2020 Research and Innovation Framework Programme (H2020). It also pushed for cPPP-driven research to build trust and enhance cooperation among the public and private sector and to better understand the danger cyber threats pose to critical infrastructure. To that end, the EU works closely with NATO's Cyber Defence Centre CoE in Tallinn and it also established its own Centre of Excellence for Countering Hybrid Threats (Hybrid CoE) in Helsinki which conducts research and training exercises and facilitates dialogue between governments, non-governmental experts and practitioners to better grasp the Russian cyber threat.

The legal framework is in place, the national CSIRTs and various platforms promoting exchange of information have been established, ENISA's mandate has been reinforced,[63] the budget for trainings and research on countering cyber security threats will be increased and several research-oriented instruments are in place. However, despite ENISA's efforts through the ongoing pilot projects

---

63 'The European Union Agency for Cybersecurity – A New Chapter for ENISA', 26 June 2019, available at: <https://www.enisa.europa.eu/news/enisa-news/the-european-union-agency-for-cybersecurity-a-new-chapter-for-enisa> (accessed 1 April 2020).

analysing critical European infrastructures[64] and the implementation of cPPP projects funded under H2020 on cyber security,[65] the EU's response is still largely focused on raising awareness, identifying threats and understanding its adversary to say the least. Lack of trust among Member States remains a major thorn. More than a year after the May 2018 deadline passed, four Member States had not completed the transposition according to the 2016 NIS Directive.

Emphasis on more cPPPs and enhanced cooperation between cyber security authorities at the EU level, national CSIRTs and the private sector is needed. The expected new European Cyber Security Competence Centre will have to be financially capable to fund projects and boost synergies that will address the skills gap in cyber security. At the same time, Member States should invest, in a coordinating manner, on interdisciplinary educational programmes combining courses from computer science and political science/international relations departments, while promoting the participation of think tanks in exchange programmes to foster international dialogue and cooperation among non-governmental organisations and academic institutions in this field.

Simultaneously, the EU can 'open its doors' to countries like Ukraine and Georgia, two which have experience with Russian state-sponsored attacks targeting every sector that ENISA considers mandatory for Member States and their Computer Security CSIRTs to protect. The EU should therefore take the time to learn lessons from the EaP countries and others. It can do so by utilising the existing clauses under the PESCO and the EU-NATO Enhanced Cooperation which allows cooperation with third countries, with the latter being able to participate in cyber-related projects, share their valuable experience and provide solutions against common threats to stability in wider Europe.

Strengthening the resilience of its institutions and Member States against cyber threats is a lengthy process that requires strategic patience and the involvement of a plethora of actors from the public, private, academic and civil society sectors. It is a long-term strategy and, to be a sustainable one, emphasis not only must be placed on building the necessary institutions now but also on investing in educating the youth.

---

64 In 2013, the European Commission evaluated the progress made by the European Programme on Critical Infrastructure Protection and suggested that the programme enter a new, more practical phase. This phase involves launching a pilot project analysing four critical European infrastructures that could be vulnerable to threats. These are: (1) the EU's electricity transmission grid, (2) the EU's gas transmission network, (3) Eurocontrol and (4) Galileo – the European programme for global satellite navigation.

65 ECSO, *op. cit.* note 61.

PART 4

Selective Engagement with Russia

∴

CHAPTER 13

Countering Transnational Security Threats

Prospects for EU-Russia Cooperation in an Era of Sanctions

Olga Potemkina

1   Introduction

The 'five principles' that currently guide the EU's policy towards Russia were launched in 2016 and basically reduce relations to those points that match EU interests contrary to Russia's proposal to make a common inventory of the accomplished work and restore cooperation. Counter-terrorism was declared as one of the spheres of 'selective engagement' with Russia, which forms the fourth principle.[1] The EU Global Strategy, which was adopted in June 2016, reproduces the five principles and displays Russia as a source of security challenges to the EU. However, similar to the five principles, the Strategy suggests pragmatic cooperation on a limited number of issues, terrorism and organised crime among them, while regarding Russia as a 'global actor' and thus recognising its role in counter-terrorism.[2]

On 11 July 2017, a year after the EU Global Strategy was adopted, Federica Mogherini, the High Representative of the Union for Foreign Affairs and Security Policy, and Sergei Lavrov, Russia's Foreign Minister, agreed in Brussels to step up regular contacts 'to increase the rhythm of exchanges at different levels on the main foreign policy issues'.[3] Since then, several meetings have been organised to discuss various issues such as the situation in Libya, tensions in the Gulf and on the Korean Peninsula, the Middle East peace process, the Western Balkans, and the conflicts in eastern Ukraine and Syria. Russia and the EU also confirmed their desire to respond to threats emanating from the Near East and Northern Africa and affecting people not only in this very region but

---

1   Council of the EU, Conclusions of the Foreign Affairs Council, Doc. 7042/16, Brussels, 14 March 2016.
2   EU External Action Service, 'Shared Vision, Common Action: A Stronger Europe. A Global Strategy for the European Union's Foreign and Security Policy. European Union. Brussels, June 2016', available at: <https://eeas.europa.eu/sites/eeas/files/eugs_review_web.pdf> (accessed 1 April 2020).
3   *Bulletin Quotidien Europe*, 2017, 11828.

in Europe and Russia as well. The meetings gave hope to the Russian Foreign Minister that the situation will gradually come back to normal.

'Coming back to normal' might mean that tensions will pass and work toward building a cooperative EU-Russia partnership resume. Alternatively, 'the emergence of a new model of bilateral relations, significantly different in character and intensity' could be expected, as the Russian International Affairs Council has suggested.[4] The EU has repeatedly stated that it is not possible to return to business as usual. Russia agrees that the relationship needs a fundamental change: only resetting will not remove its underlying systemic imperfections.[5]

Russia and the EU still understand 'business as usual' differently. It is clear that the reintegration of Crimea can formally be considered a watershed in EU-Russia relations. However, in reality, a cooling period began earlier. Russia already had long been unsatisfied by the status quo or business as usual, and had demonstrated its unwillingness to be just a passive consumer of EU norms. Therefore, today, Russia is clearly not talking about reproducing what was lost after 2014 but about creating a new formula of relations. More precisely, Russia desires to be recognised as an equal actor in the multipolar world.

The EU seems not prepared to answer Russia's desire for cooperation on an equal footing. The Global Strategy suggests that, even if the political dialogue is defrosted, Russia will not become an equal partner on counter-terrorism or fighting other global security threats. The 'new normal' does not give a clear perception of Russia's role in the European security architecture.[6] Conditionality remains the main principle in the EU's approach towards Russia – the options to resume cooperation, even in fighting terrorism, are conditioned by Russia's willingness to implement the Minsk agreements.[7]

---

4 L. Kulesa, I.Timofeev and J. Dobbs (eds.), *Special Report. Damage Assessment: EU-Russia Relations in Crisis*, European Leadership Network – RIAC, 2017, 6, available at: <https://www.europeanleadershipnetwork.org/wp-content/uploads/2017/10/170615-ELN-RIAC-Damage-Assessment-EU-Russia-Relations-in-Crisis.pdf> (accessed 14 January 2020).

5 As Permanent Representative Vladimir Chizhov stated, Russia does not need business as usual but rather more sensible, honest and open cooperation based on mutual interdependence, which must be free of a value-oriented approach. V. Chizhov, Permanent Representative of the Russian Federation to the EU, Interview to the ITAR-TASS News Agency, 24 December 2014, available at: <http://itar-tass.com/politika/1669109> (accessed 10 January 2019).

6 I. Timofeev, *Russia and the West: The New Normal* (Russian International Affairs Council 2016), 23, available at: <http://russiancouncil.ru/en/activity/workingpapers/russia-and-the-west-the-new-normal/> (accessed 14 January 2019).

7 D. Danilov, 'EU-Russia: Making up for Security Cooperation Shortfall', in O. Potemkina (ed.), *The EU- Russia: The Way out or the Way down?* (Institute of Europe, Egmont – The Royal Institute for International Relations 2018) 20–28.

Meanwhile, Russia's National Security Strategy includes a list of new threats and, among them, a threat to Russia's independent foreign policy from the side of the United States and 'its allies, who are seeking to retain their dominance in world affairs'. The Strategy states that by means of deterrence, they exert economic, political and informational pressure on Russia. Following this logic, NATO and the EU, for their part, pose a challenge to Russia. In fact, Moscow and Brussels put forward similar arguments to accuse each other of the same acts – security threats and attempts to establish the world order according to their own rules. Yet Russia 'advocates the consolidation of mutually beneficial cooperation with European states and the European Union, the harmonisation of integration processes in Europe and on the post-Soviet territory'.[8]

The goal of this chapter is to analyse the possibilities, limits and challenges of selective engagement in the sphere of counter-terrorism and organised crime. In this respect, it is noteworthy that the five principles and the EU Global Strategy identify Russia as a key strategic challenge. Thus, in the attempt to manage the situation in Syria, Russia (like China) is considered a '(challenging) interlocutor' more than a partner. However, in spite of differences in perceptions and motivations, Russia and the EU recognise a similar global challenge. Besides, as Thomas Renard states, there is 'a certain degree of threat-connectivity' between Russia and Europe which strongly motivates them to cooperate.[9]

This chapter starts by assessing the achievements and failures of past cooperation between the EU and Russia in the Common Space of Freedom, Security and Justice, and reveals the fundamental obstacles that prevented the full implementation of the road map on internal security. It describes in further detail recent developments in counter-terrorism and cooperation on fighting organised crime. It highlights that the EU Area of Freedom, Security and Justice (AFSJ) falls under the shared competence of the EU and the Member States, which gives Russia enough room for manoeuvre to develop cooperation with the Member States on an intergovernmental level under the sanctions regime. Nevertheless, the chapter argues that the current state of cooperation does not respond to the challenge of security threats.

---

8 National Security Strategy of Russian Federation, 31 December 2015, 4, 35, available at: <http://static.kremlin.ru/media/events/files/ru/l8iXkR8XLAtxeilX7JK3XXy6Y0AsHD5v.pdf> (accessed 8 October 2019).
9 T. Renard, 'Partnering for Global Security: The EU, Its Strategic Partners and Transnational Security Challenges', *European Foreign Affairs Review* 21 (1), 2016, 19.

2 Cooperation on the Common Space of Freedom, Security and Justice

After a large-scale enlargement in 2004–2007, which became a strong motivation for the partial communitarisation of Justice and Home Affairs (JHA), the EU began shaping the external dimension of internal security through the European Neighbourhood Policy (ENP). Concerned with the intrusion of illegal migration and organised crime through the new frontiers, the EU decided to tackle 'soft security' issues by exporting JHA concepts and tools to neighbouring countries. Researchers have characterised this policy as 'external governance', by means of which the EU strived to spread its internal policy principles to third states which had not participated in their design.[10]

The EU has performed functions of external governance by negotiating with third countries in matters which have traditionally belonged to their internal policy. Scholars of JHA define the embodiment of external governance as 'extraterritorialisation', illustrating this concept with an example of 'remote control' (e.g., border control), which the EU carries out far beyond its own boundaries. Thus, *external governance* is a process by which an actor regulates, manages or controls the behaviour and, in certain circumstances, identities and interests of another actor.[11]

The Road Map on the Common Space of Freedom, Security and Justice (CSFSJ), which was adopted at the EU-Russia Summit in May 2005, became an important tool for promoting EU internal security principles beyond its borders: common values of democracy and rule of law; their effective application by independent judicial systems; and respect for human rights. The Road Map fixed the priorities for cooperation: combatting terrorism, cyber crime and money laundering; promoting security of documents and trans-border cooperation; and judicial cooperation in civil cases. The very idea of the internal security space emerged due to the prospect of a visa-free regime declared as a common objective by Russia and the EU.[12]

---

10 See: S. Lavenex. 'Migration', in: A. Draude and T.A. Börzel (eds.), *The Oxford Handbook of Governance and Limited Statehood* (Oxford University Press 2018), 520–542; S.Gänzle, 'The EU's Policy towards Russia: Extending Governance beyond Borders?', in: J. DeBardeleben (ed.), *The Boundaries of EU Enlargement* (Palgrave Macmillan 2007), 53–69; F. Trauner and H. Carrapiço, 'The External Dimension of EU Justice and Home Affairs: Post-Lisbon Governance Dynamics', *European Foreign Affairs Review* 17, 2012, 165–182.

11 T. Balzacq. 'The Frontiers of Governance: Understanding the External Dimension of EU Justice and Home Affairs', in: T. Balzacq (ed.), *The External Dimension of EU Justice and Home Affairs: Governance, Neighbours, Security* (Palgrave Macmillan 2009), 2–3.

12 *Road Map on the Common Space of Freedom, Security and Justice,* available at: <http://en.kremlin.ru/supplement/3588> (accessed 26 March 2019).

In this context, Oleg Korneev and Andrei Leonov consider that the project of the CSFSJ 'has been designed in order to foster at least some degree of socialisation of the Russian internal security system with EU norms and best practices'.[13] To be more precise, while participating in the design of the common spaces, Russia – sometimes intentionally, sometimes unconsciously – has pursued the logic of social learning, trying to apply EU legislation and practice where it was appropriate. From the other side, the hope for advancing to a visa-free regime has made Russia accept the EU requirements of a value-driven approach in cooperation on the common space, thus following the EU's 'rules of the game' and conditionality. Accordingly, Russia agreed to include 'adherence to common values' and 'respect of human rights' in the preamble to the Road Map. However, security threats formed a strong motivation for both sides to create a common space. According to Korneev and Leonov, 'The internal structure of the four road maps indeed reflects some sort of balance between the EU's and Russia's interests and, prevailingly, the EU's values'.[14]

Yet Russia's role in the CSFSJ was not very clear – to serve only as a buffer zone and protect EU citizens, or to become a real partner in countering common threats. Indeed, a certain asymmetry in the relations has always existed, which could become an obstacle: Russia has seen its security risks emanating not from the EU but rather from the South, while the EU has perceived Russia among the main security threats.[15]

In 2013, Russia and the EU presented their plans in the list of 'Common Steps towards Visa Free Short-term Travel of Russian and EU Citizens'. Russia voiced no objections against 'the links among the evolution of migratory flows and the protection of human rights and fundamental freedoms as well as the respect of rule of law' to be taken into account when assessing the implementation of the Common Steps.[16] The Commission published its Report on the

---

13   O. Korneev and A. Leonov, 'Eurasia and Externalities of Migration Control: Spillover Dynamics of EU-Russia Cooperation on Migration', in: R. Zaiotti (ed.), *Externalizing Migration Management: Europe, North America and the Spread of 'Remote Control' Practices* (Routledge 2016), 154.
14   *Ibid.*
15   O. Potemkina, 'EU-Russia Cooperation on the Common Space of Freedom, Security and Justice – A Challenge or an Opportunity?', *European Security* 19 (4), 2010, 551–568.
16   Common steps towards visa-free short-term travel of Russian and EU citizens (Russia-EU visa dialogue), 13 March 2013, available at: <https://ec.europa.eu/home-affairs/sites/homeaffairs/files/what-we-do/policies/international-affairs/russia/docs/common_steps_towards_visa_free_short_term_travel_en.pdf> (accessed 27 February 2020).

implementation by Russia of the Common Steps in December 2013,[17] a few months before the EU sanctions on Russia were imposed. The Commission's Report was disappointing for Russia, as it gave no hope for cancelling short-term visas in the near future. The Report actually was not about the results of common actions but rather about Russia's achievements and failures on the way to a visa-free regime. It included several evaluations of the joint initiatives. For example, the Commission appreciated cooperation between the Federal Drug Control Service (FDCS) of Russia (since 2016, the General Administration for Drug Control) and the European Monitoring Centre for Drugs and Drug Addiction (EMCDDA) on the base of the Memorandum of Understanding signed on 26 October 2007. Establishing a permanent communication channel, which allowed information exchange on different topics of mutual interest, was considered a good result. In particular, the Commission was satisfied with participation of the Russian law enforcement agencies in various joint operations with the EU Member States. However, along with practical recommendations, the Report contained political requirements, which were conditioned by the security of EU citizens' trips to Russia. Russia was not going to adopt anti-discrimination laws; therefore, the Commission expressed fears for the safety of lesbian, gay, bisexual and transgender (LGBT) persons, when they would travel to Russia visa free. Legislation on 'foreign agents' was also regarded as an obstacle to visa-free travel of people working for non-governmental organisations (NGOs). Therefore, implementation of all recommendations in full obviously could become an endless process for Russia, and some of them were principally impracticable for political reasons. The Commission's recommendations for Russia's Operational Agreement with Europol deserve special attention. The Agreement, in the Commission's opinion, could 'further improve cooperation and exchange of information with the EU, especially regarding monitoring and combating of transnational organised crime'.[18] By the time the Report was published, the EU-Russia partnership on the fight against terrorism and organised crime was founded on a legal, political and operational basis, with various dialogues in place, which were however not always successful, 'as a result of a lack of trust as well as normative divergences'.[19] The most symbolic example is the fate of the Russia-Europol Operational Agreement.

---

17   First Progress Report on the Implementation by Russia of the Common Steps towards Visa Free Short-term Travel of Russian and EU Citizens under the EU-Russia Visa Dialogue, COM (2013) 923 final, 18 December 2013.

18   *Ibid.*, 33.

19   T. Renard, 'Partners in Crime? The EU, Its Strategic Partners and International Organised Crime', ESP Working Paper, 2014, 23, available at: <http://www.egmontinstitute.be/partners-in-crime-the-eu-its-strategic-partners-and-international-organised-crime/> (accessed 1 April 2020).

The Strategic Cooperation Agreement between Europol and Russia (Rome, 2003) constituted the legal basis for joint actions against transnational organised crime. The Agreement included exchange of information, experience and best practices, pieces of legislation and other documents, as well as study visits, expert workshops and seminars. Both the EU and Russia repeatedly expressed their clear desire to proceed to the next stage of cooperation – exchange of personal data, which would open new possibilities for common activities against terrorism and organised crime.[20]

The Europol-Russia negotiations on the Agreement on Strategic and Operational Cooperation passed four rounds with partial success. The problem, which at first sight seemed just a technical obstacle, has become a stumbling block in EU-Russia cooperation. In Russia, the Federal Service for Supervision in the Sphere of Telecom, Information Technologies and Mass Communications (*Roskomnadzor*) – established in 2007 – possessed relevant competences, and the Prosecutor General's Office fulfilled supervisory functions, including personal data protection. *Roskomnadzor*, as an authorized body, participated in negotiations on the agreements with Europol and Eurojust. However, it appeared that the additional protocol to Council of Europe (CoE) Convention 108 regarding supervisory authorities and transborder data flows (ETS No. 181), which Russia did not ratify, required the establishment of another body, under the Duma's control, that has been recognised by Russian authorities as inappropriate in practice. Therefore, by the time the sanctions were imposed, the perspective for the Operational Agreement remained unclear.

The EU recommendations on the standards of data protection did not suit Russia for rather practical reasons – and not political ones – since it was considered inappropriate to create another supervisory body in addition to the existing *Roskomnadzor* and the Prosecutor General's Office. It is worth mentioning that the EU faced the same problem in the negotiations on the USA-Europol Operational Agreement – that is, the reluctance of the United States to create an independent supervisory body to protect information. This obstacle did not prevent the partners from signing the Agreement, and it means that the EU recommendations, perhaps being reasonable, appeared to be not vitally important so as to block the Agreement. However, the United States is not a member of the Council of Europe and, therefore, is not obliged to follow the

---

20 Permanent Mission of the Russian Federation to the European Union, 'Russia and Europol Negotiate a New Cooperation Agreement', 12 January 2011, available at: <https://russiaeu.ru/en/news/russia-and-europol-negotiate-new-cooperation-agreement> (accessed 27 February 2020).

CoE Conventions and Protocols. But in the case of Russia, a major normative disconnect with the EU occurred, which renders cooperation more difficult.

The same was true for the negotiations on Russia's similar Agreement with Eurojust, which began in 2007, passed four rounds and afterwards were suspended due to discrepancies on the status of the supervisory structure in Russia. Until then, the bilateral agreements with the Member States' law enforcement bodies, as well as cooperation between the liaison officers, helped Russia to exchange information in the process of joint operations under Europol's coordination.[21] Negotiations stopped in 2014, together with a number of other dialogues in the economic and political sphere. Still, even if they restart, the existing problem of information protection remains unsolved. The Commission Progress Report emphasised 'the horizontal importance of the respect of data protection rules' and called on Russia to 'ensure the independence of the Data Protection authority'. In the Commission's opinion, this should lead as well 'to a possible swift conclusion of the cooperation agreement with Eurojust'.[22]

The absence of a perspective for a full-format information exchange narrows possibilities of common activities in fighting terrorism and organised crime. Besides, due to the sanctions, no Justice, Liberty, Security (JLS) Senior Officials meeting was expected in the format of the Permanent Partnership Council (PPC). The latest meeting was held on 17 January 2014. Therefore, the possibility to discuss further steps on concluding the Operational Agreements is limited.

The Report on the results of the EU-Russia 'common steps' demonstrated the EU's strong incentive for more conditionality than for more social learning. It is true that 'caution and suspicion towards Russia remained the EU main companions on the road to a visa-free regime'.[23] While intending to continue dialogues and consultations on security and cancelling of visas, Russia specified several points beyond the 'red line' in the EU requirements, which actually ran counter to the logic of appropriateness. The EU's approach is not accepted by Russia, which on the eve of the Ukrainian conflict showed no enthusiasm for conditionality but rather for equal partnership.

---

21 See in more detail: R. Hernández i Sagrera and O. Potemkina, *Russia and the Common Space on Freedom, Security and Justice*, Study for the European Parliament LIBE Committee, 2013, 22–23, available at: <https://www.europarl.europa.eu/RegData/etudes/etudes/join/2012/474394/IPOL-LIBE_ET(2012)474394_EN.pdf> (accessed 1 April 2020).

22 First Progress Report, *op. cit. supra* note 17, 38.

23 A. Dekalchuk, 'From Hidden "Othering" to Open Rivalry: Negotiating the EU-Russia Role Structure through the Visa Dialogue', in: T. Casier and J. DeBardeleben (eds.), *EU-Russia Relations in Crisis: Understanding Diverging Perceptions* (Routledge 2018), 93–111.

2.1 Terrorism

In the conclusions on EU External Action on Counter-terrorism of 19 June 2017, the Council of the EU emphasised the importance of effective counter-terrorism partnerships through dedicated political dialogues with priority partners in the Middle East, North Africa, the Western Balkans and Turkey.[24] Russia was not included on the list of the priority partners, although an interaction on counter-terrorism had been developed through consultations. The Council conclusions did not specify the criteria for being called 'priority partners' in counter-terrorism but they must have been selected due to the obvious threats of terrorist attacks emanating from the mentioned regions. Besides, by that time, the EU had not identified Russia as a partner in any field.

Counter-terrorism cooperation has traditionally been in the field of Russia's bilateral relations with the EU Member States. However, it was included in the EU-Russia political agenda, in both the Road Maps on internal and external security and the Permanent Partnership Council meetings. Under the sanctions regime, Russia maintains relations with the EU Member States. Their security services and law enforcement bodies have never interrupted operative contacts but, in the absence of an EU-Russia high-level dialogue, the activities have become more complicated.

On 1 September 2010, the EU-Russia agreement on the protection of classified information entered into force, according to which the sides may exchange classified information in accordance with their own laws or regulations.[25] The agreement was supposed to increase the efficiency of cooperation in fighting terrorism but it has not brought significant results due to the frozen high-level political relations. The last EU-Russia common initiative was the Joint Statement on combatting terrorism, adopted on 28 January 2014.[26] It was highly respected in both the EU and Russia, and it was the only visible result of the last EU-Russia Summit before the political dialogue was limited. In the Joint EU-Russia Statement on combatting terrorism, the sides committed to:

---

24   Council of the EU, Conclusions on EU External Action on Counter-terrorism, Doc. 10384/17, 19 June 2017.

25   The Agreement between the Government of the Russian Federation and the European Union on the Protection of Classified Information, Rostov-on-Don, 1 June 2010, available at: <http://www.russianmission.eu/sites/default/files/user/files/Agreement%20on%20classified%20information_2010_English.pdf> (accessed 14 January 2019). Experts emphasise the parity of the Agreement, which maintains autonomy of Russia's participation. See, for example, P. Koutrakos, *The EU Common Security and Defence Policy* (Oxford University Press 2013), 105.

26   Joint EU-Russia Statement on Combatting Terrorism, Brussels, 28 January 2014, available at: <http://www.consilium.europa.eu/uedocs/cms_Data/docs/pressdata/EN/foraff/140835.pdf> (accessed 14 January 2019).

- Considering possibilities for further strengthening cooperation in response to crimes committed by terrorists and organised crime, including exploring prospects of signing cooperation agreements in the future, to ensure, *inter alia*, an information exchange between Russia and the EU in the sphere of combatting terrorism in conformity with their respective internal legislation including data protection standards;
- Expanding cooperation in exchanging best practices in counter-terrorism and training experts in counter-terrorism through joint seminars, training courses and other activities,
- Intensifying cooperation in the UN framework as well as other multilateral fora such as the Group of 8 (G8), in particular the G8 Rome/Lyon Group, and the Global Counter-Terrorism Forum (GCTF), Organisation for Security and Co-operation in Europe (OSCE), and the Council of Europe, as well as other international organisations actively involved in combatting terrorism.

As Renard points out, Joint Statements do not always lead to concrete actions; they just send a political signal to start consultations and negotiations on a series of substantial agreements with partners – on extradition, mutual legal assistance, passenger name records (PNR) or financing of terrorism. Until now, the EU-US partnership is the only one that has managed to culminate in a number of these issues.[27] It was expected that, after the 2014 EU-Russia Summit, a list of activities would be adopted during the consultations on combatting terrorism within the Russia-EU political dialogue. However, this dialogue was soon limited and Russia's participation in G8 meetings suspended. The EU sanctions, announced on 26 July 2014, imposed travel bans and asset freezes on 15 people, including the Head of Russia's Federal Security Service and Head of the Foreign Intelligence Service. Four members of Russia's national Security Council are also on the list. The Russian Foreign Ministry statement denounced the sanctions, saying they show the EU is taking 'a complete turn away from joint work with Russia on international and regional security, including the fight against the spread of weapons of mass destruction, terrorism (and) organised crime'.[28] In the second half of 2020 the situation worsened due to the incident with Russian oppositioner Alexei Navalny, which

---

27 T. Renard, 'Confidential Partnerships? The EU, Its Strategic Partners and International Terrorism', ESPO Working Paper, 2014, 21, available at: <http://www.egmontinstitute.be/confidential-partnerships-the-eu-its-strategic-partners-and-international-terrorism-3/> (accessed 1 April 2020).

28 The RF Ministry of Foreign Affair's statement, 26 July 2014, available at: <http://www.mid.ru/brp_4.nsf/0/25A2BD25E3B202BD44257D1800253CCB> (accessed 10 January 2019).

resulted in EU sanctions against high-level Russian officials in October 2020 and Russian counter-sanctions in response.

The Joint Statement on combatting terrorism assured that the EU and Russia 'act on the premise that the fight against terrorism is a long-term process, requiring from the international community a complex approach and united efforts for countering terrorists striving to impose their will on states, both at national, regional and global levels'.[29] For a long time, Russia has suggested a single international legal instrument in the fight against terrorism, which would close the gaps in international law. In particular, the common approach could harmonise the terrorist lists of Russia and the EU, as well as the United States, which, in turn, would increase the effectiveness of the fight against terrorism by freezing the assets of organisations and persons involved in terrorist activities. Currently, cooperation on terrorist lists is based only on their partial coincidence, and political differences prevent a consensus on the rest of the individuals and entities. For example, the Russian Federal List includes the 'Caucasus Emirate', which is not recognised as a terrorist organisation in the European Union.[30]

However, it is not very obvious that today the world is able to rally around the fight against terrorism as in September 2001. Political disagreements on the roots of terrorism remain a serious obstacle to cooperation. Russia's position towards international terrorism has not changed: to fight terrorists, one should support those who suffer from their actions (i.e., the Iraqi and Syrian governments). Russian Foreign Minister Sergey Lavrov stressed in his speech to the 69th Session of the UN General Assembly that it is 'a key issue to resolutely counter the terrorists who are attempting to control increasingly larger territories in Iraq, Syria, Afghanistan and the Sahara-Sahel area. ... [T]his task should not be sacrificed to ideological schemes'.[31] Lavrov called for structuring the struggle against terrorists in Syria in cooperation with the Syrian government, 'which has already proven its ability to work with the international community by delivering on its obligations under the programme to dispose of its chemical weapons'. He confirmed Russia's resolution to supply the governments of

---

29 Joint EU-Russia Statement on Combatting Terrorism, *op. cit.* note 26.
30 Unified Federal List of Organisations, including Foreign and International Organisations, Recognized as Terrorist in accordance with the Legislation of the Russian Federation, updated 31 August 2020, available at: <http://www.fsb.ru/fsb/npd/terror.htm> (accessed 25 March 2019).
31 Address by Russian Foreign Minister Sergey Lavrov to the 69th Session of the UN General Assembly, New York, 27 September 2014, available at: <http://www.mid.ru/brp_4.nsf/0/CDEA7854FF002B5A44257D62004F7236> (accessed 14 January 2019).

Iraq, Syria and the other Middle East and North Africa (MENA) countries with weapons and military equipment and to continue to support their efforts to suppress terrorists.

In addition, Lavrov suggested launching, under the auspices of the UN Security Council, 'an in-depth study on the extremist and terrorist threats in all their aspects across the MENA area. This integrated approach also implies that long standing conflicts should be examined, primarily the Israeli-Arab conflict'.[32] Besides, Russia's preparations to counter terrorist activities on Russian territory provide an important incentive to cooperate with the EU and the United States by exchanging information, which has become the most important instrument of international cooperation against terrorism. Against this background, the suspended EU-Russia negotiations on an Operational Agreement with Europol are becoming even more urgent than before.

However, there is still a lack of awareness that the current situation of frozen Russia-NATO and Russia-EU mechanisms does not respond to the common interests in the fight against terrorism. The Islamic State in Iraq and Syria (ISIS) demands a more serious attitude and more resistance. Its emissaries have appeared not only in Syria and Iraq but also in Libya, Lebanon and northern Afghanistan. These areas are very close to Central Asia, from where ISIS can maintain contacts with terrorists in Europe. The Islamists in Europe have established contacts with similar terrorist groups in the Northern Caucasus. Terrorists interact on a broad front, so a response must be based on an unbiased analysis of the problem, which would demonstrate the necessity of an urgent political and diplomatic interaction, as well as cooperation of security services, the military and law enforcement bodies. These mechanisms functioned rather effectively in the past, and it was not Russia's initiative to freeze them.

In October 2017, Nathalie Tocci, Advisor to the EU High Representative, stated a need for EU-Russia cooperation against terrorism. She noted the different approaches to this challenge but, at the same time, also a common perception of the issue because terrorism does not have borders. In Tocci's opinion, Russia and the EU not only should exchange information but also should counter the roots of radicalisation.[33] It is worth mentioning that, in 2017, both the EU and Russia adopted similar legislation on strengthening penalties for those who support terrorism. The Russian law presupposes responsibility for

---

32   *Ibid.*
33   *Parlamentskaya gazeta*, 17 October 2017.

terrorism financing, as well as recruitment and any other involvement of a person in terrorist crimes.[34]

As part of the EU-Russia political dialogue, regular consultations of senior officials on anti-terrorism issues began in 2016, and as of 2017 the discussion of practical aspects of cooperation at the expert level has been resumed between the respective interagency delegations. The sides have exchanged assessments of global and regional terrorist threats and counter-terrorism experience. Russia and the EU do not exchange operational information on terrorism, while a certain exchange is maintained through national channels. Russia and the EU are each concerned about the threat of foreign terrorist fighters (FTF) returning from the zones of military conflict. They have taken the necessary legislative measures in the framework of the relevant resolution of the UN Security Council.[35] In October 2019, Moscow hosted the high-level talks on counter-terrorism cooperation between the delegations of Russia and the EU. Both sides exchanged their experiences, with an emphasis on countering FTF returning from armed conflict zones. The talks were followed by a visit of the Russian delegation to the Europol headquarters in The Hague in February 2020, where the sides discussed several aspects of bilateral cooperation in the areas of counter-terrorism, organised crime, cyber crime, drug trafficking and money laundering.

What would be needed to establish a more profound basis for cooperation? Russia rejects the EU's conditionality approach; namely, that cooperation might be restarted on the condition that Russia changes its attitude and behaviour towards Ukraine. Until now, Russia has been considered 'a partner as much as a target of European counter-terrorism efforts' and, thus, the EU 'has developed counter-terrorism programmes *on* Russia (more than *with* Russia)'.[36] The war in Syria as well as the terrorist attacks in Europe were expected to change the situation and make the EU recognise Russia's key role in fighting the global threat. The 'Mogherini issue paper', which was introduced to the Foreign Affairs Council on 19 January 2015, gave a certain hope for restarting cooperation despite 'the evident differences between Russia

---

34 The RF Federal Law on Improving Counter-terrorism Measures, 29 December 2017, available at: <http://publication.pravo.gov.ru/Document/View/0001201712290061> (accessed 14 January 2019).

35 Resolution 2178 (2014) adopted by the Security Council at its 7272nd Meeting, on 24 September 2014, available at: <https://www.un.org/ga/search/view_doc.asp?symbol=S/RES/2178%20%282014%29> (accessed 5 October 2019).

36 Renard, *op. cit.* note 27, 18.

and the EU on the Syrian crisis'.³⁷ Surely, potential cooperation is complicated by the sides' different approaches to the sources of terrorism and the political processes in the MENA. However, the paper, among other proposals, recognised the value of 'existing counterterrorism dialogue with Russia'.³⁸ Yet the conditionality approach was clearly demonstrated, which Russia rejected in the same unreserved manner. According to Oleg Syromolotov, the Russian Deputy Minister of Foreign Affairs, Russia stands for translating into practice the Russia-EU cooperation in justice and home affairs. At the same time, he believes that the lack of a legal framework for exchange of personal data between Russian law enforcement agencies and Europol is a serious obstacle.³⁹

2.2 *Organised Crime*

2.2.1 Drug Trafficking

Cooperation on preventing drug trafficking has recently seemed more important to Russia than to the EU because the trafficking routes to Europe do not go through Russia but rather through the Balkans and the Mediterranean. However, EU-Russia cooperation brought good results in consultations between the EMCDDA and the Federal Drug Control Service (FDCS). Both parties showed interest in exchanging their experience and best practices, which was demonstrated in their Memorandum of Understanding signed on 26 October 2007.⁴⁰ On 4 June 2013, in the margins of the 31st EU-Russia Summit and after several rounds of difficult negotiations, the Agreement on Drug Precursors was signed.⁴¹

In 2013, a number of Russia's joint operations with the most problematic neighbours – Estonia and Lithuania – ended in success. The joint operation with Finland and Estonia under the code name *Kuru* resulted in crushing an international criminal group involved in trafficking cannabis from Morocco. In November 2013, the FDCS ten-phase joint operation with the Lithuanian

---

37 Issue Paper on Relations with Russia, Foreign Affairs Council of January 19, 2015, available at: <https://blogs.ft.com/brusselsblog/files/2015/01/Russia.pdf> (accessed 9 January 2019).
38 *Ibid.*
39 Interview of the Deputy-Minister Oleg Syromolotov, 8 September 2019, available at: <https://tass.ru/interviews/6858459> (accessed 6 October 2019).
40 Memorandum of Understanding between EMCDDA and the Federal Service of the Russian Federation for Narcotics Traffic and Control (FDCS), 26 October, 2007, available at: <http://www.russianmission.eu/sites/default/files/user/files/memorandum_on_understanding_on_drugs_2007_english.pdf > (accessed 9 January 2019).
41 Agreement between the European Union and the Russian Federation on Drug Precursors, *OJ*, 2014, L165/7.

criminal police resulted in arresting 75 criminals of the international group *Cucumber* (*Agurkiniu* in Lithuanian), who were involved in a network covering the EU, Russia and Southeastern Asia. The new phase was discussed with senior officials of the Lithuanian police in St. Petersburg in October 2014.

Since 2014 and the reintegration of Crimea, the heroine traffic through the Black Sea has become a serious problem for Russia. The geographical position of Crimea and its developed transport infrastructure predestine its involvement as a major transit point for Afghan drugs on the northern branch of the Balkan route. Because of this situation, the FDCS has begun to establish an optimal drug police structure in Crimea, which will be able to cut drug channels short in key places of the Crimean Peninsula – the large port complexes and transport centres.

Drug police bodies of Russia, the EU and the United States have continued cooperation in spite of sanctions, although information exchange has decreased. Viktor Ivanov, the former FDCS Head, was included on the US sanctions list, but not in the EU one. In August 2014, he participated in a meeting with colleagues from Interpol and senior French police officers who, according to Ivanov's interview, 'got the directive from President Hollande to cooperate closely with Russia with no limitations'.[42]

The latest Russia-EU expert consultations on drugs were held in December 2019 in Brussels, where the participants exchanged their views on drug policies, the drug situation in Russia and EU Member States and the problem of new psychoactive substances. The implementation of the 2016 UN General Assembly Special Session final document on the world drug problem was discussed, as well as the 2009 Action Plan on countering illicit drug trafficking. On 23–24 July 2019, a delegation of the EMCDDA visited Moscow to discuss the control over new psychoactive substances and the spread of drugs through the internet with the Main Directorate for drug control of the Russian Ministry of Internal Affairs.

However, the anti-narcotic fight is not limited by the law enforcement bodies' cooperation. Planning, joint operations and information exchange form the basis for common activities, and trust between police bodies has always been relatively high. Political dialogue and, especially, political will for cooperation play a significant role. The frozen negotiations on Russia-Europol and Russia-Eurojust Operational Agreements do not cause direct damage to joint activities but they certainly complicate them.

---

42 Viktor Ivanov's interview to the 'Echo of Moscow' radio station, 6 October 2014, available at: <http://echo.msk.ru/programs/beseda/1413178-echo/> (accessed 9 January 2019).

2.2.2 Irregular Migration

Cooperation against irregular migration has been realised rather fruitfully in several formats. In May 2011, the EU and Russia launched a dialogue on migration, which was not affected much by the sanctions. Several sessions gathered senior officials from Russia, the EU, and the Member States, as well as the United Nations High Commissioner for Refugees (UNHCR), to exchange information and views on asylum and other forms of international protection, and to discuss approaches for combatting irregular migration and human trafficking. Currently, Russia is able to satisfy the EU's interest in the experience of refugee protection, which Russia acquired while regulating the inflow of displaced persons from Ukraine.[43] The dialogue seems more practical than politicised, and thus could be used to maintain EU-Russia cooperation in the spheres of common interest. Yet it will not reach an operational level under the sanctions regime.

EU-Russia cooperation on readmission is another success story. The Agreement on Readmission, which entered into force on 1 June 2007, became an important step in establishing mechanisms to combat irregular migration.[44] On the basis of this agreement, the sides will take back their citizens who have illegally entered Russia or the EU Member States. Since 1 June 2010, this procedure has also been applicable to third-country nationals and stateless persons. By 2014, Russia had signed all the bilateral protocols which were needed to implement the agreement. The EU required cooperation in readmission as a precondition for visa facilitation; therefore, it was a kind of a 'bargained conditionality', as Sandra Lavenex calls it,[45] and Russia had no objections to the EU's approach of linking readmission and visa facilitation.

In 2006, Russia was among the first states to set up contacts between its national Border Guard Service of the Federal Security Service and the European Border and Coast Guard Agency (Frontex). Russian and European border guard services cooperate intensively on the base of the Terms of Reference on the establishment of operational cooperation and of the relevant Common Action

---

43 According to the UN High Commissioner for Refugees (UNHCR), by 16 April 2015, 800,961 Ukrainians had sought asylum, residence permits or other forms of legal stay in neighbouring countries. This includes 659,143 individuals in Russia and an additional 81,023 individuals in Belarus. See: United Nations Office for the Coordination of Humanitarian Affairs (OCHA), Situation Report, 36, 17, available at: <https://reliefweb.int/sites/reliefweb.int/files/resources/ocha_ukraine_situation_report_36_-_17_april_2015.pdf> (accessed 10 October 2019).

44 Agreement between the European Community and the Russian Federation on Readmission, *OJ*, 2007, L 129/40.

45 Lavenex, *op. cit.* note 10, 520.

Plans. They organise training seminars, exchange risk analyses and carry out joint operations; the latest one took place during the Sochi Olympic Games in February 2014. The security of the 2018 FIFA World Cup was guaranteed, regardless of any sanctions and political tensions, by the cooperation of 34 states.

Russia has not been deeply involved in cooperation with the EU in fighting other spheres of organised crime. For example, its cooperation with the European Anti-Fraud Office (OLAF) on smuggling started with a dialogue in 2011 but it did not bring tangible results. Meanwhile, there are important directions where Russia has been regarded more as an object of fighting organised crime than as a partner. An example might be environmental crime and the EnviCrimeNet which became concerned, in particular, with the illegal trade in caviar to the EU and the over-exploitation of wild sturgeon stocks in Russia, as well as the involvement of criminal networks.[46]

Another potentially important field for common action is vehicle crime. In this context, the Joint Police Operation (JPO) ITACAR, which was led by Italy in October 2014 and supported by Europol, is a typical example. The aim of JPO ITACAR was to target vehicles stolen in the EU and smuggled mainly to Central and North Africa, the Middle East, Russia and Central Asia, and to track down the criminal gangs active in this area.[47] Russia could play an active role in supporting the EU Member States' and Europol's activities, as well as those of the regional organisations.

Cooperation in cyber security is a fairly new field, which has never been among the priority areas such as the fight against terrorism. Russia used to participate in several projects like 'Check the Web', and in 2008 the EU and Russia began to discuss creating a cyber space and elaborating a new common definition of 'cyber security'. Joint efforts 'to combat terrorism and other criminal threats involving the use of information and communication technology' could become the most urgent dimension of cooperation.[48] However, the current situation, where the EU speaks regularly about cyber security threats coming from Russia,[49] is hardly conducive to intensive activities. Following its

---

46 'Experts on environmental crime met at Europol', *Europol news*, 1 December 2014, available at: <https://www.europol.europa.eu/latest_news/experts-environmental-crime-met-europol> (accessed 9 January 2019).

47 '28 EU Member States join forces combating vehicle crime', *Europol news*, 14 October 2014, available at: <https://www.europol.europa.eu/content/28-eu-member-states-join-forces-combating-vehicle-crime > (accessed 9 January 2019).

48 Foreign Policy Concept of the Russian Federation, 2016, available at: <http://www.mid.ru/en/foreign_policy/official_documents/-/asset_publisher/CptICkB6BZ29/content/id/2542248> (accessed 9 January 2019).

49 See the contribution by A. Marazis (chapter 12) in this volume.

Foreign Policy Concept, Russia 'seeks to devise, under the UN auspices, universal rules of responsible behaviour with respect to international cyber security, including by rendering the internet governance more international in a fair manner'.[50] In Moscow's view, all multilateral agreements on cyber security must be concluded through the UN as the most important supranational body, and a new convention on cyber security should be elaborated to replace the Council of Europe's Budapest Convention. It would be untimely to speak about the EU's support of Russia's ambitions in this direction. To the contrary, on 30 July 2020, the EU Council decided to impose new restrictive measures against individuals and entities of Russia as well as China and North Korea for their alleged involvement in various cyber-attacks,[51] which the Russian MFA disapproved as unfounded and leading to new political confrontation and cyber chaos.[52] Russia once again called to draft effective rules for preventing conflicts in cyber space, but it is clear that today this appeal will get no answer.

3   Conclusion

The EU-Russia Common Space of Freedom, Security and Justice proved rather efficient in the presanctions period, as it was filled with real content and concrete actions, many of which brought positive results. Several agreements were concluded and implemented, and a number of provisions reached the operational level. Russia's engagement in joint operations with Europol and Frontex and its exchange of analytical information with the European agencies can be regarded as success stories.

However, the development of the common space has always depended significantly on the general framework of EU-Russia political relations. The perception of Russia as a threat was demonstrated long before 2014 by the EU's position on a visa-free regime. For its part, the Russian government has always suspected that the EU intended to use joint achievements in only its

---

50   Foreign Policy Concept of the Russian Federation, *op. cit.* note 48.
51   Council Decision (CFSP) 2020/1127 of 30 July 2020 amending Decision (CFSP) 2019/797 concerning restrictive measures against cyber-attacks threatening the Union or its Member States, *OJ*, 2020, L 246/12.
52   Comment by the Information and Press Department of the Russian MFA on the introduction of EU restrictions on Russian individuals and state entities for their alleged involvement in cyber attacks, 31 July 2020, available at <https://russiaeu.ru/en/news/comment-information-and-press-department-russian-mfa-introduction-eu-restrictions-russian> (accesed 13 September 2020).

own interest. The securitisation of visa issues did not go well with the idea of a common space.

Before the Ukraine conflict, there appeared no serious contradictions in combatting common internal security threats, although Russia's desire for being an equal partner within the common space slowed down cooperation. The lack of political willingness to apprehend the European norms in the field of internal security makes a reinvigoration of the EU-Russia common internal security space highly unlikely, even in the case that the high-level political dialogue would be relaunched. The EU does not seem to want to change its *modus operandi*, and Russia will not agree to be just a norm taker but rather suggests commonly elaborated universal norms under the UN auspices.

The multi-level approach to counter-terrorism suits Russia's interests. Currently, the EU Member States remain the main actors in the EU's counter-terrorism policy, and Russia's operational cooperation with the national special services and police has always been considered satisfactory. However, regular consultations in the framework of the EU-Russia political dialogue are being held, and the significance of information exchange between police and counter-terrorism units is growing every day; therefore, Russian law enforcement bodies are interested in information exchange at the EU level to facilitate access to integrated databases. This will be possible only on the basis of an Operational Agreement with Europol.

The EU-Russia consultations on terrorism, as well as exchange of opinions, assessments, best practices and so forth are useful. But obviously they are not enough. Besides, the process of consultations is not very stable; it remains politicised and goes through ups and downs. Ideally, resuming cooperation would suppose guidelines similar to the EU partnership on internal security with the United States, Canada, Japan and Brazil, and based on international norms. In this case, the Joint EU-Russia Statement on terrorism might be followed by a precise plan of joint activities, which would provide for deepened cooperation rather than only expert consultations.

Cooperation against drug trafficking up to now has not demonstrated significant achievements. Yet stopping drug trafficking is a global challenge. Ideally, drafting a coherent anti-drug policy in the framework of the UN Conventions and a legal base for bilateral and multilateral cooperation with the EU Member States would meet EU-Russia strategic interests. To carry out this task, Russia could further maintain bilateral cooperation with the Member States and, together with the EU, engage in international fora and develop other common initiatives.

The EU has strictly followed 'selective engagement' with Russia in fighting global security threats. But this has not led to the expected results, when the high-level political dialogue, 'the crucial part of confrontation management',[53] has been abandoned and replaced only by uncoordinated actions based on overlapping interests. Under the sanctions regime, EU-Russia consultations has remained the highest level of achievement. This was demonstrated with the latest round of sanctions and the new crisis in EU-Russia relations, which dealt a hard blow to mutual trust. A permanent channel of high-level political dialogue is still needed to make the EU and Russia understand each other's motivations, possibilities and limitations to correctly manage transnational security threats.

53 T. Frear and J. Kearns, *Defusing Future Crises in the Shared Neighbourhood: Can a Clash between the West and Russia Be Prevented?*, European Leadership Network, 2017, 24–25, at <https://www.europeanleadershipnetwork.org/wp-content/uploads/2017/10/170320-Defusing-future-crises-in-the-shared-neighbourhood.pdf> (accessed 1 April 2020).

CHAPTER 14

Conditions for Effective Selective Engagement
Greening Russia's Energy Sector

Niels Smeets

1   Introduction

In terms of energy security, assisting Russia to green its energy sector may reduce fundamental tensions between the EU's move towards a market-based renewable energy transition and Russia's currently monopolised hydrocarbon-based economy. Moreover, it is in the EU's interest to cooperate with the world's fifth-largest greenhouse gas (GHG) emitter to achieve the global goal of mitigating climate change. As the EU restrictive measures targeted Russia's oil sector and deep-sea drilling technologies, and limited access to the EU's capital markets – and Russia set up retaliatory trade restrictions – renewable energy cooperation may gradually break the vicious circle of escalation. To ensure that cooperation in the field of renewable energy is effectively contributing to these goals of climate action, energy security and economic relations, it is argued that the EU should be able to back up its engagement with actual programming of projects, including financing.

Given this clear EU interest in de-escalation through renewable energy cooperation, it is nevertheless imperative that key conditions are identified to allow for the EU to selectively engage with Russia without backtracking on its restrictive measures linked to the Minsk agreements. Selective engagement in the field of renewable energy may, by no means, imply that the EU seems to approve of Russia's acts of aggression. In addition, the conditions have to reflect the EU's interests of greening Russia's energy sector to fight climate change, induce market reform of Russia's state-controlled energy sector and respect the existing restrictive measures vis-à-vis trade and investment, which have been unanimously supported by the EU Member States as a proper answer to Russia's breach of international law and Ukrainian territorial integrity.

As a result, the main research question that this chapter addresses is: Which conditions have to be met for the EU to effectively engage with Russia in the field of renewable energy cooperation? To answer this question, the chapter draws on insights obtained through five months of participatory observation within the EU institutions (European Parliament, Commission and Council in

October-February 2018), triangulated with interviews with EU civil servants, implementing partners and Russian renewable energy companies, and examinations of key policy documents.

This chapter starts by discussing the concept of 'selective engagement' and scrutinises opportunities in the field of renewable energy cooperation. To pave the way for well-founded conditions, the third section analyses Russia's renewable energy market as to identify local needs. The subsequent section formulates three sets of conditions rooted in the actual needs of Russia's renewable energy sector. The conclusion suggests conditions under which selective engagement between the EU and Russia may be effective in the field of renewable energy, building cooperation on climate action, energy security and economic relations.

2 Selective Engagement with Russia in the Field of Renewable Energy

Of the five principles, selective engagement is arguably the only principle that may constructively rebuild EU-Russia relations. Nevertheless, the areas within which selective engagement would be possible have not been exhaustively defined. Some documents mention concrete – yet potential – areas within which selective engagement with Russia would be possible, including climate, Arctic policies, maritime security, education, research and cross-border cooperation, as well as migration, counter-terrorism and other security-related foreign policy issues with particular countries such as the Democratic People's Republic of Korea and Iran. However, there is no exhaustive list of topics on which the EU may selectively engage with Russia; rather, the EU decides on a case-by-case basis whether it is opportune to engage with Russia on a given topic.

Two necessary conditions have to be fulfilled to be eligible for selective engagement: the presence of a clear EU interest, and the necessity to engage with Russia to come to an effective solution.[1] The Iran nuclear deal serves as an example, where Russia was a necessary partner, and EU businesses and Member States had a clear interest in putting the sanction regime to an end. Another field that meets both conditions is the trilateral gas talks between Russia and Ukraine, with the European Commission as a mediator. The latter engagement became all the more pressing, as the energy dialogue was suspended after the illegal annexation of Crimea.

Selective engagement with Russia in the field of renewable energy is of particular interest because it may offer a triple dividend in terms of climate policy,

---

1 Interview with policy officer, European External Action Service (EEAS), 10 January 2019.

energy security and trade and investment relations. One of the common challenges in which the EU has a clear interest is climate change, a field in which it needs to cooperate with Russia to achieve a less than two-degree world. In particular, the EU seeks to engage major polluters, among which is Russia, to adopt climate and energy goals.[2] As Russia's energy sector accounts to 82.7% of Russia's CO_2 emissions, renewable energy cooperation may greatly reduce Russia's emissions.[3] From a Russian perspective, cooperation would mitigate climate change effects, which Russia's Hydrometereological Institute considers as significant: the energy sector may perish, given pipelines could be destabilised in melting permafrost subsoil; forest fires may become more frequent; and rising water levels threaten its northern shores.[4] Russia's government increasingly takes these threats into consideration, and opens up for international cooperation as in adopted the Paris Agreement.[5] The EU and Russia seem to share complementary interests in mitigating CO_2 emissions to which cooperation in renewable energy policies (REPs) may contribute.

With respect to energy security, Russia is mainly interested in securing its hydrocarbon exports and ensuring long-term energy revenues to its state budget,[6] while the EU seeks to reduce dependence from Russia's energy exports by diversifying routes and suppliers in combination with reducing energy intensity and developing indigenous renewable resources.[7] These seemingly contrasting interests may be overcome if the EU cooperates in accelerating Russia's REPs, thereby reducing hydrocarbon consumption in Russia. REPs would free up resources for lucrative hydrocarbon exports and reduce the depletion ratio,

---

2 EEAS, 'Shared Vision, Common Action: A Stronger Europe. A Global Strategy for the European Union's Foreign and Security Policy', 2016, available at: <https://eeas.europa.eu/archives/docs/top_stories/pdf/eugs_review_web.pdf> (last accessed 22 January 2019) 9.
3 Russian Ministry of Natural Resources and Ecology (MNRE), 'Sixth National Communication of the Russian Federation to the United Nations Framework Convention on Climate Change' (MNRE 2013), 53.
4 Ministry of Natural Resources and Ecology, 'Fifth Annual Communication of the Russian Federation to the United Nations Framework Convention on Climate Change' (MNRE 2010), 95–105.
5 Russian Government, 'Government Decree No. 1228 on the Participation in the Paris Agreement', 21 September 2019, available at: <http://government.ru/docs/37917/> (accessed 2 October 2019).
6 N. Smeets, 'Opening up the Black Box: Russia's Energy Security Concept', in: A. Heinrich and H. Pleines (eds.), *Export Pipelines from the CIS Region: Geopolitics, Securitization and Political Decision-making* (Ibidem 2014), 107–127.
7 European Parliament, 'Directive 2009/28/EC of the European Parliament and the Council of 23 April 2009 on the Promotion of the Use of Energy from Renewable Sources and Amending and Subsequently Repealing Directives 2001/77/EC and 2003/30/EC', Brussels; EU and Russia, 2013, EU-Russia Energy Cooperation until 2050 Roadmap, Brussels.

stretching exports over a longer period of time.[8] These policies would ease the current perception in Russia that EU REPs may damage Russia's hydrocarbon model in the medium run.[9] Moreover, developing the renewable energy (RE) share in Russia's energy market would reduce the increasing gap between an EU energy market, which transitions to renewable energy sources, and Russia, which sticks to a hydrocarbon model having less than 1% of its electricity generated from renewable energy sources (RES).[10] Bringing Russia's energy structure closer to the likings of the EU may constructively reduce future tensions between a renewable energy and hydrocarbon-driven economy.

With respect to trade and investment cooperation, the EU may gain new export markets for its renewable energy companies, components and technologies. Russia, on the other hand, is looking for technologies and RE investments to localise an RE industry within its borders.[11] In a later phase, Russia seeks to export RE components and renewable electricity to foreign markets to ensure energy rents in a low-carbon context.[12] In a long-term perspective where both partners embrace a low-carbon economy, RE trade may replace asymmetric hydrocarbon tensions.[13] This trade in innovative technologies and human capital may be more balanced than Russia merely being a resource exporter.[14]

In sum, cleaning and greening Russia's energy sector is a possible win-win area of selective engagement in terms of combatting climate change, providing energy security and fostering trade relations.

---

8   I. Øverland and H. Kjærnet, *Russian Renewable Energy: The Potential for International Cooperation.* (Ashgate 2009); N. Tynkkynen, and P. Aalto, *Environmental Sustainability of Russia's Energy Policies: Russia's Energy Policies. National, Interregional and Global Levels* (Edward Elgar 2012), 92–116.

9   Russian Ministry of Energy, *Project Russian Energy Strategy until 2035* (Ministry of Energy 2014).

10 RES are defined as excluding large hydropower stations, given their substantial impact on both CO_2 emissions and environmental consequences; Russian Ministry of Energy, 'On Approval of the Scheme and Development Program of the Unified Energy System of Russia in the Years 2016–2022' [Ob utverzhdenii schemy I programmy razvitiya Edinoy Energeticheskoy sistemy Rossii na 2016–2022], Ministerial Decree of 1 March 2016 No. 147.

11 A.L. Teksler, 'Interview to ITAR/TASS' (Ministry of Energy 2015), 6 December 2013, available at: <https://minenergo.gov.ru/node/4434> (accessed 27 June 2019).

12 A. Novak, 'Priorities of Russian Energy Policies: Ministry of Energy', available at: <http://minenergo.gov.ru/node/3380> (accessed 4 January 2019).

13 D. Scholten and R. Bosman, 'The Geopolitics of Renewables; Exploring the Political Implications of Renewable Energy Systems', *Technological Forecasting and Social Change* 103, 2016, 273–283.

14 T. Van de Graaf, 'Battling for a Shrinking Market: Oil Producers, the Renewables Revolution, and the Risk of Stranded Assets', in: D. Scholten (ed.), *The Geopolitics of Renewables* (Springer International 2018).

3 A Needs-Based Approach: Challenges of Russian Renewable Energy Companies

Prior to identifying conditions of effective selective engagement, this section first looks into the three main economic challenges that Russian renewable energy companies face. First, renewable electricity producers face fierce competition from gas-fired electricity generation. According to the Russian Ministry of Energy, renewable electricity generation is 20% to 30% more expensive than traditional energy sources in 2017 and will be competitive only within 10 to 12 years.[15] According to the Russian Solar Energy Association, a solar power plant generates electricity at 30 RUB/kWh (0.52 USD/kWh) and wind parks produce at 10–12 RUB/kWh,[16] whereas the average world price for solar was 0.16 USD/kWh and 0.07 USD/kWh in 2014.[17] These production costs are ten times more expensive than electricity generated on the basis of gas and nuclear energy, 3.4 RUB/kWh and 3.8 RUB/kWh respectively.

The source of this artificial 'unlevel playing field' of energy investments is the state's subsidies for traditional energy sources. The International Energy Agency (IEA) estimated that Russia's fossil fuel sector received almost 40 billion dollars in keeping end-user prices below those that would prevail in an open and competitive market in 2011.[18] Apart from these direct consumer subsidies, another 14.4 billion dollars of quantifiable federal and regional subsidies to oil and gas upstream activities have been allocated to Russia's fossil fuel sector in the form of tax breaks in 2010.[19] In comparison to these subsidies, the state support for renewables is negligible.[20]

A second, interrelated challenge is that RE investments have longer payback periods due to relatively low electricity prices. As a consequence of low input

---

15 A. Teksler, 'Interview to RBK', 23 October 2017, available at: <https://minenergo.gov.ru/node/9622> (accessed 26 January 2019).

16 T.Y. Dyatel, *Solntse na gospodderzhke*, 4 August 2017, available at: <https://www.kommersant.ru/doc/3374284> (accessed 26 January 2019).

17 International Energy Agency, 'Renewables 2017: Analysis and Forecasts to 2022', available at: <https://www.oecd-ilibrary.org/energy/market-report-series-renewables_25202774> (accessed 1 April 2020) 142.

18 International Energy Agency, World Energy Outlook 2012, 70.

19 I. Gerasimchuk, 'Fossil Fuels – At What Cost? Government Support for Upstream Oil and Gas Activities in Russia', 10, February 2012, available at: <http://www.iisd.org/gsi/sites/default/files/ffs_awc_russia_eng.pdf> (accessed 26 January 2019).

20 International Finance Corporation, *Renewable Energy Policy in Russia: Waking the Green Giant*, 26, 1 January 2011, available at: <http://documents.worldbank.org/curated/en/536181468304472759/Renewable-energy-policy-in-Russia-waking-the-green-giant> (accessed 1 April 2020).

costs,[21] the electricity price is relatively low compared with other developed countries. Average prices for Russian residential consumers were just over USD 66 per MWh, or around 38% of the Organisation for Economic Co-operation and Development (OECD) average of nearly USD 175 per MWh and around 27% of the OECD Europe average of nearly USD 245 per MWh in 2011.[22] The average Russian industrial electricity price is less subsidised but, nevertheless, remains 10% to 40% below prices for OECD industrial customers.[23] Such low electricity prices reduce the profit which renewable energy companies receive for selling green electricity to the grid, making the payback period longer for RE investments.

A third challenge relates to the monopolistic market structure, which seriously inhibits market entrance of new players such as renewable energy companies. An important indicator is Russia's low number of small and medium enterprises (SMEs) – estimated at 20% to 25% – which not only is significantly lower than in developed countries but it is incomparable to developing ones as well.[24] In the energy market, the situation is even more dominated by large business concerns. Less than 5% of SME turnover comes from the energy sector.[25] Most of the Russian interviewees in this study mentioned the flip side of this under-representation of SMEs: a highly monopolistic and state-controlled energy market as an obstacle for new firms to enter the market.[26]

As the Kremlin considers the energy sector strategic,[27] given its significance in terms of financial contributions to the state budget, the government not only has increased its state control over the energy sector[28] but also has created a

---

21 Regulated gas prices and inexpensive operational nuclear energy costs given most Nuclear Power Plants are fully amortised.
22 Russian residential prices also compared favourably with OECD countries on a purchasing power parity basis.
23 D. Cooke, 'Russian Electricity Reform 2013 Update: Laying an Efficient and Competitive Foundation for Innovation and Modernisation', 79, available at: <http://www.iea.org/publications/insights/RussianElectricityReform2013Update_FINAL_WEB.pdf> (accessed 26 January 2019).
24 European Investment Bank, 'Small and Medium Entrepreneurship in Russia', 3 November 2013, available at: <http://www.eib.org/attachments/efs/econ_study_small_and_medium_entrepreneurship_in_russia_en.pdf> (accessed 26 January 2019).
25 *Ibid.*, 11.
26 Interview with business analyst in gas sector, MOEK/Gazprom, Moscow, 5 April 2015; Interview with wind entrepreneur, Russian Association for Wind Energy, Moscow, 11 August 2014; Interview with energy expert, Greenpeace Russia, Moscow, 4 August 2014.
27 V. Putin, 'Presidential Decree on the Adoption of a List of Strategic Enterprises and Strategic Joint Stock Companies', 29 December 2018, available at: <http://docs.cntd.ru/document/901904859> (accessed 26 January 2019).
28 A. Heinrich, 'Under the Kremlin's Thumb: Does Increased State Control in the Russian Gas Sector Endanger European Energy Security?', *Europe-Asia Studies*, 60 (9), 2008, 1540.

new vertically integrated monopoly in the oil sector, Rosneft.[29] Energy giants as Gazprom, Rosneft, Rosatom and RusHydro account for the lion's share of energy production. In the electricity market the state monopoly, Unified Energy System of Russia (RAO UES), was privatised but the market was not liberalised. The wholesale market is characterised by long-term regulated electricity prices and participation in the wholesale market is limited to large generating facilities.[30] As the IEA has noted, 'consolidation into government ownership after unbundling and privatisation [of UES] is an unusual development'.[31]

The retail market is dominated by regulated 'Guaranteed Suppliers' which enjoy regional monopoly status. Moreover, limited access to information and customers as well as continuing uncertainty over the roles, responsibilities and rules applying to retail market entities and transactions inhibit new entry.[32] This market structure and financial disadvantages, combined with the government policy to control the energy sector, have resulted in renewable energy companies being feasible only within existing energy concerns such as Renova and Rosatom.[33]

Paradoxically, this monopolistic market structure has been strengthened as a result of the EU's restrictive measures. As Russia's companies lost access to long-term EU bank loans (>30 days), it became even harder for small- and medium-sized renewable energy enterprises (SMREES) to access affordable loans, which increased their dependence on Russia's bank system that mainly loans mainly to large businesses. Moreover, the devaluation of the rouble resulted in rising interest rates (up to 19%) and pushed bank loan interest rates even higher. As a result, RE investment projects with high upfront investment costs further lost economic viability in Russia. Therefore, only RE companies within large traditional energy companies were able to finance and implement projects.

In addition, Russia has turned to alternative financing to avoid the Western sanction regime. Russia cunningly substituted US-blacklisted VneshEkonomBank with the Eurasian Development Bank as an intermediary actor, allowing two Karelian small hydroprojects to be financed by the BRICS New Development Bank.[34] Selective engagement could also mitigate this unintended consequence

---

29   J. Godzimirski, *Russian Energy in a Changing World* (Ashgate 2013), 16.
30   International Finance Corporation, *op. cit.* note 20, 15.
31   Cooke, *op. cit.* note 23, 4.
32   *Ibid.*, 8.
33   N. Smeets, 'Similar Goals, Divergent Motives: The Enabling and Constraining Factors of Russia's Capacity-based Renewable Energy Support Scheme', *Energy Policy* 101, 2017, 138–149.
34   Nord Hydro, 'Bank BRIKS investiruyet v Kareliyu', 18 July 2016, available at: <http://nord-hydro.ru/press-tsentr/novosti/2016/24-07/>; N. Smeets, 'The Green Challenge: Exploring

of Russia moving towards Asia, and the increase in power of state-controlled energy concerns.

These barriers result in limited access to financing of SMREEs, especially in the case of renewable energy installations, which are characterised by high upfront costs. Currently, the most popular form of SME financing in Russia is expensive bank loans (27%), followed by loans from relatives and friends (19%).[35]

4 Conditions for Effective Selective Engagement in the Field of Renewable Energy

Taking into account these three main challenges, the EU could play an important role in supporting SMREEs as identified in the previous section.

A first set of conditions of effective selective engagement relates to facilitating access to financing of Russian SMREEs. The EU in indirect management with the European Investment Bank (EIB), guided by programming under the Partnership Instrument,[36] may organise a call for loan applications with contractually binding provisions. Such a call for intermediated loans would meet at least two EIB priority areas: developing SMEs and supporting the transition to a low-carbon and environmentally friendly economy.[37] The primary goal of these binding contractual provisions consists of ensuring that local banks[38] would exclusively finance SMREEs.

This condition avoids use of EU funds to strengthen state-controlled and oligarch-led energy concerns, as has been the case with the Partnership for Modernisation (P4M).[39] The P4M provided loans to increase energy efficiency, *de facto* financing state-controlled hydrocarbon energy companies mediated by Vnesheconombank (VEB).[40] This financial support comes at a dual

---

Explanations of Russia's Renewable Energy Policies', Dissertation No. 361, Faculty of Social Sciences, 2018, 236.

35 European Investment Bank, *op. cit.* note 24.
36 This will become part of the Neighbourhood, Development and International Cooperation Instrument (NDICI) as of 2021.
37 European Investment Bank, 'Priorities', available at: <https://www.eib.org/en/projects/priorities/index.htm> (accessed 8 March 2020).
38 Hence, intermediated loans. See 'EIB Intermediated Loans', available at: <https://www.eib.org/en/products/lending/intermediated/index.htm > (accessed 8 March 2020).
39 'Russia-EU Partnership for Modernisation Projects', available at <http://ru-eu.org/main-project/> (accessed 8 March 2020).
40 *Ibid.*

cost: strengthening existing neopatrimonial relations between political and economic elites, and allocating funds to a polluting hydrocarbon sector rather than supporting an emerging renewable energy sector. This lesson learned may be taken on board not only by contractually including an employee's cap but also by excluding seemingly small-sized companies that are subsidiaries of larger energy conglomerates as well as government-controlled intermediate banks. The latter is a necessary condition in the case of sanctioned Vnesheconombank.

By offering intermediated loans to Russian SMREEs, EU support facilitates the identified problem of access to financing of SMEs. To mitigate exchange rate fluctuation risks, it is advised to offer these loans in local currency. Similar to CSO financing, this additional contractual provision covers the exchange change risks which renewable energy companies faced in 2014–2015.[41] In October 2017, EU practice set precedent in local currency lending by using EIB financing in cooperation with an international currency exchange fund to hedge for exchange rate risks.[42]

If the EU would consider investing in Russia's RE industry to achieve progress on combatting climate change, energy security and trade relations, an exemption should be provided for the restrictive measures concerning bank loans. RE investments need long-term loans to facilitate high upfront investments; however, the current restrictive measures include the suspension of new operations by the EIB and European Bank for Reconstruction and Development (EBRD). This demonstrates the limits of effective selective engagement in which political goals of clear EU interest are backed up with financial support and concrete project funding. An exemption for RE cooperation may be politically unfeasible at the moment, and depends on the continuation of restrictive measures as decided by unanimity in the EU Council. In its turn, overcoming this serious hurdle is directly dependent on meeting the Minsk agreements. This demonstrates that the political boundaries within programming are possible.

Although RE technologies and services do not strictly fall under sensitive technologies and services that may be used for oil exploration and production,[43]

---

41   Smeets, *op. cit.* note 33, 145.
42   European Investment Bank, 'First EIB Local Currency Loan for SMEs in Ukraine Made Possible with EU Support', 26 October 2017, available at: <http://www.eib.org/en/infocentre/press/releases/all/2017/2017-288-first-eib-local-currency-loan-for-smes-in-ukraine-made-possible-with-eu-support.htm> (accessed 26 January 2019).
43   EEAS, 'EU Restrictive Measures in Response to the Crisis in Ukraine', 16 March 2017, available at: <https://www.consilium.europa.eu/en/policies/sanctions/ukraine-crisis/> (accessed 22 January 2019).

RE technologies should not be exported to Crimea. As the EU maintains a firm non-recognition policy, backed up with restrictions on economic relations with Crimea and Sevastopol, RE investments and trade in Russian-occupied Crimea's energy sector should be explicitly excluded. In particular, Council Regulation 825/2014 stipulates that any financial loan or credit specifically relating to the creation, acquisition or development of infrastructure in the area of energy in Crimea or Sevastopol is prohibited.[44] The end-use location of projects thus must be included in the proposal for financing RE projects, specifically excluding the Autonomous Republic of Crimea and the city of Sevastopol. The Siemens case, exporting gas turbines to Crimea, may serve as a precedent, by conditioning loan and grants with the end-use location which may not be changed once the project is attributed. *Ex post* changes may result in suspending the long-term loan, as well as being subjected to asset freezes and travel bans.[45] As a result, investments in Crimean renewable energy sectors should be explicitly excluded from EU-Russia cooperation.

A second set of conditions fosters competition within an emerging Russian renewable energy market. Currently, only renewable subsidiary companies of existing state-controlled hydrocarbon companies dominate the renewable submarket. In particular, state-owned nuclear energy monopoly Rosatom became the dominant investor in Russia's wind energy market, in the solar sector oligarch-led Renova controls the market and Rushydro is dominant in the small hydropower market.[46] It is important to notice that these companies not only win most of the respective renewable energy tenders but also control the market as each company is vertically integrated. This implies that Renova Group owns the dominant producer of solar panels Hevel Solar and Avelar Solar which develops most solar power plants, as well as a research and development (R&D) facility in St. Petersburg. Similarly, Rosatom localised the production of wind power components (nacelle and generators) at its factory in Volgodonsk in 2019, and seeks to develop R&D and organise certification

---

44 Art. 2a 1.(a) of Council Regulation (EU), No. 825/2014 of 30 July 2014 Amending Regulation (EU) No. 692/2014 concerning Restrictions on the Import into the Union of Goods Originating in Crimea or Sevastopol, in Response to the Illegal Annexation of Crimea and Sevastopol, *OJ*, 2014, L 226/2.

45 Council Implementing Regulation (EU) 2017/1417 of 4 August 2017 Implementing Regulation (EU) No. 269/2014 concerning Restrictive Measures in Respect of Actions Undermining or Threatening the Territorial Integrity, Sovereignty and Independence of Ukraine, *OJ*, 2017, L 203I/1.

46 N. Smeets, 'The Green Menace: Unraveling Russia's Elite Discourse on Enabling and Constraining Factors of Renewable Energy Policies', *Energy Research and Social Science* 40, 2018, 251.

and technical regulations.[47] This closed market structure is further enhanced by law, requiring renewable energy projects to be built with Russian-made components.[48] As A. Boute and A. Zhikarev argue, the main driver of Russia's renewable energy policies is to achieve economic benefits related to manufacturing of green equipment by vested business interests.[49]

Thus, even if Russia drastically raises the share of renewable energy sources in its energy mix, it would not be sufficient for the market to become more similar to EU energy markets. Therefore, it is imperative to act by developing a counterweight to these monopolistic developments by means of support to SMREEs to enter the wind, solar and small hydromarkets.

The EU can do so by providing direct loans to SMREEs to offset the comparative advantage of subsidiaries of large energy concerns: access to own financing institutions within the conglomerate.[50] This would facilitate market entrance of SMREEs in the overly monopolised energy market.

A third set of conditions relates to the network mode of governance at the background of the suspended EU-Russia energy dialogue. Russian SMREEs are weakly connected and have limited capacity for R&D. The EU has to be aware that Russia's goal as an energy-rich country is not in the first place to raise the share of renewables, as it has plenty of inexpensive fossil resources, but to establish a localised renewable industry to prevent Russia from technological backwardness. As Deputy Energy Minister A.L. Teksler formulates it: 'For us, it is crucial to obtain the necessary data from our colleagues in modern technologies for the subsequent establishment of Russian made equipment and components, as well as to adopt best practices of management in this area'.[51] EU renewable energy companies have something to offer to Russia's SMREEs: renewable energy technologies.

An important flanking measure to strengthen Russian SMREEs is to set up a horizontal Russia-EU SMREE forum to share best practices and stimulate

---

47 K. Komarov, 'Rosatom Group Wind Energy,' available at: <https://www.rosatom.ru/en/rosatom-group/wind-energy/> (accessed 22 January 2019).

48 Russian Government, Government Resolution of 28 May No. 861-r 'O vnesenii izmenenii v Osnovnye napravleniya gosudarstvennoi politiki v sfere povysheniya energeticheskoi effektivnosti elektroenergetiki na osnove ispol'zovaniya vozobnovlyaemykh istochnikov energii na period do 2020 goda, utv. Rasporyazheniem Pravitelsva RF ot 8 yanvarya 2009 g. N 1-r', Russian Government, 2013.

49 A. Boute and A. Zhikharev, 'Vested Interests as Driver of the Clean Energy Transition: Evidence from Russia's Solar Energy Policy', *Energy Policy* 133, 2019, 110910.

50 Smeets, *op. cit.* note 33, 138–149.

51 A.L. Teksler, 'Interview to ITAR/TASS', Ministry of Energy, Moscow, 22 January 2016, available at: <https://minenergo.gov.ru/node/4434> (accessed 22 January 2019).

joint investment projects, possibly under the auspices of the International Renewable Energy Agency (IRENA). To guide this process of capacity building, a road map towards RE investment facilitation in Russia should be developed and jointly monitored in the SMREE forum.

From an EU perspective, selective engagement should also be backed up by increased institutional capacity to fully develop a renewable energy programme. The EU may also have to attribute human resources to a Russian unit within the European Commission. Although a Russian division still operates within the EEAS and an EU Delegation is operational in Moscow, these officers mainly deal with diplomatic relations. To cooperate in the field of renewable energy with Russia since the breakdown of political relations, only a few programme officers are working within the European Commission who would be able to design and oversee implementation of an RE cooperation programme. In the Multiannual Financial Framework period 2014–2020, only one policy officer works on Partnership Instrument (PI) funded programming of CSOs within the Directorate-General for Neighbourhood and Enlargement Negotiations (DG NEAR),[52] with others fragmented over the remaining Directorate-Generals.[53] Thus, to manage a new RE cooperation programme with Russian SMREEs to support selective engagement, the European Commission would need to strengthen this team of programme officers within the DG NEAR in the next Multiannual Financial Framework 2021–2027. By extension to renewable energy cooperation, an informal matrix structure of all Russian experts within the Commission, meeting regularly, would already be a substantial improvement, as Russia's influence is non-negligible in the entire range of policy fields, especially within the Southern neighbourhood, the candidate countries in the Western Balkans and the frozen conflicts in the Eastern neighbourhood.

5 Conclusions

In this chapter, three sets of conditions have been identified which have to be met for the EU to effectively engage with Russia in the field of renewable

---

52　Currently, there are five PI-funded programmes to Russia in 2014–2020, three of which are on climate energy action, one on sustainable environment, and a fifth on women rights. This also indicates that climate and environmental issues have been a top priority in EU-Russia programming after 2014. Yet the programmes are limited to CSOs, while SMEs could be important economic drivers of RE investments. Detailed project information is available at: European Commission, 'Partnership Instrument World Map', 2020, <https://pivisibility.eu/index.html> (accessed 12 March 2020).

53　Interview with a policy officer, DG NEAR, Brussels, 8 January 2019.

energy cooperation. Eligibility conditions provide that there should be a clear EU interest and Russia has to be a necessary partner to achieve this goal. Selective engagement in the field of renewable energy may be such a case, as the EU has a clear interest in combatting climate change, and Russia is a necessary partner given that it represents almost 5% of global GHG emissions.

To speak of 'effective' selective engagement, operational conditions should serve the EU's interest in supporting SMREEs, market formation and trade and investment. Whereas the former two may reduce energy security risks as they reduce differences between an EU renewable energy market and a Russian hydrocarbon-fired oligarchic energy system, the latter contributes to rebuilding trade relations in the long run. To ensure that cooperation in the field of renewable energy is effectively contributing to these goals of climate action, energy security and economic relations, the EU should be able to back up its engagement with actual programming of projects, including financing.

Despite the highly unfavourable political context after 2014, with a shift of RE economic relations towards Asia and a web of restrictive measures, RE cooperation may develop under these three sets of conditions. A call for loan applications in indirect management might still be considered in which Russian SMREEs compete for low-interest rate loans. Binding contractual provisions may ensure participation of SMEs. Local currency lending would lower the main investment barrier of SMREEs in Russia; namely, access to affordable long-term loans. Nevertheless, a political exemption for EIB loans to SMREEs should be provided as long as the restrictive measures are upheld. Moreover, companies operating in or targeting investments in Crimea should be explicitly excluded from participation given the EU's non-recognition policy. Targeting SMREEs would also ease the current monopolistic market structure in the solar, wind and small hydro subsectors. Through the establishment of an SMREE forum in which EU and Russian companies share their best practices and develop joint investment projects, trade and investment relations may be stimulated.

In sum, under these conditions, small-scale RE loans directly awarded to Russian SMREEs may effectively contribute to the shared goals of fostering mutual trade and investments, reducing GHG emissions and increasing energy security in Russia and in the EU.

CHAPTER 15

The Arctic as a Micro-Cosmos for Selective Engagement between the EU and Russia?

Thomas Kruessmann

1   Introduction

The idea of selective engagement with Russia came to be known first as part of the so-called 'five guiding principles', elaborated and agreed in the framework of the EU Foreign Affairs Council in March 2016.[1] Later, in June 2016, 'selective engagement' was elevated to a key feature in EU-Russia relations by the EU Global Strategy. However, the wording in the Global Strategy is rather careful, emphasizing the possibility that selective engagement 'could' take place over matters of European interest, including the Arctic, maritime security and cross-border cooperation.[2]

Indeed, the Arctic has been drawing increasing attention of scholars and politicians alike. As a region undergoing major environmental transformations, it raises concerns about climate protection and the ability of the international community to stick to a coherent plan of action against global warming. While the receding ice caps hold out the promise of an easier access to a vast array of Arctic resources (hydrocarbons, minerals, etc.) there are concerns over the degradation of the Arctic's natural environment which is intensifying as the climate warms and which, in turn, highlights the need for sustainable development as a means of protecting the environment and improving the socio-economic well-being of the indigenous peoples. The immense natural wealth of the Arctic turns the region into a point of contention and provokes

---

1 Remarks by High Representative/Vice-President Federica Mogherini at the press conference following the Foreign Affairs Council meeting of 14 March 2016, available at: <https://eeas.europa.eu/headquarters/headquarters-homepage/5490/remarks-by-high-representativevice-president-federica-mogherini-at-the-press-conference-following-the-foreign-affairs-council_en> (accessed 23 February 2020).

2 'Shared Vision, Common Action: A Stronger Europe. A Global Strategy for the European Union's Foreign and Security Policy', published in June 2016, available at: <http://europa.eu/globalstrategy/en/global-strategy-foreign-and-security-policy-european-union> (accessed 23 February 2020).

sovereignty concerns and security threats. In the face of such a paradoxical situation, the question of the prospects for EU-Russia collaboration in the Arctic is of exceptional importance.

To assess the feasibility of the Arctic as a territory of selective engagement, this chapter proceeds in a two-step manner. First, the question of how well the EU is positioned to deliver on its ambitions as an Arctic stakeholder will be addressed. Second, the chapter will look into the current state around the Northern Sea Route (NSR) to find out whether this is an area in which the EU could, quite literally, break the ice with Russia and engage in selective cooperation. This question will be answered by examining whether the EU's actorness can be strengthened by joining forces with China as the second most emerging actor in the region. It is argued that there are grounds to believe that a common approach in the Chinese spirit of 'win-win' can be found and that both the EU and China should carefully align their positions to enable the EU to re-enter constructive relations with Russia.

2   The Various 'Arctics' and the EU's Role in General

There are a number of different 'Arctics' that the EU is dealing with, and its latest 2016 Joint Communication 'An Integrated EU Policy for the Arctic'[3] is more of an attempt to create coherence in the Arctic narrative than to deliver a precise reflection of the various areas and policy fields it is engaged in. The following frameworks should be distinguished:

(1)   The five coastal states bordering on the Arctic Ocean: the United States, Russia, Canada, Norway and Denmark (through Greenland), creating the core of Arctic countries. The 'Arctic Five' are not merely a club of states, convened by virtue of their geographical location. They also represent a thinly veiled attempt to sideline the other recognised Arctic countries: Iceland, Sweden and Finland. The latter are either EU Member States or a close partner of the EU via the European Economic Area (EEA). Indeed, Iceland has also become the preferred partner of China in the Arctic,[4] and it is known for its interest in advancing multilateralism

---

3   European Commission and High Representative of the Union for Foreign Affairs and Security Policy, Joint Communication to the European Parliament and the Council, 'An Integrated Union Policy for the Arctic', JOIN 2016 (21) final of 27 April 2016.

4   C.T.N. Sørensen and E. Klimenko, 'Emerging Chinese-Russian Cooperation in the Arctic', SIPRI Policy Paper 46, June 2017, 7, available at: <https://www.sipri.org/publications/2017/sipri-policy-papers/emerging-chinese-russian-cooperation-arctic> (accessed 23 February 2020).

and reforming governance structures. To prevent such policies from taking hold, the Arctic Five, in the Ilulissat Declaration of 2008, confirmed their intention to govern the Arctic Ocean 'by virtue of their sovereignty, sovereign rights and jurisdiction'.[5] They also flatly rejected the need to develop a new comprehensive legal regime to govern the Arctic Ocean, as might be envisioned under Article 123 of the UN Convention on the Law of the Sea (UNCLOS).[6] For the EU, this means that there is no seat at the table in this most informal and entirely unstructured club. It can hope only to be able to express some positions in line with its Member State Denmark (taking into account the complex situation around Greenland) and the EEA Member State Norway.

(2) The Arctic Council,[7] a high-level intergovernmental forum founded in 1996 to bring together the Arctic Five plus Iceland, Sweden and Finland with the six Permanent Participant Groups, representing Arctic indigenous peoples' organisations. It continued an earlier initiative of the participating states, the Arctic Environmental Protection Strategy, agreed on in 1991 in Rovaniemi.[8] It is also the only circumpolar intergovernmental organisation, and it commands a high level of respect as the premier site for multilaterally addressing Arctic issues. The EU is not a formal member but its claim to participation is underscored by the membership of Denmark, Finland and Sweden plus Iceland and Norway.

(3) The Barents Euro-Arctic Cooperation, an example of subregional intergovernmental cooperation. To be precise, it is not even one intergovernmental cooperation instrument but two: the Barents Euro-Arctic Council (BEAC) and the Barents Regional Council (BAR). Members of the BEAC are the EU Member States Denmark, Finland and Sweden, the EEA countries Norway and Iceland, the Russian Federation and the European Commission. The BAR comprises a number of regions from

---

5   The Ilulissat Declaration, Arctic Ocean Conference Ilulissat, Greenland, 27–29 May 2008, available at: <http://www.oceanlaw.org/downloads/arctic/Ilulissat_Declaration.pdf> (accessed 23 February 2020).
6   For more details, see R. Kefferpütz and D. Bochkarev, 'Expanding the EU's Institutional Capacities in the Arctic Region', *Heinrich Böll Foundation Policy Briefing and Key Recommendations*, 18 November 2008, 11, available at: <https://www.boell.de/de/node/272663> (accessed 23 February 2020).
7   See <https://arctic-council.org/index.php/en/> (accessed 23 February 2020).
8   M. Heikkilä, 'It all Started in Rovaniemi', *Shared Voices* 2016, available at <https://www.uarctic.org/shared-voices/shared-voices-magazine-2016-special-issue/it-all-started-in-rovaniemi/> (accessed 23 February 2020).

Finland, Norway and Sweden as well as the Russian Federation regions Arkhangelsk, Karelia, Murmansk, Komi and Nenets.

(4) The Northern Dimension (ND), which was relaunched in 2006 as the political and operational framework for promoting the implementation of the EU-Russia Common Spaces at the regional/subregional/local level.[9] In the official language used, there is no mention of intergovernmentalism or membership, and technical designations are avoided altogether. There are four sectorial partnerships (environment/public health and social well-being/transport and logistics/culture) in which cooperation is organised with a substantial Russian participation. This cooperation is supported in depth by a network of participants, observer states, international financial institutions, EU Member States, universities and research centres.

(5) The so-called 'European Arctic' covering those parts of EU Member States that lie beyond the Arctic circle. This includes the northernmost regions of Finland, Sweden and Denmark (although Greenland is autonomous from Denmark and decided to opt out of EU membership in 1985), as well as of Norway as an EEA country. Compared to all other aforementioned frameworks, the EU is a full player and brings its full arsenal of development funding to bear. It is primarily concerned with supporting the sparsely populated regions and engaging in structural and development work.

3 EU-Russia Relations in the 'Various Arctics'

3.1 *Definition of Actorness*

In the following overview, EU-Russia relations in the Arctic Council are juxtaposed with EU-Russia relations in the Barents Euro-Arctic Cooperation and the Northern Dimension (ND), using the concept of 'actorness' as the main analytical prism.[10] Originally a term from international relations, *actorness* is used in European studies as an analytical tool to identify those properties of the EU, or of its interaction with the external world, which in

---

9   For a comprehensive background, see P. van Elsuwege, 'The EU's Northern Dimension: A Format for Pragmatic Co-operation with the EU's Biggest Neighbour', in: S. Gstöhl (ed.), *The European Neighbourhood Policy in a Comparative Perspective* (Routledge 2016), 92–104.

10 See also the good compilation of T. Nguyen and T. Williams, *The Arctic: Organizations Involved in Circumpolar Cooperation* (Library of Parliament, Ottawa 2016).

significant way express to what degree the EU is to be regarded as an international actor.[11]

3.2   *The EU in the Arctic Council*
3.2.1   Background

From its very beginning, the Arctic Council earned respect for its so-called 'boundary work' between policy-makers, scientific communities and indigenous organisations.[12] Despite its predominantly intergovernmental character, the Arctic Council originally was not designed as an institution to develop Arctic governance. In recent years, however, there has been an increasing rush of countries developing an interest in the Arctic and presenting themselves as 'Arctic stakeholders'. This is especially true for the EU and China, which are both investing substantial amounts of funding into Arctic research and using the channels of science diplomacy to support their claims for a seat at the table. The EU in its 2016 Joint Communication held that 'many of the issues affecting the Arctic region ... can be more effectively addressed through regional or multilateral co-operation'.[13] China in its 2018 White Paper on the Arctic likewise claimed that 'the Arctic situation now goes beyond its original inter-Arctic States or regional nature, having a vital bearing on the interests of States outside the region and the interests of the international community as a whole, as well as on the survival, the development, and the shared future for mankind. It is an issue with global implications and international impacts'.[14]

The pressure brought on the Arctic Council from the EU, China and a number of other states is, of course, diametrically opposed to the view of the Arctic Five who see themselves as gatekeepers to the Arctic. In this sense, Russian Minister of Foreign Affairs Sergey Lavrov, at the 2017 Fairbanks Ministerial Meeting, reiterated that the Arctic States 'bear special responsibility for long-term development in the region'.[15] But there is also a widely shared feeling

---

11   This definition is based on G. Sjøstedt, *The External Role of the European Community* (Westmead 1977). See also C. Bretherton and J. Vogler, *The European Union as a Global Actor*, 2nd ed. (Routledge 2006).

12   See the case study by J. Spence, 'Is a Melting Arctic Making the Arctic Council Too Cool? Exploring the Limits to the Effectiveness of a Boundary Organization', *Review of Policy Research* 34, 2017, 790.

13   European Commission and High Representative, *op. cit.* note 3.

14   White Paper 'China's Arctic Policy', 26 January 2018, available at: <http://english.gov.cn/archive/white_paper/2018/01/26/content_281476026660336.htm> (accessed 23 February 2020).

15   Statement by Russian Federation Foreign Minister Sergey Lavrov at the Ministerial Meeting of the Arctic Council, Fairbanks U.S.A., 11 May 2017, available at: <https://oaarchive.arctic-council.org/handle/11374/2024> (accessed 23 February 2020).

among other participants that the Arctic Council is overstretching itself. Practically, the Senior Arctic Officials (SAO) and Ministerial Meetings, to be accessible for the representatives of indigenous peoples, are often held in rather remote Northern locations, and the few days of meetings usually offer a very tight programme. There is a fear that governance issues will deflect the attention from the substantive work that the Arctic Council is interested in delivering.

Against this background the EU has, legally speaking, two possibilities of strengthening its claim to be present at the Arctic Council: obtaining observer status and/or asking the EU Member States in the Arctic Council to act as trustees of EU interests.

3.2.2 EU Observer Status

The number of requests for observer status by non-Arctic states to the Arctic Council has been increasing ever since the Arctic became a hot topic. Currently, 13 non-Arctic states have been approved as observers, with Switzerland being the latest addition in 2017. The EU itself has had quite a chequered history with the Arctic Council, and up to this day its ambition to obtain full observer status has not been realized.

Before 2009, the Arctic Council distinguished between permanent observers (the United Kingdom, France, Netherlands, Poland, Spain and Germany) and *ad hoc* observers (including China, South Korea and the EU). There was practically no difference except that *ad hoc* observers had to apply to be able to attend Arctic Council meetings. In 2009, at the Tromsø Ministerial Meeting, it was widely expected that the *ad hoc* observers would be upgraded to permanent ones. In the case of the EU, however, there was a fair amount of discontent. On the one hand, only one month earlier the European Parliament had adopted a resolution calling for an international treaty for the protection of the Arctic in parallel to the Antarctic Treaty.[16] This move caused consternation among the Arctic Five. On the other hand, a major trade dispute between the EU and Canada had erupted concerning the import of indigenous seal products into the EU single market. Canada consequently not only vowed to block the EU's bid for observer status but also launched World Trade Organisation (WTO) dispute settlement proceedings.[17]

---

16 European Parliament Resolution on the International Treaty for the Protection of the Arctic of 26 March 2009, available at: <http://www.europarl.europa.eu/sides/getDoc.do?type=MOTION&reference=B6-2009-0173&language=EN> (accessed 23 February 2020).

17 For more details, see E. Lannon and P. van Elsuwege, 'The EU and Its Neighbourhood: A Patchwork of Regional Strategies and Institutions from the Mediterranean to the

Following the 2009 events, the Arctic Council revised its observership policy. It abolished the distinction between permanent and *ad hoc* observers and made observership conditional on a set of requirements. Among other things, observers must recognise Arctic states' sovereignty, sovereign rights and jurisdiction in the Arctic, and they must recognise that an extensive legal framework applies to the Arctic Ocean including the Law of the Sea, and that this framework provides a solid foundation for responsible management of this ocean.[18]

With this new policy in place, China, Japan, South Korea, India and Singapore were admitted as observers at the Kiruna Ministerial Meeting in 2013. By contrast, the EU's application was only 'affirmatively received', meaning that the EU was *de facto* granted observer status, with the full observer status pending until the EU had resolved its conflict with Canada. When the EU found a compromise and Canada withdrew its objections,[19] it was widely expected that the EU would finally receive its upgrade. However, at the Iqaluit Ministerial Meeting in 2015 no new observer positions were discussed, and the issue was put off until the 2017 Ministerial Meeting in Fairbanks[20] where it was not resolved either.

As the 2015 Ministerial Meeting was already overshadowed by EU sanctions against Russia, it is no wonder that Arctic Council members would rather not touch the hot potato of admitting the EU as an observer.[21] In a think tank report commissioned by the European Parliament,[22] it is assumed that the 2015 deferral of the decision on the EU observer application was due to the expectation

---

Arctic', in: R. Wessel and J. Odermatt (eds.), *Research Handbook on the European Union's Engagement with International Organizations* (Edward Elgar 2019).

18 See <https://www.arctic-council.org/index.php/en/about-us/arctic-council/observers> (accessed 23 February 2020).

19 European Parliament, Question for written answer to the Commission by Urmas Paet 'EU Efforts to Secure Arctic Council Observer Status'. Answer given by Mr. Vella on behalf of the Commission on 26 September 2016, available at: <http://www.europarl.europa.eu/sides/getDoc.do?pubRef=-//EP//TEXT+WQ+E-2016-005644+0+DOC+XML+V0//EN&language=EN> (accessed 23 February 2020).

20 Para. 51 of the Iqaluit Declaration of 24 April 2015, available at: <https://www.stjornarradid.is/media/utanrikisraduneyti-media/media/nordurslodir/ACMMCA09_Iqaluit_2015_Iqaluit_Ministerial_Declaration_2015_signed.pdf> (accessed 23 February 2020).

21 D. Depledge, 'The EU and the Arctic Council', European Council on Foreign Relations, 20 April 2015, available at: <https://www.ecfr.eu/article/commentary_the_eu_and_the_arctic_council3005> (accessed 23 February 2020).

22 European Parliament, Directorate-General for External Policies, 'EU Arctic Policy in Regional Context', Study provided by G. Stang, June 2016, 12, available at: <http://www.europarl.europa.eu/RegData/etudes/STUD/2016/578017/EXPO_STU(2016)578017_EN.pdf> (accessed 23 February 2020). See also the summary, commissioned by the same department, on the outcome of the 9th Arctic Ministerial Meeting, available at:

that Russia would veto the application. Whether this expectation was also valid in 2017 is unclear. Danish Member of the European Parliament Jørn Dohrmann, who is also President of the European Parliament's Switzerland, Norway and the EU-Iceland and European Economic Area Joint Parliamentary Committees (SINNEA) delegation, emphasized:

> The EU's ambition for more engagement in the Arctic forces it to keep on good terms with Russia. This is in particular the case in order to become a full observer in the Arctic Council, where Russia is a member with veto power, but also in general because the Arctic is one of the last remaining international fora where dialogue between the EU and Russia is still open.[23]

The EU's ambitions have thus been thwarted as a result of larger geopolitical conflicts outside the region.[24] China, by comparison, had more luck. Although its 2013 bid for observer status had not received Russian endorsement either, the Chinese were nimble enough to prevent a formal Russian veto while, at the same time, assuaging the fears of the other Arctic Council Member States. Still, it came as an unpleasant surprise to China that its newly found 'strategic partner' Russia endorsed the competing bid of Japan for observership.[25]

3.2.3 Trusteeship of Denmark, Sweden and Finland?

Denmark, Sweden and Finland, as Member States of the EU bound by the Treaty on European Union (TEU), might be legally obliged in the Arctic Council to express EU positions next to or even instead of their national ones, if matters fall under EU competences. For example, in the area of the Common Foreign and Security Policy (CFSP), 'member states shall coordinate their actions in international organisations. ... They shall uphold the Union's position in such forums'.[26] Article 34 (1) TEU also specifies that 'in international organisations

---

<http://www.europarl.europa.eu/RegData/etudes/ATAG/2015/549036/EXPO_ATA(2015)549036_EN.pdf> (accessed 23 February 2020).

23 'EU Wants to Boost Arctic Ties with Russia despite Ukraine Tensions', Euractiv, 27 April 2016, available at: <https://www.euractiv.com/section/global-europe/news/eu-wants-to-boost-arctic-ties-with-russia-despite-ukraine-tensions/> (accessed 23 February 2020).

24 J. Käpylä and H. Mikkola, 'The Promise of the Geoeconomic Arctic: A Critical Analysis', *Asia Europe Journal* 14, 2016, 215.

25 M. Pollmann, 'How Japan and Russia Cooperate in the Arctic', *The Diplomat*, 10 March 2016, available at: <https://thediplomat.com/2016/03/how-japan-and-russia-cooperate-in-the-arctic/> (accessed 23 February 2020).

26 Art. 34 (1) TEU.

... where not all the member states participate, those which do take part shall uphold the Union's position'. Furthermore, in Article 34 (2) TEU the Treaty refers to the principle of 'loyalty and mutual solidarity' of Article 24 (3) TEU, in stating that the Member States participating also have an obligation to keep other Member States and the High Representative/Vice-President 'informed of any matter of common interest'.[27]

Outside the CFSP, EU Member States are bound by the duty of sincere cooperation under Article 4 (3) TEU. The European Court of Justice (ECJ) case law reveals that this rather abstract principle implies concrete substantive and procedural obligations for EU Member States, in particular when the areas of competence of the Union and the Member States are closely interrelated and when the actions of Member States may affect the unity of the EU's external representation.[28] Hence, the EU may rely to a certain extent on its Member States to act as 'trustees' of EU positions, largely depending on the nature of the EU competences at stake.

3.2.4 The EU's Actorness in the Arctic Council

As highlighted above, the EU's claim to Arctic recognition has not been met with enthusiasm by the members of the Arctic Council. Obviously, when the Canadian veto was removed, it was due to Russia's influence that decisions on the EU's full observership were delayed. Still, the EU has not been hindered from using its *de facto* role in the Arctic Council. The most recent Arctic Council Observer Report of the EU shows that the EU has been formally represented by the European External Action Service (EEAS).[29] In addition, a number of Directorate-Generals and European Agencies have been involved.

In substance, although the Observer Report 2016 was basically an exercise in copy and paste based on the 2016 Joint Communication 'An Integrated EU Policy for the Arctic',[30] it invited a good amount of criticism regarding the coherence of the policies pursued by the EU Commission.[31] The 2016 Joint

---

27 *Ibid.*
28 See P. Van Elsuwege 'The Duty of Sincere Cooperation and Its Implications for Autonomous Member State Action in the Field of External Relations', in: M. Varju (ed.), *Between Compliance and Particularism: Member State Interests and European Union Law* (Springer 2019), 283–298.
29 For example, Arctic Council Observer Report by the EU of 5 December 2016, available at: <https://oaarchive.arctic-council.org/handle/11374/1867> (accessed 23 February 2020).
30 European Commission and High Representative, *op. cit.* note 3.
31 A. Stępień and T. Koivurova, 'Formulating a Cross-cutting Policy: Challenges and Opportunities for Effective EU Arctic Policy-making', in: N. Liu, E.A. Kirk and T. Henriksen (eds.), *The European Union and the Arctic* (Brill 2017), 10, 12.

Communication had been addressed to the European Council and Parliament but obviously no feedback had been considered. In the interview with Dohrmann cited above,[32] he notes the significant military build-up of Russia in the Arctic and criticises the fact that the 2016 Communication remained silent on this issue. This criticism is echoed in the 2016 think tank report on behalf of the European Parliament,[33] which goes even further by pointing at the lack in attention to energy issues, primarily in the field of hydrocarbons.

3.3 The EU in the Barents Euro-Arctic Co-Operation

The BEAC is widely credited with being an effective subregional network, involving both EU Member States and Russia as well as the Northern regions on both sides.[34] Interestingly, the EU is not fully engaged in this framework. Instead, there has been a 'membership' of the European Commission ever since the BEAC was launched in 1993. This so-called 'membership' poses a number of interesting questions.

After the breakup of the Soviet Union a number of Central and Eastern European countries applied for EU membership, creating concern about the future architecture of Europe. In this situation, the European Commission decided to create subregional 'training grounds' for EU membership. At the same time, it was interested in preventing development paths from becoming too divergent.[35] In this way, up until today there is a 'membership' of the European Commission in the Council of Baltic Sea States and in the BEAC.

Legally speaking, it is an anomaly to have a stand-alone 'membership' of the European Commission in an international network without formally representing the EU. In 2008, Peter van Elsuwege provided a detailed analysis of this phenomenon regarding the Council of Baltic Sea States.[36] He concluded that the legal basis for the Commission's engagement is not very clear and that even ECJ case law indicates that despite the 'unbinding and declaratory nature' of the cooperation framework where the terms of engagement are so broad, the Council and the European Parliament should be involved.[37]

---

32 Euractiv, *op. cit.* note 23.
33 European Parliament, *op. cit.* note 22.
34 A.J.K. Bailes and K. Ólafsson, 'The EU Crossing Arctic Frontiers: The Barents Euro-Arctic Council, Northern Dimension and EU-West Nordic Relations', in: N. Liu, E.A. Kirk and T. Henriksen (eds.), *The European Union and the Arctic* (Brill 2017), 48.
35 *Ibid.*, 44.
36 P. van Elsuwege, *From Soviet Republics to EU Member States: A Legal and Political Assessment of the Baltic States' Accession to the EU* (Martinus Nijhoff 2008).
37 *Ibid.*, 179.

In any case, some observers claim that in times of overall confrontation between the EU and Russia post-2014, the EEAS has been able to also use the existing channels of communication for non-Arctic matters.[38] This poses the question of how to evaluate the fact that the 'technocratic' EEAS is able to maintain channels of communication while the institutions representing the official positions within the EU are not represented. This concerns the BEAC Parliamentary Assembly where in case of full membership the European Parliament should be involved, and the positions of a number of EU Member States who are more critical than others vis-à-vis Russia.

3.4 *The Northern Dimension as an In-Between*

Between the politicised issue of EU observer status in the Arctic Council and the depoliticised role of the EU in the BEAC stands the Northern Dimension. In its new post-2006 format as a policy framework, it is characterised as a hybrid between a technical investment scheme and a regional 'partnership' similar to the Eastern Partnership but without its problems.[39] Starting from some legal observations, it needs to be acknowledged that the EU is fully engaged in this cooperative framework, that EU Member States play an important role and that there is also a ND Parliamentary Forum.

The problem with the ND is that although the four Member States (including Norway and Iceland) are formally equal, the practical work of the ND revolves around the EU-Russia relationship. Here, it had reportedly been a productive place of work as long as the ND focused on the Baltic Sea and the Northwestern regions of Russia. When things came to the Arctic, Russia had been insisting on limiting the ND framework to the European Arctic and not turning it into a back door to circumpolar Arctic policy-making.[40] In this respect, A.J.K. Bailes and K. Ólafsson point out the question of 'whether an institution combining membership of all EU states with a local focus can durably match the success of the smaller High Northern groups … in de-politicisation and crisis avoidance'.[41] Indeed, in terms of actorness, it seems that the full representation of the EU in a regional framework makes it a much less flexible player.

3.5 *Subconclusion*

Compared to the situation in the Arctic Council, the EU is recognised as a full Arctic stakeholder in the BEAC and ND. However, any attempts to use these

---

38   Bailes and Ólafsson, *op. cit.* note 34, 49 and 50.
39   *Ibid.*, 51.
40   *Ibid.*, 54.
41   *Ibid.*, 56.

regional fora for dealing with circumpolar issues are closely watched by the Arctic Five and Russia in particular. In the case study below, it is shown that both frameworks do hold some relevance to the NSR but that their significance is rather played down by Russia.

4 The NSR as a Case Study of EU-Russia Engagement

4.1 Russia's Claim to the NSR

In marked contrast to those viewing the Arctic as one of the world's last 'global commons', Russia's Arctic domain is imbued with images of national sovereignty and military as well as economic security.[42] Although this patriotic image does not 'sell' as comfortably to ordinary Russians as Crimea, the Arctic nevertheless serves as a projection of national grandeur and strength. This includes the NSR in the specific understanding that Russia developed.

At the heart of the problem is Russia's claim that the NSR represents an internal trade route to which the UNCLOS rights to free navigation and innocent passage do not fully apply. The argument behind this claim is rather complex and intriguing.[43] What it essentially means is that Russia, based on national legislation,[44] feels entitled to require any ship entering the NSR to obtain permission from the relevant Russian authorities and to comply with a host of requirements. It is this claim – similar to Canada's claim on the Northwest Passage (NWP) – that is seen in the EU and in China as an obstacle to the development of the NSR into a transit shipping route. So far, due to the limited amount of transit shipping, this issue has not become very significant[45] and

---

42 A. Makurin, 'Led tronulsya. Zachem Rossiya vkladyvaetsya v Arktiku?', Argumenty i fakty of 12 December 2018, available at: <http://www.aif.ru/money/economy/lyod_tronulsya_zachem_rossiya_vkladyvaetsya_v_arktiku> (accessed 23 February 2020).

43 For more details, see E. Broks, 'Who May Sail the Arctic: Russia's and EU's Perspectives on the Legal Status of the Northern Sea Route', in: T. Hoffmann and A. Makarychev (eds.), *Russia and the EU, Spaces of Interaction* (Routledge 2018), 207–222. See also R. Dremliuga, 'A Note on the Application of Article 234 of the Law of the Sea Convention in Light of Climate Change: Views from Russia', *Ocean Development and International Law* 48, 2017, 128; V.V. Gavrilov, 'Legal Status of the Northern Sea Route and Legislation of the Russian Federation: A Note', *Ocean Development and International Law* 46, 2015, 256.

44 Federal Act Nr. 132-FZ of 28 July 2012, 'On Amendments to Various Laws of the Russian Federation, Pertaining to State Regulation of Commercial Navigation in the Arctic Waterways of the Northern Sea Route'.

45 L.E. Flake, 'Navigating an Ice-free Arctic', *The RUSI Journal* 158, 2013, 46.

the EU has, so far, preferred to keep a low profile on this matter.[46] But from a Russian perspective, things look different.

Beyond sovereignty, to understand the significance of the NSR in the Russian world view, two interrelated interests need to be distinguished. The first one is to extract resources, primarily hydrocarbons, in the High North and to sell them to Eastern and Western customers for hard currency. In the light of depleted resources in Western Siberia, revenues from such sales are urgently needed to bolster the federal budget and to stabilise the economic and political system of the country. While economic growth in China is slowing down, thereby threatening the Communist Party's claim to be the guarantor of economic development, Russia's elite is already caught in a spiraling delegitimisation with almost zero growth, *de facto* shrinking benefits and increased hardship for ordinary people. Exploiting Arctic resources and selling them to customers in the East and West via the NSR is thus a survival strategy for the regime, not to mention the vast opportunities for corruption as Russia is not even a member of the Extractive Industries Resource Initiative (EITI). The second interest is to have the NSR strengthened by increasing the volume of goods transiting between Europe and China and other Asian economies compared to the competing trade corridors in the South. In this case, Russia may collect the fees for servicing NSR transit but, more importantly, it is in a position to create incentives for European and Asian companies to enter into direct infrastructure investments. The cost for refurbishing ports along the coastline and for establishing a safety infrastructure for transit users of the NSR is daunting. Therefore, budget financing is wholly unrealistic and hopes are pinned on public-private partnerships to bring in cash.

The urgency of the Russian need to develop the NSR can be seen in the latest string of events. On 7 May 2018, President Vladimir Putin issued Decree No. 204 'On the National Goals and Strategic Development Tasks of the Russian Federation until the Year 2024', in which he ordered the government to increase the volume of cargo transported on the NSR up to annually 80 mio. tons. By comparison, in Soviet times the NSR had reached a record of 6.7 mio. tons in 1987.[47] During the past two years, the volume of cargo transported rose from 6.9 mio. tons in 2016 to 9.93 mio. tons in 2017.[48] As a

---

46 Broks, *op. cit.* note 43.
47 E. Klimenko, 'Interdependence, Not Sovereignty, Is the Key to the Development of Russia's Arctic Region', SIPRI, 30 October 2013, available at: <https://www.sipri.org/commentary/essay/2013/interdependence-not-sovereignty-key-development-russias-arctic-region> (accessed 23 February 2020).
48 See the Russian Federation State Statistics website EMISS at <https://www.fedstat.ru/indicator/51479> (accessed 23 February 2020).

response the government adopted, on 30 September 2018, a 'complex plan for the modernisation and broadening of infrastructure corridors until the year 2024'.[49] Although not quite an Action Plan, the document breaks down the relevant tasks and determines deadlines and responsible persons in the relevant ministries and other agencies. Interestingly, by going beyond the Presidential Decree, the government also commits itself to raising the ranking of Russia in the World Bank's Logistics Performance Index from the current rank of 85[50] up to at least rank 50 by 2024. The document also introduces an important proviso. Since most projects will be funded not from the budget, but from private companies, compliance with the timetables is contingent on the private investors' capability to deliver. One of the most prominent so-called 'private companies' is Novatek,[51] which is operating the liquified natural gas (LNG) plant Yamal and is currently preparing the follow-up project Arktik LNG-2. Novatek with its two onshore LNG projects is currently the Kremlin's showcase for public-private partnership involving both the EU and China. In this context, it is interesting to note the position of Novatek's CEO Leonid Mikhelson when Prime Minister Dmitriyev, along with a number of heads of ministries and agencies, visited the port of Sabetta to attend the full opening of the LNG Yamal project on 11 December 2018. Mikhelson explained that Novatek's LNG projects will be capable of delivering 46.5 mio. tons of cargo by 2024 to be transported via the NSR, which is equivalent to 55% of the 80 mio. tons decreed by President Putin. But to achieve this goal, Mikhelson demanded federal budgetary funding for modernising the NSR infrastructure and creating the relevant objects in federal ownership.[52] This may have been an ordinary episode in lobbying but it illustrates the workings of the federal government. Reminiscent of Soviet times, an arbitrarily defined benchmark is prescribed which ought to be realized by the government at any cost. The government is aware that there is no budget funding for this, so it pins its hope on public-private partnerships. Private partners, on the other hand, return the call, asking for budgetary funding to be able to deliver their contribution.

---

49 See the Russian Federation Government website at <http://government.ru/docs/34297/> (accessed 23 February 2020).

50 See the World Bank Logistics Performance Index at <https://lpi.worldbank.org/international/aggregated-ranking> (accessed 23 February 2020).

51 See <http://www.novatek.ru/> (accessed 23 February 2020).

52 Pravitel'stvo RF. Soveshchaniye po voprosam razvitiya Arktiki 11-go dekabrya 2018 g. v poselke Sabetta, available at: <http://government.ru/news/35056/> (accessed 23 February 2020).

4.2 Engaging with Russia Multilaterally

One possibility for strengthening EU actorship is to see whether there is scope to make a positive contribution to opening up the NSR. Shorter transport routes and lower costs are in the interests of both the EU and China, as currently the EU is China's number 1 trading partner and, reversely, China ranks as the second-largest EU trading partner after the United States.[53]

First, using its *de facto* observership status, the EU could become even more active in the Arctic Council Working Group Protection of the Arctic Marine Environment (PAME) which is devoted *inter alia* to Arctic marine shipping,[54] and engage in one of the many projects on shipping and navigation. However, the EU is already using its *de facto* observership to the fullest, paying a substantial contribution to the Arctic Council working groups and task forces.[55]

Second, the EU could use its role in the BEAC to engage in its Regional Working Group on Transport and Logistics (RWGTL). According to the available documents, in 2011 a representative of the Murmansk Area Government explained the Russian expectations for developing the Murmansk transport knot as the westernmost starting point of the NSR.[56] When Russia held the BEAC chairmanship in 2015–2017, its priorities focused, *inter alia,* on transport and logistics, including 'making use of commercial advantages of the NSR'. What happened to this priority is not outwardly known. Surprisingly, the RWGTL Annual Report 2017 explains that 'most challenges were found with activity and communication with the Russian partners'.[57]

Finally, the EU could engage in the Northern Dimension Partnership on Transport and Logistics (NDTPL).[58] One of its aims is to establish a Regional

---

[53] See the 'EU-China Fact Sheet', updated June 2020, available at: <https://eeas.europa.eu/headquarters/headquarters-homepage_en/34728/EU-China%20Relations%20factsheet> (accessed 23 September 2020).

[54] See <https://pame.is/index.php/projects/arctic-marine-shipping> (accessed 23 February 2020).

[55] P. Graczyk et al., 'Preparing for the Global Rush: The Arctic Council, Institutional Norms, and Socialisation of Observer Behaviour', in: K. Keil and S. Knecht (eds.) *Governing Arctic Change* (Palgrave Macmillan 2017), 132.

[56] Theses of the Presentation of N.N. Ostapchuk at the Meeting of the Work Group on Transport in the Barents Region, held at Kayani (Finland) on 22 March 2011, available at <https://www.barentsinfo.fi/beac/docs/RWGC_Kajaani_22_March_2011_Speech_by_Mr_Ostapchuk.pdf> (accessed 23 February 2020).

[57] See Barents Regional Working Group on Transport and Logistics, Annual Report for 2017, available at <https://www.barentsinfo.fi/beac/docs/RWGTL_annual_report_2017.pdf> (accessed 23 February 2020).

[58] See <http://www.ndptl.org/home> (accessed 23 February 2020).

Transport Network to connect to the NSR to the wider European Transport Network (TEN-T).[59]

It seems doubtful, however, whether any of these activities will cut the ice with the Russian government. There is nothing new to them: many are in the areas of standard setting and knowledge building, and for the most part they do not entail significant infrastructure investment. Given that the Russian side has systematically moved to keep strategic matters such as the NSR out of regional platforms, there apparently is no chance to launch a visible initiative regarding the NSR here. 'Connecting the dots' and creating a friendly environment is not a bad strategy but it does not address the concerns of the Russian side, which are time and money.

4.3 Seeking a Joint Position with China on the NSR

4.3.1 Commonalities

The EU shares with China a Comprehensive Strategic Partnership which is now in its fifteenth year. To commemorate this event, China issued its 3rd Policy Paper on the EU on 18 December 2018, in which it reiterated its readiness 'to work with the EU to strengthen dialogue and coordination at bilateral, regional and global levels'.[60]

The Policy Paper does not mention third countries such as the United States or Russia. But in the context of the US government's increasingly confrontational stance, the paper's affirmations serve to underscore the large amount of common interests between the EU and China.[61] Arguably, one important aspect of this commonality is Europe-China connectivity. China ostensibly welcomed the recent EU Strategy for Connecting Europe and Asia and suggests using the China-EU Connectivity Platform to seek greater synergy between Belt and Road Initiative (BRI) and EU developmental plans. In particular, it proposed to 'support port and shipping companies in actively participating in each other's projects, promote all-round and mutually beneficial shipping and maritime cooperation'.[62] In parallel, China agreed with Russia to make its BRI

---

59 See <http://www.ndptl.org/ndptl-regional-transport-network> (accessed 23 February 2020).

60 Full text of China's Policy Paper on the European Union, 18 December 2018, available at: <https://chinastan.org/2018/12/25/full-text-of-chinas-policy-paper-on-the-european-union/> (accessed 23 February 2020).

61 See also G. Geeraerts, 'The EU and China. Modest Signs of Convergence?', Egmont Security Policy Brief No. 101, 19 December 2018, available at: <http://www.egmontinstitute.be/the-eu-and-china-modest-signs-of-convergence/> (accessed 23 February 2020).

62 China's Policy Paper on the EU, *op. cit.* note 60.

compatible with the Trans-Eurasian Development Plan, calling for a 'Polar Silk Route' to be established.

While scholars are increasingly criticising China for double standards and the not quite unintended divisive effects of its BRI policies,[63] the EU has begun to rephrase its China policy in a more assertive direction.[64] Nevertheless, there are grounds to assume that the EU and China will be able to find a common position on opening up the NSR, using their shared financial possibilities and offering substantial support; for example, through the Asian Infrastructure Investment Bank (AIIB).[65]

4.3.2 Differences?

In addition to the nuanced view on commonalities presented above, there are a number of real differences which mitigate against an EU-China joint position on the NSR. Most fundamentally, while the EU is an outspoken representative of sharing sovereignty for the common good, China's political discourse is rather sovereignty driven. Many studies analysing the advances of China into the Arctic emphasise that China is painstakingly observing all sensitivities that may create a backlash against its presence. Indeed, there is an expansive literature placing China's Arctic drive into its domestic policy framework and explaining why China, despite its massive interests, is treading very carefully when it comes to sovereignty issues.[66] For instance, under the current Arctic Council Observer conditions, China has vowed to 'recognise Arctic States' sovereignty, sovereign rights and jurisdiction in the Arctic', and it would be hard to imagine that China becomes a 'rogue' observer along with the EU.

One important emanation of China's careful policy with direct relevance to its position vis-à-vis Russia is the fact that China did not join the US and

---

63   See, for example, J. Parello-Plesner, 'A Health Check to Reset the EU's China Policy', German Marshall Fund Policy Brief 5/2019, available at: <http://www.gmfus.org/publications/health-check-reset-eus-china-policy> (accessed 23 February 2020).

64   See the Joint Communication of the European Commission and the HR/VP 'EU-China. A Strategic Outlook' of 12 March 2019, JOIN(2019) 5 final, available at: <https://ec.europa.eu/commission/sites/beta-political/files/communication-eu-china-a-strategic-outlook.pdf> (accessed 23 February 2020).

65   On this option, see in particular Geeraerts, *op. cit.* note 61, 3.

66   L. Xing and R.G. Bertelsen, 'The Drivers of Chinese Arctic Interests: Political Stability and Energy and Transportation Security', *Arctic Yearbook* 2013, 1–16, available at: <https://arcticyearbook.com/images/yearbook/2013/Scholarly_Papers/2.LIBERTLESON.pdf> (accessed 23 February 2020). See also Sørensen and Klimenko, *op. cit.* note 4; S. Kopra, 'China's Arctic Interests', *Arctic Yearbook* 2013, 1–16, available at: <https://arcticyearbook.com/arctic-yearbook/2013/2013-scholarly-papers/36-china-s-arctic-interests> (accessed 23 February 2020).

EU sanctions in the aftermath of the annexation of Crimea, despite Russia's blatant violation of Ukraine's sovereignty. Along with the Barack Obama Administration's sanctions, the EU sanctions of 2014[67] had a harsh effect on Russia's Arctic plans, hitting long-term cooperation with Western companies, bringing offshore oil and gas exploration to a standstill and placing the onshore Yamal LNG project on the brink of failure. In this situation, China came to the rescue by delivering not only direct investment but also loans. For Russia's 'pivot to the East', this intervention created the narrative on why Russia would survive US and EU sanctions by creating strategic partnerships with Eastern countries, particularly with China. The reality, however, is slightly more complex. It is true that after the China National Petroleum Corporation (CNPC) had taken a 20% share in the Yamal LNG project in 2013 even before the Crimea-related sanctions, it was the Chinese Silk Road Fund which stepped in after the sanctions and purchased another 9.9% of stock for more than €1 billion plus offering a loan over €730 million. In addition, in 2016 Yamal LNG announced the signing of agreements with the China Exim Bank and China Development Bank on two 15-year credit line facilities for the total amount of €9.3 billion and ¥9.8 billion to finance the project. Impressive as this may sound, observers have come to the conclusion that the Chinese investors had no intention to rush to the rescue of their 'strategic partners' but considered the situation in light of primarily US sanctions rather reluctantly, finally obtaining a deal which was highly advantageous and showed that the Russian side was rather desperate to enter into the agreement.[68]

History is now repeating itself. With uncertainty around a new US sanctions bill,[69] Novatek is scrambling to secure the capital for its second LNG project, the Arktik LNG 2. Again, there is talk about participation of investors from China.[70] However, the main question is whether Russia's hype about a

---

67 Council Regulation No. 833/2014 concerning Restrictive Measures in View of Russia's Actions Destabilising the Situation in Ukraine, *OJ*, 2014, L 229/1.
68 Sørensen and Klimenko, *op. cit.* note 4, 33.
69 Bill S. 3336 of 1 August 2018, 'Defending American Security from Kremlin Aggression Act of 2018' died in the 115th Congress, see <https://www.govtrack.us/congress/bills/115/s3336> (accessed 23 February 2020).
70 J. Corcoran, 'Novatek LNG Project Defies US Sanctions', *Petroleum Economist*, 17 October 2018, available at: <http://www.petroleum-economist.com/articles/politics-economics/europe-eurasia/2018/novatek-arctic-lng-project-defies-us-sanctions> (accessed 23 February 2020). As a background from the Russian perspective, see also the authoritative analysis by the Russian International Affairs Council (RIAC), 'Asian Players in the Arctic: Interests, Opportunities, Prospects', Report 26/2016, available at: <http://russiancouncil.ru/en/activity/publications/aziatskie-igroki-v-arktike-interesy-vozmozhnosti-perspektivy/> (accessed 23 February 2020).

strategic partnership with China[71] will actually prevent China from joining the EU in demanding the opening up of the NSR. Most observers agree that despite EU sanctions, the EU is still widely seen as Russia's natural partner, sharing a host of business interests. China, on the other hand, understands that Russia's much-heralded 'pivot to the East' is accompanied by deep mistrust and that Russia might revert back to Europe the moment that sanctions get lifted. Therefore, despite differences, it makes sense for China to remain open to long-term common positions with the EU.

4.3.3 Subconclusion

Opening up the NSR has been identified as a policy goal to which both the EU and China could subscribe in their respective trajectories. 'Opening up' can be understood as having a legal dimension, by not acquiescing with Russia's customary control over the NSR and insisting on free passage without burdensome and potentially costly Russian permits and services.[72] It can also be understood as offering financial and logistical support for modernising and updating the waterways and relevant port infrastructure. The EU and China could thus make a concerted effort to help Russia increase the amount of cargo to be transported on the NSR, thereby assisting Russian partners to meet the trade volumes prescribed by the Russian President.

5 Consequences and Possible Scenarios

A joint Chinese-EU initiative to modernise the NSR would not necessarily impact the Arctic Council. In the dominant understanding of the Arctic Five, shipping on the NSR is not by definition a circumpolar issue but a matter for Russian sovereignty alone. However, repercussions may arise because of Canada's handling of the NWP. Although Canada is running in effect only a notification system, its approach is contested by the United States. If Europe

---

71 For example, G.T. Allison, 'China and Russia: A Strategic Alliance in the Making', *The National Interest*, 14 December 2018, available at: <https://nationalinterest.org/feature/china-and-russia-strategic-alliance-making-38727> (accessed 23 February 2020).

72 According to D. Beixi, there is a discrepancy emerging between Russia's interpretation of Arctic shipping as using 'a domestic sea-lane' and China's view of 'opening of high-latitude corridor (the Northeast Passage) linking Northeast Asia with Nordic and West Europe'. See D. Beixi, 'Shipping Matters: The Role of Arctic Shipping in Shaping China's Engagement in Arctic Resource Development', *Arctic Yearbook* 2018, 68, available at: <https://arcticyearbook.com/images/yearbook/2018/China-and-the-Arctic/4_AY2018_Deng.pdf> (accessed 23 February 2020).

and China attach conditions to their offer with regard to removing the overly rigid Russian national controls over the NSR, it is quite likely that a new debate on control over the Arctic passages will emerge and that Canada will become the second focus of attention.

Indeed, many of the established players will perceive a Chinese-European initiative as a threat to Arctic governance. Both the EU and China share an interest in moving Arctic governance to a truly multilateral level. For established Arctic Council members, this might be a nightmare scenario, proving once again that Arctic Council observership is a Trojan horse and that observers are largely out of control. It would probably also trigger security reflexes in Russia, turning the political elite into a hostage of their own imperial rhetoric.[73] On the other hand, revitalising the NSR may be an attractive proposition not just for the EU and China but also for other relevant Asian economies and for India. The effect may go beyond an increase in transit by triggering interest in foreign direct investment in infrastructure and easing the access to energy and resource extraction. Eventually, Russia may stand to gain more by opening up than by treating the NSR similar to its Near Abroad in the South.

For the issue of EU actorness in the Arctic, joining forces with China may present a much-needed boost. Both countries have proved their Arctic credentials and the sincerity of their interest in improving Arctic livelihoods. In terms of dealing with Russia, however, such a move may seem difficult, if not wholly illogical. But this internal contradiction is built into the doctrine of selective engagement itself. If sanctions are seen not merely as symbolic contestation but as a move to definitely hurt the regime and its proponents, they should be straightforward and clear. Sanctions will lose their credibility if selective engagement becomes a back door. On the other hand, it is up to politicians to decide how to calibrate confrontation and collaboration. Sanctions have a tendency to spiral out of control and, for proponents of sanctions, it becomes difficult to revert back to business as usual unless the other side comes with full-fledged apologies (which is something one should never expect from Russia). So, diplomatic back doors may actually be quite useful, especially when underscored by Chinese win-win rhetoric.

---

73   The amount of sensitivity can be seen in the following RIAC end-of-year 2018 assessment: 'The forecasts of China's expansion in the Arctic under the slogan of developing the "Polar Silk Road" initiative, part of the larger "One Belt One Road", also came to naught. Beijing was quite constructive and demonstrated in every possible way its respect for the sovereignty of the Arctic nations'. See A. Sergunin, 'Back to "Normalcy"', RIAC, 28 December 2018, available at: <http://russiancouncil.ru/en/analytics-and-comments/analytics/back-to-normalcy/> (accessed 23 February 2020).

PART 5

Supporting Russian Civil Society and People-to-People Contacts

CHAPTER 16

Principled Pragmatism and Civil Society in the EU Policies towards Russia

Elena Belokurova and Andrey Demidov

1 Introduction

The EU has been an important actor for Russian civil society since the beginning of the 1990s, when it became a source of financial and political support, a promoter of norms and values and a mediator linking Russian and European civil society actors through its programmes and policy instruments. The EU has not changed its stance towards civil society even in light of noticeable deterioration of mutual relations that especially speeded up after the annexation of Crimea. Most importantly, 'support of civil society and engaging in people-to-people contacts' is one of the five guiding principles that constitute the 'principled pragmatism' that the EU announced as its main approach for managing its relations with Russia since 2016.[1] How is this principle implemented in practice, what are its concrete empirical manifestations and, most importantly, how has its introduction affected already existing practices of civil society support and EU-Russia civil society cooperation?

This chapter's analysis of the EU civil society support in Russia draws an interesting and rather complicated picture. On the one hand, there is clearly a certain legacy and continuity in the EU policy in this sphere. At present, Russian civil society actors still enjoy access to programmes and financial mechanisms established in times of friendlier EU-Russia relations. These include, for instance, several EU-Russia cross-border cooperation programmes – a segment in EU-Russia cooperation that successfully survived the recent political turmoil. Moreover, the EU did not suspend, but rather adapted to the new reality, its European Instrument for Democracy and Human Rights (EIDHR), its major democracy promotion instrument in Russia, and its programme that supports 'Civil Society Organisations as Actors of Governance and Development'.

---

[1] Council of the EU, Conclusions of the Foreign Affairs Council, Doc. 7042/16, Brussels, 14 March 2016.

On the other hand, the new reality of EU-Russia relations produced new parallel mechanisms and language of civil society support in Russia. First of all, the EU resorts to a less politically sensitive and provocative jargon of strengthening 'people-to-people contacts' through the development of the new concept of 'public diplomacy'. Second, the EU channels financial support to Russian civil society through a new financial instrument, the Partnership Instrument (PI), which has been introduced under the Multiannual Financial Framework 2014–2020 and focuses on public diplomacy as one of its key objectives. Thus, this new instrument constitutes an additional layer to the existing mechanisms of civil society support, offering new thematic and financial orientations and discourse on such support. Finally, one can see the emergence of new and previously unknown practices of civil society support such as transnational dialogue and cooperation between the EU and Russian civil society organisations. Thus, the 'fifth principle' appears to be an integral part of a more complex and historically crystallised reality of EU-Russia relations and EU policy towards civil society in Russia, which are described and explained in this chapter.

2   The EU's Policy towards Russian Civil Society before Crimea: Evolution of the Approaches

2.1   *The Cheerful 1990s: Democracy Promotion through Technical Assistance*

The basis and core ideas behind the EU's support of the Russian civil society emerged and developed in the 1990s. It was the period of active cooperation and rapprochement between the EU and Russia based on the consensus that Russia was on its way towards democratisation, and the EU was there to assist it in this process on the basis of the Partnership and Cooperation Agreement (PCA) between the two parties. In 1999, the EU Common Strategy on Russia reiterated that 'fostering a stable, open and pluralist democracy in Russia' was one of the EU strategic goals and highlighted the importance of 'promoting greater cultural exchanges and deeper contacts between societies, supporting independent NGOs [non-governmental organisations], contributing to the freedom of media and promoting equal opportunities between men and women'.[2]

---

2   Common Strategy of the European Union on Russia, *OJ*, 1999, L 157/1.

The goal of bringing Russia closer to the EU was implemented through the Technical Assistance for Newly Independent States (TACIS) programme. Unlike the Central and Eastern European countries that were preparing for accession to the EU, Russia was subject to conditionality to a lesser extent, and technical assistance was not conditioned on approximation to or compliance with the EU *acquis*. TACIS funded projects for the development of human resources, institutional reforms, infrastructure and agriculture and on combatting soft security problems. Although most funding was received by the federal, regional and local authorities, some subprogrammes of TACIS contained means to support civil society organisations through funding of projects on human rights, rule of law and solving social problems. Thus, despite being articulated as one of the intentions, democracy promotion through support of civil society got rather lost in the realm of larger technical assistance.

This EU approach to civil society support exhibited several unique features.[3] Thus, the EU focused on strengthening the social partnership between NGOs and authorities whereas, for instance, the US donors supported the newly established independent 'NGO sector'. As noted by scholars, the EU approach reflects a specific European image of civil society as a partner in governance rather than a sphere of autonomous collective action, a vision that also found its way to development and enlargement policies.[4]

Another peculiarity of the EU support of civil society in Russia was its geographic focus. While the US aid reached many 'inner' Russian regions considered to be front runners in democratisation – Novgorod, Ekaterinburg, Nizhny Novgorod – the EU located its programmes in border regions and regions with a high level of urbanization and social capital.[5] The rationale behind this was quite instrumental – to pave the way for EU trade and investment through endorsing practices of good governance and to mitigate the consequences of Russia's massive economic and social crisis for neighbouring Member States. This explains why most of the EU civil society support concentrated in the border regions of the Northwest such as Leningrad Oblast, Republic of Karelia and

---

3 S. L. Henderson, 'Selling Civil Society: Western Aid and the Nongovernmental Organization Sector in Russia', *Comparative Political Studies* 35 (2), 2002, 139–167; T. Narozhna, 'Foreign Aid for a Post-euphoric Eastern Europe: The Limitations of Western Assistance in Developing Civil Society', *Journal of International Relations and Development* 7 (3), 2004, 243–266.

4 A. Buzogany, 'Civil Society Organizations beyond the European Union: Normative Expectations and Local Realities', *Journal of Contemporary European Research* 14 (2), 2018, 187–205; A. Kutay, 'Managerial Formations and Coupling among the State, the Market, and Civil Society: An Emerging Effect of Governance', *Critical Policy Analysis* 8 (3), 2014, 247–265.

5 T. Lankina, 'Explaining European Union Aid to Russia', in: J. Newton and W. Tompson (eds.), *Institutions, Ideas and Leadership in Russian Politics* (Palgrave Macmillan 2010), 218–241.

Murmansk Oblast,[6] and why cross-border cooperation became an activity the lion's share of which was constituted by civil society cross-border cooperation.[7]

Although in general EU TACIS programmes played a big role in the establishment and further development of Russian NGOs and their cooperation with EU counterparts, they also were criticised for their low effectiveness and the excessive hegemony of EU experts over the specific recipients' needs.[8] As a result, their one-sided funding, project-orientation and top-down knowledge transfer from the EU to Russia had side effects for civil society development in Russia such as overdependence on external funding and discontinuity of cooperation practices.

Apart from TACIS, the important initiative for the Russian civil society framed explicitly as a tool of democracy promotion was the European Initiative for Democracy and Human Rights in Russia, established by the European Parliament in 1994 and launched in Russia in 1997 to support the activities of civil society working for human rights and democracy and the efforts of international organisations. It was renamed the European Instrument for Democracy and Human Rights in 2006. Unlike TACIS, the EU granted financial support directly to the Russian civil society organisations working in the fields of human rights protection and monitoring, civic education, electoral observation, prevention of torture, anti-discrimination and so forth. Since its launch in Russia in 1997 and until 2018, the EIDHR has supported over 390 projects selected on an open comparative basis, each of them between 100,000 and 1 million euros, with a duration of between 12 and 36 months.[9] The EIDHR was very important for the establishment and development of human rights organisations and it represented an attempt by the EU to move to a more locally sensitive democratisation approach.[10]

---

6   G. Yarovoy and E. Belokurova, *Evropeiskiy Sojuz dlja regionov: chto mozhno i nuzhno znat rossijskiv regionam o ES* (Saint-Petersburg Norma 2012), 368.

7   J. Scott and J. Laine, 'Borderwork: Finnish-Russian Co-operation and Civil Society Engagement in the Social Economy of Transformation', *Entrepreneurship and Regional Development* 24 (3–4), 2012, 181–197.

8   G. Mikhaleva 'The European Union and Russian Transformation', in: N. Hayouz, J. Leszke and W. Meurs (eds.), *Enlarged EU – Enlarged Neighborhood: Perspectives of the European Neighbourhood Policy* (Peter Lang 2005), 107–126.

9   Official information of the EU Delegation to the Russian Federation, 2 February 2018, available at: <https://eeas.europa.eu/delegations/russia/35939/european-union-and-russian-federation_en> (accessed 1 March 2019).

10 M. Kurki, 'Governmentality and EU Democracy Promotion: The European Instrument for Democracy and Human Rights and the Construction of Democratic Civil Societies', *International Political Sociology* 5 (4), 2011, 349–366.

The scheme represented a slight deviation from the EU general vision of civil society support in the 1990s, known for its depoliticised instrumental orientation towards effective social problem-solving rather than involving civil society in enhancing rule of law, political accountability, transparency or representation.[11]

To sum up, in the 1990s EU support of Russian civil society exhibited several peculiarities. First, it was a part of proclaimed democracy promotion in Russia, politically approved by both parties. Second, despite such articulation, in practice the bulk of financial support was provided to NGOs working on social problem-solving, especially those involved in cross-border cooperation in regions bordering the EU, thus making civil society support part of larger depoliticised technical assistance. The programmes that directly supported civil society and linked this support to political issues of rule of law, democracy, accountability and so forth – EIDHR – existed in parallel to the technical assistance and were considerably smaller in their outreach.

2.2 The 2000s: First Tensions and Separation of Civil Society Support from EU-Russia Relations

This unproblematic EU-Russia cooperation began to change with the Presidency of Vladimir Putin, more so during his second term in power in 2004 and as a result of the reorientation of Russian foreign policy.[12] Russia slowly turned from its rapprochement with the West towards pursuit of its own 'national interests'. In EU-Russia relations, the adoption of two separate strategies towards each other in 1999[13] and 2000,[14] respectively, illustrates the emerging discrepancy of foreign policy aspirations. Whereas the EU continued to define stability, democracy, rule of law, a social market economy in Russia and security in Europe as strategic goals, Russia's strategy aimed primarily at ensuring national interests and enhancing the role and image of Russia in Europe and in the world. The negotiations on the newly introduced European Neighbourhood Policy (ENP) also illustrated the drift away from each other: the Russian government refused to participate in the ENP but remained the

---

11   B. Isleyen, 'Governing the Israeli-Palestinian Peace Process: The European Union Partnership for Peace', *Security Dialogue* 46 (3), 2015, 156–271.
12   S. Fernandes, 'EU-Russia Relations and Norm Diffusion: The Role of Non-state Actors', in: R. Piet and Simão L. (eds.), *Security in Shared Neighbourhoods: New Security Challenges* (Palgrave Macmillan 2016), 75–94.
13   Common Strategy of the European Union on Russia, *op. cit.* note 2.
14   'Strategy of the Relations Development of the Russian Federation with the European Union for the Mid-Term Strategy (2000–2010)', available at: http://docs.cntd.ru/document/901773061 (in Russian, accessed 1 March 2019).

target of EU funding in the framework of the European Neighbourhood and Partnership Instrument (ENPI), yet following the principle of equal financial participation. Decision-making in this framework was shifted to the level of cross-border regions with joint bodies deciding on project priorities and selection criteria.[15] Interestingly, the priority of development of people-to-people contacts was agreed as one of the main priorities of every ENPI program along with environment and modernisation of border-crossing points.

For civil society, this change also had some implications. Although in cross-border cooperation the EU continued to follow its governance/partnership view of civil society, this time with co-funding from the Russian side, TACIS was replaced in 2007 with a number of EU-Russian Cooperation Programmes with less funding. Here, the separation of the programmes happened: some were oriented both toward the cooperation between state institutions and civil society (e.g., Institution Building Partnership Programmes), others on NGOs dealing with human rights (EIDHR) and social support (Non-State Actors Programme).[16]

Thus, the EU approach to civil society has not changed radically but started toning down its explicit democracy promotion rhetoric and distinguishing it from the general cooperation. The EU refrained from accentuating the political role of civil society in Russia, unlike in the ENP countries.[17] In the framework of broader EU-Russia relations, cooperation between Russian and European NGOs was divided into two streams. On the one hand, the NGOs worked on such depoliticised issues as environment protection and historical heritage as well as social work and social protection, connected with the new common borders with Russia in the post-enlargement context. For this stream of cross-border cooperation, the rhetoric of tackling problems of so-called 'soft security' – for example, softening of ecological or nuclear threats, overcoming of social problems and elimination of differences in social standards on both sides of the border – became important. On the other hand, the support of human rights defenders and democracy was separated from the broader EU-Russia relations and official programmes, and the EU started to channel its support directly to independent human rights NGOs.

---

15 G. Yarovoy and E. Belokurova, *Evropeiskiy Sojuz dlja regionov: chto mozhno i nuzhno znat rossijskiv regionam o ES* (Norma 2012), 368.

16 Delegation of the European Union to the Russian Federation, 'Non-State Actors Programme', available at: <https://eeas.europa.eu/sites/eeas/files/369349_brochure_en_web_0.pdf> (accessed 13 March 2020).

17 T. Rommens, 'The Eastern Partnership in Georgia: Europeanizing Civil Society?', *Communist and Post Communist Studies* 50 (2), 2017, 1–11.

The history of the EU-Russia human rights dialogue in the 2000s provides a good illustration of this trend of separation. The EU became more vocal about human rights violations in Russia already during the beginning of the 2000s. The Country Strategy Paper adopted in 2001, for instance, gave a critical account on human rights, reflected on the ongoing strengthening of the state and bureaucratic structures in Russia and referred to continuation of direct support of the Russian civil society as a natural remedy against these trends. The Country Strategy Paper of 2007 employed an even more critical tone, in light of several cases of attacks on journalists and new legislation on NGOs. Despite these occasional criticisms, by 2007 the EU and Russia were actively practicing in the Human Rights Consultations, regular semi-annual intergovernmental meetings in Brussels. The dialogue was criticised as highly ineffective as both parties accused each other of human rights violations: the EU expressed its concerns over prosecution of opposition leaders, deteriorating conditions for NGOs, increasing murders of journalists and increasing suppression of lesbian, gay, bisexual and transgender (LGBT) rights, whereas Russia continuously spoke of increasing racism and xenophobia in the EU, presence of secret detention facilities and unresolved status of non-citizens in the Baltic countries.

As a result of such an ineffective format, the EU tried to pressure the Russian government to include NGOs as regular participants in the EU-Russia Human Rights Consultations but these attempts failed. Therefore, the EU opted for additional separate consultations with Russian human rights organisations, normally a day before the official meetings, thus separating the EU's support of the Russian civil society from its official relations with Russia. This development and others finally brought the Human Rights Consultations to a closure by the end of the 2000s. In this situation, the EU resorted to two strategies: rhetorical support of the Russian NGOs affected by Kremlin's restrictive policies, and intensification of its relations with the Russian NGOs as suppliers of policy information on human rights violations, political repression and non-democratic practices.[18]

Thus, the pre-Crimea EU approach to the Russian civil society was characterised by moderate democracy promotion. The old EU approach supporting government-NGO cooperation was transformed into EU-Russia funded programmes (among them, the cross-border cooperation programmes became the

---

18 E. Klitsounova, 'Promoting Human Rights in Russia by Supporting NGOs: How to Improve EU Strategies', CEPS Working Document No. 287, April 2008, available at: <https://www.ceps.eu/ceps-publications/promoting-human-rights-russia-supporting-ngos-how-improve-eu-strategies/> (accessed 1 April 2020).

most important) with the addition of new purely NGO-supported programmes. Although this state of the art already had some elements of the transformation of the EU approach after the Crimea crisis, it gradually changed after 2012.

3 Three Sources for Change in the EU Approach

The change in the EU approach towards civil society in Russia after the Crimea crisis in 2014, which among others resulted into the introduction of the fifth principle of the EU policy towards Russia in 2016, has several sources. In the authors' opinion, it was brought about by changes in the EU foreign policy and understanding of civil society support as a foreign policy priority in general, by Russia's internal transformation and by the transformation of EU-Russia relations.

3.1 The EU's Internal Transformation: New Vision of Civil Society in External Relations

Strengthening and reshaping of the EU foreign policy in the aftermath of the Lisbon Treaty and establishment of the European External Action Service (EEAS) represented the first source of change. In 2009, the EEAS began its work with the development of its institutional and personnel structures, elaboration of EU strategies and new policy and financial instruments, including the ones related to civil society support abroad. The EU support of the Russia civil society also reflected these novelties. The Communication 'The Roots of Democracy and Sustainable Development: Europe's Engagement with Civil Society in External Relations', released in 2012, summarises how the EU approach to civil society abroad altered.[19] The Communication reflects on the reasons behind this change such as the Arab Spring and popular uprisings in neighbouring countries, unclear results of legislative approximation with the Eastern partners and gradual deterioration of relations with Russia. It also registers a gradual worsening of conditions for civil society actors worldwide and already refers to it as 'shrinking space for civil society'.[20]

The Communication makes several important moves regarding civil society. First, it breaks with a criticised view of civil society as 'organised civil society' and acknowledges a multiplicity of forms of civil society organisations

---

19 European Commission, 'The Roots of Democracy and Sustainable Development: Europe's Engagement with Civil Society in External Relations', COM (2012) 492 final.
20 Ibid., 4.

(CSOs) such as youth movements and 'fluid forms of citizens', thus hinting at youth mobilization during the Arab Spring and 'Occupy movement'. Second, it explicitly links civil society with democracy rather than with efficiency of problem-solving and efficient aid delivery, thus ascribing a more political role to civil society actors abroad.[21] Clarifying this, the Communication states that the EU will pay closer attention to the political and legal environment for CSOs in partner countries, will invest in strengthening of CSOs involved in scrutinising domestic governments and holding them to account and, overall, promises to endorse local watchdogs, thereby equating the role of civil society with ensuring political accountability.

Thus, the EU approach towards civil society abroad has shifted from a focus on depoliticised engagement with organised civil society actors as partners in state-NGO governance networks, sources of policy input and expertise to a more open endorsement of civil society actors as political actors, including cooperation with loosely organised social and popular movements. It also emphasises the issues of political accountability in the contemporary world and signals the EU intention to channel a share of its support directly to civil society actors.

These priorities found their way into the EU's approach towards civil society support in Russia, which saw the EU strengthen its programmes for NGOs and civic initiatives as well as introduce some new instruments. More generally, it was expressed in the fifth principle of the EU's five principles for its further relations with Russia, formulated in March 2016 by the Foreign Affairs Council as 'the need to engage in people-to-people contacts and support Russian civil society'.[22] Based on this fifth principle, the EU decided to continue to support Russian civil society. Support of people-to-people contacts was recognised as especially important in light of existing tensions in EU-Russia relations and the shrinking space for civil society in Russia.

3.2 *Russian Internal Transformation: Shrinking Space for Civil Society*

By 2016, Russian civil society actors had already been exposed to a range of restrictive domestic policies such as the 'foreign agents' and 'unwanted organisations' legislation, persecution of human rights defenders and critical CSOs,

---

21 A. Demidov, 'Partnership with Civil Society and the Legitimacy of EU Policymaking: Exploring Actors' Normative Arguments in Four Member States', *Journal of Contemporary European Research* 14 (2), 2018, 169–186; S. Smismans, 'European Civil Society: Shaped by Discourses and Institutional Interests', *European Law Journal* 9 (4), 2003, 473–495.

22 Council of the EU, Conclusions of the Foreign Affairs Council, Doc. 7042/16, Brussels, 14 March 2016.

and discursive delegitimisation of their existence and activities in politics and media. Although this policy was accompanied by support of the loyal socially oriented NGOs contributing to the social policy implementation, the NGOs and civic initiatives working on defence of human rights, democracy and environment were put under governmental, political and bureaucratic pressure.[23]

Even more devastating for EU-Russia relations and civil society activities has been the overall conservative trend in Russia and the predominance of an anti-Western discourse actively translated by the authorities to the population through the controlled media. The anti-Western campaign that appeals to fundamental discrepancies between Russia and the West seeks to depict the latter in general, and the EU in particular, as a space of negative political, economic and social developments exacerbated by unsolved problems of migration, financial crisis and so forth. Most importantly, the main effect of this discursive framing on practices of EU-Russia cooperation is the voluntary withdrawal of many actors, including civil society ones, from this cooperation. Cancelled projects, cut ties between Russian and European partners and experts, cancelled public events (lectures, seminars, schools etc.) on EU-related topics and disrupted networks of cooperation, not only at the level of official institutions but importantly at the level of citizens and CSOs, constitute the new reality for Russian civil society.

As a result, both Russian CSOs and their partners in the EU CSOs and international organisations strengthened their pressure on the EU institutions by demanding more solidarity and better support of the Russian civil society organisations. Under such pressure, the EU institutions expressed more endorsement for the Russian CSOs by including them in the list of priorities for support.

3.3 Transformation of EU-Russia Official Relations after the Crimea Crisis

The Crimea crisis has been the dividing line in EU-Russia official relations. Besides economic sanctions, restrictions on economic cooperation, diplomatic measures and individual restrictive measures described in other chapters of this volume, the crisis led to the gradual suspension of joint EU-Russia contacts and programmes in other areas. The EU recognised that in a situation

---

23   Y. Skokova, U. Pape and I. Krasnopolskaya, 'The Non-profit Sector in Today's Russia: Between Confrontation and Co-optation', *Europe-Asia Studies* 70(4), 2018, 531–562; S. Stewart, 'Russian Civil Society: Simultaneously Suppressed and Supported', Friends of Europe, 13 October 2017, available at: <https://www.friendsofeurope.org/insights/russian-civil-society-simultaneously-suppressed-and-supported/> (accessed 1 April 2020).

when Russia is no longer a 'strategic partner' but a 'strategic challenge', as formulated in the EU Global Strategy, the official cooperation programmes became less possible. As result, not only were the official negotiations and sectoral dialogues frozen but also the human rights dialogue and other fora.

Civil society cooperation between the EU and Russian actors was affected to a lesser extent. Although a lot of partners among EU and Russian cultural, social and educational institutions reduced their cooperation, more general relations among civil society and people from the EU and Russia continued. In this situation, people-to-people contacts remained one of the few spheres where the EU could keep its contacts with Russian actors and society. Moreover, as shown above, the EU fully acknowledged the shrinking space of civil society in Russia. As a result, through its fifth principle, the EU openly declared the prominence of people-to-people contacts and its intensions to invest in strengthening societal ties through student exchanges, civil society cooperation, research and cross-border cooperation and business contacts.

As a response, the Valdai Club, which is closely connected to the Russian government, formulated a couple of months later in 2016 its '6 principles' requiring the EU to take into account Russia's interests and relations with other countries and partners. It proposed that 'the future model of Russia-EU relations could be defined in the following way: close and adjacent to each other, rather than together'.[24] The declaration of the EU's fifth principle was reacted to most negatively by the Russian authorities as 'Russia will not tolerate any interference in its domestic affairs'.[25]

At the same time, in spite of its rhetoric, the Russian government does not prohibit EU programmes in Russia. Among the 'unwanted' organisations by mid-2019, there were no EU-based organisations (with one exception, namely the European Platform for Democratic Elections).[26] Russian CSOs can still get

---

24 Valdai Discussion Club, 'Russia and the European Union: Three Questions concerning New Principles in Bilateral Relations', available at: <http://valdaiclub.com/files/10754/> (accessed 1 March 2019).

25 Comment by the Information and Press Department on the Remarks by the High Representative of the European Union for Foreign Affairs and Security Policy Federica Mogherini Following an EU Foreign Affairs Council Meeting, The Ministry of Foreign Affairs of the Russian Federation, 15 March 2016, available at: <http://www.mid.ru/en/foreign_policy/news/-/asset_publisher/cKNonkJE02Bw/content/id/2148856> (accessed 1 March 2019).

26 This is a network of NGOs and initiatives engaged in election observation in European countries, including Russia. The organisation was included on the list just before the presidential elections of 2018. In accordance with the legislation of 2015, the list of unwanted organisations is compiled by the Ministry of Justice of the Russian Federation. See See Перечень иностранных и международных неправительственных организ

grants from the EU and can successfully implement them, and Russian citizens can freely participate in EU-organised events and activities.

4 Three Elements of the Fifth Principle in Action

Although the EU declared its support for Russian civil society and its cooperation with EU partners as crucial for both democracy promotion and people-to-people cooperation, its implementation faces some important limits and consists of three elements, as shown below.

4.1 *Strengthening the Civil Society Significance: EDIHR and Other Programmes*

The first and most visible element of the EU policy towards the Russian civil society is directly related to the legacy of the previous EU 'democracy promotion' approach and support of Russian NGOs. The well-known EU programmes and financial instruments that constituted the core of the earlier EU support remain operational: EDIHR, CSO support and cross-border cooperation programmes.

The tense EU-Russia relations did not lead to their abolishment but affected the trajectory of their implementation. Thus, the EU has strengthened and changed the EDIHR focus. In 2017, it introduced the priority of media support in response to the rising significance of social media and Russian state propaganda. At the end of 2018, one of the lots was dedicated to the support of small non-formalised grassroots initiatives in the Russian regions, which had become very important for the development of the Russian civil society in recent years, because many NGOs and civil society groups are working as unregistered initiatives to avoid repressive foreign agents and unwanted organisations legislation.

In addition to EIDHR, two calls for the programme 'Civil Society Organisations as Actors of Governance and Development' were introduced in 2015 and 2019 for support of Russian NGOs working in the social sphere. In 2019, the call was aimed at the promotion of 'the social rights and protection of disadvantaged groups' (objective 1), 'the economic and social rights/

аций, деятельность которых признана нежелательной на территории Российской Федерации [List of foreign and international non-governmental organisations, whose activity is recognised as undesirable on the territory of the Russian Federation], available at: <https://minjust.gov.ru/ru/documents/7756/>, 11 June 2020 (accessed 18 September 2020).

empowerment of women' (objective 2) and 'social economy and economic inclusiveness' (objective 3).[27] These priorities also reflect the changing situation of the oppressed and discriminated groups in Russia as well as the trend towards social entrepreneurship. For the Russian NGOs and civic initiatives, this EU support became even more important than earlier because many other previously available programmes of the United States and EU Member States were meanwhile closed for Russia because of its hostile legislation and policies. For some oppressed groups and human rights activists, the support of the European Endowment for Democracy became vital. As result, the EU support of civil society still revolves around democracy promotion and protection of human rights, freedoms and rights of different social groups.

At the same time, the content of civil society cross-border cooperation supported through EU-Russia programmes has also changed, though in the direction of greater depoliticisation. The projects became even more oriented towards tackling practical problems common on both sides of the border – environment, cultural heritage, biodiversity, infrastructure, social work and so forth – a trend captured already before the Crimea crisis. Depoliticisation keeps afloat cooperation that requires governmental support.

4.2 The Partnership Instrument and Public Diplomacy as a New Element of the EU Approach

As mentioned above, due to its own institutional development, the EU recently established new instruments of support such as the Partnership Instrument (PI). The PI is a mechanism that does not envisage support of civil society as such but has turned out to be one of the main tools of implementing the new idea of 'engaging in people-to-people contacts' through 'public diplomacy'.[28]

The PI for cooperation with third countries was introduced in 2014 as an attempt to come up with new upgraded mechanisms of EU external relations with large and developed countries. It was designed as a 'new and complementary instrument providing direct support for the Union's external policies, expanding cooperation partnerships and policy dialogues to areas and

---

27 European External Action Service, 'Civil Society Organizations as Actors of Governance and Development', 25 February 2019, available at: <https://eeas.europa.eu/delegations/russia/58613/civil-society-organisations-actors-governance-and-development-europeaid161855dhactru_sk> (accessed 13 March 2020).

28 D. Valenza and F. Bossuyt, 'A Two-Way Challenge: Enhancing EU Cultural Cooperation With Russia', CESP Policy Brief No. 2019/02, 11 June 2019, 4, available at: <https://www.ceps.eu/ceps-publications/a-two-way-challenge/>. See also the contribution by D. Valenza (chapter 17) in this volume.

subjects beyond development cooperation'.²⁹ The PI as such was conceived of as a tool that would implement the international dimension of the Europe 2020 strategy, improve access for the EU companies to markets of emerging economies and enhance visibility of the EU worldwide.

But in the Russian situation, the new foreign policy instrument turned out to be especially handy given the tremendous change in EU-Russia relations after 2014, when official relations were frozen, many projects were cancelled and mutual economic and political sanctions were introduced. There was a need for a mechanism that could assist in keeping the relations with Russia afloat without affecting the rapidly declining political dialogue. There are some references to politically sensitive topics in the official documents introducing the PI; for example, the statement that the 'Union seeks to promote, develop and consolidate the principles of democracy, equality, respect for human rights and fundamental freedoms and the rule of law on which it is founded, by means of dialogue and cooperation with third countries'.³⁰ However, these goals are outshined by such economy-centric missions as restoration of economic growth; promoting resource efficiency, employment and social policy; and tackling climate change.

By 2014, the Crimean crisis made implementation of these goals highly problematic. Therefore, the PI in Russia has acquired its own specificities of implementation. Due to the lack of opportunities for implementation of the bilateral programmes, the EU opted for shaping the civil society cooperation. At the general level, the PI does not contain direct references to civil society. However, the concept that acquires especial centrality in case of the PI and subsumes some of meanings and actions previously associated with civil society is the one of public diplomacy as a tool of promoting EU values and interests as well as improvement of the perception of the EU in the partner countries.

At the same time, in Russia these activities were already developed in the 1990s yet without any explicit public diplomacy goals. Thus, besides the regular EU-Russia Summits twice a year, a number of sectoral dialogues were signed, conducted and implemented by their joint institutions and bodies. The cooperation and exchange between the EU and Russian officials and stakeholders took place on all possible levels: from high-level officials to grassroots initiatives. Russian organisations and institutions became partners and

---

29 European Commission, 'Partnership Instrument: Multiannual Indicative Programme', available at: <https://ec.europa.eu/fpi/sites/fpi/files/pi_mip_annex_en_0.pdf> (accessed 1 March 2019).

30 *Ibid.*

received access to EU programmes such as Erasmus+, ENPI, and Framework Programmes in the research field.

Moreover, already during the 1990s-2000s, the EU Delegation to Russia established and developed different mechanisms of promoting knowledge about the EU and European values among the Russian population and different target groups. CSOs had the opportunity to participate in various support programmes, consultations and dialogues. The universities were involved in the European educational and research cooperation networks. Scholars working in the area of European studies had the possibility to join EU Documentation Centres, other EU Centres, Jean Monnet networks and other programmes. Young people and students could participate in events organised by the EU Delegation such as Europe Days, EU Study Weeks, public lectures and festivals. Informational resources became available to the Russian audience such as Europulse, websites of EU-supported programmes and projects, mailing lists and accounts on social networks. Some of these activities were implemented by the CSOs as contractors through tender procedures. Accordingly, their involvement in EU-related projects was endorsed, although the central goal of these efforts was to create and spread a positive public perception of the EU and its Member States in Russia.

So, the new public diplomacy activities of the EU in Russia were rooted in previous experiences but meant something new in terms of discourse, institutional organisation and funding. Thus, in 2015 the tender was organised for a two-year project on public diplomacy in Russia, which was won by a consortium of different organisations under the lead of the Goethe-Institut in Moscow and later extended until the end of 2020. The project includes activities for people-to-people cooperation in different fields through organisation of study trips for Russian experts to the EU, invitation of EU experts to Russian public events and dialogues between business and think-tank representatives from the EU and Russia. Interestingly, both the parties and actors involved acknowledge that there is a strong need for such dialogues and new approaches and modes of cooperation.[31]

At the same time although the project's implementation is in full swing, it is not as visible as could be expected; neither does it include the local actors and civil society organisations as would be necessary for the new instrument. The reason is the EU's institutional decision to designate a consortium of large organisations capable of demonstrating the necessary experience in handling

---

31 Dahrendorf Forum, 'Avoiding a New Cold War: The Future of EU-Russia Relations in the Context of the Ukraine Crisis', available at: <http://www.lse.ac.uk/IDEAS/publications/reports/pdf/LSE-IDEAS-Avoiding-a-New-Cold-War.pdf> (accessed 1 March 2019).

big budgets to be eligible for such a contract. No local NGOs or even national CSOs can be competitive enough to participate in such a tender. Therefore, a large state-close organisation like the Goethe-Institut is the most likely winner of such a tender. As a result only one small team, which is a part of the big organisation, is implementing the whole project, in cooperation with the EU Delegation. As a consequence, the local actors and civil society organisations are able participate in its implementation to only a very limited extent.

4.3 Support of the Transnational Dialogue: The EU-Russia Civil Society Forum

The third important element of the current EU policy towards the Russian civil society is support of the EU-Russia Civil Society Forum (CSF).[32] The CSF was established as an NGO network in March 2011, first as a network of 40 NGOs from the EU and Russia working on different issues with the goal to establish a civil society cooperation platform within the framework of EU-Russia relations. It was a quite positive period of EU-Russia relations, when the Partnership for Modernisation was developed and implemented. Therefore, the NGOs hoped to influence the EU-Russia intergovernmental dialogue to present the civil society perspectives. Since its foundation in 2011, the Forum has attracted a lot of new member organisations from the EU and Russia, amounting to more than 170 by the end of 2019.

Importantly, it was not the EU which established or even initiated the CSF, as it did in the case of the Eastern Partnership Civil Society Forum. The CSF was the initiative of NGOs themselves, which established the it with an effective self-governing institutional structure. Thus, the main decision-making institution is the General Assembly, an annual gathering of most members. It elects a board representing an equal number (four to six) of members from the EU and Russia. The permanent secretariat, situated in 2011–2012 in Prague and since 2013 in Berlin, is responsible for the management of daily activities and for the implementation of the decisions taken by the collective institutions mentioned above. The work of the CSF is organised as a platform for exchange and cooperation between different NGOs, and as a channel for advocacy and communication with different policy-makers and civil society actors in the EU and in Russia. In 2017, the new separate legal entity EU-Russia Civil Society Forum was established in Berlin.

In the beginning, discussions within the CSF concerned its potential influence on EU-Russia relations and official negotiations, so that it could become a civil society complement to the intergovernmental negotiations. Political

---

32 Official CFS webpage is available at <http://eu-russia-csf.org>.

developments, especially the strengthening of authoritarian tendencies in Russia and political conflicts between the EU and Russia, resulted in a transformation of the CSF's work.

Since 2012, the CSF has begun to pay more attention to the support of and solidarity with their members recognised as 'foreign agents' like the first of them, the association 'Voice' (*Golos*) and the Kostroma Centre for Support of Community Initiatives.[33] Moreover, due to problems with the intergovernmental dialogue between the EU and Russia in 2014, the objective of influence on this dialogue became irrelevant and was replaced by the internal cooperation among the NGOs within the CSF. As a result of this tendency, the Mid-Term Development Strategy adopted by a majority of members in the summer of 2015[34] proclaimed the following major objectives (in order of prioritisation):

1. Support and solidarity for civil society organisations and activists facing pressure and persecution.
2. Promoting cooperation between civil society organisations in Russia and the EU based on shared values, and facilitating people-to-people exchanges.
3. Efforts to promote shared values, strengthen the European legal frameworks and pan-European institutions, facilitate Russian-European integration and create a common public space.

Given the pressure on Russian NGOs participating in international relations, the CSF became one of the most important spaces for the continuation of NGO cooperation. This can explain the decision of the EU to support the CSF as part of its PI: their goals and activities were in full accordance with the priorities of the PI, the CSF's activities and participants were already known to the EU officials, and they already had shown their readiness and ability to implement big EU-funded projects. The EU support became crucially important for the CSF, keeping the transnational cooperation among EU and Russian NGOs on the basis of shared values and objectives and with a self-governed institutional structure.

5   Conclusions

The fifth principle presupposes continuation of civil society support in Russia and engaging in people-to-people contacts. At first sight, the principle

---

33 See more statements of the CSF Steering Committee/the Board, available at: <https://eu-russia-csf.org/news/statements/> (accessed 13 March 2020).

34 'Mid-Term Strategy of Development of the EU-Russia Civil Society Forum' (mid-2015-mid-2018), on file with the authors.

introduces and promises very little. The EU has always been an important supporter of Russian civil society since the early 1990s, as one of the biggest donors and suppliers of knowledge and expertise. In addition, the reference to people-to-people contacts does not sound particularly innovative. Expanding people-to-people contacts has always been mentioned as one of the goals of assisting Russia and civil society support, especially in the realm of cross-border cooperation. What does the introduction of this principle mean in terms of concrete practices of EU civil society support in Russia?

The analysis in this chapter shows that, at the level of concrete practices, three developments are significant. First, the fifth principle complements the legacy of EU civil society support. This legacy manifests itself in the form of earlier introduced programmes and mechanisms of support such as EIDHR and cross-border cooperation. Their focus and thematic orientation have undoubtedly changed as a result of the dynamic evolution of EU-Russia relations. For instance, cross-border cooperation programmes that were also initially introduced as a tool to promote democracy in Russia evolved more into a practice of depoliticised practical cooperation. One can say that that the rhetoric and discourse of democracy promotion sustained under the EIDHR Non-State Actors and European Endowment for Democracy programmes almost totally disappeared. Not only has the EU withdrawn from providing this kind of explicit democracy support but it has adapted smoothly to the new needs of the Russian civil society actors.

Second, this chapter's analysis shows the emergence of a new approach towards EU civil society support. More specifically, one can notice the EU's effort to resort to alternative mechanisms of civil society support against the background of the impossibility of introducing new official programmes and the need to keep existing ones functioning. For civil society actors, the PI, an EU foreign policy tool, became such an instrument. Interestingly, it is in the PI that the focus on people-to-people contacts is strongly present. Even more interestingly, assistance to civil society and people-to-people contacts is now wrapped in the rhetoric of public diplomacy as a set of actions aimed at improving the EU's image and public perceptions in Russia and expansion of the knowledge about the EU. Thus, the main peculiarity of existing civil society support is that these activities are justified by the EU by references to 'public diplomacy' rather than 'strengthening of civil society' or 'civil society support'. This 'safe' discourse as opposed to the politically sensitive discourse of civil society support seems to be convenient for both parties. At the same time, this change appears to have been brought about by a combination of other sources: change in the EU policy towards civil society with a new accent on engaging not only with the NGOs but also with non-formalised civic initiatives and ordinary citizens; new EU foreign policy instruments; and the complexity of official EU-Russia relations.

Finally, another peculiarity of the EU's civil society support is the support of new and previously unknown initiatives such as the transnational dialogue between European and Russian NGOs. This has happened mainly through the activities of the EU and Russian civil society organisations, their work on the maintenance of civil society in the situation of the 'shrinking space for civil society' in Russia and their advocacy efforts.

These three elements draw a rather complicated picture of multiple layers of practices of civil society support, all of them reflecting the non-linear history of EU-Russia relations, as well as the transformations of Russia's internal policy towards its civil society and of the EU's approach towards the role of civil society in general.

At the same time, although the fifth principle was introduced in 2016, its implementation at least up until 2019 has been rather limited. In essence, all three elements are not well connected to each other, the policy is not very coherent and the funding is not enough to provide for significant changes in the field. These critical points, as well as other trends in the development of civil society in Russia, are taken into consideration in the development of the relevant recommendations[35] and future EU policies and approaches towards Russia civil society.

---

35 For example, see relevant and grounded policy recommendations developed by the EU civil society leaders: B. von Ow-Freytag, 'Filling the Void: Why the EU Must Step up Support for Russian Civil Society', Policy Brief of the Wilfried Martens Centre for European Studies, April 2018, available at: <https://www.martenscentre.eu/sites/default/files/publication-files/eu-support-russian-civil-society_0.pdf> (accessed 20 July 2019).

CHAPTER 17

A Crisis or a Turning Point? EU Cultural Relations with Russia after Crimea

Domenico Valenza

1   Introduction

As the 'hidden gem' of the European Union (EU) foreign policy and a crucial tool in 'building long-term relationships',[1] culture has become a privileged area of intervention to overcome hostility in EU-Russia relations. Two major events made this shift happen in 2016. In March, the Council of the EU agreed on five principles guiding EU policy towards Russia, with the fifth principle stressing the need 'to support more and more Russian civil society and engage and invest in people-to-people contacts and exchanges and policies that are related to that'.[2] Three months later, the European Commission (EC) and the European External Action Service (EEAS) adopted the Joint Communication 'Towards an EU Strategy for International Cultural Relations' (ICR), supporting the need to incorporate culture as a strategic element in EU international policies.[3] Taken together, these two documents set the stage to further develop cultural relations with Russia. This progress was also in line with the proposals included in the EU preparatory action 'Culture in EU External Relations', recommending the use of cultural actions to improve relations with Russia and suggesting a focus on the fields of arts, heritage and mobility and on *ad hoc* large-scale events.[4]

---

1   Quotations from the European Commissioner for Education, Culture, Youth and Sport, Tibor Navracsics. European Commission, 'A New Strategy to Put Culture at the Heart of EU International Relations' (2016), available at: <http://europa.eu/rapid/press-release_IP-16-2074_en.htm> (accessed 19 February 2019).
2   European External Action Service (EEAS), 'Remarks by High Representative/Vice-President Federica Mogherini at the Press Conference following the Foreign Affairs Council' (2016), available at: <https://eeas.europa.eu/headquarters/headquarters-homepage/5490/remarks-by-high-representativevice-president-federica-mogherini-at-the-press-conference-following-the-foreign-affairs-council_en> (accessed 19 February 2019).
3   European Commission and EEAS, 'Joint Communication to the European and the Council: Towards an EU Strategy for International Cultural Relations', JOI (2016) 029 final.
4   Y.R. Isar, R. Fisher, C. Figueira, D. Helly and G. Wagner, 'Preparatory Action Culture in EU External Relations: Engaging the World: Towards Global Cultural Citizenship' (2014),

In the past years, such concepts as public diplomacy, cultural diplomacy and cultural relations have entered political debates. At the EU level, two approaches to culture in external relations have been fostered: one has aimed at showcasing European and Member States' cultures to improve their perceptions in third countries, while the other has focused on EU cultural diversity and equal exchange.[5] These two approaches have largely coexisted in EU external action. Nonetheless, the 2016 Joint Communication marked two important steps: first, an increased focus on the second approach, building on the idea that co-creation provides higher opportunities than traditional showcase; second, and as a consequence of this shift, a growing emphasis on the concept (and label) of cultural relations. In the Joint Communication, cultural relations encompass a cross-cutting range of areas, involving not just the arts or literature but also intercultural dialogue, tourism, education, heritage protection and the like. Building on these latest debates, this chapter follows this conceptualisation proposed by EU strategic documents and refers to 'cultural relations' as a practice seeking to engage with foreign citizens through cultural work.

While more recently a large number of scholars have paid attention to the features of Russia's softer tools in the EU and beyond,[6] the EU's approach to culture in Russia has been somewhat neglected within academia. Drawing on recent policy developments, this chapter attempts to fill this void and has a twofold objective. In the first place, it reviews EU cultural leadership through a quadripartite model involving: (1) the legal and policy basis of EU-Russia relations (purpose); (2) EU cultural funding instruments and managing actors (input); (3) cultural programmes, initiatives and projects (output); and (4) recognition by public opinion and relevant stakeholders (outcome).[7] As a result

---

available at:<https://www.cultureinexternalrelations.eu/cier-data/uploads/2016/12/Engaging-The-World-Towards-Global-Cultural-Citizenship-eBook-1.5_13.06.2014.pdf> (accessed 19 February 2019).

5   R. Trobbiani and L. Kirjazovaite, 'Euro-Mediterranean Cultural Relations: A Northern Current in Troubled Waters?', in: C. Carta and R. Higgott (eds.), *Cultural Diplomacy in Europe: Between the Domestic and the International* (Palgrave Macmillan 2019), 89–111.

6   See M. Laruelle, 'The Russian World: Russia's Soft Power and Geopolitical Imagination' (Center on Global Interests 2015), available at: <http://globalinterests.org/wp-content/uploads/2015/05/FINAL-CGI_Russian-World_Marlene-Laruelle.pdf> (accessed 19 February 2019); A. Sergunin and L. Karabeshkin, 'Understanding Russia's Soft Power Strategy', *Politics* 35 (3–4), 2015, 347.

7   This quadripartite model builds on previous conceptualizations of policy analyses, moving from D. Easton and further approaches. See, among others, D. Easton, *A Systems Analysis of Political Life* (University of Chicago Press 1979); M. Hill and P. Hupe, *Implementing Public Policy* (SAGE 2010); L. Neija and K. Åstrandb, 'Outcome Indicators for the Evaluation of Energy Policy Instruments and Technical Change', *Energy Policy* 34, 2006, 2662.

of this, this chapter also attempts to assess whether and how EU cultural relations have evolved since Crimea as a result of these engagements.

Overall, in spite of a strongly unfavourable legal and political background, the chapter finds that the EU has been able to devise an articulated and multi-layered approach to culture targeting Russian cultural operators and the general public in a number of different ways. In particular, the involvement of local authorities (whether in the capacity of donors, co-organisers, project applicants and partners or simple stakeholders) seems to be a prudent approach defusing their possible discomfort and scepticism, and securing cultural operators' participation in a 'protected' environment. Finally, and perhaps paradoxically, while there is no doubt that cultural actions, as much as other sectorial initiatives, have become more difficult in the current scenario, cultural methodologies have grown in importance and been used to raise awareness and mobilise individuals on sensitive topics (i.e., environment, urban planning).

However, key advancements should not hide some shortcomings. The first is unquestionably declarative: in spite of greater engagement, the EU has not yet developed a country-based strategic approach to culture in external relations, summarising lessons learned and strengthening the place of culture as the major device to overcome frosty diplomatic relations. At the input level, although the volume of activity emanating from Brussels and targeting Russia has grown, funding to cultural operators does yet not match rhetorical aspirations. Also, to deal with Russia's tighter legal framework, more creative and flexible measures should be designed to broaden the boundaries of the cultural sector beyond traditional civil society organisations (CSOs). This should include increased funding opportunities for non-recognised organisations, profit entities or individuals.

2 Purpose: Legal Basis and Declarative Commitment

To analyse EU cultural relations with Russia, legal and policy documents can provide a first overview of strategic directions and an understanding of their evolution over time. To this end, this chapter looks at official texts outlining the role of culture in EU external relations and also at those agreements and policy documents addressing cooperation with Russia.

The legal basis for EU cultural action can be traced back to the Treaty of Maastricht, which gave the EU limited competence in education (Article 165) and culture (Article 167). The treaty clarified that the Union supports and supplements Member States' actions in those fields. In spite of limited room for initiatives, in the new century different groups pressured the EU to raise its ambitions in the cultural realm. As a result of these attempts, the 2007 Communication on a European Agenda for Culture in a Globalising World emphasised the role of culture 'as a vital element in international relations'.[8] The Communication was followed one year later by the Council conclusions on the promotion of cultural diversity and intercultural dialogue in external relations.[9]

In the wake of this growing interest, in 2012 the European Parliament initiated the Preparatory Action 'Culture in EU External Relations', and a consortium of cultural institutes led by the Goethe-Institut carried out a factual mapping on the use of culture. The study also included Russia as one of the ten strategic partners of the EU.[10] The Action paved the way for the Council's call on the Commission and the High Representative to prepare a strategic approach to culture in EU external relations. In June 2016, an EC and EEAS Joint Communication designed a number of priorities for external cultural action. The Communication promotes the use of culture through existing frameworks for cooperation, and shows EU institutions' willingness to restructure its existing action and enhance cooperation among the Commission, the EEAS and Member States. Finally, in April 2019, the Foreign Affairs Council approved the Conclusions on an EU Strategic Approach to international cultural relations, integrating the latter in the range of its foreign policy instruments.[11] The Conclusions recognise a need to develop a decentralised approach to culture and to increase coordination between Member States, EU institutions and other relevant stakeholders.

At the bilateral level, EU cultural action in Russia relies on the Partnership and Cooperation Agreement (PCA), which was signed in 1994.[12] Article 1 includes culture as a key area of cooperation based on mutual advantage, responsibility and support. According to Article 85, cultural cooperation

---

8   European Commission, 'Communication from the Commission to the European Parliament, the Council, the European Economic and Social Committee and Committee of the Regions on a European Agenda for Culture in a Globalizing World', COM (2007) 242 final.
9   Conclusions of the Council and of the Representatives of the Governments of the Member States, Meeting within the Council, on the Promotion of Cultural Diversity and Intercultural Dialogue in the External Relations of the Union and Its Member States, (2008) *OJ* C320.
10 Y. Smits, 'Preparatory Action: Culture in EU External Relations. Russia Country Report' (2014), available at: <http://ec.europa.eu/assets/eac/culture/policy/international-cooperation/documents/country-reports/russia_en.pdf> (accessed 19 February 2019).
11 Council Conclusions on an EU Strategic Approach to International Cultural Relations and a Framework for Action, (2019) *OJ* C192/6.
12 Agreement on Partnership and Cooperation establishing a Partnership between the European Communities and their Member States, of one part, and the Russian Federation, of the other part, *OJ* (1997) L 327/3-69.

should address, *inter alia*, architectural heritage, exchanges of people working in the area of culture and translation of literary works. Education and training (Article 63) and tourism (Article 75) are also tackled as key areas to enhance people-to-people contacts. The year 2003 marked a new step for cultural cooperation. On the occasion of the EU-Russia Summit, it was agreed to strengthen cooperation with the objective to create in the long term four common spaces, and in particular a space of research and education, with cultural aspects.[13] Two years later, a package of four road maps to create the Common Spaces was adopted. The fourth space addressed in two different subareas education and culture, and the road map mentioned a possible development of a cooperation programme including 'the promotion of artistic and cultural projects with a European dimension'.[14] As part of this momentum, between 2007 and 2009 the EU Delegation in Moscow launched three thematic calls for grassroots projects in the framework of the Institution Building Partnership Programme (IBPP).

In the aftermath of Russia's takeover of Crimea, a comprehensive reassessment of the relations took place. On 3 March 2014, EU Foreign Ministers agreed to suspend bilateral talks on a new PCA and visa policy. This was shortly followed by the European Council's decision to cancel future EU-Russia Summits. Since then, while regular dialogue with Russian counterparts has been frozen, people-to-people initiatives and cross-border cooperation (CBC) have become key areas of intervention in a changed international environment.

In June 2015, a resolution of the European Parliament called on stronger promotion of people-to-people contacts, dialogue between EU and Russian students and researchers and increased funding 'for initiatives developing Russian-language media alternatives to Russian state-controlled media'.[15] A year later, the Foreign Affairs Council defined its five guiding principles and reiterated EU engagement on people-to-people contacts and support to civil society.

Overall, while the latest developments suggest that the place of culture in EU foreign policy is rising, this framework lacks at present a country-based strategic approach to the role of culture in external relations with Russia. Unquestionably, such a document should not emphasise an old-fashioned approach to culture, focusing on showcase of European and national cultures,

---

13 Council of the European Union, 'EU-Russia Summit. Joint Statement' (2003), 9937.
14 Council of the European Union, '15th EU-Russia Summit' (2005), 8799.
15 European Parliament Resolution of 10 June 2015 on the State of EU-Russia Relations, (2015) 2001 INI.

and pointing to the fact that 'the EU has a lot to offer',[16] to quote the Joint Communication. Declarative commitment on culture should not translate into a narrative on the EU as a 'cultural superpower'[17] or, much worse, 'the cultural superpower in the world'.[18] If generally speaking such an approach can lead to 'negative postcolonial readings',[19] this can have an even more detrimental effect on the relations with Russia, given its long-standing refusal of Western superpower assertions.

Conversely and building on the recently approved Council Conclusions, this new country-based strategic approach should adjust current policies to the aspirations and needs of cultural operators and local authorities, based on lessons learned before and especially after Crimea and the implementation of the fifth principle. This could also clarify the interplay between cultural relations and strategic communication, and whether these should be integrated in a common framework when it comes to Russia.

3   Input: Funding Instruments and Managing Actors

Two major funding mechanisms support EU cultural relations with Russia; namely, the Partnership Instrument (PI) and the European Neighbourhood Instrument (ENI). Created under the Multiannual Financial Framework 2014–2020, the PI is designed to promote EU strategic interests worldwide. The framework follows a thematic rather than geographic approach, and national programming relies on the four objectives included in the Regulation. For the period 2014–2020, the PI total budget amounts to

---

16   European Commission and European External Action Service, 'Joint Communication to the European and the Council: Towards an EU strategy for international cultural relations', JOIN (2016) 029 final.

17   European External Actions Service, 'Speech of the HR/VP Federica Mogherini at the Culture Forum in Brussels' (2016), available at: <https://eeas.europa.eu/headquarters/headQuarters-homepage/5164/speech-hrvp-federica-mogherini-culture-forum-brussels_en> (accessed 17 July 2019).

18   European External Action Service, 'Remarks by High Representative/Vice-President Federica Mogherini at the Frankfurt Book Fair Opening Ceremony', 9 October 2018, available at: <https://eeas.europa.eu/headquarters/headquarters-homepage/51895/remarks-high-representativevice-president-federica-mogherini-frankfurt-book-fair-opening_fr> (accessed 17 July 2019).

19   R. Higgott, 'EU Cultural Diplomacy: A Contextual Analysis of Constraints and Opportunities', in: C. Carta and R. Higgott (eds.), *Cultural Diplomacy in Europe: Between the Domestic and the International* (Palgrave Macmillan 2019), 19–40.

955 million euros.[20] In its fourth objective, cultural diplomacy is included alongside public diplomacy.

The PI midterm external evaluation, covering the period between 2014 and mid-2017, reported that the funds allocation for actions in Russia was lower than the sharing proposed in the planning phase.[21] However, this did not involve actions under PI objective 4 but rather projects in such sectors as trade and energy, which were suspended by the Council in 2014. For the period 2018–2020, Russia is in fact targeted as a priority country within the Action Fiche for Public and Cultural Diplomacy as part of the 2017 Partnership Instrument Annual Action Programme.[22] The Action Fiche involves a EU budget contribution of 12.4 million euros for three years and builds on previous experiences from 2015 to 'continue supporting actors globally in their endeavours to further develop the EU's soft power'.[23]

Russian entities are also eligible for the cross-border cooperation programmes funded by the ENI. For 2014–2020, the total budget for CBC Russia-related projects was 324 million euros, with about 54% of allocations coming from the EU European Regional Development Fund (ERDF, funding EU participants), and ENI which supports Russian entities. Russia co-funds CBC programmes for about 27%, while remaining contributions come from EU Member States and Norway.[24] Most of CBC programmes back cultural initiatives (see the next section).

To complement the analysis on funding instruments, one should also look at those actors involved in financial management and initiating EU cultural actions. As a result of its local presence the EU Delegation in Russia is critical to reach out to the local public within and outside the capital. Following the implementation of the Joint Communication, a cultural focal

---

20 European Commission Service for Foreign Policy Instruments, 'The Partnership Instrument, Advancing the EU's Core Interests' (2019), available at: <https://ec.europa.eu/fpi/what-we-do/partnership-instrument-advancing-eus-core-interests_en> (accessed 15 July 2019).

21 Coffey International, 'External Evaluation of the Partnership Instrument (2014-mid 2017). Final Report. Evaluation Carried out on Behalf of the European Commission' (2017), available at: <https://www.europarl.europa.eu/cmsdata/139384/PI%20Final%20Evaluation%20-%20Main%20Report.pdf> (accessed 19 February 2019).

22 European Commission, 'Annex 14 of the Commission Implementing Decision of 22.5.2017 on the 2017 Partnership Instrument Annual Action Programme for Cooperation with Third Countries to Be Financed from the General Budget of the European Union', C (2017) 3311 Final.

23 *Ibid.*

24 M. Russell, 'EU-Russia Cross-Border Cooperation', *European Parliament Think Tank* (European Parliament 2017).

point was appointed to facilitate information sharing, better disseminate best practices and meet the expectations of local stakeholders. Given the strategic significance of Russia at a time of tensions, a great share of the Delegation's information and communication budget is devoted to cultural purposes.[25]

Under CBC initiatives, financial supervision is granted to managing authorities (MA), carrying out day-to-day project administration. MAs are either national or local authorities from an EU Member State and can be supported by branch offices located in other eligible regions. An example is offered by the Karelia CBC programme, including Finland and Russia and involving a branch office at Petrozavodsk, in the Republic of Karelia. Branch offices operate in any case under MAs' guidance.

Finally, EU cultural relations in Russia also rely on the work of the European Union National Institutes for Culture (EUNIC), a coordinating mechanism created in 2006. EUNIC Cluster Funds support joint activities at the local level and are mainly financed by voluntary contributions from members. Two EUNIC Clusters are located in the country: EUNIC Russia, based in Moscow and consisting out of 17 members, and EUNIC St. Petersburg, which involves 11 organisations.[26]

4   Output: Programmes, Projects and Activities

The input review shows that EU cultural relations with Russia is significantly fragmented and multi-layered, with different actors involved in different ways and to different extents. To help the reader navigate EU cultural relations, this section looks at three categories of outputs: activities managed by the EU Delegation; CBC cultural projects; and activities implemented by EUNIC Clusters in Moscow and St. Petersburg. It ends with an analysis of EU cultural initiatives designed for awareness-raising or mobilisation aims.[27]

---

25 Interview with EU official (30 January 2019).
26 EUNIC Global, 'Clusters' (2019), available at: <https://www.eunicglobal.eu/map> (accessed 19 February 2019).
27 As noted, the EU's approach to cultural relations encompasses a cross-cutting range of areas, involving education initiatives among other things. To avoid duplications with other contributions to this volume, Erasmus+ actions in Russia are not discussed here. For an overview of current initiatives and activities, see the contribution by N. Leskina (chapter 18) in this volume.

4.1 The EU Delegation: From Europe Days to Discover Your Europe

In the past years, the EU Delegation in Moscow has attempted to devise a more structured approach to the role of culture. Although EU-driven factors have inherently played a role and provided a framework for the development of cultural relations, there is little doubt that the Ukraine crisis has represented a major shift for the Delegation's activities, making their overall outreach and communication objectives much more challenging.[28] At present, the Delegation organises regular cultural initiatives in the country and resorts to a number of service contracts, while no thematic calls for proposals on cultural cooperation have been available since 2009.

In the cultural sector, large agreement is found on the fact that Western financial disengagement is correlated to Russia's tighter measures in the civil society sector, discouraging foreign funding of Russian organisations.[29] The main example is in this regard the Foreign Agent Law. Under this framework, non-governmental organisations (NGOs) have been obliged to either become 'foreign agents', with serious legal risks for their representatives, or discontinue cooperation with international donors.[30] Scholars have seen this law as part of a broader repressive framework designed in response to the 2011–2012 protest movement.[31]

In an already shrunk space for civil society, Russia's annexation of Crimea involved a reorientation of the Delegation's cultural strategy to maintain existing bridges with Russians and build new ones where possible.[32] The clearest example is perhaps offered by the organisation of the Europe Days, a range of different events showcasing European cultures in different cities. Europe Days included film screenings, workshops, food street events and the like. In the aftermath of the crisis and EU decision to impose sanctions on Russia, members of the government voiced their discontent regarding Europe Days. Later in 2015, EU Ambassador to Russia Vygaudas Usackas

---

28   Interview with EU official (30 January 2019).
29   See D. Javeline and S. Lindemann-Komarova, 'Indigenously Funded Russian Civil Society', PONARS Eurasia (2017), available at: <http://www.ponarseurasia.org/memo/indigenously-funded-russian-civil-society> (accessed 19 February 2019).
30   S. Stewart, 'Russian Civil Society: Simultaneously Suppressed and Supported', Friends of Europe (Brussels 2017), available at: <https://www.friendsofeurope.org/insights/russian-civil-society-simultaneously-suppressed-and-supported/> (accessed 19 February 2019). See also the contribution by E. Belokurova and A. Demidov (chapter 16) in this volume.
31   See V. Gel'man, 'The Politics of Fear. How the Russian Regime Confronts Its Opponents', *Russian Politics and Law* 53 (5–6), 2015, 6; F. Daucé, 'The Government and Human Rights Groups in Russia: Civilized Oppression?', *Journal of Civil Society* 10, 2014, 239.
32   Interview with EU official (30 January 2019).

confirmed that the cancellation of the initiative was a result of domestic motives.[33]

The shutdown of this major event emphasised the need for a renewed approach. The spirit of the Europe Days was eventually revived with the 'Discover Your Europe in the Hermitage' initiative. This annual event is co-organised by the Delegation and the State Hermitage Museum in St. Petersburg, together with EU Member States' consulates and cultural institutes. It takes place in September and is linked to the European Day of Languages, which is celebrated on 26 September. In 2018, the fourth year of the event included film screenings, music performances and master classes.

If EU cultural action in Russia is clearly no easy task, some other examples suggest avoiding black-and-white thinking. The first is the EU Film Festival in Kaliningrad, which has reached its fourteenth year without any disruption after the Ukraine crisis. In 2018, the programme included 40 films and some co-productions involving both European and Russian companies, proposed by the festival direction as examples of 'fruitful collaboration which brings good films to the wide audience'.[34] Similar to 'Discover Your Europe in the Hermitage', a public body, the government of Kaliningrad Oblast, co-organises the event. A second and perhaps more powerful example is offered by the Tomsk EU Film Festival, launched in 2017. The request to replicate the Kaliningrad festival format in the city of Tomsk came from the oblast government.[35] Also, for its second year, EU Ambassadors of Member States were invited to attend the opening day. Three aspects show the significance of the festival: first, it was thought up and designed after (and in spite of) Crimea; second, local authorities contacted spontaneously the EU Delegation; third, the participation of 18 EU Member States' Embassies and 12 Ambassadors in the openings of the second year gave to the festival a more pronounced political meaning, showcasing an example of successful cultural cooperation between Russian local authorities and European counterparts.

Beside film projections, the EU Delegation has also supported the Russian language online platform Europulse, created in 2009 and implemented via

---

33   Speech by the Head of the Delegation of the European Union to the Russian Federation at the Finnish Institute of International Affairs (FIIA), Ambassador Vygaudas Ušackas at the Seminar 'The Freeze in EU-Russia Relations: Is There a Way out?' (2015), available at: <https://eeas.europa.eu/archives/delegations/russia/documents/speeches/15-05_vu_speech_fiia.pdf> (accessed 19 February 2019).

34   'Filmmakers from 25 Countries to Compete at 14th EU Film Festival in Kaliningrad', TASS (Moscow 2018), available at: <http://tass.com/society/1033471> (accessed 19 February 2019).

35   Interview with EU official (30 January 2019).

periodic service contracts. Europulse aims at promoting people-to-people contacts and shaping a 'perceptible image of the EU among the Russian general public'.[36] The project also includes video blogging with Russified video materials created by EU institutions for domestic consumption.

4.2 Cultural Relations within Cross-Border Cooperation

For the 2014–2020 period, Russia's cross-border regions are involved in eight CBC land-border programmes and also in the Baltic Sea Region, which is implemented by DG REGIO.[37] With the exception of Kolarctic, all programmes address culture-related priorities (see Table 17.1). A precise cultural focus is included in Karelia, Lithuania-Russia and Poland-Russia, which target the third CBC Thematic Objective (TO), TO3 'Promotion of Local Culture and Preservation of Historical Heritage'. Other CBC programmes support either creative industries and tourism under TO1, or education and research under TO2. Except for the Baltic Sea Region, Russian entities can be applicants of projects in all CBC programmes.

Since the first round of calls for proposals was launched in 2017 and 2018, it is not possible to provide at this stage a defined mapping of projects implemented by or involving Russian organisations. Public information available on CBC websites nevertheless provides a general overview of awarded projects for some programmes. As a result of their explicit cultural focus, Karelia, Lithuania-Russia and Poland-Russia have funded a valuable number of cultural projects. The Karelia programme launched in particular two rounds of calls for proposals in 2017 and 2018. Under TO3, funded projects cover a wide series of areas, including arts, cultural heritage, cultural services and gastronomic tourism. The majority of Russian awarded organisations are public subjects, including universities, research institutes and government-sponsored entities. Nonetheless, CSOs with a cultural focus are also eligible for funding. The best example is perhaps offered by the project 'Promotion of Local Film Capacities for Regional Development of the Bordering Territories of the Republic Karelia and Finland', launched in December 2018 and implemented by Karelian Cinematographers' Union.[38] Also, non-governmental entities

---

36 Delegation of the European Union in Russia, 'Tender Specifications No. EEAS-485-DELRUSM-SER-DIR – Contract notice in OJ 2016/S 060-100513. EU-Russia Multimedia Web Platform EUROPULSE' (2016).

37 European Commission, 'Cross Border Cooperation' (2019), available at: <https://ec.europa.eu/neighbourhood-enlargement/neighbourhood/cross-border-cooperation_en> (accessed 19 February 2019).

38 Karelia CBC Programme, 'Projects' (2019), available at: <https://www.kareliacbc.fi/en/projects> (accessed 19 February 2019).

TABLE 17.1   CBC programmes (2014–2020) with cultural objectives and involving Russian regions[a]

Programme	EU Member States and partner countries	Eligible Russian federal subjects	Cultural objectives	Funded by
Karelia	Finland	Arkhangelsk, Karelia, Leningrad, Murmansk, St. Petersburg	TO3 (local culture and historical heritage)	European Commission, Finland, Russia
South-East Finland-Russia	Finland	Leningrad, St. Petersburg	TO2 (education and research), and tourism and culture are horizontal issues	European Commission, Finland, Russia
Estonia-Russia	Estonia	Leningrad, Pskov, St. Petersburg	TO1 (support to creative industry and cultural tourism)	European Commission, Finland, Russia
Latvia-Russia	Latvia	Pskov	TO1 (support to culture and tourism)	European Commission, Latvia, Russia
Lithuania-Russia	Lithuania	Kaliningrad	TO3 (local culture and historical heritage)	European Commission, Russia
Poland-Russia	Poland	Kaliningrad	TO3 (local culture and historical heritage)	European Commission, Russia
Baltic Sea Region (managed by DG REGIO)	Denmark, Estonia, Finland, Germany, Latvia, Lithuania, Poland and Sweden. PC: Belarus, Norway	St. Petersburg, Arkhangelsk, Vologda, Kaliningrad, Karelia, Komi, Leningrad, Murmansk, Nenetsky, Novgorod and Pskov	Support to culture, creative industries and tourism under Priority 1 'Capacity for Innovation'	European Commission, Norway, Russia

Note: TO = Thematic Objective.
[a] Author's own compilation based on European Commission, *op. cit.* note 38.

working on culture and with broader priorities are the charity Mill Foundation, leading partner of a project on ethnocultural CBC in tourist industry, and the Centre for Problems of the North, Arctic and CBC, focusing on environmental resilience in natural and cultural heritage areas.[39] Besides having leading roles, Russian cultural organisations are also involved as partners in a number of projects.

Perhaps more interestingly, under the Karelia programme, the Ministry of Culture of the Russian Republic of Karelia has shown support to applications from local operators and willingness to cover the 10% co-funding requirements of the programme.[40] As already witnessed with the Delegation's initiatives, to the extent that local authorities are recognised and involved as full stakeholders, cultural cooperation can lead to positive results.

While Karelia seems to rise as a successful example of integration and participation of cultural organisations, other CBC programmes seem to provide fewer opportunities for CSOs, as applicants are mainly local authorities, including district and city councils, public museums and parks. This applies, for instance, to South-East-Finland-Russia (whose regions are also covered by Karelia), Lithuania-Russia and Poland-Russia. However, this preliminary assessment should be further reviewed as soon as at least a cycle of awarded projects has ended in all CBC programmes.

Clearly, the strength of cultural cooperation within CBC hides a major shortcoming; that is, the fact that the bulk of engagement with cultural operators take place only in neighbouring EU regions. In the absence of a bilateral framework on cultural cooperation, or of thematic calls for proposals as in the framework of IBPP between 2007 and 2009, more isolated Russian regions remain out of the scope of EU cultural action.

4.3 EUNIC

To implement cultural initiatives, EUNIC Clusters can rely on the EUNIC Cluster Fund or provide small grants to local organisations based on voluntary contributions from members. The EUNIC Cluster Fund was created in 2012 to support EUNIC activities and enhance its role as a global player in the field of culture. Between 2012 and 2016 the EUNIC General Assembly promoted a call every year, while in 2017 and 2018 a two-call approach was adopted. Two initiatives were recently funded in Russia. In 2015, EUNIC St. Petersburg implemented 'Green St. Petersburg', tackling sustainability and environmentally

---

39   *Ibid.*
40   Interview with cultural operator (6 March 2019).

friendly solutions through the promotion of green cultural products (green architecture, film, organic cuisine).[41] According to the Cluster Fund Evaluation Report, NGOs' involvement in the project did not match initial attempts as the organisations were short of funding and staff and, thus, unable to fulfil expected commitments.[42] A second initiative backed by the EUNIC Cluster Fund was approved in 2018 and promoted by EUNIC Russia. The Curatorial Exchange allows a group of Russian art curators to spend an internship period in Europe and design their own independent project.[43] EUNIC Moscow then awards and finances the best proposed idea. The project is implemented in cooperation with a selection of European museums operating as hosting organisations.

In some cases, EUNIC members have provided direct grants to relevant projects in the field of culture. This is the case of Arts4City, an initiative promoted in 2015 by the Centre for German and European Studies (CGES) and supported by EUNIC St. Petersburg. Arts4City aimed at promoting urban spaces and the value of urban culture in different areas of St. Petersburg through different formats and activities (cooking games, open space events, local artisans' workshops and the like).[44] A rotation principle was applied to fund the project: for instance, the first initiative saw the participation of Italian artists and was co-funded by CGES and the Italian Institute of Culture, while the second initiative (including German experts and stakeholders) was backed by the Goethe-Institut.[45] Grants provided by national institutes covered event costs and mobility expenses for European experts and artists, while human resources costs and fees were not eligible. As a result, some European artists declined to participate.[46]

4.4 *Cultural Work for Awareness-Raising and Social Change*
Most of the initiatives mapped in this section share one common feature: they support cultural expressions (be they movie screenings, art exhibitions or online media platforms) to enhance cultural promotion and image-building.

---

41   EUNIC Global, 'Cluster Fund 2012–2015: Evaluation Report' (2016), available at: <https://www.cultureinexternalrelations.eu/2016/09/19/eunic-cluster-fund-evaluation-report-2012-2015> (accessed 19 February 2019).
42   *Ibid.*
43   EUNIC Global, 'Exchange Programme for Young Russian Curators: EUNIC Moscow' (2018), available at: <https://www.eunicglobal.eu/projects/exchange-programme-for-young-russian-curators> (accessed 19 February 2019).
44   Interview with cultural operator (9 February 2019).
45   *Ibid.*
46   *Ibid.*

Through these actions, culture becomes a substantial component and pillar of EU's external action. While these initiatives are the core of EU cultural relations, we should also look at those cases in which cultural works and methodologies are used to raise awareness on topical questions and/or to mobilise potential activists. From being an end, culture becomes rather an engine for social change.[47]

Some examples of this second approach to culture can be found in Russia. For instance, the EU Delegation supported several editions of ECOCUP, an environmental documentary festival held in Moscow. Together with movie screenings, the festival included showcasing of eco-friendly initiatives and meetings with film directors from Europe. Since their creation, ECOCUP festivals have been organized in more than 20 cities in Russia and received support from a number of public and private entities, including the Embassy of Switzerland, the Embassy of the United States and the Heinrich-Böll-Stiftung.[48]

Examples of the use of cultural methodologies can also be found in the activity of the EU-Russia Civil Society Forum.[49] In 2013, the network launched the Working Group 'Historical Memory and Education' to facilitate ties between European and Russian organisations working on memorial issues and thus smooth out 'aspects of conflicting historical memories in Russia, the EU and other European countries'.[50] The Working Group initiated in 2014 preparations for the launch of the exhibition 'Different Wars: National School Textbooks on World War II', showcasing variations in history narrations and perceptions across Europe. Five Russian cities hosted the exhibition: Moscow, St. Petersburg, Novosibirsk, Yekaterinburg and Perm.

Beside memorial work, the Forum has also launched 'Europe Lab', a young professionals platform designed to develop networks and CBC. Under the Forum's support, some cultural projects have been proposed: among those are City Future Imaginarium, a platform involving locals, artists and designers to exchange on city planning; LOUDER, an art project raising awareness on diversity and cultural challenges; and 'After the Iron Curtain: Memory and Culture

---

47 Interview with representative of a CSO network (11 February 2019).
48 ECOCUP, 'O nas' [in Russian] (2019), available at: <http://www.ecocup.ru/ru/about-ru/> (accessed 19 February 2019).
49 This section provides only a brief overview on cultural methodologies adopted by the EU-Russia Civil Society Forum. For a broader analysis of their activities, see the contribution by E. Belokurova and A. Demidov (chapter 16) in this volume.
50 EU-Russia Civil Society Forum, 'Working Group. Historical Memory and Education' (2019), available at: <https://eu-russia-csf.org/wp-content/uploads/2019/03/2014.11.23_Historical_Memory_Flyer-1.pdf> (accessed 19 February 2019).

in Post-communist Europe', aiming at creating an oral library to map individuals' trajectories after the collapse of the Soviet Union.[51]

5 Outcome: A Vital Engagement at a Hard Time

The worsening relations between the EU and Russia have translated into more negative perceptions of the EU among Russia's public opinion. Data from the Levada Center show that, beginning in 2014, Russians' attitudes towards the EU became overwhelmingly negative, reaching the lowest point since figures started being collected (in 2003).[52] While an increase was recently observed with positive attitudes progressing from 19% in September 2014 to 36% in November 2018, the EU's reputation did not return to earlier levels. More precise observations on the significance of this shift came from N. Chaban, O. Elgström and O. Gulyaeva, who assessed Russian images of the EU before and after Maidan.[53] The study detected a significant change in Russians' labels of the EU. In 2012 the most used descriptors for the EU were modern, united, likeable and peaceful, while in 2015 the top selections were hypocritical, multicultural and arrogant.[54] Although it is hard to establish a precise correlation between worsening reputation and decline in cultural interest, it was reported that engaging with the Russian public on EU-related activities has become more challenging since 2014.[55]

On the other hand, risks of the EU's declining charm should not be overestimated. According to a study commissioned by the EC Service for Foreign Policy Instruments (FPI) in 2015 and involving public opinion surveys in ten countries, including Russia, the EU seems to remain a clear cultural partner.[56] About 72% of Russian respondents agreed that Europe should engage more in cultural exchanges with Russia,[57] while more than half saw the EU as an important partner for educational exchanges (54%).[58]

---

51 Europe Lab, 'Projects' (2019), available at: <http://europe-lab.net/projects> (accessed 19 February 2019).
52 Levada-Center, 'Indicators' (2019), available at: <http://www.levada.ru/en/ratings> (accessed 19 February 2019).
53 N. Chaban, O. Elgström, and O. Gulyaeva, 'Russian Images of the European Union: Before and after Maidan', *Foreign Policy Analysis* 13, 2017, 480.
54 *Ibid.*
55 Interview with cultural operator (28 February 2019).
56 Public Policy and Management Institute, National Centre for Research on Europe, NFG Research Group, 'Analysis of the Perception of the EU and EU's Politics Abroad' (2015), available at: <https://ec.europa.eu/fpi/showcases/analysis-perception-eu-and-eus-policies-abroad_en> (accessed 19 February 2019).
57 *Ibid.*
58 *Ibid.*

Other insights on the recognition of cultural practices come from key stakeholders. Within the cultural sector, there is agreement on the fact that the harsh post-2011 political context and the tighter legal framework compromised cultural cooperation before the takeover of Crimea.[59] The Foreign Agent Law and other measures called into question CSOs' financial authority and obliged them either to reorient their action or register as foreign agents. Self-censorship became more likely, as operators may lack the audacity to embark on international projects with European partners.[60] These concerns also apply to those operators whose activities are not overtly political: an interviewee noted that working with European artists is always delicate even when actions are purely artistic.[61]

Interestingly, in such a political context, even the work of public or mixed actors (so excluded from legislation applying to NGOs or CSOs) who engage with European partners can become challenging at times. A staff member of a publicly funded research centre working in cooperation with European counterparts lamented the very exposed position of the centre as a result of its work. Cooperation with European institutes was, in fact, seen with scepticism by central authorities. Conversely, and somewhat paradoxically, what threatens the centre – cooperation with abroad academic institutions – also secures its survival, as its international activity improves the university's reputation. As such, this makes the centre needed even when its work is quietly undesired.[62]

While the post-2011 events amplified Russian cultural operators' isolation, the Ukraine crisis dramatically compromised cooperation with the EU. Contacts with European actors have become more complicated and so have funding opportunities. Somewhat surprisingly, it was observed that the Ukraine crisis and the EU's turn of actions against Russia (ending cooperation in a number of sectors, sanctions and the like) have reinforced the role of culture and that of culture as a medium in non-cultural initiatives.[63] This perspective provides an unexpected understanding on EU action in Russia, as it puts cultural work as the major tool allowing for reconstruction of relations with Russian civil society, based on current obstacles to cooperation.

---

59   Interview with cultural operator (9 February 2019); interview with representative of a CSO network (11 February 2019).
60   Interview with representative of a CSO network (11 February 2019).
61   Interview with cultural operator (9 February 2019); interview with a member of a public higher education institution (HEI) (26 February 2019).
62   Interview with member of a public HEI (26 February 2019).
63   Interview with representative of a CSO network (11 February 2019).

Overall, cultural operators agree that the EU has increasingly become a major actor in the cultural field since Crimea, highlighting good levels of coordination among different initiatives. The EU's substantial backing and dialogue are considered as critical to support the cultural sector, and a possible withdrawal would be shattering in the current domestic context.[64] However, to further enhance the fifth principle, funding instruments should be increased and improved to provide adequate support to local organisations. As noted by several operators, most of their recent work has so far relied on volunteering, and management fees in some cases have not been covered by the donor.[65] Stronger material support, including the launch of new thematic calls, should be coupled with more creative and flexible measures allowing entities other than CSOs to be involved in the cultural field. A non-exhaustive list would include non-recognised organisations and profit entities as well as individuals operating on their own.

Finally, in the light of the long-term significance of EU cultural relations with Russia, increasing involvement of Russian authorities as co-donors, partners and/or stakeholders is seen as a solution to overstep, albeit partly, legal, political and bureaucratic obstacles.[66] This would replicate and amplify the CBC programmes' *ratio*, which is co-funded by Russia and open to local authorities and CSO participation.

6   Concluding Remarks

This chapter attempted to map EU cultural relations with Russia through an analysis of their legal and policy bases, funding instruments and programmes, and to provide an overview on the recognition of EU cultural action by public opinion and relevant stakeholders. Building on this mapping work, the chapter also sought to understand whether and to what extent the EU is following up on its fifth principle via cultural relations with Russia, based on the new legal and policy framework designed in the past years.

Against a complex domestic and international scenario, since Crimea the EU has attempted to strengthen its emphasis on the role of culture in its external relations with Russia. EU cultural action in the country is at present supported through a variety of financial instruments and programmes. Stakeholders and

---

64   Interview with cultural operator (9 February 2019); interview with cultural operator (28 February 2019); interview with member of a public HEI (26 February 2019).
65   *Ibid.*
66   *Ibid.*; interview with cultural operator (6 March 2019).

cultural operators agree that EU engagement in the cultural sphere plays a vital role in breaking civil society isolation and fostering long-term openness in Russia. Examples of stronger engagement have been provided throughout this study: for instance, for the period 2018–2020, within the PI Annual Action Programme, the Action Fiche for Public and Cultural Diplomacy has included Russia as a priority country. The EU Delegation has used an extensive share of its communication and information budget for cultural goals, and a clear cultural focus can be found in most CBC programmes targeting Russia's bordering regions. Taken together, these initiatives suggest somewhat that cooperation with local authorities is inescapable to make cultural cooperation possible in Russia. As such, triangular initiatives involving EU actors, CSOs and local authorities may circumvent disruptions or distrust of the latter and secure opportunities for cooperation between Russian cultural operators and European counterparts. Selective engagement in the sphere of culture could and should guide relations with local authorities in Russia. These can, in fact, be receptive or even proactive, as the Tomsk and Karelia cases show, and willing to engage in cultural relations.

Of course, the shortcomings highlighted in this study should not be neglected. In spite of an increased declarative commitment, the EU lacks at present a comprehensive document presenting its strategic approach to culture in Russia and adjusting its objectives to the needs of cultural operators and local authorities. Clearly, any country-based strategic approach should not emphasise EU cultural superpower, as this appears in some political statements; rather, it should restate the commitment in the cultural realm and emphasise the EU interest to strengthen cultural cooperation with Russia.

This chapter has also identified a number of weaknesses beyond declarative engagement. In fact, in spite of an increased focus, funding still does not match rhetoric engagement. Traditional instruments for CSOs should be coupled with more creative and flexible tools to circumvent current legal and bureaucratic obstacles. Also, thematic calls on culture and with a national focus – that is, targeting the whole country rather than bordering regions or the Moscow area – should also be considered.

Overall, this study reveals the existence of a paradox: frosty diplomatic relations have been both an obstacle and an opportunity to enhance EU cultural action in Russia. On the one hand, geopolitical tensions have affected EU cultural relations with Russia and reduced space for cooperation with cultural operators. On the other hand, the EU has realised that cultural relations are the major tool that can make its voice heard and counter isolation and self-censorship. Together with traditional showcasing, there is growing understanding that cultural initiatives can serve to raise awareness on non-artistic issues (i.e., environment, urban planning, diversity) and mobilise action to change people's everyday lives. Bearing in mind Russia's domestic context and the aspirations of its civil society, the transformative potential of cultural expressions should be at the core of future strategic approaches to EU-Russia relations.

CHAPTER 18

The Integration of Russia in the European Higher Education Area
Challenges and Opportunities

Natalia Leskina

1   Introduction

Higher education has always played an important role in EU-Russia relations. Following the emergence of independent Russia in the early 1990s, higher education was supported through the Trans-European Mobility Programme for University Studies (TEMPUS), which was intended to develop the capacities of Russian universities to cope with the transition from state control to a market economy and democratic society. Since the 1999 launch of the Bologna Process, which aims to create a European Higher Education Area (EHEA), Russia has made a significant effort to modernise its higher education to comply with the principles of the Process. Despite the current difficulties in EU-Russia bilateral relations, people-to-people contacts remain a priority for the EU.[1] They are covered by the fifth principle of the EU's current policy towards Russia,[2] which also includes cooperation on higher education.

To investigate how these political issues are impacting higher education, this chapter maps the developments in cooperation in higher education from the viewpoints of both the EU and Russia, identifying instances in which these developments have been in agreement with each other as well as instances in which they have been in opposition. The chapter is based on the analysis of official documents, speeches of key officials and statistical data. The relevant government departments in Russia include those of the President of the Russian Federation, the Ministry of Education and the Ministry of Foreign Affairs; from the EU side, the Education, Audiovisual and Culture Executive

---

1   'A Global Strategy for the European Union's Foreign and Security Policy 'Shared Vision, Common Action: A Stronger Europe'', 33, June 2016, available at: <http://eeas.europa.eu/archives/docs/top_stories/pdf/eugs_review_web.pdf> (accessed 5 July 2018).
2   Council of the European Union, 'Outcome of the Council Meeting', press release, 14 March 2016, available at: <https://www.consilium.europa.eu/media/22914/st07042en16.pdf > (accessed 27 July 2018).

Agency (EACEA) of the European Commission. The chapter also reviews key intellectual debates in the Russian academic community. The chapter begins with a description of higher education regionalism, which is the conceptual framework for the study, and is followed by an overview of EU-Russia cooperation in higher education in the 1990s. Then, it discusses how Russian academics have approached the country's perspectives in the Bologna Process. After that, it examines the change in the Kremlin's approach towards integration into the EHEA in the early 2010s and its underlying factors. The concurrent emergence of Moscow's independent agenda and policy efforts to foster higher education region-building in the immediate geographic neighbourhood amid increasing tensions with the EU are then analysed. Finally, changes in the EU's approach to educational cooperation with Russia are presented. In the conclusion, possible future developments in EU-Russia educational cooperation are discussed.

2   Higher Education Regionalism

The creation of the EHEA aimed to enhance the competitiveness of European higher education and to move closer to the idea of a Europe of Knowledge.[3] Although the Bologna Process was developed as an intergovernmental initiative outside the EU, there has gradually been a convergence between the wider Bologna agenda and the EU's agenda in the area of higher education.[4] Indeed, in 2005 the road map of the EU-Russia common space on research and education encouraged 'integration and a closer co-operation within the framework of the new forming European Higher Education Area in accordance with the main provisions of the Bologna Process'.[5] As for the Russian side, policy efforts to achieve so-called 'European standards' started even before the Bologna Declaration and were considered one of the dimensions of the country's strategic orientation towards the West. At the same time, Russian

---

3 European Ministers of Education, 'The Bologna Declaration of 19 June 1999', available at: <http://www.ehea.info/media.ehea.info/file/Ministerial_conferences/02/8/1999_Bologna_Declaration_English_553028.pdf> (accessed 28 August 2019).

4 P. Ravinet, 'From Voluntary Participation to Monitored Coordination: Why European Countries Feel Increasingly Bound by Their Commitment to the Bologna Process', *European Journal of Education* 43, 2008, 353–367; R. Keeling, 'The Bologna Process and the Lisbon Research Agenda: The European Commission's Expanding Role in Higher Education Discourse', *European Journal of Education* 41, 2006, 203–223.

5 'Road Map on the Common Space of Research and Education, Including Cultural Aspects', available at: <https://russiaeu.ru/userfiles/file/road_map_on_the_common_space_of_research_and_education_2005_english.pdf> (accessed 15 August 2019).

education policy has not been confined to the European project and supports the development of alternative education areas in its neighbourhood such as the Commonwealth of Independent States (CIS) and Shanghai Cooperation Organisation (SCO).

The CIS, SCO and EHEA are manifestations of regionalism in higher education,[6] which represents 'a political project of region creation involving at least some state authority (national, supranational, international), who in turn designates and delineates the world's geographical region to which such activities extend, in the higher education policy sector'.[7] Thus, the region is socially constructed by the actors involved. According to A. Hurrell, 'There are no "natural" regions, and definitions of "region" and indicators of "regionness" vary according to the particular problem or question under investigation'.[8] As there could be different perceptions of the same territory, regions may overlap. Moreover, actors may be operating strategically by imposing 'a definition of the region which places the actor as close as possible to its several cores'.[9] Thus, an actor may give preference to a regional strategy that places the former closer to its perceived 'core'. National characteristics may also be important factors when it comes to region-building. In the case of Russia, the long history of the debate over whether Russia is a European or an Asian civilization plays an important role.[10]

3   First Steps in EU-Russia Cooperation

The end of the 1980s was marked by dramatic changes in international politics, underpinned by the collapse of the Soviet bloc and the end of the Cold War. To support reforms to help the transition to a market economy and

---

6   N. Leskina, 'Is a Eurasian Higher Education Area in the Making?', *Higher Education in Russia and Beyond* 19, 2019, 12–13, available at: <https://herb.hse.ru/data/2019/04/02/1190797061/1HERB_19_view.pdf#page=12> (accessed 29 August 2019).

7   M.-H. Chou and P. Ravinet, 'The Rise of "Higher Education Regionalism": An Agenda for Higher Education Research', in: J. Huisman, H. de Boer, D.D. Dill and M. Souto-Otero (eds.), *The Palgrave International Handbook of Higher Education Policy and Governance* (Palgrave Macmillan 2015), 368.

8   A. Hurrell, 'Regionalism in Theoretical Perspective', in: L. Fawcett and A. Hurrell (eds.), *Regionalism in World Politics* (Oxford University Press 1995), 38.

9   I. B. Neumann, 'A Region-building Approach', in: F. Söderbaum and T.M. Shaw (eds.), *Theories of New Regionalism* (Palgrave Macmillan 2003), 160.

10 M. Khomyakov, 'Russia between East, West and North: Comments on the History of Moral Mapping', in: P. Wagner (ed.), *The Moral Mappings of South and North* (Edinburgh University Press 2017), 72–106.

democracy – and, in particular, reform of the education and training system – the European Community, which in 1992 became the European Union, introduced the TEMPUS programme to encourage university-university and university-industry cooperation.[11] Education was at the core of the Soviet system, providing ideological support and human resources training for the needs of the command economy. Thus, social and political reforms would not be possible without restructuring of the education and training system. TEMPUS supported the development of new curricula, interuniversity alliances and university management.[12]

The EU's intention to support transition-related reforms coincided with the aspirations of Russian political elites. To become an ordinary democratic nation, Moscow refused 'any claim to become new "centre" of the Commonwealth'[13] and agreed on the need to radically transform the Soviet educational system[14] through democratisation, decentralisation and humanitarisation.[15] Such proposals proved to be extremely complicated without external support. Just as the Soviet Union helped socialist countries for ideological reasons, former communists believed that proclaiming their way to the capitalist and democratic camp would result in massive support by new allies through a programme compared with the Marshall Plan.[16]

Indeed, the Partnership and Cooperation Agreement (PCA) of 1994, which became the basis for bilateral EU-Russia cooperation, envisaged support for reforms including the modernization of the Russian training system within TEMPUS.[17] The programme focused on people-to-people contacts to break down barriers in the minds of individuals and on the capacity building of

---

11   Council Decision (EEC) 90/233 of 7 May 1990 Establishing a Trans-European Mobility Scheme for University Studies (Tempus), [1990] OJ L 131.
12   J. Marquand, 'The EU TEMPUS TACIS Programme', in: *Development Aid in Russia: Lessons from Siberia* (Palgrave Macmillan 2009), 46–68.
13   'Osnovnye polozhenija Koncepcii vneshnej politiki Rossijskoj Federacii utverzhdeny Rasporjazheniem Prezidenta Rossijskoj Federacii B.N. El'cina ot 23 aprelja 1993 g.', *Diplomaticheskij vestnik* 1–2, 1993, 3.
14   T. Casier, 'From Logic of Competition to Conflict: Understanding the Dynamics of EU-Russia Relations', *Contemporary Politics* 22, 2016, 376–394.
15   Humanitarisation of education meant transition from a repressive Soviet system that taught in-depth knowledge that should be studied and accepted to a new differentiated approach aimed at the development of each individual student.
16   A.D. Bogaturov, 'Tri pokolenija vneshnepoliticheskih doktrin Rossii', *International Trends* 5 (1), 2007, 54–69.
17   Agreement on Partnership and Cooperation Establishing a Partnership between the European Communities and Their Member States, of One Part, and the Russian Federation, of the Other Part, [1997] OJ L 327/3.

universities by allocating funds for equipment renovation, the introduction of new study programmes and the teaching of foreign languages. As a result, international offices were established in Russian universities, and some universities gained the experience of international cooperation for the first time. The exchange of best practices led to the international socialization of academia, integration with Western educational systems and improvement of the efficiency and democratic nature of university management.[18] Given the lack of funding from the Russian government, the programme became very important for Russian academics. Despite these achievements, the bureaucratic-heavy system and the lack of previous experience in international collaboration and of language skills prevented many universities, especially small regional ones, from participation.[19] Also, TEMPUS provided a limited amount of funds for the transformation of the whole higher education system despite the aforementioned need for restructuring of the entire system.

EU-Russia cooperation had a clear unidirectional approach, where Russia was the recipient of EU reforms and funds for their implementation. It is in this light that the EU attempts to apply conditionality to funding to Russia in 1995 and 1999 because of the conflict in Chechnya can be understood. The ratification of the PCA was postponed,[20] and in 1999 the technical assistance programme was suspended.[21] These actions resulted in the perception that the EU had a highly political approach towards Russia and was playing its own game to the detriment of Russia. Furthermore, the financial support by Western partners did not meet the expectations of Russian political elites because it came not as a donation but mainly as tied loans by the International Monetary Fund (IMF) and other financial institutions, which led to the subsequent rise of the foreign debt. Aspirations of a fast transition to a market economy and rapidly reaching Western standards of living were not fulfilled.

As a result of increasing disillusionment with the West, Russia resumed its interest in cooperation with its own neighbourhood from the mid-1990s. In 1997, two years before the Bologna Process came into being, political leaders

---

18 'Evaluation of Tacis Country Programme in Russia', 136, available at: <http://ec.europa.eu/europeaid/how/evaluation/evaluation_reports/reports/tacis/951500_annex_en.pdf> (accessed 25 July 2018).

19 Marquand, *op. cit.* note 12, 46–68.

20 European Commission, 'The European Union and Russia: The Future Relationship', press release, 31 May 1995, available at: <http://europa.eu/rapid/press-release_IP-95-533_en.htm?locale=en> (accessed 27 July 2018).

21 Helsinki European Council, 'Presidency Conclusions of 10–11 December 1999, Declaration on Chechnya', available at: <https://www.consilium.europa.eu/ueDocs/cms_Data/docs/pressData/en/ec/ACFA4C.htm> (accessed 9 July 2018).

from the ex-Soviet states signed an agreement on the creation of a CIS Common Educational Area. This was defined as an 'affinity of principles of state educational policy, coherence of state educational standards, programs, coupled with equal opportunities and right on education in all educational institutions located in CIS countries'.[22] This new regional space was marked by educational legacies from the Soviet period such as high state regulation and the notion of education as a right. However, this agreement had no clear agenda and tools. Implementation as well as funding were left to the discretion of national governments, which meant it became little more than a proclamation on paper.

In sum, EU-Russia cooperation in the 1990s was driven by the Kremlin's will to become a 'normal' democracy and, to this end, to transform the Soviet system, including the higher education system that had been a core part, in line with Western standards. TEMPUS became the main programme for the transformation of higher education. Despite its positive impact on institutional practices, it was not enough to transform the whole system and did not fulfil the aspirations of Russian elites for large-scale financial aid. After the EU began to apply conditions to its funding, this led to disillusionment with the West and a growing prominence of good relations with the immediate neighbourhood, where a CIS common area was launched.

4   Debates on the Russia's Perspectives in the Bologna Process

In the 2000s, EU-Russia cooperation was given a new impetus. The politics of then new Russian President Vladimir Putin put 'national interests' at the centre. Putin's policies aimed at the economic and political stabilization of the country, as well as the development of cooperation with all interested neighbouring countries. As during the 1990s the EU was one of the country's main partners, this direction remained a priority in Russian foreign policy despite the disillusionment that had arisen in the early phase of cooperation. Russia saw its destiny within a 'Larger Europe' since 'geographical approximation with Europe was expected to lead to the economic and spiritual one'.[23] The EU welcomed the stabilization in its immediate neighbour, and intensified cooperation with Russia.

---

22   CIS, 'Koncepcija formirovanija edinogo (obshhego) obrazovatel'nogo prostranstva Sodruzhestva Nezavisimyh Gosudarstv', 17 January 1997, available at: <http://cis.minsk.by/reestr/ru/index.html#reestr/view/text?doc=665> (accessed 2 May 2018).

23   V.V. Putin, 'Poslaniye Federalnomu Sobraniyu Rossiyskoy Federatsii', 26 May 2004, available at: <http://kremlin.ru/events/president/transcripts//22494> (accessed 2 May 2018).

However, Moscow wanted the recognition of being a partner equal to the EU, and opted to cooperate through four common spaces instead of the European Neighbourhood Policy available to other countries of the region.[24] In May 2003, Russian and EU officials reached an agreement 'to reinforce co-operation with a view to creating in the long term a common economic space, a common space of freedom, security and justice, a space of co-operation in the field of external security, as well as a space of research and education, including cultural aspects'.[25] This aimed to contribute to people-to-people contacts, the promotion of common values and the competitiveness of both economies. At the same time an extended approach to the definition of 'Europe' within the intergovernmental Bologna Process, whose final objective was the establishment of the European Higher Education Area by 2010, allowing all countries that were signatories of the European Cultural Convention to join the process,[26] made the EHEA accessible to Russia which was a party to the Convention.

Exemplifying the debate this led to in the intellectual community was a heated discussion between the leaders of the country's two most prestigious universities: Ludmila Verbitskaya, Rector of Saint Petersburg State University, and Victor Sadovnichiy, Rector of Moscow State University. This reflected the two main positions on Russia's prospects in the Bologna Process. Verbitskaya insisted that if Russia remained outside the process, it would lose the reform momentum and fail to respond to the demands of global higher education. Conversely, she believed a positive decision would allow Russia to participate in shaping the future of European education. In contrast, Sadovnichiy, while acknowledging the need to integrate into the global educational arena, believed that it could be achieved in different ways. He felt it should be a two-way process – Russia not only should adopt European norms but also propose its own. In his view, Russian interests also included higher education integration in the post-Soviet space.[27]

---

24 E. Korosteleva, *The European Union and Its Eastern Neighbours: Towards a More Ambitious Partnership?* (Routledge 2012).

25 EU-Russia Summit (St.-Petersburg, 31 May 2003), '300th Anniversary of St.-Petersburg Celebrating Three Centuries of Common European History and Culture' (Joint Statement), available at: <https://www.consilium.europa.eu/uedocs/cms_data/docs/pressdata/en/er/75969.pdf> (accessed 17 September 2018).

26 Conference of Ministers Responsible for Higher Education in Berlin on 19 September 2003, 'Realising the European Higher Education Area' (Communiqué), available at: <http://www.ehea.info/media.ehea.info/file/2003_Berlin/28/4/2003_Berlin_Communique_English_577284.pdf> (accessed 3 October 2018).

27 A.E. Fominykh, 'Institucional'no-politicheskie i sociokul'turnye aspekty sotrudnichestva ES i Rossii v oblasti vysshego obrazovanija: opyt regional'nogo issledovanija' (PhD thesis, Mari State University 2003), 51.

The Russian government took the position expressed by the Rector of Saint Petersburg State University, and in 2003 Russia became the first CIS country to sign the Bologna Declaration. Despite the intergovernmental nature of the Bologna Process outside the EU, this event was perceived as 'a breakthrough in the relations of Russia with United Europe'. According to Vladimir Filippov, then Russian Minister of Education, 'Russia was not allowed in the common market, Eurozone, common customs union, either Schengen zone, we have been let in only in education'.[28] Filippov indicated that an important impact of the decision to include Russia in the Bologna Process was the position of the Russian President, who had said that it was unwarranted to build a new Berlin Wall in Europe, thus 'this decision was necessary and indispensable'.[29]

Thus, the objective to get into the EHEA was twofold: first, as part of the 'controlled' integration into the global higher education market through the modernization of the Russian higher education system; and, second, as a development of the European vector of Russian foreign policy. However, as the debate in the intellectual community showed, there already was a discussion about where Russia interests sat and whether to adopt to European standards or to develop post-Soviet integration based on the country's own strengths.

5   Evolution of Russia's Attitude towards Integration into the EHEA

Despite being intergovernmental in nature and largely outside the scope of EU competences, the Bologna Process is closely associated with the EU in Russian public opinion.[30] Indeed, EU-Russia cooperation on higher education was closely linked with the Process. The Bologna Process was incorporated into the EU-Russia road map on education, which followed the agreement on four common spaces of 2003 that also include economy, internal and external security.[31] The first aim of the road map on a common educational space was to contribute to the integration and deepening of cooperation within

---

28   V.V. Filippov, 'Vkljuchenie Rossii v Bolonskij process jeto proryv v otnoshenijah s Edinoj Evropoj', 21 October 2003, available at: <https://regnum.ru/news/170574.html> (accessed 2 May 2018).
29   V.V. Filippov, 'Interview', *Uchitelskaya Gazeta*, 7 October 2003, available at: <http://www.ug.ru/archive/1681> (accessed 2 May 2018).
30   T.V. Kruglikova, 'Bolonskij process: itogi pervogo desjatiletija. (obzor)', *Current Problems of Europe* 2, 2013, 193.
31   EU-Russia Summit (St.-Petersburg, 31 May 2003), *op. cit.*

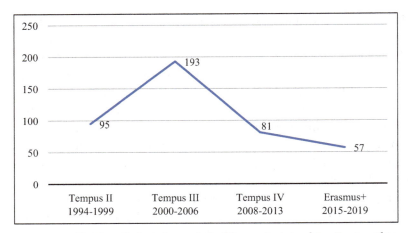

FIGURE 18.1 Number of selected capacity-building projects involving Russia within TEMPUS and Erasmus+ programmes
AUTHOR'S OWN COMPILATION BASED ON EACEA DATA, AVAILABLE AT: <HTTPS://EACEA.EC.EUROPA.EU/> (ACCESSED 8 OCTOBER 2019).

the emergent EHEA in accordance with the main provisions of the Bologna Process.[32] In the early 2000s, the EU allocated even more funds to TEMPUS by increasing the number of projects (Figure 18.1), and this actively supported the implementation of the Bologna principles.[33]

However, the Russian interpretation reduced the Bologna Process to primarily the transition from the five-year undergraduate specialist degree that had been specific to Soviet higher education to the two-tier bachelor's-master's degree system. This reform was imposed as a hard requirement because it was presented as a Russian obligation on signing the Bologna Declaration. The implementation of other action lines, such as introduction of Diploma Supplements, the European Credit Transfer System (ECTS) and changes in quality assurance, remained superficial or limited in scope. G. Telegina and H. Schwengel link the narrow interpretation of reforms with the cultural legacies of the Soviet system (lack of foreign language skills and intercultural

---

32 Russia-EU Summit (Moscow, 10 May 2005), 'Dorozhnye karty chetyreh obshih prostranstv', available at: <http://www.mid.ru/evropejskij-souz-es/-/asset_publisher/6OiYovt2s4Yc/content/id/439524> (accessed 7 September 2018).

33 'Mid-term Evaluation of Tempus in Russia – Assessing the Contribution of Tempus to the Bologna Process in Russia', Final Report, 2008, available at: <http://www.russianenic.ru/publications/DOC/3%20Mid%20term%20Evaluation%20TEMPUS%20.pdf> (accessed 12 March 2018).

experience), as well as limited autonomy and excessive bureaucratization of universities, excessive state regulation and poor resources, and the structure of the national economy.[34] In addition, the Bologna reforms continued to be accompanied by heated debates. Proponents pointed to the need for modernization, while opponents pointed out that Russia needed to retain its strong traditions to achieve leadership in higher education.

Since the transition to the two-tier system in 2009, interest in the Bologna reforms has decreased at the policy level. The Russian Ministry of Education did not even provide a country report to the Bologna Process Secretariat in 2012. Dissatisfied with its position of rule follower in the European Higher Education Area and having limited influence on decision-making, Russia adopted a 'pragmatic' approach 'to implement only provisions that will strengthen our higher education',[35] relying on the strengths stemming from its history and traditions (i.e., the strong social dimension of education and its comprehensive character). The Kremlin's rationale for education reforms changed from the necessity of integrating into the global higher education space and, to this end, complying with European standards to building its own leadership.

This position coincided with general trends in Russian politics. The 'sovereign democracy' concept developed in 2005–2006 implied the right to choose Russia's own way of development.[36] The discourse was increasingly centred on the country's need to follow its own way, to develop in compliance with national particularities and to not blindly follow Western models. Step-by-step, this developed into the idea that Russia is another type of civilization, in between Europe and Asia. According to former Russian Minister for Education Dmitry Livanov, 'Russia is not only a European country. We actively develop relations with Asia and Pacific region within the BRICS and APEC'.[37] The practical embodiments of this statement were more intense efforts in region-building with former Soviet countries and China, which are discussed in the next section.

---

34 G. Telegina and H. Schwengel, 'The Bologna Process: Perspectives and Implications for the Russian University', *European Journal of Education* 47, 2012, 37–49.

35 D. Livanov, 'Rossijskaja delegacija obsudila Bolonskij process sovmestno so stranami-uchastnikami processa na mezhdunarodnoj konferencii v Erevane', 15 May 2015 available at: <http://минобрнауки.рф/%D0%BD%D0%BE%D0%B2%D0%BE%D1%81%D1%82%D0%B8/5554> (accessed 8 May 2018).

36 V. Surkov, 'Nacionalizacija budushhego', *Expert*, 20 November 2006, available at: <https://web.archive.org/web/20061205211300/http://www.expert.ru/printissues/expert/2006/43/nacionalizaciya_buduschego/> (accessed 19 August 2019).

37 'Ministry obrazovanija obsudili Bolonskij process', 14 May 2015, available at: <https://iz.ru/news/586511> (accessed 8 May 2018).

Thus, Russia's participation in the Bologna Process in the early 2000s was closely linked with the general agenda of building an EU-Russian common space, and relevant reforms were supported by the TEMPUS programme. However, since the mid-2000s the Russian rationale changed from the need to modernise, which was accomplished within the Bologna reforms, to becoming a world leader in global higher education space. Subsequently, Russia has viewed the Bologna Process as one, instead of the only, space that could improve its competitiveness while keeping national features as a competitive advantage.

6   Russia's Independent Agenda

Wishing to restore its Soviet-era leadership in education and training and to increase its intellectual influence, Russia since the 2000s has increased its efforts to develop post-Soviet regionalisms. For example, education was included in the competences of the Eurasian Economic Community (EurAsEC) and the SCO. The EurAsEC, a major Russia and Kazakhstan–led project designed for states in the CIS that were willing to cooperate more intensively, helped make significant progress in elaborating regulatory frameworks for international educational cooperation.[38] To complement the intergovernmental level, SCO and CIS network universities were created in 2008. Both network universities are consortia of leading national universities working together to deliver joint master's degrees, foster student exchanges and undertake collaborative research.

The transformation of the EurAsEC into the Eurasian Economic Union (EAEU) in 2015 was expected to be a major project for the post-Soviet countries with the potential to consolidate previous efforts to create a higher education area.[39] Initially, this Eurasian project was designed to be a subsystem of 'Greater Europe' stretching from Lisbon to Vladivostok in Russia's Far East.

---

38   EurAsEC, 'Soglashenie o sotrudnichestve gosudarstv – chlenov Evrazijskogo jekonomicheskogo soobshhestva v oblasti obrazovanija', available at: <http://docs.cntd.ru/document/902312974> (accessed 10 November 2018); EurAsEC, 'Soglashenie o mehanizme vzaimnogo priznanija i ustanovlenija jekvivalentnosti dokumentov ob uchenyh stepenjah v gosudarstvah-chlenah Evrazijskogo jekonomicheskogo soobshhestva', available at: <http://nic.gov.ru/ru/docs/foreign/confirmation/agreem_recog_EurAsEC_2005> (accessed 10 November 2018).

39   G. Povolockij, 'Vzaimosvjaz' modernizacii nacional'nyh jekonomik stran Evrazii ochevidna', *International Affairs*, 23 June 2015, available at: <https://interaffairs.ru/news/show/13358?show_desktop_mode=true> (accessed 17 November 2018).

It was to be based on the common values of freedom, democracy and the free market, and aimed to improve the standing of each member for easier integration into Europe.[40] It had to be a supranational union, one of the poles of the world system and a link between Europe and Asia. The dialogue between the EU and Russia was therefore expected to be supplemented by an EU-Eurasian Union interchange. In this format, post-Soviet countries, and in particular Russia as a regional leader, would have had a stronger voice in promoting their national interests. But the EU refused to start direct negotiations with the EAEU, which was perceived as a neoimperialist project. Instead, the EU promoted closer relations with post-Soviet countries within its own Eastern Partnership programme.[41] Despite the emerging tensions, the Russian strategy of 2013 towards the EU still envisaged the creation of a common cultural space from the Atlantic to the Pacific Ocean.[42]

However, the EAEU ended up splitting the post-Soviet space and causing tensions between the EU and Russia. These tensions detained both the EU and Russia's region-building projects. Even Kazakhstan, which had initiated the EAEU, expressed concerns about the massive brain drain to Russia, and refused to engage in supranational as well as intergovernmental coordination of education within the EAEU.[43]

Following the EU-Russia contestation over this shared neighbourhood, the Eurasian vision was transformed by Russian elites into an anti-hegemonic project where the EU is labelled as a 'Western peninsula of Eurasia'.[44] Russia challenged the EU's role of a 'teacher' that dictates its rules and exclusive interpretation of reality. Cooperation with China as a partner in challenging Western dominance and, thus, changing the world order has gained in

---

40 V.V. Putin, 'Novyj integracionnyj proekt dlja Evrazii – budushhee, kotoroe rozhdaetsja segodnja', *Izvestia*, 3 October 2011, available at: <https://iz.ru/news/502761?page=2> (accessed 19 November 2018); V. V. Putin, 'Vystuplenija na rabochem zasedanii vstrechi na vysshem urovne Rossija – Evropejskij sojuz', 4 June 2013, available at: <http://kremlin.ru/events/president/transcripts/18251> (accessed 19 November 2018).
41 Casier, *op. cit.* note 14, 376.
42 'Ob utverzhdenii koncepcii vneshnej politiki Rossijskoj Federacii ot 12 fevralja 2013', Order of President of Russian Federation, available at: <http://www.mid.ru/foreign_policy/official_documents/-/asset_publisher/CptICkB6BZ29/content/id/122186> (accessed 10 November 2018).
43 S. M. Yun, 'Obrazovanie kak sfera sotrudnichestva v ramkah evrazijskogo jekonomicheskogo sojuza: problemy i perspektivy', *Tomsk State University Journal of History* 50, 2017, 89–92.
44 D. Efremenko, 'Rozhdenie Bol'shoj Evrazii', *Russia in Global Affairs*, 6, 28 November 2016, available at: <http://www.globalaffairs.ru/number/Rozhdenie-Bolshoi-Evrazii-18478> (accessed 17 November 2018).

prominence. As part of this 'Eastern turn' by Russia, in 2015 Russian and Chinese authorities declared their intentions to link the EAEU with the One Belt, One Road initiative.[45] In 2016, Russian President Vladimir Putin officially declared a new vision for Eurasia, also called 'Greater Eurasia' or the 'great Eurasian partnership', linking the EAEU with China, India, Pakistan, Iran, CIS members and other interested countries/regions, including the European Union.[46]

Despite the complicated relations between Brussels and Moscow, international cooperation in higher education remains prominent. Russian ministerial officials resumed their interest in the Bologna Process after 2014, as demonstrated through the participation of the Russian Minister of Education in the Bologna Process meeting in Yerevan, Armenia. Moreover, the Kremlin does not apply any restrictive measures to the participation of Russian universities in the EU's programmes.

Aspiring to become one of the leaders in higher education, and dissatisfied with the perceived position as a 'pupil' of the EU, Russia has thus spearheaded alternative region-building projects with its neighbours. Despite their initial orientation towards the European partners, these projects have been considered by Brussels to be Moscow's neoimperialist ambitions. The tensions that arose have led to a destructive influence over the shared neighbourhood and the deferment of regionalisms. The EAEU project turned into an antihegemonic one and assigned a more important role to China as a partner in changing the world order. At the same time, educational cooperation with European partners remains important for Russia.

7 A Change in the EU's Approach towards Russia: From Transformation to Public Diplomacy

A differentiation in the EU's approach towards the former Soviet countries became observable in the 2000s. First, in 2003 EU-Russia cooperation was handled as a separate strategic partnership. Then, four years later another strategy

---

45 'Sovmestnoe zajavlenie Rossijskoj Federacii i Kitajskoj Narodnoj Respubliki o sotrudnichestve po soprjazheniju stroitel'stva Evrazijskogo jekonomicheskogo sojuza i "Jekonomicheskogo pojasa Shelkovogo puti" ot 8 maja 2015 g.', available at: < http://kremlin.ru/supplement/4971> (accessed 8 September 2018).

46 'Plenarnoe zasedanie Peterburgskogo mezhdunarodnogo jekonomicheskogo foruma', 17 June 2016, available at: < http://kremlin.ru/events/president/news/52178> (accessed 8 August 2019).

was implemented towards Central Asian countries, and since 2009 the Eastern Partnership has encompassed Moldova, Ukraine, Belarus and three Caucasus republics.

In higher education, changes became observable in 2010–2012 when, parallel to the TEMPUS projects, six 'EU Centres' were established in Russian universities. These are comparable to EU Centres already established in the United States, Canada, Australia and Japan.[47] Their aim is to disseminate knowledge on the EU as well as contribute to a favourable perception of the EU. To this end, they work in close collaboration with the EU Delegations in the respective countries. Therefore, the centres put emphasis on the dissemination of information rather than capacity building of the universities or reform of higher education systems.

This shift became even more obvious in 2014 when TEMPUS was incorporated into the new Erasmus+ programme as capacity building in the field of higher education action. The EU changed the conditions for the participation of Russian universities, restricting them to joining multi-country (as opposed to bilateral) projects. In practice, this means that universities need to develop projects that fall within the overlapping priorities that are set separately for each region and country. Since Russia is a separate region, as are Central Asia and the Eastern Partnership countries – each with a list of priorities specific to them – it complicates the preparation of joint applications by institutions of post-Soviet countries. Moreover, according to the rules of the programme, Russian institutions cannot be grant holders, unlike in other post-Soviet countries. In spite of these restrictions and the relatively low success rate, Russian universities are eager to participate in capacity-building calls (Figure 18.2).

After the eruption of the Ukrainian crisis in 2014, the EU did not stop funding educational programmes in Russia as it did in 1999, and even increased funding for Jean Monnet activities between 2014 and 2015 (Figure 18.3). These projects aim to support teaching and, to a lesser extent, research on EU-related subjects. In this sense, Jean Monnet projects can be considered as an additional tool of public diplomacy that creates a direct channel of communication with the Russian academic community and through it with the society, bypassing the Russian government and official news. Indeed, the former EU Centres were transformed into Jean Monnet Centres of Excellence in 2015 and 2016. The Jean Monnet programme focuses on supporting individual academics studying or

---

47   Centry ES, available at: <http://eeas.europa.eu/archives/delegations/russia/eu_russia/tech_financial_cooperation/eu_centres/index_ru.htm> (accessed 8 November 2018).

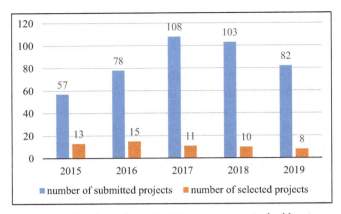

FIGURE 18.2 Russian universities in Erasmus+ capacity building in higher education

SOURCE: AUTHOR'S OWN COMPILATION BASED ON 'ERASMUS+ FOR HIGHER EDUCATION IN RUSSIA', AVAILABLE AT: <HTTP://EC.EUROPA.EU/PROGRAMMES/ERASMUS-PLUS/RESOURCES/DOCUMENTS/COUNTRY-FACTSHEET-RUSSIA_EN> (ACCESSED 8 OCTOBER 2019). EACEA, 'SELECTION RESULTS', 2019, AVAILABLE AT: <HTTPS://EACEA.EC.EUROPA.EU/ERASMUS-PLUS/SELECTION-RESULTS_EN> (ACCESSED 10 OCTOBER 2019).

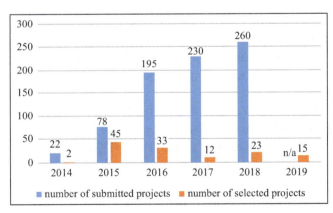

FIGURE 18.3 Participation of Russian universities in Jean Monnet activities
SOURCE: SAME AS FIG. 18.2

teaching issues related to the EU but the networking possibilities are limited in comparison with large capacity-building projects. The relatively easy submission and reporting procedure has made them accessible to many academics, and applications have increased markedly since 2014 (Figure 18.3).

In 2016, these changes were enshrined in the EU's Global Strategy.[48] Despite the recognition of Russia as 'a key strategic challenge', the EU envisaged selective engagement that included 'deeper societal ties through facilitated travel for students'.[49] The fifth guiding principle towards Russia conceived of people-to-people contacts and exchanges; in particular, among the youth. Indeed, the EU has supported exchanges of students and staff.[50] However, these exchanges remain small-scale relative to the total population. At the same time, the demands of Russian universities which have been inclined towards cooperation with European partners since the 1990s have not been met, as the disjuncture between the number of applications and funded projects demonstrates. This may result in a gradual loss of the bridging achievements from previous stages of cooperation.

As such, since the 2010s the EU's programmes have been adjusted to the growing tensions in bilateral relations at the political level. They have shifted their focus from the transformation of Russian higher education to the promotion of EU studies as a public diplomacy tool. While capacity-building projects have remained limited in scope, the general focus has shifted from the support of large institutional projects to individual academics and students. Nevertheless, levels of individual academic mobility remain low in relation to the high demand for cooperation with European partners from Russian universities.

8 Conclusion

This chapter has mapped the main developments in EU-Russia cooperation in the field of higher education since the dissolution of the USSR and has identified when they were in coherence or opposition. In the 1990s, EU aid to help transition to a market economy coincided with Moscow's aim to deconstruct the Soviet system and to modernise higher education in line with Western standards. Along with other post-Soviet countries, Russia was a recipient not only of financial aid but also of EU norms in higher education. Although this assistance was not sufficient to transform the whole system, TEMPUS projects became best practices that spearheaded Russian reforms in the European

---

48   'A Global Strategy for the European Union's Foreign and Security Policy, *op. cit.* note 1.
49   *Ibid.*
50   European Commission, 'Erasmus+ for Higher Education in Russia', available at: <http://ec.europa.eu/programmes/erasmus-plus/resources/documents/country-factsheet-russia_en> (accessed 8 October 2018).

direction and provided the groundwork for Russia's decision to join the Bologna Process in 2003. This led to the transformation of the five-year specialist degree inherited from the Soviet Union to the two-cycle bachelor's-master's degree system.

Nevertheless, from the mid-2000s onwards, the Kremlin began to demand changes in the EU's approach towards an equal partnership. At the same time, the Russian internal agenda gradually changed from needing to comply with Western standards to the goal of becoming a leader in the global higher education market. Russia fostered alternative region-building projects that placed it at the centre of a Eurasian area. The EU's reluctance to cooperate with the emergent Eurasian Union and Russia's tenacity contributed toward growing tensions and led to deadlock in bilateral relations and the suspension of region building on both sides. Yet despite the current difficulties, people-to-people contacts have remained a consistent priority in the EU's strategy towards Russia. Overall, the general focus of the EU's strategy towards Russia has shifted from the transformation of the higher education system to public diplomacy. In turn, aspiring to become a leader in educational exports, Russia has sought to diversify its international collaboration. This has led to the EU becoming one of many partners rather than the main or sole partner. Throughout this period, Russian academics and universities have shown an ever increasing interest in collaboration with European partners and participation in EU programmes, even when political relations with the EU have been troublesome.

Looking forward, it seems unlikely that Moscow will decide to remove itself from the EHEA, even though current relations between the EU and Russia are strained. First, the two-cycle bachelor's-master's degree system has become a 'gold standard' of global higher education, and changing it would mean giving up on the aspiration to become a leader in the higher education space. Second, most of the countries that Russian alternative region-building projects are aimed at have also adopted the Bologna reforms, albeit with varying degrees of success. Therefore, any reverse actions would distance Russian universities from them. Finally, the Russian academic community is more inclined towards cooperation with European colleagues who over the past three decades have become well-established partners following the support of many joint projects by the EU. Barriers to people-to-people contacts would hinder the internationalisation of universities, which would go against the proclaimed aims of the Russian government.

At the same time, there is a strong probability that Russia will continue to develop its own educational agendas. Building a common educational area in the post-Soviet space is likely to remain a priority. Even though countries of the former Soviet region have been reluctant to ally with Russia while it is isolated from the West because they do not want to share this burden, the development of an Eastern-facing cooperation may ease these tensions. At the political level, Russia will continue to focus on cooperation with Asian and BRICS countries, and especially with China as an emerging centre of power. Continued research into these future directions will demonstrate the extent to which Russia is able to enact these plans.

GENERAL CONCLUSION

The Five Guiding Principles for the EU's Relations with Russia: In Need of Revision?

Fabienne Bossuyt and Peter Van Elsuwege

1 Introduction

The aim of this volume has been to take stock of the implementation of the EU's Global Strategy and the five principles that are currently guiding the EU's policy towards Russia. In particular, it has sought to examine the implications of each of these principles for the EU's relations with Russia and aimed to identify the challenges for the further development of EU-Russia relations.

Based on the findings of the previous contributions, this concluding chapter looks into the successes and failures that the EU has encountered since the five guiding principles were launched. Moreover, it provides a number of more general reflections that can be drawn from the contributions and which critically assess the current state of EU-Russia relations. Together, they point towards the need for a qualitatively different and more constructive long-term strategy to guide the EU's policy towards Russia.

2 Success and Failures of the Five Guiding Principles

As can be derived from the preceding chapters in this volume, the EU has achieved some progress in implementing the five guiding principles defining its relations with Russia. However, the progress is not evenly spread across the five principles, with the implementation of the fifth principle being the most successful and rather mixed results for the other principles. In general, some contradictory and sometimes even counterproductive effects may be discerned.

With respect to the *first principle*, which defines that the lifting of the EU's restrictive measures against Russia is linked to the implementation of the Minsk agreements, the picture is blurred. On the one hand, it could be argued that this principle has so far been successfully implemented, in the sense that it has enabled the EU to remain firm in the face of Russian interference in Ukraine and in response to Russia's violation of international law.

Moreover, despite attempts by certain EU Member States to agree on a partial lifting of the sanctions, as highlighted by Tony van der Togt in Chapter 2, the EU has not diverted from its principled position and has continued to extend the sanctions in the absence of Russia's compliance with the Minsk agreements.

On the other hand, the continuing lack of progress in implementing the Minsk agreements casts strong doubts on the success and sustainability of the first principle. As highlighted by Sebastiaan Van Severen in Chapter 1, almost five years after the principles were introduced the Minsk peace talks find themselves in a deeply entrenched stalemate. As a result, it appears that the first principle is becoming increasingly unsustainable in the sense that it only confirms the status quo without offering concrete prospects for a more constructive relationship. This is further evidenced by the observation, put forward by Irina Petrova in Chapter 3, that the EU and Russia hold diverging views on the sequencing of the implementation process of the Minsk agreements, as well as on the responsibilities of the parties involved. As argued by Alexandra Hofer in Chapter 4, the lack of progress of the Minsk agreements shows that the first principle may even be counterproductive, as the restrictive measures have triggered Russian resentment and resulted in further alienation. Moreover, as shown in Chapter 5 by Kirill Entin and Chapter 6 by Celia Challet, the sanctions against Russian individuals and companies are increasingly contested before the Court of Justice of the European Union (CJEU), raising questions about the mechanisms of effective judicial review in the area of the Common Foreign and Security Policy (CFSP).

The *second principle* is arguably no less challenging and contested than the first one. Indeed, building strengthened relations with the EU's Eastern partners poses significant challenges, as it directly links up to the context of EU-Russia geopolitical competition in the shared neighbourhood. Nevertheless, on balance the implementation of the second principle so far seems to have progressed more smoothly than many would have expected. As indicated in the introductory chapter, the EU has sought to find a balance in accepting the Eurasian Economic Union (EAEU) as a new reality in the post-Soviet space without undermining the scope for the development of differentiated bilateral relations with these countries. In this regard, the conclusion of new bilateral agreements with EAEU Member States Kazakhstan, Kyrgyzstan and Armenia can be considered a success, as it illustrates that EAEU membership is reconcilable with close bilateral links with the EU. As Laure Delcour and Narine Ghazaryan argue in Chapter 7, the Comprehensive and Enhanced Partnership Agreement (CEPA) with Armenia has emerged as 'a litmus test for both the EU's ability to strengthen ties with its Eastern partners and Russia's acceptation thereof'.[1] Arguably, the development of bilateral ties with individual EAEU Member States may lead to constructive EU-EAEU relations in the future, depending of course on the legal and political development of the latter. Moreover, these new bilateral agreements may be used as a source of inspiration for the required upgrade of the largely outdated Partnership and Cooperation Agreement (PCA) between Russia and the EU.

Apart from the development of structural relations with its Eastern neighbours, through the conclusion of a new generation of bilateral framework agreements developments in the direction of visa liberalisation (for the associated Eastern Partnership [EaP] countries) and visa facilitation (for the non-associated EaP countries) significantly affect the broader picture of EU-Russia relations. As Igor Merheim-Eyre showed in Chapter 9, both the EU and Russia increasingly use visas as an instrument to pursue their respective region-building and foreign policy goals in the contested neighbourhood of Eastern Europe and the Southern Caucasus. As a result, visa diplomacy developed into another field of competition between the EU and Russia, leading to new challenges for the creation of a common European space of freedom, security and justice.

The limits of the EU's focus on developing strengthened bilateral relations with its Eastern neighbours is also visible with respect to the so-called 'frozen conflicts'. As Benedikt Harzl revealed in Chapter 8, the issue of conflict resolution hardly features on the EU's agenda, which may be partly explained by the EU's limited competences in this area. Hence, the EU's efforts predominantly focus on the economic integration of the EaP countries but largely ignore the delicate security question of the frozen conflicts and the reality of *de facto* states in the post-Soviet space.

With respect to *the third principle* – namely, strengthening the EU's resilience to Russian threats – some progress can be observed. Yet this principle also entails several implications for the future of EU-Russia relations which do not necessarily offer a positive prospect for overcoming the current tensions between the two.

As indicated in the introductory chapter, the longest standing threat when it comes to Russia remains the EU's energy dependence. In recent years, the EU has successfully implemented a number of measures that have helped to strengthen its energy resilience, including via the development of the third energy package and the establishment of the Energy Union. Interestingly, as demonstrated by Marco Siddi in Chapter 11, the EU could not risk compromising its energy trade with Russia; therefore, energy is also an area of selective

---

1   See the contribution by Laure Delcour and Narine Ghazaryan (chapter 7) in this volume.

engagement with Russia and thus actually falls under two principles.[2] This helps to explain why the volume of the energy trade did not decrease in the past few years and even increased in 2017 and 2018.

Another key area where the EU has been trying to strengthen its resilience against threats from Russia is cyber security. As outlined by Andreas Marazis in Chapter 12, the EU has made some progress in this regard, among other things by updating the existing legal framework for cyber security and by pushing forward the harmonisation of the Member States' legislation. Yet there is still a long way to go, considering that only a few EU Member States have completed the transposition of the legal framework into their domestic law, and cooperation and coordination between the EU Member States is only slowly developing in this field due to a lack of trust.

While it may seem essential for the EU to boost its resilience against Russian threats, the third principle in it itself is not very conducive to the improvement of EU-Russia relations. As argued by Elena Pavlova and Tatiana Romanova in Chapter 10, the third principle implies that the EU has brought its policies and norms in opposition to those of Russia, which has turned from a potential partner into a threat. This only further exacerbates the alienation between the EU and Russia that had been gradually building up in the past decade and culminated in the Ukraine crisis.

Moving to the *fourth principle*, 'selective engagement' is the principle that seems the most pragmatic of all five principles. As spelled out in the EU's Global Strategy, following the acknowledgement that the EU and Russia are highly interdependent and thus should cooperate on issues of common interest, the EU envisions selective engagement with Russia on pressing foreign policy matters such as Syria and counter-terrorism, and in other areas where there is a clear EU interest such as climate and maritime security. Yet in practice, the fourth principle has so far yielded only a few results. As Olga Potemkina showed in Chapter 13, cooperation on countering global security threats, for instance, has been limited to uncoordinated actions based on overlapping interests. While a broad range of areas could potentially qualify for selective engagement, the areas where selective engagement has materialised are mostly limited to a few major foreign policy issues, including the conflict in Syria and the Iran nuclear programme.[3] While the case of Iran could be considered a

---

2   See also, in this respect, the contribution by Niels Smeets on renewable energy as a potential area for selective cooperation (chapter 14).
3   A. Legucka, 'The Risk of Selective Engagement in Relations between the EU and Russia', Polish Institute of International Affairs, 148(1896)/2019, available at <https://www.pism.pl/publications/The_Risk_of_Selective_Engagement_in_Relations_between_the_EU_and_Russia>;

rare example of fruitful cooperation between the EU and Russia, whereby they joined forces in trying to save the Joint Comprehensive Plan of Action (JCPOA) in the face of the United States' withdrawal, cooperation on Syria has been much more cumbersome, not least due to fundamental disagreements and diverging approaches to addressing the conflict.[4]

Although the fourth principle fully reflects the spirit of 'principled pragmatism', its implementation thus turns out to be difficult, not least because the sanctions regime and the lack of trust complicate the level of engagement in practice. Moreover, in the absence of a precise definition of the fourth principle, it has been very difficult for the EU and its Member States to agree on the areas that qualify for selective engagement with Russia. Several EU Member States, including Germany and France, and institutional actors, in particular the Head of the EU Delegation to Russia, Markus Ederer, have been proposing specific areas for selective engagement, including the Arctic, the digital sphere, cooperation with the EAEU, regional infrastructure, and the Northern Dimension.[5] As Thomas Kruessmann demonstrated in Chapter 15, the Arctic is indeed an area where selective engagement could be considered, be it ideally in cooperation with China. However, other EU Member States, including Poland and Lithuania, have been fiercely opposed to extending the areas of selective engagement, mostly because they lost faith in a cooperative approach towards the Kremlin. Indeed, these are mostly EU Member States which, based on their own historical experiences with Russia, believe that the Ukraine crisis confirmed the failure of a cooperative approach towards Russia.[6]

Last but not least, it appears that the *fifth principle,* which spells out the need to support Russian civil society and engage in people-to-people contacts, is arguably the most successful of all five principles. In a context of strained diplomatic and political relations, the EU has invested significantly in strengthening societal ties through student exchanges, civil society cooperation and research and cross-border cooperation. As Elena Belokurova and Andrey Demidov showed in Chapter 16, the EU has been following a two-track

---

S. Fischer and I. Timofeev, 'Selective Engagement between the EU and Russia', Interim Report EU-Russia Expert Network on Foreign Policy, 2018, available at: <https://www.clingendael.org/sites/default/files/2018-10/2018-10-01_EUREN%20Interim%20Report%20Final.pdf>.

4   M.A. Suchkov, 'Prospects for EU-Russia Cooperation in the Middle East: A View from Moscow', *EUREN Brief*, No. 12/2020, available at: <http://188.127.251.150/wp-content/euinrussiapdf/EUREN_Brief_12_Suchkov.pdf>.

5   See 'EU Envoy Urges Bloc to Engage More with Russia over 5G and Data', *Financial Times*, 13 September 2020.

6   T. van der Togt, 'In Search of a European Russia Strategy', *Atlantisch Perspectief*, 1, 2020, 38.

approach towards support for civil society in the past few years. While continuing support for civil society under the existing instruments, the shrinking space for civil society activities in Russia led to the introduction of new, more indirect channels of civil society support. In particular, the EU has embedded civil society support within its wider cultural and public diplomacy towards Russia. As Domenico Valenza revealed in Chapter 17, this approach is paying off, in the sense that EU engagement in the cultural sphere is playing an important role in breaking civil society isolation and nurturing long-term openness in Russia. As Natalia Leskina pointed out in Chapter 18, EU-Russia relations are also witnessing fruitful cooperation in the field of research and higher education. The past few years have seen an increased interest from Russian academics and universities in collaboration with European partners and participation in EU-funded programmes. In sum, it can be concluded that the field of people-to-people contacts has become a privileged area of intervention to maintain a dialogue with Russia at the societal level.

3   The Way Forward: Time to Revise the Guiding Principles?

The mixed picture that emerges from the assessment of the five guiding principles suggests that a revision of the EU's current policy will be needed to pursue a more effective and constructive policy towards Russia. This conclusion is finding growing resonance among experts, who echo the need for a more strategic policy towards Russia.[7] As S. Fischer has shown, 'These guiding principles have earned praise for being flexible and sufficiently balanced to keep on board Member States with very different positions and interests vis-à-vis Russia. They have also been fiercely criticised for a lack of policy goals and strategic vision'[8]

The contributions to this volume largely confirm this view and point at the broader paradoxes and challenges that have characterised EU-Russia relations in recent times. Awareness of these broader trends and features is essential if the EU and Russia want to move beyond the lingering deadlock in their bilateral relations.

As several contributions to this book revealed, it has to be recognised that the current paralysis in the EU-Russia relationship did not start with the Ukraine

---

7   See, for example, van der Togt, *op. cit.* note 6; S. Fischer, 'What the New EU Leadership Should Do about Russia', *Carnegie Moscow*, 4 December 2019, available at: <https://carnegie.ru/commentary/80485>.

8   Fischer, *ibid.*

crisis in 2014 but is the result of a process of gradually worsening relations set against a longer history of mutual misunderstandings that goes back to the early 2000s. Ever since, an increasing gap between the political discourse of 'Strategic Partnership' and the reality of growing distrust and widening divergence between the positions and interests of both parties could be witnessed. While the EU's and Russia's competing paradigms for the development of relations with the so-called 'shared neighbourhood' would eventually instigate an explosive rivalry between them, the lack of progress in implementing the so-called 'four Common Spaces' had already revealed that bilateral cooperation on areas of common interest, ranging from the deepening of trade relations and energy cooperation to questions of internal and external security, proved difficult. The contributions to this volume offered further insights that help to explain the dynamics underlying the worsening relationship, which will need to be addressed to overhaul the EU's current short-term policy towards Russia in favour of a more constructive, long-term strategy.

First, the profound discord between the EU and Russia is reflected in the actors' diverging images and perceptions, which have in turn engendered a deeply ingrained misunderstanding and lack of trust. As has been argued elsewhere, diverging images and perceptions can be major obstacles to the enhancement of relations between the EU and Russia.[9] Hence, it is essential to understand how these divergences have emerged and how they have been manifested. This is important not only to be able to identify confidence-building measures to restore trust but also to develop a common vision for cooperation between the EU and Russia.

A key element is that the EU and Russia have divergent views on security, and disagree fundamentally on what constitutes and safeguards the European security order.[10] The latter has been clearly manifested in their opposing views on the Ukraine crisis. As demonstrated by Petrova (chapter 3), the EU and Russia have promoted their own interpretation of events, in which they each present the other as the opponent and hold conflicting perspectives on the sequencing of the implementation process of the Minsk agreements, as well as on the responsibilities of the parties involved. Clearly, as long as the EU and

---

9 T. Casier and J. DeBardeleben (eds.), *EU-Russia Relations in Crisis: Understanding Diverging Perceptions* (Routledge 2017).

10 See, for example, Van der Togt, *op. cit.* note 6; Fischer and Timofeev, *op. cit.* note 3; K. Raik and A. Racz (eds.), *Post-Crimea Shift in EU-Russia Relations: From Fostering Independence to Managing Vulnerabilities* (Tallinn, International Centre for Defence and Security 2019); N. Zaslavskaya and D. Averre, 'EU-Russia Political and Security Cooperation: Major Research Trends', *Journal of Contemporary European Studies* 27 (2), 2019, 147–158.

Russia interpret the Ukraine crisis so differently, no significant progress may be expected with respect to the full implementation of the Minsk agreements. As highlighted above, this raises serious doubts on the effectiveness of the first principle and signals the need for a revision of the EU's existing conditionality approach with respect to the lifting of the sanctions regime.

Another important aspect that has impeded constructive cooperation is the mismatch between the EU's ambitions as a global norm-setter, which is perceived as paternalistic from a Russian point of view, and Russia's ambitions to become a norm-setter in its own right. Several chapters, especially those by Russian authors, argued that this mismatch lies at the basis of the worsening relationship between the EU and Russia and the difficulty to engage in cooperation that has manifested itself since the 2000s.[11] This is also acknowledged in the existing literature. As N. Zaslavskaya and D. Averre pointed out, 'Russia's present path of self-exclusion from Europe arises from a refusal to adopt wholesale EU norms and values and assert the legitimacy of its domestic order and national identity, while accentuating its sovereign power as a response to the failure of Brussels to recognise Moscow as a legitimate and equal partner in the European security order'.[12]

As indicated by Pavlova and Romanova (chapter 10), Potemkina (chapter 13) and Leskina (chapter 18), Russia has no interest in cooperating with the EU if it can only be 'a passive consumer of EU norms'. Instead, it seeks recognition as an equal actor in today's multipolar world. Russia thus wants to move beyond a 'master-pupil' or 'donor-recipient' relationship which can be observed, among other things, in specific areas such as higher education and transnational security threats.[13]

So far, the EU has shown only a little readiness to answer Russia's desire for cooperation on an equal footing. As highlighted by Pavlova and Romanova (chapter 10), the EU's Global Strategy has further cemented the EU's binary logic, whereby it asks Russia to conform to the EU's vision of security and cooperation, and identifies Russia as a 'strategic challenge' as long as it does not do so. An increasing number of scholars have criticised this approach and are calling on the EU to accommodate Russia's desire for cooperation based on an equal footing.[14]

---

11   See the contributions by E. Pavlova and T. Romanova (chapter 10), O. Potemkina (chapter 13) and N. Leskina (chapter 18) in this volume.
12   Zaslavskaya and Averre, *op. cit.* note 10, 155.
13   See, respectively, the contributions by N. Leskina (chapter 18) and O. Potemkina (chapter 13) in this volume.
14   L. Deriglazova and S. Mäkinen, 'Still Looking for a Partnership? EU-Russia Cooperation in the Field of Higher Education', *Journal of Contemporary European Studies* 27 (2), 2019,

Last but not least, some of the contributions to this volume have also provided further insights into the role that the EU Member States play in the formulation and implementation of the EU's current policy towards Russia. While the EU Member States all still formally agree with the sanctions policy and the five guiding principles, and unity thus prevails on the surface, the divisions that predated the Ukraine crisis have gradually re-emerged in the past five years.[15] The lack of a common position among the Member States has always been considered the Achilles heel of the EU's policy towards Russia, especially after the Eastern enlargement of the EU.[16] The current disagreement among the EU Member States is making it difficult for the EU to find a way out of the lingering impasse in its relations with Russia. EU Member States remain deeply divided as to the most appropriate and effective approach towards Russia. Some Member States, such as France, Italy, Greece and Hungary, promote a pragmatic, instrumentalist strategy of constructive engagement while others, such as Poland and Lithuania, advocate a normative agenda and insist on a policy of containment.[17]

As demonstrated by van der Togt in Chapter 2, Germany assumed a leading role in the EU's immediate response to the Ukraine crisis and was pivotal in rallying all the Member States behind a common EU position on the sanctions. However, the support that Germany enjoyed among Central and Eastern European EU Member States started eroding in the face of Germany's determination to continue the construction of the Nord Stream 2 gas pipeline. In 2019, France tried to take over Germany's leadership position by spearheading a new effort to reanimate the talks on a settlement of the Ukraine crisis in the Normandy Format and by undertaking a new initiative to revamp EU-Russia relations based on a proposal to build an 'architecture of trust' with Russia on the European continent.[18] However, it appears that these efforts are to little avail, mostly due a lack of broader support from other EU Member

---

184–195; K. Liik, 'EU-Russia Relations: Where Do We Go from Here?', in: K. Raik and A. Racz (eds.), *Post-Crimea Shift in EU-Russia Relations: From Fostering Independence to Managing Vulnerabilities* (Tallinn, International Centre for Defence and Security 2019), 285; E. Korosteleva, 'Putting the EU Global Security Strategy to Test: 'Cooperative Orders' and Othering in EU-Russia Relations', *International Politics* 56, 2019, 304–320.

15 See, for example, van der Togt, *op. cit.* note 6; Legucka, *op. cit.* note 3; Fischer, *op. cit.* note 7.

16 See, for example, M. David, J. Gower and H. Haukkala, 'Introduction: The European Union and Russia', *Journal of Contemporary European Studies* 19 (2), 2011, 183–188.

17 See, for example, Fischer, *op. cit.* note 7.

18 See 'France's Macron Makes Russia a Top Diplomatic Priority', *Euractiv*, 28 August 2019, available at: <https://www.euractiv.com/section/global-europe/news/frances-macron-makes-russia-a-top-diplomatic-priority/>.

States.[19] Moreover, the poisoning of Russian opposition leader Alexei Navalny created new tensions in EU-Russia relations. In this context, it is noteworthy that the Foreign Affairs Ministers of France and Germany issued a joint statement calling for additional sanctions against Russia.[20]

Some observers have suggested that Brexit would tilt the centre of gravity in the EU towards a softer line on Russia.[21] So far, it seems that the UK's departure from the EU is not strongly affecting the current dynamic in EU-Russia relations. As Oksana Antonenko indicated, 'Although the UK's departure will remove a strong supporter of tough sanctions against Russia from the EU decision-making table, many like-minded countries remain, meaning EU sanctions are likely to remain in place even after the UK's departure'.[22]

Finally, the question remains as to whether the onset of a new leadership of the EU institutions will entail any significant change in the EU's policy towards Russia. Commission President Ursula Von der Leyen's proposal to lead a 'geopolitical Commission' can be seen as an attempt to reposition the EU's place and role in the world in the face of a more isolationist United States and a more assertive and powerful China.[23] However, so far, this has not resulted in a different position towards Russia. The Union's new High Representative for Foreign Affairs and Security Policy, Josep Borrell, has maintained the status quo and has expressed support for keeping the EU's sanctions on Russia in place as long as the Minsk agreements are not fully implemented.[24] Moreover, he has been an active supporter of additional sanctions following the poisoning of Alexei Navalny.[25]

19　See van der Togt, *op. cit.* note 6; Fischer, *op. cit.* note 7.

20　German Federal Foreign Office, 'Joint statement by the foreign ministers of France and Germany on the Navalny case', 7 October 2020, available at: < https://www.auswaertiges-amt.de/en/newsroom/news/maas-le-drian-navalny/2403036> (last accessed 13 October 2020).

21　See, for example, 'What Next for EU Russia Policy?', *European Council on Foreign Relations*, available at: <https://www.ecfr.eu/debate/what_next_for_eu_russia_policy> (last accessed 1 September 2020).

22　O. Antonenko, 'Why Brexit Won't Affect EU-Russia Relations', Carnegie Moscow Center, 3 February 2020, available at: <https://carnegie.ru/commentary/80957> (last accessed 1 September 2020).

23　See, for example, van der Togt, *op. cit.* note 6; Fischer, *op. cit.* note 7.

24　See 'Borrell Hard on Russia in EU Hearing', *EUobserver*, 8 October 2019, available at: <https://euobserver.com/foreign/146195>. (last accessed 1 September 2020).

25　EEAS, 'Russia – Poisoning of Alexei Navalny: Remarks by the High Representative/Vice-President Josep Borell at the EP Plenary', 15 September 2020, available at: <https://eeas.europa.eu/headquarters/headquarters-homepage/85149/russia-poisoning-alexei-navalny-remarks-high-representative-vice-president-josep-borrell-ep_en> (last accessed 13 October 2020).

4 Concluding Remarks

Almost five years after the five guiding principles were introduced, EU-Russia relations remain at an all-time low and continue to be in a state of paralysis, marked by deinstitutionalisation, inertia and estrangement. While the confrontation over the Donbas area is increasingly set to become a frozen conflict and the annexation of Crimea is unlikely to be reversed, the EU maintains its policy of principled pragmatism towards Russia as laid down in the EU's Global Strategy of 2016. This means that the EU continues to uphold its principled position regarding the implementation of the Minsk agreements as a condition for lifting the sanctions on Russia, while pragmatically allowing for cooperation with Russia in areas of common interest. Yet as even selective engagement with Russia on areas of common interests has so far remained minimal, and the conflict in eastern Ukraine is nowhere near settlement, the effectiveness and sustainability of the EU's approach have been called into question.

The assessment of the five guiding principles and their state of implementation has shown that the EU's current policy is in need of revision. The five principles can merely be seen as a short-term, intermediate framework, which needs to be reviewed in favour of a more effective and long-term policy with a clear strategic vision. As illustrated throughout this volume, some positive results can be discerned from the current policy, such as the promotion of people-to-people contacts, which should feed into any revision of the EU's policy. Overall, however, the outcome nearly five years after the five principles were introduced is meagre and a more long-term strategic framework for the future development of EU-Russia relations is needed.

Arguably, any revision of the EU's approach towards Russia needs to proceed from a broader understanding of the strained relationship. This implies, among other things, a recognition that the Ukraine crisis was only the culmination of a longer process of deteriorating bilateral relations embodied by the growing divergence between the two actors' positions and interests. The key challenge in defining a new long-term strategy for the future of EU-Russia relations will be to develop a common vision for cooperation based on mutually acceptable parameters. In this regard, the challenge is double, as the EU needs to develop a vision that is shared by its internally divided Member States as well as by Russia.

To restore trust, it seems essential to develop a 'step-by step' approach based on confidence-building measures, which – if successfully implemented – could eventually lead towards broader and longer-term cooperation. In this respect, some lessons could also be drawn from the EU's Northern Dimension (ND) policy. It constitutes a pragmatic, multilateral framework for cooperation with Russia and essentially focuses on issues of 'low politics' such as environment protection, social welfare, transport networks and cultural cooperation.[26] This has allowed the ND policy to succeed in a context of deteriorating bilateral relations.[27]

In addition, an upgrade of the legal and institutional framework for cooperation remains important. It is well known that the old PCA, which was negotiated in the 1990s, is no longer fit for purpose. Whereas the suspension of negotiations on a new legal framework agreement may be regarded as a logical, immediate response to the events in Ukraine, the long-term sustainability of this approach is questionable. A common political agenda for (selective) cooperation requires appropriate legal and institutional structures. This is one of the lessons that could be drawn from the largely failed 'Common Spaces' agenda.

In any event, a revision of joint ambitions and approaches while recognising the existence of fundamental differences is at stake. This obviously is not an easy exercise but Russia's geographical position as well as its geopolitical significance in today's multipolar world simply cannot be ignored. The high degree of interdependence means that the EU and Russia are bound to cooperate in certain areas, as the case of energy security shows. At the same time, there are also areas where cooperation is more difficult such as the field of cyber security. Even in the event of improving EU-Russia relations, the EU's resilience towards cyber threats and disinformation campaigns will remain relevant. Moreover, the unsolved conflict in the Donbas region and Russia's annexation of Crimea imply that a simple return to business as usual is impossible. That said, a revision of the five guiding principles in the direction of a more comprehensive and strategic approach should allow for at least a move beyond the current paralysis.

---

26   P. Van Elsuwege, 'The Northern Dimension: A Format for Pragmatic Cooperation with the EU's Biggest Neighbour', in: S. Gstöhl (ed.), *The European Neighbourhood Policy in a Comparative Perspective* (Routledge 2016), 92–104.

27   For instance, in October 2014, at a time of strained EU-Russia relations and mutual sanctions due to the crisis in Ukraine, Russian Foreign Minister Sergey Lavrov praised the ND as a guiding example of how the EU and Russia can develop their cooperation in a sphere of partnership. See 'Speech and Replies to Questions by Foreign Affairs Minister Sergey Lavrov at the Meeting with the Heads of the Member Companies of the Association of European Businesses in the Russian Federation', Moscow, 14 October 2014, available at: <http://russian-embassy.org/en/?p=1202> (last accessed 1 September 2020).

Studies in EU External Relations

Edited by

Marc Maresceau

1. *The European Union at the United Nations: The Functioning and Coherence of EU External Representation in a State-centric environment*, Maximilian B. Rasch (2008)
2. *From Soviet Republics to EU Member States: A Legal and Political Assessment of the Baltic States' Accession to the EU* (2 vols), Peter van Elsuwege (2008)
3. *The EU and Cyprus: Principles and Strategies of Full Integration*, Stéphanie Laulhé Shaelou (2009)
4. *Evolving Practice In EU Enlargement With Case Studies In Agri-Food And Environment Law*, Kirstyn Inglis (2010)
5. *International Law as Law of the European Union*, Edited by Enzo Cannizzaro, Paolo Palchetti, and Ramses A. Wessel (2011)
6. *The European Union's Emerging International Identity: Views from the Global Arena*, Henri de Waele (2013)
7. *EU Peacebuilding in Kosovo and Afghanistan: Legality and Accountability*, Martina Spernbauer (2014)
8. *EU Management of Global Emergencies: Legal Framework for Combating Threats and Crises*, Edited by Inge Govaere and Sara Poli (2014)
9. *Good Neighbourliness in the European Legal Context*, Edited by Dimitry Kochenov and Elena Basheska (2015)
10. *The EU-Ukraine Association Agreement and Deep and Comprehensive Free Trade Area: A New Legal Instrument for EU Integration Without Membership*, Guillaume Van der Loo (2016)
11. *European External Action Service: Promoting Coherence through Autonomy and Coordination*, Mauro Gatti (2016)
12. *The EU and the Security-Development Nexus Bridging the Legal Divide*, Hans Merket (2016)
13. The EU as a Global Actor – Bridging Legal Theory and Practice Edited by Jenő Czuczai and Frederik Naert 2017
14. *The Future of International Competition Law Enforcement: An Assessment of the EU's Cooperation Efforts*, Valerie Demedts (2018)

15 *The External Dimension of EU Social Security Coordination: Towards a Common EU Approach,* Pauline Melin (2019)
16 *EU External Relations Post-Lisbon: The Law and Practice of Facultative Mixity,* Merijn Chamon and Inge Govaere (eds.), (2020)
17 *The European Union and the Use of Force,* Julia Schmidt, (2020)
18 *Law and Practice of the Common Commercial Policy: The first 10 years after the Treaty of Lisbon,* Michael Hahn, Guillaume van der Loo, (2021)

Index

Abkhazia 3–4, 165–167, 166–167n13, 168–169, 172–173n39, 173n45, 173–174n47, 174, 174n53, 176–178, 177–178n64
Actorness 291, 293–294, 298, 300, 309
Annexation (*see also* Crimea) 6, 7, 12, 17–18, 46, 47–48, 49–50n19, 54, 58, 86–87, 96–97, 164–165, 171n35, 175, 180, 185–186, 186n24, 190, 193, 196, 202, 233, 235, 251, 253, 306–307, 313, 340–341, 380, 381
  Illegal annexation 70, 73–74, 211, 278
Approximation 4, 145, 146, 153–154, 155, 161–162, 163–164n2, 173, 315, 320
Arctic (*see also* Northern Dimension) 11, 278, 290–294, 297, 298–299, 300, 301, 306, 308n72, 309, 309n73, 342–344, 374
  Arctic Council 292–298
  Arctic Five 291, 292, 294–295
  Barents Euro-Arctic Cooperation (BEAC) 292, 293–294, 299, 300–301, 308–309
Area of Freedom, Security and Justice (AFSJ) 259
Armenia 5, 9–10, 11, 143, 145, 148–152, 153–161, 166, 167n17, 168–169, 168–169n23, 170–171n29, 170–171n32, 171nn33–35, 172–173, 180n4, 182, 192–193, 194
Azerbaijan 158, 163–164n3, 166, 168–169, 168–169n3, 169–170nn28, 170–171n32, 171n33, 172–173, 177–178, 180n4, 189, 194, 364, 371–372

Belarus 5, 59, 101, 114–115, 180n4, 183, 185, 186, 187, 189, 192n51, 192–193, 194, 195n68, 222, 230, 233n43, 343, 364–365
Belgium 83–84
Bologna Process 352–354, 356–357, 358–361, 362, 364, 367–368
BRICS 100–101, 283–284, 361, 368–369

Capacity-building 247, 360, 365–366, 367
Caucasus
  North Caucasus 166–167, 268

South Caucasus 173–174, 180, 196, 364–365, 372
Central Asia 8–9, 180n4, 183–184, 183–184n15, 205, 208, 268, 273, 364–365
China 61, 100–101, 102–103, 222–223, 226, 259, 273–274, 291, 294–295, 296, 297, 301–303, 304, 305–309, 361, 363–364, 368–369, 374, 379
Civil society 11, 12, 44–46, 53–54, 105n8, 115, 149–150n45, 151, 186, 189, 192, 254, 313–329, 332, 336, 340, 348, 349–351, 374–375
  Civil Society Organisation (CSO) 151, 288, 288n52, 314, 315, 316, 320–322, 323–325, 327–328, 329, 331, 334, 342–344, 348, 349–350
  Civil society support 313–314, 315–316, 317, 320, 321, 329–331
  EU-Russia Civil Society Forum (CSF) 328, 346
Climate change 7, 277, 278–279, 280, 285, 288–289, 326
Collaboration 248, 290–291, 309, 341, 355–356, 365, 368, 374–375
Common Foreign and Security Policy (CFSP) 1–2, 5–6, 8, 40, 106, 108, 109–110, 114, 124, 126, 128–129, 136–137, 138–140, 151–152, 164, 170, 297–298, 371–372
Common neighbourhood 180n4, 181–182, 183, 192–193
Common Spaces 2–4, 44, 261, 293, 335–336, 358, 359–360, 375–376, 381
Common Strategy on Russia (CSR) 1–3, 44, 314
Commonwealth of Independent States (CIS) 195, 353–354, 355, 356–357, 359, 362, 363–364
Comprehensive and Enhanced Partnership Agreement (CEPA) 9–10, 143–145, 148–155, 157, 159, 160–162, 371–372
Connectivity 249–250, 259, 305–306
Counter-terrorism 11, 257, 258, 259, 265, 269–270, 275, 278, 373–374

Court of Justice of the European Union (CJEU) 105–107, 109, 111, 112, 120, 121–124, 125–126, 129, 134–135, 136–138, 140, 371
   European Court of Justice (ECJ) 110–111, 116–117, 120–121, 167–168n18, 175–176, 298, 299
   General Court (GC) 105, 106, 110–112, 113–115, 118–119, 120–122, 137, 138–139
Crimea 5, 6, 7, 12, 17–18, 40–41, 46, 47–48, 48n16, 54, 58, 68–69, 70, 73–74, 80, 84–85, 86–87, 90–91, 96–97, 99–100, 104–105, 116, 118, 119, 164–165, 164–165n5, 164–165n7, 169–170n27, 171n35, 175, 180, 185–186, 190, 193, 211, 233, 235, 251, 253, 258, 271, 278, 285–286, 289, 301, 306–307, 313, 319–320, 322–323, 325, 333–334, 336, 337, 340–341, 348, 349–350, 380, 381
Critical Discourse Analysis (CDA) 63–64, 203
Cross-Border Cooperation (CBC) 11, 12, 35–36, 244n28, 278, 290, 313, 315–316, 317–318, 319–320, 324, 325, 329–330, 336, 338, 339, 342, 346–347, 349, 374–375
Culture 2–3, 332–337, 340–341, 342–346, 348, 349–350
   Cultural diplomacy 333, 337–338, 349–350, 374–375
   Cultural exchanges 314, 347
   Cultural relations 12, 332–334, 335, 337–338, 339–340, 339n27, 342, 349–351
Cyber security 207, 208, 235, 239–245, 244n28, 246, 248, 250, 251–254, 273–274, 373, 381
   Cyber operations 234, 235–236, 239–243
   Cyber resilience 239, 247, 248, 251
Cyprus 60–61, 81, 83–84, 167–168n18, 177–178

Decision-making 40–41, 57–58, 59, 60, 61, 65, 96, 213, 317–318, 328, 361, 379
De facto states 10, 163–164, 167, 169–170, 173–174, 176–177, 178–179, 372
Democracy promotion 313, 314, 318, 319–320, 324–325, 330
Discourse 12, 19–20, 72, 83–84, 85, 120–121, 167n17, 168–169, 203, 205, 206, 207–208, 214, 306, 314, 322, 327, 330–331, 361, 375–376

Donbas(s) 5–6, 12, 17–18, 19–21, 23, 24, 28–29, 32–36, 37–39, 42, 48, 49, 50–51, 54, 65, 66, 68–69, 75–76, 77–78, 119–120, 169–170n27, 180, 181n8, 190–191, 193, 194, 196, 380, 381
Donetsk/ Donetsk People's Republic (DPR) 5, 10, 20–21, 22, 23, 24, 26–27, 29, 31–32, 33, 35–36, 77–78, 164–165, 169–170n27

Eastern Europe 53, 171, 180, 196, 223, 372
   Eastern European (member) states 42–43, 52, 59, 218, 223–224, 299, 315, 378–379
Eastern Partnership (EaP) 4, 4n7, 5, 9–10, 143–144, 145–146, 148, 163–165, 169–170, 173, 180, 181–182, 187, 190, 195, 196, 254, 300, 328, 362–363, 364–365, 372
Eastern neighbourhood 168, 187–188, 288
Enemy image 72, 84–85
Energy
   Energy dependence 10, 52, 372–373
   Energy relations(hip) 10, 40–41, 42–43, 44, 49, 53–54, 57–58, 216, 217, 218–219, 220, 221–222, 223, 225–226, 227–228, 232–233
   Energy resilience 220, 372–373
   Energy security 10, 147–148, 210–211, 216, 218–219, 220, 222–223, 224, 225–226, 230, 231–232, 233, 277, 278–280, 285, 289, 370
ENISA 242–243, 246, 252, 253–254
Enhanced Partnership and Cooperation Agreement (EPCA) 143–144, 149–150, 149–150n39, 151
Enlargement 202, 260, 288, 315
   2004 enlargement 183, 187
   DG Near 288
   Eastward/Eastern enlargement 1–2, 12, 163–164, 378
Erasmus\+ 326–327, 360, 365, 366
Eurasian Economic Community (EurAsEC) 362–363
Eurasian Economic Union (EAEU) 4, 4n7, 5, 8–10, 143–145, 143–144n4, 148–149, 151–155, 156–157, 159, 160–162, 180, 195, 362–364, 371–372, 374
Euromaidan *see* Maidan

INDEX

European Commission 3–4, 42–43, 48, 49–50, 57, 72, 191–192, 218–221, 222, 223–224, 228–229, 232–233, 242–243, 244, 247, 248–249, 278, 288, 292, 299, 332, 343, 352–353
European Convention on Human Rights and Fundamental Freedoms (ECHR) 114–115, 126–127, 129–130, 165–166n7
European Council 1–2, 3–4, 8, 48, 50–51, 55, 63–64, 87, 107, 298–299, 336
European Court of Justice, *see* Court of Justice of the EU
European Court of Human Rights (ECtHR) 111, 114–115, 129, 165–166n7
European External Action Service (EEAS) 63–64, 76, 242–243, 288, 298, 300, 320, 332, 335
European Higher Education Area (EHEA) 12, 352–354, 358, 359–360, 368
Europeanisation 52, 163–164, 163–164n2, 175, 178
European Neighbourhood Policy (ENP) 4, 12, 143–144, 146, 171–172, 173, 201–202, 208, 260, 317–318
  European Neighbourhood and Partnership Instrument (ENPI) 317–318, 326–327
  European Neighbourhood Instrument (ENI) 337–338
European Parliament 72, 186, 277–278, 295, 296–297, 298–299, 300, 316, 335, 336
European Union National Institutes for Culture (EUNIC) 339, 344
EU-Russia summit 2–4, 75, 260, 265–267, 270, 326–327, 335–336

France 22, 26–27, 37–38, 42–43, 48–49, 64, 81–84, 226, 227–229, 232–233, 295, 374, 378–379
Frozen conflicts 10, 168, 168n20, 170–174, 175, 177–178, 237, 288, 372, 380
Fundamental rights 112, 113, 115–116, 123, 127–128, 134–135, 139–140

Gas 10, 42–43, 49, 52, 57, 59, 160, 210–211, 217, 218–221, 223, 226–228, 230, 232, 233, 245, 278, 281, 378–379
  Liquified natural gas (LNG) 218, 220–223, 225, 232–233, 302–303, 306–308

Gazprom 53, 98, 130–131, 147–148, 219–221, 222–224, 225–227, 228, 229–231, 232–233, 282–283
Geneva statement 18, 24, 37–38
Georgia 2–4, 143–144, 148–150, 158, 159, 163–164n3, 165–167, 168–169, 170–171n32, 171, 171n33, 172–174, 175–179, 186–187, 188–189, 190–191, 191n42, 192–193, 192–193n53, 194, 254
Germany 20–21, 22, 26–27, 28, 37–38, 40–47, 53–55, 57, 58, 59, 64, 81–84, 194, 227–229, 232–233, 246, 252, 295, 374, 378–379
Global Strategy 7–8, 11, 12–13, 72, 201–204, 205, 207–210, 211, 213, 257–258, 259, 290, 322–323, 367, 370, 373–374, 377, 380

Higher education 178–179, 352, 353, 355–356, 357, 358, 359–361, 362–363, 364, 365, 367–368
Hollande 22, 49–51, 271
Hungary 60–61, 81–84, 92–93, 220, 378
Hybrid operations 235–236, 237

Identity 71, 74, 84–85, 89–90, 101–102, 148, 206, 214, 377
Information operations 235–236, 237
Institutions 42–43, 109–110, 205–206, 237–239, 246, 249, 252–253, 254, 287, 300, 318, 322, 323, 326–327, 328, 329, 348, 356–357, 365
  EU institutions 40, 42–43, 59, 61, 68n18, 106, 228, 229, 239, 277–278, 322, 335, 341–342, 379

Jean Monnet
  activities 365–366
  Centres of Excellence 365–366

Kaliningrad 2, 184, 341
Kazakhstan 5, 9–10, 100–101, 143–144, 149–151, 362, 363, 371–372
Kyrgyzstan 9–10, 100–101, 371–372

Lavrov 18–19, 24–26, 77, 160–161, 257–258, 267–268, 294–295, 380n27
Luhansk/ Luhansk People's Republic (LPR) 5, 20–21, 23, 24, 26, 29, 31–32, 33, 35–36, 77–78

Macron 29, 42–43, 60, 238–239
Maidan 5, 5n20, 12, 41, 47, 190–191, 347
Merkel 22, 29, 38–39, 41–42, 48–52, 59
MH17 (Malaysian airlines flight) 5–6, 22, 40–41, 42, 49, 50, 54–56, 58, 59–60, 87–88, 104–105, 130, 180, 185–186
minorities 1–2, 193n60, 194
Minsk agreements 8, 17–19, 22, 26–28, 30–32, 33–35, 36–37, 41, 51, 55, 58, 61, 62, 64, 65–66, 67, 68–70, 73, 74, 75–76, 77–78, 81–84, 87–88, 99–100, 106–107, 126, 258, 277, 285, 370–371, 376–377, 379–380
    Minsk process 29
    Minsk protocol 20, 22, 23, 24–27, 28–30, 33–34, 50–51, 60
mirror narratives 64, 71–72, 76
Mogherini 6, 51, 58, 72, 210–211, 216, 220, 257–258, 269–270

Nagorno-Karabakh 152, 165–166, 168–169, 169–170n28, 172–173, 180
Navalny 59, 266–267, 378–379
Netherlands 40–43, 45, 53–58, 59–60, 83–84, 222, 227–228, 252, 295
Network and Information Security Directive 242–243, 244–245, 246–247, 249–250, 251–252, 253–254
Newly Independent States 43–44, 315
Nord Stream 42–43, 52, 57, 59–60, 219, 220–221, 222, 224–225, 226–228, 229–230, 231–232, 233, 378–379
Normandy format 20, 22, 26–27, 29, 37–39, 41, 48–49, 50–52, 58, 60, 65, 378–379
Normative power Europe 203, 205–206, 207–208, 209–210
North Atlantic Treaty Organisation (NATO) 11, 36, 54–55, 96–97, 147, 234, 242–243, 246, 247–248, 252, 253, 254, 259, 268
Northern Dimension (ND) 25n27, 293–294, 300–301, 304–305, 374, 380–381
Northern Sea Route 291, 300–301, 304–305, 306, 307–309

Obama 18–19, 49–50, 58, 306–307
Office for Democratic Institutions and Human Rights (ODIHR) 31–32
Organisation for Economic Co-operation and Development (OECD) 203–204, 281–282
Organisation for Security and Co-operation in Europe (OSCE) 18–19, 20–21, 22–23, 24–28, 29, 31–32, 34, 36, 37–38, 41, 43, 47–48, 51–52, 54–55, 65, 86–87n3, 169–170, 172–173
    Minsk group 152, 172–173n42
    Special Monitoring Mission 22, 30, 36
    Trilateral Contact Group 20–22, 23

Partnership and Cooperation Agreement (PCA) 1, 2–4, 5–6, 8–9, 12, 44, 98–99n73, 105–106, 120–121, 122–123, 126–127, 149–150, 156, 163–164n2, 171–172, 173, 202, 314, 335–357, 371–372, 381
Partnership for Modernisation 3–4, 44–45, 202, 281, 328
people-to-people contacts 12, 87–88, 106–107, 118–119, 181, 188, 189, 313, 314, 317–318, 321, 323, 325, 327, 329–331, 332, 335–336, 341–342, 352, 355–356, 358, 367, 368, 374–375, 380
Permanent Structured Cooperation (PESCO) 252, 254
Polar Silk Road 305–306, 309n73
Poroshenko 20–22, 24–26, 37–38, 49–50, 190
post-Soviet space 9–10, 160, 168n20, 171, 180n4, 183, 187, 190, 192–193, 195, 196–197, 208, 214–215, 358, 363, 368–369, 371–372
pragmatism 203, 210
    principled pragmatism 7, 11, 12–13, 86–87, 89–90, 101–103, 178–179, 202–203, 208–210, 214, 313, 374, 380
principles
    five guiding principles 7–8, 12–13, 17–18, 106–107, 126, 163–164, 201–202, 210–211, 290, 313, 336, 370–375, 378, 380, 381
public diplomacy 12, 314, 325, 326–327, 330–331, 333, 337–338, 364, 365–366, 367, 368, 374–375
Putin 8–9, 20–22, 29, 38, 44–46, 48, 49–50, 53–54, 60, 77, 81, 96–97, 99–100, 102–103, 117, 158, 160, 202, 226, 302–303, 317–318, 357, 363–364

region-building 180, 182, 187–188, 190, 195, 196–197, 352–353, 354, 363, 364, 368
renewable energy 277–280, 281–282, 283, 284–289
reunification
  German reunification 43–44
  De facto states 178–179
resilience
  the concept of resilience 7, 10, 56–57, 201–202, 203–206, 207–209, 210–211, 212–215, 216, 372
  cyber resilience 235, 239, 247, 248, 249–250, 251, 253, 254, 373, 381
  energy resilience 217–218, 222–223, 224, 225–226, 231–232, 233, 372–373
  environmental resilience 342–344
restrictive measures (see also: sanctions) 5–6, 8, 11, 12, 17–18, 86–87, 88–91, 95–96, 99–100, 101–102, 104–107, 109, 110, 112, 113, 114–116, 117–118, 119–124, 126, 127–129, 130–132, 134–138, 149–150, 273–274, 277, 283, 285, 289, 322–323, 364, 370–371
Rosneft 99–100n73, 105–106, 108, 109–112, 114, 119–123, 126–127, 137–139, 282–283
Russia
  Duma 45–46, 263
  Federal Migration Service of Russia 193
  Foreign Ministry 19–20, 266–267
  Military intelligence unit (GRU) 20
Russian-speaking minorities 1–2, 194

sanctions (see also restrictive measures)
  EU sanctions 6, 7–8, 11, 12–13, 17–18, 20, 38–39, 41, 47–52, 54, 55, 57, 58, 59, 60–61, 62, 66–68, 69–70, 73–74, 75–76, 78–80, 81, 83–84, 86–90, 91, 92–93, 94–96, 98–102, 104–105, 106–107, 110–111, 180, 185–186, 202–203, 218, 221–222, 258, 259, 261–262, 263, 264, 265, 266–267, 275–276, 296–297, 306–308, 309, 322–323, 340–341, 348, 370–371, 374, 376–377, 378–380
  Counter-sanctions 97–98
  Judicial review 108, 112–115, 116–117, 118–119, 120–121, 124–129, 130–140
  US sanctions 226, 229–230, 271, 306–308
Sberbank 113, 119–120, 131–132

selective engagement 10, 11, 51–52, 61, 207, 216, 217–218, 220, 255, 259, 275–276, 277, 278–279, 280–281, 283–284, 290, 291, 309, 349–350, 367, 372–374, 380
shared neighbourhood 4, 141, 203, 363–364, 371–372, 375–376
South Ossetia 3–4, 165–167, 173n45, 174, 176–177, 180, 190–191, 202
Steinmeier formula 28–30, 32–33, 36, 37–39, 44–45, 51–52n26
strategic narrative 62–65, 66, 67, 68–69, 70, 71, 73, 74, 75–80, 81–84
Strategic Partnership
  EU-Russia 1–2, 4, 12, 107, 364–365, 375–376
  EU-China 305, 306–308

Technical Assistance for Newly Independent States (TACIS) 315, 316, 318
Trans-European Mobility Programme for University Studies (TEMPUS) 352, 354–356, 357, 359–360, 362, 365, 367–368
Transnistria 165–167, 176–177, 180
TurkStream 222, 225, 226, 231

Ukraine
  Constitution 118
  constitutional reform 20–21, 24, 35–36, 38–39, 66
  eastern Ukraine 6, 7, 8, 10, 17–21, 24–26, 30, 34, 37–38, 41, 46, 54, 58, 70, 78–79, 86–88, 104–105, 118, 130, 175, 211, 257–258, 380
  Ukrainian crisis 5, 6, 7–8, 10–11, 12, 40–42, 43, 45–46, 47, 50–52, 53, 57–58, 59, 60, 67, 68, 71, 74, 216–217, 218, 340, 341, 348, 373, 374, 375–377, 378–379, 380
United Nations (UN) 74, 169–170, 172–173, 203–204, 210, 273–274, 275
  Charter 86–87, 88–89, 97–98, 100–101, 121
  Convention on the Law of the Sea (UNCLOS) 228, 291, 301–302
  General Assembly 17–18, 86–87n3, 267–268, 271
  High Commissioner for Refugees (UNHCR) 272

United Nations (UN) *(cont.)*
  Peacekeeping   38
  Security Council   27–28, 55–56, 112, 120–121, 268, 269
United States (US)   18–20, 24, 34, 45–46, 47, 49–50, 52, 57, 61, 64–65, 66, 69, 71, 73, 81–83, 86–87, 89–91, 94–95, 96–98, 102–103, 180, 202, 220–221, 222–223, 229, 237–238, 259, 263–264, 266–267, 268, 271, 275, 291, 304, 305–307, 308–309, 315–316, 324–325, 346, 365, 373–374, 379

Velvet Revolution   143–144, 159, 161–162
visa
  bans   180, 182–183, 185–187
  dialogue   5–6, 91, 104–105, 107
  diplomacy   10, 181–182, 183, 187–188, 189, 190–192, 194, 195, 196–197, 372
  facilitation   182–184, 272, 372
  liberalisation   159, 181–188, 189, 194, 372
  visa-free regime   182, 184–185, 188–191, 193, 196, 202, 260–262, 264, 274–275

World Trade Organisation (WTO)   8–9, 98–99, 100–101, 105–106, 120–123, 153–155, 202, 220–221, 223, 224–225, 295

Yanukovych   5, 47–48, 64–65, 132–134

Zelenskiy   28–30, 32–33, 36–38, 60

Printed in the United States
by Baker & Taylor Publisher Services